DEVELOPMENTAL PSYCHOLOGY:
AN ADVANCED TEXTBOOK
Second Edition

DEVELOPMENTAL PSYCHOLOGY:
AN ADVANCED TEXTBOOK
Second Edition

Edited by
Marc H. Bornstein
Michael E. Lamb
*National Institute of Child Health
and Human Development*

LAWRENCE ERLBAUM ASSOCIATES, PUBLISHERS
1988   Hillsdale, New Jersey   Hove and London

Lawrence Erlbaum Associates, Inc., Publishers
365 Broadway
Hillsdale, New Jersey 07642

Library of Congress Cataloging-in-Publication Data

Development psychology.
  Includes indexes.
  1. Developmental psychology.   I. Bornstein, Marc H.
II. Lamb, Michael E., 1953–   . [DNLM: 1. Human
Development.   2. Psychology.   BF 713 D488]
BF713.D465   1988   155   87-13719
ISBN 0-89859-969-5

Printed in the United States of America
10   9   8   7   6   5   4   3   2   1

Contents

v

3. Measurements and Analysis   85
Donald P. Hartmann

PART II: PERCEPTUAL, COGNITIVE, AND LINGUISTIC DEVELOPMENT

4. Perceptual Development Across the Life Cycle   151
Marc H. Bornstein

5. Cognitive Development   205
Deanna Kuhn

List of Contributors

Thomas M. Achenbach
Departments of Psychiatry and
  Psychology
University of Vermont
Burlington, VT 05405

Marc H. Bornstein
Section on Child and Family Studies
National Institute of Child Health and
  Human Development
Bethesda, MD 20892

Roger A. Dixon
Department of Psychology
University of Victoria
Victoria, British Columbia
CANADA

Nancy Eisenberg
Department of Psychology
Arizona State University
Tempe, AZ 85287

Matia Finn-Stevenson
Department of Psychology
Yale University
New Haven, CT 06520

Lila Gleitman
Department of Psychology
University of Pennsylvania
Philadelphia, PA 19104

Donald P. Hartmann
Department of Psychology
University of Utah
Salt Lake City, UT 84112

Martin L. Hoffman
Department of Psychology
New York University
New York, NY 10003

Deanna Kuhn
Department of Psychology
Teachers College
Columbia University
New York, NY 10027

Michael E. Lamb
Section on Social and Emotional
  Development
Laboratory of Comparative Ethology
National Institute of Child Health and
  Human Development
Bethesda, MD 20892

Richard M. Lerner
Department of Individual and Family
  Studies
Pennsylvania State University
University Park, PA 16802

Diane N. Ruble
Department of Psychology
New York University
New York, NY 10003

Victoria Seitz
Department of Psychology
Yale University
New Haven, CT 06520

Robert J. Sternberg
Department of Psychology
Yale University
New Haven, CT 06520

Eric Wanner
Sloane Foundation
New York, NY 10111

Edward F. Zigler
Department of Psychology
Yale University
New Haven, CT 06520

Preface

Developmental psychology is a unique, comprehensive, and important aspect of psychology for at least three reasons. First, developmental psychologists adopt a vital perspective on psychological theory and research. When psychologists conduct experiments in perception, investigate language, or study personality, they usually concentrate on perception, language, or personality in individuals of a particular age, be they children, college students, or the elderly. In so doing they may gain important knowledge about perception, language, or personality. To study psychological phenomena at only one point in the life cycle, however, is to limit knowledge about those phenomena by failing to consider the continuity or change in psychological phenomena that are the province of developmental psychology. Indeed, it could be argued that when we undertake the psychological study of any phenomenon, we must—wittingly or unwittingly—do so in a developmental context. The chapters in this volume on substantive areas of psychology, like perception, cognition, and language, by Bornstein, Kuhn, Sternberg, and Glietman and Wanner, and those on personality and social psychology by Lamb, Eisenberg, Hoffman, Ruble, and Achenbach, all demonstrate that the developmental perspective transcends and enriches any focus on particular points in the life span. One purpose of this volume, then, is to provide the inescapable and valuable developmental perspective on all substantive areas in psychology.

Second, developmental psychology is also a major subdiscipline in its own right. It has its own history and systems, as Dixon and Lerner point out; its own methodologies, as Seitz shows; its own tradition of measurement and analysis, as Hartmann demonstrates; and its own perspectives, as each of the authors illustrate. If studying psychology comprehensively involves attending to developmental psychology, then, there are systems, methodologies, and perspectives to be learned, and a second purpose of this volume is to clarify those systems, methodologies, and perspectives for the would-be student of psychology.

Third, the many aspects of developmental psychology have obvious and immediate relevance in applied issues and problems. Each of the chapters in this book illustrates the relevance of developmental psychology through reviews of the history, theory, and substance of the subdiscipline. In addition, questions about application are specifically emphasized in the chapter by Zigler and Finn-Stevenson.

In summary, developmental psychology provides a perspective that bears on all substantive phenomena in psychology, that applies across the life span, that has its own internal value, and that has manifest relevance to everyday life. It is for these reasons that we, the editors, have taken up the study of developmental psychology and have organized this introduction to developmental psychology for the advanced student of psychology.

This volume meets a need for texts in this area that can be used at the advanced undergraduate and introductory graduate levels. We knew of no other work available to the instructors of such courses when the first edition was prepared. Sadly, it is not possible today for any one or two individuals to convey, with proper sensitivity, the breadth of contemporary developmental psychology at this level. For that reason we invited several experts to prepare original, comprehensive, and topical treatments of the major areas of developmental psychology. We then organized and edited these chapters, with their cooperation and good will, into a single coherent volume. The success of this first edition encouraged us to prepare an updated second edition to which we have added chapters on measurement and statistics, and information processing, while expanding the purview of several other chapters.

Developmental Psychology has many purposes. We hope that readers will obtain a new perspective on psychology, a greater appreciation of the varied phenomena that constitute psychology, and a fundamental grounding in developmental psychology itself.

Work on this book was conducted in our private capacities, largely before we joined the NICHD staff. Our institutional affiliation is listed for informational purposes only, and no official support is implied or intended.

January 1988

Marc H. Bornstein
Michael E. Lamb
Bethesda, Maryland

FOUNDATIONS OF DEVELOPMENTAL PSYCHOLOGY

The three chapters in this first section focus on the intellectual history of developmental study, and the manner in which empirical research is conducted.

In Chapter 1, Roger Dixon and Richard Lerner summarize the philosophical and intellectual history of developmental psychology as an empirical science. Consistent with many other commentators, they place great emphasis on Darwin's role in transforming what would become developmental psychology from a largely speculative and descriptive discipline into a theoretically grounded empirical science. Since Darwin's seminal contributions, developmental psychology has been the primary battleground for contests among sets or families of theories concerned with explaining development. Shifts over time in both the definitions of development proposed within each type of theory, and in the manner in which central issues in development (e.g., nature vs. nurture, continuity vs. discontinuity) are portrayed, are explained by Dixon and Lerner.

In Chapters 2 and 3, Victoria Seitz and Donald Hartmann discuss the ways in which evidence is gathered and analyzed by developmental psychologists. Developmental psychologists, as these contributors show, are a methodologically eclectic breed, willing to rely on systematic or unsystematic observations, on interviews or questionnaires, and on manipulative experiments to obtain data. They use an array of descriptive and inferential statistical techniques to reduce those data and reach conclusions based

1

on them. Because most studies conducted by developmental researchers involve children, a unique array of ethical issues attend developmental research, as Seitz points out in her chapter.

1 A History of Systems in Developmental Psychology

Roger A. Dixon
University of Victoria

Richard M. Lerner
Pennsylvania State University

INTRODUCTION

A student beginning the advanced study of developmental psychology is probably all too aware of the vast array of theories, methods, and ideas present in the field. Such an array may suggest a picture of formidable complexity, or even anarchy. Closer inspection, however, reveals some identifiable clusters of theories, methods, and ideas, and shows that although these clusters differ in important ways, they also share certain foci, themes, and—most important for the purposes of this chapter—historical roots. Accordingly, we examine some of the key historical bases of the major modern systems of developmental psychology. In considering this history we trace early connections among what have evolved into major theoretical orientations toward development. In addition, we specify some major similarities and differences in these approaches to understanding development. By referring to the field's history, we are able to understand much of the contemporary scene in developmental psychology.

Today there are two major conceptual features in developmental psychology that can be identified by an analysis of the field's history. First, developmental psychologists are now more concerned with, and better prepared to address, the explanation of developmental change (in terms of both the methods and concepts available to assist in the specification of the causes or antecedents of development) as opposed to just the description of development (i.e., the depiction or representation of change). Second, because it has been recognized that one's explanation of development derives from one's theory of development, developmental psychologists have recently begun to attend to one or more of the viable theories or systems of interpretation that are available (e.g., Baldwin, 1980;

Lerner, 1986). Much current, exemplary developmental research is aimed at theory or model testing as opposed, for example, to the mere generation of developmental norms.

What led to these current emphases? We begin this chapter by tracing some of the recent events that have led to today's emphasis on theory and explanation. Next we find that, although the current emphasis on theory has been associated with the recognition of the range of systems that may be used to account for development, there has also been a concern with explaining the presence of several viable theories of development. In other words, why is there more than one theory of psychological development? Are these theories mutually compatible or do they compete in some way with one another? Although we shall see that the answers to such questions depend on philosophical differences among psychologists, we will also see that another answer exists. Distinct in many important ways, today's major theoretical systems of developmental psychology can be linked historically to a common intellectual "source": The intellectual context of the nineteenth century, including especially the historical and evolutionary theories of Charles Darwin and others. Thus, one explanation for the presence of distinct theories of development is that different scientists devised their accounts of development by emphasizing different aspects of such prominent accounts of historical change as Darwin's theory of evolution (Dixon & Lerner, 1985; White, 1968; Wohlwill, 1973). We return to this point later. In addition to observing the existence of several relatively adequate "families" of developmental theories, we discuss the recent surge of interest in the history of developmental psychology (e.g., Borstelmann, 1983; Cairns, 1983; Eckardt, Bringmann, & Sprung, 1985; Smuts & Hagen, 1986). Finally, we summarize the history and the major features of one of the most pervasive contemporary perspectives within developmental psychology; that is, the life-span approach. Let us turn now to the bases of the trend toward addressing issues of explanation.

SOME BASES OF THE CONTEMPORARY CONCERN WITH THE EXPLANATION OF DEVELOPMENT

In the early decades of this century, and continuing through at least the beginning of the 1940s, much of developmental psychology was descriptive and normative. Instrumental in promoting this emphasis was the research of Arnold Gesell (1880–1961). Gesell (1929, 1931, 1934, 1946, 1954) emphasized that maturationally based changes unfold independently of learning, and his research stressed the need for the careful and systematic cataloging of growth norms. His work provided the field with useful information about the expected sequence for, and normative times of, the emergence of numerous physical and mental developments in infants and children. Conceptually, Gesell's work is related to one side of what has been a continuing debate in the history of developmental psychology: the *nature–nurture* controversy. This controversy pertains to a consideration of where the sources of development lie, whether in inborn (or heredi-tary) mechanisms or in acquired (or learned) processes. By stressing that matura-tion rather than learning is the prime impetus for developmental change, Gesell (1929) was taking a "nature," as opposed to a "nurture," stance. Historically, other terms associated with the nature position are *preformationism, nativism,* and *innateness;* some terms associated with the nurture position are *learning, conditioning, experience,* and *socialization.*

It is important to recognize that the differences in views of the source of development are associated with differences regarding the nature–nurture issue because, although Gesell's (1929, 1931, 1934) work emphasized the descriptive and normative nature of the field, there was indeed work occurring in other areas of psychology that countered Gesell's emphasis (White, 1970). For example, some experimental psychologists stressed the applicability of learning principles to the study of childhood (e.g., Dollard, Doob, Miller, Mowrer, & Sears, 1939; Miller & Dollard, 1941; Watson, 1924). One consequence of this activity was to provide evidence that nurture-based learning phenomena, as opposed to nature-based maturation phenomena, could account for some features of children's behavior and development. These learning psychologists emphasized less the facts of development per se (e.g., "What is the age at which an infant sits, stands, walks, or has a two-word vocabulary?") than the explanation of those facts (e.g., "What mechanisms—nature or nurture—need to be referred to in order to explain these facts?").

This alternative emphasis was furthered in the 1940s by events leading up to and including World War II (Lerner, 1983). Nazi persecution led many Jewish intellectuals to flee Europe, and many sought refuge and a new start for their careers in the United States. Many of these refugees were able to secure positions in American universities and associated institutions, despite the fact that they often brought with them ideas counter to those that were typical of the American scene (e.g., behaviorism and learning theory). For instance, although Freud himself settled in London (and died there in 1939), many psychoanalytically oriented psychologists, some trained by Freud or his daughter Anna, emigrated to North America (e.g., Peter Blos and Erik Erikson).

One reason that so many psychoanalytically oriented professionals were able to secure faculty positions in America may be related to the fact that the federal government was contributing large amounts of money to universities to support the training of clinical psychologists. Such psychologists were needed to conduct the testing of soldiers for both psychological and physical fitness (Misiak & Sexton, 1966). This infusion of psychoanalysis resulted in the introduction of a nature-based perspective into numerous psychology departments, some of which had been dominated by nurture-based theorists (Gengerelli, 1976). Nevertheless, the psychoanalytic orientation represented just one of many different theoretical accounts of human functioning—accounts that stressed either nature or both nature and nurture as sources of behavior and development—that were now making inroads into American thinking.

For similar reasons, nativistic ideas about perception and learning, introduced by psychologists who believed in the holistic aspects of behavior, began to appear more frequently on the American scene. The gestalt (meaning "form," "shape") views represented by some Europeans (people like Max Wertheimer, Kurt Koffka, Wolfgang Köhler, Kurt Goldstein, and Kurt Lewin) were shown to be pertinent also to areas of concern such as brain functioning, group dynamics, and social problems (Henle, 1977; Sears, 1975). European perspectives relevant to human development also were being introduced. For the most part, as we shall see later, these views also emphasized maturational (nature) components and, to some extent, clinical, nonexperimental methods. Heinz Werner (e.g., 1948) and Jean Piaget (e.g., 1923) were especially influential.

The outcome of this cross-fertilization of ideas about development was to reinforce, if not redefine, the evolving ideas about development in North America. Any given behavior, patterns of behaviors, or systematic changes in behavior could be explained by a number of different theories, and these various theories were advanced by respected advocates often working in the same academic contexts (Gengerelli, 1976). Thus, in American departments of psychology, developmentalists were confronted with a range of perspectives. We suggest that such fundamental differences in approaches to, and interpretations of, behavior may have led to more serious efforts to articulate one position over another. In this way, the pluralistic situation in American academia may have fostered or strengthened interest in the issues surrounding the explanation of human development. That is, the simultaneous presentation of diverse interpretations further promoted a more serious concern with theoretical interpretations of development. In subsequent decades conceptual and historical reviews of "child development" or "child psychology" reflect this trend (e.g., Anderson, 1956; English, 1950; Frank, 1935, 1962). This focus on theoretical and explanatory concerns continued in the post-World War II era, in the late 1950s and 1960s. The pluralism of ideas about development is especially evident in the now-classic publication, *The Concept of Development,* a collection of thematic chapters which was edited by Dale Harris (1957).

In an early review of the history of developmental science, Bronfenbrenner (1963) noted that from the 1930s to the early 1960s there was a continuing shift away from studies involving the mere collection of data, a shift toward research concerned with abstract processes and constructs. Some books and essays published during this period epitomized this trend by calling for the study of developmental processes and mechanisms (e.g., Harris, 1956, 1957; McCandless & Spiker, 1956; Spiker & McCandless, 1954). Accordingly, describing the status of the field in 1963, Bronfenbrenner wrote that "first and foremost, the gathering of data for data's sake seems to have lost in favor. The major concern in today's developmental research is clearly with inferred processes and constructs" (p. 527).

Similarly, in a review almost a decade later, Looft (1972) found a continuation of the trends noted by Bronfenbrenner. Looft's review, like Bronfenbrenner's, was based on an analysis of major handbooks of developmental psychology published from the 1930s to 1972. Looft noted that a shift toward more general, integrative concerns occurred by 1945 (after World War II), and that the trend continued through 1963 (Bronfenbrenner, 1963) to 1972. As a case in point we may note that the editor of a 1970 handbook (Mussen, 1970) points out: ''The major contemporary empirical and theoretical emphases in the field of developmental psychology, however, seem to be on explanations of the psychological changes that occur, the mechanisms and processes accounting for growth and development'' (p. vii).

Since the early 1970s, this trend toward attending to both the description and explanation of developmental processes has continued in a number of ways. For example, considerable interest has come to be focused on a variety of theories, on explanations, and on processes of development. Such foci have led to the recognition that there are multiple adequate ways (theories) of accounting for the facts (descriptions) of development. This pluralistic perspective implies further that theoretical concerns may guide the collection and interpretation of data, and that theory and data should be evaluated in terms of each other. A second aspect of this trend toward explanation may be seen in an examination of the most recent compilations of research and theory. For example, in the fourth edition of the *Handbook of Child Psychology,* the first volume (Mussen & Kessen 1983) is devoted to historical, theoretical, and methodological issues, topics not even juxtaposed in a single section of previous editions.

Indeed, the interest in conceptual and methodological issues has itself generated considerable scholarship. In particular, the theoretical and metatheoretical bases upon which individual development is studied and interpreted became a focus of investigation (e.g., Overton, 1984; Overton & Reese, 1973; Reese & Overton, 1970). Following the work of such philosophers as Kuhn (1970) and Pepper (1942), Reese and Overton (1970; Overton & Reese, 1973, 1981) identified two major philosophical models that provide the basis for many extant assumptions about human development. These models provide a set of assumptions, or metatheoretical ideas, about human nature and thereby influenced lower order theoretical and methodological statements.

The two models discussed by Reese and Overton (1970) were termed *organicism* and *mechanism*. The organismic position stresses the qualitative features of developmental change and the active contribution of the organism's processes in these changes. The theories of Piaget (e.g., 1970) and to some extent of Freud (e.g., 1954) are examples of such organismically oriented approaches. In contrast, the mechanistic position stresses quantitative change and the active contribution of processes lying outside the primary control of the organism (e.g., in the external stimulus environment) as the major source of development. The behavioral analysis theory of Bijou (1976) and of Bijou and Baer (1961) is a major example of such mechanistically oriented approaches. (We discuss these metatheories in greater detail later.)

Again, on the basis of some well-known philosphical ideas, discussions occurred concerning the "family of theories" associated with each model (Reese & Overton, 1970). For instance, as we previously noted, there are at least two types of organismically oriented theories, those of Freud and those of Piaget. Although there are differences among family members (Freud emphasized social and personality development and Piaget emphasized cognitive development), there is greater similarity among the theories within a family (e.g., the common stress on the qualitative, stagelike nature of development) than there is between theories associated with different families (e.g., mechanistically oriented theories would deny the importance, indeed the reality, of qualitatively different stages in development). Due to the philosophically based differences between families of theories derived from the organismic and the mechanistic models, the period since the early 1970s has involved several discussions about the different stances regarding an array of key conceptual issues of development. Examples are the nature and nurture bases of development (Lehrman, 1970; Lerner, 1978; Overton, 1973); the quality, openness, and continuity of change (Brim & Kagan, 1980; Looft, 1973); appropriate methods of studying development (Baltes, Reese, & Nesselroade, 1977; Nesselroade & Baltes, 1979); and ultimately, the alternative truth criteria for establishing the "facts" of development (Dixon & Nesselroade, 1983; Overton & Reese, 1973; Reese & Overton, 1970).

This awareness of the philosophical bases of developmental theory, method, and data contributed to the consideration of additional models appropriate to the study of psychological development. In part, this consideration developed as a consequence of interest in integrating assumptions associated with theories derived from organismic and mechanistic models (Looft, 1973). For instance, Riegel (1973, 1975, 1976) attempted to apply an historical model of development that seemed to include some features of organicism (e.g., active organism) and some features of mechanism (e.g., active environment). However, interest in continual, reciprocal relations between an active organism and its active context (and not in either element per se) and the concern with these relations as they have existed on all phenomenal levels of analysis have formed a basis for proposing such related conceptions of human development as the *dialectical* (Riegel, 1975, 1976), *transactional* (Sameroff, 1975), *relational* (Looft, 1973), or *dynamic interactional* (Lerner, 1978, 1979). In a similar way, a number of theorists have explored the application of a change-oriented contextual model to the collection and interpretation of developmental (and other psychological) data (Beilin, 1984; Lerner, Hultsch, & Dixon, 1983; see especially the volume on contextualism edited by Rosnow & Georgoudi, 1986).

By the end of the 1970s, developmental psychology had evolved into a field marked by not one but several explanatory theories. This theoretical pluralism (or multiplicity of reasonable theoretical alternatives) continues to exist today (Dixon & Nesselroade, 1983). An interesting paradox exists, however, that leads to both similarities and differences among the present major theoretical systems in developmental psychology. Although these systems differ in the superordinate philosophical models that they represent, as well as in their respective definitions of development, variables and problems of interest, and their methods of research, to a great extent all share a common intellectual heritage: All have been influenced by theories of temporal progression or evolution, with perhaps the most dominant exemplar being Darwinism.

In the next section of this chapter, we suggest that historical and evolutionary theories (and in particular Darwinism) have provided some intellectual basis for five different theoretical systems in developmental psychology. This is the case despite the frequent misuse and misunderstanding of Darwinism evident in the early literature (e.g., Charlesworth, 1986; Dixon & Lerner, 1985; Ghiselin, 1986). First, the influence of nineteenth-century evolutionary thought on the *organismic model* may be traced from the work of G. Stanley Hall, James Mark Baldwin, Pierre Janet, and Arnold Gesell, to the continuing influential work of Jean Piaget and Heinz Werner. Second, the related *psychoanalytic model* developed in a less direct fashion from the work of Sigmund Freud and Carl Jung to that of Erik Erikson. Third, Wilhelm Preyer and Sir Francis Galton, as well as (some later aspects of) G. S. Hall and John B. Watson were the early contributors to the development of the *mechanistic model. Contextualism* derived from the turn-of-the-century American pragmatic philosophers, most notably William James, Charles Sanders Peirce, John Dewey, and G. H. Mead. Finally, the *dialetical model,* influenced by G. W. F. Hegel and Karl Marx, was later developed more specifically by Lev S. Vygotsky and Klaus F. Riegel. Thus, one way in which we can understand the present meaning of each of the different theoretical systems in developmental psychology is to appreciate their relatively common intellectual heritage and the historical trajectories they followed in developing away from one another. To understand the influence of evolutionary theories on developmental psychology it is useful first to consider the historical setting within which Darwin developed his theory.

EVOLUTIONARY THEORY AND THE EMERGENCE OF DEVELOPMENTAL PSYCHOLOGY

Early Work on the Concept of Development

It is impossible to understand either the genesis or the eventual impact of evolutionary theory (and in particular, Darwinism) without understanding the interest among eighteenth- and nineteenth-century intellectuals in the topic of history (Dixon & Lerner, 1985; Eiseley, 1958; Vidal, Buscaglia, & Voneche, 1983; Wertheimer, 1985). In his intellectual history of the nineteenth century, Mandelbaum (1971) observed:

> It is generally agreed that one of the most distinctive features of nineteenth-century thought was the widespread interest evinced in history. The manifestations of this

interest are not only found in the growth and diversification of professional historical scholarship, but in the tendency to view all of reality, and all of man's
achievements, in terms of the category of development. (p. 41)

The category of development implies that an adequate understanding of any
phenomenon (biological or philosophical) requires that it be considered in terms
of its position in the present situation and its role in a continuous developmental
or historical process. As Mandelbaum (1971) described it, the concern is not
with the "nature of the event itself, [but] . . . with its place in some process of
change" (p. 46). Events have no autonomous existence (and, especially, no
independent meaning) outside of the role they play in the stream of history. In the
human sciences, where the events of concern are sociohistorical in nature (e.g.,
wars and plagues), the province of general human history is indicated; where the
events are of an individual nature (e.g., the onset of logical thinking, puberty, or
marriage), the province of individual human history, or developmental psychology, is implied.

In general, during the late eighteenth and early nineteenth centuries, the
concept of development received attention on two fronts, both of which helped to
influence the emergence of developmental psychology. The thrust of the interest
in the idea of development (and individual development in particular) was an
ongoing attempt by researchers in a variety of disciplines to understand humanity
in a temporal and historical context. On the philosophical front, this involved a
dynamic, dialectical theory of history, such as the ideal philosophy of G. W. F.
Hegel (1770–1831) and the material philosophy of Karl Marx (1818–1883). On
the scientific front, the interest in development was manifested in two mutually
influential areas of investigation. On the one hand, there were the notions of
natural history informed by research in geology; of particular note in this regard
was the gradual and developmental method of Sir Charles Lyell (1797–1875).
On the other hand, there were various biological theories of evolution, especially
those of Jean Baptiste de Lamarck (1744–1829), Charles Darwin (1809–1882),
and Herbert Spencer (1820–1903).

Prior to the nineteenth century, most efforts to understand human development did not result in sustained developmental psychologies. Many such efforts
derived primarily from philosophical, literary, or theological domains. From
Aristotle (384 B.C.–322 B.C.) through St. Augustine (354–430) to William
Shakespeare (1564–1616) and Jean-Jacques Rousseau (1712–1778), many
important thinkers wrote about the ages or stages of human life, often speculating
on their unique needs and purposes (Dennis, 1972). It was not until the eighteenth and the early nineteenth century, however, that these theoretical perspectives were attached to systematically empirical investigations.

The nineteenth century has often been viewed as a formative period in the
emergence of developmental psychology (Baltes, 1983; Cairns, 1983; Dixon &
Lerner, 1985; Groffman, 1970; Reinert, 1979; Wertheimer, 1985). In addition to
the influence of evolutionary theory, several advances occurred in this and in the

late part of the preceding century. Especially notable early contributors are the following: (a) Dietrich Tiedemann (1748–1803), who, in 1787, produced the first psychological diary of the growth of a young child (see Murchison & Langer, 1927); (b) Friedrich August Carus (1770–1808), who endeavored to develop a comprehensive age-oriented science; (c) Carl Gustav Carus (1789–1869), who argued for the application of the developmental method to a broad range of psychological issues (Köhler, 1985); (d) Adolphe Quetelet (1796–1874), who produced highly advanced methods to disentangle the multiple influences on the course of human development; and (e) Johann Nikolas Tetens (1736–1807), who argued for natural scientific methods to guide the search for general laws regarding human development from birth to death. In the nineteenth century numerous "baby biographies" began to appear. Such ontogenetic observational studies often took the form of diaries written by scientist-parents describing the successive achievements of a child (often their own). For example, Darwin kept such a diary of his infant son's growth during the years 1840–1841; this was not published, however, until 1877, when it appeared as an article, "Biographical Sketch of an Infant," in the journal, *Mind*. Many other baby biographies appeared around the turn of the century (e.g., Braunshvig & Braunshvig, 1913; Champneys, 1881; Hall, 1891; Moore, 1896; Perez, 1878; Prior, 1895; Shinn, 1893–1899, 1900; Simpson, 1893; Sully, 1903). Shinn's (1893–1899, 1900) work with her niece was perhaps especially well known, for she made comparisons with the methods and results of other, similar research. This biographically oriented activity continued through (and in some cases beyond) the 1930s (Bühler, 1930; Dennis, 1949, 1951; Jaeger, 1985).

In the next section we describe more completely the impact of evolutionary theory (and especially Darwin) on the study of psychological development (see also the collection edited by Butterworth, Rutkowska, & Scaife, 1985). Before doing so, however, it may be useful to point out that developmental psychology obviously did not arise solely as a function of evolutionary theory. As Peters (1965) suggested, evolutionary theory was useful in preparing the way for a scientific analysis of change (or progress) and of continuity, both between human and animal and between adult and child. But there was also a quite practical social influence, which consisted of pressure applied by educational administrators and social planners concerned with the large-scale education of a growing population of children (see also Borstelmann, 1983). Such a development served to focus institutional attention on the practical issues of ontogenesis (Sears, 1975). These practical concerns continued to be influential in the twentieth century, as evidenced by the founding of numerous child welfare and research centers (Frank, 1962; Sears, 1975).

Darwin and the Theory of Evolution

Charles Darwin played perhaps the exemplary role in the emergence of evolutionary thinking in the nineteenth century, but even he was not without intellectual antecedents (Eiseley, 1958). He was influenced by a number of different people, ideas, and experiences, but two major interrelated strands should be noted. On the one hand, it has been shown that Darwin gathered from his own family, his life history, and his early cultural context much of the intellectual disposition that is apparently necessary to effect a massive scientific revolution and to effect the precise kind of revolution with which he was associated (Gillespie, 1979; Gruber, 1974; Manier, 1978). On the other hand, it is quite clear that Darwin was part of an intellectual lineage that stemmed from more formal or academic sources. For example, it is well known that Darwin's views about evolution were influenced by the English geologist Sir Charles Lyell, who was among the first to view natural phenomena from a historical and developmental perspective.

Darwin's model of nature, and especially his theory of evolution, served as a conceptual impetus for many fields of scholarly inquiry, including biology, philosophy, and developmental psychology (Dewey, 1910; Dixon & Lerner, 1985; Toulmin & Goodfield, 1965; Vidal et al., 1983). It is also apparent that Darwin developed his theory in the context of the extant philosophical and scientific models of human behavior, activity, and development. It may be inferred that there was a bidirectional relation between Darwin's theory and the theoretical ideas that have shaped developmental psychology (Vidal et al., 1983). Given that evolutionary biology and developmental psychology have similar—if not parallel—missions, it is not surprising that Darwinism had a notable impact on the emergence of the latter.

Some selected features of Darwin's theory of evolution deserve specific attention. Darwin proposed a theory of evolution in which species development occurs in gradual, continual, and adaptive steps. In other words, Darwin (1859) believed that new species emerge gradually over long periods of time; thus, there is a continuous chain of being from our now-extinct ancestors to us, a chain built on the concepts of natural selection and survival of the fittest. Briefly, let us explain this theory by noting the meaning of these key ideas.

The environment may be portrayed as placing demands on the members of a given species. In effect, it selects individuals who possess some characteristic that contributes, for example, to the successful gathering of available nourishment. If the individual has that characteristic, the individual will fit in with its environment, obtain nourishment, and survive. If not, it will either move to another ecological setting or die. The weakest or least adaptable members of the species are unable to reach maturity and therefore to mate (Morgan, 1902). Thus, the natural setting determines which characteristics of the organism will lead to survival, and will therefore be passed on genetically. This action of the natural environment, selecting organisms for survival, is termed *natural selection* (Loewenberg, 1957; Mayr, 1977).

Hence Darwin proposed the idea of *survival of the fittest*. Organisms that possess characteristics that fit the survival requirements for a particular environmental setting will "survive" in the sense of successfully passing on their genes. In other words, certain characteristics in certain settings have fundamental biological significance; that is, they allow the organism to survive. Characteristics that meet the demands of the environment (and so allow survival) are adaptive, or functional, characteristics.

In an evolutionary sense, something is functional if it is adaptive; that is, if it aids survival. Thus, the structure of an organism (its physical makeup, its constitution, its morphological or bodily characteristics) may be functional. Although Darwin emphasized the function of physical structures of species in 1859, he later (Darwin, 1972) pointed out that behavior too has survival value. Showing the emotion of fear when a dangerous bear approaches and being able to learn to avoid certain stimuli (e.g., poisonous snakes) and to approach others (e.g., food) are examples of behaviors that would be adaptive; they would further the individual's chances for survival.

Thus, mental activity and behavior also have a function (Stout & Baldwin, 1902). The function of behavior became the focus of much social scientific concern. This concern was reflected not only in the ideas of those interested in the phylogeny of behavior; additionally, the idea was promoted that those behavior changes characterizing ontogeny could be understood on the basis of adaptation. Although occasionally misrepresented and misunderstood, the adaptive role of behavior thus became a concern providing a basis for all American psychology (White, 1968); it has played a major part in the ideas of theorists as diverse as Hall (1904), Freud (1954), Piaget (1950), Erikson (1959), and Skinner (1938, 1950). Indeed, a functional and neofunctional view of developmental psychology continues to reflect this concern (e.g., Beilin, 1984; Dixon & Baltes, 1986).

Peters (1965) indicated that, prior to Darwin, emphasis was placed on differences between human and animal on the one hand, and adult and child on the other. After Darwin's argument for continuity in the former case, emphasis in human study shifted to the detection and consideration of similarities between adult and child. Peters (1965) summarized the sentiment of this period: "And if under the influence of theology, men had tended to say before Darwin: 'What a piece of work is man,' they would now tend to say, under the influence of biology: 'How wonderful are children and the beasts of the field' " (p. 732). Darwin (1871) suggested that there is substantial similarity (as well as dissimilarity) and continuity (as well as discontinuity) among several species and between the adult and child of a given species. For this reason, the absolute, ahistorical view of both present species and the adult form of a given species was called into question (Richards, 1982). Whether on the species or individual level, it became theoretically and methodologically important to consider a present form (or phenomenon) as having developed from a succession of earlier forms, and being likely to continue to develop into future forms. We refer to this perspective as the developmental tradition or approach. Although Darwin's own view emphasized continuous or gradual change, other evolutionary theories emphasized discontinuous or qualitative change (e.g., Costall, 1986; Toulmin & Goodfield, 1965).

We now consider how the general impetus provided by the active intellectual milieu of the nineteenth century, and especially evolutionary theory, led to the multiplicity of theories we find in developmental psychology today.

ROOTS OF CONTEMPORARY THEORIES IN DEVELOPMENTAL PSYCHOLOGY

To some extent, all extant metatheoretical, and derivative theoretical, views about human development were influenced by, or progressed through, the prism of nineteenth-century evolutionary thinking. We have noted that there are presently at least five major models of developmental psychology, and we suggest that these models share some common historical heritage. That is, although there is no single originative figure in developmental psychology, the ideas of Darwin—whether accurately or inaccurately understood, whether accepted entirely or rejected in part—were considered by the major early representatives of many modern theories in the discipline (Angell, 1912; Dixon & Lerner, 1985; Kirkpatrick, 1909; Misiak & Sexton, 1966; Vidal et al., 1983 White, 1968; Wohlwill, 1973).

Some Important Caveats

There are a number of ways to represent the history of a complex science such as developmental psychology. Histories of sciences can be (and have been) written in numerous ways, ranging from conceptual histories (histories of ideas and concepts where personalities may play a subservient role) to ''great-person'' or ''great-event'' histories (emphasizing the major characters or events populating the centuries). We have chosen a middle ground, in that we have adopted one broad conceptual organization of the field (the five major models) consistent with some recent theoretical treatments (e.g., Lerner, 1986). We have identified some (but not all) of the major thinkers active within each of the conceptual categories, and discussed briefly (a) their major ideas and research emphases, and (b) where they might fit in the chronological history of the model. A detailed history of each conceptual category would, of course, be a worthwhile endeavor, but this is beyond the mission of our chapter. Thus, our historical treatment of each of the metatheories is incomplete; learned observers of given models are advised that it is possible to note occasional omissions of people, ideas, or events. For example, our discussion of philosophers who contributed to the conceptual foundations of the various models of development has been curtailed (see Pepper, 1942; Reese & Overton, 1970).

On the other hand, we have tried to minimize the errors of commission. To this end, we would like to clarify our focus on the nineteenth century and, in particular, Darwinism as a ''starting point'' in the history of developmental psychology. Several important reservations should be noted.

First, we have already mentioned the fact that Darwin is by no means the original evolutionist (Ruse, 1979; Toulmin & Goodfield, 1965). It appears, however, that he may be the evolutionist with the single greatest influence on the emergence of a scientific developmental approach to studying humans. Second, and related to the first reservation, we have seen that several "developmental psychologists" antedated Darwin; for the most part, however, these figures were not major influences in the emergence of the field of developmental psychology. Third, it is not proposed that Darwin is the single generative figure in developmental psychology; rather, the intellectual climate of historical or evolutionary thinking—a climate that, as we have seen, both preceded Darwin and gained impetus from him and that, in some ways, was epitomized by him—is the originative intellectual core of developmental psychology. That is, on some occasions we indeed generalize our use of the name *Darwin* (and the term *Darwinism*) to indicate the temporalizing of scientific theories and methods that occurred during the career of Charles Darwin. Fourth, we do not propose that all present versions of developmental psychology embrace a Darwinian evolutionism, for, as we shall see below, this is simply not the case. Nevertheless, in the developmental "tradition" there is a stress on the history of the organism, a focus on the functional, adaptive features of behavioral and mental ontogeny, and an interest in the study of the role of the environment or context in such ontogeny (see Lerner, 1986). This is a tradition propagated in part by Darwin, and it is present in all current major systems. Thus, although the present (or even early) representatives of the existing models may not have produced (or even endorsed) developmental theories that are "truly" Darwinian (Dixon & Lerner, 1985; Ghiselin, 1986) an influence may still be identifiable. Indeed, it is the connection between what we see as key features of the developmental tradition— a tradition we believe is identifiable in all the models of development we discuss—and the ideas propagated by Darwin that allows us to argue for his seminal role. Fifth, we should note that there were, of course, other sources of influence on today's developmental theories and metatheories. These other influences account for many specific features of the different approaches to developmental psychology. This is an important caveat, for some researchers may argue, for example, that Darwinian mechanisms are largely irrelevant to their views of developmental psychology. Others (e.g., those interested in aging) may argue that Darwinian mechanisms are less active agents of change in adulthood (and thus less influential in the development of their field) than other more sociocultural or individual goal-directed models of change (some of which, indeed, predate Darwin). This latter qualification may apply especially to the recent life-span approach to developmental psychology, which we treat in a later section. In addition to nineteenth-century influences, the roots of this approach may extend both to some of the earlier European developmental scientists mentioned previously and to philosophers of cultural and social change (Baltes, 1983; Collingwood, 1956; Nisbet, 1980; Toulmin & Goodfield, 1965).

Despite these disclaimers, we should note that other, earlier reviewers have also depicted Darwin as a point of origin for several of the major lines of thought in contemporary developmental psychology (White, 1968; Wohlwill, 1973). However, consistent with our earlier suggestions, White (1968) noted that each of these lines of thought apparently selected something different from the writings of the evolutionist, and it is partly due to this selection that they all developed in different fashions. As White (1968) noted, "Within 50 years after the publication of Darwin's *The Origin of Species* in 1859, the theory of evolution has crystallized its influence upon developmental psychology not once but several times. As happens with a broad and powerful idealogy, different people took different messages from evolutionism and occasionally those messages could come into conflict" (p. 187). Wohlwill's (1973) views about the originative nature of Darwin's thought are somewhat distinct from those of White (1968), in that Wohlwill stressed not Darwin's influence on developmental theories per se, but the contribution of Darwinian thinking to the development of metatheories.

Although we sketched the intellectual connections for the five metatheories on an earlier page, it may be useful to provide a more detailed overview prior to addressing each of the models separately. Although all models started with philosophers (as, for example, *world views*), we concentrate on the developmental and empirical aspects stimulated during the nineteenth century. The first metatheoretical line of thought we will consider is the *organismic* model. In addition to the influence of Darwin and such philosophers as Hegel, it developed out of the early work of G. Stanley Hall (1846–1924) and James Mark Baldwin (1861–1934), through Arnold Gesell (1880–1961) and Pierre Janet (1859–1947) to Jean Piaget (1896–1980) and Heinz Werner (1890–1964). A second, organismically oriented line of thought is the *psychoanalytic*. Philosophically related to the work of F. W. Nietzsche (1844–1900), it stemmed from the work of Sigmund Freud (1856–1939) through Carl Jung (1875–1961) and Erik Erikson (b. 1902). The third metatheoretical line, the *mechanistic* model, is philosophically related to the work of, for example, John Locke (1632–1704) and David Hume (1711–1776). It developed from the works of Wilhelm Preyer (1841–1897) and Sir Francis Galton (1822–1911) to those of the later G. Stanley Hall and John B. Watson (1878–1958). In addition, a fourth line of thought, *contextualism*, may also be traced to Darwinism; this line was promoted by William James (1842–1910), Charles Sanders Peirce (1839–1914), John Dewey (1859–1952), and George Herbert Mead (1863–1931), the major figures of pragmatic philosophy. Further, a fifth line that is described has its principal roots in both the philosophy (Hegel, Marx) and the biology (Darwin) of the nineteenth century; it culminates in the *dialetical* model of developmental psychology as it was proposed by such Soviet psychologists as Lev S. Vygotsky (1894–1934) and A. R. Luria (1902–1977) and, more recently in America, by Klaus F. Riegel (1925–1977). Although we noted some of the general features of some of these metatheoretical positions earlier, it is useful to treat them in more detail here. For heuristic purposes we present the history of each model as an historical lineage; however, the lineages represent more the flow of ideas since Darwin than the impact of one individual upon another.

Organicism

As described by Pepper (1942; see also Lerner, 1986; Overton & Reese, 1973; Reese & Overton, 1970), the organismic model was patterned after the view of biological growth that prevailed in the preceding century. That is, psychological development was thought to be goal-directed and teleological in character. Developmental change, according to this model, is characterized as qualitative rather than (or, in isolated cases, in addition to) quantitative, and as unidirectional and irreversible. Following the emphasis on qualitative changes a stage pattern is often employed, resulting in a conception of development that is discontinuous and universal in sequence and pattern. The organism is seen as relatively active, constructing a relatively passive environment. The major figures in the emergence of this tradition of developmental psychology are thought to be linked, as shown in Row A of Fig. 1.1.

G. Stanley Hall is one initial figure linking the elaboration of an organismically derived theory with the Darwinian evolutionism. Hall organized the American Psychological Association and became its first president. He started the first American journal of psychology (aptly called *The American Journal of Psychology*), as well as the first scientific journal devoted to human development (first entitled *Pedagogical Seminary,* and then given its present name *The Journal of Genetic Psychology*). Hall (1883) contributed one of the earliest papers on child psychology and also wrote the first text on adolescence (a two-volume work, entitled *Adolescence,* 1904), as well as an often overlooked text on old age (*Senescence,* 1922). The latter testifies to his ground-breaking life-span perspec-

Tradition	19th Century Origins (Darwin, Evolutionary Theory, Historical Perspective)	Into the 20th Century	Late 20th Century
A. Organismic	● ————	► (early) Hall ‹ Baldwin ► Piaget, Werner ———► / Gesell Janet	*Contemporary neo-Piagetians*
B. Psychoanalytic	● ————	► Freud ———► Jung ———► Erikson ———► / Hall	*Contemporary Ego and Depth Psychologists*
C. Mechanistic	● ————	Galton ‹ ► (later) Hall ———► Watson ———► ► Preyer	*Contemporary Mechanistic Psychologists*
D. Contextual	● ————	James ‹ ↑ ► Dewey ———► Mead, Bartlett ———► ► Peirce	*Contemporary Contextual Psychologists*
E. Dialectical	● ————	► Marx ———► Vygotsky, Luria ———► Riegel ———► / Hegel	*Contemporary Soviet and Dialectical Psychologists*

Fig. 1.1   Heuristic scheme representing the nineteenth-century origins of five metatheoretical traditions in developmental psychology.

tive but is also an example of his later mechanistic tendencies, as described further on.

One of the most prominent and influential psychologists at the turn of the century, Hall had his most specific (but not enduring) influence on developmental psychology. Hall saw development from a nativistic (nature, or hereditary) point of view. Although not many people (including his students) adopted his specific nature-based theory of development as such, some did follow the general nature orientation he espoused. Consequently, Hall's influence was to direct scientific concern to human development, but to do so from a predominantly nature perspective.

In devising his nature viewpoint, Hall was profoundly influenced by Darwin. In fact, fancying himself the "Darwin of the mind" (White, 1968), Hall attempted to translate Darwin's phylogenetic evolutionary principles into conceptions relevant to ontogeny. He did this by adapting ideas derived from those of the embryologist, Ernst Haeckel (1834–1919). Haeckel believed that an embryo's ontogenetic progression mirrored the phylogenetic history—the evolution—of its species. Thus, when one looks at the changes characterizing an individual member of a species as it progresses across its embryological period, one sees a recapitulation of the evolutionary changes the species went through. In short, Haeckel was one of the prominent proponents of the notion that "ontogeny recapitulates phylogeny."

Hall applied to postnatal life the recapitulationist idea that Haeckel used for prenatal, embryological development. Arguing that during the years from birth to sexual maturity a person was repeating the history of the species, as had been done prenatally, Hall believed that the postnatal recapitulation was somewhat more limited (Gallatin, 1975). Furthermore, although an ardent evolutionist and a strong proponent of recapitulation theory, and so an exemplar of organismic theories, Hall nevertheless placed considerable emphasis on environmental, especially social, factors in later ontogenesis. That is, at separate points, recapitulation theory and environmental influences were incorporated into Hall's perspective, becoming one that encompassed the life span. In his attempt to extend the work of previous developmentalists beyond childhood, Hall (1904) argued that until adolescence the developing child repeats (through both play and fear) the evolution of human society. During adolescence, however, environmental factors increase their developmental significance (McCullers, 1969); this gives the latter part of Hall's ideas the mechanistic tone that is discussed later. Indeed, Hall believed that during adolescence genetic changes could be effected by the environment (Charles, 1970).

Arnold Gesell, whose work we described earlier, was for a time a student of Hall's at Clark University. Like Hall's other prominent student, Lewis Terman, Gesell was his heir but not his descendant (Kessen, 1965). That is, Gesell was an ardent student of child development and, although convinced of the importance of biological considerations, he distanced himself from Hall's recapitulationist ideas. Gesell's positive regard for Darwin's impact on developmental psychology can be read in his article "Charles Darwin and Child Development" (Gesell, 1939, 1948). In this article, Gesell (1948) pays tribute to Darwin's "perception of the gradual genesis of all living things, including the genesis of the human mind" (p. 44). This "developmental outlook . . . led to profound revisions in the interpretation of childhood" (p. 44). The new revolutionary formulations, Gesell argues, influenced his own former teacher, G. S. Hall.

As pointed out in an earlier part of this chapter, Gesell's own contributions are notable for three major reasons. First, his approach was consistent with the assumptions of organicism in that it focused on the biological, maturational, growthlike aspects of psychological development. In the 1920s, when the heredity–environment (or nature–nurture) issue was actively debated, Gesell (1928, 1929) argued for the predominance of nature (heredity), even adopting some teleological (goal-directed and -oriented) language. Second, Gesell, who was a thorough methodologist, was an assiduous observer of change patterns, and thus a prodigious contributor of normative growth tables and descriptions. In this way, his theoretical contributions—his efforts at explanation or interpretation— are no longer very influential. Third, it should be noted that Gesell, as a methodologist, made at least two lasting contributions: (a) he was an early and active proponent of the use of "cinema records" (a forerunner of videotapes) in the study of children, and (b) he was an early advocate of twin studies in disentangling the influences of nature and nurture. For these reasons, Gesell continues to be remembered in contemporary treatments of the history (e.g., Cairns, 1983) and theories (e.g., Lerner, 1986) of developmental psychology.

Like Hall, James Mark Baldwin is difficult to classify in purely organismic terms. There are two major intellectual sources to Baldwin's (e.g., 1895, 1906) developmental psychology. Fundamentally a Darwinian evolutionist, he was also influenced by British empiricism/associationism (see Baldwin, 1913). The former influence is manifested most positively by Baldwin's devotion to a Darwinian psychology (Baldwin, 1909; Russett, 1976) and, less positively, by his endorsement of recapitulation theory, although some authors suggest that Baldwin managed to avoid a thorough parallelism (Reinert, 1979). The British influence is revealed through his stimulus–response system based on pleasure and pain. Baldwin saw the child as developing from the simple to the more complex, first through an instinctive biological stage and second through a plastic or learning stage. The social system, especially the interactions between the child and this system (Cairns & Ornstein, 1979), was seen as a critical feature of ontogenesis.

Although some of Baldwin's work appears to be antithetical to organismic theory, his endorsement of the developmental method (Baldwin, 1930), and his leadership (with G. S. Hall) of the developmental psychology movement, assure him a place in the history of organicism. Moreover, much of his work prefigures the assimilation–accommodation theory of Piaget (Broughton, 1981; Piaget,

1982; Reinert, 1979; Ross & Kerst, 1978) and has been firmly placed in the history of genetic epistemology, the theory of knowledge most appropriate to organismic thinkers (Wozniak, 1982). Several recent reviewers have explored the influence of Baldwin on Piaget (e.g., Broughton, 1981; Cahan, 1984; Cairns, 1980; see also several contributors to a book on Baldwin's cognitive developmental psychology edited by Broughton & Freeman-Moir, 1982). Although there is considerable overlap in the assumptions and approaches of Baldwin and Piaget, Cahan (1984) pointed also to some important differences. Although both proffer models of developmental sequences (or stages), Baldwin's approach was more attentive to the dialectical interplay between the social and individual aspects of intellectual development. This attention is not sufficient to remove him from the organismic camp, for he was less mechanistic and dialectical than his contemporaries. For example, his speculations on the biological nature of at least early behavioral development often led to criticism from (mechanistic) experimentalists who thought that his questionnaires and experimental studies were not a sufficient basis on which to found a developmental psychology. In complementary fashion, Baldwin expressed doubt that a mechanistic account would ever succeed.

Rather more isolated from mainstream developmental psychology than either Hall or Baldwin, Pierre Janet developed a historical (or developmental) clinical psychology (Mayo, 1952). He viewed the life course as a succession of adaptive moments, each of which could influence the long-range adjustment of the individual (Janet, 1930). An evolutionary concept of psychic tension, together with the developmental method of, for example, Baldwin, informed Janet's approach to the study of the development of human action and behavior (Sjövall, 1967). To understand the psychological conditions of adulthood, according to this approach, the investigator must also explore the childhood and adolescent history of the individual (Mayo, 1952). The mental life of the organism is seen as both active and passive (reflective). Piaget took courses from Janet, and it has been noted that Janet had an active appreciation of Baldwin (Mueller, 1976). Indeed, it may have been through Janet that Piaget was most influenced by Baldwin (Cairns & Ornstein, 1979; Mueller, 1976; Piaget, 1978). It should be noted that Janet also had an impact on Freud.

Although only some of Piaget's early work cites Baldwin (see Piaget, 1923, 1932), his later publications contain ample acknowledgment of Baldwin's influences (Cairns & Ornstein. 1979; Evans, 1973; Langer, 1969; Piaget, 1978, 1982; White, 1977; Wozniak, 1982). Piaget may have taken from Baldwin an interest in such processes as imitation and play. Further, according to McCullers (1969), Piaget's early work contains some endorsement of a modified recapitulation theory (later termed *correspondence theory;* Gould, 1977). Like Baldwin, Piaget proposed a qualitative stage model of the development of the individual's interpretation of reality. But, as alluded to earlier, Piaget's stage model was more completely organismic than Baldwin's, for Piaget emphasized the active, unfolding nature of intellectual development. Nevertheless, numerous reviewers have noted that Piaget's (1972) developmental psychology was anticipated by Baldwin (Wozniak, 1982). Still, it is important to note that the early Piaget accords less emphasis to the influence of the social environment on individual development.

As noted earlier, Piaget's theory of the development of cognition was known in America in the 1920s (Piaget, 1923). It is unclear why his theory and research were generally ignored until the late 1950s (Flavell, 1963). Some observers have speculated that the reason may lie in the "clinical," nonexperimental nature of his research methods, his nonstatistical style of data analysis, or the abstract constructs with which he was concerned, all of which ran counter to predominant trends in the United States. Perhaps due to the European intellectual influences on American thinking occurring from events related to World War II, greater attention was given by Americans to the intellectual resources coming from and present in Europe. Thus, Piaget was "rediscovered," and in the 1960s achieved prominence in American developmental psychology. Indeed, to some extent his influence continues to the time of this writing, as a result both of further substantiation of portions of his theory, and of promoting discussions of alternative (but still organismic) theoretical conceptualizations (Brainerd, 1978; Kuhn, this volume; Overton & Newman, 1982; Siegel & Brainerd, 1977). For example, theoretical issues of the relationship between cognitive development and epistemology (or theory of knowledge) have been explored by several contributors to books edited by Mischel (1971) and by Kitchener (1986). In addition, that oft-cited gap in Piaget's theory—pertaining to the relation between social and individual-cognitive development—has been explored recently (e.g., Flavell & Ross, 1981; Overton, 1983; Wapner, Kaplan, & Cohen, 1973).

Due to Piaget's centrality in modern organismic metatheory, most of the introductory comments to this section are directly applicable to his developmental psychology (see also Kuhn, this volume). In the present context we cannot completely represent the thinkers who influenced him (they range from philosophers such as Hegel and Kant to biologists such as Lamarck and Darwin). Indeed, it should be noted that partly because of his affinity to Hegel, some aspects of his thought are distinctly dialectical (Reese, 1986). Piaget wrote voluminously, and his work has served as a framework for his many followers in the United States and Europe (see Kuhn, this volume). His influence has been felt in educational practice (primarily dealing with young children), psychological research (on cognitive development through adolescence), and philosophy (e.g., epistemology). Although continually criticized, amended, and extended, the Piagetian organismic model has become somewhat institutionalized in contemporary developmental psychology (Liben, 1981). One unresolved issue is whether Piaget's (1983) theory is a life-span theory. Recently, some notable efforts have been made to examine the Piagetian perspective in terms of its application to adult cognitive development (e.g., Labouvie-Vief, 1980, 1982). A critical issue is whether there is additional qualitative (or structural) change after formal operations, the final stage in Piaget's model.

Werner's (1948) orthogenetic principle—that development proceeds from a lack of differentiation to increasing differentiation, integration, and hierarchic organization—was anticipated by Baldwin and supported by embryology (Langer, 1969). His early work (e.g., his introductory book on developmental psychology, first published in German in 1926) was influenced by the developmental-holistic psychology of Felix Krueger (Baltes, 1983; Werner, 1948, 1957). In keeping with his conviction that it is not appropriate to systematize developmental theory (because it was a way of viewing behavior in general), Werner did not generate a methodical scheme of developmental psychology. In his later writing (e.g., 1957), he considered recapitulation theory (in particular, G. S. Hall's version) and rejected it. He was, however, willing to accept a parallel between evolutionary development and ontogenetic development, but not a one-to-one correspondence (see Brent, 1978). Nevertheless, his concept of development is clearly biological and maturational. The orthogenetic principle implies that development is directional and unilinear (Werner, 1957). Werner argues, as well, that any evolutionary or developmental process tends toward stabilization, thus adding a teleological (goal-oriented) component to his model. It is apparent, however, that Werner (1957) considered as well a number of contextual, non-organismic factors to be influential in change (see Lerner, 1986; Wapner et al., 1973).

Although Freud was eclectic, his theoretical position (Freud, 1954) is, in many ways, an organismic one akin to that of Piaget (1970; see also Fast, 1985). Nevertheless, it is sufficiently distinct to merit attention as a line of thought independent of organicism per se (Wohlwill, 1973).

The Psychoanalytic Tradition

The organismic, dynamic psychology of Sigmund Freud (1954) did not emerge until the last few years of the nineteenth century (Freud, 1910, 1938). Developmental change is viewed as qualitative and stagelike, proceeding through tension resolution from one stage to the next. Generally, a direction of development is implied; i.e., there is an end-state toward which development progresses. The psychoanalytic tradition shares this teleological perspective with organicism. Unlike the typical organismic model, however, regression (movement back through earlier stages) is possible and, in some cases, frequent. The focus of attention is on emotional or personality development (especially abnormal personality), with only secondary interest given to cognitive progression (Wolff, 1960). The proposed line of influence is shown in Fig. 1.1 (Row B).

According to Groffman (1970), "The psychoanalysts were usually outsiders [to the developmental tradition]. As physicians they were confronted mainly with the psychological disorders of adult persons. . . . It is doubtful whether [Freud] was influenced by early developmental psychology'' (p. 62). Somewhat to the contrary, however, McCullers (1969) argued that Freud may have been influenced by G. S. Hall, especially in light of the former's active endorsement of recapitulation theory in such seminal works as *Totem and Taboo* (Freud, 1961; first published in 1913), *Introductory Lectures on Psychoanalysis* (Freud, 1966; first published in 1916), and *Moses and Monotheism* (Freud, 1939), and the fact that Freud visited Hall in 1909, at the twentieth anniversary of Clark University (of which Hall was then president). This was the only time that Freud visited the United States, and it resulted in the establishment of a long-term correspondence between Hall and Freud (Freud, 1938). It appears that Freud was influenced by Darwin, at least in some respects; for example, he credited Darwin (along with the German philosopher and poet Goethe) for his decision to enter medical school (Schur, 1972). By his own account the theories and methods of both Darwin and Goethe inspired him (see, e.g., Jones, 1961).

Sulloway (1982) explored specifically the biological influences on Freud's theory of psychosexual development. Sulloway argued that Freud's former friend and colleague, Wilhelm Fliess (1858–1928) was instrumental in articulating the relevance of evolutionary theory to Freud. Again, like G. S. Hall, Freud was an adherent to Haeckel's recapitulation theory (the biogenetic law). Freud's endorsement of this law was in part a result of his early training as a biologist when this perspective was influential (Gould, 1977). Indeed, in his first year of medical school, Freud enrolled in a class on biology and Darwinism taught by Carl Claus, an adherent of Darwin and of Haeckel's theory (Schur, 1972). Although the biogenetic law was discredited as being justified more by Lamarckian than by Darwinian evolutionary theory (Gillispie, 1968; Lovejoy, 1968), Freud's developmental theories had already absorbed certain features. For example, Sulloway (1982) argued that the universal character of Freud's developmental theories can be attributed to his understanding of the biogenetic law. It was virtually impossible to abandon, even if he had wanted to, certain features of his theory that were influenced by biogenetic assumptions. Moreover, Sulloway (1982) asserted that it is possible

> to trace many of the most basic psychoanalytic concepts to Freud's prior thinking along biological lines. Included among these psychobiological aspects of Freudian theory are the notion of infantile sexuality, particularly its polymorphously perverse and periodic (schubweise) nature; the theory of erotogenic zones; sexual latency; sublimation; reaction formation; critical stages in psychosexual development; and the theories of fixation, regression, the death instinct, and organic repression. (p. 212)

In addition, Groffman (1970) pointed out that although it was Quetelet who helped make it clear that behavioral changes were, in part, a result of the interaction between the individual and his or her social and cultural context, it was psychoanalysis that brought this relation into focus in developmental research. It is worth noting that such a characterization of environment–organism interaction (minus the Lamarckian view of inheritance) is not antithetical to Darwin's evolutionary theory (Lerner, 1986). Certainly Freud adopted a developmental approach to understanding his preferred domain of psychological phenomena. In addition, psychoanalytic theory delineates two major mechanisms (fixation and regression) through which early events influence or determine later behavior (Cairns & Ornstein, 1979).

Another potential, albeit indirect, Darwinian connection may also exist in that Galton appears to have anticipated Freud in one important way. Galton (1883) described mental operations and incidents that may appear in childhood and then lie dormant for years, until roused to consciousness. Alternatively, permanent traces of these incidents may continually influence the development of mental operations throughout life. This notion, which appeared prior to Freud, bears a striking resemblance to Freud's theory of the unconscious. It should be noted, however, that the notion of the unconscious had been around at least since the time of the philosopher, Arthur Schopenhauer (1788–1860), with a major nineteenth-century work devoted to this topic appearing first in 1868 with several subsequent editions (Hartmann, 1931). One other indirect linkage between Darwin and Freud can be noted. It has been claimed that Darwin influenced Baldwin, who in turn influenced Janet and Piaget. As it happens, Freud is a minor figure in this equation, for he shared a direct intellectual ancestor with Janet. Both Freud and Janet studied under Jean Martin Charcot (1825–1893) in Paris (Flugel, 1933).

Groffman (1970, p. 61), following G. S. Hall and Lindzey (1957), viewed Freud's psychosexual theory of development as partly mechanistic and partly Darwinian: "[Freud's] theory of personality development was basically a theory of the development of the libido, which he attempted to explain in terms of both a phylogenetic and ontogenetic process." Significant events in the life course (or significant confrontations) disposed people to particular developmental paths.

One of Freud's early followers, Carl Jung, became one of his most distinguished critics, and one of the most notable contributors to psychoanalytic developmental theory. According to Havighurst (1973), "Disciples of Jung generally claim that his personality theory was more 'developmental' than that of Freud" (p. 19). Although Havighurst (correctly) disputed the developmental claim with regard to Jung—calling Jung's theories more a "philosophy of life than a theory of life-span development" (p. 61)—he did not question the aptness of the comparison. Jung's developmental psychology was more explicit, if not more refined, than Freud's.

Jung, criticizing both Freud's model of psychosexual development (as too reductionistic) and the Christian view of personal transformation (as lacking applicability to rational modern man), proposed an individuation process consisting of four stages. Based on this rather teleological perspective, such development has as its goal the emergence of self. Jung, taking an explicit life-course perspective and also adopting a recapitulation view, was seen by McCullers (1969) as more closely parallel to Hall than to Freud.

Like Freud, Jung was a lifelong supporter of recapitulation theory (Gould, 1977; Jung, 1916). For Jung, few psychopathologies were developed during the childhood period of recapitulation. As did Freud, Jung had a potential source of Darwinian thinking inculcated through a reliance on the work of Galton (Darwin's cousin). In his early work Jung employed the method of associative word reaction, which had been invented by Galton and Wundt (Flugel, 1933). Whereas the latter two researchers were primarily interested in intellectual factors related to word association, Jung demonstrated that the affective dimension was also influential.

Jung was one of several major revisionists of Freudian psychoanalytic theory. Other influential figures include Alfred Adler (1870–1937), Karen Horney (1885–1952), Eric Fromm (1900–1980), and Harry Stack Sullivan (1892–1949). Modern psychoanalytic views of development are represented by Erik Erikson (b. 1902), who developed a life-span theory of personality. His theory, revolving around a set of sequential psychosocial tasks (note again the confrontation between organism and environment), is also a stage theory (see Emmerich, 1968; Erikson, 1950, 1959). His organismically oriented views have begun to influence some conceptions of cognition in later adulthood. His view of wisdom, for example, suggests that wisdom is a virtue emerging after the successful mastery of earlier life tasks (Erikson, 1968). Although it is clearly clothed in developmental terms—because it may appear in earlier stages of life as an expression of the contingencies of that level of development—wisdom, like most concepts in the psychoanalytic model, is largely restricted to the realm of personal and emotional development. Nevertheless, Erikson's perspective has inspired some generalized inquiry into the cognitive aspects of wisdom and other such potentially progressive forms of adult development (e.g., Clayton & Birren, 1980). Much psychoanalytically inspired life-span developmental work has appeared in recent years. For example, both Levinson and colleagues (Levinson, Darrow, Klein, Levinson, & McKee, 1978) and Gould (1978) have made considerable progress in understanding the dynamics of personal change in adulthood.

Mechanism

The mechanistic model represents the organism as analogous to a machine in that it is composed of discrete parts interrelated by forces in a space–time field (see Overton & Reese, 1973; Pepper, 1942; Reese & Overton, 1970). Behavioral change or development depends on the level of stimulation, the kind of stimulation, and the history of the organism. The organism is seen as relatively passive (or reactive), whereas its environment is considered relatively active. In this way, behavioral functioning is a result more of environmental forces than of intrinsic (organismic, psychodynamic) causes. Moreover, behavioral change is more quantitative, additive, and continuous, than purposive, qualitative, and structural. The major figures in the progression of this model are shown in Row C of Fig. 1.1.

It is to Preyer (1882, 1893), Galton (1883), and Watson (1924, 1926) that the origin of the mechanistic view of the science of developmental psychology is usually traced. Preyer's 1882 German publication, later translated as *The Mind of the Child,* was the first book devoted to a systematic consideration of the development of the mental faculties of the child; and it is the one (despite its somewhat mixed reviews) to which responsibility for the advent of developmental psychology is often assigned (Eckardt, 1985; Hardesty, 1976; Reinert, 1979). Although he devoted much attention to patterns of physical development, Preyer also commented on such psychological phenomena as reflexes, language, spatial knowledge, and memory. Primarily a physiologist, Preyer was also influenced by extant work in psychoanalysis and evolutionary theory (Eckardt, 1985; Jaeger, 1982; Tobach, 1985). Late in his life, Preyer (1896) published a biography of Darwin, in which he extolled the discovery of the developmental method; that is, the attempt to understand current phenomena through an examination of the processes through which they came to be. The influence of evolutionary theory can be seen, however, not only in the developmental approach of his research, but also in the comparative methods he adopted. Preyer (1882) argued for intra-individual (longitudinal), interindividual (e.g., cross-sectional), and interspecies comparisons. The influence of the biology of the day can also be seen in Preyer's work insofar as it reflected consideration of several organismic features (e.g., maturational, nativistic thinking) as well as, to some extent, the biogenetic law. Some observers have argued that, because of his wide range of influences and writings, Preyer was not a "pure" mechanist (Eckardt, 1985). Although this may be accurate, it is important to note that incorporating variables normally associated with a different model of development does not in itself make him less a mechanist. In contrast to the early G. S. Hall, Preyer emphasized individual differences in child development (Tobach, 1985). In addition, as a function of his interest in psychophysics, Preyer attended to the role of stimulus-experience relations in child development. Furthermore, as Dennis (1972) noted, Preyer's method of response management anticipates much of the reinforcement theory of modern mechanistic psychology. Although Preyer (1893) upheld a basically voluntaristic position, the organism must exert some effort to overcome immediate environmental contingencies. Thus, development is viewed as a struggle for freedom or emancipation.

Darwin's influence on the work of his cousin Sir Francis Galton is quite apparent. Galton's investigations of individual differences in psychology form an intellectual bridge between Darwinian evolutionism and individual psychology. His well-known work on heredity (e.g., *Hereditary Genius,* first published in

1869) is one of the earliest scientific formulations of one of the basic issues of developmental psychology, the nature–nurture question (Galton, 1978). Galton's (1876) early study, in which he used twins in an attempt to disentangle nature and nurture influences, is still considered a classic. Galton's consuming interest in this issue, however, was practical as well as theoretical and thus led to the founding of *eugenics,* the applied science of heredity (Hearnshaw, 1964). In addition, his classic treatise on human development (Galton, 1883) contained an array of essays that anticipated both experimental and correlational developmental psychology (although some of his methods and statistics were apparently influenced by Quetelet). Galton's views on the predominance of nature (inheritance) over nurture in the development of mental trait was, according to Buss (1975), partly ascribable to the prevailing political orientation of the time, which, in effect, demanded a "nature" interpretation. As Bronfenbrenner and Crouter (1983) pointed out, Galton qualified carefully his nature-oriented conclusions. Indeed, Galton argued that nature is a more predominant influence than nurture only within a restricted range of environmental variation. Beyond that range, when more environmental factors are allowed to vary, nurture becomes considerably more influential (Bronfenbrenner & Crouter, 1983).

   G. S. Hall, who wrote the introduction to the American edition of Preyer's (1888) *The Mind of the Child,* placed considerable emphasis in his later work on environmental, especially social, factors in postchildhood behavioral ontogenesis. Thus, at separate points in the life span, nature *and* nurture components were incorporated into Hall's perspective. As a developmental psychologist, Hall lacked a systematic program of thought. In this respect he fits neither the mechanistic nor the organismic model perfectly. Hall's somewhat loose eclecticism is revealed by his simultaneous attachment to correlational, experimental, and psychoanalytic traditions, in addition to his a priori dedication to recapitulation theory (Cairns & Ornstein, 1979). Regarding the latter, Hall actually represents the peak of the influence of recapitulation theory in psychology; as it was being increasingly discredited in embryology, the foundation of its application to psychology was crumbling (Gould, 1977; Thorndike, 1904).

   Although John B. Watson is not normally identified as a developmental psychologist, he had a lasting impact on the emergence of behavioral (learning theory) developmental psychology. His atomistic, reductionistic framework (Watson, 1924) has a diminished influence on the contemporary scene, and his subsequent view of development as tantamount to cumulative learning (Watson, 1926) could hardly contrast more with the biological, organismic view of Baldwin and Piaget (Cairns & Ornstein, 1979). Further, Watson modified James' contextual interest in the stream of consciousness to a more empirical interest in stream of behavior (White, 1968).

   Today, the mechanistic tradition in developmental psychology is best represented by those adopting a behavior-analytic approach to studying change across life, as for example in the work of Donald M. Baer and Sidney W. Bijou (see

Reese, 1986, for a comparison of the Watsonian and Skinnerian views of behavioral psychology). The concepts, methods, and principles of behavior analysis (e.g., Skinner, 1953) were extended to child developmental psychology in a series of articles by Bijou and in a landmark text by Bijou and Baer (1961). As with all approaches to development, the behavior-analytic approach has evolved in the nearly 30 years since Bijou and Baer's (1961) seminal work (see the collection edited by Lipsitt & Cantor, 1986). Such evolution can be observed by consulting the more recent versions of child development textbooks (Bijou, 1976; Bijou & Baer, 1978), as well as recent theoretical statements (e.g., Bijou, 1979; Morris, 1982; Reese, 1986; Spiker, 1986). Morris and Hursh (1982) indicated that behavior-analytic developmentalists have become increasingly concerned with metatheoretical issues (e.g., Bijou, 1979; Skinner, 1974), and in this regard they have examined the usefulness of key developmental concepts and issues such as those pertinent to the nature of change (continuous), the usefulness of age (descriptive) as a variable in developmental research, model of the organism, and the role of the environment (Baer, 1970, 1973, 1976; Baltes & Lerner, 1980; Reese, 1980, 1986). Bijou (1979) appeared to distance the behavior-analytic approach from extreme positions on several issues fundamental to the mechanistic viewpoint. For example, he rejects both reductionism (explaining behavioral phenomena with, for instance, chemical phenomena) and a passive model of the organism. The rejection of a purely passive model of the organism is consistent with Skinnerian behaviorism (Reese, 1980, 1986; Skinner, 1974).

Despite the apparent movement toward the center among contemporary behavior analysts regarding developmental issues—and despite parallel movements among, for example, organicists—it is unlikely that harmonious relations between these two approaches will ever be established (Baer, 1982; Molenaar & Oppenheimer, 1985; Reese, 1982b). (Indeed, the philosopher Pepper, 1942, warned against eclecticism among the world views.) Clear differences exist on a number of fundamental issues and assumptions (Baer, 1982; Lerner, 1986). However, it is possible to note several similarities between the mechanistic behavioral-analytic approach to studying individual development and some aspects of the contextual model (see following section).

The behavior-analytic approach to development is not the only one that can be identified within contemporary developmental psychology as consistent with a mechanistic tradition. Current applications to life-span developmental psychology of both the operant approach and learning theory can be seen in Hoyer (1980). Current cognitive social learning approaches to development (e.g., Bandura, 1977; Mischel, 1977) also have features consistent with a mechanistic orientation. These latter positions have also been revised, and they now include ideas pertinent to reciprocal, person–context interaction models of development (Bandura, 1978). As such, these cognitive social learning approaches share common elements with contextualism.

Contextualism

Contextualism derives in part from such pragmatic philosophers as Charles S. Peirce, William James, John Dewey, and George Herbert Mead. The contextual model of psychology was also influenced by such functional psychologists as James Rowland Angell, Harvey Carr, and, of course, James and Dewey. Much of the formative activity occurred in the early part of this century, and thus contextualism, as a philosophical position, is quite advanced (Pepper, 1942). It has been recently revived in psychology (e.g., Rosnow & Georgoudi, 1986) and applied to such research areas as cognition and cognitive development (e.g., Dixon, 1986; Jenkins, 1974) and social and personality development (Blank, 1986; Lerner & Lerner, 1986; Sarbin, 1977). Its basic metaphor is change or the historic event. The individual and the social environment are viewed as mutually influential, acting upon one another in dynamic interaction. The proposed line of influence is presented in Fig. 1.1 (Row D).

William James was considerably influenced by Darwin's natural selection theory of evolution. James' (1890) psychology was nonreductionistic in character; that is, he argued against the analysis (or reduction) of complex mental events into primitive or elementary parts. Instead, experience consists of a stream of events, each of which possesses a unique quality or meaning. The novelty of each event is assured by the stream metaphor. The implication James developed was that the meaning or significance of a mental event is inseparable from the context of its occurrence, which is itself in flux. Development is continuous, "without breach, crack, or division" (1890, p. 237); it is composed of quantitative differences rather than qualitatively distinct stages. His approach to psychology may be characterized as historical in that "mental reaction on every given thing is really a resultant of our experience of the whole world up to that date" (1890, p. 234).

As had Darwin, James viewed the human mind as both dynamic (active) and functional, continuously involved in the process of adaptation to a changing ecology. Both James and Peirce sought to infuse the developmental stream (at the individual, phyletic, and cosmological levels) with the element of chance (e.g., Peirce's "tychism") so integral to the Darwinian hypothesis. Eschewing the directional or teleological focus of Lamarckian evolutionists and psychologists, these early contextualists sought to develop a generally nonteleological, Darwinian-based developmental method. According to the Darwinian interpretation, a chance event, while not wholly determined by the past, does reflect the character of preceding events (Russett, 1976). In this way, teleological characteristics are avoided, but both novelty and developmental continuity are maintained (James, 1977).

The concept of function was critical to the early contextual approach to psychology; indeed, this concept represents a clear conduit through which Darwinian thinking entered into American psychology. The biological version of this concept suggested that anatomical structures, shaped as they were by natural selection, functioned so as to further the survival of the organism (Ghiselin, 1969). Early contextualists applied this concept to psychology in a straightforward manner (Bawden, 1910; James, 1890; Wiener, 1949). The mind, they argued, is an "organ" selected for its utility in promoting the successful adaptation of the complex, changing human organism to the complex, changing environment. This approach to psychology is often dated to John Dewey's (1896) classic paper "The Reflex Arc Concept in Psychology." However, even in his earlier work in psychology, Dewey had already demonstrated a strong dynamic and practical orientation to the study of mental phenomena. In this earlier period, however, Dewey had cast developmental questions in the framework of a Hegelian *telos,* or necessary movement to a final end-state. But Dewey soon fell under the influence of Darwinism (see Dewey, 1910) and his subsequent psychological writings stressed the developmental method, the continuous model of developmental change, as well as the Darwinian view of the dynamic organism–environment transaction (Russett, 1976). Like James, Dewey offered a relatively active organism (and active environment) model of this transaction. Finally, like so many of the early figures we have discussed, Dewey (1910) attributed the discovery of the historical (or developmental) method to Darwin.

No modern contextual developmental psychologist has produced a system as complete as that of James and his colleagues. Certainly, with the exception of areas pertinent to language development, Peirce and Mead have not had a major effect on contemporary developmental psychology. Indeed, with the exception of the work of F. C. Bartlett (1932) and perhaps Vygotsky (1934/1962), a dialectician (discussed later) who at least cited James, contextual developmental psychology appears to have lain dormant for several decades. However, several prominent psychologists, normally associated with other models, espoused some tenets of contextualism. For example, Reese (1986) argued that Skinner's (e.g., 1974) philosophy of science is pragmatic (contextual), even though the model of the organism is mechanistic. Other notable mechanists/contextualists are J. R. Kantor (1888–1984) and E. C. Tolman (1886–1959). On the other hand, Lerner (1986) has linked contextualism to organicism and thus to such organicists as Werner (1948). Nevertheless, numerous psychologists have recently rediscovered contextual thinking and have attempted to articulate its methodological implications (Beilin, 1984; Bronfenbrenner, 1977; Bruce, 1985; Dixon & Hertzog, in press; Dixon & Nesselroade, 1983; Hultsch & Pentz, 1980; Jenkins, 1974; Lerner et al., 1983; Petrinovich, 1979; Sarbin, 1977).

At the risk of oversimplification, psychological development for the contextual psychologist is portrayed as a continuing, adaptive lifelong process, related to other internal or mental processes, and interacting with external activities and sociohistorical processes. In principle, both the internal and external conditions of behavioral ontogenesis are examined with respect to a given psychological process. A corresponding interest is evident in examining a dependent measure in conditions approximating those that occur in the natural ecology of the individual. This interest has resulted in a concern for such attendant methodological issues as ecological representativeness and external validity (Bronfenbrenner, 1977; Hultsch & Hickey, 1978). Put simply, in the assessment of psychological development, it is both theoretically and methodologically profitable to use measures that are representative of (or drawn from) the population of related psychological activities that individuals could encounter in their everyday lives. In this respect, performances on experimental tasks may be generalized to cognitive adaptiveness and efficiency in the familiar ecology of the individual.

With a slightly different emphasis, Sarbin (1977) has adapted the dramaturgical model of G. H. Mead (1934), one of the important figures in the development of contextualism. Assuming that individuals carry on their activities and interactions in an episodic, changing way, Sarbin argued for an *emplotment* methodology. That is, Sarbin suggested that psychologists develop a taxonomy of plots; action is temporal, occurring in historical, concurrent, and future contexts. Further examples of the appplication of contextualism to personality development may be found in the collection edited by Rosnow and Georgoudi (1986). For example, Lerner and Lerner (1986) describe a contextual goodness-of-fit model of child temperament development, and Blank (1986) describes a contextual approach to adult social development. With regard to cognition, Jenkins (1974) arqued for a contextual approach (reminiscent of both William James and F. C. Bartlett) to memory research. According to this view, a memory is not an item, a thing, or a spot in the cortex (all of which appear in some alternative accounts); nor is memory separable from other processes, much less the environment (as some accounts often suggest); rather, "what memory is depends on context" (Jenkins, 1974, p. 786). As the context is ever-changing, so is the memory. Several other researchers have explored the relevance of a contextual approach to life-span cognitive development (e.g., Bruce, 1985; Dixon, 1986; Dixon & Hertzog, in press; Neisser, 1978). In sum, contextualism turns attention not only to the external context of psychological development, but also to the internal context (e.g., affective processes, motivation, other skills or schemata). It especially focuses attention on the coordination or interaction of these aspects of the organism, and on opportunities for and constraints on change promoted by both organism and context (Lerner, 1986; Lerner & Kauffman, 1985).

Dialecticism

The dialectical materialism of the nineteenth century has significantly influenced one modern approach to developmental psychology. Under the contemporary dialectical model, the basic metaphor appears to be contradiction or conflict (Riegel, 1975, 1976; see also collection edited by Datan & Reese, 1977). As with the contextual model, the activities of the individual are here viewed as being in dynamic interaction with the activities of the environment. Some dialecticians represent the individual, like the society, as developing through a continuous process of thesis, antithesis, and synthesis (Wozniak, 1975a, 1975b). This perspective emphasizes the continuing nature of change, as well as the fact that change occurs at multiple levels (Reese, 1982a; Riegel, 1975, 1976; Tolman, 1983; Vygotsky, 1978). Thus the interactional nature of individual and social development becomes a prime concern (Lerner, 1978; Overton, 1973; Riegel & Meacham, 1976). In addition, the dialectical model generally represents both the organism and the environment as inherently active. A schematic representation of the line of influence is presented in Row E of Fig. 1.1.

Although neither Hegel nor Marx proposed a specific program of individual development, their views on both ideational and social change have been adapted for the individual psychological level. Hegel was unquestionably an influence on Marx, although in certain respects his ideas were rejected by the much younger revolutionary. The important point of commonality between them is the dialectic itself. The influence of Darwin on Marx is difficult to assess completely, but some writers have suggested that Marx wanted to dedicate *Das Kapital* to the evolutionist (Berlin, 1978; but see also Fay, 1978). Further, it is known that Marx warmly inscribed a copy of the second edition of his magnum opus to Darwin (Huxley & Kettlewell, 1965). And Marx's own intellectual companion, Friederich Engels (1820–1895), portrayed a certain intellectual kinship between Darwin and Marx in his notes read at the latter's graveside. Several of Marx's letters to Engels in the years immediately following the 1859 publication of Darwin's *Origins* indicated that he believed evolutionary thinking to be consonant with his own dialectical materialism (see Padover, 1978).

In some respects, however, Marx's own evolutionism may have more closely resembled Spencer's or Lamarck's than Darwin's. For example, unlike Darwin's view of development, Marx wrote occasionally as though social change was directed toward an ultimate endstate, and as though development occurred in a revolutionary rather than evolutionary manner. Nevertheless, both Darwin and Marx shared a concern, emerging on multiple fronts in the nineteenth century, with a historical and developmental perspective. It is this shared fundamental concern that forms a critical link between the two. This focus on change entailed developmental methods. It may not be widely known by students of developmental psychology that Marx believed his theory to be scientific, and strongly supported enlightened empirical enquiry.

After the Bolshevik revolution in 1917, dialectical psychology in the Soviet Union burgeoned. The most influential of these dialetical developmentalists was Vygotsky (1929, 1934/1962, 1978). Through such junior colleagues as A. R. Luria (e.g., Luria, 1971, 1976, 1979) and A. N. Leontiev (e.g., Leontiev, 1978; Leontiev & Luria, 1968), a dialectical approach to psychology developed. Several features of this approach are notable. For example, it inherited from Marxism a strongly developmental approach and a focus on individual activity (e.g., Leontiev, 1978). It may also be characterized as sociocultural in that it attends closely to the impact of cultural change (and extant cultural differences) on individual development (e.g., Luria, 1976). Luria (1979) recounts his own view on the emergence of many of these ideas in his history of Soviet psychology. (As discussed earlier, Vygotsky also influenced contextual developmental psychology.)

For both intellectual and political reasons, dialectical developmental psychology was not until recently a noticeable, much less a prominent, force on the American scene (Riegel, 1972). Thus, there is little explicit linkage between Soviet and American developmental psychology until after the mid-twentieth century. The leading figure in contemporary developmental dialectics was Klaus Riegel (e.g., 1979). Wozniak (1975a, 1975b) has described the following three laws of developmental change based on Marxist dialectics: (a) the unity and opposition of contradictory principles; (b) the possibility of transforming quantitative change into qualitative change and vice versa; and (c) the negation of a negation. Developmental psychology is viewed dialectically as the study of the changing individual in a changing world (Riegel & Meacham, 1976). As with the historical methods of Marx's dialectical materialism, the utility of the methods involved in a dialectical approach to the study of human development, insofar as they vary from more traditional methods, is an issue deserving further attention. Several efforts have been made to examine the implications of this approach for psychological research (e.g., see the collections edited by Datan & Reese, 1977; Hultsch, 1980). The implications of Soviet psychology for cross-cultural developmental research have been articulated by Michael Cole and colleagues (e.g., Cole, Gay, Glick, & Sharp, 1971; Laboratory of Comparative Human Cognition, 1983). In this research the cultural relativism of developmental patterns is emphasized.

Summary

Contemporary developmental psychology is marked by a diversity of theoretical systems that are nevertheless linked by a common intellectual heritage. The contemporary scene in developmental psychology is not a static one. Indeed, to illustrate this dynamism, we turn now to a discussion of one currently central perspective, an orientation which not only reflects a concern for the developmental tradition but which, as well, represents a concern with the major issues of development (such as nature–nurture) brought to the fore by the diversity of theoretical systems present in contemporary developmental psychology. The perspective on which we focus in the next section is the life-span view of human development.

THE LIFE-SPAN PERSPECTIVE WITHIN
CONTEMPORARY DEVELOPMENTAL PSYCHOLOGY

Earlier, we noted that the developmental "tradition," promoted by the contributions of evolutionary theory and the historical perspective of the nineteenth century stresses the necessity of knowing something about an organism's history in order to understand the organism's present situation or behavior. Although the developmental tradition is present (albeit in different ways) in each of the five models we have discussed, there arose in the late 1960s a "life-span perspective" of development that not only emphasized this developmental approach, but also constituted an attempt to integrate compatible ideas derived from the several models we have discussed.

Many writers within the current life-span orientation (e.g., Dixon, 1986; Dixon & Baltes, 1986; Lerner, 1984, 1986) note the links between evolutionary thinking and the set of concepts found within this perspective. However, these writers note as well that this theoretical influence does not necessarily imply that the features of an individual's development across life are entirely the product of Darwinian mechanisms (e.g., natural selection). Especially in the postreproductive mature adult and aged years, it may be the social context (which is shaped by evolving social institutions and cultural conditions) that provides primary impetus for the content and direction of life-span change (Featherman & Lerner, 1985; Lerner, 1984). The consequence of our evolutionary heritage is to have the potential for a period of life—indeed, a relatively extensive one—extending beyond the point of reproduction; however it is the social context, involving such elements as medical technology and institutional support for the health and welfare of the person, which across history has allowed the evolutionary potential for plasticity of functioning into late adulthood to be realized. Thus, social interactional factors supplement biological ones to provide the breadth and content of the human life course. This emphasis underscores the link between the life-span perspective we discuss in this section and the evolutionary thinking just described. Once again the notion of organism–environment interaction is emphasized.

What is the life-span perspective? It should be noted immediately that it does not constitute a theory, a collection of theories, or a metatheory of development; rather, it offers a perspective on psychology based on the proposition that the changes (growth, development, aging) shown by people from the time of their conception, throughout their lives, and until the time of their death are usefully conceptualized as developmental (Baltes, Reese, & Lipsitt, 1980). This developmental conceptualization can occur without necessarily prejudging several fundamental assumptions and conceptual issues on which the models of development clearly differ.

The point of view currently labeled as "life-span developmental psychology"

34

or as the "life-span view of human development" (Baltes, 1979; Baltes et al., 1980) became crystallized as a set of interrelated ideas about the nature of human development and change. In their combination, these ideas present a set of implications for theory building, for methodology, and for scientific collaboration across disciplinary boundaries. There are perhaps two key propositions or assumptions of the life-span perspective. These have been labeled *embeddedness* and *dynamic interaction* (Lerner, 1986). From these propositions an interrelated set of implications may be derived, and these propositions and implications constitute the key concepts in current life-span thinking.

The idea of embeddedness is that the key phenomena of human life exist at multiple levels of being (e.g., the inner-biological, individual-psychological, dyadic, social network, community, societal, cultural, outer-ecological, and historical). Thus, at any one point in time variables from any and all of these levels may contribute to human functioning. However, the reason it is important to have a perspective about human development that is sensitive to the influences of these multiple levels is that the levels do not function as independent domains; rather, the variables at one level influence and are influenced by the variables at the other levels. In other words, there is a dynamic interaction among levels of analysis. As such, each level may be a product and a producer of functioning and change at other levels (Lerner, 1986).

How can the dynamic interaction between person and environment emphasized in the life-span perspective be explained? Baltes et al. (1980) suggest three major influence patterns that affect this relationship: (a) normative age-graded influences; (b) normative history-graded influences; and (c) non-normative, life-event influences. Normative age-graded influences consist of biological and environmental determinants that are correlated with chronological age. They are normative to the extent that their timing, duration, and clustering are similar for many individuals. Examples include maturational events, such as menarche and the initiation of the growth spurt, and socialization events, such as entrance into parenthood. Normative history-graded influences consist of biological and environmental processes occurring at a particular historical time. They are normative to the extent that they are experienced by most members of a cohort. In this sense they tend to define the developmental context of a given cohort. Examples include historical events (epidemics and periods of economic depression or prosperity) and sociocultural evolution (changes in sex-role expectations, the educational system, and child-rearing practices). Several contributions to a collection edited by McCluskey and Reese (1984) explore the conceptual and methodological issues involved in research on such topics and describe the present state of empirical evidence. Both age-graded and history-graded influences covary with time. Non-normative, life-event influences (e.g., accidents, sudden illnesses)—the third system—are not directly indexed by time because they do not occur for all people, or even for most people. In addition, when non-normative influences do occur, they are likely to differ across people in terms of their clustering, timing, and duration. Examples of non-normative events relevant to life-span development include such items as illness, divorce, or death of a spouse.

Baltes et al. (1980) have speculated that these three sources of influence exhibit different profiles over the life cycle. Normative age-graded influences may be particularly significant in childhood and early adolescence, and again in old age, whereas normative history-graded influences are thought to be more important throughout adolescence and the years immediately following it; this is believed to reflect the importance of the sociocultural context as the individual begins adult life. Finally, non-normative, life-event influences are postulated to be particularly significant during middle adulthood and old age, reflecting increasing diversity among individuals produced by each person's experience of unique life events.

In summary, two key assumptions of the life-span perspective—embeddedness and dynamic interactionism—suggest, first, that individual developmental phenomena occur in the context of the developmental and nondevelopmental changes at other levels of analysis; second, the assumptions suggest that developments and/or changes on one level both influence and are influenced by developments and/or changes at these other levels. There are at least three major implications of these ideas.

First, the potential for plasticity indicates that changes at one level are reciprocally dependent on changes at other levels. This suggests that there is always some possibility for altering the status of a variable or process at any or all levels of analysis. However, we must emphasize that this potential for plasticity is not construed by life-span developmentalists to mean that there are no limits or constraints on change. For instance, by virtue of its structural organization, a system delimits the range of changes it may undergo and such a structural constraint holds for any level of analysis. In addition, the possibility that developmental and nondevelopmental phenomena at one point in life may influence functioning at later points is explicitly recognized by life-span developmentalists in the concept of developmental embeddedness (Lerner, 1986). Second, the potential for intervention derives from the plasticity of developmental processes. Given potential plasticity, it follows that means may be designed to prevent, ameliorate, or enhance undesired or nonvalued developments or behavior. Third, the person as a producer of his or her own development suggests that any level of analysis can influence phenomena at other levels of analysis. For individual psychological development this means that people may affect the social or physical context that affects them (Lerner, 1986).

The life-span perspective is often associated with a call for interdisciplinary research on human development. That is, attempts have been made to integrate ideas from the many disciplines involved in the study of human lives (e.g., anthropology, biology, sociology). The generality of the perspective—its tolerance for multiple metatheoretical positions and methodological approaches—promotes openness to such interdisciplinary contact and sometimes generates ambiguity and controversy (Dannefer, 1984). Lifelong change occurs on multiple levels of analysis (e.g., biological, psychological, social), and changes on one level often influence changes on other levels. The life-span psychologist argues that, given this complex set of change patterns, the student of human development is well served by collegial contact with neighboring disciplines.

Although the life-span perspective is often dated to the late 1960s, a number of historical observers (e.g., Baltes, 1979; Dixon & Nesselroade, 1983; Havighurst, 1973) have identified instances of precursors from much earlier periods: for example, the aforementioned Tetens (1777), Carus (1808), and Quetelet (1835). In the early twentieth century contributions from both Europe and the United States are noteworthy: for example, Sanford (1902); Hall (1922); Hollingworth (1927); Bühler (1933); and Pressey, Janney, and Kuhlen (1939). Work conducted by the Committee on Human Development at the University of Chicago (e.g., Havighurst, 1948; Neugarten, 1964; Neugarten & Guttman, 1958) was quite influential in bringing a multidisciplinary perspective to the study of individual and social development across life.

As interest burgeoned in multidisciplinary perspectives and, in particular, problems of adult development and aging, new theoretical (e.g., Baltes, in press; Lerner, 1986) and methodological (e.g., Baltes et al., 1979; Nesselroade & Baltes, 1979) advances were required. The nature of the life-span orientation has become somewhat clearer through the publication of several conference proceedings, symposia, and a series of annual volumes, as well as numerous empirical and theoretical papers (e.g., Baltes, in press; Baltes et al., 1980). For example, an annual series of conferences at West Virginia University on conceptual, methodological, and empirical issues has been held since 1969 (e.g., Baltes & Schaie, 1973; Datan & Ginsberg, 1975; Datan & Reese, 1977; McCluskey & Reese, 1984; Nesselroade & Reese, 1973). The annual research series, *Life-Span Development and Behavior,* edited by Paul B. Baltes and colleagues (Orville G. Brim, Jr., David L. Featherman, and Richard M. Lerner), began publication in 1978 (e.g., Baltes, 1978; Baltes & Brim, 1984; Baltes, Featherman, & Lerner, 1986). Perhaps the greatest testimony to its impact is that not only do numerous contributors to these and other volumes come from disciplines other than psychology, but that the following summary of this perspective applies as well to most of the other chapters in this particular textbook. The summary is: From the life-span perspective, the potential for developmental change is seen to be present across all of life; the human life course is held to be potentially multidirectional and necessarily multidimensional. In addition, the sources of the potentially continual changes across life are seen to involve both inner-biological and outer-ecological levels of the context within which the organism is embedded. Indeed, although it is an orientation *to* the study of development rather than a specific theory *of* development (Baltes, 1979), life-span developmental psychology is disposed to a reciprocal model of organism–context relations. In this way, it establishes and maintains contact with such neighboring fields as life-course sociology.

CONCLUSIONS

Developmental psychology has come to be characterized by an emphasis on explanation and process, and by a concern with several theoretical systems and their philosophical bases. We have described how from a common intellectual source—nineteenth–century evolutionary theory and historical perspectives—numerous figures drew sustenance and then turned to face the fresh demands of their own context. These demands were sufficiently varied to propagate views about human development that today appear mutually distinct. Perhaps one of the greatest contributions of evolutionary theory to the emergence of developmental psychology derives from its accentuation of the underlying general issues pertaining to ontogeny. Among these abiding problems are such classical polarities as nature versus nurture (Lerner, 1978), continuity versus discontinuity of development (Brim & Kagan, 1980), and unidirectionality versus non- or multi-directionality of temporal progression (Lerner, 1986). All of these are addressed throughout this volume.

It is reasonable to assert that the structure of the five major contemporary developmental metatheories described in this chapter cut across these salient issues in qualitatively different ways. Thus, contemporary developmental theories may share a certain intellectual lineage, embrace a generalized historical or developmental approach to human phenomena, and at the same time represent relatively distinct metatheoretical positions, resulting in relatively specific methods and unique interpretations of data.

ACKNOWLEDGMENT

This chapter has been revised to reflect the historical coverage of an earlier chapter of the same title in the first edition of this volume (by the present authors), and to summarize the contemporary life-span movement as covered in another chapter of the same volume, *The Life-span Perspective in Developmental Psychology* (by Baltes and Reese). The present chapter benefited from several valuable discussions with Paul B. Baltes and from careful commentaries on previous drafts by Hayne W. Reese. The authors wish to thank also Marc Bornstein and Michael Lamb for their many helpful suggestions on an earlier draft. Richard M. Lerner's work on this chapter was supported in part by grants from the William T. Grant Foundation and by NIMH grant MH29957.

REFERENCES

Anderson, J. E. (1956). Child development: An historical perspective. *Child Development, 27,* 181–196.

Angell, J. R. (1912). *Chapters from modern psychology.* New York: Longmans, Green.

Baer, D. M. (1970). An age-irrelevant concept of development. *Merrill-Palmer Quarterly, 16,* 238–245.

Baer, D. M. (1973). The control of developmental process: Why wait? In J. R. Nesselroade & H. W. Reese (Eds.), *Life-span developmental psychology: Methodological issues.* New York: Academic Press.

Baer, D. M. (1976). The organism as host. *Human Development, 19,* 87–98.

Baer, D. M. (1982). Behavior analysis and developmental psychology: Discussant comments. *Human Development, 25,* 357–361.

Baldwin, A. L. (1980). *Theories of child development* (2nd ed.). New York: Wiley.

Baldwin, J. M. (1895). *Mental development in the child and the race.* New York: Macmillan.

Baldwin, J. M. (1906). *Mental development in the child and the race: Methods and processes* (2nd ed.). New York: Macmillan.

Baldwin, J. M. (1909). *Darwin and the humanities.* Baltimore: Review Publishing.

Baldwin, J. M. (1913). *History of psychology: A sketch and interpretation: (Vol. 2). From Locke to the present time.* London: Watts.

Baldwin, J. M. [Autobiography]. (1930). In C. Murchison (Ed.), *A history of psychology in autobiography* (Vol. 1). Worcester, MA: Clark University Press.

Baltes, M. M., & Lerner, R. M. (1980). Roles of the operant model and its methods in the life-span approach to human development. *Human Development, 23,* 362–367.

Baltes, P. B., & Brim, O. G., Jr. (Eds.). (1984). *Life-span development and behavior* (Vol. 6). Orlando: Academic Press.

Baltes, P. B. (1979). Life-span developmental psychology: Some converging observations on history and theory. In P. B. Baltes & O. G. Brim, Jr. (Eds.), *Life-span development and behavior* (Vol. 2). New York: Academic Press.

Baltes, P. B. (1983). Life-span developmental psychology: Observations on history and theory revisited. In R. M. Lerner (Ed.), *Developmental psychology: Historical and philosophical perspectives.* Hillsdale, NJ: Lawrence Erlbaum Associates.

Baltes, P. B. (in press). Theoretical propositions of life-span developmental psychology: On the dynamics between growth and decline. *Developmental Psychology.*

Baltes, P. B., & Brim, O. G., Jr. (Eds.). (1984). *Life-span development and behavior* (Vol. 6). Orlando: Academic Press.

Baltes, P. B., & Cornelius, S. W. (1977). The status of dialectics in developmental psychology: Theoretical orientation versus scientific method. In N. Datan & H. W. Reese (Eds.), *Life-span developmental psychology: Dialectical perspectives in experimental research.* New York: Academic Press.

Baltes, P. B., Featherman, D. L., & Lerner, R. M. (Eds.). (1986). *Life-span development and behavior* (Vol. 7). Hillsdale, NJ: Lawrence Erlbaum Associates.

Baltes, P. B., & Nesselroade, J. R. (1984). Paradigm lost and paradigm regained: Critique of Dannefer's portrayal of life-span developmental psychology. *American Sociological Review, 49,* 841–847.

Baltes, P. B., Reese, H. W., & Lipsitt, L. P. (1980). Life-span developmental psychology. *Annual Review of Psychology, 31,* 65–110.

Baltes, P. B., Reese, H. W., & Nesselroade, J. R. (1977). *Life-span developmental psychology: Introduction to research methods.* Monterey, CA: Brooks/Cole.

Baltes, P. B., & Schaie, K. W. (1973). *Life-span developmental psychology: Personality and socialization.* New York: Academic Press.

Bandura, A. (1977). *Social learning theory*. Englewood Cliffs, NJ: Prentice-Hall.

Bandura, A. (1978). The self system in reciprocal determinism. *American Psychologist, 33*, 344–358.

Bartlett, F. C. (1932). *Remembering*. Cambridge: Cambridge University Press.

Bawden, H. H. (1910). *The principles of pragmatism: A philosphical interpretation of experience*. Boston: Houghton Mifflin.

Beilin, H. (1984). Functionalist and structuralist research programs in developmental psychology: Incommensurability or synthesis? In H. W. Reese (Ed.), *Advances in child development and behavior* (Vol. 18). Orlando: Academic Press.

Berlin, I. (1978). *Karl Marx: His life and his environment* (4th ed.). Oxford: Oxford University Press.

Bijou, S. W. (1976). *Child Development: The basic stage of early childhood*. Englewood Cliffs, NJ: Prentice-Hall.

Bijou, S. W. (1979). Some clarifications on the meaning of a behavior analysis of child development. *Psychological Record, 29*, 3–13.

Bijou, S. W., & Baer, D. M. (1961). *Child development, Vol. I: A systematic and empirical theory*. New York: Appleton-Century-Crofts.

Bijou, S. W., & Baer, D. M. (1978). *Child development: A behavior analysis approach*. Englewood Cliffs, NJ: Prentice-Hall.

Blank, T. O. (1986). Contextual and relational perspectives on adult psychology. In R. L. Rosnow & M. L. Georgoudi (Eds.), *Contextualism and understanding in behavioral science*. New York: Praeger.

Borstelmann, L. J. (1983). Children before psychology: Ideas about children from antiquity to the late 1800s. In P. H. Mussen & W. Kessen (Eds.), *Handbook of child psychology: Vol. 1. History, theory, and methods*. New York: Wiley.

Brainerd, C. J. (1978). The stage question in cognitive-developmental theory. *The Behavioral and Brain Sciences, 2*, 173–182.

Braunshvig, M., & Braunshvig, G. (1913). *Notre enfant: Journal d'un père et d'une mère* [Our child: Journal of a father and a mother]. Paris: Hachette.

Brent, S. B. (1978). Individual specialization, collective adaptation and rate of environmental change. *Human Development, 21*, 21–33.

Brim, O. G., Jr., & Kagan, J. (1980). Constancy and change: A view of the issues. In O. G. Brim, Jr., & J. Kagan (Eds.), *Constancy and change in human development*. Cambridge, MA: Harvard University Press.

Bronfenbrenner, U. (1963). Development theory in transition. In H. W. Stevenson (Ed.), *Child psychology. Sixty-second yearbook of the National Society for the Study of Education, part 1*. Chicago: University of Chicago Press.

Bronfenbrenner, U. (1977). Toward an experimental ecology of human development. *American Psychologist, 32*, 513–531.

Bronfenbrenner, U., & Crouter, A. C. (1983). The evolution of environmental models in developmental research. In P. H. Mussen & W. Kessen (Eds.), *Handbook of child psychology: Vol. 1. History, theory, and methods*. New York: Wiley.

Broughton, J. M. (1981). The genetic psychology of James Mark Baldwin. *American Psychologist, 36*, 396–407.

Broughton, J. M., & Freeman-Moir, D. J. (Eds.). (1982). *The cognitive-developmental psychology of James Mark Baldwin*. Norwood, NJ: Ablex.

Bruce, D. (1985). The how and why of ecological memory. *Journal of Experimental Psychology: General, 114*, 78–90.

Bühler, C. (1930). *The first year of life*. New York: John Day.

Bühler, C. (1933). *Der menschliche Lebenslauf als psychologisches Problem*. [The human life course as a psychological problem]. Leipzig: Hirzel.

Buss, A. R. (1975). The emerging field of the sociology of psychological knowledge. *American Psychologist, 30,* 988–1002.

Butterworth, G., Rutkowska, J., & Scaife, M. (Eds.). (1985). *Evolution and developmental psychology.* New York: St. Martin's.

Cahan, E. D. (1984). The genetic psychologies of James Mark Baldwin and Jean Piaget. *Developmental Psychology, 20,* 128–135.

Cairns, R. B. (1980). Developmental theory before Piaget: The remarkable contributions of James Mark Baldwin. *Contemporary Psychology, 25,* 438–440.

Cairns, R. B. (1983). The emergence of developmental psychology. In P. H. Mussen & W. Kessen (Eds.), *Child psychology: Vol. 1. History, theory, and methods.* New York: Wiley.

Cairns, R. B., & Ornstein, P. A. (1979). Developmental psychology. In E. Hearst (Ed.), *The first century of experimental psychology.* Hillsdale, NJ: Lawrence Erlbaum Associates.

Carus, F. A. (1808). *Psychologie. Zweiter Theil: Specialpsychologie.* [Psychology. Second part: Differential psychology.] Leipzig: Barth & Kummer.

Cavanaugh, J. C. (1981). Early developmental theories: A brief review of attempts to organize developmental data prior to 1925. *Journal of the History of the Behavioral Sciences, 17,* 38–47.

Champneys, E. H. (1881). Notes on an infant. *Mind, 6,* 104–107.

Charles, D. C. (1970). Historical antecedents of life-span developmental psychology. In L. R. Goulet & P. B. Baltes (Eds.), *Life-span developmental psychology: Research and theory.* New York: Academic Press.

Charlesworth, W. R. (1986). Darwin and developmental psychology: 100 years later. *Human Development, 29,* 1–4.

Clayton, V. P., & Birren, J. E. (1980). The development of wisdom across the life span: A reexamination of an ancient topic. In P. B. Baltes & O. G. Brim, Jr. (Eds.), *Life-span development and behavior* (Vol. 3). New York: Academic Press.

Cole, M., Gay, J., Glick, J. A., & Sharp, D. W. (1971). *The cultural context of learning and thinking.* New York: Basic Books.

Collingwood, R. G. (1956). *The idea of history.* London: Oxford University Press.

Costall, A. (1986). Evolutionary gradualism and the study of development. *Human Development, 29,* 4–11.

Dannefer, D. (1984). Adult development and social theory: A paradigmatic reappraisal. *American Sociological Review, 49,* 100–116.

Darwin, C. (1859). *On the origin of species.* London: John Murray.

Darwin, C. (1871). *Descent of man.* London: John Murray.

Darwin, C. (1872). *The expression of emotions in man and animals.* London: John Murray.

Darwin, C. (1877). Biographical sketch of an infant. *Mind, 2,* 285–294.

Datan, N., & Ginsberg, L. H. (Eds.). (1975). *Life-span developmental psychology: Normative life crisis.* New York: Academic Press.

Datan, N., & Reese, H. W. (Eds.). (1977). *Life-span developmental psychology: Dialectical perspectives on experimental research.* New York: Academic Press.

Dennis, W. (1949). Historical beginnings of child psychology. *Psychological Bulletin, 46,* 224–235.

Dennis, W. (Ed.). (1951). *Readings in child psychology.* New York: Prentice-Hall.

Dennis, W. (Ed.). (1972). *Historical readings in developmental psychology.* New York: Appleton-Century-Crofts.

Dewey, J. (1896). The reflex arc concept in psychology. *Psychological Review, 3,* 357–370.

Dewey, J. (1910). The influence of Darwinism on philosophy. In J. Dewey (Ed.), *The influence of Darwin on philosophy and other essays on contemporary thought.* New York: Henry Holt.

Dixon, R. A. (1986). Contextualism and life-span developmental psychology. In R. L. Rosnow & M. Georgoudi (Eds.), *Contextualism and understanding in behavioral science.* New York: Praeger.

Dixon, R. A., & Baltes, P. B. (1986). Toward life-span research on the functions and pragmatics of intelligence. In R. J. Sternberg & R. K. Wagner (Eds.), *Practical intelligence: Nature and origins of competence in the everyday world*. Cambridge: Cambridge University Press.

Dixon, R. A., & Hertzog, C. (in press). A functional approach to memory and metamemory development in adulthood. In F. E. Weinert & M. Perlmutter (Eds.), *Memory development across the life span: Universal changes and individual differences*. Hillsdale, NJ: Lawrence Erlbaum Associates.

Dixon, R. A., & Lerner, R. M. (1985). Darwinism and the emergence of developmental psychology. In G. Eckhardt, W. G. Bringmann, & L. Sprung (Eds.), *Contributions to a history of developmental psychology*. Berlin: Mouton.

Dixon, R. A., & Nesselroade, J. R. (1983). Pluralism and correlational analysis in developmental psychology: Historical commonalities. In R. M. Lerner (Ed.), *Developmental psychology: Historical and philosophical perspectives*. Hillsdale, NJ: Lawrence Erlbaum Associates.

Dollard, J., Doob, L. W., Miller, N. E., Mowrer, O. H., & Sears, R. R. (1939). *Frustration and aggression*. New Haven: Yale University Press.

Eckardt, G. (1985). Preyer's road to child psychology. In G. Eckardt, W. G. Bringmann, & L. Sprung (Eds.), *Contributions to a history of developmental psychology*. Berlin: Mouton.

Eiseley, L. (1958). *Darwin's century*. Garden City, NY: Doubleday.

Emmerich, W. (1968). Personality development and concepts of structure. *Child Development, 39,* 671–690.

English, H. B. (1950). Child psychology. In J. P. Guilford (Ed.), *Fields of psychology: Basic and applied*. Princeton, NJ: D. Van Nostrand.

Erikson, E. H. (1950). *Childhood and society*. New York: Norton.

Erikson, E. H. (1959). Identity and the life cycle. *Psychological Issues, I,* whole volume.

Erikson, E. H. (1968). *Identity, youth and crisis*. New York: Norton.

Evans, R. I. (1973). *Jean Piaget: The man and his ideas*. New York: Dutton.

Fast, I. (1985). *Event theory: A Piaget-Freud integration*. Hillsdale, NJ: Lawrence Erlbaum Associates.

Fay, M. A. (1978). Did Marx offer to dedicate *Capital* to Darwin? *Journal of the History of Ideas, 39,* 133–146.

Featherman, D. L., & Lerner, R. M. (1985). Ontogenesis and sociogenesis: Problematics for theory and research about development and socialization across the life span. *American Sociological Review, 50,* 659–676.

Flavell, J. H. (1963). *The developmental psychology of Jean Piaget*. Princeton, NJ: C. Van Nostrand.

Flavell, J. H., & Ross, L. (Eds.). (1981). *Social cognitive development: Frontiers and possible futures*. Cambridge: Cambridge University Press.

Flugel, J. C. (1933). *A hundred years of psychology*. New York: Macmillan.

Frank, L. K. (1935). The problem of child development. *Child Development, 6,* 7–18.

Frank, L. K. (1962). The beginnings of child development and family life education in the twentieth century. *Merrill-Palmer Quarterly, 8,* 207–227.

Freud, S. (1910). The origin and development of psychoanalysis. *The American Journal of Psychology, 21,* 181–218.

Freud, S. (1938). The history of the psychoanalytical movement. In A. A. Brill (Ed. and trans.), *The basic writings of Sigmund Freud*. New York: Random House.

Freud, S. (1939). *Moses and monotheism*. (K. Jones Trans.). New York: Knopf.

Freud, S. (1954). *Collected works, standard edition*. London: Hogarth Press.

Freud, S. (1961). *Totem and taboo*. (J. Strachey Trans.). London: Routledge & Paul.

Freud, S. (1966). *Introductory lectures on psychoanalysis*. (J. Strachey Trans. (Ed.)). New York: Liveright.

Gallatin, J. E. (1975). *Adolescence and individuality*. New York: Harper & Row.

Galton, F. (1876). The history of twins as a criterion of the relative power of nature and nurture. *Anthropological Institute Journal, 5*, 391–406.

Galton, F. (1883). *Inquiries into human faculty and its development.* London: Macmillan.

Galton, F. (1978). *Hereditary genius: An inquiry into its laws and consequences.* New York: St. Martins.

Gengerelli, J. A. (1976). Graduate school reminiscence: Hull and Koffka. *American Psychologist, 31*, 685–688.

Gesell, A. (1928). *Infancy and human growth.* New York: MacMillan.

Gesell, A. L. (1929). Maturation and infant behavior pattern. *Psychological Review, 36*, 307–319.

Gesell, A. L. (1931). The individual in infancy. In C. Murchison (Ed.), *Handbook of child psychology.* Worcester, MA: Clark University Press.

Gesell, A. L. (1934). *An atlas of infant behavior.* New Haven: Yale University Press.

Gesell, A. (1939). Charles Darwin and child development. *Scientific Monthly, 49*, 548–553.

Gesell, A. (1948). *Studies in child development.* Westport, CT: Greenwood.

Gesell, A. L. (1946). The ontogenesis of infant behavior. In L. Carmichael (Ed.), *Manual of child psychology.* New York: Wiley.

Gesell, A. L. (1954). The ontogenesis of infant behavior. In L. Carmichael (Ed.), *Manual of child psychology* (2nd ed.). New York: Wiley.

Ghiselin, M. T. (1986). The assimilation of Darwinism in developmental psychology. *Human Development, 29*, 12–21.

Gillespie, N. C. (1979). *Charles Darwin and the problem of creation.* Chicago: University of Chicago Press.

Gillispie, C. C. (1968). Lamarck and Darwin in the history of science. In B. Glass, O. Temkin, & W. L. Straus, Jr. (Eds.), *Forerunners of Darwin: 1745–1859.* Baltimore: The Johns Hopkins Press.

Gould, S. J. (1977). *Ontogeny and phylogeny.* Cambridge, MA: Harvard University Press.

Groffman, K. J. (1970). Life-span developmental psychology in Europe: Past and present. In L. R. Goulet & P. B. Baltes (Eds.), *Life-span developmental psychology: Research and theory.* New York: Academic Press.

Gruber, H. E. (1974). *Darwin on man: A psychological study of scientific creativity.* New York: Dutton.

Hall, C. S., & Lindzey, G. (1957). *Theories of personality.* New York: Wiley.

Hall, G. S. (1883). The contents of children's minds. *Princeton Review, 11*, 249–272.

Hall, G. S. (1891). The contents of children's minds on entering school. *The Pedagogical Seminary, 1*, 139–143.

Hall, G. S. (1891). Notes on the study of infants. *The Pedagogical Seminary, 1*, 127–138.

Hall, G. S. (1904). *Adolescence: Its psychology and its relations to physiology, anthropology, sociology, sex, crime, religion, and education* (2 vols.). New York: D. Appleton.

Hall, G. S. (1922). *Senescence: The last half of life.* New York: D. Appleton.

Hardesty, F. P. (1976). Early European contributions to developmental psychology. In K. F. Riegel & J. A. Meacham (Eds.), *The developing individual in a changing world.* Chicago: Aldine.

Harris, D. B. (September 3, 1956). *Child psychology and the concept of development.* Presidential address to the Division of Developmental Psychology, American Psychological Association.

Harris, D. B. (Ed.). (1957). *The concept of development.* Minneapolis, MN: University of Minnesota Press.

Hartmann, E. von (1931). *Philosophy of the unconscious: Speculative results according to the inductive method of physical science.* London: K. Paul, Trench, Trubner.

Havighurst, R. J. (1948). *Developmental tasks and education.* New York: David McKay.

Havighurst, R. J. (1973). History of developmental psychology: Socialization and personality development through the life span. In P. B. Baltes & K. W. Schaie (Eds.), *Life-span developmental psychology: Personality and socialization.* New York: Academic Press.

Hearnshaw, L. S. (1964). *A short history of British psychology 1840–1940.* New York: Barnes & Noble.

Henle, M. (1977). The influence of gestalt psychology in America. *Annals of the New York Academy of Sciences, 291,* 3–12.

Hollingworth, H. L. (1927). *Mental growth and decline: A survey of developmental psychology.* New York: Appleton.

Hoyer, W. J. (Ed.). (1980). Conceptions of learning and the study of life-span development: A symposium. *Human Development, 23,* 361–399.

Hultsch, D. F. (Ed.). (1980). Implications of a dialectical perspective for research methodology. *Human Development, 23,* 217–267.

Hultsch, D. F., & Hickey, T. (1978). External validity in the study of human development: Theoretical and methodological issues. *Human Development, 21,* 76–91.

Hultsch, D. F., & Pentz, C. A. (1980). Encoding, storage, and retrieval in adult memory: The role of model assumptions. In L. W. Poon, J. L. Fozard, L. S. Cermak, D. Arenberg, & L. W. Thompson (Eds.), *New directions in memory and aging: Proceedings of the George A. Talland Memorial Conference.* Hillsdale, NJ: Lawrence Erlbaum Associates.

Huxley, J., & Kettlewell, H. B. D. (1965). *Charles Darwin and his world.* New York: Viking.

Jaeger, S. (1982). Origins of child psychology: William Preyer. In W. R. Woodward & M. G. Ash (Eds.), *The problematic science: Psychology in nineteenth-century thought.* New York: Praeger.

Jaeger, S. (1985). The origin of the diary method in developmental psychology. In G. Eckhardt, W. G. Bringmann, & L. Sprung (Eds.), *Contributions to a history of developmental psychology.* Berlin: Mouton.

James, W. (1890). *The principles of psychology* (Vol. 1). New York: Dover.

James, W. (1977). *A pluralistic universe.* Cambridge, MA: Harvard University Press.

Janet, P. (1930). [Autobiography]. In C. Murchison (Ed.), *A history of psychology in autobiography* (Vol. 1). Worcester, MA: Clark University Press.

Jenkins, J. J. (1974). Remember that old theory of memory? Well, forget it! *American Psychologist, 29,* 785–795.

Jones, E. (1961). *The life and works of Sigmund Freud.* London: Hogarth.

Jung, C. G. (1916). *Psychology of the unconscious.* London: Kegan Paul, Trench, Trubner.

Kessen, W. (1965). *The child.* New York: Wiley.

Kirkpatrick, E. A. (1909). *Genetic psychology: An introduction to an objective and genetic view of intelligence.* New York: Macmillan.

Kitchener, R. F. (1986). *Piaget's theory of knowledge: Genetic epistemology and scientific reason.* New Haven: Yale University Press.

Köhler, U. (1985). The concept of development and the genetic method of C. G. Carus. In G. Eckhardt, W. G. Bringmann, & L. Sprung (Eds.), *Contributions to a history of development psychology.* Berlin: Mouton.

Kuhn, T. S. (1970). *The structure of scientific revolutions* (2nd ed.). Chicago: University of Chicago Press.

Laboratory of Comparative Human Cognition. (1983). Culture and cognitive development. In P. H. Mussen & W. Kessen (Eds.), *Handbook of child psychology: Vol. 1. History, theory, and methods.* New York: Wiley.

Labouvie-Vief, G. (1980). Beyond formal operations: Uses and limits of pure logic in life-span development. *Human Development, 23,* 141–161.

Labouvie-Vief, G. (1982). Dynamic development and mature autonomy: A theoretical prologue. *Human Development, 25,* 161–191.

Langer, J. (1969). *Theories of development.* New York: Holt, Rinehart & Winston.

Leontiev, A. N. (1978). *Activity, consciousness, and personality.* Englewood Cliffs, NJ: Prentice-Hall.

Leontiev, A. N., & Luria, A. R. (1968). The psychological ideas of L. S. Vygotsky. In B. B. Wolman (Ed.), *Historical roots of contemporary psychology.* New York: Harper & Row.

Lehrman, D. S. (1970). Semantic and conceptual issues in the nature–nurture problem. In L. R. Aronson, E. Tobach, D. S. Lehrman, & J. S. Rosenblatt (Eds.), *Development and evolution of behavior: Essays in memory of T. C. Schneirla.* San Francisco: W. H. Freeman.

Lerner, R. M. (1978). Nature, nurture, and dynamic interactionism. *Human Development, 21,* 1–20.

Lerner, R. M. (1979). A dynamic interactional concept of individual and social relationship development. In R. L. Burgess & T. L. Huston (Eds.), *Social exchange in developing relationships.* New York: Academic Press.

Lerner, R. M. (Ed.). (1983). *Developmental psychology: Historical and philosophical perspectives.* Hillsdale, NJ: Lawrence Erlbaum Associates.

Lerner, R. M. (1986). *Concepts and theories of human development* (2nd ed.). New York: Random House.

Lerner, R. M., & Busch-Rossnagel, N. A. (1981). Individuals as producers of their development: Conceptual and empirical bases. In R. M. Lerner & N. A. Busch-Rossnagel (Eds.), *Individuals as producers of their development: A life-span perspective.* New York: Academic Press.

Lerner, R. M., Hultsch, D. F., & Dixon, R. A. (1983). Contextualism and the character of developmental psychology in the 1970s. *Annals of the New York Academy of Sciences, 412,* 101–128.

Lerner, R. M., & Kauffman, M. B. (1985). The concept of development in contextualism. *Developmental Review, 5,* 309–333.

Lerner, R. M., & Lerner, J. V. (1986). Contextualism and the study of child effects in development. In R. L. Rosnow & M. Georgoudi (Eds.), *Contextualism and understanding in behavioral science.* New York: Praeger.

Levinson, D. J., Darrow, C. N., Klein, E. B., Levinson, M. H., & McKee, B. (1978). *Seasons of a man's life.* New York: Knopf.

Liben, L. S. (1981). Individuals' contributions to their own development during childhood: A Piagetian perspective. In R. M. Lerner & N. A. Busch-Rossnagel (Eds.), *Individuals as producers of their development: A life-span perspective.* New York: Academic Press.

Lipsitt, L. P., & Cantor, J. H. (Eds.). (1986). *Experimental child psychologist: Essays and experiments in honor of Charles C. Spiker.* Hillsdale, NJ: Lawrence Erlbaum Associates.

Loewenberg, B. J. (1957). *Darwin, Wallace and the theory of natural selection.* Cambridge, MA: Arlington.

Looft, W. R. (1972). The evolution of developmental psychology: A comparison of handbooks. *Human Development, 15,* 187–201.

Looft, W. R. (1973). Socialization and personality throughout the life span: An examination of contemporary psychological approaches. In P. B. Baltes & K. W. Schaie (Eds.), *Life-span developmental psychology: Personality and socialization.* New York: Academic Press.

Lovejoy, A. O. (1968). Recent criticism of the Darwinian theory of recapitulation: Its grounds and its initiator. In B. Glass, O. Temkin, & W. L. Straus, Jr. (Eds.), *Forerunners of Darwin: 1745–1859.* Baltimore: The Johns Hopkins University Press.

Luria, A. K. (1971). Towards the problem of the historical nature of psychological processes. *International Journal of Psychology, 6,* 259–272.

Luria, A. R. (1976). *Cognitive development: Its cultural and social foundations.* (Trans. by M. Lopez-Morillas & L. Solotaroff; ed. by M. Cole). Cambridge, MA: Harvard University Press.

Luria, A. R. (1979). *The making of mind: A personal account of Soviet psychology.* Cambridge, MA: Harvard University Press.

Mandelbaum, M. (1971). *History, man, and reason.* Baltimore: The Johns Hopkins University Press.

Manier, E. (1978). *The young Darwin and his cultural circle.* Dordrecht, Holland: D. Reidel.

Mayo, E. (1952). *The psychology of Pierre Janet.* Westport, CT: Greenwood.

Mayr, E. (1977). Evolution through natural selection: How Darwin discovered this highly unconventional theory. *American Scientist, 65,* 321–328.

McCandless, B. R., & Spiker, C. C. (1956). Experimental research in child psychology. *Child Development, 27,* 78–80.

McCluskey, K. A., & Reese, H. W. (Eds.). (1984). *Life-span developmental psychology: Historical and generational effects.* Orlando: Academic Press.

McCullers, J. C. G. (1969). G. Stanley Hall's conception of mental development and some indications of its influence on developmental psychology. *American Psychologist, 24,* 1109–1114.

Mead, G. H. (1934). *Mind, self, and society.* Chicago: University of Chicago Press.

Miller, N. E., & Dollard, J. (1941). *Social learning and imitation.* New Haven: Yale University Press.

Mischel, T. (Ed.). (1971). *Cognitive development and epistemology.* New York: Academic Press.

Mischel, W. (1977). On the future of personality measurement. *American Psychologist, 32,* 246–254.

Misiak, H., & Sexton, V. S. (1966). *History of psychology in overview.* New York: Grune & Stratton.

Molenaar, P., & Oppenheimer, L. (1985). Dynamic models of development and the mechanistic–organismic controversy. *New Ideas in Psychology, 3,* 233–242.

Moore, K. C. (1896). The mental development of a child. *Psychological Review Monograph,* (Supplement, Vol. 1, No. 3).

Morgan, C. L. (1902). Selection. In J. M. Baldwin (Ed.), *Dictionary of philosophy and psychology* (Vol. 2). New York: Peter Smith.

Morris, E. K. (1982). Behavior analysis and developmental psychology. *Human Development, 25,* 340–364.

Morris, E. K., & Hursh, D. E. (1982). Behavior analysis and developmental psychology: Metatheoretical considerations. *Human Development, 25,* 344–349.

Mueller, R. H. (1976). A chapter in the history of the relationship between psychology and sociology in America: James Mark Baldwin. *Journal of the History of the Behavioral Sciences, 12,* 240–253.

Murchison, C. (Ed.) (1931). *Handbook of child psychology.* Worcester, MA: University Press.

Murchison, C., & Langer, S. (1927). Tiedemann's observations on the development of the mental faculties of children. *Journal of Genetic Psychology, 34,* 205–230.

Mussen, P. H. (Ed.). (1970). *Carmichael's manual of child psychology* (3rd ed.). New York: Wiley.

Mussen, P. H., & Kessen, W. (Eds.). (1983). *Handbook of child psychology: Vol. 1. History, theory, and methods.* New York: Wiley.

Neisser, U. (1978). Memory: What are the important questions? In M. M. Gruneberg, P. Morris, & R. H. Sykes (Eds.), *Practical aspects of memory.* New York: Academic Press.

Nesselroade, J. R., & Baltes, P. B. (Eds.). (1979). *Longitudinal research in the study of behavior and development.* New York: Academic Press.

Nesselroade, J. R., & Reese, H. W. (Eds.). (1973). *Life-span developmental psychology: Methodological issues.* New York: Academic Press.

Neugarten, B. L. (1964). *Personality in middle and late life.* New York: Atherton Press.

Neugarten, B. L., & Guttman, D. L. (1958). Age-sex roles and personality in middle age: A thematic apperception study. *Psychological Monographs, 72,* No. 470.

Nisbet, R. (1980). *History of the idea of progress.* New York: Basic Books.

Overton, W. F. (1973). On the assumptive base of the nature–nurture controversy: Additive versus interactive conceptions. *Human Development, 16,* 74–89.

Overton, W. F. (Ed.). (1983). *The relationship between social and cognitive development.* Hillsdale, NJ: Lawrence Erlbaum Associates.

Overton, W. F. (1984). World views and their influences on psychological theory and research: Kuhn-Lakatos-Lauden. In H. W. Reese (Ed.). *Advances in child development and behavior* (Vol. 18). New York: Academic Press.

Overton, W. F., & Newman, J. L. (1982). Cognitive development: A competence-activation/utilization approach. In T. Field, A. Huston, H. Quay, L. Troll, & G. Finley (Eds.), *Review of human development.* New York: Wiley.

Overton, W. F., & Reese, H. W. (1973). Models of development: Methodological implications. In J. R. Nesselroade & H. W. Reese (Eds.), *Life-span developmental psychology: Methodological issues.* New York: Academic Press.

Overton, W. F., & Reese, H. W. (1981). Conceptual prerequisites for an understanding of stability–change and continuity–discontinuity. *International Journal of Behavioral Development, 4,* 99–123.

Padover, S. K. (Ed.). (1978). *The essential Marx: The non-economic writings.* New York: New American Library.

Pepper, S. C. (1942). *World hypotheses.* Berkeley: University of California Press.

Perez, B. (1878). *Les trois premières anne'es de l'enfant* [*The child's first three years*]. Paris: Ballieze.

Peters, R. S. (Ed.). (1965). *Brett's history of psychology.* Cambridge, MA: The MIT Press.

Petrinovich, L. (1979). Probabilistic functionalism: A conception of research method. *American Psychologist, 34,* 373–390.

Piaget, J. (1923). La pensée symbolique et la pensée de l'enfant. *Archives of Psychology, 18,* 273–304.

Piaget, J. (1923). *Le langage et la pensée chez l'enfant.* [*The language and thought of the child.*] Neuchatel: Delachaux & Niestlé.

Piaget, J. (1932). *The language and thought of the child.* New York: Harcourt, Brace.

Piaget, J. (1950). *The psychology of intelligence.* London: Routledge & Kegan Paul.

Piaget, J. (1970). Piaget's theory. In P. H. Mussen (Ed.), *Carmichael's manual of child psychology* (Vol. 1). New York: Wiley.

Piaget, J. (1972). *Problémes de psychologie génétique.* [Problems of genetic psychology]. Paris: Denoel.

Piaget, J. (1978). *Behavior and evolution.* New York: Pantheon.

Piaget, J. (1982). Reflections on Baldwin. In J. M. Broughton & D. J. Freeman-Noir (Eds.), *The cognitive-developmental psychology of James Mark Baldwin: Current theory and research in genetic epistemology.* Norwood, NJ: Ablex.

Piaget, J. (1983). Piaget's theory. In P. H. Mussen & W. Kessen (Eds.), *Handbook of child psychology: Vol. 1. History, theory, and methods.* New York: Wiley.

Pressey, S. L., Janney, J. E., & Kuhlen, R. G. (1939). *Life: A psychological survey.* New York: Harper & Row.

Preyer, W. (1882). *Die Seele des Kindes.* [*The mind of the child.*] Leipzig: Fernau.

Preyer, W. (1888). *The mind of the child: Part I. The senses and the will* (H. W. Brown, Trans.). New York: D. Appleton.

Preyer, W. (1893). *Mental development in the child* (H. W. Brown, Trans.). New York: D. Appleton.

Prior, M. D. (1895). Notes on the first three years of a child. *Pedagogical Seminary, 3,* 339–341.

Quetelet, A. (1835). *Sur l'homme et le développement de ses facultés.* [*On man and the development of his faculties.*] Paris: Bachelier.

Reese, H. W. (1976). Conceptions of the active organism (introduction). *Human Development, 19,* 69–70.

Reese, H. W. (1980). A learning theory critique of the operant approach to life-span development. *Human Development, 23,* 368–376.

Reese, H. W. (1982a). A comment on the meanings of 'dialectics.' *Human Development, 25,* 423–429.

Reese, H. W. (1982b). Behavior analysis and developmental psychology: Discussant comments. *Human Development, 25,* 352–357.

Reese, H. W. (1986). Behavioral and dialectical psychologies. In L. P. Lipsitt & J. H. Cantor (Eds.), *Experimental child psychologist: Essays and experiments in honor of Charles C. Spiker.* Hillsdale, NJ: Lawrence Erlbaum Associates.

Reese, H. W., & Overton, W. F. (1970). Models of development and theories of development. In

L. R. Goulet & P. B. Baltes (Eds.), *Life-span developmental psychology: Research and theory*. New York: Academic Press.

Reinert, G. (1979). Prolegomena to a history of life-span developmental psychology. In P. B. Baltes & O. G. Brim, Jr. (Eds.), *Life-span development and behavor* (Vol. 2). New York: Academic Press.

Richards, R. J. (1982). Darwin and the biologizing of moral behavior. In W. R. Woodward & M. G. Ash (Eds.), *The problematic science: Psychology in nineteenth-century thought*. New York: Praeger.

Riegel, K. F. (1972). Influence of economic and political ideologies on the development of developmental psychology. *Psychological Bulletin, 78,* 129–141.

Riegel, K. F. (1973). Developmental psychology and society: Some historical and ethical considerations. In J. R. Nesselroade & H. W. Reese (Eds.), *Life-span developmental psychology: Methodological issues*. New York: Academic Press.

Riegel, K. F. (1975). Toward a dialectical theory of development. *Human Development, 18,* 50–64.

Riegel, K. F. (1976). The dialectics of human development. *American Psychologist, 31,* 689–700.

Riegel, K. F. (1979). *Foundations of dialectical psychology*. New York: Academic Press.

Riegel, K. F., & Meacham, J. A. (Eds.). (1976). *The developing individual in a changing world* (2 vols.). Chicago: Aldine.

Rosnow, R. L., & Georgoudi, M. (Eds.). (1986). *Contextualism and understanding in behavioral science*. New York: Praeger.

Ross, B. M., & Kerst, S. M. (1978). Developmental memory theories: J. M. Baldwin and Piaget. In H. W. Reese (Ed.), *Advances in child development and behavior* (Vol. 12). New York: Academic Press.

Ruse, M. (1979). *The Darwinian revolution*. Chicago: University of Chicago Press.

Russett, C. E. (1976). *Darwin in America: The intellectual response 1865–1912*. San Francisco: W. H. Freeman.

Sameroff, A. J. (1975). Transactional models in early social relations. *Human Development, 18,* 65–79.

Sanford, E. C. (1902). Mental growth and decay. *American Journal of Psychology, 13,* 426–449.

Sarbin, T. R. (1977). Contextualism: A world view for modern psychology. In J. K. Cole & A. W. Landfield (Eds.), *Nebraska Symposium on Motivation* (Vol. 24). Lincoln: University of Nebraska Press.

Schur, M. (1972). *Frued: Living and dying*. New York: International Universities Press.

Sears, R. R. (1975). Your ancients revisited: A history of child development. In E. M. Hetherington (Ed.), *Review of child development research* (Vol. 5). Chicago: University of Chicago Press.

Shinn, M. W. (1893–1899). *Notes on the development of a child* (Vol. 1). Berkeley: University of California Press.

Shinn, M. W. (1900). *The biography of a baby*. Boston: Houghton Mifflin.

Siegel, L. S., & Brainerd, C. J. (Eds.). (1977). *Alternatives to Piaget: Critical essays on the theory*. New York: Academic Press.

Simpson, W. G. (1893). A chronicle of infant development. *Journal of Mental Sciences, 39,* 378–389, 498–505.

Sjövall, B. (1967). *Psychology of tension: An analysis of Pierre Janet's concept of "tension psychologique" together with an historical aspect* (Alan Dixon, Trans.). Norstedts, Sweden: Scandinavian University Books.

Skinner, B. F. (1938). *The behavior of organisms*. New York: Appleton.

Skinner, B. F. (1950). Are theories of learning necessary? *Psychological Review, 57,* 211–220.

Skinner, B. F. (1953). *Science and human behavior*. New York: Macmillan.

Skinner, B. F. (1974). *About behaviorism*. New York: Macmillan.

Smuts, A. B., & Hagen, J. W. (Eds.). (1986). History and research in child development. *Monographs of the Society for Research in Child Development* (Vol. 30, Nos. 4–5).

Spiker, C. C. (1986). Principles in the philosophy of science: Applications to psychology. In L. P. Lipsitt & J. H. Cantor (Eds.), *Experimental child psychologist: Essays and experiments in honor of Charles C. Spiker*. Hillsdale, NJ: Lawrence Erlbaum Associates.

Spiker, C. C., & McCandless, B. R. (1954). The concept of intelligence and the philosophy of science. *Psychological Review, 61*, 255–266.

Stout, G. F., & Baldwin, J. M. (1902). Adaptive (mental processes). In J. M. Baldwin (Ed.), *Dictionary of philosophy and psychology* (Vol. 1). New York: Peter Smith.

Sulloway, F. J. (1982). Freud and biology: The hidden legacy. In W. R. Woodward & M. G. Ash (Eds.), *The problematic science: Psychology in nineteenth-century thought*. New York: Praeger.

Sully, J. (1903). *Studies of childhood*. New York: D. Appleton.

Tetens, J. N. (1777). *Philosophische Versuche über die menschliche Natur und ihre Entwicklung.* [Philosophical research on human nature and its development.] Leipzig: Weidmanns Erben und Reich.

Thomson, K. S., & Rachootin, S. P. (1982). Turning points in Darwin's life. In R. J. Berry (Ed.), *Charles Darwin: A commemoration 1882–1982*. London: Academic Press.

Thorndike, E. L. (1904). The newest psychology. *Educational Review, 28*, 217–227.

Tobach, E. (1983). The relationship between Preyer's concept of psychogenesis and his views of Darwin's theory of evolution. *Zeitschrift für Psychologie, 191*, 387–395.

Tobach, E. (1985). The relationship between Preyer's concept of psychogenesis and his views of Darwin's theory of evolution. In G. Eckhardt, W. G. Bringmann, & L. Sprung (Eds.), *Contributions to a history of developmental psychology*. Berlin: Mouton.

Tolman, C. (1983). Further comments on the meaning of "dialectic." *Human Development, 26*, 320–324.

Toulmin, S., & Goodfield, J. (1965). *The discovery of time*. Chicago: University of Chicago Press.

Vidal, F., Buscaglia, M., & Voneche, J. J. (1983). Darwinism and developmental psychology. *Journal of the History of the Behavioral Sciences, 19*, 81–94.

Vygotsky, L. S. (1929). The problem of the cultural development of the child. *Journal of Genetic Psychology, 36*, 415–434.

Vygotsky, L. S. (1962). *Thought and language*. Cambridge, MA: The MIT Press. (Originally published 1934)

Vygotsky, L. S. (1978). *Mind in society* (Ed. by M. Cole, V. John-Steiner, S. Scribner, & E. Souberman). Cambridge, MA: Harvard University Press.

Wapner, S., Kaplan, B., & Cohen, S. B. (1973). An organismic-developmental perspective for understanding transactions of men and environments. *Environment and Behavior, 5*, 255–289.

Watson, J. B. (1924). *Behaviorism*. New York: W. W. Norton.

Watson, J. B. (1926). What the nursery has to say about instincts. In C. Murchison (Ed.), *Psychologies of 1925*. Worcester, MA: Clark University Press.

Werner, H. (1948). *Comparative psychology of mental development*. New York: International Universities Press.

Werner, H. (1957). The concept of development from a comparative and organismic point of view. In D. B. Harris (Ed.), *The concept of development*. Minneapolis: University of Minnesota Press.

Wertheimer, M. (1985). The evolution of the concept of development in the history of psychology. In G. Eckhardt, W. G. Bringmann, & L. Sprung (Eds.), *Contributions to a history of developmental psychology*. Berlin: Mouton.

White, S. H. (1968). The learning–maturation controversy: Hall to Hull. *Merrill-Palmer Quarterly, 14*, 187–196.

White, S. H. (1970). The learning theory tradition and child psychology. In P. H. Mussen (Ed.), *Carmichael's manual of child psychology* (3rd ed.). New York: Wiley.

White, S. H. (1977). Social proof structures: The dialectic of method and theory in the work of psychology. In N. Datan & H. W. Reese (Eds.), *Life-span developmental psychology: Dialectical perspectives on experimental research.* New York: Academic Press.

White, S. H. (1983). The idea of development in developmental psychology. In R. M. Lerner (Ed.), *Developmental psychology: Historical and philosophical perspectives.* Hillsdale, NJ: Lawrence Erlbaum Associates.

White, S. H. (1985). Presidential address: Developmental psychology at the beginning. *Developmental Psychology Newsletter, 7,* 27–39.

Wiener, P. P. (1949). *Evolution and the founders of pragmatism.* Cambridge: Harvard University Press.

Wohlwill, J. F. (1973). *The study of behavioral development.* New York: Academic Press.

Wolff, P. H. (1960). The developmental psychologies of Jean Piaget and psychoanalysis. *Psychological Issues, 2* (1, Monograph No. 5).

Wozniak, R. H. (1975a). A dialectical paradigm for psychological research: Implications drawn from the history of psychology in the Soviet Union. *Human Development, 18,* 18–34.

Wozniak, R. H. (1975b). Dialectics and structuralism: The philosophical foundations of Soviet psychology and Piagetian cognitive developmental theory. In K. F. Riegel & G. Rosenwald (Eds.), *Structure and transformation: Developmental aspects.* New York: Wiley.

Wozniak, R. H. (1982). Metaphysics and science, reason and reality: The intellectual origins of genetic epistemology. In J. M. Broughton & D. J. Freeman-Noir (Eds.), *The cognitive-developmental psychology of James Mark Baldwin: Current theory and research in genetic epistemology.* Norwood, NJ: Ablex.

2 Methodology

Victoria Seitz
Yale University

INTRODUCTION

There is no one best method for studying human development. Occasionally, theoreticians will promote one particular method as the ideal against which all others should be viewed as inadequate. Laboratory experimentation has sometimes been championed in this manner; naturalistic observation has also had its surprisingly vociferous adherents. When one considers, however, the astonishing breadth of subject matter studied by developmental psychologists, it is easier to defend the proposition that developmental researchers need a corresponding breadth of methodology. Studying the elderly will almost inevitably require different procedures from those suitable for studying infants. Hypotheses about the determinants of physical growth may necessitate the use of biochemical laboratory tests, whereas hypotheses about the development of moral reasoning probably would not. Even within a single topical domain—sex role differentiation for example—one researcher might focus on hormonal influences while another scientist might study cultural differences in how adults socialize boys and girls. In short, developmental psychology provides so diverse and rich a topical terrain that a very broad spectrum of methodology is necessary to do justice to it. The present chapter provides an overview of these methods. In the following three sections, we consider procedures by which data are gathered, including naturalistic observations, experiments, and correlational studies. Then, we consider the ways in which people are selected for study and the problem of obtaining representative individuals from whose behavior valid generalizations can be made. Finally, we consider ethical issues involved in performing research. Statistical issues are discussed by Donald Hartmann in Chapter 3.

OBSERVATIONAL METHODS OF OBTAINING DATA

By naturalistic observations, we mean simply observations of events occurring in nature. Sometimes these observations are made with a clear hypothesis in mind; sometimes they are made to gain a better understanding of the kinds of events that would be interesting to study further. There are many observational methods (Boehm & Weinberg, 1977; Flanders, 1970; Wright, 1960). Wright (1960) has classified them as *open* methods in cases where the observer does not have any preconceived idea of what to look for, and as *closed* methods in cases where the observer decides in advance exactly what and when to observe.

Open Methods

The *case history,* or *diary,* is one example of an open observational method. In a case history, information is recorded with no fixed plan about events that seem interesting to the observer. If a preschool child offers a visitor objects at "a dime for each one. Or you can have two for a nickel," the child's mother may be so amused by this evidence of quantitative confusion that she may record it in a diary. The case history provides rich and detailed information, but it is also an unsystematic and subjective source of data. Consider, for example, the following record written by the parent of an 18-month-old:

> She broke a plastic highball spoon the other day. The loud snap scared her and perhaps a small piece stung when it hit her. Anyway, she cried and cried "back!" and pushed the broken pieces on me. I tried to demonstrate that they would not go "back" and at last she seemed to get the idea. Maybe she was just tired and gave up for that reason. (Peterson, 1974, p. 74)

As this description shows, case histories often suggest interesting hypotheses, but it is difficult—if not impossible—to test hypotheses by referring to case history data.

A second open method is *specimen description.* Here the observer tries to record everything that is happening, in effect, trying to be a camera. With the advent of ever more sophisticated technological devices, observers can increasingly approximate the ideal of simply recording what is there. Although this is a more systematic approach than the case history, the chief problem is that specimen description yields too much information if it is continued for very long. One investigator, for example, followed an 8-year-old child for a single day, recording everything the child said and did. The resulting output, called *One Boy's Day,* required a 435-page book (Barker & Wright, 1951).

Closed Methods

Closed observational methods are based on the strategy of choosing only some aspects of behavior to record. Closed methods lose much of the richness of detail that can be obtained in case histories and specimen descriptions, but what they lose in richness they gain in precision of measurement. It is usually much easier to test a scientific hypothesis using data from systematic sampling methods than from narrative descriptions.

Event sampling is a procedure for recording certain behaviors each time they occur. For example, an observer could record instances of crying in a group of preschool children, or instances of quarrels among children at a day care center. Usually the observer records additional descriptive information as well. In studying quarrels, for example, the investigator might note the number of children involved, their sexes, who began the incident, how long it lasted, and whether it terminated spontaneously or required adult intervention. Usually, event sampling takes place over a relatively long time period. *Trait rating* is similar to event sampling, except that instead of recording events, the observer records a judgment. The observer may thus rate a child's friendliness, aggressiveness, cheerfulness, and so forth.

In a procedure called *time sampling,* the occurrence of specific kinds of behavior is observed during preselected time periods. The rationale behind time sampling is that people continue to behave in more or less the same way for relatively long periods of time, and that examining behavior only occasionally will yield a valid overall estimate of normal behavior. The length of each time interval may be only a few seconds, for some kinds of behavior, or several minutes or hours for others. The key feature is that the same time span is used according to a predetermined plan. During these times, the observer records either a single check mark (if the behavior of interest occurred) or a tally of the number of times the behavior occurred. To use the quarreling example again, the researcher might decide to observe for the first 10 minutes of four successive hours, tallying the number of quarrels that occurred during these periods. Rich information, such as why these quarrels occurred, would not be obtained by this method. But time sampling would probably permit a better comparison of the harmoniousness of two different preschoolers than would the event sampling procedure.

In a method called *field unit analysis,* the observer uses "behavior units" rather than time or events as the basis for segmenting behavior. A new behavior unit is said to begin whenever either the child's behavior or the child's environment changes. If a child who is playing in a sandbox suddenly puts sand in another child's hair, for example, or if a child is hit by another child, a new behavior unit is scored. For each behavior unit, the observer records both whether the child's behavior has changed and whether the child's environment has changed. When the observation period is completed, the observer examines the behavior units in order to analyze them.

An example of the field unit analysis method is provided in a study of 2- and 3-year-old children's responses to each other in an interracial nursery school (Stevenson & Stevenson, 1960). The investigators recorded behavior units, then found that these units could be classified into eight categories. Examples were "friendliness," where the child actively sought out the company of others, and "lack of social participation," where the child played in a solitary manner. Analyzing the behavior units, these investigators discovered that even though these young children were sensitive to the sex of other children in their social interactions, they were surprisingly insensitive to race. As the observers put it, "They might as well all be blue" (Stevenson & Stevenson, 1960, p. 370).

Special Considerations in Observing

Reliability.   In all observational methods, an important goal is to achieve inter-observer reliability. If two or more observers watch the same behavior, it is important that they be able to produce accounts that coincide. As trial lawyers know, untrained observers are often unreliable. One eyewitness to a crime may assure the jury that the criminal was "tall—about 6'4"—with sandy hair" while another contends that the culprit was "about medium height, with brown hair, and shifty eyes." Unless observers could be trained to see and report the same events in the same manner, observational data would be purely subjective and therefore worthless for scientific purposes. In general, it is easier to achieve inter-observer reliability with closed than with open observational methods. In psychological research, observers are usually given practice before the study begins until they can score behavior with nearly perfect (at least 90%) agreement. It is also a common practice to have two or more observers in observational studies. When films, videotapes, or tape recordings have been made, the investigator can refer to the original behavior if there are disagreements about what happened. Before beginning a study, a researcher can also use such recorded data for pilot subjects to establish good coding systems and thereby increase inter-observer reliability.

Functions of Observations.   Observational studies may serve two different purposes. The first is a *hypothesis-generating function,* which is most useful when one knows relatively little about the subject being observed. When first studying a particular population, such as preschool children, or a particular topic, such as aggression or play, a good strategy is to observe by using an open method. After a period of open observation, one is more likely to have a better idea of what could be worth studying systematically. One might then use observations in their second capacity; that is, in their *hypothesis-testing function,* employing a time sampling procedure or selecting certain individuals or behaviors for more concentrated observation.

If one were to observe infants in their homes, for example, one might notice that fathers seemed to be more playful with babies than mothers. One might then formulate a hypothesis that the nature of an infant's social interactions differs depending on the sex of the parent. To test this, one could systematically observe interactions, using event sampling, for example, to study all those episodes in which adults hold their infants. One would then confirm the hypothesis, finding that mothers most often hold infants to perform caretaking acts, such as feeding or changing diapers, while fathers most often hold babies to play with them (Lamb, 1977).

EXPERIMENTAL STUDIES

Definition and Examples

While it is impossible to draw a clear line between experimental and nonexperimental methods, generally speaking, experimental procedures imply the ability to *create* the event to be studied and to *control* factors that would interfere with the interpretability of the study's results. Before performing an experiment, a researcher formulates a hypothesis, which is a statement of how constructs in a theory are related. For example, a researcher might hypothesize that the exposure to violence increases children's aggression. The researcher then translates the hypothesis into a specific, measurable prediction, such as "if children see an hour of TV violence every day for a month, they will behave more aggressively than if they do not see the violence." To test the prediction, the experimenter could randomly assign some children to see an aggressive television program for an hour every day and other children to see a nonaggressive program (such as a nature program).[1] The assumption in using random assignment is that other factors that might cause aggressive behavior, such as the hours of violent TV programs children watch at home will be similar in randomly assigned groups and, being similar, will not be the cause of any differences between the groups at the end of the experiment. The prediction would be confirmed if the two groups were initially equivalent in aggression, but after a month of seeing the daily hour of televised violence the first group had become more aggressive than the second.

The causal part of the hypothesized relationship, televised violence, is called an *independent variable*. The consequence, children's aggressive behavior, is called a *dependent variable*. In general, to perform an experiment, a researcher creates conditions that represent different levels of the independent variable and assigns groups of subjects to receive each different condition. An experiment therefore requires a minimum of two groups: an *experimental group,* which receives some kind of special treatment, and a *control group,* which is initially equivalent to the experimental group but which does not receive the treatment. In the example just given, the experimental group received one hour's worth of the independent variable—televised violence—per day for a month whereas the control group received none. Sometimes there are several experimental groups, as when some children see films with many aggressive episodes and others see films with only a few. There can also be several control groups, as when a nature

---

[1]We discuss ethical issues in how such research might be conducted later in this chapter.

film is shown for one group and no film at all is shown for another group. The critical part of the experimental method, however, is that all of the groups must be exactly the same with the exception of the kind of treatment they receive during the experiment. If this ideal can be achieved (and random assignment to groups is the usual method of trying to accomplish it), then changes in the dependent variable (aggression) can reasonably be believed to have been caused by changes in the independent variable (TV violence).

Threats to Experimental Validity

Although the experimental method is the most powerful means of testing whether a cause-effect relationship exists, there are some special problems raised by the method. One problem is that just being part of an experiment evidently changes the behavior of some individuals. When this occurs, the results of an experiment may not be valid for real-life events (Roethlisberger & Dickson, 1939). In medical research, this problem is called the *placebo effect*. As amazing as it may seem, almost any kind of symptom can be alleviated in some individuals by giving them a placebo—a treatment that theoretically should not have curative properties, such as a sugar pill or an injection of saline solution. Once regarded as a nuisance, the placebo is now viewed by many medical researchers as an alternative treatment, reflecting the action of some not yet well-understood mechanism by which people's feelings affect their physical well-being. Often, special control groups of people who believe they are receiving a treatment, but who actually are not, are therefore included in an experiment to assess this effect.

A second problem is that random assignment to conditions may cause negative reactions to being a part of an experiment. *Resentment* at being denied a desired service can lead to a subject's refusal to participate in or to an early withdrawal from a study. Changes in control groups, such as demoralization or compensatory rivalry (the John Henry effect), may arise from having been denied a treatment rather than as a reflection of its simple absence. Thus, rather than improving the validity of a study, random assignment can sometimes create attitudes that threaten it. This may be especially true in the realm of social intervention projects, such as the provision of day care services to poor, working families (Seitz, 1982).

A third problem of the experimental method is that the apparatus and conditions in the experiment may cause people to believe that they are supposed to behave in a particular manner (Orne, 1962). In effect, certain experimental arrangements almost demand a certain kind of response that is not actually what the person would do when not participating in the experiment. An example of this *experimental demand* problem is making available a large number of aggressive toys, such as knives and guns, and very few nonaggressive toys. Such a procedure could cause children to behave more aggressively than they normally do. Even the most docile child is unlikely to play "house" or "tea party" with guns and knives.

A fourth problem is that the *experimenter's expectations* may influence the results of the experiment (Rosenthal, 1963). A researcher who believes strongly in his or her hypothesis may unwittingly create conditions confirming that hypothesis. The experimenter may, for example, give subtle cues to the subjects, causing them to behave in the expected manner. For this reason, experiments are often conducted in a "double-blind" manner. In such a procedure, neither the subjects nor the person who observes the subjects knows who is receiving a particular treatment until the study is completed.

Quasi-Experimental Studies

In cases where true experiments cannot be performed, it is often possible for a researcher to introduce some degree of control over potentially interfering extraneous factors and to approximate the conditions of an experiment. A number of such approximate or "quasi-experimental" designs exist, and there is now considerable literature on their advantages and disadvantages (Bryk & Weisberg, 1977; Cook & Campbell, 1979; Cronbach, 1982; Glass, Willson, & Gottman, 1975; Schaie, 1977). Suppose, for example, that an investigator wishes to study the effects of day care on children's social development. Conducting a true experiment would require that the independent variable (day care versus no day care) come under the researcher's control: children would be randomly assigned either to receive day care or to remain at home under parental care for the duration of the experiment. Most parents would be unwilling or unable to permit their children to participate in an experiment of this kind, and most studies of such potentially important socializing events as day care, preschool intervention programs, or public versus private schooling cannot be conducted with true experiments. Quasi-experimental studies sometimes permit a more controlled approach to such problems than do simple correlational studies.

Quality. Quasi-experimental designs vary greatly in quality. One of the best of these designs involves using people who are on waiting lists for the treatment or program in question as control subjects. Cochran (1977), for example, has studied the effects of day care with a waiting list design, and Zigler and Butterfield (1968) used this kind of quasi-experimental design to study the effects of Project Head Start. While waiting list subjects may differ in some ways from the people who actually receive the program (perhaps they are procrastinators, or somewhat less well informed about scarce community resources), they are comparable in that they are a self-selected group of people who explicitly desire to receive the program. Therefore, they provide a far superior alternative to using a group of "no day care" or "no Head Start" subjects whose families have not attempted to enroll them in the programs. Parents who choose to enroll their children in day care may be presumed to differ in many ways from parents who do not (Hock, 1980; Sibbison, 1973). Some of these differences—perhaps family size, family income, or parental educational level—could easily be more important than the day care itself in producing differences later observed between children who receive day care and those who do not.

At the opposite end of the spectrum are very poor quasi-experimental procedures that often produce misleading results. One example is the matched group design, in which the researcher compares two groups that are matched on a variable on which they normally differ and that might have a causal influence on the dependent variable. For example, if children who are receiving day care come from families who are poorer than those of children who are not receiving day care, an investigator might attempt to "match" the groups by selecting nonday-care families who have the same income level as does the day-care sample. Comparing two such groups is, unfortunately, likely to yield results that cannot be interpreted as a reflection of the true effects of day care on the children. Because it is so commonly encountered, we discuss the matching problem more extensively later in this chapter.

On the "Relevance" of Experiments

Artificiality.   One criticism of experimentation is that it is often conducted in such artificial settings with such a restricted range of conditions that we cannot apply it to the complex, real world. A great deal of research in developmental psychology has been conducted in university laboratories where children are taken into a quiet room by an adult and given tests or other psychological tasks to perform. This kind of laboratory research has been criticized as being too far removed from the children's real-life experiences to give a good picture of how they actually behave (Bronfenbrenner, 1977, 1979; Brooks & Baumeister, 1977). As Bronfenbrenner has phrased it, such research can produce a "science of the strange behavior of children in strange situations with strange adults for the briefest possible periods of time" (1977, p. 513).

This criticism has its merits. Nevertheless, controlled studies conducted in artificial settings can be very useful. The critical point is that where and how one chooses to study development depends on the questions one is asking. Some types of experiments can only be performed in a laboratory, yet the information obtained is almost certainly valid in real-life situations. If one wishes to know how well infants see color, one needs to use precision equipment that can deliver light of exactly the right brightness and wavelength (e.g., Bornstein, Kessen, & Weiskopf, 1976). The way in which infants respond to color in the laboratory is almost certainly the same way they would respond elsewhere, but the laboratory setting is necessary to measure their responses with scientific accuracy. If one is studying social behavior, however, it is possible that children do behave differently in familiar and unfamiliar places. The place where behavior is studied probably matters more for some kinds of behaviors than for others.

It is useful to think of studies as falling along a *continuum of naturalness* (Parke, 1976). Naturalistic observations usually represent studies at one end of the continuum, while controlled experiments are usually at the other end, representing relatively contrived situations. However, there is nothing about the experimental method that *requires* that experiments be conducted in artificial settings or in laboratories. To return to the example of studying the effects of televised aggression, Friedrich and Stein (1973) have established a very naturalistic setting for an experiment. Children were shown television programs as part of the ordinary activities of a nursery school session. Familiar programs (e.g., "Batman" and "Mister Roger's Neighborhood") were used. The routine of the nursery school allowed a greater degree of control over the children's activities than would have been possible if the study was conducted in the children's homes. Yet the conditions were neither artificial nor laboratorylike. As we will see in later chapters, many psychologists are turning to procedures that combine the control and precision possible in experiments with the advantages of observing children in their everyday surroundings.

Theory Testing.   It is also important to recognize that experiments that seem trivial and irrelevant to real life can provide an important test of a theory. A scientist may have a very complex theory, yet the predictions based on the theory may be quite simple: either a given event will occur under specified circumstances or it will not. Physicists employ this approach when they create in a cyclotron particles that cannot exist under ordinary conditions but that their theory predicts should exist if those conditions are made proper. Finding these particles is extremely important, because it suggests that the theory is correct—it is a "go-ahead" signal for applying the explanatory theory to events in the real world. In psychology, an example of this kind of experiment is one in which language researchers have created nonsense words to study young children's acquisition of grammatical rules. When a child is shown a drawing of a strange animal and told that it is a "wug," psycholinguists have been interested to discover how the child refers to two of them (Berko, 1958). When children reply "wugs," the researcher can be confident that they have learned a linguistic rule they can apply correctly, and that they are not simply remembering a word they have heard others use. Such nonsense words do not exist in the natural language, but the way the child responds to them provides information that can be important in theory testing.

CORRELATIONAL STUDIES

Definition and Examples

In a correlational study, the researcher measures at least two variables and calculates the degree of relationship between (or among) them. Correlational studies are often performed with only one group of subjects. For example, an investigator could ascertain the number of hours of homework that children complete nightly and the children's scores on an academic achievement test in order to determine the relationship between these two variables. Correlational studies are also frequently used to compare groups, as discussed below.

There are two important features to notice about a correlation coefficient: its size and its sign. The *size* of the correlation indicates the strength of the relationship, while the *sign* indicates whether the relationship is positive or negative. Several illustrations might be helpful. The size of a correlation is always a value between −1 and +1. Ignoring the sign, the closer the value is to 1, the stronger the relationship, and the closer to zero, the weaker the relationship. The sign shows the direction of the relationship. A positive sign means that the high values of one variable are associated with the high values of the other, and that low values similarly occur together. An example of a moderate-sized positive relationship is the correlation of +.57 between height and weight in mature teenage girls (Faust, 1977). This correlation reflects the fact that taller girls tend to weigh more and shorter girls less, but that there are some exceptions to the rule. A negative correlation signifies that the high values of one variable are associated with the low values of the other. An example would be temperature and the amount of clothing worn; the lower the temperature, the more clothing people wear, and the higher the temperature, the less clothing they wear.

Interpretational Problems

Correlation coefficients can be deceptively simple. A number of factors affect whether a particular correlation coefficient is a good or a poor estimate of the true degree of relationship that exists between two variables. One of the most common problems is that an investigator has sampled too narrow a range of one or both variables. *Restriction of range* reduces the size of the correlation coefficient from the value that would be found with a more representative sample. For example, there would be little relationship between age and size of vocabulary in a group limited to children who were between 10 and 11 years old. If a relationship is *curvilinear* (for example, the average daily temperature over the months of March through November), an ordinary correlation coefficient would underestimate the true degree of predictability of temperature from the calendar date. *Reliability of measurement* affects the interpretation of correlations. Correlations between unreliably measured variables underestimate the true degree of relationship. As correlations are the basis of many analyses performed in developmental research (such as multiple regression and factor analysis), it is a good idea to become familiar with these and other technical factors affecting their interpretation. Guilford (1965) and Cohen and Cohen (1975) are two good sources of such discussions; this information can also be found in many basic statistical textbooks.

Causality—A Special Problem

Correlational evidence tells us *whether* certain events are related to each other, but not *why* they are. For example, watching aggressive television programs is correlated with the amount of aggression children display: the more hours of aggressive television the child watches, the more aggressive the child is when playing with other children (Stein & Friedrich, 1975). The problem with correlational information such as this is that the cause of the relationship is not evident. Does television incite children to violence, or do aggressive children like to watch violent programs when they aren't occupied with hitting their playmates? Or does some unknown event cause children both to become aggressive and to enjoy watching violent TV programs?

Although correlations do not prove causation, they can often suggest its probable nature. It is usually more plausible to believe that the cause runs in one direction rather than the other. For example, a number of years ago, social psychologists discovered that the price of cotton and the number of lynchings in the South were negatively correlated. It is certainly more plausible that the price of cotton is the cause and the lynchings the effect, rather than vice versa. It is hard to see how having more lynchings could cause prices to drop, whereas a drop in the price of the main commodity of a region might cause hard times, anger and frustration, and so more violence.

Naturally Formed Groups and Correlational Studies

There are many occasions when investigators compare naturally existing groups in order to discover factors affecting development. For example, children from industrialized, Western societies can typically memorize isolated pieces of information more easily than can non-Westernized children. Non-Westernized children, however, excel when they are asked to recall complex three-dimensional scenes. Cross-cultural researchers have pointed out that children in nonindustrialized societies are expected to learn by observing others in everyday activities. In contrast, children in industrialized countries spend long hours in school learning verbally presented information. The memory differences that have been found may therefore be due to the extensive cultural differences in the ways children are taught.

The study of this kind of developmental factor (cultural influences) is not experimental. One cannot randomly assign one group of children to be born to parents in a village in the Mexican highlands and another to parents living in New England. Neither can one assign people to be boys rather than girls, or infants rather than adolescents. Such factors as ethnic heritage, gender, and age are, as Kenny (1975a) aptly puts it, variables that are "attached to rather than assigned to" the organism (p. 888).

Because people are not assigned to naturally formed groups, it is never possible for such groups to be truly comparable in the way that experimentally formed groups are. Thus, studies of naturally formed groups are always *methodologically* correlational (even though one can choose statistical procedures other than correlations to analyze results from them). The challenge for the researcher in studying these important kinds of factors is to attempt to eliminate rival explanations for group differences in order to make causal inferences based on the variable of interest (e.g., age or culture).

Obtaining Comparable Groups.   As Cole and Means (1981) point out, the more scientists know about the subject populations they are studying, the better control they can exercise over important sources of unwanted differences between the groups. Consider the comparison of normal and retarded children on intellectual development, for example. Ideally, one wishes to study two groups that differ only in the variable of interest—retardation. As Zigler (1969) remarks, however, comparisons have often been made between retarded children who live in an institution and children of normal intellect who live with their own families. It is therefore unclear whether any differences that are found are due to retardation or to institutionalization. The latter experience is known to affect children's motivation in testing situations: institutionalized children are often especially wary of strangers and tend to perform more poorly than their actual cognitive abilities would permit. Knowing the importance of institutionalization, researchers can attempt to obtain groups that are comparable on this factor; for example, by studying only noninstitutionalized subjects. (Care must be exercised, however, not to fall into the matching problem, described in the following section of this chapter, when trying to equalize groups on nuisance variables.)

Obtaining Equivalent Treatments for Different Groups.   Before differences between groups can be interpreted, it is necessary that the materials, procedures, and instructions they receive be equally motivating and equally well understood by all of the groups. In the example of retarded children given above, an attempt could be made to reduce the motivational differences likely to exist between such children and the normal children with whom they are to be compared. An extra period of warm-up interactions with the examiner, for example, could be employed with retarded children, or with any children suspected of having motivational problems related to being tested by unfamiliar adults. In one study using this strategy (Zigler, Abelson, & Seitz, 1973), lower-class preschool children who received a 10-minute play period with the examiner performed better than similar children who were tested without a play period. Middle-class children's performance, however, was unaffected by this experimental manipulation, suggesting that comparisons of children from different social classes should always be made with an allowance for possible motivational differences between them.

The Group X Task Strategy for Group Comparisons.   In the comparison of naturally formed groups, Cole and Means (1981) suggest searching for Group X Task interactions using at least two tasks. These tasks should be chosen in such a way that, if the hypothesis about the underlying causes of the group differences is correct, the groups will perform equivalently on one of the tasks and differently on the other. This equivalent task condition provides a kind of control condition, in that a number of potential rival explanations (group differences in motivation, understanding instructions, etc.) are less plausible when equivalence is found on at least one task. The Cole and Means (1981) book provides numerous examples of how this strategy can be employed.

Combining Methods

The most productive strategy for studying development will often be an eclectic one. In their examination of culture and thought, Cole and Scribner (1974, 1975) call attention to the many advantages of merging the "complementary and mutually enriching research approaches" of experimentation (the psychologist's traditional method) and observation (the anthropologist's). The three steps they recommended are particularly applicable to situations where naturally occurring groups are to be compared:

1. First, analyze a proposed or actual experiment to determine the possible task-specific sources of difficulty for the subjects. Become familiar with how the subject understands the experimental tasks and his or her role as a subject. Does the experiment seem reasonable to the subject (foreigner/child)? Are the tasks sufficiently familiar and performable?

2. Second, see if there are naturally occurring situations in which the subjects perform well, even though they may have performed poorly in an experiment. Determine how these situations differ from the laboratory.

3. Third, integrate observation and experimentation: "experiment with the experiment." Try variations of the research procedures designed to test specific hypotheses about what causes good performance in naturally occurring situations.

For example, consider this study of young children's memory. Istomina (1975) found that 3- and 4-year-olds performed poorly when they were asked to recall objects that were placed in view on a table. Yet, in naturalistic observations, children this young showed much better recall, sometimes even remembering aspects of events that adults had forgotten. Istomina hypothesized that the poor performance in the laboratory recall task had occurred because 3- and 4-year-olds were unlikely to consider recall an abstract skill. Rather, for young children, remembering things is a means to an end. Thus, tailoring the experiment to fit into the normal expectations of the children might improve their performance. Istomina therefore "experimented with the experiment," embedding the children's task within a meaningful, realistic situation. She set up a "store" in the children's preschool and equipped it with merchandise, play money, a cash register, and a "salesperson." The children were sent on a "shopping trip" by their teacher, who slowly named five items for the child to buy before sending him or her to the "store" in the next room. Recall was much better—almost twice as high for the youngest children—in the store situation than it had been in the laboratorylike task.

Summary

In developmental studies, data can be obtained through naturalistic observations, experiments or quasi-experiments, or correlational studies. Naturalistic observations may be made either with a predetermined plan (closed methods) or with no such plan in mind (open methods). Open methods are particularly suitable for suggesting hypotheses, while closed methods are superior for testing them. In both cases, interobserver reliability is a necessity if the observations are to be valid.

Experimental methods are those in which investigators attempt to create the event they wish to study. Experiments require a minimum of two groups; an experimental group that receives a specific treatment and a control group that does not. Random assignment is used to attempt to make the groups comparable at the time the study begins. If the groups differ at the end of the experiment, there is strong reason to believe that the experimental treatment caused the difference.

Although it is easier to draw causal inferences from experiments than from other kinds of studies, problems can occur that reduce experimental validity. Attitudinal changes in subjects, the expectations of the experimenter, and the constraints placed on the subjects during the experiment can cause outcomes that are not true reflections of the experimental treatment.

Quasi-experiments are designs that do not provide the full control possible in experiments. These designs vary greatly in quality, with the best of them approximating true experiments when used appropriately.

Even though experiments have been criticized for their lack of naturalness, they vary in the degree to which they resemble real-life situations. Psychologists are becoming increasingly creative in designing experiments that have a natural, rather than a laboratory, quality. While this is often an advantage, even artificial experiments have an important place in psychological research, because they do play a role in testing theories.

In correlational studies, the investigator's interest lies in the relationship between variables. These relationships can be studied within a single group, as in the examination of how intelligence and creativity are related. They can be studied in the context of comparing groups, as in determining whether children's gender is related to their aggressiveness. Correlations can establish the magnitude and direction of relationships, but they do not provide information on causality.

Many studies in developmental psychology involve comparing naturally formed groups to which subjects could not possibly be assigned (such as boys versus girls). Because these are correlational studies, the causative role of the difference between the groups is difficult to establish. Some guidelines for dealing with this fact of developmental research were discussed, with the recommendation that searching for Group X Task interactions is a particularly good strategy.

If we contrast the methods of research, we find that the experimental method is powerful but narrow. It is a spotlight that brightly illuminates a small portion of the stage: We can see everything in that portion very clearly, but we can see nothing else. Natural observation and correlational methods are more like dim lights that permit us to see only shadows, but they illuminate a large portion of the stage. The usual sequence in scientific method is to begin with naturalistic observations, progress to correlational methods, and then use experiments. Non-experimental methods are the best source of hypotheses for a young science. Without knowing where to look, one could easily perform an elaborate experiment only to find that one has an excellent view of a very empty corner of the stage.

THE SELECTION OF PEOPLE TO STUDY

Representativeness

The most important question a researcher asks about the people being studied is: How *representative* are they? Ideally, one would like to be able to conclude that what is true of the subjects studied is true of others as well. In practice, however, research is usually conducted with groups of people who may easily be unrepresentative in some way. They may, for example, all be from a university community or from middle-class families.

In order to reconcile the limitations of information from particular samples with the ideal of studying people in general, a common strategy is to repeat a study (to *replicate* it) with new groups of subjects. Suppose we find in one study that middle-class, American 13-year-olds from San Francisco can reason abstractly while their 8-year-old brothers and sisters cannot. We can be more confident that we have described a genuine developmental change in logical thinking if someone replicates the study with other children, such as American children from other locales and social class backgrounds, and especially with children from other countries.

Some research involves subjects who are unusual in some way, such as juvenile delinquents or infants who were born blind. The study of unusual development is valuable in illuminating the nature of normality. The study of blind infants, for example, has taught us much about the role of smiling in normal social development (Fraiberg, 1977). Because blind children smile at the same age as do sighted children, it is clear that some kind of maturational mechanisms must be involved and that the children are not simply imitating their caregivers. In the study of unusual people, representativeness remains important in the sense that we try to study individuals who are typical of others like themselves. Studying blind children, for example, we would try to be sure that they were not unusual in some other way as well, such as being physically disabled or mentally retarded.

Comparing Individuals of Different Ages

Cross-Sectional Studies. One way to compare the behavior of individuals of different ages is by conducting a *cross-sectional* study in which the subjects are of different ages. The major advantage of such a study is that it produces information about typical age differences relatively quickly. By studying emotional behavior in people of different ages, we could discover that temper tantrums are common among 2-year-olds but unusual in 12-year-olds without having to wait ten years for the 2-year-olds to mature. Because of this key advantage, cross-sectional studies are very common in developmental research.

The results from cross-sectional studies, however, must always be interpreted cautiously. In a cross-sectional study, there is no assurance that the younger subjects would actually come to resemble the older subjects as they develop. There are two main reasons for this. First, there may be sampling problems, especially if it is harder to obtain representative groups of individuals at one age than at another. Finding typical 12-year-olds, who are likely to be attending a local school, may be easier than finding typical 2-year-olds, some of whom are at home, some with babysitters, and some in day care centers. Cross-selectional sampling error often occurs when researchers choose their subjects by grade level rather than by age. Because children are not necessarily promoted to a new grade each year, children in a classroom can differ in age and life history (in having experienced school failure). It is, therefore, a poor idea to compare "first graders" with "fourth graders" without checking the children's ages and school records. The percentage of children who have failed a grade is likely to be higher among the fourth graders, since they have had more opportunity to fail than have the first graders. Any cause of unrepresentativeness in the sample for any age group will bias the results of a cross-sectional study.

A second problem with cross-sectional study designs is that societal changes may be responsible for some of the differences observed in persons of different ages. If IQ tests are given to adults, groups of older adults almost always score lower than do younger ones (Kimmel, 1974). Results from cross-sectional studies suggest that IQ begins to drop at about age 45 and declines slowly but continuously thereafter. However, in many of these studies, the older adults tested grew up during a time when few people attended college, and many did not even complete high school. Lack of education may have made them perform less well than the more educated younger adults, who may continue to score well on IQ tests as they grow older. Other studies of IQ test performance, in fact, show that when the *same* individuals are tested as they grow older, there does not appear to be a drop in IQ until very late in life (Botwinick, 1967). Due to the difficulties in interpreting results from cross-sectional studies, the results are often tested by other means as well, in order to permit us to be confident of the findings.

Longitudinal Studies. In a *longitudinal* study, the same people are studied as they grow older. Although the advantage of this approach is that it yields a convincing picture of how particular individuals change over time, an obvious disadvantage is the long time required to complete it. One investigator, Lewis Terman, began a study of intellectually gifted children in 1921. Now, over half a century later, information about what became of these children is still being analyzed and reported (P. Sears & Barbee, 1978; R. Sears, 1977). A longitudinal study need not continue for an entire lifetime, but even if it continues for only a year or two, it is relatively costly in time and effort.

The most serious methodological limitation of longitudinal research is that it produces results specific to a particular *cohort* measured at particular times. (The term "cohort" was the Roman name for legions of soldiers who fought together; to present-day demographers, it refers to persons born in the same year and thus, figuratively, marching through the life span together.) The group one chooses to study longitudinally may differ, for both genetic and environmental–cultural reasons, from other groups one might instead have studied. Considering societal changes, for example, gifted children in the 1980s—particularly girls and minority group children—may have different opportunities from those that were available to them when Terman began his study sixty years ago. A new longitudinal study to determine what becomes of such individuals might yield quite a different set of findings from Terman's.

Another problem in longitudinal work is that subjects may cease to be available for study. People move, or become tired of participating. As a result of the loss of subjects from a study, which is called *attrition,* the subjects still participating at the end of the project may be unusual. They may be more cooperative, healthier, or better educated than people in general, and therefore not a good group upon which to base conclusions about human development. Problems also arise from measuring the same people many times. Taking IQ tests every year might cause people to become better at them. One might therefore erroneously conclude that people's IQs increase as they grow older.

Despite its limitations, longitudinal research is a very useful method in developmental psychology. As we will see later, a number of longitudinal studies have now been completed, and from them we now know a great deal about change and constancy in people's lives (Bloom, 1964; Jones, Bayley, MacFarlane, & Honzig, 1971; Thomas & Chess, 1977). As is the case with cross-sectional studies, researchers usually try to test the conclusions from longitudinal research by other means.

Cohort Sequential Designs.   One good test of the validity of the findings from a longitudinal study is simply to repeat the study at a different time and with a different group of individuals. If the same results continue to be obtained, then we can have a great deal of confidence in them. The *cohort sequential* method refers to performing a replication of a longitudinal study with subjects from a new cohort. For example, suppose social development was studied over a 10-year period beginning in 1980 with people who were 15 years old when the study began. At some later time, say five years later, the researcher would repeat the identical procedures using a new group of subjects who were 15 years old. The two different cohorts of subjects would each be studied from ages 15–25, but one of the groups would have been born in 1965 and the other in 1970. If the two groups showed similar age changes in social behavior from ages 15–25, this would strengthen the case for interpreting the changes as age-specific.

Cross-Sequential Designs. Cross-sectional designs can also be extended into *cross-sequential* designs by re-measuring each subject in at least one follow-up test. The value of this kind of design is illustrated in a study of adult cognitive abilities conducted by Schaie and Labouvie-Vief (1974). These investigators measured subjects at three separate times over a 14-year time span. Using the cross-sequential method, several different kinds of information were obtained, providing an overall picture that is very informative. Figure 2.1, for example, presents the cross-sectional findings from Schaie and Labouvie-Vief's study using a test of Spatial Reasoning Ability from the Primary Mental Abilities Test (Thurstone, 1958).

As the data in Fig. 2.1 show, in each of the three years that the study was conducted, cross-sectional comparisons suggested a steady decline in spatial ability with age. In contrast, however, consider Fig. 2.2, where the data represent a 14-year picture of performance on this test by the same subjects retested longitudinally. These data suggest that, across almost the whole adult life span, a person's ability in this area will remain constant, or may even improve. What these data—and most of the data on other tests used by these investigators—also show is cohort differences. On a wide range of intellectual tests, subjects who were born earlier were less competent as adults than were subjects born later. A summary of this kind of information is shown in Fig. 2.3, for the Space test as well as for a composite IQ measure and for a test of educational aptitude (Thurstone, 1958).

From these data, the authors conclude "that most of the adult life span is characterized by an absence of decisive intellectual decrements. In times of rapid cultural and technological change it is primarily in relation to younger populations that the aged can be described as deficient . . ." (Schaie & Labouvie-Vief, p. 317). As computer usage becomes more generalized in our society, this trend for young adults to outperform the levels reached by their parents on many kinds of cognitive tests when they were the same age may well be even greater than was true for the cohorts studied by Schaie and Labouvie-Vief.

Numerous other refinements of the longitudinal and cross-sectional methods exist. Discussions of these variations and statistical methods of analyses appropriate for disentangling cohort, age, and time of measurement effects may be found in Schaie (1977) and in Nesselroade and Baltes (1978).

Representativeness in Naturally Formed Groups

Thus far, we have discussed representativeness primarily in terms of age group comparisons. As noted earlier, a common problem in the comparison of any naturally formed groups is the existence of correlated "nuisance" variables. It is

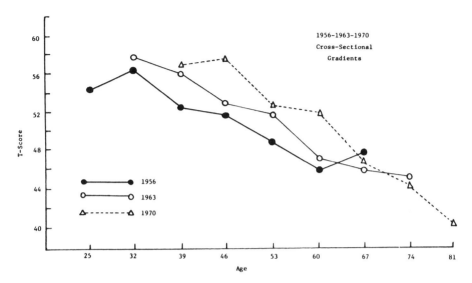

FIG. 2.1. Spatial Ability for Subjects of Different Ages (Cross-Sectional Methodology). (From K. W. Schaie and G. Labouvie-Vief, *Developmental Psychology,* 1974, Volume 10, p. 309. Reprinted by permission of the publisher and authors.)

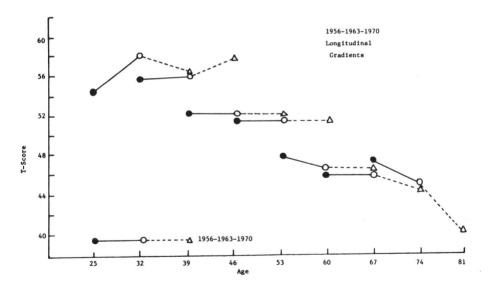

FIG. 2.2. Spatial Ability for Subjects of Different Ages (7 Longitudinally Studied Groups). (From K. W. Schaie and G. Labouvie-Vief, *Developmental Psychology,* 1974, Volume 10, p. 309. Reprinted by permission of the publisher and authors.)

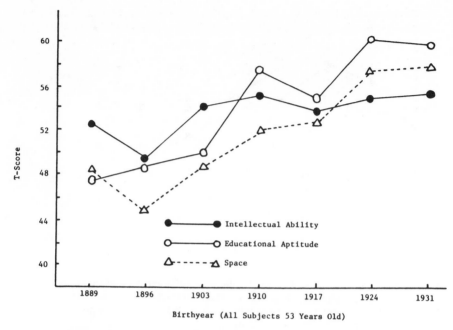

FIG. 2.3. Cohort Effects: Comparison for 53-Year-Old Persons Born in Different Years. (From K. W. Schaie and G. Labouvie-Vief, *Developmental Psychology,* 1974, Volume 10, p. 316. Adapted and reprinted by permission of the publisher and authors.)

important to consider how this fact affects the representativeness of samples. Suppose one wishes to compare children from two social classes on a measure of creativity. It is likely that children from different socioeconomic backgrounds will differ significantly on IQ test scores. If creativity test performance is influenced by general cognitive level, as indexed by the IQ, some method is needed to deal with this correlated nuisance variable. One strategy is to match the groups on IQ and compare the performance of the resulting *matched samples.* Another strategy is to sample randomly from the two populations, and then employ some form of *statistical "correction"* for the known difference. In one case one controls procedurally, in the other statistically. This choice can make a considerable difference in the results.

Matching.   If a variable is distributed in a different way in two populations, the chief problem with matching on it is that the resulting samples are unrepresentative of the populations (Campbell & Erlbacher, 1970; Cook & Campbell, 1979; Meehl, 1970, 1971). For example, IQ is typically distributed differently in lower- and middle-class populations, with the mean for the latter group being higher than that for the former. If lower- and middle-class children are selected for a study only if their IQs are between 90 and 110, the result will be a group of lower-class children who have relatively high IQs compared with their class-mates, and a group of middle-class children for whom the reverse is true. To whom, one may wonder, could the results of such a study be generalized? Although one might wish the answer to be "children of average intellect who happen to have been raised in different socioeconomic circumstances," it is clear that this may not be true. The effects of years of social comparisons with their peers, for example, might have given both groups of children somewhat odd life experiences for children of their social class group.

A related problem is that the atypical samples created by matching are likely to be subject to unequal *regression* effects that make it difficult to study change over time. In this context, "regression" refers to the tendency for any group that is selected on the basis of extreme performance to perform in a more average manner when retested. (Furby, 1973, provides a relatively nontechnical explana-tion of the regression problem and the reasons it occurs.) The more extreme the sample is, relative to its parent population, the greater is the expected regression. For example, taking a cutoff point of 145 on an IQ test and defining such children as "gifted" is a procedure virtually guaranteed to result in a group that will perform more poorly when retested.

Typical Samples.   Rather than risking unrepresentative sampling, it is almost always better to obtain representative samples and to attempt to deal with a nuisance variable statistically. Covariance analyses, multiple regression analy-ses, and techniques based on partial correlations can be helpful. This is a very complex, problematical area in statistical analysis, however, and no general principle that will cover all cases can be given. Reichardt (1979) devotes a chapter to the problem and possible solutions involved in attempting to perform such statistical adjustments, and there are a number of useful articles on the problem (Bryk & Weisberg, 1977; Kenny, 1975a; Linn & Werts, 1977; Lord, 1960, 1967; Overall & Woodward, 1977; Werts & Linn, 1970).

Dual Sampling Strategies.   A final approach to the nuisance variable prob-lem is to employ both matched and representative samples and to compare the results, a strategy suggested by Meehl (1970, 1971). The consequences of Meehl's strategy can be seen in results from a study of personality and moti-vational characteristics in lower- and middle-class children (Yando, Seitz, & Zigler, 1979). With samples of children matched on age and IQ, there were few differences among social class and ethnic groups on a large battery of measures. With typical samples and a covariance analysis there were many differences. Some variables showed significant group differences regardless of the sampling procedure employed. The effort needed for such a double approach can some-times be rewarded by the strength of the generalizations that emerge from it. As Meehl comments, "we know more if we have both to think about" (1971, p. 147).

Summary

Representative samples are important in order to be able to generalize validly from their performance. As truly representative samples usually cannot be obtained, replicating a study's results with new samples is the usual procedure to test whether a finding can be generalized or not.

The nature of age changes in behavior can be studied either cross-sectionally (using different subjects at each age level) or longitudinally (measuring the same subjects at different ages). Both methods are vulnerable to sampling error and societal change, although in different ways. Both methods can be strengthened by combining their best features in either a cohort-sequential or a cross-sequential design.

Obtaining equally representative samples for two or more naturally formed groups is usually complicated by the existence of correlated nuisance variables. Matching on such variables is usually a poor idea, resulting in unrepresentative samples.

DEVELOPMENTAL ISSUES AND STATISTICS

Aims of Developmental Research

Developmental Functions.   One common aim of developmental psychologists is to establish the "developmental function" for a behavior (McCall, 1981; Wohlwill, 1973). This is the process of describing what is typical, average behavior at different ages. The data shown in Figs. 2.1 and 2.2 are examples of developmental functions for cognitive abilities during adulthood. The documentation of basic developmental functions was a key interest early in the history of developmental psychology. Normative patterns for physical growth, language development, and so forth are now a standard feature of developmental textbooks.

Individual Differences.   Another common developmental research aim is the study of individual differences and the stability or instability of a trait across time. For example, is IQ stable: is a bright child always a bright child? Will an unusually tall 12-year-old girl become an equally unusually tall woman?

Statistical Implications of the Two Aims.   The first of these two aims is usually addressed statistically by methods that allow the comparison of means. If there are two times of measurement, the means can be compared with a *t*-test. If there are three or more measurement occasions, some possible choices are an analysis of variance (ANOVA), multivariate analysis of variance (MANOVA), planned trend analysis, or a repeated measures ANOVA. If the data are obtained longitudinally, there will usually be significant positive correlations between the scores for any two times. The procedure chosen should therefore be one that takes this fact into consideration (e.g., a t-test for correlated observations). For three or more times of measurement, either a MANOVA or a repeated measures ANOVA can be used for longitudinal data (see McCall & Appelbaum, 1973, for comparisons of the procedures). With a repeated measures ANOVA, it is usually necessary to introduce a correction for the fact that correlations between tests given close together in time are found to be higher than correlations between the same tests given a long time apart; Winer (1971) provides the necessary information for doing so.

With three or more age levels, a planned trend analysis is a more powerful procedure for detecting age effects and interactions with age than is a standard ANOVA. If developmental change can reasonably be expected to be in the same direction—the scores are either steadily increasing or decreasing, but not both—across the age span in question, trend analysis is more appropriate (Hale, 1977). Hays (1963), Kirk (1968), and Winer (1971) all counsel the use of planned comparisons when justified by reasonable theoretical expectations, rather than the use of an overall ANOVA F-test. Winer (1971, pp. 482–485) specifies how to explore interactions in trend analysis.

The second aim requires information about correlations at each time. As McCall (1977) points out, correlational methods are of little value in determining developmental functions, because correlations are insensitive to differences in mean values across time. Correlational methods are fundamental to the individual differences approach because they preserve information about rank order for all testings. Ordinary correlations, partial correlations, and multiple regression procedures can provide efficient descriptions of the relationships of interest (see Cohen & Cohen, 1975; Draper & Smith, 1981; Kerlinger & Pedhazur, 1973).

Comparison of Groups

Sometimes both aims interest the researcher simultaneously. For example, the investigator may wish to determine whether there are meaningful individual differences in developmental functions. It is also possible to use the data to identify groups of individuals who have recognizably different patterns of development. For example, an investigator might wish to determine if children born to teenage mothers show a different pattern of cognitive development from that of children born to older mothers.

Although comparisons for naturally formed groups are correlational, the statistical analyses applied to the data from such studies need not be. The choice of method depends on whether the researcher's primary interest lies in the group means or in the percentage of variance that is accounted for by group membership status. One can compare the mean from a group of boys with the mean from a group of girls by a t test. It is equally feasible to calculate a correlation coefficient to describe the relationship between sex and performance. All that is necessary is to assign numerical values to the sex "variable" (e.g., 0 = male, 1 = female, or vice versa), and to compute the correlation between sex coded in this manner and performance scores. Similarly, analysis of variance (ANOVA) problems can be analyzed as multiple regression problems (an extension of simple correlational analysis) by assigning numerical values to different levels of the classifying variables. A Sex X Race ANOVA design might thus be recast as a multiple regression predicting performance from sex and racial group membership.

As Cohen and Cohen (1975) point out, a comparison of means is most informative when measures impart a direct sense of the magnitude of the effect. Dollars of welfare costs, age at first childbearing, height, and number of ounces of alcohol consumed daily are directly meaningful numbers. To be told that teenage mothers had an average age of 16 years at the birth of their first child, while a control sample had an average age of 22 would be immediately understandable. Many social science data are based on arbitrary units of measurement, however. To be told that teenage mothers had an average "family conflict" score of 10 while the control sample had an average value of 2 would not be readily interpreted. If one were told, however, that the younger–older mother distinction in the sample accounted for 50% of the variance in family conflict scores, it would be much more easily understood. Cohen and Cohen (1975) argue that multiple regression analysis tends to be more useful, therefore, with data of this kind.

Measuring Change

The single issue that is perhaps the most basic interest in developmental research—the assessment of change over time—is also one of the most difficult problems to address statistically. The principal reason for this fact is that detecting change requires highly reliable measures. (Unreliability, by its very definition, means that scores are likely to be different the next time a measurement is taken.) Using completely reliable measures, it is legitimate to calculate a simple difference score between time 2 and time 1 and to analyze these difference scores. Physicists can calculate changes in temperature, or pressure, or volume, with exactitude. Data in psychological research are usually only moderately reliable, and psychologists cannot measure change so easily.

Psychological change is also difficult to study because a trait can be differently manifested at different ages, and its causes may not remain constant. Aggression, for example, is not likely to be displayed in the same way by a 10-year-old as by a 2-year-old, nor are the causes of aggressive behavior (considered relatively normal in 2-year-olds) the same for the two ages. Change scores comparing the number of times someone bites a peer would thus not only be statistically ill-advised, but also psychologically ridiculous. Studying developmental change requires the researcher to deal both with problems of reliability of measurement and with changing manifestations of, and causes of, the traits the researcher is tracking.

There are technical reasons, deriving from measurement theory, why the difference between unreliable scores is even more unreliable. Discussions of these reasons may be found in many textbooks and in some specialized articles (Cronbach & Furby, 1970; Reichardt, 1979; Werts & Linn, 1970) as well as in Chapter 3. As a concrete illustration, consider what scores should be like if children receive an IQ test at two different times, about a week apart. If one were asked to place a bet on a child's second score, based on one's knowledge of the first score, one might be willing to do so within a range of 5 points or so. But if one were asked to bet on the specific number of points the score would change and whether the direction would be up or down, it would be much riskier. One has a much better (more reliable) idea of what the child's basic cognitive level is than one does of how much it will change from one testing occasion to another. Even with quite reliable variables ($r = .80$), it is easy for the difference score between them to have a reliability as low as .50. Cohen and Cohen (1975) describe the situation well: "the danger in using difference scores is a real one, since they frequently cannot be expected to correlate very substantially with anything else, being mostly measurement error" (p. 64).

A number of alternative procedures to difference scores have been suggested for studying change. Cohen and Cohen's recommendation (1975, chapter 9) is to use regressed change scores. Sociologists and economists likewise tend to favor methods based on multiple regression or partial correlation (Goldberger, 1971; Heise, 1970). Kenny (1975a) points out that cross-lagged panel correlation can be a good choice for ascertaining possible causes of change in a longitudinally studied sample. As Kenny points out, multiple regression presumes causative relationships between predictors and the criterion for study and is vulnerable to measurement error and to unmeasured third variables. Cross-lagged panel correlation presumes both measurement error and unmeasured third variables and attempts to deal with them. This method, along with suggestions for when it should and should not be used, is described in several sources (Cook & Campbell, 1979; Kenny, 1973, 1975a; Rickard, 1972; Rozelle & Campbell, 1969). In practice, it is usually necessary to have relatively large samples to use cross-lagged panel correlation effectively.

There are also a number of procedures that can be applied to the more complex problem of comparing the amount of change in two or more groups. Discussion of these procedures is beyond the scope of this chapter; interested readers may consult Kenny (1975b) and Reichardt (1979) for details.

The choice of a method for analyzing change depends on how the data are gathered (e.g., as judgments in a scaling procedure or scores on tests), on the reliability of the measures, on the underlying pattern of change (increasing or decreasing, linear or not), and on whether the causes of the behavior are assumed to be the same at each time of measurement. Choosing a method is not necessarily as difficult as it sounds. Some simple scatterplots of performance at time one versus time two, and graphs showing the mean performance of each group at each time, can be useful aids in determining what kind of situation the data fit into. By comparing these diagrams with the theoretical ones shown in Reichardt (1979) or Kenny (1975b), it may be possible to decide on an appropriate treatment of the data.

As suggested above, the better the investigator's understanding of the causes and measurement problems involved, the better the statistical analysis of the results is likely to be. What is really needed to study change intelligently is a good working model of causality (Blalock, 1964; Kenny, 1979). As more substantive information becomes available on an issue and a better theory is developed, it is possible to develop increasingly plausible causal models and to use statistical procedures to test them. As Kenny notes, "Ideally the researcher starts with a model or formulates one. Then the researcher determines if the data to be analyzed can estimate the parameters of the model and if the data can falsify the model. Such estimation and testing reveal whether the model is too general, too simple, or just plain wrong" (1979, p. 6).

Kenny's book on nonexperimental causal inference (1979) shows that estimates of causal parameters can be made in a number of ways, including regression coefficients, partial correlations, factor loadings, and canonical coefficients. Nonexperimental causal inference has long been of interest to economists and sociologists, who are generally unable to manipulate the variables—such as interest rates, money supply, crime rates, or urban density—that are important in their theory development. In many cases, developmental psychologists may find these methods useful as well.

Summary

The two chief aims in developmental research are determining what is typical behavior at different ages (establishing the "developmental function") and studying the stability of behavior across time. Statistical procedures for the former involve comparisons of means; addressing the second aim requires methods based on correlations.

The measurement of change is of particular interest to developmental psychologists; yet it is complicated due to the unreliability of measurement, and because of normal developmental changes in the causes and expression of traits. There is no simple solution to these problems. A number of approaches that are sometimes appropriate were discussed. It is likely that causal modeling will prove to be the best strategy for conceptualizing change and that, as substantive knowledge and theory improve in an area, so also will the measurement of change.

ETHICAL ISSUES IN DEVELOPMENTAL RESEARCH

Historical Reasons for Concern

Human beings are not guinea pigs to be experimented with at will. The history of science, however, contains some chilling episodes of science run amok. In the 1920s, medical investigators allowed a group of prisoners suffering from syphilis to remain untreated to prove the effectiveness of the penicillin cure they provided to others (U.S. Public Health Service, 1973). In the 1930s, two psychologists raised a pair of infant twin girls in a single room, rarely speaking to or playing with them, to see if they would develop normally despite these deprivations (Dennis & Dennis, 1941). It is now recognized that the potential emotional and intellectual damage to the children was much too great to permit such a study to be attempted. Due to a growing awareness of ethical issues in research, studies such as these would never be permitted today.

A more recent study that raised the ethics issue in public awareness was performed by Stanley Milgram (Milgram, 1965). Milgram designed the study because of his concern about the obedience Nazi officials had shown in carrying out inhumane acts during World War II. In an effort to learn more about this frightening phenomenon, Milgram studied it in a laboratory, having American college students perform the role of "simply following orders." The results were disturbing: Many students continued to press buttons that had been described as delivering painful electrical shocks, even when they could see the "victim" in the next room, evidently suffering and finally becoming unconscious. Although the subjects were later told the truth—that no shock had been employed and that the "victim" was an actor—the possibility of psychological damage to these subjects was clearly present. This study raised a storm of controversy (see Baumrind, 1964).

Due to the potential for harm, there are some who feel that research with human subjects should never be performed. This extreme position, however, also carries risks for society. Advances in the treatment of diseases such as rabies and yellow fever are clear examples of how scientific knowledge has reduced human misery, and research with human subjects was essential to produce this knowledge. Similarly, practices such as placing children in institutions were once more common than they are today because research has demonstrated that alternative methods of care are usually less harmful. Society needs the knowledge that science can produce, although it must always be careful of the cost.

It is also now recognized that special ethical problems arise when young children are subjects for research. There are many important questions about child development that research might answer to the benefit of all children. But children are vulnerable and may suffer more extensively than an older person from any negative effects of experimental procedures. Children are also unlikely to be able to weigh the potential risks and benefits of participating in a study.

There is no simple solution to the problem of how to balance the benefits of research against the risks involved. A common approach is to have special ethics committees examine proposed research before it is conducted to determine whether it might pose risks and, if so, whether it should be conducted. Federal regulations now require that institutions receiving governmental support for research have an ethics committee screen all proposals for research involving human subjects. There are a number of guidelines that these ethics committees must employ (National Commission for the Protection of Human Subjects of Biomedical and Behavioral Research, 1977).

Guidelines for Ethics in Research

One guideline for ethics in research is that the research should be *scientifically sound and significant*. People have a right not to be asked to participate in studies that are so trivial or poorly designed that they cannot yield useful information. The first decision of an ethics committee, therefore, is whether or not the research is worth doing from a scientific point of view.

A second guideline is *justifiable risk*. The ethics committee must decide whether there are any potential risks and, if so, how serious these risks are. In developmental psychology, most research involves what is called "minimal risk"; that is, no more likelihood of harm than the child normally encounters in daily life. When the risk is more than minimal, however, ethics committees must wrestle with the question of whether the risks are justifiable. If the subjects are likely to receive important benefits, such as a cure for an illness or psychological disturbance, and if the researcher is using the safest possible method, the committee may decide that the risks are justified in that case.

A third ethical principle is the necessity for *informed consent*. People have a right to know exactly what will happen to them if they agree to participate in a study, the nature of any possible risks, and the manner in which the results of the study will be reported. They also have the right not to be coerced in any way and to withdraw from the research at any time. The principle of informed consent does not mean that deception can never be practiced in an experiment. If the deception is mild and is necessary for the purpose of the study, the committee may decide it is permissible. In order to study gambling behavior, for example, it might be necessary to "rig" apparatus so that what the subject thinks is a game of skill is actually a game of chance. If any deception is employed, the researcher is required to provide the truth before the subject leaves the experimental setting.

Obtaining informed consent from children poses special problems, as they are less able to understand the purpose and nature of the research than are adults. Law and longtime practice therefore dictate that the consent for children's participation in a study be obtained from the child's parents or legal guardians. When children are old enough, their own assent is also required, and, as with adults, they must always be allowed to discontinue participating if they wish to do so. As children become adolescents, their best interests sometimes require that they, rather than their parent, should be the only people asked for consent. Ethics committees have special guidelines as to how researchers should obtain consent for participation in programs dealing with drug addiction, teenage pregnancy, and other areas in which the requirement of parental permission might cause the adolescent to avoid participating in a program that he or she would otherwise like to be a part of.

Another guideline is the *right to privacy*. The results of a subject's performance should not be publicized in any way unless the person does not object. In most developmental research, this is not a problem, as results are reported as averages or correlations from groups of subjects. Reporting an individual's performance would require the individual's permission if that person could be identified in any way.

A final guideline is that *principles of justice* must be followed in choosing subjects. If there are any risks in research, they should be borne equally by all members of a society. People who are especially weak or vulnerable, such as children, the sick, and the poor, should not be participants in research more often than other groups of people unless the research is especially designed to benefit them.

In summary, balancing competing ideals in performing research is often not easy. On the one hand, freedom of inquiry is a basic scientific ideal that deserves to be vigorously defended. On the other hand, the protection of individual rights is equally basic. Although there is probably no one "best" solution to the problem of weighing the alternatives, the trend toward ethics committees is a welcome one that should help to maximize the information science can produce, while minimizing its risks and costs.

SUMMARY AND CONCLUSIONS

In this chapter, a number of methods used by developmental psychologists to gather their data and to analyze their results have been discussed. A key emphasis throughout has been the need for flexibility and breadth in locating and adapting methodology. There is no single, best method to study all of the issues that are important in development. The contributions of ethologically trained researchers to our understanding of children's attachment and emotional development has been enormous. These researchers have extensively favored observational methods, rather than experiments, for good and practical reasons. The contributions of cognitive psychologists to our understanding of children's learning has also been enormous. Many of these researchers have used carefully controlled experiments in laboratory settings, again because the method was reasonable and appropriate. It is simply not possible to single out one method of choice for all cases.

REFERENCES

Barker, R. G., & Wright, H. F. (1951). *One boy's day: A specimen record of behavior.* New York: Harper & Row.

Baumrind, D. (1964). Some thoughts on ethics of research: After reading Milgram's "Behavioral study of obedience." *American Psychologist, 19,* 421–423.

Berko, J. (1958). The child's learning of English morphology. *Word, 14,* 150–177.

Blalock, H. M. (1964). *Causal inferences in non-experimental research.* Chapel Hill, NC: University of North Carolina Press.

Bloom, B. S. (1964). *Stability and change in human characteristics.* New York: Wiley.

Boehm, A. E., & Weinberg, R. A. (1977). *The classroom observer: A guide for developing observation skills.* New York: Columbia Teacher's College.

Bornstein, M. H., Kessen, W., & Weiskopf, S. (1976). Color vision and hue categorization in young human infants. *Journal of Experimental Psychology: Human Perception and Performance, 2,* 115–129.

Botwinick, J. (1967). *Cognitive processes in maturity and old age.* New York: Springer.

Brazelton, T. B., Koslowski, B., & Main, M. (1974). The origins of reciprocity: The early mother-infant interaction. In M. Lewis & L. G. Rosenblum (Eds.). *The effect of the infant on its caregiver.* New York: Wiley.

Bronfenbrenner, U. (1977). Toward an experimental ecology of human development. *American Psychologist, 32,* 513–531.

Bronfenbrenner, U. (1979). *The ecology of human development.* Cambridge, MA: Harvard University Press.

Brooks, P. H., & Baumeister, A. A. (1977). A plea for consideration of ecological validity in the experimental psychology of mental retardation. *American Journal of Mental Deficiency, 81,* 407–416.

Bryk, A. S., & Weisberg, H. I. (1977). Use of the nonequivalent control group design when subjects are growing. *Psychological Bulletin, 84,* 950–962.

Campbell, D. T., & Erlbacher, A. (1970). How regression artifacts in quasi-experimental evaluations can mistakenly make compensatory education look harmful. In J. Hellmuth (Ed.), *Compensatory education: A national debate.* Vol. 3 of *The disadvantaged child.* New York: Brunner/Mazel.

Cochran, M. (1977). A comparison of group day and family child-rearing patterns in Sweden. *Child Development, 48,* 702–707.

Cohen, J., & Cohen, P. (1975). *Applied multiple regression/correlation analyses for the behavioral sciences.* Hillsdale, NJ: Lawrence Erlbaum Associates.

Cole, M., & Means, B. (1981). *Comparative studies of how people think: An introduction.* Cambridge, MA: Harvard University Press.

Cole, M., & Scribner, S. (1974). *Culture and thought: A psychological introduction.* New York: Wiley.

Cole, M., & Scribner, S. (1975). Theorizing about socialization of cognition. *Ethos, 3,* 249–268.

Cook, T. D., & Campbell, D. T. (1979). *Quasi-experimentation: Design and analysis issues for field settings.* Chicago: Rand-McNally.

Cronbach, L. J. (1982). *Designing evaluations of educational and social programs.* San Francisco: Jossey-Bass.

Cronbach, L. J., & Furby, L. (1970). How we should measure "change"—or should we? *Psychological Bulletin, 74,* 68–80.

Dennis, W., & Dennis, M. G. (1941). Infant development under conditions of restricted practice and minimum social stimulation. *Genetic Psychology Monographs, 23,* 147–155.

Draper, N., & Smith, H., Jr. (1981). *Applied regression analysis* (2nd ed.). New York: Wiley.

Faust, M. S. (1977). Somatic development of adolescent girls. *Monographs of the Society for Research in Child Development, 42*, No. 1. (Serial No. 169).

Flanders, N. (1970). *Analyzing teacher behavior*. Reading, MA: Addison-Wesley.

Fraiberg, S. (1977). *Insights from the blind: Comparative studies of blind and sighted infants*. New York: Basic Books.

Friedrich, L. K., & Stein, A. H. (1973). Aggressive and prosocial television programs and the natural behavior of preschool children. *Monographs of the Society for Research in Child Development, 38* (Serial No. 151).

Furby, L. (1973). Interpreting regression toward the mean in developmental research. *Developmental Psychology, 8*, 172–179.

Glass, G. V., Willson, V. L., & Gottman, J. M. (1975). *Design and analysis of time-series experiments*. Boulder, CO: Associated University Press.

Goldberger, A. S. (1971). Econometrics and psychometrics: A survey of communalities. *Psychometrika, 36*, 83–107.

Guilford, J. P. (1965). *Fundamental statistics in psychology and education* (4th ed.). New York: McGraw-Hill.

Hale, G. A. (1977). On the use of ANOVA in developmental research. *Child Development, 48*, 1101–1106.

Hays, W. L. (1973). *Statistics for the social sciences* (2nd ed.). New York: Holt, Rinehart & Winston.

Heise, D. R. (1970). Causal inference from panel data. In E. F. Borgatta & G. W. Bohrnstedt (Eds.), *Sociological methodology 1970*. San Francisco: Jossey-Bass.

Hock, E. (1980). Working and nonworking mothers and their infants: A comparative study of maternal caregiving characteristics and infant social behavior. *Merrill-Palmer Quarterly, 26*, 79–101.

Istomina, Z. M. (1975). The development of voluntary memory in preschool-age children. *Soviet Psychology, 13*, 5–64.

Jones, M. C., Bayley, N., MacFarlane, J. W., & Honzig, M. P. (1971). *The course of human development*. Waltham, MA: Xerox Publishing.

Kenny, D. A. (1973). Cross-lagged and synchronous common factors in panel data. In A. S. Goldberger & O. D. Duncan (Eds.), *Structural equation models in the social sciences*. New York: Seminar Press.

Kenny, D. A. (1975a). Cross-lagged panel correlation: A test for spuriousness. *Psychological Bulletin, 82*, 887–903.

Kenny, D. A. (1975b). A quasi-experimental approach to assessing treatment effects in the nonequivalent control group design. *Psychological Bulletin, 82*, 345–362.

Kenny, D. A. (1979). *Correlation and causality*. New York: Wiley.

Kerlinger, F. N., & Pedhazur, E. J. (1973). *Multiple regression in behavioral research*. New York: Holt, Rinehart & Winston.

Kimmel, D. C. (1974). *Adulthood and aging*. New York: Wiley.

Kirk, R. E. (1968). *Experimental design: Procedures for the behavioral sciences*. Belmont, CA: Brooks/Cole.

Lamb, M. E. (1977). Father-infant and mother-infant interaction in the first year of life. *Child Development, 48*, 167–181.

Linn, R. L., & Werts, C. E. (1977). Analysis implications of the choice of a structural model in the nonequivalent control group design. *Psychological Bulletin, 84*, 229–234.

Loftus, G. R. (1978). On interpretations of interactions. *Memory and Cognition, 6*, 312–319.

Lord, F. M. (1960). Large-sample covariance analysis when the control variable is fallible. *Journal of the American Statistical Association, 55*, 307–321.

Lord, F. M. (1967). A paradox in the interpretation of group comparisons. *Psychological Bulletin, 68*, 304–305.

McCall, R. B. (1977). Challenges to a science of developmental psychology. *Child Development*, *48*, 333–344.

McCall, R. B. (1981). Nature–nurture and the two realms of development. *Child Development, 52*, 1–12.

McCall, R. B., & Appelbaum, M. I. (1973). Bias in the analysis of repeated-measures designs: Some alternative approaches. *Child Development, 44*, 401–415.

Meehl, P. E. (1970). Nuisance variables and the ex post facto design. In M. Radner & S. Winokur (Eds.), *Minnesota studies in the philosophy of science* (Vol. 4). Minneapolis, MN: University of Minnesota Press.

Meehl, P. E. (1971). High school yearbooks: A reply to Schwartz. *Journal of Abnormal Psychology, 77*, 143–148.

Milgram, S. (1963). Behavioral study of obedience. *Journal of Abnormal and Social Psychology, 67*, 371–378.

National Commission for the Protection of Human Subjects of Biomedical and Behavioral Research. (1977). *Report and recommendations: Research involving children*. Washington, DC: Superintendent of Documents, U.S. Government Printing Office.

Nesselroade, J. R., & Baltes, P. B. (Eds.). (1978). *Longitudinal research in human development: Design and analysis*. New York: Academic Press.

Orne, M. T. (1962). On the social psychology of the psychological experiment: With particular reference to demand characteristics and their implications. *American Psychologist, 17*, 776–783.

Overall, J. E., & Woodward, J. A. (1977). Nonrandom assignment and the analysis of covariance. *Psychological Bulletin, 84*, 588–594.

Parke, R. D. (1976). Issues in child development: On the myth of the field-lab distinction. *Newsletter of the Society for Research in Child Development*, 2–3.

Peterson, C. C. (1974). *A child grows up: Watching a child develop through a baby-diary and an annotated text*. New York: Alfred Publishing.

Reichardt, C. S. (1979). The statistical analysis of data from nonequivalent group designs. In T. D. Cook & D. J. Campbell (Eds.), *Quasi-experimentation*. Chicago: Rand-McNally.

Rickard, S. (1972). The assumptions of causal analysis for incomplete causal sets of two multilevel variables. *Multivariate Behavioral Research, 7*, 317–359.

Roethlisberger, F. L., & Dickson, W. J. (1939). *Management and the worker*. Cambridge, MA: Harvard University Press.

Rosenthal, R. (1963). On the social psychology of the psychological experiment: The experimenter's hypothesis as an unintended determinant of experimental results. *American Scientist, 51*, 268–283.

Rozelle, R. M., & Campbell, D. T. (1969). More plausible rival hypotheses in the cross-lagged panel correlation technique. *Psychological Bulletin, 71*, 74–80.

Schaie, K. W. (1977). Quasi-experimental research designs in the psychology of aging. In J. E. Birren & K. W. Schaie (Eds.), *Handbook of the psychology of aging*. New York: Van Nostrand Reinhold.

Schaie, K. W., & Labouvie-Vief, G. (1974). Generational versus ontogenetic components of change in adult cognitive behavior: A fourteen-year cross-sequential study. *Developmental Psychology, 10*, 305–320.

Sears, P. S., & Barbee, A. H. (1978). Career and life satisfaction among Terman's gifted women. In J. Stanley, W. George, & C. Solano (Eds.), *The gifted and the creative: Fifty-year perspective*. Baltimore, MD: Johns Hopkins University Press.

Sears, R. R. (1977). Sources of life satisfaction of the Terman gifted men. *American Psychologist, 32*, 119–128.

Seitz, V. (1982). A methodological comment on the problem of infant day care. In E. Zigler & E. Gordon (Eds.), *Day care: Scientific and social policy issues*. Boston, MA: Auburn House Publishing.

Sibbison, V. H. (1973). The influence of maternal role perceptions on attitudes toward and utilization of early child care services. In D. Peters (Ed.), *A summary of the Pennsylvania day care study*. University Park, PA: Pennsylvania State University Press.

Stein, A. H., & Friedrich, L. (1975). Impact of television on children and youth. In E. M. Hetherington (Ed.), *Review of child development research* (Vol. 5). Chicago: University of Chicago Press.

Stern, D. (1977). *The first relationship*. Cambridge, MA: Harvard University Press.

Stevenson, H. W., & Stevenson, N. G. (1960). Social interaction in an interracial nursery school. *Genetic Psychology Monographs, 61*, 37–75.

Thomas, A., & Chess, S. (1977). *Temperament and development*. New York: Brunner/Mazel.

Thurstone, T. G. (1958). *Manual for the SRA Primary Mental Abilities 11–17*. Chicago: Science Research Associates.

U.S. Public Health Service. (1970). *Final report of the Tuskeegee Syphilis Study Ad Hoc Advisory Panel*. Washington, DC: U.S. Public Health Service.

Werts, C. E., & Linn, R. L. (1970). A general linear model for studying growth. *Psychological Bulletin, 73*, 17–22.

Winer, B. J. (1971). *Statistical principles in experimental design* (2nd ed.). New York: McGraw-Hill.

Wohlwill, J. F. (1973). *The study of behavioral development*. New York: Academic Press.

Wright, H. F. (1960). Observational child study. In P. H. Mussen (Ed.), *Handbook of research methods in child development*. New York: Wiley.

Yando, R. M., Seitz, V. R., & Zigler, E. F. (1979). *Intellectual and personality characteristics of children: Social class and ethnic group differences*. Hillsdale, NJ: Lawrence Erlbaum Associates.

Zigler, E. (1969). Developmental versus difference theories of mental retardation. *American Journal of Mental Deficiency, 73*, 536–556.

Zigler, E., Abelson, W. D., & Seitz, V. (1973). Motivational factors in the performance of economically-disadvantaged children on the Peabody Picture Vocabulary Test. *Child Development, 44*, 294–303.

Zigler, E., & Butterfield, E. C. (1968). Motivational aspects of changes in IQ test performance of culturally deprived nursery school children. *Child Development, 39*, 1–14.

3 Measurement and Analysis

Donald P. Hartmann
University of Utah

INTRODUCTION

Developmental research encompasses a broad range of investigative strategies, from the correlational studies performed by traditional developmentalists to the experiments more typically associated with the psychology of learning, sensation, and perception. Whichever of these or other hybrid strategies is followed, techniques of measurement and analysis play crucial roles in both the conduct and the interpretation of the research.

Measurement includes the operations that are used to obtain scores for subjects in developmental research. These scores assess more than just dependent variable performance. They also evaluate subjects' independent variable status, as well as their standing on other variables that might be used to describe a research sample or to control for differences among individual subjects or groups of subjects.

Some methodologists, particularly those who are measurement specialists, might argue that measurement is the *sine qua non* of science; other methodologists, particularly those of an experimental bent, might argue that manipulation of the independent variable deserves that lofty status. Because developmental investigations employ a diversity of research methods, developmentalists would not likely hold a uniform position on this issue. All would agree, however, that measurement (or *scaling,* as it is sometimes called) is a critical research ingredient—one that requires mastery for success as an investigator.

Analysis refers to those procedures, largely although not exclusively statistical in nature, that are applied to the products of measurement (scores) in order to describe them and assess their meaning. Methods of analysis, because they are equated with sometimes difficult and obscure aspects of mathematics, seem to distress students (and some professionals as well) more than any other aspect of scientific inquiry. This chapter discusses some of the technical aspects of statistical analysis—as well as more friendly graphic methods.

Victoria Seitz repeatedly emphasizes, in Chapter 2 of this volume, the dependence of methodology on the questions motivating the empirical investigation. This same point—that the substantive dog should wag the methodological tail, and not the other way around—is equally true of measurement and analysis. The question to be answered should determine, usually in very specific and detailed ways, the measures which will be needed and the forms of analysis that should be applied to the resulting scores. Questions determined solely or even largely by available measuring instruments (e.g., "What question could I ask of these 2,491 WISC-Rs?") tend to be unsystematic, atheoretical, and of dubious use in advancing the science of development. Likewise, techniques of analysis chosen because of their familiarity or availability are unlikely to answer the precise questions addressed by the researcher. The dependence of measurement and analysis on the substance of the experimental questions places an additional burden on investigators: They must find—or, if unavailable, develop—*the* measurement operations and *the* methods of analysis that are uniquely suited to their research questions.

The aspects of measurement and analysis presented in this chapter are not intended to qualify individuals to select, let alone develop, their own measurement and analysis procedures. Those tasks typically require entire *series* of graduate courses. Instead, this chapter is intended to serve as a guide for those individuals who are seriously entering the domain of developmental research; to show them how measurement and analysis work in this area of investigation, by specifying commonly used methods, indicating major issues, noting more serious pratfalls, and suggesting where additional information might be obtained.

MEASUREMENT: OBTAINING SCORES

Scores are the product of measurement and come in a bewildering assortment of types. At one extreme are scores that are expressed in basic units of measurement such as length, frequency, and duration (see Johnston & Pennypacker, 1980). At the other extreme are scores expressed in more complicated, constructed units— IQ, grade-equivalence, percentiles, and "alphabet scores" (T- and z-scores)— which come with additional interpretive baggage.

Whatever the type, the purpose of obtaining these scores is to assist developmental investigators in decision making (e.g., Cronbach, 1970). When applied to empirical research, these decisions concern the validity of individual experiments and studies. Decisions or inferences regarding validity are enormously important to developmental investigators in charting their future research activities, as well as to consumers of developmental research, such as theoreticians, legislators, educators, pediatricians, and parents. These validity decisions are based on the quality as well as the appropriateness and extent of the measurements employed in the research in question, and on a variety of theoretical, logical, and other methodological considerations.

The assessment of measurement quality, not surprisingly, depends on the nature of the research and the specific questions put forward for investigation. Nevertheless, certain criteria generally are relevant to judgments of quality, including whether or not the measurement device is applied in a standard fashion, and whether or not the resulting scores are replicable (reliable) and measure what they are suppose to (valid). Still other criteria may be imposed by the nature of the statistical or other quantitative methods that are to be applied to the resulting scores.

Precisely how these criteria or standards are applied, and which of them are relevant, may also depend on various measurement considerations—sometimes referred to as measurement *facets* and *sources* (e.g., Messick, 1983). The *facets* include the nature of the characteristics assessed; whether they are stable traits or changing states, structures, or functions; and competence or typical performance. Other facets involve whether the scores are used for interindividual (normative) or intraindividual (ipsative) comparisons, and whether they depend for their interpretation on norms (norm-referenced) or upon objective performance standards (criterion-referenced).

The *sources* of measurement include whether the assessment responses are based on children's self-reports, or constitute test responses, or are reports made regarding the children in naturalistic settings by participant or independent observers. These measurement issues are examined in subsequent sections, which conclude with a more extensive discussion of the direct observations of children's social behavior.

Types of Scores

Most scores obtained from subjects in developmental research will be straightforward and understandable either from reading the description of the study's procedures or from examining the study's tables or figures. Examples include frequency and duration scores obtained from observational systems, and many aggregate scores resulting from performance on questionnaires and tests. These scores need not concern us further.

Other scores pose slight interpretive problems because they are transformations of the original scores that are designed either to meet the assumptions of statistical tests or to remedy some perturbation, such as skewness, in the original distribution of scores. Such scores are described in Table 3.1, as are the defects they are intended to remedy and the interpretive warnings with which they are associated.

TABLE 3.1
Transformed Scores, Their Purposes, and Qualifications to Their
Interpretation

Transformation	Purpose	Interpretive Qualifications
$[X+1]^{1/2}$, log X, arc sin X	Regularize (e.g., normalize) distributions for analytic purposes	Interpretation must be applied to transformed scores
Proportion of X_1, X_2, etc.	Control for variation in subject productivity	All subjects have the same total score (across all variables)[a]
Standard score: $z=(X-M)/SD$	Control for disparate Ms and/or SDs for variables	All variables have Ms$=0$ and SDs$=1.0$[b]
Percentile rank of X	Reduce the disparity of extreme scores	All variables are given identical ranges (i.e., 1 to 99)

Note: The original raw scores are symbolized X.

[a]See the later discussion of ipsative scores.

[b]Distributions of standardized scores can be generated with any convenient mean and standard deviation. For example, if the transformed score distribution has a mean of 50 and a standard deviation of 10, the scores are referred to as T-scores. T-scores are generated by the following equation: $T=50+z(10)$.

Still other scores represent more complicated transformations of the original data; such scores must be treated with some caution. Perhaps the most troublesome of these are simple difference scores, X(post-treatment or time 2) − X(pre-treatment or time 1), used to index change over some period of development or as a result of treatment. (Problems associated with change-of-difference scores are discussed by Seitz in Chapter 2; also see Achenbach, 1978; Cronbach & Furby, 1970; Rogosa, Brandt, & Zimowski, 1982.) Other problematic scores are age- (or grade-) equivalent and age-adjusted scores, such as MA and IQ. The former, age-equivalent scores are, of course, only as good as the normative groups on which they are based. In addition, they may vary in meaning at different locations on the measurement scale. For example, during periods when skills and abilities are improving dramatically, the performance differences between adjacent age or grade groups may be appreciable; yet during periods of sluggish growth, performance differences between adjacent groups may be minimal. To take a somewhat farfetched example, contrast the differences in temper outbursts or tantrums between 2- and 5-year-old children and between 7- and 10-year-old children. In the former case the differences would likely be substantial; in the latter case they would likely be trivial. Thus, developmental researchers need to exercise caution in interpreting differences expressed in age equivalents.

Age-adjusted scores such as IQ scores are not only encumbered by the surplus meanings attributed to them (e.g., that IQ scores are fixed, similar to the way eye color is fixed—see Hunt, 1961), but also by the special measurement properties shared by all such age-adjusted scores. Equal scores for children of different ages do not indicate equal skill or ability, but instead indicate equivalent statuses for the children in their respective age groups. Thus, groups of 8-year-olds and 10-year-olds with equal mean IQs of 115 do not have equivalent cognitive skills. Indeed, the 10-year-olds clearly are the more skillful. What the two groups of subjects do have in common is that they are both one standard deviation above their age-group means with respect to IQ (Anastasi, 1978). Age-adjusted scores, similar to age-equivalent scores, must be interpreted with care.

Functions of Measurement

According to Cronbach's decision-making analysis (1970), measurement assists in the classification and selection of individuals and in the evaluation of treatments. Each of these activities occupies developmental researchers, particularly evaluation of the myriad forms of treatments administered to children. (Treatments in this context refer to life experiences, such as attending kindergarten or being hospitalized for surgery, and to levels of some manipulated independent variable, such as alternative methods of stimulating sympathetic responding [Staub, 1979].) Evaluation of these activities involves complex judgments of their validity. Campbell and his associates (Campbell & Stanley, 1966; Cook & Campbell, 1979) have distinguished four validity types that developmental researchers must confront. Each of these forms of validity implicates measurement, and many of them also involve analysis:

1. *Statistical conclusion validity.* Are the statistical tests conducted on the data valid? Or is (statistical conclusion) validity threatened by failure to meet the assumptions of the test, or by insensitivity (low power) of the investigation caused by such factors as small N (sample number), unreliable measurement, or ineffective manipulation of the independent variable?

2. *Internal validity.* Can the observed findings be attributed to the independent variable(s)? Or is (internal) validity threatened by some methodological confound, such as history, maturation, instrumentation changes, testing, or regression toward the mean?

3. *Construct validity.* Do the independent and dependent variables manipulate and measure the intended constructs? Or is (construct) validity threatened by a methodological artifact such as experimenter expectations, social desirability, or the "guinea pig effect" (Selltiz, Jahoda, Deutsch, & Cook, 1959)?

4. *External validity.* Can the results of the investigation be generalized broadly? Or is (external) validity threatened by contrived settings, unusual subjects, or other factors that limit the generality of the results of the study?

These validity issues are particularly acute in developmental investigations because of the vicissitudes of measurement with subjects occupying the ends of the developmental spectrum. Youngsters in particular present problems "of

establishing rapport and motivation, of ensuring that instructions are well understood, of maintaining attention, and of coping with boredom, distraction, and
fatigue'' (Messick, 1983, p. 479). These problems can harbor threats to all of the
four major validity types. In addition, because of children's rapid changes in
many cognitively based activities, it may be difficult to capture their transient
performances levels. This is a problem of reliability that represents a potential
threat to statistical conclusion validity and to internal validity via regression
toward the mean. (Regression is exacerbated by poor reliability.) Furthermore,
the meaning of test scores may change in concert with changes in the children's
development. Thus, at one age, test scores may reflect understanding, and at a
slightly later age primarily reflect motivation (e.g., Hofstaetter, 1954)—a possible threat to construct validity. As a result of these problems in measuring
children's performance, developmental investigators have additional demands
placed upon them to demonstrate that their measures are indeed adequate.

Criteria for Evaluating Scores

The quality of scores usually is judged by their conformity to standard psychometric criteria. These criteria include the standardization of administration and
scoring procedures and the demonstration of acceptable levels of reliability and
of validity (e.g., APA, 1985). Some of these criteria require modification due to
the nature of the variable under investigation. For example, because many performance variables, such as children's social skills, are assumed to be consistent
over at least a few weeks, scores that assess these variables must demonstrate
temporal reliability or stability over that time period. On the other hand, a
measure of some transient characteristic, such as mood, would be suspect if it
produced scores displaying temporal stability over a 2-week period.

   Standardization.   Standardization is intended to insure that procedurally
comparable scores are obtained for all of the subjects who take part in assessments using the device. Thus, standardization requires the use of equivalent
administrative procedures, materials—such as items for tests or questionnaires
and for the timing and the setting for observations—and methods of recording
responses and of arriving at scores. In addition, it may be necessary to provide
directions on how to develop and maintain rapport, whether to terminate or
modify instruction for children with special deficiencies or handicaps, when to
present assessment materials and social commentary, and how to insure that
children understand necessary instructions (e.g., Miller, 1987). The absence of
standardized procedures can introduce substantial noise into data and hence
ambiguity into the interpretation of individual studies or even groups of studies,
as has occurred, for example, in the literature on the assessment of children's
fears using behavioral avoidance tests or BATs (see Barrios & Hartmann, in
press).

Reliability.   Reliability concerns the dependability, consistency, or generalizability of scores (e.g., Cronbach, Gleser, Nanda, & Rajaratnam, 1972). Reliability may be assessed in a number of ways, including across a measure's internal or constituent parts (internal consistency); across observers, scorers, or forms (e.g., interobserver reliability or agreement); across time (stability or temporal reliability); and possibly across settings (situational consistency or generalizability).

The former two types of reliability, *internal consistency* and *interobserver agreement,* are required for most uses of assessment instruments. The scores obtained from an instrument composed of internally consistent parts assess a single characteristic or a set of interrelated characteristics. In contrast, assessment procedures containing internally inconsistent items, time periods, or analogous constituent parts measure a hodgepodge; as a result, scores obtained from them will not be comparable. Two children who obtain identical total scores on an internally inconsistent measure will perform very differently on many of the instrument's parts.

Interobserver reliability likewise is a requisite for the minimal interpretability of scores. Without adequate agreement between observers, the very nature of the phenomenon under study is unclear (e.g., Hartmann & Wood, 1982).

The remaining forms of reliability, *situational consistency* and *temporal stability,* are required when the researcher wishes to generalize, respectively, across settings and time. Such would be the case if, for example, infants' attachment to their mothers assessed in the laboratory at age 10 months was used to infer their attachment in the home at age 10 months (situational consistency or setting generalizability), or their attachment in the laboratory at age 24 months (temporal stability). Temporal stability often is related to the time between assessments. The decreasing stability with increasing interassessment time (sometimes described as *simplex* in structure) has been observed so commonly in investigations of stability that it has assumed the character of a basic law of behavior. Temporal consistency typically increases with age during childhood (e.g., Jones, 1954); and brief temporal consistency often exceeds situational consistency (e.g., Mischel & Peake, 1983), although this finding is open to some dispute (e.g., Epstein & Brady, 1985).

Despite the quite different meanings of the various forms of reliability, they are often assessed in much the same manner—by correlating children's paired scores (e.g., Mitchell, 1979). The scores may be paired across items, observers, time, or settings depending on the type of reliability assessed. The statistics commonly used to summarize reliability data are noted in Table 3.2. The advantages and disadvantages of various statistics for summarizing reliability analyses are described in Hartmann (1982).

Reliability gains general importance because it places a very specific limit on an instrument's empirical validity. If validity is indexed by an instrument's correlation with a criterion (r_{xy}), and the instrument's reliability is expressed at

TABLE 3.2
Commonly Used Methods for Summarizing Reliability Data

Method	Primary Use
Coefficient Alpha	Describes internal consistency reliability.
Intraclass Correlation	General method of summarizing reliability data. Accommodates a variety of data types and forms of reliability. Indicates the ratio of subject to total variance.
Kappa	Summarizes the reliability of categorical data. An agreement statistic corrected for chance agreement. Frequently recommended.
Kuder-Richardson	Assesses the internal consistency reliability of a device composed of dichotomous items.
Product Moment Correlation	General method of summarizing reliability data. Will accommodate all manner of data or type of reliability with one of its many forms. Indicates the ratio of true score to total variance.
Raw Agreement	Most frequently used method of summarizing interobserver reliability data. Frequently criticized.
Spearman-Brown Prophesy Formula	Used for estimating the internal consistency reliability of lengthened or shortened assessment devices.

Note: For more extended lists of statistics used for summarizing reliability data, see Berk (1979), Fleiss (1975) and House, House, and Campbell (1981).

r_{xx}, the upper limit of r_{xy} is $r_{xx}^{1/2}$. That is, $|r_{xy}| \leq r_{xx}^{1/2}$—which is a form of the well-known correction-for-attenuation formula (e.g., Nunnally, 1978).

Validity. Although all of the aforementioned psychometric criteria involve the interpretation or meaning of scores, validity is the psychometric criterion most directly relevant to their meaning. Instruments, and the scores that they produce, may have various forms of validity: they may *appear* valid as would a measure of altruism which asked children about the amount of money they donated to starving Africans (*face* validity); they may be useful for *predicting* certain criteria such as academic success (*predictive* validity); or their content may constitute a *representative sample* of some substantive domain such as junior lifesaving (*content* validity). Perhaps the most basic, and at the same time most inclusive form of validity is *construct* validity—the extent to which the scores assess some *theoretical construct,* such as concrete operational reasoning, anxiety, or self-efficacy.

The extent of an instrument's construct validity depends upon the congruence between the pattern of results it provides and the theoretical superstructure for the construct it presumably measures (Cronbach & Meehl, 1955). The demonstration of congruence usually involves numerous sources of information. For example, the scores obtained from a construct-valid measure of children's interpersonal self-efficacy expectations (Bandura, 1977) presumably would distinguish socially successful from less successful children; show reasonable temporal stability except when following treatments intended to improve children's self-efficacy expectations; and correlate modestly with traditional measures of intelligence and moderately with peer-based measures of popularity and self-perceived competence. The more extensive and collaborative the interconnections between theory and measure, the stronger the evidence of the validity of the measure for assessing the construct (e.g., Kerlinger, 1986).

Wise investigators provide evidence for the construct validity of their measures, evidence that is independent of the results of the study which uses the measures to answer substantive questions. The failure to do so may result in a serious interpretive dilemma, particularly if the investigation does not work out as predicted. Critics may ask: Did the assessment instrument inadequately assess the construct? Was the theory supporting the construct faulty? Or did the study itself contain fatal validity threats? Without independent support for the construct validity of the measures, it may not be possible to decide among these three vastly different possibilities.

Other Criteria. With some interpretations of scores, the standard psychometric criteria must be supplemented with additional quantitative requirements. The scores may be required to have a meaningful zero point; the differences between scores may be required to have direction; and the differences between scores may have to be scaled (e.g., Nunnally, 1978). For example, if the differences between popularity scores are scaled, interpretations such as ''Suzy is as different from Chen in popularity as Sigerdur is from Abdul'' are possible. If, in addition, the popularity scale has a meaningful zero point, interpretations such as ''Ling is twice as popular as Danielle'' also are possible. Whichever of these criteria are met establishes the *level* of measurement obtained by the assessment instrument's scores. The level of measurement relates not only to the interpretations that can be applied to the scores, but also to the statistics that are most commonly used with them (e.g., Stevens, 1968). The typically distinguished levels of measurement, along with illustrations, interpretations, and statistics typically used with them, are summarized in Table 3.3.

Data Facets

Measurement specialists and personality theoreticians have described an array of conceptualizations or facets of measurement that concern developmental investigators. The more important of these facets concern the nature of the constructs assessed—their organization, stability, and content; the targeted response characteristics; and the standards against which scores are compared. These facets are generally noteworthy because they influence the planning, execution, analysis, and interpretation of developmental investigations. More specifically, they deter-

TABLE 3.3
Typically Distinguished Levels of Measurement

Level	Example	Interpretation	Typical Statistics
Nominal	Gender	= or not =	Counts; chi square
Ordinal	Best friends	< or >	Centiles and rank-order correlations
Interval	Grade equivalent	differences are =, <, or >	Ms, SDs, rs and ANOVAs; t and F
Ratio	Height	ratios	Geometric and harmonic means; coefficient of variation

Note: The interpretations and typical statistics appropriate for more primitive levels of measurement also are applicable to higher levels of measurement.

mine which of the psychometric standards are relevant to judging the adequacy of scores. These considerations are touched upon in the following pages; also see Messick (1983).

Nature of the Measurements. The scores which developmentalists target in their empirical investigations invariably represent classes or categories. These categories may be narrow and seemingly simple, such as bar presses (see Bijou & Baer, 1960); or they may be broad and encompassing, such as social behavior. These response categories may be conceptualized as *traits,* which are relatively enduring, internally organized patterns of responding (e.g., Cattell, 1957); as *response classes,* which are sets of responses that are elicited and/or maintained by similar environmental contingencies (Skinner, 1971); or as assessing relatively transient conditions or *states* of the organism (e.g., Hertzog & Nesselroade, 1987). Whichever of these conceptualizations is adopted has implications for both the internal consistency and the temporal stability of the scores used in an investigation. For example, behaviors composing a trait should display internal consistency and temporal stability; but only internal consistency would be expected of behaviors constituting a response class or state (see Gewirtz, 1969).

The responses assessed can also be considered as *samples* of the behavior of interest or as *signs* of some substrate not directly accessible (Goodenough, 1949). Children's eye contact, for example, might be a sample of an important aspect of social skill, or reflect the underlying trait of introversion. In the former case, the investigator must be concerned about the representativeness of the sample of eye contact obtained, and in the latter case about the extent to which eye contact scores predict the trait of introversion.

The substrate assessed need not be some relatively enduring, organized *structure,* such as a trait, but could instead be a *process* or function, such as social problem solving. And either children's *competence* or their *performance* on these structures or processes could be targeted for assessment. According to Messick, "competence embraces the structure of knowledge and abilities, whereas performance subsumes as well the processes of accessing and utilizing those structures and a host of affective, motivational, attentional, and stylistic factors that influence the ultimate responses" (1983, p. 484). The distinction between competence and performance is particularly important for developmental researchers, as it is tempting to imply that subjects are incompetent based on their inadequate performance. However, it may be erroneous to imply, for example, that young children do not have the concept of conservation because they fail to solve Piaget's water-glass problem, or that they do not have a particular linguistic structure because they do not use the structure in their spontaneous verbalizations (e.g., Flavell & Wohlwill, 1969). Instead, the failure may belong to the investigator, who did not elicit competent responses because of faulty selection of test stimuli or setting, or because of the use of inadequately motivating instructions (e.g., Overton & Newman, 1982).

Responses also can be conceptualized in terms of whether they assess behavior, attitudes and images, or physiological responding (Lang, 1968). This triple response *mode* distinction has been particularly useful for the assessment of the constructs of fear and anxiety, which are construed as being represented in varying degrees by different individuals through the three modes (e.g., Barrios & Hartmann, in press).

Response Characteristics.   There are many properties of responses that could form the basis for scoring systems. Some of these properties are simple and easy to measure such as number, duration, and amplitude. Other characteristics of responses are more complex, and must be inferred or judged by some standard that exists beyond the response itself, such as the *correctness* or the *goodness* of the response. In assessing correctness, scoring of responses usually occurs by comparing the responses to a list of acceptable alternatives, and a total score is obtained simply by accumulating all correct or partially correct responses. This is the procedure that is typically followed in scoring achievement tests. Response goodness may be substantially more difficult to judge (see, for example, Cronbach, 1970), and to summarize. To illustrate this latter difficulty, consider the situation in which children's block play is scored for the uniqueness of their constructions (Goetz & Baer, 1973). The children may use quite different building strategies, with some of them generating few, highly elaborated constructions, others many simple ones, and still others some mixture of these two strategies. Thus, a summary response score may need to be based on some weighting of response number, complexity, and uniqueness, even though the latter is of primary interest. This example illustrates a ubiquitous characteristic of performance—that responses differ not only in *substance,* but also in *style.* The stylistic aspects of responding initially captured the attention of measurement specialists because they were a nuisance; differences in style were targets of control as they colored judgments of substance. Later, when the ugly duckling had turned into the Prince Charming (McGuire, 1969, p. 20), and style became the focus, measurement specialists were faced with the opposite task—of assessing style untainted by substance! This latter focus on the manner or style of responding has led to the creation of a number of major style constructs, including social desirability, cognitive tempo, and field dependence (e.g., Wiggins, 1973).

Comparison Standards.   Because most scores are not meaningful in themselves, they must be compared to some standard in order to achieve meaning. Traditionally, scores have acquired meaning by comparison with the average performance of some relevant group of subjects, called a norm group. Such scores, not surprisingly, are called *normative* scores. Typical standard scores and percentile ranks are normative scores. *Ipsative* scores, in contrast, are obtained by comparing the scores to other scores obtained by the same individual (Cattell, 1944).[1] The proportion scores obtained from observational measures of children's social behavior are ipsative scores; they indicate, for example, what proportion of the *individual's* total behaviors was assigned to each of the score categories. Ipsative scores can be perplexing and sometimes troublesome: First, they have unusual statistical properties; for example, the mean of a set of k ipsative subscales is $1/k$, their average intercorrelation is $-1/(k-1)$, and their average correlation with a criterion is exactly zero (Hicks, 1970). Second, ipsative scores pose very knotty problems of interpretation when investigators use both normative and ipsative comparisons. For example, one could be in the difficult position of having to explain how a child who scores consistently below par (normatively) on an IQ test, could score higher (ipsatively) on the vocabulary subscale than another child scoring consistently above average (normatively) on the very same test.

Another possible method of inducing meaning in scores is to compare them with a criterion or a behavioral referent. Using this *criterion-referenced* approach, a child might be said to have mastered the ability to add two-digit numbers, or to have mastered 80% of the tasks necessary to replace the rear wheel of a bicycle. Instruments that are constructed with the intent of using criterion-referenced scoring have substantially different statistical properties than have instruments developed with the intent of employing normative scoring. The primary statistical differences between these two approaches to test construction are summarized in Table 3.4.

---

[1]A somewhat related distinction is made between whether the methods and procedures of investigation are designed to discover general laws (the *nomothetic* approach) or designed to discover laws that may be unique to the individual (the *idiographic* approach); see, for example, Allport (1937) and West (1983). This distinction is one of those that separates behavioral assessment from more traditional branches of assessment (e.g., Hartmann, Roper, & Bradford, 1979).

TABLE 3.4
Distinguishing Features of Criterion-Referenced from
Norm-Referenced Assessment Instruments

Method	Purpose	Statistical Characteristics
Criterion-referenced	Determining what a child can do, or what a child knows	Truncated, sometimes dichotomous score distributions. Items with variable intercorrelations; many easy or difficult items
Norm-referenced	Determining how a child compares to other children	Highly variable, often normal score distributions. Items are moderately intercorrelated. No very easy or very difficult items

Sources of Data

Assessment data on subjects come from a number of sources: from the subjects themselves, from objective tests, and from observations of the subjects in more-or-less natural settings (e.g., Cattell, 1946). These three sources can be further subdivided. For example, self-reports can be open-ended or provided in response to standard questions, their content can be narrowly focused or far-ranging, and they can be intuitively judged or formally scored.

Each of the sources is associated with a relatively unique set of distortions. The presence of these method-specific distortions prompted Campbell and Fiske (1959) to propose that all scores should be conceived of as trait- or behavior-method units: Both the construct assessed and the method of measurement contribute to the resulting scores. As a consequence, total score variation is sometimes decomposed into two variance components: "construct variance" and "method variance". In order to avoid research results that are limited in generality by method variance, investigators assess their major constructs with multiple measures that differ in method-specific variation.

The primary distortions (contributors to method variance) associated with the three sources are summarized in Table 3.5. It is important to note in interpreting this table that the distortions lose their unique associations with the sources if, for example, the child is aware of the purpose of an objective-test assessment, or is even aware that an observational assessment is underway. In these two cases, the distortions produced by deception, defensiveness, and impression management are shared by all three sources.

It is not uncommon in assessment research to confound *mode* (behavior, images, and physiological responses) with *source* in examining the consistency of responding in the three modes. For example, fearful behavior measured with observations might be compared with fearful images and physiological response assessed by means of self-report (Cone, 1979). It would not be surprising in these comparisons to find greater correspondence between self-reports of fearful

TABLE 3.5
Sources of Method Variance for Children's Self-Report, Objective-
Test, and Observational Sources of Assessment Data

	Sources of
Data	Distortions
Self-Report	Misinterpretations; atypical use of descriptors (differing "anchor points")
	Degree of relevant self-knowledge; self-observational skills; memory; verbal skills
	Reactive effects such as deception, defensiveness, and impression management
Objective-Test[a]	Cognitive styles such as impulsivity and field dependence
	Response styles such as acquiescence or position preferences
	Instrumentation effects such as differential familiarity with various item formats and content selection biases
Observations[a]	Observer biases and expectancies
	Observer distortions including memory loss and leveling (Campbell, 1958)
	Instrumentation effects such as halo error, leniency error, and central tendency errors (Guilford, 1954)
	Reactivity effects, such as defensiveness

[a]I am assuming that the child is unaware of the purpose of the assessment for objective-test assessment, and is unaware that the assessment is being conducted for observational assessment.

images and those of physiological responses, than between either of these two responses and observed fearful behavior. This pattern of responding may not reflect greater synchrony between imaginal and physiological response systems. Instead, it may be attributable to the self-report method variance shared by the imaginal and physiological response measures.

To illustrate the variety of issues associated with obtaining scores once a measurement source has been selected, the following section discusses the assessment of children's social behavior by means of observations.

Observations of Children's Social Behavior

Observational assessment of children's social behavior has a long history (e.g., Arrington, 1943), and continues to be popular in both the clinical and the developmental investigations of children (e.g., Cairns, 1979; Lamb, Soumi, & Stephenson, 1979; Sackett, 1978). Observations have been used to assess a variety of human (and infrahuman) social behaviors including infants' attachments (e.g., Ainsworth, Blehar, Waters, & Wall, 1978), children's play (Parten, 1932) and emotional expression (Ekman, 1972), and coercive parent–child interactions (Patterson, 1982). The popularity of this method is due, in part, to the inadequacies of other sources: Young children have limited capacity for describing their own behaviors, and retrospective reports of their behavior by primary socializing agents such as parents tend to be inaccurate (e.g., Goodwin & Driscoll, 1980). Other, more proactive reasons for the popularity of behavioral observations include their flexibility, simplicity, and wide range of applicability (Yarrow & Waxler, 1979). Methodological behaviorism also has emphasized the direct observation of behavior (Hartmann, 1984), as have current research interests in peer interactions and in the microanalysis of children's social behavior (e.g., Messick, 1983; Wasik, 1984).

Choosing What to Observe.   Before observations can be made of children's social behavior, the investigator must answer a series of questions involving the what, where, when, and how of the data collection system. The first question, logically, concerns the behaviors to be observed, and the answer obviously depends largely on the theoretical questions to be asked of the data. Investigators also must make other decisions regarding the following: (a) whether the observation system is to catalogue all responses—in which case it would be called *exhaustive;* (b) whether the response classes are to be mutually exclusive or can occur concomitantly (Sackett, 1978); (c) which response characteristics are to be assessed; and (d) what level of inference is to be required of the observers. As regards the last category, global or *molar* response categories such as "cooperative play," "kvetch," or "empathize" may require substantial inferences from the observers (Hutt & Hutt, 1970). As a result, observational systems using molar responses may require the use of unusually talented observers (Boice, 1983) who are trained extensively. In contrast, so called *molecular* responses— responses narrowly defined in terms of sequences of movements—such as "smile" may require less observer training and nevertheless produce reliable data (e.g., Hawkins, 1982). This is so because of the greater objectivity and operational precision of molecular response definitions.

The Context of Observations.   Next, investigators must select the context of their observations. Observations can be conducted in analogue or laboratory settings, or in either tampered or untampered natural settings such as summer camps, playgrounds, and shopping centers (e.g., Cone & Foster, 1982). Observations conducted in natural settings have the advantage of ecological validity (Bronfenbrenner, 1979), but may be associated with excessive dross—time during which relevant behaviors are not occurring. Contrived settings are usually more efficient of observer time, as investigators can structure their settings to insure that the behaviors of interest occur with adequate frequency. However, as a consequence of structuring observational settings the inferences drawn may be specific to the data obtained in that setting (e.g., Kazdin, 1979).

If observations are conducted in natural settings, investigators may have the choice of using participant observers, such as teachers or counselors, instead of employing independent observers. The former have the advantages of convenience and of unobtrusiveness, but they may be less dependable, more subject to biases, and more difficult to train and evaluate than are independent observers (e.g., Nay, 1979). When behavior cannot be scored *in situ*—perhaps because the presence of observers would cause serious reactive effects or because the scoring system requires repeated exposure to the stream of behavior—observational data can be collected by means of video- or audio-recorder and scored later at the observers' convenience (e.g., Weick, 1968).

Next, unless data are collected by participant observers in institutional or home settings (so that observations can be conducted continuously), observation sessions must be scheduled. Haynes (1978) suggests that more (and perhaps longer) sessions are required when rates of the targeted behavior are low, variable, or changing in some systematic manner; when setting or other contextual events vary; and when complex coding systems are used. Larger numbers of sessions or longer sessions are required also when more than one individual is being observed in the same setting, and when chains of behavior are being studied (see Arrington, 1943).

Finally, investigators must decide on how the behavioral stream will be described. The observations can be relatively unstructured (*open*) (Wright, 1967), or clearly focused (*closed*). Illustrative of an open format are the running accounts, narrative recordings, or specimen records of activities, such as Barker and Wright's (1951) description of a day in a boy's life.[2] Open methods have as their primary functions the generation of hypotheses and the capacity of serving as preliminary techniques in the development of closed methods. Open methods are also useful when a set of observations will later be subject to a variety of scoring systems for quite different purposes.

Closed methods are sometimes called "sampling procedures," perhaps because they refer to various methods of segregating or sampling the behavioral stream. Among the closed methods are real-time recording, event recording, scan sampling, and interval recording (Altmann, 1974). With *real-time recording,* the frequency and duration of the targeted events are recorded as they are occurring. Because of the complexity of this method, real-time recording either is limited to simple observation systems or else requires the aid of special equipment, such as a hand-held electronic recording device (e.g., Simpson, 1979). Such devices are virtual necessities for gathering the fine-grained (or microanalytic) data required for many forms of sequential analysis (Bakeman & Gottman, 1986).

Event recording scores the initiation of events, and is appropriate when only the count of events or chains of events is of interest (Wright, 1960). Because event sampling or recording breaks up the continuity of behavior, it is sometimes supplemented with some form of narrative recording, particularly during the early phases of investigation.

---

[2]This specimen record of the activities of a single day required a 435-page monograph.

Scan sampling refers to a technique that extracts brief "snapshots" from the behavior stream. The observer might glance at the subjects every three minutes and note whether preselected behaviors are included in each "snapshot." This approach provides unbiased estimates of the duration of the targeted responses. Because of its simplicity, scan sampling can even be used when an entire group of children is observed for the occurrence of some response such as hitting or "being near."

The final sampling method is referred to as *interval recording*. This method divides the observation period into brief intervals, each of which is scored if the behavior occurs during any portion of the interval. Although popular (Kelly, 1977), interval recording is problematic as it provides biased estimates of both frequency and duration (Hartmann & Wood, 1982, p. 115). The direction and extent of the bias varies as a function of the interval size and the behavior's frequency and range of durations (e.g., Ary, 1984). Ary and Suen (Ary & Suen, 1983; Suen & Ary, 1986) have developed somewhat complicated methods for retrieving frequency and duration data from interval recordings, but these methods have limited utility.

If the questions motivating the investigation require knowledge of the order of occurrence of behaviors, and knowledge of their frequencies and durations, then real-time recording is required. However, if less complex information is needed, simpler and less expensive methods of "sampling" the behavioral stream can be used. For example, if duration is unimportant, event recording should prove to be adequate. On the other hand, if frequency and order are not relevant to the investigative question, scan sampling should provide acceptable data. And finally, in some intervention programs, the (unknown) mixture of duration and frequency data provided by the interval method might be functional.

Insuring the Quality of Observational Data.   Unless observational data are of high quality, they may be of little use in investigations of children's behavior. Quality can be improved by means of a number of the methods already mentioned, including the use of objective and clear operational definitions of the target behaviors, and by gathering sufficient data for each subject (cf. Hartmann, 1982). Other important methods of insuring that observational data will be of high quality are to select competent and motivated observers, to train them thoroughly, and to assess their performance regularly and unobtrusively. Yarrow and Waxler (1979) suggest that good observers have the ability to sustain their subjects' attention without habituation and to manage high levels of environmental stimulation without confusion; have a compulsive regard for detail and precision and an overriding commitment to scientific detachment; and are intense, analytical, and introspective. Boice (1983), in a review of the observer literature, suggests that in general females appear to make better observers than do males.

Once potential observers are selected, they must be trained. Hartmann and Wood (1982) have described seven steps for training observers. The first step includes an introduction to the importance of objectivity and of ethical principles such as confidentiality in the conduct of observational research. Subsequent steps involve learning the observational manual, scoring enacted observations, learning the rules of courtesy, practicing *in situ,* and conducting retraining-recalibration sessions. In the final step, that of postinvestigative debriefing, the expectations of observers that might have affected their performance are assessed. As Reid (1982) suggests, maintenance of high observer morale throughout these steps is a critical component in insuring high-quality data.

Evidence that observers are adequately trained is disclosed in the results of interobserver reliability checks. (If an incontrovertible standard is available, such as a criterion video tape, observer accuracy as well as observer reliability can be assessed [e.g., Cone, 1981]). These reliability checks require that two or more observers simultaneously and independently code the same stream of behavior, preferably without the observers being aware that their reliability is being assessed. This latter requirement has been added since Reid (1970) demonstrated that announced ("overt") reliability assessments can produce greatly inflated estimates of data quality. Interobserver reliability assessments should be conducted during observer training in order to reveal those behaviors that continue to produce disagreements and hence require additional training, and to indicate when the observers are ready to begin formal data collection. They also should be conducted periodically during regular data collection in order to determine if the observers have deteriorated in their performance and hence need further training (e.g., Taplin & Reid, 1973), and to provide a general assessment of the quality of the data.[3]

If both the investigator and the data collection system survive these steps, the data should be appropriate for primary data analysis. Primary data analysis is directed at answering the substantive questions that motivated the study or experiment. It is this topic to which we next turn. Students who require more specific information on the development of observational procedures for class projects might consult Boehm and Weinberg (1977), Gelfand and Hartmann (1984), or Mendinnus (1976).

ANALYZING DATA

Once scores have been obtained, preliminary operations typically are performed on them so that they will be suitable for formal analysis. These operations include adjusting the data for missing scores and outliers. (*Outliers* are extreme scores that indicate either errors in handling data or atypical subject responses.) These preliminary operations also include any additional measurement manipula-

---

[3]The methods of summarizing reliability assessment data so that they achieve these purposes are a matter of some controversy, and are beyond the scope of this chapter. The interested reader may consult Hartmann (1982) for a moderately technical discussion of these issues.

tions that need to be completed such as the construction of composite scores—difference scores, ratio scores, or total scores—and transformations of the scores in cases where they fail to meet the assumptions of the statistical tests that will be performed on them. With intractable or otherwise troublesome data sets, these adjustments—sometimes referred to as "cleaning" or "laundering" the data—may occur repeatedly and at various points during the data analysis process.

Another important goal of preliminary analysis is to become familiar with the data through hands-on experience with them. This familiarization process often occurs as part of, preceding, or following adjustments of the data. It may involve careful study of plots of means, as well as graphs of univariate and bivariate frequency distributions. It also usually includes the scrutiny of descriptive statistics calculated on the scores, such as measures of central tendency, variability, and association.

Once the data have become old friends, and their general meaning understood, the investigator conducts formal inferential tests on them. These tests function as decision aids that supplement the "binocular" tests conducted during the familiarization stage. The statistical tests determine which of the hypothesized effects, as well as those merely noted, are unlikely due to chance variation in the data; that is, which effects are statistically significant or reliable.

The statistical analysis, whether intended to describe the data or to test hypotheses relevant to them, will differ depending primarily on the research question, and secondarily on the nature of the data.[4] Most research questions can be conceived as belonging to one or both of two analytic classes. In one class are research questions that involve either the correlates of individual differences or the consistency of individual differences across time, settings, or behaviors. The data from these studies require some form of Pearsonian or correlational analysis. Correlational analysis includes simple, part, partial, and multiple regression analysis, and factor analysis, as well as structural equation modeling. In the other class are questions about longitudinal changes or cross-sectional differences in average performance. The data from these studies are subjected to some form of Fisherian analysis, such as the analysis of variance. While both analytic classes are based on the general linear model (e.g., Kirk, 1982), the distinction between Pearsonian and Fisherian approaches to data analysis has been associated with design, subject matter, and other aspects of research strategy (Cronbach, 1957).

As has already been indicated, scores differ in a variety of ways. Two of these dimensions have particular relevance for the selection of statistical tests. The first dimension is whether the scores are qualitative or quantitative in nature. Qualita-

---

[4]These analyses will have been planned, perhaps in detail, much earlier during development of the research proposal. This plan will be based partly on one's general background obtained from course work and readings in statistics, measurement, design, and computer analysis; from the careful study of related research work with particular attention given to the analysis sections of this work; from reading special statistical articles from content-specific journals as well as from the *Psychological Bulletin;* and from consultation with knowledgeable colleagues.

tive scores include binary (e.g., yes–no) and other few-categoried discrete scores, such as "like-neutral-dislike" scales. Quantitative scores are continuous and multipointed, and include ratio, interval, and near-interval scores such as ratings on five-point Likert scales. Qualitative scores often require some form of contingency table analysis, not unlike common chi-square analyses, whereas quantitative scores usually are analyzed using some form of the analysis of variance or traditional regression analysis.

The second dimension concerns the number and type of scores contributed by each sampling unit (sampling units usually are composed of individual subjects, but sometimes a dyad or a larger group such as a classroom constitutes a sampling unit). If each sampling unit contributes (a) one score, then a univariate analysis is performed; (b) one score repeatedly assessed over time or setting, then a repeated-measures univariate analysis may be conducted; or (c) multiple scores, ordinarily obtained during the same time period, then a multivariate analysis is conducted.

Preliminary Analyses

Scores, like toddlers, require our constant vigilance and repeated intervention if they are to stay out of trouble. Some subjects will have missing scores, and we must decide whether estimated scores should be derived for them or whether those subjects should be omitted from some or all of the analyses. Other scores may be incorrectly transcribed on data sheets or mistakenly entered into the computer. Most of these errors can be avoided if investigators emphasize accuracy in their scientific work, provide instructions in how to attain error-free data, institute frequent accuracy checks, and provide incentive for accurate results (Hartmann & Wood, 1982; Reid, 1982).

Still other data inaccuracies may reflect subjects' misunderstandings of instructions, their incorrect use of answer sheets, or even faking or cheating on their part. If these and other errors cannot be avoided by suitable instructions or by performance monitoring, they might be detected—and either corrected or eliminated—if the erroneous data are sufficiently atypical. Unusual scores are detectable if they are substantially different in value from those of neighboring scores. For example, a child who scored two standard deviations either above or below his or her nearest scoring classmate on an observational assessment of aggression would certainly be a candidate for further investigation, and for possible removal from the data set. Incorrect scores also may be detectable because they represent an improbable *pattern* of responding. Examples include responding to the same question differently when it is asked twice; missing three very easy problems but answering correctly four more difficult ones; and admitting to taking birth control pills by someone who indicates being a 10-year-old boy. Detection of errors of this sort requires close scrutiny of the data by members of the research team, perhaps supplemented by computer programs developed to detect unusual responses or patterns of responses (e.g., Hill, 1981; Mickey, 1981).

Still other adjustments may have to be made to the data before they are suitable for analyses. For example, it is not uncommon for scores to be combined or aggregated prior to major data analysis. The item or other subpart scores may be combined based upon purely theoretical considerations—all items measure the same construct, and so the item scores are simply summed to generate a composite total score. Or instead, the item scores may be combined on empirical bases, including the item intercorrelations, their reliability, or their correlations with a criterion (cf. Nunnally, 1978, for a discussion of these alternative empirical strategies for combining assessment information). Finally, and most often, scores may be combined with an eye to both theoretical and empirical considerations. Simultaneously serving more than one criterion need not be troublesome, unless of course the criteria suggest opposite courses of action, as may happen when theoretically appropriate items are inconsistently correlated with one other. In that case, after suitable digging into the data in an effort to make sense of the inconsistencies, investigators must rely upon their good judgment and perhaps the good judgment of their colleagues.

Another common preliminary manipulation of the data involves equating scores for differences in the opportunity to behave. For example, children may be evaluated on the number and kinds of errors they make in solving math problems, but may differ in the number of problems attempted. In such cases, investigators adjust scores by prorating, by shifting to proportion or percentage scores, or by employing other ratios such as rate per unit of time.

Still other transformations of scores, such as square root, log, and arc sin transformations may be required because the original scores violate the assumptions of statistical tests that will be performed on them. These transformations and their effects were outlined earlier in the section entitled "Types of Scores."

Following such laundering operations, or as part of or sometimes interspersed between them, investigators are well advised to construct graphs of their data and to calculate descriptive statistics on them. It is these data-familiarization tactics to which we next turn.

Becoming Familiar with Data

Informal or exploratory data analysis—consisting of constructing graphs, charts, and plots, and calculating simple descriptive statistics—is critically important to understanding the meaning of data. Indeed, some investigators argue that these procedures, particularly the scrutiny of graphic displays, constitute the *primary* method of judging the outcomes of experiments (e.g., Baer, 1977).

Whether these methods are primary or merely contributory methods for judging the outcomes of experiments, there is little doubt of their importance. Unfortunately, it seems that too often novice investigators omit all or the greater portion of the preliminary stage of data analysis: The excitement of having completed data collection is quickly followed by the need to know if the data contains anything "statistically significant." And so the data are prematurely formally analyzed, oftentimes using only standard or "canned" computer programs—and often with results that unnecessarily support the adage "garbage in, garbage out." This misplaced enthusiasm deprives investigators of the opportunity to experience a sense of intimacy with their data—the kinds of "hands-on" experiences from which serendipidous findings and otherwise new perspectives are discovered. Unfortunately, there is not a large literature on useful methods for gaining familiarity with data, and so the procedures tend to be idiosyncratic and perhaps needlessly artistic in nature. Generally, however, they involve constructing graphic displays and calculating standard as well as "quick and dirty" descriptive statistics (e.g., Tukey, 1977).

Graphing Data.   Useful graphic displays range from freehand sketches of univariate and bivariate frequency distributions to computer-crafted, publication-ready, three-dimensional drawings of multiple time series (cf. Parsonson & Baer, 1978). The concern during preliminary data analysis is not with esthetics, however, but with utility. For example, when groups are being compared, simple bar graphs (see Fig. 3.1) of each group's performance can readily be drawn. If there are many groups or many dependent variables, a master graph containing the labeled ordinate and abscissa can be constructed and duplicated, perhaps on sheets of acetate. If different colored pens are used for plotting each group's data, the groups can be easily compared for differences in average responding or

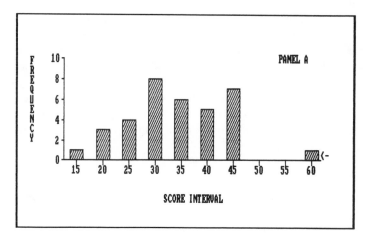

FIG. 3.1. Univariate frequency distributions illustrating the presence of an outlier (Panel A), a bimodal distribution (Panel A), a positively skewed distribution with a pronounced floor effect (Panel B), and an approximately normal distribution in which the estimated and calculated values of the mean (*M*) and standard deviation (*SD*) are in reasonable agreement (Panel C).

Panel A. Illustration of a bimodal frequency distribution containing an outlier (see arrow). With the outlier, *M* = 34.3, *SD* = 9.56, and *N* = 35; without the outlier, *M* = 33.5, *SD* = 8.57, and *N* = 34.

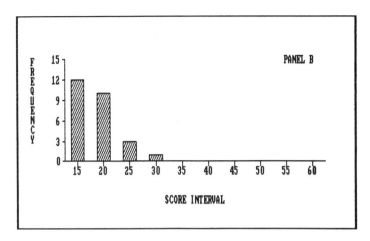

Panel B. Illustration of a positively skewed frequency distribution with a distinct floor effect. For this distribution, M = 18.7, SD = 4.14, and N = 26.

variability of responding by stacking the graphs and holding them up to a light source.

Before graphs are compared with one another, they should be examined individually. Each display might be checked for atypical performances (see Panel A of Fig. 3.1) if this has not already been done in some other way, and a decision made concerning how unusual respondents should be handled. Other aspects of the data also might be noted, such as the modality or peakedness of the

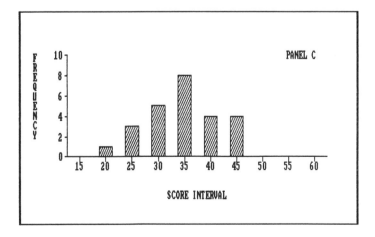

Panel C. Illustration of an approximately normal frequency distribution for which rules of thumb provide close approximations to the M and SD of the distribution. M = 34.6 (estimated M = 35), SD = 6.8 (estimated SD = range/3.8 = 25/3.8 = 6.6), N = 25.

distribution of scores (see the bimodal distribution in Panel A of Fig. 3.1), their symmetry (see the positively skewed distribution in Panel B of Fig. 3.1), and whether floor and ceiling effects are present (also see Panel B of Fig. 3.1). Bimodal distributions are found when a sample is composed of scores for two quite different types of subjects, such as a distribution of birth weights for a sample composed of full-term and preterm infants. Skewness, or lack of symmetry in the scores, might occur for a variety of reasons, including the presence of floor or ceiling effects. These latter forms of asymmetry are observed when a preponderance of subjects receives either the lowest scores (floor effect) or the highest scores (ceiling effect) on the assessment instrument. In ability testing, the presence of a floor effect suggests that the test was too difficult for the subjects, while a ceiling effect suggests that the test was too easy for them.

If the data are approximately normal in their distribution, both the mean and the standard deviation can be readily estimated from graphic displays. The mean will lie approximately in the center of the distribution, and the standard deviation will be between one sixth and one half of the group's range, depending on the size of the sample (see Table 5.6 in Guilford, 1965, p. 81). With the data shown in Panel C of Fig. 3.1, the standard deviation for a sample of $N = 25$ is estimated to be 1/3.8 of the range of scores ($= 25/3.8 = 6.6$).

When investigations employ more than one dependent variable it often proves useful to cross-tabulate the scores or to sketch their bivariate frequency distribution (see Fig. 3.2). The resulting displays—sometimes referred to as *scatter diagrams*—can be examined for a number of disturbances, including the presence of outliers. When outliers are present, they can dramatically change the magnitude of the correlation between the variables. (Compare the value of r for the data in Panel A of Fig. 3.2 when the outlier is included, and when the outlier is excluded.)

Scatter diagrams also can be checked for the extent to which the regressions between the variables are linear. Nonlinear regression is illustrated in Panel B of Fig. 3.2. Because the product moment correlation (r) assesses the linear part of the relation between variables, r will underestimate the relations between variables that are nonlinearly related. Compare, for example, the value of r and of eta (the curvilinear correlation coefficient) for the data shown in Panel B of Fig. 3.2.

In addition to disclosing the presence of outliers and nonlinear regressions, scatter diagrams can indicate *heteroscedasticity* or unequal dispersion of scores about the regression line. Heteroscedasticity indicates that errors of prediction vary depending upon the value of the predictor score. With the data displayed in Panel C of Fig. 3.2, Y-scores are less accurately predicted for individuals with high X-scores than for individuals with low X-scores.

Scatter diagrams and other graphic plots serve both as important detection devices and as judgmental aids in the hands of experienced investigators. Indeed, after substantial experience with well-behaved bivariate displays, visual analysts

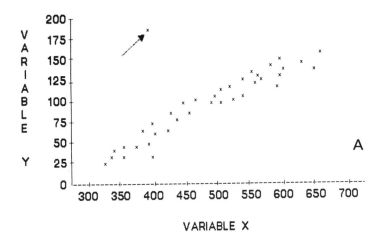

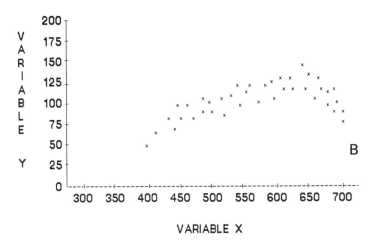

FIG. 3.2.   Bivariate frequency distributions illustrating an outlier (see arrow in Panel A), linear regression (Panel A), curvilinear regression (Panel B), homoscedasticity (Panel A and the regression of Y on X for Panel B), and heteroscedasticity (Panel C and the regression of X on Y for Panel B).

Panel A.   Illustration of positive linear relation between variables X and Y. Outlier indicated by arrow. With the outlier included, $r = +.81$; with the outlier omitted, $r = +.94$. The dispersion of scores with each X-array is approximately normal (homoscedasticity). $N = 38$.

Panel B.   Illustration of curvilinear relation between X and Y. The value of the linear correlation is $+.54$, whereas the value of eta, the curvilinear correlation, is $+.94$. The disperson of scores within each X-array is approximately equal (homoscedasticity). $N = 40$.

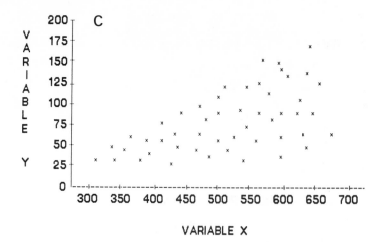

VARIABLE X

Panel C. Illustration of heteroscedasticity (unequal dispersion of scores within each X-array). $r = +.57$ and $N = 50$.

may be able to estimate the magnitude of the correlation between variables with less than $\pm.05$ margin of error. Such estimates can serve as convenient checks on the accuracy of computer calculations.

More on Descriptive Statistics.   Although means, standard deviations, and correlation coefficients are the most commonly used descriptive statistics, a number of other statistics are sufficiently common to deserve brief mention.

First we consider a number of the many descriptive statistics related to r, the correlation coefficient: part and partial correlation, kappa, and conditional probability. *Part* and *partial correlations* are ordinary product–moment correlations that deserve special names because of the nature of the scores to which they are applied: either one (part) or both (partial) of the scores correlated are corrected for heterogeneity with respect to a third variable. For example, in a three-variable regression problem involving height, weight, and age, the correlation between height and weight with age controlled is called the partial correlation, and is symbolized $r_{hw \cdot a}$. This partial correlation—between height and weight—is equal to the correlation between these two variables when calculated in a homogeneous age group. If age was partialed out of weight, but not out of height, the resulting correlation would be the part correlation between height and weight. This part correlation is symbolized $r_{h(w \cdot a)}$. Part correlations play an important role in multiple regression, as they indicate the overlap of the criterion with the unique portion of each of the predictors. In a three-predictor variable problem, the unique relation between the criteria (c) and predictor variable three (p_3) is given by $r_{c(p_3 \cdot p_1 p_2)}$.

Kappa (Cohen, 1960) is an agreement statistic that is used increasingly to

| | | Observer 1 Child Interacts With | | | |
Observer 2		Peer	Teacher	No one	Totals
Child Interacts With	Peer	95	05	10	110
	Teacher	05	25	00	30
	No one	20	00	40	60
	Totals	120	30	50	200

FIG. 3.3 Joint but independent observations of a child's interactions by Observer 1 and Observer 2 used to illustrate the calculation of interobserver reliability using Cohen's kappa.

summarize interjudge reliability data, particularly for observationally gathered data. Assume that two observers each independently classified the same 200 10-sec observation intervals into whether a target child interacted with her peers, or with her teacher, or failed to interact. The resulting data might resemble those given in Fig. 3.3. A typical, older, and flawed method of summarizing these data is simply to tabulate the proportion of intervals for which the two observers agreed. For the data in Fig. 3.3, the observers agreed on 95 intervals scored as "interacted with peers," 25 intervals rated as "interacted with teacher," and 40 intervals classified as "no interaction". These 160 intervals, when divided by 200 (the total number of intervals during which observations were taken), gives a proportion of agreement of .80. When kappa is calculated on these same data, a somewhat lower estimate of agreement is obtained, as kappa corrects for agreements that might have occurred by chance (e.g., Hartmann, 1977). Kappa is equal to

$$(p_o - p_c), \text{ where}$$

p_o is the proportion of observed agreements, and

p_c is the proportion of chance agreements.

For the data in Fig. 3.3, p_o is .80, as we have already determined in the calculation of the simple agreement statistic; and p_c is equal to the sum of the expected values[5] for each of the agreement cells in Fig. 3.3 divided by the total number of observation intervals. The expected value for the agreement cell for "interacts with peers" is $120 \times 110/200 = 66$; for the agreement cell "interacts with teacher" it is $30 \times 30/200 = 4.5$; and for the agreement cell "no interaction" it

---

[5]The expected values are determined in exactly the same manner as they typically are for chi square tables; that is, by summing the products of corresponding marginal values and dividing by N.

is $50 \times 60/200 = 15$. Summing these values and dividing by N yields $p_c = (66 + 4.5 + 15)/200 = .4275$. Kappa is then equal to

$$(.80 - .4275)/(1 - .4275) = .65.$$

The final common descriptive statistic related to r is the *conditional probability*. Conditional probabilities play an important role in analysis of fine-grained interactional data. These probabilities can perhaps best be understood by examining 2×2 table data, such as those shown in Fig. 3.4. The data in Fig. 3.4 describe the temporal patterning of talking by a mother and her child. These data can be summarized in various ways, including a correlation statistic such as the phi coefficient, or by means of a conditional probability. The conditional probability of the child talking, given that her mother talked in the prior interval, is equal to the joint probability that the child talked and the mother talked in the previous interval divided by the probability that the mother talked in the previous interval (e.g., Allison & Liker, 1982). For the example given in Fig. 3.4, the conditional probability of the child talking at time $t + 1$ given that her mother talks in the previous interval—$(\Pr[C_{t+1} = 1 \mid M_t = 1])$—is equal to $B/(A + B) = 40/(10 + 40) = .80$. The conditional probability is oftentimes compared with its *unconditional probability*. The unconditional probability of the child talking—$\Pr[C_t = 1]$ or $\Pr[C_{t+1} = 1]$—is, again with reference to the symbols used in Fig. 3.4, $(B + D)/(A + B + C + D) = (40 + 20)/(10 + 40 + 30 + 20) = .60$. Thus, the mother's talking in the previous interval increases the likelihood that the child will talk in the following interval from .60 to .80.

Another common descriptive statistic, this one similar to an ordinary variance, is the characteristic root or *eigen value*. Eigen values are to matrices what the variance is to a distribution of numbers. Not surprisingly then, eigen values (symbolized as gammas), are frequently encountered in multivariate analysis, where one deals with matrices of scores. For example, in principle component analysis, a factoring technique, the eigen value for each principle component may be thought of as the amount of variance in the original standardized variables associated with that principle component. In canonical correlation analysis, the multivariate analogue of r, the eigen value associated with each set of

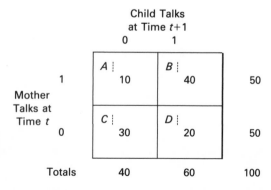

FIG. 3.4. Temporal sequence of mother and child talking (mother talking at time t and child talking at time $t + 1$) used to illustrate the calculation of conditional probabilities.

		Child Talks at Time $t+1$		
		0	1	
Mother Talks at Time t	1	A — 10	B — 40	50
	0	C — 30	D — 20	50
Totals		40	60	100

TABLE 3.6
Illustration of the Calculation of Standard
Normal Deviates

	N	M	SD	Pooled SD
Girls	357	5.7	4.4	5.01
Boys	399	6.1	5.2	

$$d = [M(\text{girls}) - M(\text{boys})]/SD(\text{pooled})$$
$$= [5.7 - 6.1]/5.01$$
$$= -.08$$

Note: Data obtained from Hartshorne, May, and Maller (1929).

canonical variables indicates the variance shared by the variables. And in multi-variate analysis of variance the eigen value can be thought of as the variance between the group centroids.[6]

The final descriptive statistic is the *standard normal deviate*. We briefly alluded to the standard normal deviate in Table 3.1 under another name—the standard score or z-score. A standard score is defined as the signed deviation of a raw score from the mean score measured in standard deviation units; that is, $z = (X - M)/SD$. Standard scores, by definition, have a mean equal to zero and a standard deviation equal to 1.0; in a normal distribution of scores, z-scores range from approximately -3.0 to $+3.0$.

Standard scores are used in a variety of statistical and measurement operations. For example, item scores often are transformed to z-scores before they are added together to form a composite or total score. This transformation is undertaken in order to insure more equal weighting of items. A type of standard score called a *d*-score is increasingly used in quantitative summaries of research literatures, called *meta analyses* (see the penultimate section of this chapter). A *d*-score is defined as the difference between two group means divided by a standard deviation, usually the pooled within-group standard deviation. The calculation and meaning of *d* is illustrated with data obtained by Hartshorne, May, and Maller (1929), and included in a recent meta analysis of gender differences in children's altruism (Abbott & Hartmann, 1986). The data are summarized in Table 3.6. The value of *d* for "Donating school supplies to needy others" is $-.08$. This value indicates that the mean donation for the boys exceeds the mean donation for the girls by .08 standard deviations; it is equivalent to a correlation between gender and donating of about .05. Furthermore, if we could assume that the distributions of both the girls' and the boys' donation scores were normal with equal standard deviations, one could also state that the average boy donated more than about 54% of the girls (Cohen, 1977).

---

[6]A centroid is to multiple dependent variables what a mean is to a single dependent variable.

Inferential Statistical Tests

Following the calculation of descriptive statistics, investigators employ one or more methods to judge the significance of the statistics. Significance in this context refers to whether or not the effects of interest, which are presumably reflected in the data and in the summary descriptive statistics applied to the data, could have arisen by chance. The primary method that developmentalists use to judge the statistical significance of their results is *null hypothesis testing*. Preference for this method of assessing statistical significance exists despite the very substantial criticism directed at null hypothesis testing procedures (e.g., Meehl, 1978; Morrison & Henkel, 1970).

Null Hypothesis Testing.   Null hypothesis testing is a multistep process that begins with the development of two models or hypotheses about the data. One model, sometimes called the experimental model, contains the putative effect of interest to the investigator, such as treatment, age, or gender. The other model, often called the null or restricted model, either does not contain this effect or states that the effect of interest equals zero. Null models or hypotheses often are stated in one of two forms.[7] In one form of the null hypothesis, some effect or parameter is assumed to equal zero in the population under investigation. The parameter, for example, may be a beta weight in a multiple regression analysis or an interaction term in a multivariate analysis of variance; the population may be defined by any number of independent variables. In another form of the null hypothesis, the values of the parameter of interest for two or more populations are assumed to be equal. The parameters to be compared most often include population means, correlation coefficients, or variances.

In the second step of null hypothesis testing the investigator decides how unlikely the obtained results must be before concluding that the null hypothesis is probably false. The logic implied here is that if the sample data are unlikely to have occurred under the null model, then that model must not be true. This step is sometimes referred to as "selecting an alpha level." Alpha levels (or probabilities) of .05 or .01 are the conventional ones used by investigators in deciding whether to reject their null models or hypotheses. However, it is important to add that the selection of alpha should be based on the consequences of making a type I error versus the consequences of accepting a false null hypothesis, and not based on convention. If the consequences of making a type I error are substantial—say millions of dollars may be spent in changing an existing social pol-

---

[7]These are the forms for two-tailed tests. For one-tailed null hypotheses, substitute for the word "equal" either the phase "equal or less than" or the phrase "equal or greater than." Which of the two phases is used depends upon the direction of the investigator's prediction. For example, if the investigator expected the correlation to be greater than zero, then the first form of the null hypothesis would be used with the phrase "equal or *less* than" substituted for the word "equal."

icy—and the consequences of accepting a false null hypothesis are minor, a very, very small alpha level, such as .0001, might be employed.

In the third step, the investigator uses the sample data to compute the value of a test or inferential statistic. This test statistic measures the extent of the deviation of the sample data from that expected on the basis of the null hypothesis. Traditional univariate test statistics are the z (normal curve) test, the t test, the F-test, and the chi-square test. Multivariate test statistics include Wilk's lambda, Roy's theta, and the Pillai–Bartlett trace criterion (e.g., Marascuilo & Levin, 1983).

In the fourth step, the investigator determines the probability associated with the test statistic, often by reference to statistical tables or computer output. In order for these sources to provide appropriate probability values, the sample data must be consistent with a set of assumptions required by the statistical test. While each statistical test has its own set of assumptions, some assumptions are common to many inferential tests. Typical among these shared assumptions are the assumptions that scores (usually error or residual scores) must be distributed normally, homogeneously, and independently. Violation of these assumptions— particularly that of independence and to a lesser degree that of homogeneity— can result in highly erroneous probability values (e.g., Kirk, 1982; Lewis & Burke, 1949; Scheffé, 1959). In order to insure the correctness of probability values that result from the major statistical analyses, the tenability of critical assumptions is assessed by means of their own statistical tests (see, for example, Kirk, 1982).

In the final step of null hypothesis testing, the probability value associated with the statistical test is compared with the alpha value selected by the investigator (see step two). As a result of this comparison, the null hypothesis, and the model on which it is based, is either accepted or rejected. These five steps are summarized and illustrated with a fictitious sample correlation coefficient in Table 3.7.

As I have already suggested, investigators may err in two different ways using the null hypothesis testing approach. A type I error is made when a correct null hypothesis is rejected. The probability of a type I error is given by the value of alpha selected by the investigator, such as $p < .05$. A type II error is made when an incorrect null hypothesis is accepted. The probability of a type II error cannot so easily be determined, as type II errors depend on a number of factors. Some of these factors include the magnitude of the parameter (such as a correlation coefficient) tested, the reliability and variability of scores, the statistical test conducted on the data, and the value of alpha selected by the investigator (see, for example, Cohen, 1977).

Just as two types of incorrect decisions are possible, so also are two types of correct decisions possible. Correct decisions are made when a true null hypothesis is accepted and when a false null hypothesis is rejected. The probability of the former correct decision is 1.0 minus the value of alpha. The latter proba-

TABLE 3.7
Illustration of Null Hypothesis Testing

Step (1)

An investigator explores the relation between the number of observed positive social requests and sociometric status in a group of 3-year-old children. The null hypothesis states the following about the population correlation (rho):

$$rho = .00.$$

This null hypothesis is contrasted with an alternative hypothesis that states that

$$rho \text{ is not equal to } .00$$

Step (2)

Alpha, the probability associated with rejection of the null hypothesis, is set at $p<.05$. Therefore the obtained finding must have a probability of occurrence of less than .05 before the null hypothesis will be rejected and the alternative hypothesis accepted.

Step (3)

The obtained correlation is tested with the z-test for the significance of r using Fisher's r to z_r transformation. With $r = .50$, and $N = 19$,

$$z = z_r(N-3)^{1/2}, \text{ where } z_r \text{ for } r = .50 \text{ is } .549$$
$$= .549(19-3)^{1/2} = .549(4) = 2.20$$

Step (4)

The probability value associated with $z = 2.20$, according to the normal curve table, is approximately $p = .028$.

Step (5)

Because $p = .028$ meets the criterion established in Step (2) where alpha was set at $p<.05$, the null hypothesis is rejected. Therefore, it is concluded that positive social requests and sociometric status are significantly correlated in 3-year-old children.

---

bility, referred to as the power of the statistical test, is 1.0 minus the probability of a type II error. Power has increasingly been recognized as a critical consideration in the design of investigations (e.g., Cohen, 1977). Adequate power, say in excess of .80, can be insured during the design of a study by selecting large subject samples and by using reliable measures of the dependent variables and cleanly manipulated and powerful independent variables. The calculation of power for the example given in Table 3.7 and a summary of the decisions involved in null hypothesis testing are presented in Table 3.8.

The statistical testing procedures just outlined differ in detail depending on a variety of considerations. These considerations include the descriptive statistic that answers the investigator's question. For example, questions answered by examining means may require different testing procedures than do questions concerned with variability or correlation. Another consideration involves

TABLE 3.8
Illustration of a Power Calculation and Summary of the Decisions
Resulting from Null Hypothesis Testing

A. Summary of Decision Making:

	State of Nature: H_o	
	Correct	Incorrect
Reject H_o	Type I Error (Alpha)	Correct Rejection [Power]
Investigator's Decision		
Accept H_o	Correct Acceptance (1 − alpha)	Type II Error

Note: H_o is the commonly used symbol for the null hypothesis.

B. Illustration of a power calculation using the data from Table 3.7.

Assume that the value of the correlation in the population is .30. The z_r corresponding to an r of .30 is .309. With samples of size 19, and a population z_r = .309, the distribution of sample z_rs centers at .309 and has a standard deviation of $17(n-3)^{1/2}$ = 1/4 = .25. On the other hand, the sampling distribution under the null hypothesis centers at 0.0 with a standard deviation of .25. These two sampling distributions are depicted below.

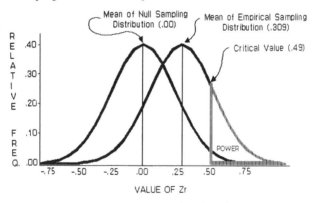

If alpha is set at .05, a sample $z_r \geq$ ┊ 1.96(.25) ┊ $\geq$ ┊ .49 ┊ is required for significance. The critical value of +.49 is indicated on the figure above.

The probability of obtaining a sample $z_r \geq$ +.49 is found by determining the proportion of area in the empirical sampling distribution (the one centering at .309) that lies to the right of the critical value of +.49 for rejecting the null hypothesis. (The area in that distribution lying to the left of the critical value of −.49 can be disregarded, as sample values that small are very unlikely to occur in this problem.) This is the area that lies to the right of the z-score of (.49−.309)/.25 = .724 (see shaded area in figure above). This area includes all sample values of z_r which would have resulted in rejection of the null hypothesis.

About a quarter of the area of the empirical sampling distribution lies to the right of the z-score of .724. Thus, the probability of correctly rejecting the null hypothesis is .25 (1 out of 4)— *if* the value of the population correlation is .30, a sample of size 19 is drawn, and the sample correlation is tested using Fisher's r to z_r transformation and the z test for the significance of a correlation. Most investigators would find this level of power too low. Hence, they probably would have designed the investigation differently, perhaps using more subjects.

whether each independent experimental unit[8] receives a score for a single dependent variable (univariate analysis), more than one score for a single dependent variable (repeated measures analysis), or one or more scores for more than one dependent variable (multivariate analysis). Still another consideration is whether qualitative or quantitative data are tested for significance. The following sections address significance testing in these various circumstances. Because of the large number of combinations of circumstances involved, however, only those commonly occurring are discussed.

Qualitative Analysis

The analysis of categorical data, the most common form of qualitative data, typically has involved some form of *chi-square analysis*. Less frequently used are other nonparametric tests, such as Fisher's Exact Test, and parametric tests which are more appropriate for quantitative data. Chi-square tests serve a variety of uses in the statistical testing of categorical data. For example, they are used to determine whether proportions or frequencies differ from one another, whether categorical variables are correlated, and whether distributional assumptions, such as normality, hold. These uses of chi-square and of other traditional nonparametric testing procedures have been ably described in a number of books, including those by Conover (1971), Hollander and Wolfe (1973), Fienberg (1980), Fleiss (1973), and the perennial favorite of psychologists, Siegel (1956), and are not catalogued here. Instead, I note some common errors made in these analyses and then briefly describe relatively new methods for analyzing complex categorical data.

Perhaps not surprising in view of their general utility, chi-square tests have long been a favorite for abuse. The sources of this abuse are clearly spelled out in a sequence of critical papers, including the classic papers by Lewis and Burke (1949, 1950) and the recent paper by Delucchi (1983). Perhaps the most serious of the many errors made in the use of chi-square is violation of the independence assumption. This error frequently occurs when investigators shift experimental units from subjects to the events engaged in by these subjects.

Consider a set of fictitious data gathered to assess a prediction derived from a theory of moral development: that 4-year-olds would cheat more frequently in turn-taking than would 6-year-olds. The data gathered to test this hypothesis might take the form of the number of violations of turn-taking observed during 10-minute samples of free play for fifteen 4- and fifteen 6-year-old children. If

---

[8]The number of independent experimental units usually, though not always, is equal to the number of subjects. Exceptions occur when the responses of subjects affect one another, as when subjects interact as dyads, as families, or as larger social units such as classrooms. In those cases, the independent experimental units are given by the number of dyads, families, and classrooms, respectively. See, for example, discussion of interacting or "nested" subjects by Anderson and Ager (1978) and by Cairns (1983).

the number of cheating incidents totaled 25, and individual scores ranged from 0 to 3, some investigators might be tempted to conduct the chi-square analysis summarized in Part A of Fig. 3.5. It is apparent from inspection of this figure that the investigator has shifted experimental units from children ($N = 30$) to some combination of children and cheating incidents ($N = 40$). The 19 entries in cell A represent the number of incidents of cheating engaged in by the nine 4-year-old children who engaged in some cheating. It is difficult to argue that these cheating incidents were independent, as individual children contributed as many as three entries to this cell.

A correct analysis of the data shown in Fig. 3.5, maintaining children as the unit of analysis, is given in Part B of that figure. As can be seen from this latter analysis, the two age groups do not differ significantly in the *proportion* of children who are observed cheating (.6 vs. .4). Comparing the results of the

	Age of child		
	4	6	
Occurrences	A 19	B 6	25
Nonoccurrences	C 6	D 9	15
Totals	25	15	40

Part A.

Chi square $= \Sigma\Sigma(o_{i_j}-e_{i_j})^2/e_{i_j}$,

where o_{i_j} is the observed frequency in the ith row and jth column, e_{i_j} is the expected frequency in the ith row and jth column, and e_{i_j} = the product of the ith row frequency and the jth column frequency divided by N

$$= [(19-25\times25/40)^2]/25\times25/40+[(6-25\times15/40)^2]/25\times15/40+$$
$$[6-25\times15/40)^2/25\times15/40=[9-15\times15/40)^2]/15\times15/40$$
$$= 5.184, \text{ which, with 1 degree of freedom, has } p<.05.$$

Part B.

Chi square $= 2\times[(9-15\times15/30)^2/15\times15/30+$
$$2\times[(6-15\times15/30)^2]/15\times15/30$$
$$= 1.20, \text{ which, with 1 degree of freedom, has } p>.20.$$

FIG. 3.5. Incorrect (Part A) and correct (Part B) applications of chi-square analyses to the occurrences of cheating during turn-taking in fifteen 4-year-old and fifteen 6-year-old children. Note that even though some of the cells in the correct (Part B) analysis included small expected values, no correction for continuity was included. Recent research indicates that the correction usually is unnecessary as long as N exceeds 20; indeed, use of the correction produces overly conservative probabilities (e.g., Delucchi, 1983).

appropriate and inappropriate analysis indicates that violating the independence assumption can produce serious distortions in chi-square probabilities.[9] Similar distortions of chi-square probabilities have been noted by Gardner, Hartmann, and Mitchell (1982) in the analysis of dyadic time series data when an interacting dyad provides all of the data entries (see Fig. 3.4 for an example of data of this type).

The newer methods of analyzing categorical data are variously called *log-linear analysis* and (multidimensional) *contingency table analysis*. These approaches allow investigators to analyze complicated cross-classified categorical data, such as the data presented in Fig. 3.5 made more complex with the addition of independent as well as dependent variables. The analytic approach is similar to that used in the analysis of variance. As in ANOVA, a linear model is developed which expresses a score as a function of main and interaction effects. Multidimensional contingency table analysis differs from ANOVA in that, in the former case, the *logarithms* of the putative effects are summed. Because the equation is linear in its log form, the approach is referred to as log-linear. In addition, testing procedures resemble those used with data from unbalanced ANOVA designs. That is, a hierarchical model-testing procedure is followed in which an experimental model, simplified by the omission of one or more parameters, is tested. A small value of the test statistic indicates acceptance of this model, whereas a high value of the test statistic indicates that additional parameters must be included in the model. The test statistic used for multidimensional contingency table analysis is either the ordinary chi-square statistic or the likelihood ratio statistic, G^2. G^2 involves the logarithm of the ratio of observed and expected frequencies, rather than the squared discrepancy between observed and expected frequencies as does the ordinary chi-square test.

These techniques for analyzing multidimensional table data have the advantages of the analysis of variance: They provide omnibus tests of main and interaction effects in factorial investigations, allow for subsequent contrast tests, and control for type I error rates. These advantages come with some cost, however. According to Appelbaum and McCall (1983) multidimensional contingency analysis requires large numbers of subjects, particularly when repeated-measures versions of this approach are used.

When these as well as other methods of statistical analysis are used for the first time, the computer program as well as the user should be tested by replicat-

---

[9]The cheating data summarized in Fig. 3.5 also illustrate another aspect of data analysis: that analyses of means and of correlations are not as dissimilar as they may seem. The analyses given in Fig. 3.5 can be viewed as a test of the difference between independent proportions. That is, is the proportion of 4-year-olds who engage in cheating different from the proportion of 6-year-olds who engage in cheating? As such, the analysis is one of the difference between independent means (as the two group proportions in this problem are really group means). The analysis can also be viewed as one of the correlation between group status (age) and cheating. Thus, in an important sense, differences between means and correlations are but two alternative ways of viewing data analysis.

ing a textbook example. After an example from any of the standard texts—such as Fleiss (1981), Kleinbaum and Kupper (1978), or Landis and Koch (1979)—is successfully analyzed, the new data set is ready for analysis. Additional useful material on multidimensional table analysis can be found in Bishop and Holland (1975) and Knoke and Burke (1980).

Quantitative Analysis

More often, data are multipoint and ordered, such as Likert scale data, and can be analyzed with one or another of the general methods of quantitative analysis. The more common of these are the analysis of variance and regression/correlation analysis. Both methods are based on the general linear model, in which a score is conceived of as a linear combination of main and interaction effects, plus error. While in many respects ANOVA and regression analysis can be thought of as alternative approaches to the analysis of quantitative data, certain problems are more closely tied to one approach than to the other. Consequently, the following material will discuss the two approaches separately. However, it is important to recognize that the problems discussed under one or the other approach do not disappear when one shifts from regression analysis to the analysis of variance, or vice versa. The problems, such as lack of independence of the predictor variables (referred to as nonorthogonality in the analysis of variance), inflating type I error by conducting many tests of significance on the same set of data, and the like must be dealt with whatever the form of analysis.

Regression Analysis.   Regression analysis is the most general approach for the analysis of quantitative data. It accommodates data aimed at answering the two general types of questions asked by developmentalists: questions regarding group trends and those involving individual differences (see the chapter by Seitz in this volume). Most readers will be familiar with the latter use of regression analysis, for example to explore the correlates of popularity in a group of 8-year-old children. That regression analysis can also evaluate group trends may be less familiar—but review the discussion of the data shown in Fig. 3.5. This discussion indicates that differences in the average rate of cheating for 4- and 6-year-olds was equivalent to showing that cheating was *correlated* with age.

In both of its major applications regression analysis is plagued with difficulties for the unwary. Many of these difficulties are primarily interpretive in nature, rather than involving problems in conducting statistical tests. Nevertheless, they seem worthy of note, and the conditions responsible for these difficulties are summarized in Table 3.9. Additional information on the foibles associated with the interpretation of regression/correlation analysis can be found in McNemar (1969, chap. 10) and in Cohen and Cohen (1975).

The effects tested in regression/correlation analysis involve either correlation coefficients (bivariate rs or multiple Rs) or statistics such as path coefficients and

TABLE 3.9
Disturbing Factors in Regression and Correlation Analysis

Disturbing Factors	*Consequences*
Unreliable measurement	Correlation is underestimated
Restricted score range	Correlation typically underestimated
Non-normal distributions	Maximum correlation less than ┆ 1.0 ┆ unless correlated variables are identically non-normal
Large IV to N ratio	R overestimated; R regresses toward zero when cross-validated
Correlated IVs	$r(xy)^2$ does not give the proportion of variance in Y (the DV) uniquely associated with X; $\Sigma r(x_i y)^2$ does not equal R^2
Highly correlated IVs (multiple collinearity)	Beta weights (βs) unstable[a]

[a]Highly correlated IVs produce complicated issues of statistical testing when correlated (non-orthogonal) independent variables are analyzed by means of the analysis of variance. The problem of correlated independent variables in the analysis of variance is discussed by Kahneman (1965) and by Cohen (1968). Appelbaum and his associates (Appelbaum & Cramer, 1974; Appelbaum & McCall, 1983) have presented methods of analyzing these data.

beta weights that are a function of correlation coefficients. Tests of these statistics most often employ the F distribution (after Fisher), but in certain simple or unusual cases the t-test or the normal curve (or z) test may be used.

As in many uses of statistical testing, problems occur when investigators are insufficiently sensitive to violations of independence assumptions when conducting statistical tests in conjunction with regression/correlation analysis. Nonindependence (dependence) affects statistical tests in regression analysis in at least two ways. First, tests may be conducted on nonindependent statistics from a regression analysis, but the testing procedure may only be appropriate for independent statistics. This may occur whenever investigators attempt to answer the generic question "Is X more highly correlated with Y than S is correlated with Z?"[10] and both r_{xy} and r_{sz} are obtained from the same subjects. Because they are obtained from the same subjects, such correlation coefficients are likely to be themselves correlated, and their testing requires adjustments to accommodate the dependency between the coefficients (see Steiger, 1980).

The second dependency problem occurs when the pairs of scores on which the correlation coefficient is calculated are not independent. (A similar problem was discussed with respect to the data shown in Fig. 3.5.) This dependency problem occurs, for example, when members of the same family all contribute pairs of

---

[10]A simpler version of this question in which X and S are identical occurs even more commonly. For example, is the IQ of children (X) more highly correlated with the IQ of their mothers (Y) or of their fathers (Z)? That is, is r_{xy} different from r_{xz}?

scores to the correlation analysis, or when the same individual contributes all of the scores entering into the analysis.

A final problem in testing correlational statistics occurs when a large number of variables are intercorrelated, and the correlation between each pair of variables is tested for significance in the usual manner. When this is done, the probability of making one or more type I errors (see Table 3.7) may approach 1.0. For example, assume an investigator obtains scores on $k = 8$ variables for a group of subjects, and correlates each variable with every other one. If the 28 resulting correlations—$k(k - 1)/2$—are each tested for significance with alpha equal to .05, the probability of one or more type I errors may be as large as $1 - (1 - .05)^{28} = .76$, and the expected number of type I errors as large as $28 \times .05 = 1.4$. In order to avoid the problem of inflating the type I error with a large matrix of intercorrelations, the entire matrix is first tested to insure that some significant covariation exists in the matrix as a whole. If that test proves to be significant, then statistical tests are conducted on the individual correlations with alpha adjusted so as to hold the probability of a type I error for the entire collection of tests to some specified level (see Larzelere & Mulaik, 1977). This procedure has the effect of using a much more conservative alpha (e.g., .05/28 = .0018) for tests of the significance conducted on the individual correlations.

The Analysis of Variance.   The analysis of variance (ANOVA) is most often the approach used to assess differences in means for the variables investigated in developmental research, such as age and time of measurement. ANOVA, like regression, is a general approach to data analysis that can accommodate the data from a wide variety of experimental designs. ANOVA can be used when all design facets involve any of the following: (a) between-subject effects (completely randomized designs); (b) within-subject effects (randomized block or repeated measures designs); or (c) both within- and between-subject effects (mixed or split-plot designs). Analysis of variance procedures can also be applied when additional measured variables are included to statistically control unwanted sources of variation (the analysis of covariance or ANCOVA), and when the design employs multiple dependent variables (MANOVA).

The analysis of variance is illustrated with a 4 (age) by 2 (gender) by 3 (time of measurement) split-plot factorial design shown in Part A of Table 3.10. The analysis of variance of the data from that design might be used to test whether the means for the group defined by age, gender, and time of testing, alone and in combinations, vary significantly. These tests require that the subject scores that are used in the analysis meet certain assumptions, including those of normality, homogeneity (equivalence) of variance, and "homogeneity" of covariance or correlation between the repeated measures. The analysis of variance is relatively robust (insensitive) to violations of the former assumptions as long as each group contains approximately the same number of subjects, and sample sizes are not very small (e.g., Glass, Peckham, & Sanders, 1972). It is not robust, however,

TABLE 3.10
Schematic, Structural Equation, and ANOVA Summary Table
for an Age by Sex by Time of Testing Factorial Design

Part A. Design:

Age	Testing Period:	Girls			Boys		
		1	*2*	*3*	*1*	*2*	*3*
4	S_1				S_1		
	S_2				S_2		
	S_3				S_3		
	S_4				S_4		
	S_5				S_5		
6	S_1				S_1		
	S_2				S_2		
	S_3				S_3		
	S_4				S_4		
	S_5				S_5		
8	S_1				S_1		
	S_2				S_2		
	S_3				S_3		
	S_4				S_4		
	S_5				S_5		
10	S_1				S_1		
	S_2				S_2		
	S_3				S_3		
	S_4				S_4		
	S_5				S_5		

Part B. ANOVA Summary Table:

Source	df	MS	F	p	
Between Group					
Age (A)	$a-1=4-1=3$	25.0	5.00	$<.05$	
Gender (B)	$b-1=2-1=1$	5.5	1.10	$>.25$	
AxB	$(a-1)(b-1)=3$	10.0	2.00	$<.25$	
Error (S)	$(a-1)(b-1)(n-1)=12$	5.0			
Within Group					
Assessments (D)	$d-1=3-1=2$	10.6	4.24	$<.05$	$(<.10^a)$
DxA	$(d-1)(a-1)=6$	10.0	4.00	$<.01$	$(<.05^b)$
DxB	$(d-1)(b-1)=2$	2.8	1.12	$>.25$	$(>.25^a)$
DxAxB	$(d-1)(a-1)(b-1)=6$	3.1	1.24	$>.25$	$(>.25^b)$
Error (SxD)	$(d-1)(a-1)(b-1)(n-1)=24$	2.5			

Note: In Part A, S designates a subject. S_1 in age group 4 for girls is not the same subject as any of the other S_1 designations.

[a]Tested with 1 and 12 degrees of freedom (Geiser-Greenhouse correction).

[b]Tested with 3 and 12 degrees of freedom (Geiser-Greenhouse correction).

Note: In Part B, the lower case letters in the source table equal the number of levels for the source indicated in the corresponding upper case letter. For example, there are four ages, so the source age (A) has four level (a=4). In generating *F*-tests, age, gender, and time of testing are considered fixed so that all between-group and within-group effects are tested with their respective subject—S or SxD—error terms (e.g., Kirk, 1982).

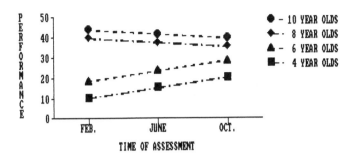

FIG. 3.6. Illustration of the interaction between age and time of assessment for the design shown in Table 3.9.

to violations of the requirement concerning the correlation between the repeated measures (e.g., Kirk, 1982). And this requirement is likely to be violated whenever more than two times of testing are employed. This is so because the essence of the assumption is that all of the repeated measures are equally correlated. However, scores almost always correlate more highly with measures that are adjacent in time, and less highly with temporally more remote measures. Hence, with even three repeated measures, the correlations between the first two and the last two measures are likely to exceed the correlation between the first and third measures.

When the assumption of "homogeneity" of covariance is violated, the probability values obtained from ordinary statistical testing are too small (i.e., "too significant"). A number of procedures have been developed to remedy the biasing of probability values when this assumption may be violated, the most popular of which is the procedure developed by Geiser and Greenhouse (1958).

The Geiser–Greenhouse adjustment was applied to all of the within-subject tests conducted in Part B of Table 3.10. That is, the degrees of freedom used in calculating the probability values for the tests were reduced by dividing the usual degrees of freedom by the degrees of freedom associated with the repeated measure, $(d - 1)$. The resulting statistical tests indicate that age and the interaction between age and time of assessment significantly "determine" performance.[11]

The interaction between age and time of assessment is shown in Fig. 3.6.

_____

[11]Time of assessment is significant using the ordinary degrees of freedom for determining probability values, and insignificant using Geiser–Greenhouse adjusted degrees of freedom. Given these inconsistent outcomes, the remainder of the Geiser–Greenhouse procedure would have been conducted. That is, the probability value associated with the main effect of time of testing would have been determined with an "exact" degree of freedom adjustment, an adjustment based on the degree to which the "homogeneity" of covariance assumption was violated. However, because the age by time-of-testing interaction effect was significant, thus calling into question the meaning of a time-of-testing main effect under even the best of circumstances, the need for this more precise test was obviated.

From an inspection of this figure, it can be discerned that the interaction—also indicated by the lack of parallelism of the four data lines—is largely due to the performance of the two older age groups of children in comparison with that of the two younger age groups. That is, the 8- and 10-year-olds slightly deteriorate in performance across time, whereas the 4- and 6-year-olds improve somewhat with each repetition of the assessment procedures.

The omnibus tests conducted by the analysis of variance are supplemented (and sometimes replaced) by other statistical tests under at least two sets of circumstances. First, additional tests usually are conducted to determine exactly what level(s) of a factor differ from which other level(s) following a significant ANOVA test involving more than one degree of freedom. (More than one degree of freedom means that more than two groups are being compared.) The procedures used for these follow-up tests involve some form of trend test, or test of simple main effects, or other comparisons between combinations of means. Generically, these tests are referred to as *multiple comparison tests*. Their intent is to determine which specific levels of the independent variables included in the omnibus test are significantly different, while maintaining some control of type I error rate produced by conducting multiple tests of significance on a set of data. (See the related discussion in the "Regression Analysis" section.) Of course, neither these nor any other form of significance testing are appropriate for "test hopping"—that is, hopping from one inferential testing procedure to another until "significant" results are found. Test hopping is never a legitimate procedure.[12]

Many multiple comparison tests are available, including the Dunnett D' test, Tukey's *HSD* test, Scheffé's *S* test, and the Newman–Keuls test (e.g., Games, 1971). The selection among tests is based on a number of considerations, including whether the comparisons were planned prior to data analysis (a priori comparisons) or selected after examining the data (a posteriori comparisons), whether pairwise or more complex comparisons among means are conducted, and whether all condition means are contrasted with a control group mean; see, for example, Kirk (1982, Table 3.61).

The second basis for not relying on omnibus tests from the analysis of variance relates to a message repeatedly emphasized in this chapter: that the analysis should suit the question. And the standard tests performed by the analysis of variance may not adequately evaluate the comparisons between means that are involved in a priori hypotheses. Consider the interaction illustrated in Fig. 3.7 among the four levels from a 2 × 2 completely randomized factorial design. (In a

---

[12]A subtle and common, but nonetheless illegitimate variant of test hopping involves switching the form of the data as well as the method of analysis. For example, an investigator interested in differences in prosocial behavior between children of different ages may initially analyze donation rate data with a *t*-test, and finding the test insignificant, switch to a chi-square analysis conducted on the transformed data of whether or not each child donated.

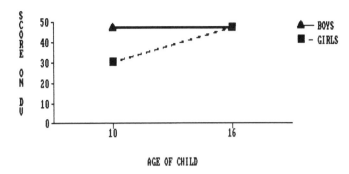

FIG. 3.7. Illustration of a predicted interaction between gender and age not adequately assessed using standard omnibus ANOVA tests.

completely randomized design, all effects involve between-group comparisons.) The variation associated with this interaction would be split between the main effects of age and of gender, and the age × gender interaction. All of the tests of these effects may be insignificant, yet a contrast written specifically for this *expected* pattern of interaction might be highly significant. And of course this is exactly the approach that should be taken with "atypical" a priori hypotheses: the contrast for the expected effect should be constructed and then tested.[13] These a priori contrast tests may be conducted prior to, or even instead of the traditional analysis of variance tests (see, for example, Rosenthal & Rosnow, 1985).

In addition to these general issues associated with the use of the analysis of variance, specific concerns accrue to the use of special, commonly used ANOVA designs. Two of these designs are the *hierarchical analysis of variance* and the *analysis of covariance*.

Hierarchical Designs. Formally, hierarchical designs are those in which the levels of one factor are nested within the levels of another factor. The design would be hierarchical, for example, if both second- and fourth-grade girls and boys were taught spelling using mnemonic devices, but different procedures were used for the second graders and for the fourth graders. Such obvious examples of nesting (think of the grades as nests, and the mnemonic devices as eggs within the nests) are unlikely to be mistakenly analyzed. Mistakes do occur, however, when nuisance variables such as classrooms, play groups, or families are nested within an experimental factor. Consider the case in which child aggression comprises the dependent variable, sex is the independent variable,

---

[13]The numerator for the contrast for this expected interaction is the mean for 10-year-old girls minus the average of the remaining three means. Assuming that all groups are of equal size, the contrast weights for the four means would be $+1$, $-\frac{1}{3}$, $-\frac{1}{3}$, and $-\frac{1}{3}$, respectively.

and children are assessed within same-sex play groups. A particularly aggressive group member might instigate counteraggression from other group members. As a result, the scores for members of the play group not only would be *interdependent,* but play group may be a substantial source of nuisance variation. Thus, the dependency between scores for members of a group and the effect of the group itself must be accommodated in the data analysis—or else serious inferential errors may be made. Various methods for integrating nested variables into the statistical analysis are discussed by Anderson and Ager (1978) and by Kraemer and Jacklin (1979); also see Kirk (1982, chapter 10).

Analysis of Covariance.   The analysis of covariance (ANCOVA) is involved when one or more measured variables are used to control unwanted sources of variance through statistical means in any of the standard ANOVA designs. For example, in an experiment on methods of teaching reading, children's IQ scores might be used as a covariate to reduce uncontrolled differences in "reading potential" for the children participating in the experiment. Because unwanted sources of variability can be reduced statistically when they cannot be controlled experimentally, ANCOVA is a popular means of increasing power. However, its use requires strict attention to a rigorous set of requirements (see, for example, Huitema, 1980).

Two particularly serious problems can occur as a result of using ANCOVA incorrectly: One problem results from violating the analysis of covariance assumptions; the other occurs when ANCOVA is asked to perform roles for which it is ill suited. the ANCOVA assumption that can be particularly problematic when violated is the assumption of independence between treatment and scores on the covariate. In the reading example mentioned above, the IQ scores must be independent of treatment—that is, obtained prior to implementation of the treatment for reading. The second problem occurs when investigators employ the analysis of covariance to adjust for initial differences between preexisting treatment groups, such as classrooms. Such an experimental strategy is a clear violation of random assignment procedures. Furthermore, initial biases typically cannot be undone by ANCOVA procedures (Overall & Woodward, 1977).

Multivariate Extensions.   Various multivariate extensions of the analysis of variance and of regression analysis are used by developmental investigators. In what follows, I briefly describe—in alphabetical order—the more popular of these extensions, indicate their primary functions or uses, list their most common problems, and note where the interested reader can find out more about them. Before doing so, it is important to note a few similarities between the various multivariate techniques. Most important, all of the multivariate procedures *apply weights to the subjects' scores on the original variables to form one or more new composite variables; the weights are selected to optimize some function.* The process is similar to forming the composite variable, total score, for a classroom achievement test. The total score is based upon a linear combination of weighted item scores. The item scores are weighted in order to maximize individual differences in performance on the test. In multivariate analysis, the weights may be selected, for example, to maximize the correlation between two sets of variables (*canonical correlation*), to minimize the number of independent dimensions necessary to characterize a set of variables (*factor analysis*), or to maximize the differences between two or more groups (*discriminant analysis*).

All multivariate techniques also share a number of common weaknesses. Foremost among these weaknesses is that they eschew perfectly (or near perfectly) correlated variables. Perfectly correlated variables comprise one kind of problem to multivariate analysis called *linear dependency*. Highly correlated variables pose a slightly different problem called *multicollinearity*. Both conditions are undesirable for all forms of multivariate analysis. Second, the multivariate procedures require substantial numbers of subjects. If these techniques are used when the ratio of variables to subjects is so unfavorable that it approaches 1.0, the optimizing algorithm used to generate weights will exploit chance differences in the data. As a consequence, the results of the study will not replicate.

Canonical Correlation.   The aim of canonical correlation is to explore the interrelations between two sets of variables. It is the multivariate analogue of bivariate correlation. Instead of single predictor and criterion variables, canonical correlation is used when sets of predictor and criterion variables are obtained. The technique generates composite scores from a weighted linear combination of each of two sets of variables; the weights are selected to maximize the correlation between the two composite scores. The linear combinations of variables generated by this procedure are called canonical variates; hence, the correlation between canonical variates is called a canonical correlation. Following the construction or extraction of the first canonical variates from the predictor and criterion sets of variables, and the calculation of their correlation, additional canonical variables may be extracted and correlated. The weights used in forming these subsequent canonical variates are chosen with an additional criterion: The new variates must be independent of the canonical variates already constructed.

Canonical correlation is used when an investigator intends to explore the relations between variables in separate domains—for example, between nursery school children's social interaction behaviors and their performance on cognitive tasks. Unless the ratio of variables to subjects in such an investigation is quite small, say less than .10, the specific optimum weights used are unlikely to cross-validate in subsequent investigations. The variable-to-subject ratio does not, however, affect the meaning of significance tests associated with the canonical correlations. Those tests "correct" for the ratio of variables to subjects. Additional information on canonical correlation can be found in Thompson (1984), and in the multivariate textbooks by Marascuilo and Levin (1983) and by Tabachnick and Fidell (1983).

Discriminant Analysis. The purpose of discriminant analysis is to assign individuals to the group to which they belong. Assignments are based upon the individual's standing on one or more weighted linear composites of their scores on a set of predictor variables. The weights are selected so that the predictor variables maximize differences between the groups. For example, a discriminant analysis might be used to assign children to popular, average, or rejected groups based upon composite scores formed by weighting their scores on the scales of the Child Behavior Checklist (Achenbach & Edelbrock, 1981). This problem, involving as it does classification into one of three groups, requires the construction of two (one less than the number of groups) composite variables.

The composite variables formed in discriminant analysis are called *discriminant functions.* Typical discriminant analysis output provides the weights for the predictor variables that are used in constructing the discriminant functions; that is, the weights for the variables that aid in the prediction of group membership. The output also includes information on which categories individual children are assigned to, based on their scores on the discriminant functions, as well as the proportion of children correctly classified. The standard multivariate texts previously mentioned, as well as the manuals for standard computer data analysis software such as BMDP (Dixon et al., 1985), SAS (SAS, 1985), and SPSS^x (SPSS, 1986) might be consulted for additional information on discriminant analysis.

Factor Analysis. Factor analysis, and related techniques such as principle component analysis, have as their purpose the discovery of the minimum dimensions underlying a set of variables. These dimensions, referred to as factors or *components,* are constructed by forming weighted linear composites of the original variables. The weights applied to the variables in the construction of each factor vary depending upon the factor technique used. In general, however, the weights are chosen to "explain" the maximum variation in the entire set of variables as yet "unexplained." Thus, the weights assigned the variables in the construction of the first factor are chosen so as to maximize the correlation of that factor with the original variables. The weights for the variables in the construction of the second factor are chosen so that factor has the highest correlation with that part of the original variables not accounted for by the first factor, and so on.

Investigators have a number of factoring techniques from which to choose, including principle components and image analysis. After factors are extracted, they often are rotated. Rotation refers to the transformation of factors by modifying the weights for the variables from which they were constructed. The purpose of rotation is to facilitate description, and hence understanding, of the factors extracted from a set of data. In Fig. 3.8, the two original factors extracted (I and

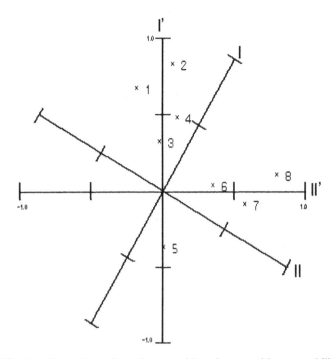

FIG. 3.8.   Illustration of rotation to achieve improved interpretability of factors. The correlations between the original eight variables and the factors, I and II, are indicated by finding the coordinates of the ×s used to represent the eight variables. For example, variable 1 (see × 1) has correlations of about |.5| with both factors I and II. The original factors were rotated approximately 30° counterclockwise to form the new factors, I′ and II′. As a result, the five verbal tests (numbered 1 through 5) defined the first rotated factor (I′), and the three quantitative tests (numbered 6 through 8) defined the second rotated factor (II′). While rotation has no effect upon the correlations between the variables, it does change the loadings (correlations) of the variables with the factors. For example, variable 7 now correlates in excess of .6 with factor II′, and slightly negatively with factor I′.

II) from eight verbal and quantitative tests were rotated (clockwise) some 45° to promote understanding of the factors. The new factors (labeled I′ and II′) appear to be relatively pure measures of verbal and quantitative skills, respectively.

Just as investigators have a number of factor extraction methods from which to choose, so also are there a number of factor rotation methods. The most common methods for rotating orthogonal (independent) factors are *varimax* and *quartimax*. If oblique (correlated) factors are to be rotated, *oblimax* and *biquartimin* are popular methods. Readers interested in learning more about factor analysis and related techniques might consult the articles by Comrey (1978) and by Rummel (1967), and the readable texts by Gorsuch (1974) and McDonald (1985).

Multivariate Analysis of Variance.   Multivariate analysis of variance (MAN-OVA) is the extension of the analysis of variance to investigations employing more than one dependent variable. As in the case of ANOVA, MANOVA determines whether the differences in performance found between levels of the independent variables are due to chance sampling variation, or whether they represent "real" differences. MANOVA forms one or more weighted composites of the dependent variables that maximize the differences between the levels of the independent variables. If two or more composites (also called *discriminant functions*) are formed, each discriminant function is independent of the discriminant functions already formed.

MANOVA has a number of advantages when compared with conducting separate ANOVAs on each dependent variable. First, MANOVA provides better control over type I error. Subsequent statistical tests (e.g., ANOVAs) are only conducted if MANOVA indicates that at least one independent variable produces an effect on some linear combination of the dependent variables. (This rule is relaxed when a priori predictions are advanced.) Second, MANOVA may detect differences that would not be found if a separate ANOVA was conducted on each dependent variable—this occurs when a weak effect is distributed over each of a number of correlated dependent variables. Thus, in some circumstances, MAN-OVA may be a more powerful method of analysis than are separate ANOVAs.

Other Statistical Techniques

A number of other, newer forms of analysis confront developmental researchers. Two of these—structural equation modeling and meta analysis—are sufficiently common and important to deserve mention.

Structural Equation Modeling.   Structural equation modeling (SEM, structural modeling, linear structural equations, or covariance structural modeling) is a multiple regressionlike statistical methodology for testing causal models. In contrast to more typical descriptive interpretations of, say, the regression coefficients in a multiple regression analysis, SEM hypothesizes that the coefficients indicate the rate with which the independent variables *cause* changes in the dependent variable. Structural equation modeling is perhaps most closely associated with the computer program LISREL, developed by Joreskog and his associates (e.g., Joreskog & Sorbom, 1983) for estimating the parameters for structural models. (LISREL is an acronym for *li*near *s*tructural *rel*ations.) However, other approaches to structural model testing than those developed by Joreskog and his associates are available (see, for example, Bentler, 1980; Heise, 1975; Kenny, 1979).

Structural modeling is particularly attractive to developmentalists. The reasons for this popularity are easily understood. The technique is well adapted for use with nonexperimental data, and it makes its strongest case with multiple wave longitudinal data—the kind of data that are traditionally associated with developmental investigations. In fact, manuscripts using (as well as misusing) structural modeling have increased at such a dramatic rate that a prominent developmental journal, *Child Development,* recently devoted much of an entire issue "to illuminate the nature and possible applications of this statistical technique to developmental data" (Bronson, 1987, p. 1).

Structural modeling employs a somewhat different vocabulary than do more traditional forms of design and analysis. In SEM, the variable set is divided into two classes, *exogenous* variables and *endogenous* variables. Exogenous variables are those variables that are hypothesized to produce changes in other (endogenous) variables in the model, although the causes for the exogenous variables themselves are not included in the model. Endogenous variables, in contrast, are those variables that are presumably changed as a result of changes in other variables in the model. Thus, exogenous variables are always independent variables, whereas endogenous variables are dependent variables but also can serve as independent variables. A variable serving both independent and dependent variable status is sometimes referred to as an *intervening* variable.

Variables included in some structural models also may be classified as *measured variables* or *latent variables.* Measured variables, as the name suggests, are variables that are directly assessed; latent, or hypothetical variables, are merely estimated—perhaps by measured variables. As this vocabulary exercise suggests, a structural model (the multiple regressionlike part of structural modeling) is often joined with a measurement model (the factor analyticlike part of SEM). When these two models are joined, as in LISREL, a good part of the Greek alphabet and parts of the English one are required in order to symbolize the components of the model and their interconnecting equations. Fortunately, models typically are expressed pictorially, in the form of path diagrams, in addition to being expressed as a series of equations.

A path diagram illustrating the structural relations among four variables is displayed in Panel A of Fig. 3.9. In path diagrams such as this one, exogenous variables are placed at the far left of the diagram, intervening variables in the middle, and other endogenous variables at the far right. Once the data have been obtained, the path coefficients (correlations and regression coefficients) often are placed on the arrows, and the values of R^2s (the proportion of "explained" endogenous variable variance) are included in the circles. Panel B of Fig. 3.9 illustrates the measurement submodel for the Panel A latent variable of child social skills. This latent variable is indexed with three measurement operations, independent observations of the child, teacher ratings, and peer sociometrics.

Each variable in path diagrams that is touched by an arrow head is included as the dependent variable in a structural equation. Each variable attached to the dependent variable by the end of an arrow is included on the right-hand side of the same structural equation as an independent variable. For example, in the rudimentary model described in Fig. 3.9, child social skills would be expressed

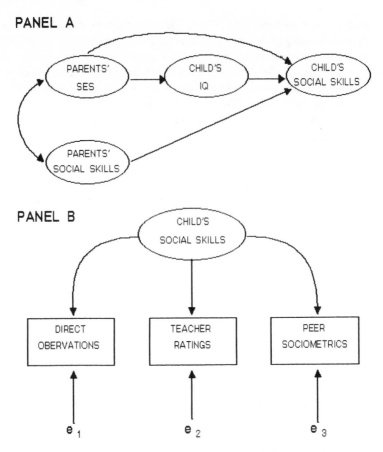

FIG. 3.9. Path diagrams. The diagram in Panel A illustrates the structural relations between the exogenous variables of parental SES and social skills, and the endogenous variables of child's IQ (an intervening variable) and social skills. Disturbance components are not included. The diagram in Panel B illustrates a measurement model for the latent variable, child's social skills.

as a function of child IQ and parental SES and social skills; whereas the observational measure of social skill would comprise the dependent variable in an equation including the latent variable of child social skill and error.[14]

SEM testing requires a number of reasonably complicated steps or phases. The first step involves formulation of the structural model, in which the hypothesized causal relations between a set of variables are formulated. James, Muliak, and Brett (1982) indicate that this step involves some seven substeps, including

---

[14]This latter expression may be recognized as a variant of the decomposition of obtained score into true score and error score from classical reliability theory.

provision of a theoretical rationale for the causal hypotheses and specification of causal order and direction. The second step involves operationalization of the variables and collection of data relevant to the test of the model. Because causes require time to produce their effects, longitudinal data involving a time lag suitable for "capturing" the causal connections stipulated in the model typically are required. After the data have been gathered—and structural modeling requires substantial data, as do all multivariate statistical techniques—they are summarized in a form appropriate for testing the goodness of fit of the model. This form typically requires the calculation of the variances and covariances between the variables included in the model. These variances and covariances are then operated upon, often with rather complex statistical programs such as LISREL, to produce estimates of the model parameters and tests of statistical significance. One or more of these tests of significance are conducted on the model as a whole (e.g., Anderson, 1987). A statistically *nonsignificant* (typically, chi square) test indicates that the model adequately fits the data, whereas a statistically *significant* test suggests that the model requires revision—that significant amounts of variability in the data are not accounted for by the model. Statistical tests also are conducted on the individual model components, such as the regression weights relating putative effects to their causes and indicators to their latent variables. For these statistical tests of predicted relations, a nonsignificant (typically an F) test indicates that the subpart of the model tested has been disconfirmed—that the expected relation is not reliably different from zero.

It is important to recognize the nature of the causal inferences that can be drawn from confirmation of a structural model. As anyone who has survived an elementary course on statistics has repeatedly heard, correlation does not prove causation. (Nor, it might be added, does any other statistic.) It is true, however, that causation implies correlation (e.g., Muliak, 1987). Thus, finding that the predicted correlations between the variables included in the model fit the data increases the credibility of the causal model and of the theory on which it was based. This increased credibility resulting from model confirmation assumes, of course, that the model was potentially disconfirmable by the data gathered (Popper, 1962).

Following testing of the model to determine whether it can be confirmed, or must be disconfirmed, further *exploratory* analyses may be conducted on the model. These analyses are performed in order to assess how the model might be revised to better fit the empirical results. The revised model produced as a result of this exploratory work requires additional empirical testing, with a new sample of data, in order to determine whether it will pass a reasonable test of disconfirmation.

While structural equation modeling is a powerful approach for the analysis of nonexperimental data, the power comes with some cost. The model requires a careful balance of variables to subjects (not more than $[N/10]-2$ variables), multiple measures or indicators for its latent variables, appropriate lags between the waves of the longitudinal data that are gathered, and assurance that certain statistical assumptions, including that of linear relationships between the variables, are upheld (e.g., Biddle & Marlin, 1987; Martin, 1987; Tanaka, 1987).

Very readable accounts of structural modeling can be found in the special issue of *Child Development* (Bronson, 1987) devoted to that topic, in Bentler (1980), and in the monographs by Dwyer (1983), Heise (1975), James et al. (1982), and Kenny (1979). More technical presentations are available in Joreskog and Sorbom (1981) and in Long (1983).

Meta Analysis.   Meta analysis is a systematic, quantitative method of summarizing the results of studies composing a research literature (Strube & Hartmann, 1983). Traditional narrative reviews of the literature have been criticized for their subjectivity, imprecision, and neglect of important information contained in primary studies (e.g., Jackson, 1980). These concerns, coupled with the relative explosion of scientific information, have suggested the need for better methods of summarizing research literatures.

Meta-analytic techniques serve a variety of functions involved in reviewing a research literature. From the very beginning of operationalizing the review, they include methods for systematically collecting the studies composing the literature to ensure that the "raw data" for the analysis will not be biased (e.g., Hunter, Schmidt, & Jackson, 1982, chapter 7). The heart of meta analysis, however, contains the statistical methods for summarizing the results of the primary studies composing the literature. Foremost among these statistical methods are techniques for combining probabilities across studies (Rosenthal, 1980). While a number of probability-combining techniques are available, they all have, as their principal purpose, determining whether the set of results composing a literature could have occurred by chance. The combination of effect sizes represents another major approach to summarizing results across studies. The methods of determining average effect size assist the reviewer in determining the importance of the findings in a literature. While a number of effect size indicators are available for accomplishing this goal, the correlation coefficient and Cohen's *d* statistic, a standard score variant previously discussed (see Table 3.6), are most commonly used for this purpose (Smith, Glass, & Miller, 1980).

Beyond the computation of a combined probability and of an average effect size, meta analysis also provides methods of determining the stability of results. Stability is often assessed using Rosenthal's (1979) fail-safe method. This method estimates the number of unpublished studies with zero effect size that would have to be contained in the file drawers of investigators in order to "wash out" the results of the available studies included in the review.

Finally, because the probability values and effect sizes of the individual studies composing a literature are likely to vary substantially, a number of procedures and strategies have been proposed for identifying those factors associated with variation in outcome across studies. Such factors include any number of primary study characteristics that might be coded during the review; examples are the subjects studied, the methods of operationalizing independent and dependent variables, and how adequately any validity threats (see earlier discussion on function of measurement) were handled in the study. These factors are then treated as independent variables (the p-values and effect sizes serve as dependent variables) in analyses using regression or analysis of variance techniques, or methods of analysis especially developed for meta analyses. (e.g., Hedges & Olkin, 1985).

A number of research literatures of interest to developmentalists have been reviewed using meta-analytic procedures. Among these are reviews of the relation between perspective-taking and altruisim (Underwood & Moore, 1982); of gender differences in helping behavior (Eagly & Crowley, 1986), in aggression (Eagly & Steffen, 1986), and in cognitive skills (Hyde, 1981); and of only child effects on a variety of cognitive and personality variables (Falbo & Polit, 1986). Meta-analytic procedures themselves have been recently reviewed (Bangert-Drowns, 1986)—though, perhaps ironically, using traditional rather than meta-analytic techniques. Understandable technical presentations of meta analyses are given in Glass, McGaw, and Smith (1981), in Hunter et al. (1982), and in Rosenthal (1980). The monograph by Hedges and Olkin (1985) is a quantitatively sophisticated presentation of recent meta-analytic techniques.

Interpreting Statistics

The statement regarding probability associated with each application of an inferential statistical test, the "p is less than" statement, has a clear but often misunderstood meaning. Consider a two-group experiment study in which $n_1 = n_2 = 20$, the difference between group means is 5 points, $t(38) = 2.03$, and $p < .05$. Which of the following conclusions can appropriately be made based upon this statement?

1. The relationship between the DV and the IV is large or important.

2. The probability of this result being replicated is .05.

3. The probability is .95 that the difference between the two population means is 5.

4. The probability is .05 that the difference between the two population means is 0.

5. If the experiment is run again and a nonsignificant outcome is obtained ($p > .05$), this necessarily means that the two studies are inconsistent.

If you endorsed any of these alternatives you are not interpreting the results of significance tests correctly (see Huitema, 1986). However, you are in good company, as even statisticians frequently err in interpreting the probability values from experiments (e.g., Tversky & Kahneman, 1971). In fact, none of the alternative interpretations is even approximately correct. The correct interpretation should read as follows: If a two-group experiment with $n_1 = n_2 = 20$ is conducted, and the true difference between the population means is 0, a difference of at least five points would occur fewer than five times in 100 (i.e., with a probability less than .05).

Let us briefly consider each of the alternatives to determine why they are incorrect.

Perhaps alternative #1 represents the most serious misinterpretation of significance tests. Probability values indicate neither effect size nor importance. Effect *size* is appropriately indexed by the correlation between independent and dependent variables, or some variant of the standardized difference statistic (d) previously discussed, or a measure of overlap between the two distributions (Cohen, 1977).[15] These effect size indicators are a function of the difference between means in comparison to some measure of within-group variability, while probability values are a function of effect size *and* sample size. Thus, given the same value of d in two studies differing only in sample size, the study with the larger sample size will be associated with a smaller probability value. *Importance* is a concept even more elusive, or at any rate more difficult to quantify. Importance is dependent not only on effect size, but possibly also on the effect sizes produced by competing variables, on substantive theory concerning the variables, and on the measurement theory associated with the operationalization of the variable (Mitchell & Hartmann, 1981; O'Grady, 1982).

Alternative #2 is substantially incorrect. The probability of precisely replicating the results of the first study are very, very small. The probability of replicating the study in the sense of rejecting the null hypothesis at a similar level of significance is dependent on the design of the subsequent study and on the true difference between the population means (see Cohen, 1977). In general, the larger the difference between the two population means, the better the design of the second study; and the larger that study's sample size, the greater the probability of rejecting the null hypothesis in that study. However, it is unlikely for that study to have a power of exactly .95.

Alternative #3 specifies the probability of a particular difference between the two population means. That interpretation is blatantly incorrect. The difference between two population means is a specific value; the value does not define a probability distribution. Our best (and only) estimate of the difference between the two population means is five points, and a particular probability cannot readily be associated with the correctness of that estimate.

Alternative #4, which stated that the probability is .05 that the difference between the two populations is 0, perhaps sounds like it may be the closest of the lot to a correct interpretation of our original finding. This interpretation has no

---

[15]Other candidates for assessing effect size have also been suggested (e.g., Jacobson, Follette, & Revenstorf, 1984).

meaning in the current problem, however. It is true that a confidence interval, say the .95 confidence interval, can be established about the obtained difference. Over the long run, such intervals would include the true mean difference 95% of the time. But that is certainly not the equivalent of stating that there is a .05 probability of the true difference being exactly zero. It is important to note, however, that in the present case the .95 confidence interval would not include the mean difference of 0. Rejection of a null hypothesis at some p is equivalent to establishing the $1 - p$ confidence interval about the obtained difference, and finding that the value of 0 lies outside of that interval.

Alternative #5—that repetition of the experiment with a $p > .05$ outcome necessarily means that the two studies are inconsistent—is one of those incorrect interpretations to which even trained statisticians fall prey. If the experiment is run a second time, the probability of rejecting the null hypothesis (or power, see Table 3.6) in the second study can be determined with some precision once the characteristics (e.g., sample size, reliability of the dependent measure, and potency of the independent variable) are determined. If the characteristics are poorly chosen, it can be *expected* that the null hypothesis will not be rejected. That is, failure to reject the null hypothesis in the second study is entirely consistent with rejection of the null hypothesis in the first study. In fact, if the difference found in the first study is exactly equal to the true population difference, and if the first study is conducted as an exact or operational replication (Lykken, 1968), the probability of rejecting the null hypothesis, as in the first study, is exactly .50!

SUMMARY

This chapter has served as a guide for two critical ingredients in the conduct of developmental research: measurement and analysis. I have repeatedly emphasized that these two methodological domains should be viewed as subservient to the substantive issues raised in developmental investigations: Theoretically driven questions should determine methodology, and not the reverse.

In examining measurement issues and techniques, and pitfalls in the implementation of the techniques, I discussed the purposes of measurement, the types of scores generated by developmental investigators, and the criteria used for judging the worth of these scores. Validity issues loomed large for assessing scores—as well as for evaluating experiments and other forms of investigation. Next, I noted the many aspects of measurements—facets (such as *trait*like vs. *state*like measures), response characteristics, and comparison standards—that determine how measurements are operationalized, as well as judged. This somewhat abstract discussion was supplemented with the examination of a concrete measurement problem—that of observing children's social behaviors.

The discussion of measurement then gave way to considerations of analysis. I noted a variety of analysis issues and procedures, beginning with the laundering and familiarization procedures that serve critical preliminary roles for more formal data analysis. I emphasized the utility of graphic displays in performing these preliminary roles.

Formal statistical analysis was viewed as serving two interrelated functions: describing data by means of various indices of typical performance, variability, and relationship; and testing whether the value of these indices varied from null, or other hypothetical values—that is, whether the data were statistically significant. A substantial number of techniques for serving these functions were described, with brief mention made of pitfalls and problems in their use and of the sources for learning more about them. These techniques of analysis include those for assessing individual differences as well as those for assessing trends in average performance. I separately targeted univariate and multivariate analytic techniques that are particularly appropriate for qualitative data and those that are more suitable for quantitative data. I singled out two relatively new and increasingly popular techniques for special attention: structural modeling and meta analysis. This section ended with a discussion of the frequent misunderstandings of the results of statistical testing, particularly the confusion between statistical significance and importance.

REFERENCES

Abbott, C., & Hartmann, D. P. (1986, April). *Meta analysis of children's prosocial behavior.* Paper presented at the annual meetings of the Rocky Mountain Psychological Association, Tucson.

Achenbach, T. (1978). *Research in developmental psychology: Concepts, strategies, methods.* New York: The Free Press.

Achenbach, T. M., & Edelbrock, C. S. (1981). Behavioral problems and competencies reported by parents of normal and disturbed children aged four through sixteen. *Monographs of the Society for Research in Child Development, 46* (Whole No. 188).

Ainsworth, M. D. S., Blehar, M. C., Waters, E., & Wall, S. (1978). *Patterns of attachment.* Hillsdale, NJ: Lawrence Erlbaum Associates.

Allison, P. D., & Liker, J. K. (1982). Analyzing sequential categorical data on dyadic interaction: A comment on Gottman. *Psychological Bulletin, 91,* 393–403.

Allport, G. W. (1937). *Personality: A psychological interpretation.* New York: Holt.

Altmann, J. (1974). Observational study of behavior: Sampling methods. *Behaviour, 49,* 227–267.

American Psychological Association. (1985). *Standards for educational and psychological tests.* Washington, DC: American Psychological Association.

Anastasi, A. (1978). *Psychological testing* (4th ed.). New York: Macmillan.

Anderson, J. G. (1987). Structural equation models in the social and behavioral sciences: Model building. *Child Development, 58,* 49–64.

Anderson, L. R., & Ager, J. W. (1978). Analysis of variance in small group research. *Personality and Social Psychology Bulletin, 4,* 341–345.

Appelbaum, M. I., & Cramer, E. M. (1974). Some problems in the nonorthogonal analysis of variance. *Psychological Bulletin, 81,* 335–343.

Appelbaum, M. I., & McCall, R. B. (1983). Design and analysis in developmental psychology. In P. H. Mussen (Ed.), *Handbook of child psychology: Vol. 1. History, theory, and methods* (4th ed., pp. 415–476). New York: Wiley.

Arrington, R. E. (1943). Time-sampling in studies of social behavior: A critical review of techniques and results with research suggestions. *Psychological Bulletin, 40,* 81–124.

Ary, D. (1984). Mathematical explanation of error in duration recording using partial interval, whole interval, and momentary time sampling. *Behavioral Assessment, 6,* 221–228.

Ary, D., & Suen, H. K. (1983). The use of momentary time sampling to assess both frequency and duration of behavior. *Journal of Behavioral Assessment, 5,* 143–150.

Baer, D. M. (1977). Reviewer's comment: Just because it's reliable doesn't mean that you can use it. *Journal of Applied Behavior Analysis, 10,* 117–119.

Bandura, A. (1977). Self-efficacy: Toward a unifying theory of behavioral change. *Psychological Review, 84,* 191–215.

Bangert-Drowns, R. L. (1986). Review of developments in meta-analytic method. *Psychological Bulletin, 99,* 388–399.

Barker, R. G., & Wright, H. F. (1951). *One boy's day: A specimen record of behavior.* New York: Harper & Row.

Barrios, B., & Hartmann, D. P. (in press). Fears and Anxieties. In E. J. Mash & L. G. Terdal (Eds.), *Behavioral assessment of childhood disorders* (2nd ed.). New York: Guilford.

Bentler, P. M. (1980). Multivariate analysis with latent variables: Causal modeling. *Annual Review of Psychology, 31,* 419–456.

Berk, R. A. (1979). Generalizability of behavioral observations: A clarification of interobserver agreement and interobserver reliability. *American Journal of Mental Deficiency, 93,* 460–472.

Biddle, B. J., & Marlin, M. M. (1987). Causality, confirmation, credulity, and structual equation modeling. *Child Development, 58,* 4–17.

Bijou, S. W., & Baer, D. M. (1960). The laboratory-experimental study of child behavior. In P. H. Mussen (Ed.), *Handbook of research methods in child development* (pp. 140–197). New York: Wiley.

Bishop, Y. M. M., & Holland, P. W. (1975). *Discrete multivariate analysis: Theory and practice.* Cambridge, MA: MIT Press.

Boehm, A. E., & Weinberg, R. A. (1977). *The classroom observer: A guide for developing observation skills.* New York: Teachers College Press.

Boice, R. (1983). Observational skills. *Psychological Bulletin, 93,* 3–29.

Bronson, W. C. (1987). Forward (Special section on structural equation modeling: Introduction). *Child Development, 58,* 1.

Bronfenbrenner, U. (1979). *The ecology of human development.* Cambridge, MA: Harvard University Press.

Cairns, R. B. (Ed.). (1979). *The analysis of social interactions: Methods, issues, and illustrations.* Hillsdale, NJ: Lawrence Erlbaum Associates.

Cairns, R. B. (1983). Sociometry, psychometry, and social structure: A commentary on six recent studies of popular, rejected, and neglected children. *Merrill-Palmer Quarterly, 29,* 429–438.

Campbell, D. T. (1958). Systematic error on the part of human links in communication systems. *Information and Control, 1,* 297–312.

Campbell, D. T., & Fiske, D. W. (1959). Convergent and discriminant validation by the multitrait–multimethod matrix. *Psychological Bulletin, 56,* 81–105.

Campbell, D. T., & Stanley, J. C. (1966). *Experimental and quasi-experimental designs for research.* Chicago: Rand McNally.

Cattell, R. B. (1944). Psychological measurement: Normative, ipsative, interactive. *Psychological Review, 51,* 292–303.

Cattell, R. B. (1946). *The description and measurement of personality.* New York: World Book.

Cattell, R. B. (1957). *Personality and motivation structure and measurement*. New York: Harcourt, Brace, & Jovanovich.

Cohen, J. (1960). A coefficient of agreement for nominal scales. *Educational and Psychological Measurement, 20,* 37–46.

Cohen, J. (1968). Multiple regression as a general data-analytic system. *Psychological Bulletin, 70,* 426–443.

Cohen, J. (1977). *Statistical power analysis for the behavioral sciences* (2nd ed.). New York: Academic Press.

Cohen, J., & Cohen, P. (1975). *Applied multiple/correlation analysis for the behavioral sciences*. Hillsdale, NJ: Lawrence Erlbaum Associates.

Comrey, A. L. (1978). Common methodological problems in factor analytic studies. *Journal of Consulting and Clinical Psychology, 46,* 648–659.

Cone, J. D. (1979). Confounded comparisons in triple response mode assessment. *Behavioral Assessment, 1,* 85–95.

Cone, J. D. (1981). Psychometric consideration. In M. Hersen & A. S. Bellack (Eds.), *Behavioral assessment* (2nd ed., pp. 38–68). New York: Pergamon Press.

Cone, J. D., & Foster, S. L. (1982). Direct observation in clinical psychology. In J. N. Butcher & P. C. Kendall (Eds.), *Handbook of research methods in clinical psychology* (pp. 311–354). New York: Wiley.

Conover, W. J. (1971). *Practical nonparametric statistics*. New York: Wiley.

Cook, T. D., & Campbell, D. T. (1979). *Quasi-experimentation: Design and analysis issues for field settings*. Chicago: Rand McNally.

Cronbach, L. J. (1957). The two disciplines of scientific psychology. *American Psychologist,* 671–684.

Cronbach, L. J. (1970). *Essentials of psychological testing* (3rd. ed.). New York: Harper & Row.

Cronbach, L. J., Gleser, G. C., Nanda, H., & Rajaratnam, N. (1972). *The dependability of behavioral measurements*. New York: Wiley.

Cronbach, L. J., & Furby, L. (1970). How should we measure change—or should we? *Psychological Bulletin, 74,* 68–80.

Cronbach, L. J., & Meehl, P. E. (1955). Construct validity in psychological tests. *Psychological Bulletin, 52,* 281–302.

Delucchi, K. L. (1983). The use and misuse of chi-square: Lewis and Burke revisited. *Psychological Bulletin, 94,* 166–176.

Dixon, W. J., Brown, M. B., Engelman, L., Frane, J. W., Hill, M. A., Jennrich, R. I., & Toporek, J. D. (1985). *BMDP statistical software: 1985 printing*. Berkeley CA: University of California Press.

Dwyer, J. H. (1983). *Statistical models for the social and behavioral sciences*. New York: Oxford University Press.

Eagly, A. H., & Crowley, M. (1986). Gender and helping behavior: A meta-analytic review of the social psychological literature. *Psychological Bulletin, 100,* 283–308.

Eagly, A. H., & Steffen, V. J. (1986). Gender and aggressive behavior: A meta-analytic review of the social psychological literature. *Psychological Bulletin, 100,* 309–330.

Ekman, P. (1972). Universals and cultural differences in facial expressions of emotions. *Nebraska Symposium on Motivation, 19,* 207–283.

Epstein, S., & Brady, E. J. (1985). The person–situation debate in historical and current perspective. *Psychological Bulletin, 98,* 513–537.

Falbo, T., & Polit, D. F. (1986). Quantitative review of the only child literature: Research evidence and theory development. *Psychological Bulletin, 100,* 176–189.

Fienberg, S. E. (1980). *The analysis of cross-classified categorical data* (2nd ed.). Cambridge, MA: MIT Press.

Flavell, J. H., & Wohlwill, J. F. (1969). Formal and functional aspects of cognitive development.

In D. Elkin & J. H. Flavell (Eds.), *Studies in cognitive development: Essays in honor of Jean Piaget*, 67–120. New York: Oxford University Press.

Fleiss, J. L. (1973). *Statistical methods for rates and proportions.* New York: Wiley.

Fleiss, J. L. (1975). Measuring agreement between two judges on the presence or absence of a trait. *Biometrics, 31,* 651–659.

Fleiss, J. L. (1981). *Statistical methods for rates and proportions* (2nd ed.). New York: Wiley.

Games, P. A. (1971). Multiple comparisons of means. *American Educational Research Journal, 8,* 531–565.

Gardner, W., Hartmann, D. P., & Mitchell, C. (1982). The effects of serial dependency on the use of X^2 for analyzing sequential data. *Behavioral Assessment, 4,* 75–82.

Geiser, S., & Greenhouse, S. W. (1958). An extension of Box's results on the use of the *F* distribution in multivariate analysis. *Annals of Mathematical Statistics, 29,* 885–891.

Gelfand, D. M., & Hartmann, D. P. (1984). *Child behavior analysis and therapy* (2nd ed.). New York: Pergamon.

Gewirtz, J. L. (1969). Mechanisms of social learning: Some roles of stimulation and behavior in early human development. In D. A. Goslin (Ed.), *Handbook of socialization theory and research,* (pp. 57–212). Chicago: Rand McNally.

Glass, G. V., McGaw, B., & Smith, M. L. (1981). *Meta-analysis in social research.* Beverly Hills, CA: Sage.

Glass, G. V., Peckham, P. D., & Sanders, J. R. (1972). Consequences of failure to meet assumptions underlying the analysis of variance and covariance. *Review of Education Research, 42,* 237–288.

Goetz, E. M., & Baer, D. M. (1973). Social control of form diversity and the emergence of new forms in children's block-building. *Journal of Applied Behavior Analysis, 6,* 123–128.

Goodenough, F. L. (1949). *Mental testing.* New York: Rinehart.

Goodwin, W. L., & Driscoll, L. A. (1980). *Handbook for measurement and evaluation in early childhood education.* San Francisco: Jossey-Bass.

Gorsuch, R. L. (1974). *Factor analysis.* Philadelphia: Saunders.

Guilford, J. P. (1954). *Psychometric methods* (2nd. ed.). New York: McGraw-Hill.

Guilford, J. P. (1965). *Fundamental statistics in psychology and education.* New York: McGraw-Hill.

Hartmann, D. P. (1977). Considerations in the choice of interobserver reliability estimates. *Journal of Applied Behavior Analysis, 10,* 103–116.

Hartmann, D. P. (1982). Assessing the dependability of observational data. In D. P. Hartmann (Ed.), *Using observers to study behavior: New directions for methodology of social and behavioral science,* (pp. 51–65). San Francisco: Jossey-Bass.

Hartmann, D. P. (1984). Assessment strategies. In M. Hersen & D. H. Barlow (Eds.), *Single case experimental designs: Strategies for studying behavior change* (2nd ed., (pp. 107–139). New York: Pergamon Press.

Hartmann, D. P., Roper, B. L., & Bradford, D. C. (1979). Some relationships between behavioral and traditional assessment. *Journal of Behavioral Assessment, 1,* 3–21.

Hartmann, D. P., & Wood, D. D. (1982). Observation methods. In A. S. Bellack, M. Hersen, & A. E. Kazdin (Eds.), *International handbook of behavior modification and therapy,* (pp. 109–138). New York: Plenum.

Hartshorne, H., May, M. A., & Maller, J. B. (1929). *Studies in service and self-control.* New York: Macmillan.

Hawkins, R. P. (1982). Developing a behavior code. In D. P. Hartmann (Ed.), *Using observers to study behavior: New directions for methodology of social and behavioral science,* (pp. 21–35). San Francisco: Jossey-Bass.

Haynes, S. N. (1978). *Principles of behavioral assessment.* New York: Gardner.

Hedges, L. V., & Olkin, I. (1985). *Statistical methods for meta-analysis.* New York: Academic Press.

Heise, D. R. (1975). *Causal analysis.* New York: Wiley.

Hertzog, H. F., & Nesselroade, J. R. (1987). Beyond autoregressive models: Some implications of the trait–state distinction for the structural modeling of developmental change. *Child Development, 58,* 93–109.

Hicks, L. E. (1970). Some properties of ipsative, normative, and forced-choice normative measures. *Psychological Bulletin, 74,* 167–184.

Hill, M. (1981). Using P1D to identify and list cases containing special or unacceptable values. In W. J. Dixon et al. (Eds.), *BMDP statistical software, 1981 edition,* (pp. 704–705). Los Angeles: University of California Press.

Hofstaetter, P. R. (1954). The changing composition of intelligence: A study of the *t*-technique. *Journal of Genetic Psychology, 85,* 159–164.

Hollander, M., & Wolfe, D. A. (1973). *Nonparametric statistical methods.* New York: Wiley.

House, A. E., House, B. J., & Campbell, M. B. (1981). Measures of interobserver agreement: Calculation formulas and distribution effects. *Journal of Behavioral Assessment, 3,* 37–57.

Huitema, B. E. (1980). *The analysis of covariance and alternatives.* New York: Wiley.

Huitema, B. E. (1986). Statistical analysis and single-subject designs. In A. Poling & R. W. Fuqua (Eds.), *Research methods in applied behavior analysis: Issues and advances.* New York: Plenum Press.

Hunt, J. M. (1961). *Intelligence and experience.* New York: Ronald Press.

Hunter, J. E., Schmidt, F. L., & Jackson, G. B. (1982). *Meta-analysis: Cumulating research findings across studies.* Beverly Hills, CA: Sage.

Hutt, S. J., & Hutt, C. (1970). *Direct observation and measurement of behavior.* Springfield, IL: Charles C. Thomas.

Hyde, J. S. (1981). How large are cognitive gender differences? A meta-analysis using w^2 and d. *American Psychologist, 36,* 892–901.

Jackson, G. B. (1980). Methods for integrative reviews. *Review of Educational Research, 50,* 438–460.

Jacobson, N. S., Follette, W. C., & Revenstorf, D. (1984). Psychotherapy outcome research: Methods for reporting variability and evaluating clinical significance. *Behavior Therapy, 15,* 336–352.

James, L. R., Muliak, S. A., & Brett, J. M. (1982). *Causal analysis: Assumptions, models, and data.* Beverly Hills: Sage.

Johnston, J. M., & Pennypacker, H. S. (1980). *Strategies and tactics of human behavioral research.* Hillsdale, NJ: Lawrence Erlbaum Associates.

Jones, H. E. (1954). The environment and mental development. In L. Carmichael (Ed.), *Handbook of child psychology,* 631–696. New York: Wiley.

Joreskog, K. G., & Sorbom, D. (1983). *Lisrel V and Lisrel VI: Analysis of linear structural relationships by maximum likelihood and least squares methods* (2nd ed.). Uppsala, Sweden: University of Uppsala Department of Statistics.

Kahneman, D. (1965). Control of spurious association and the reliability of the controlled variable. *Psychological Bulletin, 64,* 326–329.

Kazdin, A. E. (1979). Situational specificity: The two-edged sword of behavioral assessment. *Behavioral Assessment, 1,* 57–75.

Kerlinger, F. N. (1986). *Foundations of behavioral research* (3rd ed.). New York: Holt, Rinehart & Winston.

Kelly, M. B. (1977). A review of the observational data-collection and reliability procedures reported in *The Journal of Applied Behavior Analysis. Journal of Applied Behavior Analysis, 10,* 97–101.

Kenny, D. A. (1979). *Correlation and causality.* New York: Wiley.

Kirk, R. E. (1982). *Experimental design: Procedures for the behavioral sciences* (2nd ed.). Monterey, CA: Brooks/Cole.

Kleinbaum, D. G., & Kupper, L. L. (1978). *Applied regression analysis and other multivariable methods.* North Scituate, MA: Duxbury.

Knoke, D., & Burke, P. J. (1980). *Log-linear models.* Beverly Hills, CA: Sage.

Kraemer, H. C., & Jacklin, C. N. (1979). Statistical analysis of dyadic social behavior. *Psychological Bulletin, 86,* 217–224.

Lamb, M. E., Suomi, S. J., & Stephenson, G. R. (Eds.). (1979). *Social interaction analysis: Methodological issues.* Madison: University of Wisconsin Press.

Landis, J. R., & Koch, G. G. (1979). The analysis of categorical data in longitudinal studies of development. In J. R. Nesselroade & P. B. Baltes (Eds.), *Longitudinal research in the study of behavior and development,* (pp. 233–261). New York: Academic Press.

Lang, P. J. (1968). Fear reduction and fear behavior: Problems in treating a construct. In J. M. Shlien (Ed.), *Research in psychotherapy* (Vol. 3), 90–103. Washington, DC: American Psychological Association.

Larzelere, R. E., & Mulaik, S. A. (1977). Single-sample tests for many correlations. *Psychological Bulletin, 84,* 557–569.

Lewis, D., & Burke, C. J. (1949). The use and misuse of the chi-square test. *Psychological Bulletin, 46,* 433–489.

Lewis, D., & Burke, C. J. (1950). Further discussion of the use and misuse of the chi-square test. *Psychological Bulletin, 47,* 347–355.

Long, J. S. (1983). *Covariance structure models: An introduction to LISREL.* Beverly Hills, CA: Sage.

Lykken, D. T. (1968). Statistical significance in psychological research. *Psychological Bulletin, 70,* 151–159.

Marascuilo, L. A., & Levin, J. R. (1983). *Multivariate statistics in the social sciences: A researcher's guide.* Monterey, CA: Brooks/Cole.

McDonald, R. P. (1985). *Factor analysis and related methods.* Hillsdale, NJ: Lawrence Erlbaum Associates.

McGuire, W. J. (1969). Suspiciousness of experimenter's intent. In R. Rosenthal & R. L. Rosnow (Eds.), *Artifact in behavioral research,* (pp. 13–57). New York: Academic Press.

McNemar, Q. (1969). *Psychological statistics* (4th ed.). New York: Wiley.

Meehl, P. E. (1978). Theoretical risks and tabular asterisks: Sir Karl, Sir Ronald, and the slow progress of soft psychology. *Journal of Consulting and Clinical Psychology, 46,* 806–834.

Mendinnus, G. R. (1976). *Child study and observation guide.* New York: Wiley.

Messick, S. (1983). Assessment of children. In P. Mussen (Ed.), *Handbook of child psychology: Vol. 1. History, theory, and methods* (4th ed.), 477–526. New York: Wiley.

Mickey, M. R. (1981). Detecting outliers with stepwise regression (P2R). In W. J. Dixon (Ed.), *BMDP statistical software, 1981 edition,* (p. 698). Los Angeles: University of California Press.

Miller, S. A. (1987). *Developmental research methods.* Englewood Cliffs, NJ: Prentice-Hall.

Mischel, W., & Peake, P. K. (1983). Analyzing the construction of consistency in personality. In M. M. Page (Ed.), *Personality—current theory and research: 1982 Nebraska symposium on motivation,* (pp. 233–262). Lincoln, NE: University of Nebraska Press.

Mitchell, C., & Hartmann, D. P. (1981). A cautionary note on the use of omega squared to evaluate the effectiveness of behavioral treatments. *Behavioral Assessment, 1981, 3,* 93–100.

Mitchell, S. K. (1979). Interobserver agreement, reliability, and generalizability of data collected in observational studies. *Psychological Bulletin, 86,* 376–390.

Morrison, D. E., & Henkel, R. E. (Eds.). (1970). *The significance test controversy.* Chicago: Aldine.

Muliak, S. A. (1987). Toward a conception of causality applicable to experimentation and causal modeling. *Child Development, 58,* 18–32.

Nay, W. R. (1979). *Multimethod clinical assessment.* New York: Gardner Press.

Nunnally, J. C. (1978). *Psychometric theory* (2nd ed.). New York: McGraw-Hill.

O'Grady, K. E. (1982). Measures of explained variance: Cautions and limitations. *Psychological Bulletin, 92,* 766–777.

Overall, J. E., & Woodward, J. A. (1977). Nonrandom assignment and the analysis of covariance. *Psychological Bulletin, 84,* 588–594.

Overton, W. F., & Newman, J. L. (1982). Cognitive development: A competence/utilization approach. In T. Field, A. Houston, H. Quay, L. Troll, & G. Finley (Eds.), *Review of human development,* (pp. 217–241). New York: Wiley.

Parsonson, B. S., & Baer, D. M. (1978). The analysis and presentation of graphic data. In T. R. Kratochwill (Ed.), *Single subject research: Strategies for evaluating change,* (pp. 101–165). New York: Academic Press.

Parten, M. B. (1932). Social participation among preschool children. *Journal of Abnormal Psychology, 27,* 243–269.

Patterson, G. R. (1982). *A social learning approach: Vol. 3. Coercive family process.* Eugene, OR: Castalia.

Popper, K. R. (1962). *Conjectures and refutations.* New York: Basic Books.

Reid, J. B. (1970). Reliability assessment of observation data A possible methodological problem. *Child Development, 41,* 1143–1150.

Reid, J. B. (1982). Observer training in naturalistic research. In D. P. Hartmann (Ed.), *Using observers to study behavior: New directions for methodology of social and behavioral science,* (pp. 37–50). San Francisco: Jossey-Bass.

Rogosa, D., Brandt, D., & Zimowski, M. (1982). A growth curve approach to the measurement of change. *Psychological Bulletin, 92,* 726–748.

Rosenthal, R. (1979). The "file-drawer problem" and tolerance for null results. *Psychological Bulletin, 85,* 185–193.

Rosenthal, R. (Ed.). (1980). *Quantitative assessment of research domains.* San Francisco: Jossey-Bass.

Rosenthal, R. (1980). Summarizing significance levels. In R. Rosenthal (Ed.), *Quantitative assessment of research domains,* (pp. 33–46). San Francisco: Jossey-Bass.

Rosenthal, R., & Rosnow, R. (1985). *Contrast analysis: Focused comparisons in the analysis of variance.* Cambridge: Cambridge University Press.

Rummel, R. J. (1967). Understanding factor analysis. *The Journal of Conflict Resolution. XI,* 444–480.

Sackett, G. P. (1978). Measurement in observational research. In G. P. Sackett (Ed.), *Observing behavior: Vol. 2. Data collection and analysis methods,* (pp. 25–43). Baltimore: University Park Press.

Sackett, G. P. (Ed.). (1978). *Observing behavior: Vol. 2. Data collection and analysis methods.* Baltimore: University Park Press.

SAS Institute Inc. (1985). *SAS^R user's guide: Statistics* (5th ed.). Cary, NC: SAS Institute Inc.

Scheffé, H. (1959). *The analysis of variance.* New York: Wiley.

Selltiz, C., Jahoda, M., Deutsch, M., & Cook, S. W. (1959). *Research methods in social relations.* New York: Holt.

Siegel, S. (1956). *Nonparametric statistics for the behavioral sciences.* New York: McGraw-Hill.

Simpson, M. J. A. (1979). Problems of recording behavioral data by keyboard. In M. E. Lamb, S. J. Suomi, & G. R. Stephenson (Eds.), *Social interaction analysis: Methodological issues,* (pp. 137–156). Madison: University of Wisconsin Press.

Skinner, B. F. (1938). *The behavior of organisms.* New York: Appleton-Century.

Skinner, B. F. (1971). *Beyond freedom and dignity.* New York: Knopf.

Smith, M. L., Glass, G. V., & Miller, T. I. (1980). *The benefits of psychotherapy.* Baltimore, MD: Johns Hopkins University Press.

SPSS Inc. (1986). *SPSS^X user's guide* (2nd. ed.). Chicago: SPSS Inc.

Staub, E. (1979). *Positive social behavior and morality: Socialization and development* (Vol. 2). New York: Academic Press.

Steiger, J. H. (1980). Tests for comparing elements of a correlation matrix. *Psychological Bulletin, 87,* 245–251.

Stevens, S. S. (1968). Measurement, statistics, and the schemapiric view. *Science, 161,* 849–856.

Strube, M. J., & Hartmann, D. P. (1983). Meta-analysis: Techniques, applications, and functions. *Journal of Consulting and Clinical Psychology, 51,* 14–27.

Suen, H. K., & Ary, D. (1986). A post hoc correction procedure for systematic errors in time sampling duration estimates. *Journal of Psychopathology and Behavioral Assessment, 8,* 31–38.

Tabachnick, B. G., & Fidell, L. S. (1983). *Using multivariate statistics.* New York: Harper & Row.

Tanaka, J. S. (1987). ''How big is big enough?'': Sample size and goodness of fit in structural equation models with latent variables. *Child Development, 58,* 134–146.

Taplin, P. S., & Reid, J. B. (1973). Effects of instructional set and experimental influences on observer reliability. *Child Development, 44,* 547–554.

Thompson, B. (1984). *Canonical correlation analysis: Uses and interpretation.* Beverly Hills, CA: Sage.

Tukey, J. W. (1977). *Exploratory data analysis.* Reading, MA: Addison-Wesley.

Tversky, A., & Kahneman, D. (1971). Belief in the law of small numbers. *Psychological Bulletin, 76,* 105–110.

Underwood, W., & Moore, B. (1982). Perspective-taking and altruism. *Psychological Bulletin, 91,* 143–173.

Wasik, B. H. (1984). Clinical applications of direct behavioral observation: A look at the past and the future. In B. B. Lahey & A. E. Kazdin (Eds.), *Advances in clinical child psychology* (Vol. 7, (pp. 153–193). New York: Plenum Press.

Weick, K. E. (1968). Systematic observational methods. In G. Lindzey & E. Aronson (Eds.), *The handbook of social psychology* (Vol. 2, 2nd. ed.), 357–451. Menlo Park, CA: Addison-Wesley.

West, S. (Ed.). (1983). Personality and prediction: Nomothetic and idiographic approaches. *Journal of Personality, 51* (Whole No. 3).

Wiggins, J. S. (1973). *Personality and prediction: Principles of personality assessment.* Reading, MA: Addison-Wesley.

Wright, H. F. (1960). Observational child study. In P. Mussen (Ed.), *Handbook of research methods in child development,* (pp. 71–139). New York: Wiley.

Wright, H. F. (1967). *Recording and analyzing child behavior.* New York: Harper & Row.

Yarrow, M. R., & Waxler, C. Z. (1979). Observing interaction: A confrontation with methodology. In R. B. Cairns (Ed.), *The analysis of social interactions: Methods, issues, and illustrations,* (pp. 37–65). Hillsdale, NJ: Lawrence Erlbaum Associates.

II PERCEPTUAL, COGNITIVE, AND LINGUISTIC DEVELOPMENT

The focus shifts, in the four chapters that comprise this section, from foundations and methods to substance. In Chapter 4, Marc Bornstein reviews the controversies and issues that continue to make the study of perceptual development central to understanding psychological functioning. More than any other aspect of psychology, perceptual development was the forum for debates between nativists and empiricists—the fundamental battle that began with philosophical dissertation and continues to this day as the driving force of research in perceptual development, particularly in infancy. Now, however, sophisticated techniques have supplemented, if not supplanted, introspection and speculation, enabling researchers to empirically address questions concerning the origins of perception.

In Chapter 5, Deanna Kuhn moves from the registration and initial evaluation of sensory information to its interpretation. Kuhn summarizes a succession of perspectives that have appeared to explain the transformation of information into understanding, with an emphasis on Piagetian and neo-Piagetian approaches. Such theories place emphasis on developmental changes in the modes of understanding reality, rather than on the gradual accretion of information. From this perspective, individuals are seen as active interpreters of their experiences, with failures to incorporate new experiences from time to time prompting reorganizations in the individual's perspective in order to render new experiences explicable and consistent with the individual's frame of reference.

In Chapter 6, Robert Sternberg discusses attempts to describe, analyze, and explain individual differences in intellectual functioning. Psychometric issues of measurement have traditionally been emphasized by students of intelligence, but in recent years information-processing specialists have attempted to explain the basis of intelligence and individual continuity by analogy with mechanized systems of information acquisition and interpretation.

In Chapter 7, the last of this section, Lila Gleitman and Eric Wanner confront issues in the acquisition of language. Of all the hurdles faced by the young infant, cracking the linguistic code is perhaps the most impressive in the eyes of parents and observers. One cannot help but marvel at the speed with which preverbal infants, equipped with specialized abilities to segment the speech stream, learn not only how to articulate meaningful statements, but also how to understand the speech of others. Because language is purely symbolic, furthermore, its acquisition serves as the basis for advanced and abstract problem solving and cognition.

4 Perceptual Development Across the Life Cycle

Marc H. Bornstein
New York University
and The National Institute of Child Health and Human Behavior

> all that a mammal does is fundamentally dependent on . . . perception,
> past or present.
>
> —D. O. Hebb (1953, p. 44)

INTRODUCTION

Perception constitutes a necessary "first step" in experiencing and interpreting the world, and for this reason philosophers, psychologists, physiologists, and physicists have been motivated to study it. Our everyday experiences provoke many challenging questions about perception. Some are quite general: How similar to our perceptions of them are properties or objects or events in the real world? How different? How is a stable world perceived amidst continuous environmental fluctuation? How are perceptual aspects of the world invested with meaning? Other questions which perceptual experience provokes are specific: How does the quality of *bitter* differ from the quality of *red?* How is a three-dimensional world seen when visual processing begins with only a two-dimensional image in the eye? How are the individual features of things synthesized into wholes?

Another reason for studying perception is epistemological and derives from questions about the origins and nature of human knowledge. Extreme views have been put forward by *empiricists,* who have asserted that all knowledge derives from the senses and grows by way of experience; and by *nativists,* who have reasoned that some kinds of knowledge could not possibly rely on experience and thus that humans enter the world with a sensory apparatus equipped at the very least to order and organize rudimentary knowledge.[1] These positions define the classic *nature–nurture* debate.

Philosophy focused attention especially on the development of perception near the beginning of life, since this was the period at which epistemologically meaningful issues, related to the origins of knowledge, could be most directly addressed. Thus, the study of perceptual development originally captured the philosopher's imagination since it promised to reveal what kind and how much of knowledge was inborn and what kind and how much of knowledge had to be learned. In this sense, studies of early perception essentially constitute experimental tests of nativist and empiricist theories of knowledge.

Developmental studies of perception provide many important kinds of information on normative processes in early perception concerning, for example, the quality, limits, and capacities of the sensory systems as they function and first develop. Textbooks in pediatrics portrayed the infant as "perceptually incompetent"; more recent studies of perception at the beginning of life contradict the validity of this characterization. Determining how the senses function in infancy also helps to specify the perceptual world of babies. If a substance tastes sweet to adults they may suppose that it tastes that way for infants too, and even that infants like it; in fact, however, taste receptors for sweetness may not even be present in infants or, if present, may not function or signal the same perception to infants as to adults. Defining normative capacity in early life also permits developmental comparisons of mature versus immature perceptual function, and studies of perception in infancy provide baseline data against which the normal course of maturation and the effects of experience over time can be assessed.

For these reasons, much of the impetus to study perceptual development has derived from philosophy, and much perceptual study has focused on infancy. Further, in the study of perceptual development both theory and methodology have played critical roles. The discussion of perceptual development in this chapter begins with a consideration of philosophical foundations and motivations for studying perceptual development experimentally, and then turns, almost immediately, to the contribution that theory—in particular, the nature–nurture controversy—has made to the understanding of perceptual development. The

---

[1]Early empiricists and nativists were interested in epistemology for both philosophical and theological reasons. Empiricism as championed by Locke, Berkeley, and Hume arrived in the eighteenth century and was greeted into a milieu of strong religious dogma: If ideas—faith and morals—were inborn in men, then God would transcend. But the empiricists rejected this supposition on epistemological grounds, and thereby inadvertently questioned articles of faith. If the mind of the babe is a *tabula rasa,* they reasoned, knowledge (even of God) must be acquired through sense experience. But no one has witnessed God or can know God this way. (Moreover, in Berkeley and Hume's analyses even mind degenerated into frail perceptions, memories, and feelings.) Kant parried for science as well as for religion: Perhaps skepticism is not an ultimate but a limited authority, and there is room for instinct and emotion alongside the knowledge and morality inherent in the mind's nature and structure.

next section of the chapter overviews perceptual development cum a taxonomy of methodologies used in studying it. This scheme of psychophysiological and behavioral methods is organized both to reflect different contemporary strategies of addressing major questions in perceptual development, and to underscore the fact that different perceptual methodologies require different degrees of inference. Although the chapter focuses on perceptual development in early life, reflecting the evolution of theory and of contemporary research, some significant principles of perceptual development in later childhood and in old age are also reviewed. Following the history of developmental research, this chapter emphasizes the "higher" senses of sight and hearing, but also includes some data about the "lower" senses—taste, smell, and touch—and about how sensory abilities interrelate and coordinate. The chapter concludes with a brief evaluation of the developmental effects engendered by altered perceptual worlds.

PHILOSOPHICAL UNDERPINNINGS

Among all of the different subject disciplines of developmental psychology, perception has historically been the one most intimately tied in with nature–nurture questions. What do we know before we have any experience in the world? How do we acquire knowledge about the world? The two main positions are *empiricism* and *nativism*.

Empiricism

The empiricist argument is described in several steps: Empiricists assert, first, that there is no endowed knowledge at birth; second, that all knowledge comes through the senses; and third, that perceptual development proceeds through associative experience. In specific, empiricists argue that stimuli in the world naturally provoke bodily sensations which, occurring close together in space or in time, give rise to more global "ideas" and thereby begin to invest the perceptual world with meaning. It is through association, empiricism explains, that separate raw sensations aggregate into meaningful perceptions. The empiricist's view of the nature of the mind was fostered by two separate, if similar, schools of thought. One derived from John Locke (1632–1704) who is reputed to have expressed the opinion that the infant mind is a *tabula rasa*: Mental life begins with nothing, and understanding of the world depends wholly on the accretion of experiences. A slightly different empiricist view can be attributed to William James (1842–1910): The world of the infant is a "blooming, buzzing confusion" out of which, presumably, the infant's experience helps to organize and create order and knowledge. According to empiricist belief, the naive infant does not share the perceptual world of the experienced adult. Empiricism is inherently developmental because, by whatever mechanism is postulated, children develop from perceptually naive to perceptually sophisticated beings.

Nativism

The belief that human beings begin life empty-headed, so to speak, is to many both philosophically intolerable and logically indefensible. Nativists originally argued that God did not create human beings as mindless, and that the knowledge which humans possess could not be achieved by learning alone in so short a span of time as childhood. As a consequence, philosophers like René Descartes (1596–1650) and Immanuel Kant (1724–1804) conceived of humans as endowed from birth with ideas or categories of knowledge that assist perceptual functions. They postulated innate perceptual categories for size, form, position, and motion, as well as for the more abstract conceptions of space and time. The nativist argument, contrary to the empiricist, holds that the mind naturally and from the beginning of life imposes order on sensory input, thereby transforming sensations into meaningful perceptions. According to the nativist account, the infant and adult share many of the same perceptual capacities, and the two perceive the world in much the same way. For abilities that are congenital, nativism is not a developmental theory; for abilities that mature, nativism is developmental in outlook.

Reflecting on the extreme nativist and empiricist opinions that have been championed and the vigor with which they have been argued, many have observed that perceptual development stands as a kind of battleground between nativists and empiricists on how the mind works. We can examine one exemplary skirmish, the question of how depth in space is perceived. This example is suitable for several reasons. First, depth perception is crucial to determining the spatial layout of the environment, to recognizing objects, and to guiding motor action. Second, the study of depth perception addresses an interesting psychophysical question, namely how the three-dimensional layout of the environment is constructed when the retina first codes only two-dimensional information. Third, debate on this question exemplifies the typical historical course: It originates with hotly contested nativist–empiricist philosophical debates that spanned the seventeenth to nineteenth centuries and culminates with experimentation in infancy and with contributions of animal physiology in the twentieth century.

A Nativist–Empiricist Debate

How Do Human Beings Come to Perceive Depth in Visual Space?

The Phase of Philosophy.   Writing in *La Dioptrique* in 1638, René Descartes offered a straightforward answer to this question that assumed the mind's intuitive grasp of basic mathematical relations. Descartes believed that human thought operated as a system driven by natural law; knowledge was inborn. Thus Descartes introspected: Our two eyes form the base of a triangle whose apex is the object under our gaze. When we look at a faraway object, our eyes are nearly parallel and the base angles of the triangle approach 90°; whereas when our eyes converge on a nearby object, the base angles are acute. The closer the object, the more acute the angles. Descartes (1638/1824) concluded that distance is given by "an act of thinking which, being simple imagination [pure thought], does not entail [explicit] reasoning" (pp. 59–66). All of us are born with two eyes, and our eyes converge more for near than for far points of interest. But are we born with trigonometric tables in our heads?

A counterexplanation for depth perception (that actually built on Descartes') was put forward by empiricist George Berkeley (1685–1753) in his *Essay Towards a New Theory of Vision* of 1709. Berkeley (1709/1901, sect. xix) argued that humans do not deduce distance by "natural geometry":

> Since I am not conscious, that I make any such use of the Perception I have by the Turn of my Eyes. And for me to make those Judgments, and draw those Conclusions from it, without knowing that I do so, seems altogether incomprehensible.

Rather, Berkeley argued (sect. iii) that we come to know depth and distance through experience. He reflected:

> . . . when an *Object* appears Faint and Small, which at a near Distance I have experienced to make a vigorous and large Appearance; I instantly conclude it to be far off. And this, 'tis evident, is the result of *Experience;* without which, from the Faintness and Littleness, I should not have infer'd any thing concerning the Distance of *Objects.*

In essence, Berkeley claimed, we associate the large apparent size of objects (their "vigorousness") with bringing our two eyes close together in conjunction with the small cost of small arm movements when we reach for nearby objects; and we associate the small apparent size of objects (their "faintness") with the parallel position of our two eyes in conjunction with the large cost of large arm movements when we reach for faraway objects. Berkeley hypothesized that infants' consistent reaching in association with convergence of the eyes and the appearance of objects eventuates in their visual understanding of depth and distance.

Nativists objected to this experiential argument on logic. In the *Critique of Pure Reason* of 1781, Kant asserted that the human mind does not rely on experience for meaning, but innately organizes sensations into meaningful perceptions. Kant (1781/1924) argued that "Space is a necessary a priori idea":

> Space is not an empiricial conception, which has been derived from external experiences. For I could not be conscious that certain of my sensations are relative to something outside of me, that is, to something in a different part of space from that in which I myself am. . . . . No experience of the external relations of sensible

things could yield the idea of space, because without the consciousness of space there would be no external experience whatever. (pp. 22–29)

Kant buttressed his theoretical argument with two compelling observations: First, that depth perception arises early in life and could not wait for extensive experience and learning; and, second, that individuals with limited experience give evidence that they perceive depth. The philosopher Arthur Schopenhauer (1788–1860), in support, invoked the case of Eva Lauk: Born without limbs and consequently restricted in her experience, Eva reportedly possessed normal intelligence and perceptions of space. (Eva could, of course, still move about. Modern studies of profoundly handicapped infants, like thalidomide babies, demonstrate that the inability to act motorically does not inhibit the development of normal perception and cognition; see Décarie, 1969.) Fueled thus, nativists deduced that (at least) some capacity to perceive depth must be inborn or directly given. This deduction impelled some investigators to seek specific biological substrates which might underlie the ability to perceive depth. At first such mechanisms were only postulated, as for example by the notable nineteenth-century physiologist Ewald Hering (1834–1918). In more modern times, sensory physiologists recording from single cells in the cortex of the brain have found evidence for them.

Immediately after Kant, however, the debate continued with a defense of empiricism. In his classic 1866 *Handbook of Physiological Optics,* Hermann von Helmholtz (1821–1894) rebutted nativism with the logical and rational argument that "intuition theory is an unnecessary hypothesis." Helmholtz (1866/1925, Vol. III, sect. 26) asserted that it is uneconomical to assume mechanisms of innate perception, especially when:

> It is not clear how the assumption of these original *"space sensations"* can help the explanation of our visual perceptions, when the adherents of this theory ultimately have to assume in by far the great majority of cases that these sensations must be overruled by the better understanding which we get by experience. In that case it would seem to me much easier and simpler to grasp, that all apperceptions of space were obtained simply by experience.

After that blow by Helmholtz, gestalt psychologists restored credibility to the nativist views of Kant primarily by appealing to experimentation. At that time in scientific history, experimental investigation began to supplant philosophical speculation. In fact, psychology, which began in that century, was specifically organized to address just such issues. Given the enormous significance attributed to these questions, and the power of an argument supported by the test of trial, it is hardly surprising that an experimental psychology of perceptual development captured the imagination, effort, and energy of subsequent generations of researchers.

Some Science.   Three lines of investigation exemplify how developmental researchers have addressed the question of the origins of depth perception. The three together are valuable since no one alone provides definitive information, but as a group they converge to suggest how depth perception develops. The starting point for one is familiar:

> Human infants at the creeping and toddling stage are notoriously prone to falls from more or less high places. They must be kept from going over the brink by side panels on their cribs, gates on their stairways, and the vigilance of adults. . . . Common sense might suggest that the child learns to recognize falling-off places by experience—that is, by falling and hurting himself. But is experience really the teacher? Or is the ability to perceive and avoid a brink part of the child's original endowment?

Faced with this lingering conundrum, Gison and Walk (1960) began to investigate depth perception experimentally in human infants using a ''visual cliff'' (p. 64). Babies were placed on a centerboard to one side of which was an illusory precipitous drop, whereas the other side clearly continued the support of the centerboard. In fact, however, a glass sheet provided firm support for the babies on *both* sides of the centerboard. Gibson and Walk found that a majority of infants between 6 and 14 months crawled across the ''shallow'' side of the apparatus from the centerboard when the mothers called them, but only a few crawled across the ''deep'' side. On this basis, Gibson and Walk concluded that depth perception must be present in infants as young as 6 months of age. However, the method used in these studies to assess depth perception is obviously limited by the capacity of infants to locomote, which they begin to do only in the second half of the first year of life. By this time the child may have plenty of experience with depth. To meet the challange of this critique, Campos, Langer, and Krowitz (1970) monitored a different activity, heart rate, in precrawling babies suddenly exposed either to the deep or to the shallow drop. By 2 months of age, babies who were exposed to the apparently deep side showed a heart-rate change, whereas babies exposed to the shallow side showed no comparable heart-rate change. These differences suggest that babies may perceive depth long before they locomote. Of course, the two depths may stimulate babies differently and thereby affect their sensitivity differently without yielding a *perception* of depth.

The ''visual cliff'' experiments constitute one way investigators have sought to explore the infant's capacity to perceive depth. A related situation that taps perception of depth in space is ''looming.'' Looming describes the motion of an object moving directly toward us on a ''hit path,'' and our reaction normally is to avoid impending collision as the object moves closer in space. Bower, Broughton, and Moore (1970) and Ball and Tronick (1971) reported that babies only a few weeks old show an ''integrated avoidance response'' to impending collision:

They observed that infants threw back their heads, shielded their faces with their hands, and even cried when an object moved at them along a hit path, but that babies failed to show these defensive reactions when the same object moved along a "miss path" or receded in space. In the experimental situation these investigators created, infants were not actually threatened with a solid object, but viewed a translucent screen onto which a silhouette of the three-dimensional object was cast. This technique cleverly avoids cueing infants with air changes on the face as an actual approaching object would. However, Yonas (1981) insightfully reasoned that, insofar as magnification of an object's outline is the optical cue to impending collision, the object's upper contour naturally moves upward in the field of view as an object advances. In "throwing their heads back," infants may simply be tracking the rapidly changing upward contour of the advancing image, giving only an impression of "avoidance." Yonas therefore conducted a series of control experiments involving babies of different ages under conditions in which the object's image remained on a hit path but its upper contour either remained at a constant level or rose. He determined that babies probably do track upper contours and that the "looming response" could not be demonstrated reliably in babies less than approximately 4 months of age. However, Yonas also observed that babies as young as 1 month showed a reasonably consistent eye-blink response to approaching objects.

A third line of infant research that bears on the question of depth perception involves infants' sensitivities to isolated visual cues of depth. Psychophysicists traditionally categorize binocular convergence and accommodation as "primary" cues, and linear perspective, texture gradient, and shading as "secondary" cues (e.g., Hochberg, 1978). Convergence, for example, depends on an organism's capacities to fixate an object binocularly and to fuse the two separate retinal images into one. If infants rely on convergence of the eyes to respond to depth, as Descartes and Berkeley proposed, theorists need to show that the eyes indeed *can* converge. We have all noted, however, that in some babies one eye wanders, and many seem unable to fix an object with both eyes consistently. Empirical studies of infants' tracking stationary and dynamic targets have revealed only minimal convergence at 1 month, but more regular convergence by 2 to 3 months (e.g., Banks, 1980; Fox, Aslin, Shea, & Dumais, 1980). It is at this time that infants also first display sensitivity to the deep side of the visual cliff (Campos et al., 1970). Secondary cues do not seem to be available to infants before 6 months of age. One study showed that infants older than 6 months would direct their reaching to the apparently closer side of a photograph of a window rotated in depth, whereas infants only 1 month younger would not direct their reaching to the pictorially nearer side of the display although they would reach directionally when presented with a real window rotated in depth (Yonas & Granrud, 1985). When Granrud, Yonas, and Pettersen (1984) directly compared monocular and binocular cues for depth perception in a similar reaching experiment, they found that infants' perceptions of object distances were more ver-idical under binocular viewing than under monocular viewing.

Studies of the visual cliff, looming, and monocular and binocular sensitivity in human babies together suggest that depth perception is relatively poor up until about 2 months after birth, at which time this perceptual ability rapidly develops. We still do not know, however, precisely when depth perception arises or what course it follows in early development. Nor do these findings mean that the development of depth perception is complete by 4 to 6 months of age. They only show that infants have the capacity for *relative* distance perception by this time. Although binocularity, for example, provides an organism with information about *absolute* distance, it can do so only for known interocular distances; the rapidly changing distance between the eyes in growing infants would require frequent recalibration. Consequently, some investigators have argued that achieving absolute distance calibration may depend on nonvisual sources of information. Echoing Berkeley, they suggest that reaching is one valuable source of calibrating absolute distance, and that self-produced locomotion is another. More specifically, theorists such as Piaget (1954) have argued that infants can tell the absolute distance of objects in near space only after they have had experience with reaching, and the distance of objects in far space (i.e., beyond reach) only after having crawled.

When perceptual psychologists studying infancy reach an impasse in their efforts to resolve such questions, they frequently resort to other argumentation and data such as behavioral and physiological information provided by in-frahuman animals. Animals offer special circumstances for research since they lend themselves to experimentation and manipulation that are sometimes not possible with humans. So, for example, animals have provided valuable behav-ioral information about the ontogeny of depth perception. A variety of species has been tested in the visual cliff; some of these, like chicks, move about on their own within a day after birth. All show avoidance of the cliff, suggesting that depth perception may develop very early and independent of motor experience. Of course, it is still possible that depth perception is innate and congenital in some species but not in others, including human beings.

The general premise of the developmentalist's appeal to physiological data is that perceptions ought to have identifiable neural substrates, and if those sub-strates are found they can contribute evidence to the nativist–empiricist argu-ment. Continuing the example from depth perception: The fusion of two separate images such as are produced by the two eyes to yield one image (stereopsis) enhances depth perception. Hubel and Weisel (1970) and Barlow, Blakemore, and Pettigrew (1967) identified single cells in the visual systems of cats and of monkeys which are exquisitely sensitive to such fusion. Although these sorts of results suggest some physiological basis for perception, developmentalists usu-ally exercise caution about reductionism of this sort. Because such cells exist in other mature species does not mean that they exist in infant forms of those species; because such cells exist in lower species does not mean that they exist in human beings; and because such cells exist at all, of course, does not mean that they signal ''depth'' in a psychologically or functionally meaningful way.

A Conclusion.   Although empirical studies such as these clearly advance the understanding of perceptual function beyond philosophical debate, scientific investigation does not necessarily guarantee resolution. Researchers on both sides of the issue are quick to point out that there can be no final triumph for nativism or for empiricism. *No matter how early in life depth perception can be demonstrated, the ability still rests on some experience; no matter how late its emergence, it can never be proved that only experience has mattered.*

Looking back over this example, it is clear that theoretical, philosophical, and even theological differences of opinion about epistemology have burned like embers in the minds of men for centuries, now and again igniting into flaming controversy over whether human ideas, abilities, and capacities are innately given or the products of experience. The sparks of speculation which flew in bygone days generated more heat than light. In modern times, science has added experimental behavioral evidence, in addition to observations from animals and from physiology, to fan the ancient fires.

Summary

By far the two most prominent themes in perceptual study have been nativism and empiricism—opinions about how much or how little organisms are capable of before they have had experience, and what sorts of roles experience plays in development. Indeed, in no other area of psychology has the nativism—empiricism controversy been perceived as so meaningful or legitimate as in the study of perceptual development. One connected line of thought and research, extending from Locke and Berkeley down to modern empiricists like D. O. Hebb, holds that perceptions arise out of experiencing the world. A parallel line, extending from Descartes and Kant down through modern nativists like Max Wertheimer, holds that perceptions are competences already a part of the armamentarium of even the very young child. Different theorists' arguments for depth perception exemplify these divergent points of view: Nativists see the child as immediately capable of perceiving depth because of how the nervous system functions, whereas empiricists see the child as capable of that only after repeated experience in associating movements of the eyes, arms, and body with small and large images of objects. Thus, constructionist theories such as Piaget's assume that the two-dimensional retinal image must be supplemented with movement to give a scale of depth; but direct perception theories, such as James and Eleanor Gibsons', maintain that space is automatically perceived in those relations among higher-order variables (such as texture) to which the sensory systems have evolved acute sensitivity. Not every theory or theorist fits neatly into a nativist or an empiricist perspective; there are elements of both in all developmental theories. More important, despite the fact that they are sometimes conceived as either-or contributors to development, nature and nurture interact.

NATURE AND NURTURE

The potential ways in which the forces of nature and nurture may interact in the course of development can be conceptualized in a simple and comprehensive manner. Figure 4.1 shows different possible courses of development before the onset of experience, and the several possible ways experience may influence eventual perceptual outcomes after. First, there is the possibility that perceptual abilities or functions develop fully before the onset of experience, after which they require experience only to be maintained—and that, without relevant experience, these abilities or functions may be lost. Second, perceptual abilities or functions may develop only partially before the onset of experience, after which experience operates in one of three ways: Relevant experience may facilitate further development of an ability or function or may attune that ability or function; experience may serve to maintain the ability or function at the partial level of development it attained before the onset of experience; or, without relevant

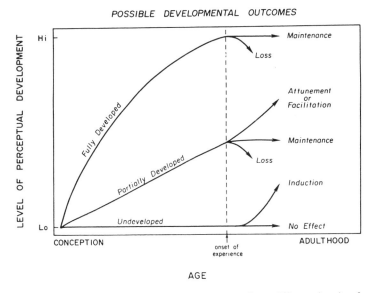

FIG. 4.1. Possible developmental outcomes given different levels of perceptual development before the onset of experience and different experiences afterward. (From Aslin, 1981. Copyright Academic Press. Reprinted with permission.)

experience, the ability or function may be lost. (Of course, experience per se may not be altogether necessary where the perceptual ability or function would continue to mature as a reflection of the genetic blueprint.) Finally, third, a perceptual ability or function undeveloped at the onset of experience may be induced by relevant experience; again, without such experience, the function or ability may not emerge.

To flesh out this skeletal introduction to how nature and nurture may interact in perceptual development, we can examine, however briefly, a perceptual domain in which these several possibilities occur. This domain is the narrow but perennially important one of *speech perception*. Just a bit of background is required before going into the scheme itself. Recall that sounds are essentially different sine-wave frequencies produced simultaneously, and that speech is the complex array of different frequencies produced at different intensities over time. Languages abstract particular subsets from the universe of all possible speech sounds (phonetics), which they invest with meaning (phonemics). One dimension along which certain phonemes in many languages are distinguished is their "voicing." Differences in voicing are heard when a speaker produces different frequencies of sound waves at slightly different times. In voicing, a sound like /b/ (pronounced "ba") is produced by vibrating the vocal cords and producing higher frequencies *before* or *at* the time the lips are opened and low-frequency energy is released—/b/ is a voiced phoneme. By contrast, for sounds like /p/ (pronounced "pa") the vocal cords do not begin to vibrate higher frequencies until some *after* the lips release lower frequencies. Thus, high-frequency components of a sound may precede low-frequency components, components may begin simultaneously, or high-frequency ones may come after low-frequency ones. The relative onset times of low and high frequencies cue phonemic perception. Physically, the relative onsets of low- and high-frequency components of a sound may vary *continuously;* however, adults perceive differences in voicing more or less *categorically.* That is, although we can distinguish among many differences in relative onset times of low- and high-frequency sounds, we classify some different sounds as similar while discriminating others. English distinguishes voiced and voiceless /b/ from /p/. Of course, different people say /b/ and /p/ in different ways, yet adult listeners seldom misidentify these speech sounds, as they employ implicit category definitions to allot a sound to the /b/ and /p/ categories. Interestingly, cross-language research has revealed that adults in nearly all cultures hear only one, two, or three categories of voicing: The three are called *prevoiced, voiced,* and *voiceless.* Categorical perception means that across a nearly infinite spectrum of possibilities, only three tokens are functionally distinguished; and they are distinguished by nearly all peoples despite wide language differences.

Many researchers speculate that phenomena so ubiquitous, consistent, circumscribed, and significant in human behavior as perceptual categories of speech might have a biological foundation. To test this assumption, Eimas,

Siqueland, Jusczyk, and Vigorito (1971) sought to discover whether preverbal human infants would perceive acoustic changes in voicing categorically; that is, in a manner parallel to adult phonemic perception. Using a technique called *habituation* that relies on babies first getting bored when the same sight or sound is presented over and over again, and then expressing interest in a novel sight or sound, these investigators arranged to "ask" infants some simple same–different questions about their auditory perceptions. They found that 1- and 4-month-olds behaved as though they perceived speech sounds in the adultlike categorical manner: Babies distinguished /b/ from /p/, but not examples of two different /b/s. That is, babies categorize different sounds as either voiced or voiceless long before they use language or even have extensive experience in hearing language. This might suggest that categorical perception is essentially innate. Returning to Fig. 4.1, it would seem that categorical perception of phonemes most closely fits the topmost developmental function.

However, this experiment did not in fact conclusively rule out the role of experience in development. The subjects were born into monolingual English-speaking families in which the voiced–voiceless distinction they discriminated is common, as in *baby* versus *papa*. It could be that categorical perception is partially developed at the onset of experience, and facilitated or attuned over the 1 to 4 months of experience these babies had prior to the experiment. It could also be that categorical perception is undeveloped at the onset of experience, and that experience with the language, however little, quickly induces sophisticated auditory perceptions.

Recall that surveys of the world's languages show that only three categories of voicing are common—prevoiced, voiced, and voiceless—but that not all languages use all these categories. Eimas et al. (1971) had only tested an English category in their babies. Are all or only some of these categories universal among infants? That is, do infants from communities where different patterns of voicing prevail in the adult language make the same categorical distinctions? If infants everywhere had some or all of the same three categories, although the adults in their cultures did not, the data would go a long way toward classifying the possible developmental courses of categorical perception of speech. To address this question, Lasky, Syrdal-Lasky, and Klein (1975) tested infants from Spanish-speaking (Guatemalan) monolingual familes. Spanish was chosen because the voiced–voiceless distinction is not quite the same as in English. The 4- and 6-month-olds from Spanish-speaking families discriminated the English voiced–voiceless sound contrast rather than the Spanish one. Likewise, Streeter (1976) found that Kenyan 2-month-olds from families that speak Kikuyu categorized the English voicing contrast that is not present in Kikuyu as well as a Kikuyu prevoiced–voiced contrast that is not present in English. These two studies confirm that at least some perceptual capacities develop before the onset of experience; and the Kikuyu study also suggests that perceptions can be induced with just two months of experience (unless Kikuyu babies and American babies are biologically different in some way). Interestingly, Spanish-speaking and Kikuyu-speaking adults perceive (though they do not use) the universal English voicing contrast, but they perceive it only weakly. Between infancy and maturity, therefore, a perceptual discrimination that is present at birth atrophies because of lack of experience, although it is not wholly lost. Similarly, American infants only 2 to 3 months of age discriminate /r/ from /l/ (Eimas, 1975), and so presumably do Japanese babies; yet Japanese adults fail to discriminate these sounds (Goto, 1971; Miyawaki, Strange, Verbrugge, Liberman, Jenkins, & Fujimura, 1975). Without experience to maintain it, this discrimination, too, appears to be lost.

These phenomena have been investigated systematically and confirmed in other languages. One study found that English 6-month-olds could discriminate pairs of Hindi speech contrasts (not used in English) as well as Hindi adults do, although English speakers 4 years of age and older could not. A follow-up study tested the generalizability of these findings and attempted to pinpoint the developmental period when the loss of this discriminative ability occurred. English 6-month-olds distinguish pairs of Thompson (native Indian) speech contrasts not used in English as well as Salish (Thompson-speaking) adults, but this ability is lost in the first year of life: 6- to 8-month-olds were found to perform the discrimination, 8- to 10-month-olds were found to do so more poorly, and 10- to 12-month-olds were found to be as poor at discriminating as were older children and adults (Werker, Gilbert, Humphrey, & Tees, 1981; Werker & Tees, 1983).

The literature in categorical perception of phonemes has developed so as to illustrate almost fully the scheme depicted in Fig. 4.1. Certain perceptions seem to be universal and developed at birth; they are maintained by linguistic experiences of the child, but may be lost if absent from the language heard by the child. Other perceptions, present at birth, can be altered by experience. Still other perceptions can be induced in children through immersion in a particular linguistic environment.

PERCEPTUAL DEVELOPMENT
AND THE METHODOLOGIES USED TO STUDY IT

In practice, the study of perceptual development is virtually synonymous with studies of infancy. This is so for three reasons. First, as we learned, perceptual study as a whole was given strong impetus by the nature–nurture debate. To study perception was to address this controversy, and to do so effectively was to study perception near the beginning of life. Second, by the time human beings reach toddlerhood their perceptions are (thought to be) reasonably mature. Thus, much of the "action" in perceptual development seems to take place in infancy. The third reason that the study of perceptual development has been circumscribed to early life is that perceptual study in the balance of the life cycle, predominantly in adulthood, normally falls outside the province of developmental psychology; it belongs to a different area in psychology—the study of sensation and perception proper. Research on adults is included in studies of perceptual development only when certain ontogenetic comparisons are called for. However, the early developmental focus of perceptual study challenges research investigators formidably; the reason is clear.

Perception is private. There is no way for one person to know what other people's perceptions of *red, C-sharp, sweet, pungent,* or *soft* are like without drawing inferences from their reports or from their behaviors. From a developmental point of view, the study of perception from young adulthood through old age poses little difficulty in this respect since mature individuals can readily be instructed to report about or to behave in certain ways that communicate their perceptions. In childhood and especially in infancy, however, the communication barrier poses a fundamental impediment to perceptual study. Moreover, infants are motorically underdeveloped. As a consequence, therefore, our knowledge of early perception must be inferred from reports and behaviors of varying fidelity and credibility.

Different methodologies available for the study of perception vary in the power of *inference* they allow about another observer's perceptions. Some methods yield only weak inference, whereas others yield stronger inference. The term can best be defined with reference to an illustration. If we ascertain that a sound applied at the ear of an observer produces a regular pattern of electrical response in the brain, then we can feel certain that some internal connections between the peripheral sensory system (the ear) and the central nervous system (the brain) are present. However, regularity of brain response tells us nothing, unfortunately, about how or even whether the observer actually *perceives* the sound; hence, inference about perception based on electrophysiological data is weak. (Even if two different stimuli gave rise to two distinctly different patterns of electrical activity in the brain, we still would not know whether the two stimuli were perceived, or whether they were perceived as different.) If, however, we were able to instruct or train the observer to respond behaviorally to a sound, or in one way to one sound and in another way to another sound, our inference would be so strong that, barring artifact, we would possess incontrovertible evidence of perception. The two main response systems for the study of perception in nonverbal observers that have been explored are psychophysiological and behavioral; several different techniques within each have been developed. For purposes of comparison, the methodologies reviewed here are ordered along a hypothetical continuum roughly in terms of the strength of inference they permit. For purposes of illustration, examples are drawn mainly from the now extensive literature on infancy.

It is interesting to note that despite important differences among methodologies, virtually all techniques developed to study perception have been engineered to address a surprisingly small number of perceptual questions. Two important questions have to do with whether the observer detects the presence of a stimulus—in the psychophysicist's terms, whether the stimulus passes above an *absolute threshold*—and whether the stimulus is meaningful for perception. A third, related question has to do with whether the observer detects the difference between two stimuli—whether the stimuli surpass a *difference threshold*.

To forecast, this section of the chapter summarizes and illustrates main principles and findings in early perceptual development. To do so, it is necessary to view the data in different substantive domains of perception as inextricably linked with common methodologies used to obtain them.

The Foundations of Perceiving and Psychophysiological Techniques

Psychological investigations of perceptual development that have adopted physiological techniques have approached the study of development via assessment of both the central and autonomic nervous systems.

CNS Function.   Research efforts related to perceptual development focused in the central nervous system (CNS) have been pitched at three general levels—neurological anatomy, single-cell physiology, and gross cortical electrical activity. Questions asked at the level of anatomical investigation concern the structural ontogeny of the perceptual apparatus, with a view to its relation to function. A presumption of this research strategy is that structure (anatomy) is necessary for function (perception), and so understanding function is, in a sense, enriched by the knowledge of underlying structure. (Perceptual theorists have on occasion turned this argument on its head and postulated the existence of structures based on known function; an example is Teller & Bornstein, 1986.) Note, however, that structure is a necessary but not a sufficient condition for function: Babies have legs but do not walk. Thus, insofar as inference about perception is concerned, evidence based on anatomical structure alone is very weak.

The course of anatomical development of the sensory systems has received more than modest attention, leading to the conclusion that human beings are reasonably well prepared for perception once extrauterine life begins. By the midtrimester of prenatal life, the eye and the visual system (Bronson, 1974; Maurer, 1975), the ear and the auditory system (Hecox, 1975), the nose and the olfactory system (Tuchmann-Duplessis, Auroux, & Haegel, 1975), and the tongue and the gustatory system (Bradley & Stearn, 1967; Humphrey, 1978) are on their way to being structurally and functionally mature. In general, two principles of development operate within and among sensory systems. Within systems, maturation tends to proceed from the periphery to the center so that, for example, the eye differentiates structurally and reaches functional maturity before the visual cortex does (e.g., Abramov, Gordon, Hendrickson, Hainline, Dobson, & LaBossiere, 1982; Conel, 1939–1959). Among systems in all species of birds and mammals, different senses tend to come into functional maturity in sequence (Gottlieb, 1983): vestibular, cutaneous, olfactory, auditory, and visual. Turkewitz and Kenny (1982, 1985) have persuasively argued the biopsychological advantages of this staggered program of development in terms of reduced mutual competition as well as heightened organization and integration.

The second level of psychophysiological investigation has focused even more narrowly on the development and specificity of individual neurons in different sensory systems. Since the advent of microelectrode recording techniques in physiology, it has been possible to study the sensitivities of single neurons in the brain. Such neurophysiological recording reveals that individual cells code specific characteristics of the environment. So-called "trigger features" of environmental stimulation to which individual neurons in the visual system, for example, have been found to be sensitive include wavelength of light, orientation of form, direction of movement, and others. Though this area of research is exciting and very provocative for the study of perceptual development, several questions render it of limited current value and indicate that findings in the area can be adopted only with caution. For example, although single neurons are sensitive to properties of environmental stimulation, their actual rule (if any) in perception is largely undefined. Further, since virtually all studies of single units have been conducted in infrahuman species, usually in the cat or monkey, the direct relevance or applicability of single-unit studies to human perception is still open to question. Finally, a very intriguing but still largely open question for perceptual development in this field is whether single units are innately sensitive to their "trigger features"; it could be that sensitivity grows with or reflects experience.

The third level of research into central nervous system contributions to perception addresses perceptual development most directly in intact human beings, and derives from measures of overall electrical activity of the developing brain. The principal electrophysiological technique involved is the cortical evoked potential (CEP). The CEP derives from the complex sequence of electrical currents that are normally produced in the brain and can be derived from the electroencephalograph (EEG). When a stimulus is presented to the eye or to the ear, for example, it gives rise to a characteristic waveform of activity in particular parts of the brain. Through computer averaging techniques, this waveform can be isolated from the EEG as a whole.

Studies of the development of the CEP show that the waveform begins simply, is slower to start in response to a stimulus in infancy than in adulthood, but has a relatively stable amplitude across the life cycle. As is shown in the top panel of Fig. 4.2, the CEP for a visual stimulus can be detected in preterm babies when it assumes a simple form, and it is already relatively complex at birth. The waveform remains quite variable up to 3 years of age, however. As can be seen in the bottom panel, the time between stimulus onset and the appearance of the major positive crest (P_2) of the CEP shows a reasonably orderly decrease with age until it reaches adult values. The amplitude of the CEP (not shown) follows a more complex course of development: It diminishes with age up to birth, then increases to 3 years of age, then decreases again so that, in essence, adult and

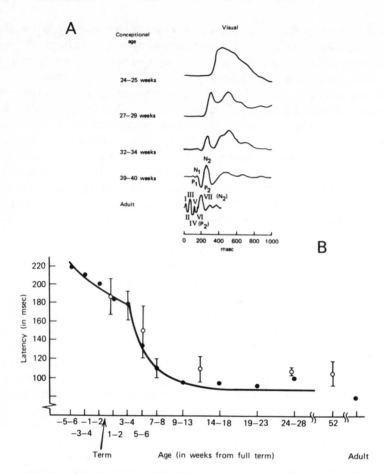

FIG. 4.2. Development of the form and latency of the cortical-evoked potential before and after term. A: Cortical responses evoked by visual stimuli in preterm infants, term newborns, and adults. (Derivations are bipolar: Oz-Pz for the visual response. Surface negatively in plotted upwards.) B: Latency (in msec) of the major positive component of the visual cortical-evoked response as a function of age (in weeks from term). (The solid and open dots represent data from two different experiments. The vertical lines passing through the open dots signify ± 1 SD for a group of 21 subjects.) (From Berg & Berg, 1979. Copyright John Wiley. Reprinted with permission.)

newborn show similar amplitudes. It is important to note that these principles, though broad (Berg & Berg, 1979), are descriptive of normal infants shown particular visual stimuli; variations among infants or stimuli compromise these generalizations.

Sound sensitivity in infants has also been measured via the CEP. Indeed, through unique placement of a miniature loudspeaker next to the ear and an electrode clipped to the scalp of the fetus *in utero,* Scibetta, Rosen, Hochberg, and Chik (1971) recorded auditory-evoked potentials in the last trimester of pregnancy. Since the middle ear reaches maturity in structure by the sixth month after conception (Hecox, 1975) and at this time fetuses respond to auditory stimuli behaviorally (Birnholz & Benacerraf, 1983), it may be that babies still in the womb can "overhear" parental conversations (Spence & De Casper, 1984). Of course, it is important to consider that human voice qualities may be altered for the fetus, given acoustic transduction characteristics of the uterus, amniotic fluid, and abdominal wall of the mother.

Studies of anatomy, single-cell physiology, and gross electrical activity of the brain all contribute to our understanding of perception, its bases, and its development. Perhaps evoked potential studies have provided the most useful data thus far.

ANS Function.   A second widely applied psychophysiological approach to gaining information about perception early in life has developed through monitoring infants' autonomic nervous system (ANS) responses in perceptual tasks. Orientation reflexes, respiration, and heart rate are commonly measured, even with the youngest observers. Figure 4.3 shows a newborn baby "wired" for perceptual study.

Among several measures, heart rate has proved to be particularly useful in the research on early perception (Berg & Berg, 1979; Porges, 1974). Heart rate has

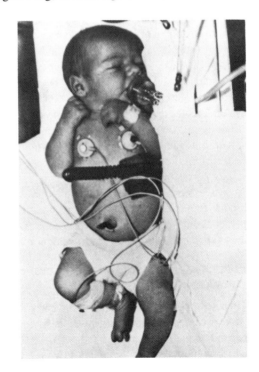

FIG. 4.3. Measurement of autonomic nervous system activity in the newborn. Two-day-old infant with heart rate electrodes attached (two on chest, and the indifferent electrode on right leg), pneumobelt between the abdomen and chest [to measure respiration], and an automatic nipple in place [to deliver fluid and measure amplitude and frequency of suckling]. (From Lipsitt, 1977.)

been substituted for crawling in testing young infants' perceptions of depth on the visual cliff; heart rate has been widely used to assess other visual, auditory, gustatory, and olfactory perceptions in infants. Further studies have even connected heart rate to more complex social-cognitive perceptions. Campos (1976), for example, collected heart-rate data in the context of 5- and 9-month-old infants' global responses in unstressed and distressed situations. Infants in this age range are beginning to fear strangers. As a stranger enters, approaches, intrudes, and then departs from them, infants' facial expressions change, going from simple interest and becoming increasingly negative; they go from a frown to a wimper to a cry; and concomitantly their heart rates first decelerate from a resting level (a common index of interest) and then accelerate during distress (as much as 30 beats per minute in 9-month-olds). Thus, heart rate accompanies changes of affect and serves, as here, as a converging measure of perception.

Our understanding of the foundations of perception has been enhanced considerably by studies of nervous system structure and function. They inform us as to the existence and operation of structures, and of the connections among structures, that underpin perception. In immature organisms, psychophysiological indices often substitute valuably for behavioral ones as objective and sensitive measures of perception, though many factors other than those under experimental scrutiny can influence psychophysiological responses. The psychophysiological approach has also proved valuable for the light it sheds on atypical development. For example, the evoked potential has been used successfully to diagnose the etiology of deafness in infancy: If the infant does not respond to sound, the evoked potential can at least indicate whether or not brain pathways are intact (Hecox & Galambos, 1974; Schulman-Galambos, 1979).

Despite these several virtues, the contributions of psychophysiology to the understanding of perception have been limited, and they require the highest degree of inference. That a cortex exists, and a stimulus presented to the sensory system creates an identifiable pattern of cortical activity, is no guarantee that the stimulus registers in *perceptually meaningful and functional ways* for the observer, whether infant or adult. Some autonomic system measures fare somewhat better in this regard, but they still do not provide convincing evidence of *conscious perception* since the body may respond in the absence of awareness. Access to conscious perceptual function is only obtainable through behavioral report. Behavioral techniques constitute the second main class of approaches to perceptual development, and from the point of view of understanding perception they represent a profound improvement over psychophysiological techniques.

Perceptual Development in Different Modalities and Behavioral Techniques

To assess perceptual development early in life, developmental psychologists have invented a wide variety of behavioral techniques. Prominent measures depend on natural responses and reactions, preferences, and learning. Again, this list is at least implicitly ordered according to the strength of inference each paradigm yields about perception. Perception in infancy and early childhood can be illustrated with data from studies that use each of these techniques.

First Vision and Corneal Reflection.   In the 1960s, Kessen, Haith, and Salapatek argued in a series of experimental reports that it ought to be possible to assess visual function at birth simply by "looking at looking." These investigators photographed the reflection of a stimulus in the cornea of the baby's eye. They assumed that "perceiving" is in some degree implied by the infant's "fixating" the stimulus—voluntary visual orienting so as to bring a stimulus into the line of visual regard—and that where a baby looks thus indicates visual selectivity and, hence, visual perception. Until these studies, basic questions such as whether or not newborn babies see were unanswered. In more than 20 years since the technique was introduced, many experimenters have adopted the logic of this inquiry and its methodology (see Fig. 4.4), but the original findings are still among the most provocative and still demonstrate many basic principles: Even in the first hours after birth, infants tend to look at parts of stimuli where there is information (usually high-contrast features such as the angles and along the contours of figures) instead of scanning randomly about the background or over the central part of a figure. Scan patterns seem to indicate that infants from the first days of life consistently and actively orient to visual information in the environment, and studies of such patterns indicate not just what babies look at,

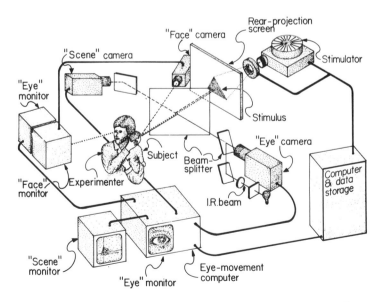

FIG. 4.4. A schematic representation of an eye movement recording system designed for use with infants. (From Hainline & Lemerise, 1982. Copyright Academic Press. Reprinted with permission.)

but how scan patterns develop and are distributed over different visual patterns. For example, scanning faces versus geometric forms speaks directly to perceptual processing (Hainline & Lemerise, 1982; Haith, 1980; Maurer, 1975, 1985).

Preferences and Natural Reactions in Different Modalities. One day while playing with his daughter, James Mark Baldwin, one of the founders of modern developmental psychology, observed that the young girl would consistently reach for a yellow cube over a blue one. The girl preferred one to the other independent of where the toy cubes were located. From this Baldwin deduced that young Helen saw color because her preferential reaching gave evidence that she discriminated yellow from blue. Although at the time Baldwin's logic met with some resistance, in the late 1950s and early 1960s Fantz revived Baldwin's argument, grounding it this time in infant *looking* rather than reaching. Fantz argued that if a baby looked preferentially at one stimulus over another in a paired-choice design, irrespective of the spatial location of the two stimuli, that preference could be taken to indicate detection or discrimination. Today Fantz's argument is the bedrock of the most popular infant research techniques. Infants visually prefer and discriminate faces over nonfacial configurations of the same elements, some pattern organizations over others, and some colors over others; and they orient and attend preferentially and discriminatively to select sounds and smells.

Studies of organized scanning indicate at a minimum *that* newborns and young infants see something when they look at patterns, but do not reveal *how well* they see. In their study of acuity, Fantz, Ordy, and Udelf (1962) capitalized on the observation that infants prefer heterogeneous to homogeneous patterns. They posted pairs of patterns for babies to look at, in which one member of the pair was always gray and the other a set of stripes that varied systematically in width. (The two stimuli were always matched in overall brightness.) If pattern is consistently preferred, the stripe width which fails to evoke a preference for the baby is the one that marks the limit of the baby's ability to tell stripes from the solid gray. (At some point, stripe width can become so fine as to fade into homogeneity for all of us.) By this measure, 2-week-olds showed 20/800 vision (in Snellen notation), whereas $5\frac{1}{2}$-month-olds showed 20/70 vision. Acuity improves steadily from infancy, until adult (20/20) levels are reached at about 5 years of age. In the 20 years since Fantz's original study, techniques for measuring infant visual acuity have grown in sophistication (e.g., Teller, 1979). Fortunately, measures of visual acuity by behavioral and electrophysiological methods agree well with Fantz's findings and also converge with one another (see Dobson & Teller, 1978).

Preferential looking and reaching have been used to investigate a wide variety of perceptual abilities in infancy, especially in pattern vision (Karmel & Maisel, 1975; Yonas & Granrud, 1985) and in color vision (Bornstein, 1981; Teller & Bornstein, 1986). Other sorts of preferences and reactions have been used to study perceptual development in other sensory systems as well. We know from experience that soothing pats can quiet a fussy infant, whereas the sharp stab of paper causes them distress; newborns can clearly feel, but research has not progressed far in helping us understand how acutely infants perceive stimuli by touch. Ruff (1984) filmed infants of 6, 9, and 12 months of age and later scored both general behaviors (e.g., touching) as well as specific ones (e.g., alternating between looking and mouthing). She found that mouthing decreased over the second half of the first year, whereas both fingering and more precise forms of manipulation increased (accompanying the further development of fine motor coordination). Ruff also found that infants vary their manipulatory activities to match the object being explored. When she changed stimuli for the infants once they had had the chance to explore them in some detail, Ruff found that infants changed in their patterns of tactual exploration so as to maximize the acquisition of information about the new stimulus. For example, they responded to a change in an object's shape by rotating it more, and to a change in its texture by fingering it more; and in both cases they threw, pushed, and dropped new stimuli less than familiar ones.

One of the clearest demonstrations of preference belongs to Steiner (1977, 1979), who investigated newborns' differential reactions to tastes and smells by their facial expressions. Psychophysical evidence is compelling that four basic qualities together exhaust taste experience: sweet, salt, sour, and bitter (Cowart, 1981). Tastes are, as we know, very powerful stimuli in learning: A single experience of nausea associated with a particular taste is enough for someone to avoid that taste virtually forever (Garcia & Koelling, 1966). Steiner gave newborn infants sweet, sour, or bitter substances to taste, and he photographed their "gustofacial" reactions—all prior to the very first time any of the babies ate. Figure 4.5 shows the results. A sweet stimulus evoked an expression of "satisfaction," often accompanied by a slight smile and by sucking movements. A sour stimulus evoked lip-pursing, often accompanied or followed by wrinkling of the nose and blinking the eyes. A bitter stimulus evoked an expression of dislike and disgust or rejection, often followed by spitting or even by movements preparatory to vomiting. These taste discriminations are organized at a primitive level of the brain, since they also appear, as Steiner reported, in babies who have no cortex.

Davis (1928) conducted a classic "cafeteria" study with babies. She reported on the food preferences of three infants allowed to choose what they wanted to eat beginning at 8 months when they were still exclusively breast-fed. At each meal, infants were served a tray with a variety of meats, vegetables, cereals, fruits, and liquids. Infants began by trying everything that was available; then they chose what they liked (though different babies developed different preferences). Although they went on food binges and strikes from time to time, on the whole the babies selected a variety and amount of food adequate for good nutrition. One baby who had rickets reportedly drank cod liver oil until he was well!

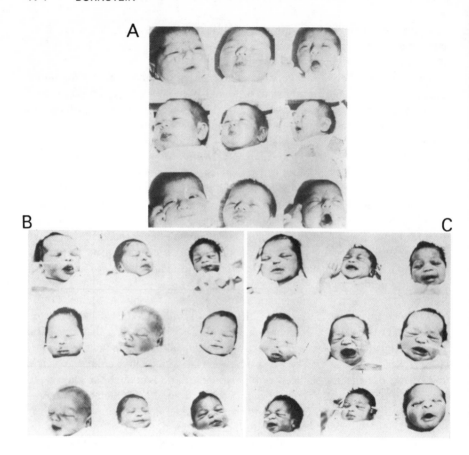

FIG 4.5. Gustatory and olfactory sensitivity in newborn babies. A: Infants' gustofacial response to the taste of sweet (left column), sour (middle column), and bitter (right column). B: Infants' nasofacial response to the smell of vanilla (B columns) and raw fish (C columns). (After Steiner, 1977.)

Steiner (1977, 1979) also observed neonates' "nasofacial" expressions and their attempts to withdraw from odors placed on cotton swabs held beneath the nose. Steiner found that newborns respond in qualitatively different ways to different food odors. Butter and banana odors elicit positive expressions; vanilla, either positive or indifferent expressions; a fishy odor, some rejection; and the odor of rotten eggs, unanimous rejection.

Cernoch and Porter (1985) systematically compared breast-fed with bottle-fed infants only 12 to 18 days old for their olfactory recognition of mother, father, and stranger. Babies were photographed while exposed to pairs of gauze pads worn in the underarm area by an adult on the previous night, and the infants' durations of orienting were recorded. Only breast-feeding infants oriented prefer-entially and exclusively to their own mothers' scents, thereby giving evidence of discriminating their mothers. Infants from neither group recognized their fathers preferentially, nor did bottle-fed infants recognize their mothers. This pattern of results suggests that, while they are breast-feeding, infants are exposed to and learn unique olfactory signatures. Similarly, the suckling young of nonhuman species are uniquely attracted to chemical signals (pheromones) produced by their lactating mothers (Porter & Doane, 1976); and, reciprocally, human moth-ers can recognize the scents of their babies after only 1 or 2 days (Porter, Cernoch, & McLaughlin, 1983; Russell, Mendelson, & Peeke, 1983).

Demonstrable preferences offer good evidence for the existence of absolute and discriminative thresholds; unfortunately, the preference paradigm suffers from a major shortcoming. It is that the observer's *failure to demonstrate* a preference is fundamentally ambiguous about the observer's ability *to detect* or *to discriminate* stimuli. A child in the laboratory, for example, may orient to mother and stranger equally, but still be able to smell them apart . . . and know which to prefer under particular circumstances. This is a nontrivial meth-odological drawback, and for this reason many investigators have turned to paradigms that draw even more actively on definitive behavioral acts to study absolute and difference thresholds in perception. Among the most widely used such paradigms today are conditioned head rotation and habituation.

Auditory Perception and Conditioned Head Rotation.   Physical development tends to proceed cephalocaudally (from the head downward) and proximodistally (from the center of the body outward); as a consequence, the eye, head, and neck regions of the body are the most highly developed earliest in ontogenesis. Many of the response procedures discussed thus far call upon children's looking or orienting or sucking for use in the analysis of perceptual function.

One paradigm that taps infants' voluntary motor control to assess perceptual development is conditioned head turning. The baby sits on the mother's lap, otherwise unencumbered. There is a loudspeaker to one side. When a sound (tone or speech syllable) is played through the speaker and the baby responds by orienting to it, the baby is rewarded by activation of a colorful mechanical toy located just above the speaker. In recent years, developmental psychoacousti-cians have defined the growth of several abilities basic to sound perception—the detection of sounds of different frequencies, discrimination among frequencies, and localization of sounds in space—as well as responsiveness to complex sounds that specify speech. Head rotation has proved valuable in the study of each.

How loud must a sound be to be heard? For adults, the amount of energy defining the auditory threshold varies with the frequency of the sound across the hearing range (approximately 20 to 20,000 hertz [Hz] or cycles per second). Both low and high frequencies (above or below 1,000 Hz) require more energy than middle frequencies (around 1,000 Hz). Schneider, Trehub, and Bull (1980; Trehub, Schneider, & Endman, 1980) found that infant thresholds for complex noises (as opposed to pure tones) vary substantially with frequency; that they are higher than those of adults for very low frequencies (200 Hz), approach adult levels for middle frequencies (1000 Hz), are again higher than those of adults at high frequencies (10,000 Hz), and finally are nearly equivalent at very high frequencies (19,000 Hz). Further, they observed nearly continuous developmental improvements in hearing at low and high frequencies during the first two years. Maturation of the ear or the CNS could account for this increasing developmental sensitivity. Whatever the reason, infants appear to be more sensitive to high-frequency than to low-frequency sounds. In complementary studies, Olsho (1984; Olsho, Schoon, Sakai, Turpin, & Sperduto, 1982a, 1982b) explored frequency discrimination and found that for infants in the same age range difference thresholds were about twice those of adults at low (250–1,000 Hz) and middle (1,000–3,000 Hz) frequencies, whereas they were virtually the same as adults' at higher frequencies (3,000–8,000 Hz).

Vision and Audition through Habituation-Test.   The conditioned head rotation technique provides reasonably secure data about infant perception since babies actively, voluntarily, and definitely respond in that way and thereby directly "communicate" their perceptions to the experimenter. An equally demonstrative and reliable technique, and one that has been adopted widely in experimental studies of perception in the first years of life, is habituation–test. This procedure has the advantage that it can and has been used to investigate perception in every modality; for purposes of this exposition, vision will serve as the main example (Bornstein, 1985, provides a comprehensive review).

In habituation, a baby is shown a stimulus and the baby's visual attention to the stimulus is monitored. Typically, when placed in an otherwise homogeneous environment, the infant will orient and attend to the novel stimulus on its initial presentation. If the stimulus is available to the infant's view continuously, or if it is presented repeatedly, the infant's attention to the stimulus will wane. This decrement in attention, called *habituation,* presumably reflects two component processes: the infant's developing a mental representation of the stimulus, and the infant's continuing comparison of whatever stimulus is present with that representation. If external stimulus and mental representation match and the baby "knows" the stimulus, there is little reason to continue to look; mismatches, however, maintain the infant's attention. A novel (and discriminable) test stimulus, introduced after habituation to a familiar one, will typically re-excite infant attention. Habituation to familiarity and recovery to novelty have proved to be most versatile and fruitful infant testing methods, permitting investigators the wherewithal to assess myriad aspects of perception in infancy. In particular, developmental researchers have focused on ontogeny of perception of form, orientation, location, movement, and color.

Consider first *form* perception. The fact that an infant scans an angle of a triangle and even resolves contour well does not mean that the infant perceives the triangle (or even an angle of it) as a triangle. Until recently, the problem of form perception proved remarkably resistant to solution because almost any discrimination between two forms (e.g., a triangle from a circle) can be explained as a discrimination on some simpler, featural basis (as between an angle and an arc) without whole form perception being implicated (e.g., Pipp & Haith, 1984). Bornstein (1982) tested infants' sensitivity to symmetry, which is usually perceived in terms of a whole form. In one study, 4-month-olds were found to habituate to vertically symmetrical patterns efficiently (where both featural discriminations and contour explanations were controlled among comparison stimuli), thereby indicating their perception of symmetry as form (Bornstein, Ferdinandsen, & Gross, 1981); in subsequent studies, infants were found to use the global composition of symmetry in discriminating forms (Fisher, Ferdinandsen, & Bornstein, 1981), and vertical symmetry was found to be a general organizing principle of whole form perception (Bornstein & Krinsky, 1985).

Another strong source of evidence that infants perceive pattern wholes derives from demonstrations of form invariance (Bornstein, 1984). Form invariance arises through the perceived stability of an object despite variations in its sensory representations. For example, shape constancy describes the tendency for perceived object shape to remain stable even through the orientation of the object's image on the retina varies. Definitive studies of shape constancy have been conducted by Caron, Caron, and colleagues (1978; Caron, Caron, & Carlson, 1978 Caron, Caron, & Carlson 1979); they show that infants as young as 3 months of age treat as familiar a shape with which they have had diverse experience, even though they are seeing it in a new orientation or slant. Bornstein and his associates (Bornstein, Gross, & Wolf, 1978; Bornstein, Krinsky, & Benasich, 1986), Fagan (1979), and Gibson, Owsley, Walker, and Megaw-Nyce (1979) have provided converging evidence for the perceived constancy of simple and complex *shapes* in 2- to 7½-month-olds; McKenzie, Tootell, and Day (1980) have provided evidence for the perceived constancy of *size* in 4- to 8-month-olds. These several lines of research provide converging evidence that babies still only in the first year of life can perceive form *qua* form.

Objects are specified not only by their form, but also by their coordination in space; that is, by their orientation, location, and movement. Physical space extends outward from the central ego equally in all directions, yet perceived orientation is not uniform: For adults, vertical holds a higher psychological status than does horizontal, and horizontal is generally higher in status than oblique (Bornstein, 1982; Essock, 1980). We accept the statement that "5° is almost vertical" as somehow truer than the statement that "vertical is almost 5°." Vertical is the reference point for *orientation* (Rosch, 1975; Wertheimer, 1938).

Studies of detection, discrimination, and preference suggest that this hierarchy among orientations exists in early life for artificial geometric forms as well as for more meaningful patterns like the human face, and for static as well as for dynamic forms. Over the first year infants detect patterns aligned vertically or horizontally more readily than they do the same patterns aligned obliquely, and visual acuity for vertical and horizontal patterns increases more rapidly than does acuity for oblique patterns (Gwiazda, Brill, Mohindra, & Held, 1978; Leehey, Moskowitz-Cook, Brill, & Held, 1975). Babies know and like the vertical: 2- to 4-month-olds strongly prefer the normal vertical orientation of a face, compared to upside-down and left and right orientations along the horizontal axis, as measured by their smiling as well as by their looking (Hayes & Watson, 1981; Watson, 1966). Bornstein and his associates have shown both preference and perceptual advantages for vertical and horizontal early in life: 4-month-olds prefer to look at a simple grating pattern aligned on the vertical and horizontal (Bornstein, 1978a), and 12-month-olds prefer vertically symmetrical patterns to matched horizontal or oblique ones (Bornstein et al., 1981). A moving vertical or horizontal pattern also evokes significantly greater heart-rate deceleration (orienting) from a 4-month-old than does the same pattern oriented on the diagonal (Ivinskis & Finlay, 1980). Finally, babies still in the first half-year of life habituate more quickly when a given stimulus is oriented on the vertical than when it is oriented on the horizontal, regardless of whether the stimulus is static (Bornstein et al., 1981) or dynamic (Gibson, Owsley, & Johnston, 1978).

Young babies seem able to discriminate orientation well, not only in the discrimination of vertical from horizontal (Bornstein et al., 1978; Fisher et al., 1981; McKenzie & Day, 1971), but also when tested using variants of the habituation design: 5-month-olds discriminate horizontal from 35° off horizontal (Weiner & Kagan, 1976), 4-month-olds vertical from 45° off vertical (Bornstein et al., 1978), and 5- to 6-month-olds a vertical face from the same face at a 45° diagonal (Fagan, 1979). Four-month-olds discriminate even finer differences involving only obliques: a 50° disparity from 20° to 70° (Bornstein et al., 1978) and a 10° disparity from 5° to 15° (Bornstein et al., 1986).

We know, from studies of the kind reviewed in the introductory section of this chapter, that young babies perceive depth in space. They can also *locate* stimuli in space. Von Hofsten (1984) submitted babies' reaching for objects to longitudinal study, beginning at 4 months when babies first make reliable contacts. Recording their following motions, goal-directed behaviors, and types of reaches to objects located at different distances and moving at different velocities, he found that infants as young as 4½ months will reach and contact an object even if it is moving (von Hofsten & Lindhagen, 1979), and that their reaching is accomplished in a way that indicates sophisticated predictive targeting of location (von Hofsten, 1980).

Infants also locate things in large-scale spaces. In anticipation of an event, infants in the second half of their first year incorrectly look in the same direction as was appropriate before they were moved to a different spot in the environment (Acredolo, 1978; Acredolo & Evans, 1980; Cornell & Heth, 1979); that is, they give priority to subjective (so-called *egocentric*) information in recalling spatial location. Toddlers in the second year of life rely on landmarks and possess an objective (so-called *allocentric*) knowledge of coordinated perspectives of space. These results give rise to speculation about a major developmental change over the first year with regard to the child's understanding of spatial location. It could also be, of course, that both egocentric and allocentric codes are available to babies at both ages, but that babies of the two ages elect to use or rely on different codes. In this connection, some researchers have speculated that the infants' own beginning locomotion in crawling and walking motivates their adopting a more mature, objective understanding of space (Benson & Užgiris, 1985; Bremner & Bryant, 1985). Pertinently, infants who crawl or have experience in a "walker," versus those who do not, extract form from a fluctuating display (Campos, Bertenthal, & Benson, 1980) and avoid the deep side of the visual cliff (Campos, Svejda, Bertenthal, Benson, & Schmidt, 1981); and infants who crawl to a search location find hidden objects more frequently than infants who are carried to the search location (Benson & Užgiris, 1985).

It has long been recognized that even newborns are attracted by *movement* (Haith, 1966): They fixate dynamic patterns and faces longer than static ones (Kaufmann & Kaufmann, 1980), and they visually lock onto moving heads and blinking eyes (Samuels, 1985). Research shows that the infant's perception of motion is quite acute. Ruff (1985) tested the abilities of young infants to recognize and to discriminate different motions of rigid objects. For example, she first habituated babies to a series of objects each one of which moved the same way (say, from side to side), and she then tested the same infants with a novel object moving in the familiar motion and with a novel object moving in a novel way (say, from side to side and rotating). Both $3\frac{1}{2}$- and 5-month-olds discriminated side-to-side from side-to-side plus rotation, and by 5 months infants discriminated side-to-side from rotation alone, rotation from oscillation around the vertical, and left versus right rotation. Finally, Slater, Morison, Town, and Rose (1985) showed that newborns perceive similarity between a stimulus when moving and stationary, can transfer what is learned between moving and stationary stimuli, and on these bases possess the potential for identity constancy.

One of the most basic aspects of the object environment revealed through motion is "figural coherence," the perceptual grouping of elements having an invariant set of spatial relations that may be extracted from coordinated relative motions among the elements. A compelling example of figural coherence is the so-called point-light walker display that specifies motion typical of humans. People perceive displays of lights attached to the joints of a human being shown in the dark not as an unrelated swarm of randomly moving dots, but as biochemical motion giving evidence of figural coherence. Johansson (1975) and Cutting, Profitt, and Kozlowski (1978) have demonstrated that adults observing such a dynamic light display can identify the motion and the object in less than 200 msec, whereas static displays of the same information are essentially uninterpretable. Infants, too, are sensitive to biomechanical motion (Fox & McDaniels, 1982). Bertenthal (Bertenthal, Profitt, & Cutting, 1984; Bertenthal, Profitt, Spetner, & Thomas, 1986) used habituation to evaluate infants' sensitivity to figural coherence in such dynamic point-light displays. He uncovered sensitivity to structural invariance in dynamic displays (but not in static ones) in infants as young as 3 months, and sensitivity to the three-dimensional structure of the human form at 9 months.

Objects in the environment not only have form and spatial coordination that help us to distinguish and identify them, they also have *color*. Additionally, color is an intellectually impressive and aesthetically attractive kind of physical information. Infants see colors and seem to do so pretty well. Charles Darwin (1877; see Bornstein, 1978b) speculated on children's seeing color in the 1870s, but real progress toward understanding the development of color vision only began in the 1970s. Studying color vision presents particularly formidable technical problems (Teller & Bornstein, 1986). For example, for both adults and infants, hue and brightness—the two major components of color—covary so that whenever the color of a stimulus changes, both its hue and brightness are changing. In order to compare two stimuli on the basis of hue alone, therefore, it is necessary to match the two in brightness. With adults, this is relatively easy since there exists a formula that relates the amount of change or difference in hue to the amount of change or difference in brightness; alternatively, adults can match colored stimuli for brightness directly. In babies, however, the precise relation between brightness and color was for a long time elusive, and babies certainly cannot be asked to match brightness. The anatomy of the immature eye is also different enough to suggest some perceptual differences between infants and adults (e.g., Abramov et al., 1982). As a consequence, an understanding of infant color vision needs to begin with studies of the infant's perception of brightness, and, on the basis of proper brightness controls, proceed to test discrimination, preference, and organization of hue.

Babies are nearly as acute as adults are when the task is to compare brightness differences between stimuli presented simultaneously (Peeples & Teller, 1978), although they are much less acute if comparison stimuli are separated in space or time (Kessen & Bornstein, 1978). Experiments comparing chromatic or spectral sensitivity using electrophysiological (Dobson, 1976; Moskowitz-Cook, 1979) and behavioral (Peeples & Teller, 1978) techniques agree that, across a broad range of conditions and across most of the visible spectrum, the infant's sensitivity is reasonably similar to the adult's. Thus, in studies where the task is hue discrimination per se, it is possible to adopt several different strategies to unconfound hue and brightness. It is possible to match colors in brightness by an adult standard in specific spectral regions where infant and adult are known to correspond, or in testing discriminations displaced in time (as did Chase, 1937, and Bornstein, 1975); to vary brightness against hue systematically or unsystematically so that brightness is not an influential factor in discrimination (as did

Peeples & Teller, 1975, and Schaller, 1975). Peeples and Teller (1975) cap-italized on the preference babies have for heterogeneity by showing 2- and 3-month-olds two screens, one white and the second white with either a white or a red bar projected onto it. They then systematically varied the brightness of the bar around the adult match to the brightness of the background screen. When the white bar was darker or brighter than the screen, it created the bar pattern that babies favored relative to the homogeneous white comparison; at the bar–screen brightness match point, however, the babies did not show a preference. Thus, just a shade of difference between the white bar and white screen engaged the babies to look: Babies' brightness sensitivity is acute. However, babies preferred the red bar–white screen combination at all brightness levels, demonstrating that even when the red bar matched the white screen in brightness, they still distinguished its hue.

''Color-blind'' people are called so because they make identifiable color discrimination errors; they also confuse certain hues with white. To assess the status of color vision in infancy, Bornstein (1976) studied both these characteristics using a habituation-test technique. Infants 3 months of age discriminated blue-green from white, and they discriminated between yellow and green; these are two sets of discriminations that individuals with the two major types of red–green blindness fail. Teller and her colleagues later confirmed these findings using the choice-preference procedure, extending them to infants as young as 1 month (Hamer, Alexander, & Teller, 1982; Packer, Hartmann, & Teller, 1985; Teller, Peeples, & Sekel, 1978). Thus, infants are not red-blind or green-blind. Adams, Maurer, and Davis (1986) showed essentially the same capacity in neonates only hours old. Teller also found that 1-month-olds give evidence they are not blue-blind, the rarer third kind of color-blindness (Varner, Cook, Schneck, McDonald, & Teller, 1984). The development of color vision right after birth has not been studied so well, and is doubtlessly immature. Yet infants 1 month and certainly 2 months of age and older are known to possess largely normal color vision, based on their discrimination of color stimuli in the absence of brightness cues.

Adults perceive the color spectrum as organized qualitatively into categories of hue: We commonly distinguish blue, green, yellow, and red as distinct hues, although we recognize blends in between. In specific, we normally see blue when the wavelength of light falls around 450 nm, green around 530 nm, yellow around 580 nm, and red around 630 nm; and we tend to regard lights of wave-lengths around 450 nm all as blue, even though we see them as different blues; see Fig. 4.6. It could be that the way that the visual system functions lends vision this organization, or it could be that children learn to organize the color world, perhaps when they acquire language. Bornstein, Kessen, and Weiskopf (1976a, 1976b) studied infants' categorization of color using a habituation-test strategy. They found that 4-month-olds who were habituated to a light of one color readily noticed when a light of a different color was shown on a test trial following

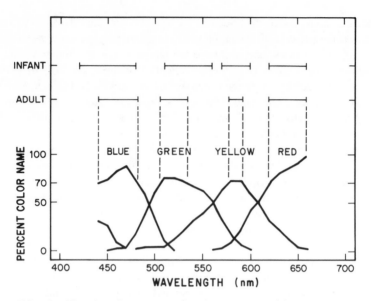

FIG. 4.6. Wavelength groupings (I.e., hue categories) for 4-month-old infants and for adults. *Bottom:* Percentage color name as a function of wavelength for the color names blue, green, yellow, and red (after Boynton & Gordon, 1965). The rising function at very short wavelengths is for red. *Top:* Summary results for hue categories for infants and adults. The infant summary is derived from Bornstein, Kessen, and Weiskopf (1976a). The adult summary reflects a projection from the color-naming data at a psychophysical criterion of 70%. Infant and adult grouping patterns are highly similar, suggesting that by 4 months infants' hue categories are similar to those of adults.

habituation, even when the two lights were matched in brightness. These investigators then proceeded to determine whether babies regard two different blues, for example, as more similar qualitatively than a blue and a green. Babies were habituated to 480 nm, a blue near the boundary between blue and green, and on test trials following habituation the babies were shown lights of 450 nm, 480 nm, and 510 nm, all matched for brightness. Thus one test stimulus was the familiar hue, and two differed from the familiar hue by identical physical amounts; however, one new test light was blue (like the familiar stimulus) whereas the other was green. Babies shown the new blue stimulus treated it and the familiar blue as the same, whereas they treated the green stimulus as different. This result along with parallel results from other groups showed that preverbal infants categorize the visible spectrum into relatively discrete basic hues of blue, green, yellow, and red, which are similar to those of adults (Fig. 4.6); even though infants, like adults, can discriminate among colors within a given category (Bornstein, 1981).

Habituation has also been combined with learning in the study of infant perception. Siqueland and DeLucia (1969) observed that babies would suck with greater force more frequently than their baseline rate if their forceful sucks brightened a visual image or produced a sound. However, repeated presentation of the same image or sound would not maintain the babies' new high rate of sucking, but would eventually result in a decrement in the frequency of their high-amplitude sucking and in a return to their baseline. The introduction of a new discriminable stimulus, however, would re-excite infant sucking. An advantage of this paradigm is that it has proved to be applicable to the study of audition as well as of vision. This was the habituation procedure Eimas and colleagues (1971) adapted to study the speech perception of infants (discussed earlier in the chapter), and the technique has now been used to investigate a host of perceptions of speech and nonspeech sounds (see Jusczyk, 1985).

For example, very young infants are attracted to the global character of speech, and seem to find it reinforcing: Trehub and Chang (1977) found that the presentation of human speech contingent on infants' sucking would increase their sucking, whereas the withdrawal of speech, the noncontingent presentation of speech, and the presentation of nonspeech had equivalent and equally uneventful effects on infants' motivation to suck.

Intermodal Perception.   When we are by the ocean we see waves, hear the surf pound, smell salt air, and these sensations go together naturally to evoke an integrated experience. Seeing, hearing, and smelling are different percepts, but work in concert. There are many stimuli and events about which the different modalities provide integrated and consonant information, even though those stimuli and events may be specified in any of several modes. Some are relatively simple, like shape; some more complicated, like approach.

Cross-modal transfer reflects observer recognition of shape information across modalities. Meltzoff and Borton (1979) found that infants as young as 1 month of age would look more at a shape that matched a shape they had previously mouthed without seeing than at a shape they had not previously mouthed. Other studies of cross-modal transfer from touch to vision (see Rose & Ruff, 1987, for a summary) confirm that infants readily recognize object shape between modalities.

Approach is specified by an object getting both larger and louder, and recession by an object getting both smaller and softer. Young infants seem to be sensitive to coherence of intermodal information specifying such change, even when different senses are stimulated in distinctly different ways. Schiff, Benasich, and Bornstein (1986) tested infants' sensitivity to conjoint information of this type using the habituation technique. They found that 5-month-olds habituated more efficiently to coherent approach and coherent recession information (when both sound and image specified the same motion) than to incoherent information (when sound approached but image receded, or vice versa).

An engaging dispute has arisen among students of perceptual development concerning the origins of such multimodal sensitivity, a dispute that contests whether different sensations are initially integrated or initially differentiated. On the integrationist side, Bower (1977) proposed that newborns actually cannot distinguish among sensory inputs arriving at the brain via different sensory modalities. Bower (1977) wrote, "It seems that a very young baby may not know whether he is hearing something or seeing something. . . . Very rapidly, [however,] babies develop the ability to register not only the place, but also the modality of an input" (pp. 68–69). Some studies support this integrationist view, at least insofar as they show that newborns and very young infants respond in a similar fashion to, or treat as equivalent, visual and auditory or tactual stimuli. For example, Lewkowicz and Turkewitz (1980) habituated infants only 3 weeks old to a light of given luminance, and afterward divided infants into different groups and then tested them with different intensity levels of sound. Adults match certain sounds and lights at relatively fixed loudness and brightness levels. Lewkowicz and Turkewitz found that babies treated loudnesses that matched brightnesses as equivalent, at just the intensity levels that adults choose in cross-modality matching. Meltzoff and Borton (1979) were brought to an integrationist conclusion as well by their finding (described above) that infants in the first month of life visually identify a shape they have only experienced tactually. The fact that very young babies match cross-modally in these ways certainly supports the integrationist position, but does not supply evidence that infants do not or could not distinguish sensations—that they actually "think" that a sound and a light are the same.

A separate school of thought argues that the ability to coordinate information across the senses develops over the first year of life. The work of Rose, Gottfried, and Bridger (e.g., 1978) on the development of class-modal transfer in infancy supports this view. They studied full-term and preterm infants on tasks that called for visual recognition of a shape that had been previously seen (*intra*modal recognition) or previously touched (*inter*modal recognition). They found that preterm 6-month-olds could perform neither the intramodal nor intermodal transfers successfully; that preterm 12-month-olds and full-term 6-month-olds could perform the intramodal transfer but still failed on the intermodal task, and that only full-term 12-month-olds could pass both the intramodal and intermodal transfer tasks.

Substance and Methodology of Early Perceptual Development

Investigators of early perception have overcome the major impediment their youngest subjects present to experimental research—silence—by establishing communication with infants in a variety of ingenious ways. Some investigators have relied on psychophysiological measurements of the central and autonomic nervous systems; others have employed behavioral measures of attention, response and reaction, and learning. Through the development of sophisticated methodologies developmentalists have glimpsed the perceptual world of the infant. In précis, what is that world like?

At birth, infants can see, hear, taste, feel, and touch; through these senses, they are well prepared for the new world that surrounds them. An important general aspect of sensation is that even from the very beginning of life babies actively seek out information in their environment. Moreover, they show distinct preferences for some kinds of information over other kinds: For example, soon after birth, newborns concentrate on contours and edges, where visual information is rich, and they prefer saturated colors, sweet tastes, and pleasant odors. Babies in the first month of life appear to discriminate among many physical stimuli that signify different sensory qualities. They can also recognize their mothers by voice and by scent. By 1 month of age, an infant's perceptual world is coming to be clearer and more organized in many ways. Babies' visual acuity and convergence are rapidly developing, and they are beginning to appreciate complex as well as simple visual patterns. At this age, babies see color and hear speech (although perhaps not yet as meaningful communication). By the end of their third month, their vision has much developed: They can focus on near or far objects, and they possess the rudiments of shape and size constancies. By 4 to 5 months of age, babies perceive gestalts and recognize objects in two or in three dimensions; they can discriminate sound differences at the beginning, in the middle, and at the end of syllables; they show sensitivity to all sorts of spatial coordination, including depth, orientation, location, and movement. By 6 months of age, their visual-auditory and visual-tactual information processing is already integrated so as to fuse perceptual wholes.

Most research in infant perception has focused on the related goals of, first, determining whether or not single particular perceptual capacities are present; and, second, tracing the emergence and the stability or change in those capacities over time. This was the logical and necessary point at which to begin basic developmental research, and the last twenty years have witnessed considerable progress in reaching these goals. Investigators of infant perception have progressed so far as to understand that the basic sensory systems are functioning and providing infants at a very early age with highly sophisticated information. In this way, modern investigators have systematically and forever eradicated the view of the perceptually incompetent infant, and are now moving on to new questions concerned with how information arriving at the different senses is processed into integrated precepts.

The exciting, sometimes startling results of these observations of infants does not mean that newborn perceptual capacities are fully developed. Even if rudimentary function is present, qualitative distinctions are often still lacking. In some systems, technical problems limit access to knowledge; in others, it is clear that development simply has not yet occurred. Some perceptual development remains to take place in the period after infancy, and much of this development, as is well known, is bound up with more comprehensive developments in cognition. An overview of these developments occupies the next section.

PERCEPTION IN CHILDHOOD, ADULTHOOD, AND OLD AGE

Historically, infancy has captured much of the attention of perceptual developmentalists for reasons already elaborated, and the most significant developments in perception seem to take place during this period. Nevertheless, two periods in the life span other than infancy hold considerable interest for perceptual developmentalists. Childhood and old age provide important basic information, and both provide further testing grounds for theories. Understanding perceptual capacity at these times is significant in a practical sense; in childhood because of the signal role of perception in learning to read (e.g., Gibson & Levin, 1975; Kavale, 1982), and in old age because of the significance of perceptual capacity to people's autonomy and self-reliance (Bromley, 1974). Comparing perception between childhood and old age is also theoretically important to determining whether deterioration of perceptual capacity follows a course parallel to its evolution (Comalli, 1970).

Childhood

Children are subjects of perceptual study for basic as well as for applied reasons. An example of the former is to trace cerebral specialization. In most right-handers, the left hemisphere of the brain is thought to be principally responsible for processing language, and the right hemisphere for processing visuospatial information. When do these specializations develop? Wittelson (1976) found them to be in place by 6 years of age; but more recently Rose (1984) found that 2- and 3-year-olds possess a left-hand (right hemisphere) superiority for shape recognition, though 1-year-olds do not.

Most applied investigators have been interested in perceptual development in childhood primarily because of its relation to schooling. How do children attend to and process perceptual information? The significance of these questions is truly brought home when children begin to learn how to read. For example, research shows that selective attention, visual integration of shape, and speed of visual information-processing vary enormously among individuals but nevertheless generally increase over childhood, reaching an adult asymptote around the onset of adolescence (e.g., Enns & Girgus, 1985, 1986; Nettlebeck & Wilson, 1985). Although visual perception per se may be mature by school age, visual functioning is not. Younger children are most distractible, less efficient, and slower than are older children.

Among the best-known experiments on the development of form perception in childhood are those conducted by the Gibsons to test a "differentiation" theory of perceptual learning. E. J. and J. J. Gibson (e.g., 1979, 1982) proposed that perceptual development involves increasingly efficient abstraction of invariants or constant stimulus features from an environmental array. Perceptual life begins as diffuse and through experience it differentiates, becoming more selective and acute. The Gibsons (1955) demonstrated perceptual differentiation of form in one cross-sectional experiment comparing children of 6 to 8 and of 8.5 to 11 years of age with adults. Each subject was shown a coil-like figure (ξ) and then asked to point it out again when shown a series of similar coils one at a time. The foils or distractors in the test looked very much like the original standard coil, except that they differed in number of turns, degree of compression, or orientation. Thus, successful identification depended on perceiving distinctive features of coils on these dimensions. There were 18 standards in all. Among the three age groups, adults initially scored the highest number correct and reached 100% recognition after only three exposures to each standard stimulus; older children scored fewer correct at first and took longer than adults to reach perfect recognition; and the youngest children scored the fewest correct initially and never met a learning criterion. Both measures give a good indication of children's increasing ability to differentiate perceptual features with age. In perception, we learn what to look for and what is distinctive versus what is irrelevant.

The Gibsons and their colleagues later applied this finding directly to the educational question of children's letter learning (Gibson, Gibson, Pick, & Osser, 1962). In this experiment, the investigators wanted to assess how children of 4 to 8 years learn to distinguish letterlike forms, a basic problem for shape constancy and a prerequisite for reading. This experiment also used a matching task, only this time letterlike forms were used (Ⅳ), and foils varied systematically from the standard to assess what specific confusions children might make and whether their confusions might vary with age. Twelve types of foils were used; they included breaks (ⵏ), rotations (Ⲗ), reversals (Ⲍ), and perspectival transformations (Ⓗ), Across ages, children detected figural breaks best, rotations and reversals less proficiently, and perspectival transformations least proficiently of all. Regardless of transformation, the children's performance improved with age. The fact that youngsters have particular difficulty with reversals reminds us of their common left–right reading and writing confusions (e.g., ɿ for s, b for d, and so forth). Bornstein et al. (1978) offered a perceptual interpretation for this phenomenon: Because left–right reversals only occur in nature when they are twin aspects of the same thing (e.g., an object and its silhouette), they ought to be treated as the same (like a constancy) and need not be differentiated. In support of this hypothesis, Bornstein et al. showed that under many conditions very young infants treat left-right reversals as similar, although they distinguish other rotations of a stimulus. In the case of reversals in letters, children seemingly must *un*learn a natural perceptual constancy.

Bornstein and his coworkers have looked at the continuity of one reading-related aspect of form perception across the life cycle. In a study of symmetry perception in children, Bornstein and Stiles-Davis (1984) found a clear developmental progression among 4- to 6-year-olds: Vertical symmetry possessed the highest perceptual advantage (as in discrimination and memory), then horizontal, then oblique. Fisher and Bornstein (1982) also found vertical and horizontal to be special vis-à-vis oblique in adults. Although the literature concerned with children's perception of form frequently has practical questions regarding reading in the background, few results have been directly applicable (Gibson & Levin, 1975). It is still not known how children gain perceptual access to this important symbol system. Some success rests on cognitive and social factors (Vellutino, 1977); clearly, however, achievement in reading depends as well on children's visual perception skills (e.g., Kavale, 1982): Fisher, Bornstein, and Gross (1985) found that, even with IQ controlled in the study, children who possess advanced visual skills read at higher levels. The practical importance of this area of research cannot be overemphasized, and there is clear need for continuing study.

The findings of children's perceptions of symmetry also address a question often posed to developmental investigators outside of infancy studies: Can studies of children converge with those of adults to advance our understanding of perceptual processes generally? It has frequently been suggested that development might parallel adult perceptual processing; unfortunately, few concrete examples exist. One may be the parallel between order of perceptual processing in symmetry by adults and development of children's learning or memory for symmetry. Many prominent models of symmetry perception postulate that adults process orientation in symmetry hierarchically, beginning with vertical, proceeding next to horizontal, and ending with oblique; empirical data support this hierarchy (e.g., Fisher & Bornstein, 1982; Palmer & Hemenway, 1978; Royer, 1981). The child studies show that detection and reproduction of symmetry follow the same orientation hierarchy ontogenetically (Bornstein & Stiles-Davis, 1984). In symmetry, perceptual biases that characterize stages of adult information processing seem equally apt to describe stages of perceptual development.

Old Age

One of the main principles of aging is that through a complex sequence of changes the body dies a little every day from its peak in early adulthood. Select intellectual functions and almost all bodily or vegetative functions decline in this way (Bromley, 1974). The consequences include changes and deterioration in perceptually related structures and functions: Brain weight reduces, cells in the CNS die and do not regenerate, nerve conduction velocity slows. Across the senses, perceptual deterioration is common and often regular.

A major question surrounding this decline of sensory–perceptual function in old age turns on the relative contributions of organ impairment, nervous system degeneration, and reduction of psychological judgment. Some poor performance in old age seems clearly to be based on physiological change. For example, conduction velocity of nerve fibers slows approximately 15 % between 20 and 90 years of age, and simple reaction time to lights and sounds concomitantly lengthens 50% over the same period (Bromley, 1974). Similarly, the lens of the eye grows like an onion over the entire course of the life span, adding layer upon layer. Each layer is pigmented, and as the lens grows light must traverse more and more absorptive material before it reaches the retina to be effective in vision. Since lens pigment selectively absorbs short-wavelength (blue) visible light, perception of blue systematically attenuates in old age; see Fig. 4.7. Other performance declines in old age may reflect a combination of central nervous system or anatomical deterioration with adverse changes in judgment.

The study of perception in aging is also of interest for the theoretical information it provides on the question of change across the life cycle. Some evidence supports progressive–regressive patterns in the life-span development of psychological abilities (Strauss, 1982). For example, many perceptual functions seem to improve during childhood, reach a peak or high plateau during adulthood, and subsequently decline in old age: Judgments of illusion magnitude, the apparent horizon, the rod-and-frame test, part–whole differentiation, visual span, and

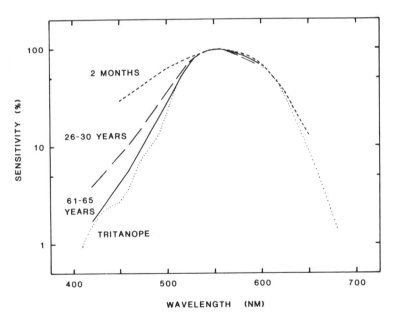

FIG. 4.7. In normal aging, the eye loses sensitivity to short wavelengths (blue light). Photopic spectral sensitivities measured near birth, at midlife, and near the end of life, in comparison with that of the average tritanope (blue-blind observer). (From Bornstein, 1977.)

tachistoscopic form discrimination are reported thus to wax and then wane during the life cycle (see Comalli, 1970). There is a need to determine how real these perceptual changes are versus how much they reflect criterion shifts in judgment.

Reprise: Nature and Nurture

The discussion of old age permits the opportunity to reconsider, if only briefly, the roles of nature and nurture in perception, this time in a somewhat different light. Consider the following.

Auditory sensitivity is measured by assessing absolute thresholds for sounds of different frequencies. One of the consequences of aging is deterioration in auditory sensitivity. In essence, the elderly require more energy to hear certain frequencies than do younger people. As the top panel of Fig. 4.8 shows, among Americans hearing loss in aging is more pronounced at higher frequencies. One prominent and straightforward explanation for this finding has been that aging entails the natural and regular deterioration of anatomical and physiological mechanisms that subserve hearing. An alternative hypothesis is that cumulative exposure to noise over the course of the life span deleteriously affects perception of high frequencies and is the first cause of the physiological change. How can we decide between the nature and nurture explanations?

Additional data—first, from individuals in other cultures with other experiences and, second, from individuals in our own society who have distinctive life histories of exposure to noise—help to distinguish between these two explanations. As the bottom panel in Fig. 4.8 shows, older American women experience less hearing loss than older American men; and Sudanese Africans, who show no sex differences in hearing with aging, sustain even less hearing deterioration than Americans of either sex. Contrary to the original biological hypothesis, gender and cultural data suggest that physiological aging alone is probably not the key factor in hearing loss. (It could still be, however unlikely, that sexes or races differ biologically in the integrity or susceptibility of their auditory mechanisms.) The data on elderly American men exposed to different amounts of noise over the course of their lifetimes lend further support to the experiential interpretation. Findings from this third research source—on noise history—strongly support the view that hearing loss in old age is related to amount of exposure to noise and less to natural physiological processes. The three research programs together supplement the original "descriptive evidence" with "explanatory evidence" and lend credence to a nurture view. Of course, the fact that noise history selectively affects high frequencies indicates that nature and nurture interact in development.

The influences of nature and nurture are often difficult to disentangle in developmental theory. Yet assessment of their differential contributions is critical to understanding the ontogeny of sensory and perceptual as well as other psychological processes. An especial virtue of developmental investigations de-

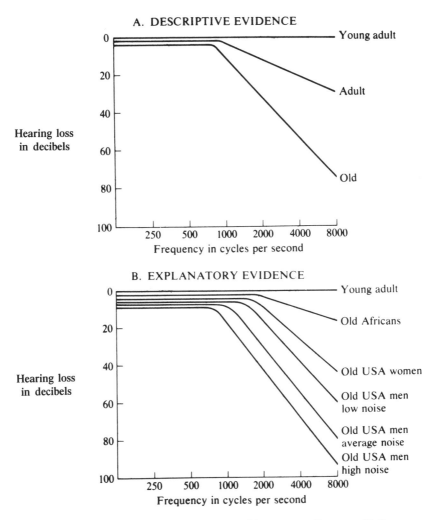

FIG. 4.8.   Descriptive and explanatory evidence on auditory sensitivity in adulthood. (From Baltes, Reese, & Nesselroade, 1977. Copyright Wadsworth Publishing Company. Reprinted with permission.)

rives from information they afford regarding *prevention:* Whereas the descriptive evidence alone strongly implicates physiological deterioration, the alleviation of which might best be achieved through specialized hearing aids for the elderly, the explanatory evidence which derives from diverse biological and experiential comparisons of development suggests more productive intervention strategies that would effectively prevent sensory deterioration and hearing loss in the first place.

PERCEPTUAL MODIFICATION, ENRICHMENT, AND DEPRIVATION IN DEVELOPMENT

How do special rearing circumstances—modification, enrichment, and deprivation—affect perceptual development? As developmental research has evolved, this single question has reformulated itself into two. The first is quite literal: How do these factors affect perceptual development per se? Two opposite views have competed—without clear resolution—in answer to this question. Consider, for example, how deprivation in one perceptual system might affect development of other systems. One view is that by way of compensation the unaffected senses literally develop to a higher level of function, or that people develop a heightened level of awareness through them. Thus, according to this view, true auditory function in the blind is enhanced as some sort of physiological compensation for blindness; or, being visually deprived, blind people attend more closely to information arriving via other sensory channels, or analyze that information more efficiently. The second view is that an absence of information processing in one modality adversely affects the level of perceptual development or awareness other modalities achieve. On the first view, psychophysics has developed techniques (e.g., signal detection theory) which help to distinguish differences in sensory function from differences in psychological judgment. There is no good evidence, based on these procedures, that surviving systems reach a higher perceptual level, although there is good evidence that attention, awareness, or strategy can be enhanced in surviving perceptual systems (Hoemann, 1978; Warren, 1978). Of course, the degree to which enhanced attention in one modality compensates for loss of another varies. On the second view, research suggests that perceptual deprivation is specifically debilitating to a sensory system and to the information processing directly involved, but need not necessarily be detrimental to sensory systems generally.

The second formulation of the original question on how special rearing circumstances might affect perceptual development has been much more general. The question has been put this way: What effects do perceptual modification, enrichment, and deprivation early in life have on the later development of perceptual, cognitive, or social capabilities? Two separate approaches to this question have evolved as well. The first has involved the study of congenitally handicapped populations; and the second has involved normal populations who, by chance, have experienced special rearing circumstances, either in institutions, natural ecologies, or cultures that vary widely in the perceptual experiences they provide. In evaluating effects of perceptual modification of development on these diverse populations, it is imperative to bear in mind that other extraordinary conditions in these populations may surpass in significance their different perceptual experiences. Blindness, deafness, or other handicaps as well as institutionalization or cultural variation can have such profound social and emotional influences on development as to render studies of perception per se problematic.

192

For example, practical research problems revolve around defining the severity of a handicap, determining at what age the handicap began, disentangling physical, emotional, and intellectual disabilities the handicap has produced, and separating the handicapped child's limited general experience from his or her limited perceptual function. Unfortunately, there are no ready replies to these criticisms. As a consequence, what we have learned about perception from investigations of the handicapped is much more limited and uncertain than is commonly supposed.

For obvious reasons, studies of the effects of deprivation on perceptual development have usually involved animals; however, analogous effects may occur in humans in "natural experiments." Lewis, Maurer, and Brent (1985) capitalized on such a natural experiment in infants born with dense cataracts in one eye to study the effects of early light deprivation on visual development. Cataracts permit only diffuse light to be seen. They studied a number of visual functions in children who had such cataracts removed at different points in childhood, and found that, for example, visual acuity was better in those who had their cataracts removed after living with them the shortest amounts of time or who were visually deprived after 3 years of age, rather than from birth; indeed, acuity was worst in children deprived for the longest amounts of time and beginning at birth.

Other special populations present different solutions but new problems as well. Understandably, most studies involving institutionalized individuals have been concerned principally with elucidating the effects of deprivation on the development of cognitive and social skills. Although perception impresses us as a natural outgrowth of biological sensory processing, in the 1960s several theorists and researchers argued that early perceptual experience was critical for normal pscyhological growth and development (see Bornstein, 1987). For example, White and Held (1966) found that simply introducing a visually interesting stabile into institutionalized infants' otherwise bland environments at 1 month of age nearly doubled their visually directed reaching and visual attentiveness over that of comparable infants not enriched in this way. Similarly, Greenberg, Užgiris, and Hunt (1968) found that 1-month-olds who had a stabile strung over their cribs developed a visually defensive response to its sudden approach in half the time of matched-aged babies without comparable experience.

Though some have argued that such circumstances matter only inasmuch as they are accompanied by the absence of human beings in the child's life (Clarke-Stewart, 1973), several major investigations have yielded direct associations between perceptual experiences (or lack thereof) and cognitive development (e.g., Parke, 1978; Wohlwill, 1983). For example, Wachs and his associates (1979, Wachs, Užgiris, & Hunt, 1971) conducted studies attempting to overcome SES, institutional, and other confounds to delimit how exposure to inanimate physical stimulation—via perception—influences cognitive development in the first three years of life. Their findings support an "optimal match hypothesis" which posits that understimulation and overstimulation as well as disorganized stimulation are equally deleterious to development.

Bornstein initiated a series of studies designed to evaluate the positive effects on perceptual development of specific experiences in infants' natural ecologies. In one longitudinal study of 2- to 5-month-olds, Bornstein and Tamis-LeMonda (1987) examined the relation between mothers' prompting their infants' attention to themselves versus properties, objects, or events in the environment and their infants' visual and tactual exploration. Several specific experience-related associations were observed: Infants whose mothers encouraged attention to themselves had babies who attended more to them and less to the environment, whereas infants whose mothers encouraged attention to the environment had babies who explored objects more and their mothers less. Further, these effects were greater among infants whose mothers engaged in physical as opposed to verbal prompting. In a second experiment, Kuchuk, Vibbert, and Bornstein (1986) assessed how mothers' didactic interactions with their 3-month-olds influenced infants' perceptions: In the laboratory, infants displayed individual differences in sensitivity to a series of smiles that graduated in intensity; and concurrent observations of mother–infant interactions at home revealed that the mothers who more frequently encouraged their infants to attend to the mothers themselves when the mothers were smiling had infants who showed the greatest sensitivity to smiling.

The third human group to whom researchers have turned to address questions of how perceptual experiences may influence development includes children reared in contrasting perceptual environments. Indeed, one of the major ways in which extremes of perceptual experience have been investigated safely in humans has been to take advantage of such natural experiments (Bornstein, 1980). Since all human beings are believed to be endowed with roughly the same anatomy and physiology, it is reasonable to expect that most perceptual systems or abilities are essentially universal and that human beings all begin life on much the same footing. Do varying rearing circumstances influence perceptual development differently? Some perceptions seem to be affected, others not. For example, consider how the literature on the categorical perception of speech has evolved. As discussed earlier (see Fig. 4.1), prelinguistic infants distinguish certain categories of speech but not others, whereas adults sometimes distinguish the same categories but sometimes distinguish different ones. It must be the case, therefore, that a dearth of experience with certain distinctions fails to maintain some speech categories, just as experiences with other distinctions may facilitate or attune the development of other categories, or even induce new speech discriminations (Bornstein, 1979; Gottlieb, 1983).

In many ways our perceptual systems are unperturbed by large but normal variation in environmental stimulation. There can be little doubt, however, that experiences, or a lack thereof, play important roles in maintaining, facilitating and attuning, and inducing perceptions in infants' seeing and hearing, and in their tasting, smelling, and touching. Perception is somewhat malleable to experience, and future research will determine the limits of that plasticity as well as which experiences are most influential. Overall, our physical and perceptual experiences seem to be sufficiently common so as to render perceptions nearly the same for everyone everywhere.

SUMMARY AND CONCLUSIONS

Perception is among the oldest and most venerable fields in psychology and among the most closely tied to psychology's origins in philosophy. It is also among the most popular in developmental study. Studies of infancy constitute the bulk of research in perceptual development, and studies of perceptual development have, until recently perhaps, constituted the bulk of research in infancy for the many reasons outlined at the inception of this chapter.

In recent years, many perceptual secrets of infants and children—formidable and intractable as they once seemed—have been penetrated through a variety of ingenious techniques. Research shows that even the very young of our own species perceive beyond simply sensing. But several traditional and important questions about perceptual development are still open, left unanswered even by a wealth of research amassed in the last two decades. Moreover, many of the startling revelations that spring to mind even from our simplest introspections continue to spark curiosity about perceptual development. How do we develop from sensing patterns received and transduced at the surface of the body to effortlessly perceiving objects and events in the real world? How does a world that is constantly in flux come to be perceived as stable? As context is so influential in perception, how does selective attention to signal and figure develop in coordination with selective elimination of noise and ground? How do perceived objects come to be invested with meaning?

The study of perception in childhood is also very practical. For example, the relevance of perceptual research to social and emotional development as well as to medicine and education is readily apparent. Physical and social stimulation are perceptual stimulation, and many aspects of social development depend initially on perceptual capacity. Specific examples abound—from the neonate's perception and consequent ability to imitate facial expressions (Meltzoff & Moore, 1983), to the toddler's acceptance of photographs to mediate separation stress from his or her mother (Passman & Longeway, 1982), to perceptual prerequisites for reading in the child (Gibson & Levin, 1975).

In the past, many investigators expressed reluctance at adding a developmental perspective to the formal study of sensation and perception—developmental psychology often being treated as a different field—and the experimental study of sensation and perception was confined largely to adults and to infrahuman animals. Today, research progress with infant, child, and aged populations demonstrates the broadly informative contribution of the developmental point of view. Developmental study is now esteemed by all enlightened students of sensation and perception.

Perceptual development could serve as a model of developmental studies as good as that of any field described in this text. It encompasses philosophy and methodology, and it confronts all of the overarching theoretical and empirical issues in developmental study. Some perceptual capacities are given congenitally—even, apparently, in the basic functioning of the sensory systems— whereas other perceptual capacities develop between infancy and maturity. This ontogenetic change, in turn, has several possible sources: Development may be genetically motivated and transpire largely as a reflection of maturational forces, or it may be experiential and largely reflect the influences of the environment and of particular events. Perceptual development after birth (or whenever the onset of experience takes place) is doubtlessly some complex transaction of these two principal forces. At one time or another each of these possibilities has been proposed as determinative. Modern studies have informed a modern view, however. Through their systematic efforts in infancy and early childhood, perceptual developmentalists have determined that basic mechanisms in many cases can impose perceptual structure early in life, but that perceptual development is determined and guided by a transaction of these structural endowments in combination with experience. Thus, neither nativism nor empiricism holds sway over perceptual development; rather, innate mechanisms and experience together co-determine how children come to perceive the world veridically.

ACKNOWLEDGMENTS

Preparation of this chapter was partly supported by a research grant from the National Science Foundation (BNS 84-20017) and by research grants (HD20559 and HD20807) and a Research Career Development Award (HD00521) from the National Institute of Child Health and Human Development. I thank H. Bornstein, L. Hainline, and G. Turkewitz for valuable comments.

REFERENCES

Abramov, I., Gordon, J., Hendrickson, A., Hainline, L., Dobson, V., & LaBossiere, E. (1982). The retina of the newborn human infant. *Science, 217,* 265–267.

Acredolo, L. P. (1978). Development of spatial orientation in infancy. *Developmental Psychology, 14,* 224–234.

Acredolo, L. P., & Evans, D. (1980). Developmental changes in the effects of landmarks on infant spatial behavior. *Developmental Psychology, 16,* 312–318.

Adams, R. J., Maurer, D., & Davis, M. (1986). Newborns' discrimination of chromatic from achromatic stimuli. *Journal of Experimental Child Psychology, 41,* 267–281.

Aslin, R. N. (1981). Experiential influences and sensitive periods in perceptual development: A unified model. In R. N. Aslin, J. R. Alberts, & M. R. Peterson (Eds.), *Development of perception: Psychobiological perspectives. Vol. 2: The visual system.* New York: Academic Press.

Ball, W., & Tronick, E. (1971). Infant responses to impending collision: Optical and real. *Science, 171,* 818–820.

Baltes, P. B., Reese, H. W., & Nesselroade, J. R. (1977). *Life-span developmental psychology: Introduction to research methods.* Monterey, CA: Brooks/Cole.

Banks, M. S. (1980). The development of visual accommodation during early infancy. *Child Development, 51,* 646–666.

Barlow, H. B., Blakemore, C., & Pettigrew, J. D. (1967). The neural mechanism of binocular depth discrimination. *Journal of Physiology, 193,* 327–342.

Benson, J. B., & Užgiris, I. C. (1985). Effect of self-initiated locomotion on infant search activity. *Developmental Psychology, 21,* 923–931.

Berg, W. K., & Berg, K. M. (1979). Psychophysiological development in infancy: State, sensory function, and attention. In J. D. Osofsky (Ed.), *Handbook of infant development.* New York: Wiley.

Berkeley, G. (1901). *An essay towards a new theory of vision.* Oxford: Clarendon Press. (Originally published, 1709)

Bertenthal, B. I., Proffitt, D. R., & Cutting, J. E. (1984). Infant sensitivity to figural coherence in biomechanical motions. *Journal of Experimental Child Psychology, 37,* 1072–1080.

Bertenthal, B. I., Profitt, D. R., Spetner, N. B., & Thomas, M. A. (1985). The development of infant sensitivity to biomechanical motions. *Child Development, 56,* 531–543.

Birnholz, J. C., & Benacerraf, B. R. (1983). The development of human fetal hearing. *Science, 222,* 516–518.

Bornstein, M. H. (1975). Qualities of color vision in infancy. *Journal of Experimental Child Psychology, 19,* 401–419.

Bornstein, M. H. (1976). Infants are trichromats. *Journal of Experimental Child Psychology, 21,* 425–445.

Bornstein, M. H. (1977). Developmental pseudocyananopsia: Ontogenetic change in human color vision. *American Journal of Optometry and Physiological Optics, 54,* 464–469.

Bornstein, M. H. (1978a). Visual behavior of the young human infant: Relationships between chromatic and spatial perception and the activity of underlying brain mechanisms. *Journal of Experimental Child Psychology, 26,* 174–192.

Bornstein, M. H. (1978b). Chromatic vision in infancy. In H. W. Reese & L. P. Lipsitt (Eds.), *Advances in child development and behavior* (Vol. 12). New York: Academic Press.

Bornstein, M. H. (1979). Perceptual development: Stability and change in feature perception. In M. H. Bornstein & W. Kessen (Eds.), *Psychological development from infancy: Image to intention.* Hillsdale, NJ: Lawrence Erlbaum Associates.

Bornstein, M. H. (1980). Cross-cultural developmental psychology. In M. H. Bornstein (Ed.), *Comparative methods in psychology.* Hillsdale, NJ: Lawrence Erlbaum Associates.

Bornstein, M. H. (1981). Psychological studies of color perception in human infants: Habituation, discrimination and categorization, recognition, and conceptualization. In L. P. Lipsitt (Ed.), *Advances in infancy research* (Vol. 1). Norwood, NJ: Ablex.

Bornstein, M. H. (1982). Perceptual anisotropies in infancy: Ontogenetic origins and implications of inequality in spatial vision. In H. W. Reese & L. P. Lipsitt (Eds.), *Advances in child development and behavior* (Vol. 16). New York: Academic Press.

Bornstein, M. H. (1984). A descriptive taxonomy of psychological categories used by infants. In C. Sophian (Ed.), *Origins of cognitive skills.* Hillsdale, NJ: Lawrence Erlbaum Associates.

Bornstein, M. H. (1985). Habituation of attention as a measure of visual information processing in human infants: Summary, systematization, and synthesis. In G. Gottlieb & N. A. Krasnegor (Eds.), *Measurement of audition and vision in the first year of postnatal life: A methodological overview.* Norwood, NJ: Ablex.

Bornstein, M. H. (1987). *The multivariate model of interaction effects in human development: Categories of caretaking.* Unpublished manuscript, New York University.

Bornstein, M. H., Ferdinandsen, K., & Gross, C. G. (1981). Perception of symmetry in infancy. *Developmental Psychology, 17,* 82–86.

Bornstein, M. H., Gross, J., & Wolf, J. (1978). Perceptual similarity of mirror images in infancy. *Cognition, 6*, 89–116.

Bornstein, M. H., Kessen, W., & Weiskopf, S. (1976a). The categories of hue in infancy. *Science, 191*, 201–202.

Bornstein, M. H., Kessen, W., & Weiskopf, S. (1976b). Color vision and hue categorization in young human infants. *Journal of Experimental Psychology: Human Perception and Performance, 2*, 115–129.

Bornstein, M. H., & Krinsky, S. (1985). Perception of symmetry in infancy: The salience of vertical symmetry and the perception of pattern wholes. *Journal of Experimental Child Psychology, 39*, 1–19.

Bornstein, M. H., Krinsky, S. J., & Benasich, A. A. (1986). Fine orientation discrimination and shape constancy in infants. *Journal of Experimental Child Psychology, 41*, 49–60.

Bornstein, M. H., & Stiles-Davis, J. (1984). Discrimination and memory for symmetry in young children. *Developmental Psychology, 20*, 639–649.

Bornstein, M. H., & Tamis-LeMonda, C. (1987). *Mother-infant interaction: The selectivity of encouraging attention.* Unpublished manuscript, New York University.

Bower, T. G. R. (1977). *A primer of infant development.* San Francisco: Freeman.

Bower, T. G. R., Broughton, J. M., & Moore, M. (1970). Infant response to approaching objects: An indication of response to distal variables. *Perception & Psychophysics, 9*, 193–196.

Boyton, R. M., & Gordon, J. (1965). Bezold-Brüke hue shift measured by color-naming technique. *Journal of the Optical Society of America, 55*, 78–86.

Bradley, R. M., & Stearn, I. B. (1967). The development of the human taste bud during the fetal period. *Journal of Anatomy, 101*, 743–752.

Bremner, J. G., & Bryant, P. E. (1985). Active movement and development of spatial abilities in infancy. In H. M. Wellman (Ed.), *Children's searching: The development of search skill and spatial representation.* Hillsdale, NJ: Lawrence Erlbaum Associates.

Bromley, D. B. (1974). *The psychology of human ageing.* Harmondsworth, England: Penguin Books.

Bronson, G. W. (1974). The postnatal growth of visual capacity. *Child Development, 45*, 873–890.

Campos, J. J. (1976). Heart rate: A sensitive tool for the study of emotional development in the infant. In L. P. Lipsitt (Ed.), *Developmental psychobiology: The significance of infancy.* Hillsdale, NJ: Lawrence Erlbaum Associates.

Campos, J. J., Bertenthal, B., & Benson, N. (1980). *Self-produced locomotion and the extraction of form invariance.* Paper presented at the meetings of International Conference on Infant Studies, New Haven, CT.

Campos, J. J., Langer, A., & Krowitz, A. (1970). Cardiac responses on the visual cliff in prelocomotor human infants. *Science, 170*, 196–197.

Campos, J. J., Svejda, M., Bertenthal, B., Benson, N., & Schmidt, D. (1981). *Self-produced locomotion and wariness of heights: New evidence from training studies.* Paper presented at the meetings of the Society for Research in Child Development, Boston, MA.

Caron, A. J., Caron, R. F., & Carlson, V. R. (1978). Do infants see objects or retinal images? Shape constancy revisited. *Infant Behavior and Development, 1*, 229–243.

Caron, A. J., Caron, R. F., & Carlson, V. R. (1979). Infant perception of the invariant shape of objects varying in slant. *Child Development, 50*, 716–721.

Caron, R. F., & Caron, A. J. (1978). Effects of ecologically relevant manipulations on infant discrimination learning. *Infant Behavior and Development, 1*, 291–307.

Caron, R. F., Caron, A. J., & Myers, R. S. (1982). Abstraction of invariant face expressions in infancy. *Child Development, 53*, 1008–1015.

Cernoch, J. M., & Porter, R. H. (1985). Recognition of maternal axillary odors by infants. *Child Development, 56*, 1593–1598.

Chase, W. (1937). Color vision in infants. *Journal of Experimental Psychology, 20*, 203–222.

Clarke-Stewart, K. A. (1973). Interactions between mothers and their young children: Characteristics and consequences. *Monographs of the Society for Research in Child Development, 38,* (6–7, Serial No. 153).

Comalli, P. E. (1970). Life-span changes in visual perception. In L. R. Goulet & P. B. Baltes (Eds.), *Life-span developmental psychology.* New York: Academic Press.

Conel, J. L. (1939–1959). *The postnatal development of the human cerebral cortex* (Vols. 1–6). Cambridge, MA: Harvard University Press.

Cornell, E. H., & Heth, C. D. (1979). Response versus place learning by human infants. *Journal of Experimental Psychology: Human Learning and Performance, 5,* 188–196.

Cowart, B. J. (1981). Development of taste perception in humans: Sensitivity and preference throughout the lifespan. *Psychological Bulletin, 90,* 43–73.

Cutting, J. E., Proffitt, D. R., & Kozlowski, L. T. (1978). A biomechanical invariant for gait perception. *Journal of Experimental Psychology: Human Perception and Performance, 4,* 357–372.

Darwin, C. (1877). A biographical sketch of an infant. *Mind, 2,* 286–294.

Davis, C. J. (1928). Self selection of diet by newly weaned infants. *American Journal of Diseases of Children, 36,* 651–679.

Décarie, T. G. (1969). A study of the mental and emotional development of the thalidomide child. In B. M. Foss (Ed.), *Determinants of infant behavior* (Vol. 4). London: Methuen.

Descartes, R. (Paris: np, 1824.) *La dioptrique.* In V. Coursin (Ed.), *Oeuvres de Descartes* (M. D. Boring, trans.). (Originally published, 1638)

Dobson, V. (1976). Spectral sensitivity of the 2-month-old infant as measured by the visually evoked cortical potential. *Vision Research, 16,* 367–374.

Dobson, V., & Teller, D. (1978). Visual acuity in human infants. A review and comparison of behavioral and electrophysiological studies. *Vision Research, 18,* 1469–1483.

Eimas, P. D. (1975). Speech perception in early infancy. In L. B. Cohen & P. Salapatek (Eds.), *Infant perception: From sensation to cognition* (Vol. 2). New York: Academic Press.

Eimas, P. D., Siqueland, E. R., Jusczyk, P., & Vigorito, J. (1971). Speech perception in infants. *Science, 171,* 303–306.

Enns, J. T., & Girgus, J. S. (1985). Developmental changes in selective and integrative visual attention. *Journal of Experimental Child Psychology, 40,* 319–337.

Enns, J. T., & Girgus, J. S. (1986). A developmental study of shape integration over space and time. *Developmental Psychology, 22,* 491–499.

Essock, E. A. (1980). The oblique effect of stimulus identification considered with respect to two classes of oblique effects. *Perception, 9,* 37–46.

Fagan, J. F. (1979). The origins of facial pattern recognition. In M. H. Bornstein & W. Kessen (Eds.), *Psychological development from infancy: Image to intention.* Hillsdale, NJ: Lawrence Erlbaum Associates.

Fantz, R. L., Ordy, J. M., & Udelf, M. S. (1962). Maturation of pattern vision in infants during the first six months. *Journal of Comparative and Physiological Psychology, 55,* 907–917.

Fisher, C. B., & Bornstein, M. H. (1982). Identification of symmetry: Effects of stimulus orientation and head position. *Perception & Psychophysics, 32,* 443–448.

Fisher, C. B., Bornstein, M. H., & Gross, G. G. (1985). Left–right coding skills related to beginning reading. *Journal of Developmental and Behavioral Pediatrics, 6,* 279–283.

Fisher, C. B., Ferdinandsen, K., & Bornstein, M. H. (1981). The role of symmetry in infant form perception. *Child Development, 52,* 457–462.

Fox, R., & McDaniels, C. (1982). The perception of biological motion by human infants. *Science, 218,* 486–487.

Garcia, J., & Koelling, R. (1966). Relation of cue to consequence in avoidance learning. *Psychonomic Science, 4,* 123–124.

Gibson, E. J. (1982). The concept of affordances in development: The renascence of functionalism.

In W. A. Collins (Ed.), *The Minnesota symposia on child psychology* (Vol. 15). Hillsdale, NJ: Lawrence Erlbaum Associates.

Gibson, E. J., Gibson, J. J., Pick, A. D., & Osser, H. (1962). A developmental study of the discrimination of letter-like forms. *Journal of Comparative and Physiological Psychology, 55,* 897–906.

Gibson, E. J., & Levin, H. (1975). *The psychology of reading.* Cambridge, MA: MIT Press.

Gibson, E. J., Owsley, C. J., & Johnston, J. (1978). Perception of invariants by five-month-old infants: Differentiation of two types of motion. *Developmental Psychology, 14,* 407–415.

Gibson, E. J., Owsley, C. J., Walker, A., & Megaw-Nyce, J. (1979). Development of the perception of invariants: Substance and shape. *Perception, 8,* 609–619.

Gibson, E. J., & Walk, R. D. (1960). The "visual cliff." *Scientific American, 202,* 64–71.

Gibson, J. J. (1979). *The ecological approach to visual perception.* Boston, MA: Houghton Mifflin.

Gibson, J. J., & Gibson, E. J. (1955). Perceptual learning: Differentiation or enrichment? *Psychological Review, 62,* 32–41.

Goto, H. (1971). Auditory perception by normal Japanese adults of the sounds "L" and "R". *Neuropsychologia, 9,* 317–323.

Gottlieb, G. (1983). The psychobiological approach to developmental issues. In P. H. Mussen (Ed.), *Handbook of child psychology (Vol. 2).* M. M. Haith & J. J. Campos (Vol. Eds.), *Infants and developmental psychobiology.* New York: Wiley.

Granrud, C. E., Yonas, A., & Pettersen, L. (1984). A comparison of monocular and binocular depth perception in 5- and 7-month-old infants. *Journal of Experimental Child Psychology, 38,* 19–32.

Greenberg, D., Užgiris, I. C., & Hunt, J. McV. (1968). Hastening the development of the blink response with looking. *Journal of Genetic Psychology, 113,*167–176.

Gwiazda, J., Brill, S., Mohindra, I., & Held, R. (1978). Infant visual acuity and its meridional variation. *Vision Research, 18,* 1557–1564.

Hainline, L., & Lemerise, E. (1982). Infants' scanning of geometric forms varying in size. *Journal of Experimental Child Psychology, 32,* 235–256.

Haith, M. M. (1966). The response of the human newborn to visual movement. *Journal of Experimental Child Psychology, 3,* 235–243.

Haith, M. M. (1980). *Rules that babies look by,* Hillsdale, NJ: Lawrence Erlbaum Associates.

Hamer, R. D., Alexander, K., & Teller, D. Y. (1982). Rayleigh discriminations in young human infants. *Vision Research, 20,* 575–584.

Hayes, L. A., & Watson, J. S. (1981). Facial orientation of parents and elicited smiling by infants. *Infant Behavior and Development, 4,* 333–340.

Hebb, D. O. (1953). Heredity and environment in mammalian behavior. *British Journal of Animal Behavior, 1,* 43–47.

Hecox, K. (1975). Electrophysiological correlates of human auditory development. In L. B. Cohen & P. Salapatek (Eds.), *Infant perception: From sensation to cognition* (Vol. 2). New York: Academic Press.

Hecox, K., & Galambos, R. (1974). Brain stem auditory evoked responses in human infants and adults. *Archives of Otolaryngology, 99,* 30–33.

Helmholtz, H. von. (1925). *Handbook of physiological optics* (J. P. C. Southall, Trans.). New York: Optical Society of America. (Originally published 1866)

Hochberg, J. E. (1978). *Perception.* Englewood Cliffs, NJ: Prentice-Hall.

Hoemann, H. W. (1978). Perception by the deaf. In E. C. Carterette & M. P. Friedman (Eds.), *Handbook of perception* (Vol. 10). New York: Academic Press.

Hofsten, C. von. (1980). Predictive reaching for moving objects by human infants. *Journal of Experimental Child Psychology, 30,* 369–382.

Hofsten, C. von. (1984). Developmental changes in the organization of prereaching movements. *Developmental Psychology, 20,* 378–388.

Hofsten, C. von., & Lindhagen, K. (1979). Observations on the development of reaching for moving objects. *Journal of Experimental Child Psychology, 28,* 158–173.

Hubel, D. H., & Weisel, T. N. (1970). Binocular interaction in striate cortex of kittens reared with artificial squint. *Journal of Physiology, 206,* 419–436.

Humphrey, T. (1978). Function of the nervous system during prenatal life. In U. Stave (Ed.), *Perinatal physiology.* New York: Plenum.

Ivinskis, A., & Finlay, D. C. (1980). *Cardiac responses in four-month-old infants to stimuli moving at three different velocities.* Paper presented at the International Conference on Infant Studies, New Haven, CT.

Johansson, G. (1975). Visual motion perception. *Scientific American, 232,* 76–88.

Jusczyk, P. W. (1985). The high amplitude sucking technique as a methodological tool in speech perception research. In G. Gottlieb & N. A. Krasnegor (Eds.), *Measurement of audition and vision in the first year of postnatal life: A methodological overview.* Norwood, NJ: Ablex.

Kant, I. (1924). *Critique of pure reason* (F. M. Müller, Trans.). New York: Macmillan. (Originally published 1781)

Karmel, B. Z., & Maisel, E. B. (1975). A neuronal activity model for infant visual attention. In L. B. Cohen & P. Salapatek (Eds.), *Infant perception: From sensation to cognition* (Vol. 1). New York: Academic Press.

Kaufmann, R., & Kaufmann, F. (1980). The face schema in 3- and 4-month-old infants: The role of dynamic properties of the face. *Infant Behavior and Development, 3,* 331–339.

Kavale, K. (1982). Meta-analysis of the relationship between visual perceptual skills and reading achievement. *Journal of Learning Disabilities, 15,* 42–51.

Kessen, W. (1967). Sucking and looking: Two organized congenital patterns of behavior in the human newborn. In H. W. Stevenson, E. H. Hess, & H. L. Rheingold (Eds.), *Early behavior: Comparative and developmental approaches.* New York: Wiley.

Kessen, W., & Bornstein, M. H. (1978). Discriminability of brightness change for infants. *Journal of Experimental Child Psychology, 25,* 526–530.

Kuchuk, A., Vibbert, M., & Bornstein, M. H. (1986). The perception of smiling and its experiential correlates in 3-month-old infants. *Child Development, 57,* 1054–1061.

Lasky, R. E., Syrdal-Lasky, A., & Klein, R. E. (1975). VOT discrimination by four- to six-and-a-half-month-old infants from Spanish environments. *Journal of Experimental Child Psychology, 20,* 215–225.

Leehey, S. C., Moskowitz-Cook, A., Brill, S., & Held, R. (1975). Orientational anisotropy in infant vision. *Science, 190,* 900–901.

Lewis, T. L., Maurer, D., & Brent, H. P. (1985). The effects of visual deprivation during infancy on perceptual development. *British Journal of Ophthalmology, 70,* 214–220.

Lewkowicz, D. J., & Turkewitz, G. (1980). Cross-modal equivalence in early infancy: Auditory-visual intensity matching. *Developmental Psychology, 16,* 597–607.

Lipsitt, L. P. (1977). Taste in human neonates: Its effects on sucking and heart rate. In J. M. Weiffenbach (Ed.), *Taste and development.* Bethesda, MD: DHEW.

Maurer, D. (1975). Infant visual perception: Methods of study. In L. B. Cohen & P. Salapatek (Eds.), *Infant perception: From sensation to cognition* (Vol. 1). New York: Academic Press.

Maurer, D. (1985). Infants' perception of facedness. In T. Field & N. Fox (Eds.), *Social perception in infancy.* Norwood, NJ: Ablex.

McKenzie, B. E., & Day, R. H. (1971). Orientation discrimination in infants: A comparison of visual fixation and operant training methods. *Journal of Experimental Child Psychology, 11,* 366–375.

McKenzie, B. E., Tootell, H. E., & Day, R. H. (1980). Development of visual size constancy during the first year of human infancy. *Developmental Psychology, 16,* 163–174.

Meltzoff, A. N., & Borton, R. W. (1979). Intermodal matching by human neonates, *Nature, 282,* 403–404.

Meltzoff, A. N., & Moore, M. K. (1983). The origins of imitation in infancy: Paradigm, phenomena, and theories. In L. P. Lipsitt (Ed.), *Advances in infancy research* (Vol. 2). Norwood, NJ: Ablex.

Miyawaki, K., Strange, W., Verbrugge, R. R., Liberman, A. M., Jenkins, J. J., & Fujimura, O. (1975). An effect of linguistic experience: The discrimination of [r] and [l] by native speakers of Japanese and English. *Perception & Psychophysics, 18*, 331–340.

Moskowitz-Cook, A. (1979). The development of photopic spectral sensitivity in human infants. *Vision Research, 19*, 1133–1142.

Nettlebeck, T., & Wilson, C. (1985). A cross-sequential analysis of developmental differences in speed of visual information processing. *Journal of Experimental Child Psychology, 40*, 1–22.

Olsho, L. W. (1984). Infant frequency discrimination. *Infant Behavior and Development, 7*, 27–35.

Olsho, L. W., Schoon, C., Sakai, R., Turpin, R., & Sperduto, V. (1982a). Preliminary data on frequency discrimination. *Journal of the Acoustical Society of America, 71*, 509–511.

Olsho, L. W., Schoon, C., Sakai, R., Turpin, R., & Sperduto, V. (1982b). Auditory frequency discrimination in infancy. *Developmental Psychology, 18*, 721–726.

Packer, O., Hartmann, E. E., & Teller, D. Y. (1985). Infant color vision: The effect of test field size on Rayleigh discriminations. *Vision Research, 24*, 1247–1260.

Palmer, S. E., & Hemenway, K. (1978). Orientation and symmetry: Effects of multiple, rotational, and near symmetries. *Journal of Experimental Psychology: Human Perception and Performance, 4*, 691–702.

Parke, R. D. (1978). Children's home environments: Social and cognitive effects. In I. Altman & J. F. Wohlwill (Eds.), *Children and the environment: Vol. 3. Human behavior and environment.* New York: Plenum.

Passman, R. H., & Longeway, K. P. (1982). The role of vision in maternal attachment: Giving 2-year-olds a photograph of their mother during separation. *Developmental Psychology, 18*, 530–533.

Peeples, D. R., & Teller, D. Y. (1975). Color vision and brightness discrimination in two-month-old human infants. *Science, 189*, 1102–1103.

Peeples, D. R., & Teller, D. Y. (1978). White-adapted photopic spectral sensitivity in human infants. *Vision Research, 18*, 49–53.

Piaget, J. (1954). *The construction of reality in the child.* New York: Basic Books.

Pipp, S., & Haith, M. M. (1984). Infant visual responses to pattern: Which metric predicts best? *Journal of Experimental Child Psychology, 38*, 373–399.

Porges, S. W. (1974). Heart rate indices of newborn attentional responsivity. *Merrill-Palmer Quarterly, 20*, 231–254.

Porter, R. H., & Doane, H. M. (1976). Maternal pheromone in the spiny mouse (*Acomys cahirinus*). *Physiology and Behavior, 16*, 75–78.

Porter, R. H., Cernoch, J. M., & McLaughlin, F. J. (1983). Maternal recognition of neonates through olfactory cues. *Physiology and Behavior, 30*, 151–154.

Rosch, E. (1975). Cognitive reference points. *Cognitive Psychology, 7*, 532–547.

Rose, S. A. (1984). Developmental changes in hemispheric specialization for tactual processing in very young children: Evidence from cross-modal transfer. *Developmental Psychology, 20*, 568–574.

Rose, S. A., Gottfried, A. W., & Bridger, W. H. (1978). Cross-modal transfer in infants: Relationship to prematurity and socioeconomic background. *Developmental Psychology, 14*, 643–652.

Rose, S. A., Gottfried, A. W., & Bridger, W. H. (1979). Effects of haptic cues on visual recognition memory in full-term and preterm infants. *Infant Behavior and Development, 2*, 55–67.

Rose, S. A., Gottfried, A. W., & Bridger, W. H. (1981). Cross-modal transfer and information processing by the sense of touch in infancy. *Developmental Psychology, 17*, 90–98.

Rose, S. A., & Ruff, H. A. (1987). Cross-modal transfer. In J. D. Osofsky (Ed), *Handbook of infant development* (2nd ed.). New York: Wiley.

Royer, F. L. (1981). Detection of symmetry. *Journal of Experimental Psychology: Human Perception and Performance, 7,* 1186–1210.

Ruff, H. A. (1984). Infants' manipulative exploration of objects: Effects of age and object characteristics. *Developmental Psychology, 20,* 9–20.

Ruff, H. A. (1985). Detection of information specifying the motion of objects by 3- and 5-month-old infants. *Developmental Psychology, 21,* 295–305.

Russell, M. J., Mendelson, T. & Peeke, H. V. S. (1983). Mothers' identification of their infants' odors. *Ethology and Sociobiology, 4,* 29–31.

Samuels, C. A. (1985). Attention to eye contact opportunity and facial motion by three-month-old infants. *Journal of Experimental Child Psychology, 40,* 105–114.

Schaller, J. (1975). Chromatic vision in human infants: Conditioned operant fixation to "hues" of varying intensity. *Bulletin of the Psychonomic Society, 6,* 39–42.

Schiff, W., Benasich, A., & Bornstein, M. H. (1986). *Infants' sensitivity to audio-visual coherence.* Unpublished manuscript, New York University.

Schneider, B. A., Trehub, S. E., & Bull, D. (1980). High-frequency sensitivity in infants. *Science, 207,* 1003–1004.

Scibetta, J. J., Rosen, M. G., Hochberg, C. J., & Chik, L. (1971). Human fetal brain response to sound during labor. *American Journal of Obstetrics and Gynecology, 109,* 82–85.

Schulman-Galambos, C., & Galambos, R. (1979). Brain stem evoked response audiometry in newborn hearing screening. *Archives of Otolaryngology, 105,* 86–90.

Siqueland, E. R., & DeLucia, C. A. (1969). Visual reinforcement of nonnutritive sucking in human infants. *Science, 165,* 1144–1146.

Slater, A., Morison, V., Town, C., & Rose, D. (1985). Movement perception and identity constancy in the new-born baby. *British Journal of Developmental Psychology, 3,* 211–220.

Spence, A. J., & De Casper, A. J. (1984). *Human fetuses perceive maternal speech.* Paper presented to the International Conference on Infant Studies, Austin, TX.

Steiner, J. E. (1977). Facial expressions of the neonate infant indicating the hedonics of food-related chemical stimuli. In J. M. Weiffenbach (Ed.), *Taste and development.* Bethesda, MD: DHEW.

Steiner, J. E. (1979). Human facial expressions in response to taste and smell stimulation. In H. Reese & L. Lipsitt (Eds.), *Advances in child development and behavior* (Vol. 13). New York: Academic Press.

Strauss, S. (Ed.) (1982). *U-shaped behavioral growth.* New York: Academic Press.

Streeter, L. A. (1976). Language perception of 2-month-old infants shows effects of both innate mechanisms and experience. *Nature, 259,* 39–41.

Tamis-LeMonda, C., & Bornstein, M. H. (1986). *Mother-infant interaction: The selectivity of encouraging attention.* Paper presented at the International Conference on Infancy Studies, Los Angeles, CA.

Teller, D. Y. (1979). The forced-choice preferential looking procedure: A psychophysical technique for use with human infants. *Infant Behavior and Development, 2,* 135–153.

Teller, D. Y., & Bornstein, M. H. (1986). Infant color vision and color perception. In P. Salapatek & L. B. Cohen (Eds.), *Handbook of infant perception.* New York: Academic Press.

Teller, D. Y., Peeples, D. R., & Sekel, M. (1978). Discrimination of chromatic from white light by two-month-old infants. *Vision Research, 18,* 41–48.

Trehub, S. E., & Chang, H. (1977). Speech as reinforcing stimulation for infants. *Developmental Psychology, 13,* 121–124.

Trehub, S. E., Schneider, B. A., & Endman, M. (1980). Developmental changes in infants' sensitivity to octave-band noises. *Journal of Experimental Child Psychology, 29,* 283–293.

Tuchmann-Duplessis, H., Auroux, M., & Haegel, P. (1975). *Illustrated human embryology* (Vol. 3). New York: Springer-Verlag.

Turkewitz, G., & Kenny, P. A. (1982). Limitations on input as a basis for neural organization and perceptual development: A preliminary theoretical statement. *Developmental Psychology, 15,* 357–368.

Turkewitz, G., & Kenny, P. A. (1985). The role of developmental limitations of sensory input on sensory/perceptual organization. *Journal of Developmental and Behavioral Pediatrics, 6,* 302–306.

Varner, D., Cook, J. E., Schneck, M. E., McDonald, M., & Teller, D. Y. (1984). Tritan discriminations by 1- and 2-month-old human infants. *Vision Research, 25,* 821–832.

Vellutino, F. R. (1977). Alternative conceptualizations of dyslexia: Evidence in support of a verbal-deficit hypothesis. *Harvard Educational Review, 47,* 334–354.

Wachs, T. D., Užgiris, I. C., & Hunt, J. McV. (1971). Cognitive development in infants of different age levels and from different environmental backgrounds: An exploratory investigation. *Merrill-Palmer Quarterly, 17,* 283–317.

Warren, D. H. (1978). Perception by the blind. In E. C. Carterette & M. P. Friedman (Eds.), *Handbook of perception* (Vol. 10). New York: Academic Press.

Watson, J. S. (1966). Perception of object orientation in infants. *Merrill-Palmer Quarterly, 12,* 73–94.

Weiner, K., & Kagan, J. (1976). Infants' reaction to changes in orientation of figure and frame. *Perception, 5,* 25–28.

Werker, J. F., Gilbert, J. H. V., Humphrey, K., & Tees, R. C. (1981). Developmental aspects of cross-language speech perception. *Child Development, 52,* 344–355.

Werker, J. F., & Tees, R. C. (1983). Developmental changes across childhood in the perception of nonnative speech sounds. *Canadian Journal of Psychology, 37,* 278–286.

Wertheimer, M. (1938). Numbers and numerical concepts in primitive peoples. In W. D. Ellis (Ed.), *A source book of gestalt psychology.* New York: Harcourt.

White, B. L., & Held, R. (1966). Plasticity of sensorimotor development. In J. F. Rosenblith & W. Allinsmith (Eds.), *The causes of behavior.* Boston, MA: Allyn & Bacon.

Wittelson, S. F. (1976). Sex and the single hemisphere: Specialization of the right hemisphere for spatial processing. *Science, 193,* 425–427.

Wohlwill, J. (1983). Physical and social environment as factors in development. In D. Magnusen & V. Allen, (Eds.), *Human development: An interactional perspective.* New York: Academic.

Yonas, A. (1981). Infants' responses to optical information for collision. In R. N. Aslin, J. R. Alberts, & M. R. Peterson (Eds.), *Development of perception: Psychobiological perspectives* (Vol. 2). New York: Academic Press.

Yonas, A., & Granrud, C. E. (1985). Reaching as a measure of infants' spatial perception. In G. Gottlieb & N. A. Krasnegor (Eds.), *Measurement of audition and vision in the first year of postnatal life: A methodological overview.* Norwood, NJ: Ablex.

5 Cognitive Development

Deanna Kuhn
Columbia University

INTRODUCTION

The primary aim of this chapter is to examine the succession of ways in which the study of cognitive development has been approached during the relatively brief historical period of its existence. Such an approach is based on the premise that an examination of this sort affords the greatest insight into the topic itself. The study of cognitive development, it can be claimed, has consisted of an overlapping historical succession of conceptualizations: (a) what it is that develops; (b) the process by means of which development occurs; and (c) how the study of this development is best conducted. These conceptualizations have dictated both the questions that are selected for investigation and how the products of those investigations are understood. They have thus provided a series of "windows" through which the topic might be viewed, and it is only by examining these windows themselves—these conceptual and methodological frameworks—that one can gain a sense of how our knowledge of cognitive development has progressed.

One thing a reader new to the field is likely to gain from this chapter is an appreciation of why the study of cognitive development has not yielded simple, straightforward answers to seemingly simple, straightforward, empirically researchable questions, such as, "Does basic memory capacity increase or remain constant as the individual develops?" The reader should come to appreciate why such questions themselves, as well as their answers, turn out to be considerably more complex than they appear on the surface. While the reader new to the field may be disillusioned to learn that the field is not comprised of simple, easily answered research questions or an accumulated body of perspective-free facts, there is actually considerable reason to be optimistic regarding the field's past and prospective progress. In fact, the field is in many ways at a turning point in its own development, with considerable promise for future progress. A number of longstanding polarities, controversies, and preoccupations that have detracted attention from the central questions crucial to an understanding of cognitive development have in recent years either been resolved, set aside, or recast; the result is that attention is now focused more directly on these key questions. Some might take the negative view that through the succession of those windows in terms of which the field has proceeded, it has done no more than repeat itself and thus in effect stand still. In this chapter I suggest instead ways in which these windows are becoming larger and clearer as the perspectives they entail increase in explanatory power.

THE COORDINATION OF MIND AND REALITY: BASIC PERSPECTIVES

An adequate account of cognitive development must, at a minimum, contain answers to two basic questions: First, what is it that develops? Second, how does this development occur? The answer to the first question, at least, might appear obvious: The profound differences in the intellectual functions exhibited by the newborn infant and the mature adult are evident to the most casual observer. It is this development that is the obvious object of concern. In fact, however, different theoretical and methodological approaches to the study of cognitive development represent a wide variety of views as to what is developing, ranging from individual stimulus–response connections to discrete, context-linked skills, to a smaller set of more general cognitive functions, to a single broad system of cognitive operations that underlies all more specific intellectual abilities and behaviors.

The second question also harbors greater complexity than is suggested on the surface. There is more to be explained than how it is that intellectual functioning, or mind, is transformed during the course of development, although formulating such an explanation is in itself a formidable challenge. The full question that must be addressed, rather, is how it is that mind comes to develop *in the particular direction,* or toward the particular end, that it does (rather than in the host of other possible directions in which it might develop) so as to become well adapted to the external world of which the developing individual is a part. The two questions are of course not independent. The answer to the second question to a large degree determines the answer to the first, although the reverse is less true. The following discussion, then, focuses on answers to the second question, while noting their implications with respect to the first.

Three broad answers to the second question have appeared and reappeared throughout the history of developmental psychology. All three have roots in classical philosophical traditions that predate psychology as a field of scientific study. Each of the perspectives can be classified in terms of which of these three answers it reflects.

The first answer, rooted in the philosophical tradition known as *rationalism,* is that mind and reality exist in preestablished coordination with one another. In other words, the development of the mind in a particular direction is predetermined, presumably through some form of genetic coding unique to the species. The second answer, whose roots lie in the philosophical tradition known as *empiricism,* is that the nature of reality is imposed on the mind from without during the course of development, and it is for this reason that mind and reality come to coordinate with one another. The third answer, rooted in the philosophical tradition known as *interactionism,* is that the mind is neither in preestablished coordination with reality nor molded by it from without; that rather, through a lengthy series of interchanges between individual and environment, the coordination is gradually achieved.

Maturationism

The first of the three answers is reflected in the first theoretical perspective to have a major guiding influence on the study of child development by North American psychologists, the doctrine of *maturationism.*[1] Until the appearance of the work of Arnold Gesell, the major advocate of maturationism, studies of children's development had been conducted largely within the atheoretical "child study movement," which had flourished in America during the early part of the twentieth century. It can be argued that the myriad of descriptive studies of children's knowledge and interests produced by the child study movement did not make a lasting contribution to our understanding precisely because these investigations were not guided by an overarching conceptual framework. Gesell's studies, in strong contrast, adhere clearly to a mold dictated by his theoretical view.

Gesell was struck by the regularity he observed in the emergence of various motor abilities during the first years of life, despite huge variability in environmental circumstances. These observations led him to the thesis that new skills emerge according to a regular sequence and timetable that are the product of a predetermined genetic code, similar, for example, to the code that governs the appearance of secondary sexual characteristics at puberty. Maturation, Gesell proposed, is the internal regulatory mechanism that governs the emergence of all new skills and abilities, cognitive as well as behavioral, that appear with advancing age. According to such a view, then, a sequence of discrete skills develops by means of predetermined unfolding.

---

[1]The theories of James Baldwin, as we note later, had an influence largely confined to Europe, despite the fact that Baldwin was an American.

Gesell and his coworkers engaged in meticulous cross-sectional and longitudinal observations of infants, which enabled them to describe in precise detail the sequence and timetable in terms of which early motor abilities appeared. Subsequent research of this sort in developmental psychology has been criticized as "merely descriptive," but one cannot lodge this criticism against Gesell's work, for there is a logical link between his research strategy and his theory: If the appearance of new behaviors is the product of an innate genetic code, the researcher's task is merely to provide a precise description of this unfolding; no further explanation is necessary.

An experimental methodology would seem to have no place in Gesell's work. One experiment Gesell performed, however, has become a classic. Gesell (1929) conducted the experiment for the purpose of demonstrating the secondary role of the environment, relative to the central role he believed to be played by the process of maturation. Quite unlike most modern experiments, Gesell's experiment had only two subjects, 11-month-old twin girls. At the onset of the experiment, neither twin exhibited any proficiency in the skill that was to be the focus of the experiment, stair-climbing. Gesell proceeded to subject one of the twins to daily training sessions on a specially constructed staircase, for a period of six weeks. At the end of this period, the trained twin was a proficient stair-climber, while the control (untrained) twin still showed no ability.

At this point, the experiment would appear to show exactly the opposite of what Gesell held; that is, it appears to show that the acquisition of motor skills is highly susceptible to environmental influence. The experiment did not end at this point, however. Several weeks later, the control twin spontaneously began to exhibit some stair-climbing proficiency. At this point, Gesell instituted a 2-week period of training of the same type that had been administered to the experimental twin. At the end of this period, the control twin equalled her experimental twin in stair-climbing proficiency, and the two remained equivalent in proficiency from then on.

What Gesell wished to demonstrate by this experiment, of course, is that the environment, or "experience," plays at most a superficial, secondary role in temporarily accelerating the emergence of a skill that is destined by the maturational code to appear at a later time. Although these results were initially accepted by some as evidence of the correctness of Gesell's maturational doctrine, a major criticism of the experiment was raised. Did the experimental design adequately control for the effects of experience? The untrained twin continued to have a variety of kinds of experience, even if not specifically stair-climbing, during the period the experimental twin was being trained. Could this experience legitimately be ruled out as having contributed to the eventual appearance of the untrained twin's skill?

At first, the issue appeared to be a problem in research design. Were it feasible on ethical and technical grounds to restrict totally the experience of the control twin during the training period, then experience could be ruled out as a contributing factor. Ultimately, however, the problem was recognized as a logical, not a methodological, one. As long as an organism has life, it is undergoing some experience, by the very definition of what it is to be alive. Thus, a process of maturation can be observed only in the case of a living organism that is undergoing experience of some sort during the period of observation. One cannot, in turn, rule out the possibility of this experience having played a role in the emergence of new behaviors exhibited by the organism.

Following this recognition of the impossibility of eliminating experience as a factor contributing to development, interest in the maturational doctrine declined, and attention turned instead toward investigating *how* experience influences development. Few if any current developmental psychologists would categorize themselves as maturationists. The modern-day theorist to whom the maturationist (or the more common modern term, *nativist*) view is often attributed is the linguist Noam Chomsky. It is important to note, however, that Chomsky does not subscribe to a nativist doctrine in anything like the strong sense that Gesell did. Chomsky regards the *capacity* to acquire language as an innate capacity unique to the human organism (in contrast to Jean Piaget, who regards the capacity for language as evolving out of sensorimotor activity during infancy). Chomsky (as well as Piaget), however, regards experience as an essential aspect of the *process* of the language acquisition.

The pure doctrine of maturationism, then, is significant because of its historical influence, rather than as a guiding perspective in the present-day study of cognitive development. However, it should be emphasized that rejection of a doctrine of maturationism does not imply rejection of underlying biological changes as critical to the emergence of new cognitive or behavioral skills. On the contrary, developments in the brain and nervous system that appear to be critical for behavioral development have become a topic of intense interest and research effort. Such physical developments, however, do not by themselves initiate related behavioral developments. At most, they are enabling conditions that make it possible for the behavioral developments to take place; the process of behavioral development itself remains to be explained.

Empiricism

Although Gesell's studies were theoretically motivated, his descriptions of developmental patterns were attended to more for their practical than their theoretical significance, most likely because the field at this point—under the influence of the child study movement—was still very practically oriented. In fact, the series of books by Gesell and his coworkers describing developmental norms are still referred to today. It is probably accurate to say, then, that when the empiricist movement that had come to occupy the mainstream of academic psychology by the middle of the century embraced the field of child development, it was the first time that the field's research efforts became dominated by an overarching theoretical framework.

The empiricist view represented a striking counterinfluence following Gesell's maturationism. If developmental change does not arise from within the organism, then perhaps it is imposed from without by the environment. This solution represents the second of the three answers presented earlier: Mind and reality come to be coordinated with one another because reality imposes itself on and hence shapes the mind over the course of development. Mind, then, is in the beginning John Locke's classic *tabula rasa,* or blank slate.

The name of B. F. Skinner is the one most closely identified with the empiricist doctrine of behaviorism. Skinner explored the full implications of the Law of Effect originally proposed by E. L. Thorndike at the turn of the century: Organisms tend to repeat those behaviors that have satisfying consequences and to eliminate those that do not. Thus, the behaviors an organism comes to exhibit are a function of the behaviors' environmental consequences. The organism is thereby shaped by its environment.

Bijou and Baer are the two theorists most widely known for applying Skinner's doctrine to child development. The child, they have proposed, is best conceptualized as "a cluster of interrelated responses" (Bijou & Baer, 1961); and development, in turn, consists of the progressive shaping of these responses by the environment. Like Skinner, Bijou and Baer claimed as one of their most important tenets that the temptation of relying on unobservable internal constructs to explain behavior must be avoided. Only external, observable behaviors are the proper object of scientific study in their view, and in turn these observable behaviors are a function of observable external events. They believed that speculation about processes internal to the individual only obscures the direct connection between external behavior and the external stimuli that control it.

One might wonder what relevance such a doctrine could have for the study of cognition and its development, as cognition almost by definition is a process internal to the individual. Bijou and Baer take the position, however, that cognition is nothing more than a particular class of behavior and as such is under the same environmental control as any other behavior. For example, consider what (mistakenly) might be regarded as an internal concept that a young child has of, say, *animals.* What this so-called "concept" actually consists of, Bijou and Baer held, is a common behavioral response the child has learned to exhibit (as a function of external reinforcement) in the presence of objects or events that have a certain set of properties (e.g., movement, four legs, eyes, nose, mouth, perhaps fur or a tail). It is thus not fruitful to regard the concept as either inside the child's head or existing in nature. Rather, such "conceptual" behavior is under the control of the environmental agents who administer the appropriate reinforcement contingencies (i.e., signify approval if the child emits the proper response when the defining properties are present). It could well be a different set of properties (and hence a different "conceptual" behavior) that the agents choose to reinforce. (See Bijou, 1976, Chapters 3 and 4, for an elaboration of this view of concept development.)

A few fundamental principles have governed research in cognitive development carried out within the empiricist framework; the most important are the principle of reductionism, the related principle of parsimony, and the principle of experimental control. *Reductionism* has been influential both as a theoretical principle and as a research strategy. As a theoretical principle, reductionism is the assertion that any complex behavior is in fact a constellation of very simple behaviors. As a research strategy, reductionism dictates that the smallest possible behavioral units that make up a complex behavior be isolated and investigated individually. Once the process governing each of these individual units is understood, explanations of more complex forms of behavior should follow.

The related principle of *parsimony* holds that an explanatory mechanism that accounts for the broadest range of phenomena is to be preferred over one that accounts for a narrower range of phenomena. In the case of behaviorist theory, this had meant that more complex explanations must be rejected if a behavior can be accounted for in terms of the simple mechanism of operant conditioning, or control by means of external reinforcement. Applied in the field of developmental psychology, the major implication is that developmental phenomena can (and should) be regarded as the accumulated effects of the operation of the simple conditioning (or learning) mechanism. In other words, development can be reduced to the simpler process of learning. Hence, there is no need to retain the more complex term.

The parsimony principle is also reflected in the assumption that the basic learning mechanism functions in an identical way throughout the individual's development. An implication of this assumption with respect to research strategy is that there is no need to compare individuals at different points in development. If a particular learning process is observed to operate at one age level, it is assumed that it will operate in the same way at any other age level. Thus, researchers studying cognitive development within an empiricist framework have tended to utilize a single age group in their studies. Rarely have they engaged in the cross-sectional and longitudinal age comparisons characteristic of much developmental research.

The principle of *experimental control* has led to the almost exclusive choice of an experimental laboratory method. Because the laboratory provides a controlled environment, the researcher can introduce the environmental variable believed to control a particular behavior, with reasonable assurances that some other (uncontrolled) variable has not actually produced the behavior, as might be the case in a natural setting.

A research program conducted within the empiricist framework that illustrates all of these principles is the laboratory study of paired-associate learning that was prevalent in the 1950s and 1960s. In a paired-associate learning experiment, a subject is exposed to pairs of nonsense syllables (e.g., PIF and LER) until the subject establishes a connection between the two members of the pair, such that presentation of one syllable enables the subject to recite the other. The choice of arbitrary (nonsensical) material to be learned is not itself arbitrary but rather is an important part of the research strategy, dictated by the objective of experimental control. Arbitrary associations between meaningless syllables will be completely, and therefore equally, new to all learners. Individual differences in past learning and reinforcement are thus controlled for.

Paired-associate learning experiments were conducted both with children and adults as subjects. The purpose of these experiments, however, was not to compare the performance of different age groups. Rather, the large number of studies conducted were all devoted to identifying the variables (for example, exposure time or distinctiveness of syllables) that affect the learning process; it was assumed that these variables would function in an identical way for all subjects at all ages.

The tremendous effort devoted to the study of paired-associate learning was justified on the assumption that it represents one of the simplest, most basic forms of learning, and that an understanding of how it operates would provide a key to understanding more complex and significant forms of learning that occur in schools and other natural settings. To critics who argue that it would be preferable to devote research effort to studying these more complex forms of learning directly, proponents of the reductionist strategy counter that the learning that occurs in natural contexts is simply too complex to be amenable to investigation. The reductionist strategy, they would claim, provides the only avenue to eventual understanding. The controversy between pro- and antireductionist positions has continued in various forms within the field of psychology to the present day. Later, we shall examine further how the reductionist strategy has fared in the study of cognitive development.

The maturationist and empiricist perspectives that have been described in this section reflect two of the three answers to the basic question posed at the outset: How does the mind develop so as to become coordinated with the external world it inhabits? The answers that underlie these two perspectives are diametrically opposed. The maturationist answer is that this coordination is preestablished within the individual, whereas the empiricist answer is that this coordination is imposed on the individual from without by the external world. Let us turn now to the perspective that reflects the third of these answers.

PIAGET AND CONSTRUCTIVISM

Rediscovering the Child's Mind

American developmental psychology was in many ways ripe for its "discovery" of Piaget in the 1950s. The Piagetian influence brought something that was new—and that many would argue had been conspicuously absent in the study of the child's cognitive (as well as social) development: the "rediscovery of the child's mind," as one observer (Martin, 1959/60) put it at the time. Some would go so far as to claim that the study of cognitive development began with Piaget;

before Piaget, there existed a psychology of learning, not a psychology of development. Many of Piaget's ideas are evident in the work of the philosopher and psychologist James Mark Baldwin (Wozniak, 1982), as well as Piaget's contemporary, Heinz Werner (1948). Yet it was Piaget who was to have the major influence on the study of cognitive development in American psychology, even though his scholarly career had been underway in Europe for several decades before American psychologists became interested in his work.

Piaget's descriptions of "childish" thought intrigued a wide audience of psychologists and educators. His revelations of the beliefs of young children—that liquid changes when poured into a differently shaped container, that names are a part of the objects they represent, that the sun follows one around and thinks and feels as humans do, that one's own thoughts and dreams are material objects apparent to observers, to cite a few of the most well-known examples—were startling to many who regarded themselves as knowledgeable about children. Such features of children's thought had evidently been "there to be seen" for centuries, but in most cases had never been noted before.

Yet Piaget himself found these observations of childish thought significant not so much for their own sake as for their implications regarding the mechanisms by means of which the mind develops. Consider, for example, the container of liquid portrayed in Fig. 5.1. If asked to draw the liquid as it would appear while the container is tilted at a 45-degree angle, young children tend not to represent the liquid by a line parallel to the true horizontal (left side of Fig. 5.1). Instead, they draw the line representing the liquid as parallel to the top and bottom of the container (right side of Fig. 5.1). No child has ever seen liquid in a container in this way. The child's drawing, therefore, cannot be a direct reflection of his or her experiences with objects and events in the physical world. Instead, Piaget argued, it must be an intellectual construction—the child's understanding of what he or she sees.

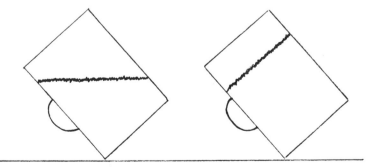

FIG. 5.1.   When asked to draw a line indicating the level of liquid in a tilted container, young children typically draw the line parallel to the top and bottom of the container (right) rather than on the true horizontal (left).

Each observation of this sort was significant in Piaget's view as testimony to the fact that the child is engaged in an extended intellectual "meaning-making" endeavor. In other words, the child is attempting to construct an understanding of self, other, and the world of objects. "Childish" beliefs, such as nonconservation (e.g., of the true horizontal, following a perceptual alteration such as tilting of the container, or of quantity, following transfer to a differently shaped container), are significant for the reason that they cannot have been directly internalized from the external world. Nor is it plausible that such beliefs are innate and simply appear, uninfluenced by the child's experience in the world.

In discounting these opposing alternatives, Piaget proposed at least the general form of a third solution to the question posed earlier of how mind and reality come to be coordinated with one another. Through a process of organism–environment, or subject–object, interchanges, the child gradually constructs an understanding of both its own actions and the external world. The most important feature of these interchanges is that they are bidirectional: The organism and the external world gradually come to "fit" one another; neither makes any radical or unilateral accommodations to the other. Each new "childish belief" that is discovered—that is, each new belief that directly reflects neither the external world nor the child's innate disposition—provides further evidence of the occurrence of some such bidirectional interchange and hence constructive process.

The Doctrine of Stages

It has been suggested that the single most central idea in Piaget's wide-ranging theorizing is that the intellectual effort to understand one's own actions and their relation to the world of objects—that is, the individual's extended "meaning-making" enterprise—motivates or energizes a constructive process directed toward progressively greater equilibrium between individual and environment. Thus, when Piaget's influence became prominent in American psychology, one might have expected that it would be this constructive meaning-making enterprise, or at the very least the "rediscovery of the child's mind," that Piaget would come to stand for.

Instead, it was the derivative doctrine of *stages* that Piaget's theory became identified with in American developmental psychology. The individual's meaning-making effort, Piaget believed, was marked by a striving for coherence, with the result that the individual's ideas had a unity to them, even if the ideas were largely incorrect by external, or mature, standards. In other words, stated more formally, these ideas were reflections of a broad, unified cognitive system that had its own unique form and that mediated all of the more specific manifestations of the individual's cognitive functioning.

Furthermore, it was this system as a whole that allegedly underwent developmental change. As a result of the interactive process directed toward adaptation, or greater equilibrium between organism and environment, the cognitive system underwent a series of major reorganizations each reflecting an improved equilibrium; that is, mind and reality were better coordinated with one another than they had been previously. These newly and better organized mental structures, or "stages," were held to appear in an invariant sequence universal to the human species, each new structure reflecting the most probable organization to emerge from the organism–environment interactions that characterized the preceding level. Each new structure represented a new set of principles or rules that governed the interaction between organism and environment. One reason the doctrine of stages may have become the focus of attention for American developmental psychologists, then, is that it respresented a challenge (and what looked like an empirically testable one) to prevailing empiricist theories, as it implied both the inevitability of the sequence of stages and their resistance to environmental influence.

Following from this structuralist theoretical perspective is an inductive research strategy, aimed at inferring the nature of the underlying cognitive system by observing a varied sampling of intellectual behaviors and postulating a model of mental structure that might underlie them. Implied in this strategy is the view that any one of these individual behaviors cannot be fully understood and appreciated in isolation. It is only by understanding their relation to each other, and to the underlying mental structure they reflect, that their true nature can be appreciated.

Following from the theoretical claim that the cognitive system undergoes a series of major transformations, is a developmental research strategy. The functional rules that describe interaction between organism and environment do not remain constant, as assumed from the empiricist perspective. Rather, these rules themselves undergo transformation, as part of the transformation of the cognitive system as a whole. Each new structure is unique, and consequently the individual at each new stage of development must be studied as a unique organism, different from what it was earlier and from what it will be at a later stage of development.

In Piaget's work these postulated structures are represented in the symbolic medium of formal logic, and each of the major structures—sensorimotor, preoperational, concrete operational, and formal operational—is regarded as a broad system of logical operations that mediates and hence unites a whole range of more specific intellectual behaviors and characteristics (Piaget, 1970). The most appropriate structure for us to examine as an example of Piagetian stage structures is the structure labelled *concrete operations,* alleged to emerge in the age range of 6 to 8 years, since it is the one that has received the most attention both in Piaget's own work and in subsequent research by others.

The central feature that defines the concrete operational thought structure and differentiates it from the earlier preoperational thought structure, Piaget claimed, is the reversibility of mental operations. Mental acts emanating from the preoperational thought structure are irreversible; they cannot be reversed and performed in the opposite direction. Thus, judging that A is smaller than B does not entail the identical judgment made from the reference point of B rather than A, that is, that B is larger than A. For this reason, the child conceptualizes phenomena in absolute rather than relative terms. For example, a young child who regards a ball as *large* is likely to find it difficult to subsequently regard this same ball as *small*, relative to another, larger ball.

The underlying irreversibility of preoperational thought, Piaget claimed, is what is responsible for many of the unique features of young children's thinking described in his investigations. Most central are the absence of operations reflecting the logic of *relations*, as just illustrated; and the logic of *classes*—that is, the ability to conceptualize elements as having multiple membership in a set of hierarchical classes (e.g., living things, human beings, man, father). It is this absence of class logic to which Piaget attributed one of his most widely cited examples of preoperational reasoning: A young child, asked if there are more roses or more flowers in a set of four roses and three tulips, is likely to reply "more roses." Such a reply, Piaget claimed, reflects the child's inability to simultaneously (and hence reversibly) regard the roses as both a subclass and a part of the larger class (flowers). Hence, the child compares the subclass *roses* to its complement *tulips*, rather than to the class *flowers*.

The complete system of operations proposed by Piaget as the concrete operational thought structure is an integrated system of the reversible operations of (a) *classification*—the combining of elements into groups based on their equivalence; and (b) *relation*—the linking of one element to another in an equivalence relation of symmetry (A is to B as B is to A, as in the case of two brothers), or in a difference relation of asymmetry (A is less than B and B is greater than A). The evolution of this structure was also postulated by Piaget to underlie the attainment of conservation: With concrete operations the child can mentally reverse the transformation (for example, the pouring of the liquid from the original to a differently shaped container), and hence deduce that the quantity must remain invariant despite its altered appearance. In addition, the irreversibility of thought prior to the evolution of the concrete operational structure was alleged by Piaget to underlie all of the characteristics of young children's thinking that he labeled "egocentric": inability to assume another perspective (role-taking), attribution of one's one psychological characteristics to material objects (*animism*), and elevation of the products of one's own psyche (thoughts, dreams) to the status of real, material events visible to others (*realism*).

Summary: Constructivism and Empiricism

In summary, the constructivist perspective that has just been described and the empiricist perspective described previously have been the two major guiding theoretical influences leading up to the present-day study of cognitive development. The two perspectives differ from one another on a number of major dimensions. The constructivist views what it is that develops as the *internal cognitive system as a whole*, the central feature of which is the individual's "meaning-making" effort to understand his or her own actions and the external world. The empiricist views what it is that develops as independent *units of external, observable behavior,* each under the individual control of environmental variables.

With respect to how development occurs, the empiricist posits a *cumulative* process in which each new behavior unit is acquired independently through operation of the same basic mechanism of shaping by the environment. The constructivist posits a *bidirectional interaction* between individual and environment, leading to a series of major qualitative reorganizations in the cognitive system as a whole and reflecting progress in the individual's "meaning-making" enterprise.

The research strategy employed by the empiricist is a nondevelopmental experimental laboratory strategy devoted to examining the process by means of which an individual behavior is shaped by environmental contingencies. Empirical investigations are therefore devoted to detailed analysis of a single simple behavior. The research strategy employed by the constructivist is inductive, as well as developmental. The researcher samples a wide range of behaviors as a basis for hypothesizing the nature of the underlying cognitive system as a whole that is presumed to generate these behaviors. Cross-age comparisons are conducted as a basis for inferring changes that occur in the cognitive system.

It is probably because the two perspectives are so diametrically opposed that the study of cognitive development during the 1960s to a large extent became polarized into two camps, with a good deal of the research and theoretical writing during this period directed toward demonstrating the merits of one of the approaches and deficiencies of the other. Since then, serious weaknesses have become apparent in each of the approaches. As a result, at most only a few theorists or researchers studying cognitive development today would classify themselves as adhering to either the empiricist or constructivist perspectives in the pure forms in which they have described here. In turn, several new perspectives have evolved and gained adherents; while each of these new perspectives retains certain aspects of empiricism or constructivism, none is in such polar opposition to another as were the original constructivist and empiricist perspectives that preceded them. Let us turn now to the weaknesses that became apparent in the empiricist and constructivist perspectives.

THE LIMITS OF EMPIRICISM

It has been suggested by some observers that researchers who conducted studies of children's learning and memory in the 1950s within the empiricist tradition that dominated at the time had no interest in childhood per se, but rather used children as subjects of convenience to investigate the processes of learning that were the real focus of their interest. Whether this claim is justified or not, a sizeable accumulation of such research supported a conclusion that gained wide acceptance: The basic mechanisms of learning function in an identical way across species and across humans of different ages. A psychology of learning is therefore applicable to children and adequate to explain development.

The Study of Learning

Subsequent research has forced a modification of this basic conclusion. The most influential series of studies, by Kendler and Kendler, originated directly in the discrimination-learning paradigm prevalent at the time. (See Kendler & Kendler, 1975, for an interesting historical review of this work.)

An example of the stimuli and reinforcement contingencies used in the basic experimental paradigm is shown in the left column of Fig. 5.2. Reinforcement is always administered if the response is made in the presence of either of the two top stimuli (designated +) and is never administered if it is made in the presence of either of the bottom stimuli (designated −). This initial "training" phase of the experiment continues until the subject reaches a preestablished criterion of some number of errorless trials—that is, repeated presentations of the four stimuli during which the subject always makes the response in the presence of a reinforced (+) stimulus and never in the presence of a nonreinforced (−) stimulus. This basic experimental paradigm was employed with quite diverse types of subjects, and so the response and reinforcement themselves might be anything from a lever press and a food pellet in the case of an animal to verbal responses and reinforcers in the case of a college student.

At this point the training phase of the procedure ends and the test phase

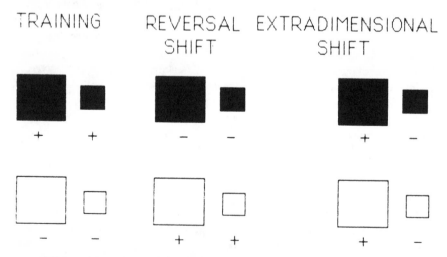

FIG. 5.2. An example of the stimuli and reinforcement contingencies used in the basic experimental paradigm.

begins. The stimuli remain unchanged during the test phase; only the reinforcement contingencies associated with them change. The contingencies are changed in one of two ways. One of the ways (labeled *reversal shift*) is portrayed in the center column of Fig. 5.2. The other (labeled an *extradimensional shift*) is portrayed in the right column of Fig. 5.2. The question of interest is how long it takes the subject to learn the new response so as to reattain the criterion of errorless responding; that is, to respond consistently in the presence of the + stimuli and never in the presence of the − stimuli. In particular, which of the two altered contingency patterns portrayed in Fig. 5.2 should result in more rapid learning, in other words more rapid reattainment of the criterion? Readers unacquainted with this research may wish to study Fig. 5.2 and make their own prediction before reading on.

Classical empiricist theories of learning yield a clear prediction. The response (or nonresponse) to each stimulus is regarded as an associative bond that is built up as a function of the reinforcement contingencies. When the shift to the test phase occurs, at least some of these bonds must be relearned. The number of such bonds that need to be relearned, however, depends on the type of shift. The reader can verify from Fig. 5.2 that in one case (extradimensional shift), only two bonds must be relearned; the other two remain unchanged. In the other case (reversal shift), in contrast, all four must be relearned. It can be predicted, therefore, that the former will be easier to master.

Kendler and Kendler compiled substantial evidence confirming this prediction in the case of animals and young human subjects (less than 6 years of age). Uncharacteristic of researchers studying learning, however, they also studied subjects at a range of different age levels, including adulthood. They discovered that older subjects performed contrary to the learning theory prediction: For them, the reversal shift was easier to relearn than the extradimensional shift.

The inability of traditional learning theory to account for the performance of older subjects in these experiments led the Kendlers to develop a new, modified theory that they termed *mediation theory*. What the older subject is learning in the training phase of the experiment, the Kendlers proposed, is not a set of discrete associations between stimuli and responses, but rather a covert (internal) "mediational" response. In the instance portrayed in Fig. 5.2, for example, a subject may in effect say to herself, "Oh, it's the color that matters; the size has nothing to do with it." This covert response mediates, or controls, the overt responses (that is, responding in the presence of the black stimuli and inhibiting response in the presence of the white stimuli). The Kendlers initially emphasized the verbal nature of these mediating responses; that is, it was verbal labels that could be applied to the stimuli (size, color; black, white) that older subjects had learned and verbalized to themselves during the experiment. Subsequently, however, the Kendlers broadened their theory somewhat to regard mediating responses as any covert symbolic responses the subject makes to common features of the stimuli.

If older subjects do indeed make mediational responses during the training phase, then the predicted relative difficulty of the two kinds of shift changes. In the extradimensional shift, not only the overt responses but the covert mediating response must be relearned (e.g., size instead of color). In the reversal shift, only the overt responses must be relearned (e.g., respond to white, not black). Therefore, the reversal shift should be easier, exactly what the Kendlers found for subjects above the age of 5 or 6.

The Kendlers therefore proposed what was in effect a developmental theory of learning. The traditional model of formation of discrete stimulus–response bonds characterizes the learning of children until the age of 5 or 6. At about this age children develop mediational learning capacity, and at this point the mediational model becomes a more accurate description of the learning process. The historical significance of the Kendlers' formulation of mediation theory is twofold. First, their theory represented a refutation of the behaviorist maxim that the basic learning process functions in an identical way across the life cycle. How an individual learns, the Kendlers' work indicates, depends on the individual's developmental level; as a result learning cannot be studied independent of development.

Second, mediation theory represented a departure from the behaviorist maxim that observable behavior is the only proper object of scientific study, and that it is not fruitful to postulate unobservable internal constructs that mediate this observed behavior. The Kendlers' work indicated that speculating about internal processes was in this case the only route to an adequate conceptualization of the external behavior that was observed. By not doing so, one ran the risk of serious misinterpretation. In the shift experiments, the achievement of laboratory rats, 5-year-olds, and college students appears equivalent at the end of the training phase (though one group may require more trials to reach the criterion than another). Performance of the respective subject groups during the test phase, however, indicates that the learning that takes place during the training phase, though it appears equivalent in its external manifestations, is actually quite different across subject groups. A theory that makes reference to the processes underlying these seemingly equivalent observable performances seemed the only way to explain the differences in performance that the subsequent test phase revealed to be present. In other words, the Kendlers' work pointed to the importance of a distinction that would become critical in future work in cognitive psychology: the distinction between product (performance) and the process that generated it.

The Study of Memory

Some notable parallels exist between historical developments in the study of learning and historical developments in the study of memory, to which we now turn our attention.

Memory as Storage. From the empiricist perspective that dominated psychology in the 1940s and 1950s, learning and memory were two sides of a single coin. As an example, recall the paired-associate paradigm discussed earlier. *Learning* refers to the process by which the associative bond (between the two nonsense syllables) is formed; *memory* refers to the retention or storage of that bond, once it has been formed. Because the stimuli are meaningless to the subject—that is, because the subject has no prior history of associations to them—they were considered as the ideal medium through which to study the basic processes of learning and retention in their pure form. By employing these elementary, "neutral" stimuli, basic properties of the human learning and memory apparatus might be identified. For example, how many exposures are required for an association to be formed, and what is the organism's storage capacity for associations, once formed? From such a perspective, the only role that development might play in the operation of memory processes is to increase the individual's storage capacity. Memory, then, could be regarded as a set of storage compartments that become larger with age.

Memory as Construction. Memory became a popular research topic in the 1960s, and many laboratory studies of it were conducted with both children and adults as subjects. The findings from much of this research, however, were difficult to reconcile with the concept of memory as a storage of associations, or of development as the expansion of storage space. Consider, for example, memory for an arrangement of chess pieces on a chessboard after a subject studies the board and it is then removed. One might anticipate that studies of this nature would provide indices of the capacity of the human visual memory system. Such estimates, however, have been found to be dependent on the subject's familiarity with the stimulus material, and on the constraints imposed on the stimulus material to be remembered; that is, whether the pieces are arranged on the board randomly or in a pattern conforming to the rules of chess. If the arrangement is random, chess experts and nonchess players show equal memory capacity; if the arrangement is legitimate, however, chess experts display greater memory capacity than nonchess players, even when the chess experts are children and the nonplayers adults (Chi, 1978). Other studies have shown exceptional memory capacity in very young children within domains in which they have a great deal of knowledge and experience (Chi, 1985, in press; Chi & Koeske, 1983). Thus, one cannot speak of any absolute memory capacity, even one that increases in an age-linked manner. It all depends on what it is that is being remembered, relative to the rememberer's existing cognitive system.

A great many other studies have suggested that, when processing a piece of information to be remembered, an individual does not store it in its intact form as an isolated unit. Instead, the individual assimilates the new information into a framework provided by the individual's existing knowledge, often altering or elaborating the new information in a way consistent with this existing knowledge base. In a series of studies, Paris and his coworkers asked children simple questions to assess their memory of short narratives. Even young children were willing to reply "yes" to a question such as "Did she use a broom?", the story having stated only, "She swept the kitchen floor" (Paris & Carter, 1973). Moreover, by the age of 9, children were able to recall a sentence such as the preceding one from the cue "broom" as effectively as from the cue "swept" (Paris & Lindauer, 1976), even though one had been explicitly and the other only implicitly present.

It appears, then, that individuals integrate new material into a framework provided by their existing knowledge and draw on this existing knowledge to make inferences that go beyond what is explicitly presented. As a result, newly acquired material cannot be clearly separated from what is already known. Memory, then, is more aptly conceptualized as a process of construction, or reconstruction, than as a process of storage. As such, it cannot be strictly separated from broader processes of reasoning and comprehension; that is, from the individual's more general "meaning-making" activity.

Memory and Development.   If memory is part of the broader cognitive system, then developmental changes in this system ought to have implications for memory functions. That this is the case has been demonstrated in both a narrow and a broad sense. In the narrow sense, the level of a subject's comprehension of material to be remembered should affect how and how well it is remembered. A simple demonstration of this influence has been provided by studies of children's ability to draw an ordered set of sticks of graduated length after they have viewed it and it is then removed (Inhelder, 1969; Liben, 1977). Children who do not comprehend the logic of asymmetrical relations (as indicated by their inability to construct a seriated array from a set of randomly ordered sticks of different lengths) have been found less able to draw a seriated array from memory after viewing one; instead they report very different-looking configurations as what they "remember" having seen (Fig. 5.3).

In the broad sense, transformations of the cognitive system ought to affect the memory function itself. A wide range of studies has been conducted indicating such developmental changes. The bulk of these have centered around the utilization of strategies to enhance memory. Organization of material to be remembered into conceptual categories, and rehearsal, for example, are both strategies that aid memory. Children below the age of Piaget's concrete operational stage show negligible use of these or other strategies to aid memory (Brown, Bransford, Ferrara, & Campione, 1983). For example, given a list of items to memorize containing foods, animals, toys, and items of clothing in a random order, older children and adults tend to recall the individual items within these superordinate categories; young children show no such organizational tendency in their recall. The absence of strategic devices in young children's performance on memory

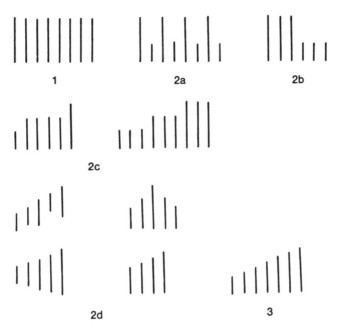

FIG. 5.3. Various arrays produced by subjects in Inhelder's studies of memory development in children (Inhelder, 1969).

tasks is further substantiated by the finding that young children perform equivalently in a memory task whether they are instructed to try to remember the presented items or simply to look at them (Flavell, Beach, & Chinsky, 1966). Later we consider further what governs the development and utilization of memory strategies and other kinds of cognitive strategies. The most important implication to note here is that, as the Kendlers' work demonstrated with respect to learning, memory functions cannot be studied without regard to the developmental status of the subject.

Summary: The Limits of Reductionism

In summary, we have traced the ways in which both the study of learning and the study of memory came to take on both a more cognitive and a more developmental cast. Neither learning nor memory can be studied profitably as a basic process that functions uniformly, independent of what it is that is being learned or remembered and of its relation to what the learner already knows. Given this to be the case, there are the two following implications for the study of the development of learning and memory, each of which has received considerable empirical support (Brown, Bransford, Ferrara, & Campione, 1983; Paris & Lindauer, 1982; Paris, Newman, & Jacobs, 1985; Siegler, 1983; Siegler & Klahr, 1982). First, developmental change in the cognitive system influences learning and memory performance in the narrow sense that the level of comprehension of new material affects how and how well it is both learned initially and remembered. Second, developmental change in the cognitive system affects learning and memory in the broad sense of influencing the learning or memory function itself, that is, the strategies the individual utilizes in executing the task.

Perhaps the most telling indicator of the evolution that has been described is that in contrast to the 1950s and 1960s, few current psychologists classify their work as devoted exclusively to the study of learning or memory. Instead, they tend to classify themselves as cognitive psychologists, interested in the study of the cognitive system as a whole. In some ways the evolution described here might be interpreted as a failure on the part of the principle of reductionism. As described earlier, the principle of reductionism and the related principle of parsimony led to the invocation of a single basic mechanism to account for acquisition of new behavior, irrespective of the behavior, the organism, or the relation between the two. The research reviewed here indicates that this assumption is incorrect. As a research strategy, reductionism dictated that very simple behaviors be isolated and studied independently. Once the acquisition mechanism governing these very simple isolated behaviors was understood, understanding of more complex and significant forms of behavior would follow. It is fair to say that this promise has not been realized. It is now largely accepted that the search for a single content- and context-free acquisition mechanism will not be fruitful, and that mastery of new cognitive material cannot be investigated independent of the broader context of the meaning the subject attributes to the material and to the task.

The implications for methodological practice are substantial. In the case of the paired-associate research paradigm described earlier, strong critics (e.g., Riegel, 1978) have characterized the studies themselves, not just the task material, as nonsensical and bound to have failed on the grounds that the learning that is observed is of no meaning or relevance to the learner; because such learning occurs completely out of any context, it cannot possibly provide insight into natural context-bound processes of learning. At a minimum, it has been established that context and meaning have a profound effect on performance (Paris, Newman, & Jacobs, 1985), an issue we shall further explore later on. Thus, studying the acquisition of arbitrary (meaningless) material in artificial settings offers at best limited insight into the acquisition of meaningful material as it occurs in complex, meaning-rich contexts. This limitation has been particularly severe in the study of memory development, in which work has been confined largely to the laboratory study of memory for arbitrary stimuli (Brown & DeLoache, 1978; Brown et al., 1983). The last decade, however, has seen an increasing concern with the investigation of cognitive functions and their development in contexts that are meaningful to the individuals being studied; this is a trend we shall have more to say about later on.

Even a rejection of reductionism, and the resulting theoretical and methodological concepts of a context-free acquisition mechanism, however, does not force a total repudiation of the empiricist view. A few theorists, such as Bijou and Baer, have retained an orthodox behaviorist perspective. More common, however, are the "neobehaviorist" formations proposed by the Kendlers and several others (Gagné, 1968; Gholson, 1980; Rosenthal & Zimmerman, 1978). Largely abandoned by the neobehaviorists are the refusal to speculate about internal processes, reductionism in its radical form, and the nondevelopmental research strategy. Common to all of the neobehaviorist formulations, however, is endorsement of the empiricist solution to the question of mechanism: Mind is shaped from without by the unidirectional effects of the environment.

THE LIMITS OF CONSTRUCTIVISM

Empirical evidence incompatible with the theory brought into focus the limitations of orthodox behaviorism as an explanatory framework for cognitive development. During the 1960s and 1970s, American developmental psychologists conducted extensive research related to Piaget's work, much of it disconfirming predictions derived from Piagetian theory. One might have expected, then, that this work would, in a similar way, have brought into focus the limitations of constructivism as an explanatory framework for cognitive development. In this case, however, matters are more complex, for it was not constructivism to which researchers principally addressed their studies, but rather Piaget's doctrine of stages.

Stages

The most straightforward prediction derived from stage theory is that the various behaviors that are the alleged manifestations of the underlying stage structure ought to emerge in synchrony, as indicators of the emergence of the underlying structure. In the case of the various behaviors alleged to be manifestations of the concrete operational structure, a large number of studies were performed that replicated Piaget's findings that these behaviors emerge in the age range of 6 to 8 years. Researchers then went on to investigate whether, within individual children, the behaviors appear synchronously at some point during this age period—an issue with respect to which Piaget himself had not reported empirical data. A substantial amount of data has now been collected; none of it has yielded strong evidence that concrete operational concepts, such as hierarchical classification, seriation, transitivity, conservation, and various forms of perspective-taking, emerge synchronously, even though they all appear during the same general age range.

In the face of such findings, some developmentalists came to Piaget's defense, objecting that Piagetian theory did not proclaim a precise synchrony but rather only emergence during a broader period of several years, by the end of which the various abilities had consolidated into the structured whole specified by the theory. Others objected on methodological grounds to the studies showing lack of synchrony: The set of tasks administered to a subject to assess the various concepts, they claimed, had not been equated with respect to their more superficial performance demands, having little to do with the concept itself. One assessment task, for example, may have been presented in such a manner that it made greater demands on the subject's verbal skills than did the other tasks, and for this reason display of the concept being assessed by this task was delayed relative to the concepts assessed by the other tasks.

This second objection, however, points to what is an even more fundamental problem for stage theory: Even slight and what one would expect to be insignificant modifications in task format can drastically alter the likelihood that subjects will exhibit the concept being assessed. For example, whether children will recognize the subclass as part of the class (class inclusion) in the example of roses and flowers given earlier is affected by the numerical ratio between the two. Thus, even *within* a single task or concept domain, whether the concept is judged to be present or absent depends to a considerable extent on particulars of the assessment procedure. The sizeable literature that accumulated on children's attainment of Piagetian concepts showed this to be the case for every one of the concepts investigated. Using one assessment procedure, for example, 30% of 6-year-olds might be assessed as having attained a particular concrete operational concept. Using a slightly different procedure, perhaps 70% of the same group of 6-year-olds would be assessed as having attained the concept. On what basis does one decide which procedure yields the "true" incidence of attainment?

These demonstrations of so-called task variance were particularly significant because they suggested that Piagetian assessment tasks were not "pure" measures of an underlying reasoning competency, in the way that Piaget's descriptions of them implied. Rather, a number of distinguishable skills appeared to be involved in successful performance on a task, many of which were not an integral part of the reasoning competency that was the focus of the assessment. Consider, for example, the concept of *transitivity*, alleged to be part of the concrete operational structure. Piaget theorized that once the child's mental actions involving relational comparisons of the form $A > B$ are organized into a reversible mental structure, such that $A > B$ is recognized as entailing $B < A$, this reversibility should enable the child mentally to construct a seriated array— that is, $A > B > C > D$—as well as to derive additional order relations from those given. For example, given $A > B$ and $B > C$, the child should be able to make the inference $A > C$. Because B is understood as participating in dual relations, in one as less than A and in another as greater than C, it can serve as the mediator linking A and C. Piaget referred to this inference as the inference of transitivity.

A number of subsequent studies of the transitivity inference, however, by

Trabasso, Bryant, and others (Bryant & Trabasso, 1971; Trabasso, 1975) aimed to demonstrate that there is more involved in making an inference of transitivity than the inference itself. Each of the individual relations—that is, A > B and B > C—must first of all be attended to and encoded by the subject. Each relation must then in some manner be represented and retained in the subject's cognitive system. Failure with respect to any of these steps would be sufficient to prevent the inference from being made, for example if the subject forgot one of the initial relations. The studies by Trabasso and Bryant endeavored to show that, if successful execution of these initial components were insured (for example, by exposing subjects to extended training with respect to the initial relations), children several years younger than the ages reported by Piaget would show successful performance on a transitivity task. Similar analyses of other concrete operational concepts have been proposed, such as, for example, an analysis of the class inclusion concept by Trabasso et al. (1978).

In addition to suggesting that multiple skills enter into performance on a Piagetian reasoning task, the Trabasso and Bryant studies were examples of the numerous so-called "training" studies conducted in the 1960s and 1970s; these are examined in more detail later, in a discussion of methods for studying developmental change. In these studies, attempts were made to induce a particular concept alleged to be part of the Piagetian stage structure by exposing children who had not yet attained the concept to some form of training in an experimental laboratory session. Whether the changes from pretest to posttest assessment that occurred in many of these studies were superficial or genuine became the topic of extended debate. At the very least, however, the studies demonstrated that with relatively minimal instruction children could be taught to display some of the behaviors characteristic of the stage structure they had not yet attained naturally, bringing into question the claim that such behaviors are integral parts of a structured whole.

All the forms of evidence described so far—evidence of asynchrony in emergence, of heterogeneous skills contributing to performance on assessment tasks, and of susceptibility of this performance to environmental influences—contributed to an increasing disenchantment with the Piagetian doctrine of stages during the 1970s. Positing a single, unified structure, the evolution of which is totally responsible for all of the more specific changes in intellectual functioning that occur over the course of development, appeared an oversimplification that did not fit with a growing body of research data. In a certain sense, stage doctrine in its strong form appeared to be a kind of reductionism of an opposite sort to that adopted by those working within the empiricist framework: Instead of the accumulation of large numbers of individually governed small behavioral units, development could be reduced to the evolution of a single, unitary, all-encompassing structure. For further discussion of the debate surrounding stage theory, the reader is referred to articles by Brainerd (1978) and Flavell (1982), and a volume by Levin (1986).

Further disenchantment with stage theory arose from the fact that Piaget's descriptions of the major stage structures such as concrete operations were not closely linked to the actual mental processes in which a subject might engage when responding to one of the typical assessment tasks. Rather, as was illustrated earlier, these structures were described in terms of formal logical models sufficiently abstract and removed from surface behavior that readers of Piaget's descriptions were left uncertain as to how such models might ever be validated as true portrayals of the individual's mental structure.

In the absence of satisfying answers to such questions, large numbers of developmental psychologists turned away from stage theory, in search of what they hoped would be more promising models of cognitive development. The problem came, however, in articulating what might replace stage theory. To conclude that the positing of a single unified structure as what develops is an oversimplification does not dictate the opposite extreme: that discrete competencies develop entirely independent of and unrelated to one another. The truth is almost certain to lie between these two extremes (Flavell, 1982). The central theoretical and research challenge, then, becomes one of characterizing the interdependencies that exist between developments that occur within distinct domains. But note that the question being posed is a question about developmental process: To what extent and in what manner do developmental changes that occur within domains interact with one another as they take place?

In many ways, theorists and researchers in cognitive development were not in a particularly strong position at that point to formulate theoretical models or research hypotheses regarding developmental process. As we have observed, Piaget's views with respect to developmental process had received relatively little attention from American developmental psychologists in favor of the derivative theory of stages. The tendency in many circles, then, was to discount Piaget's theory in its entirety in rejecting the stage doctrine. On the other hand there was little enthusiasm, following American developmental psychology's absorption with Piaget, to return to an empiricist conception of mechanism, which had become widely perceived as inadequate to deal with the complexity of human cognition and cognitive development.

I describe later in this chapter the directions in which the study of cognitive development did turn, following the disillusionment with Piaget's stage doctrine. First, however, it is important to consider the evolution that has occurred with respect to the understanding of developmental process, for during the field's preoccupation with stage theory, a few developmentalists continued to focus their attention on questions of process, or mechanism, and therefore on an examination of the merits of Piaget's constructivist hypothesis.

Constructivism

Questions about structures, it has been suggested, are really questions about the process of construction of such structures. It can be argued that the study of stages within American developmental psychology came to the dead end it did because one cannot study structures apart from the constructive processes that give rise to them.

Piaget, however, portrayed the constructive process in somewhat the same manner as he did structures, that is, in a very general, abstract form, and to some extent this mode of characterization has given rise to a similar set of problems. The process Piaget described was one in which the individual's own actions on the external world generate feedback that leads to the modification of those actions and their reorganization into new interrelations with one another. In other words, individuals themselves produce their own development (Lerner, 1982; see also Dixon & Lerner this volume). To many, this conception of developmental change seemed a welcome and desirable corrective to the empiricist view of the individual as the passive recipient of effects produced by the environment.

The effort of those who undertook to explore Piaget's constructivist model, either theoretically or empirically, however, led to articulation of two related weaknesses in the model. First, the actions generated by the individual's cognitive system that give rise to change are described by the model in such general abstract terms that it is not easy to draw on the model in conceptualizing the varieties of more specific, cognitively salient acts the individual engages in, and their likely influence on cognitive development. For example, cross-cultural findings indicating that conservation of quantity develops more rapidly in cultures that emphasize certain kinds of experiences (Newman, Riel, & Martin, 1983) are not incongruent with Piaget's model, but the model offers no way of predicting the effects of such specific variations in experience.

The second limitation, related closely to the first, is that in emphasizing the role of the individual's own self-generated actions, the constructivist model neglects the social context in which these actions, and therefore cognitive development, necessarily occur. The constructive process, whatever its precise nature, does not take place in a vacuum. In the course of their everyday experience, children encounter all sorts of implicit or explicit examples of the higher level concepts which they themselves will acquire. That does not imply that they internalize the examples to which they are exposed in any direct or automatic way. But it is equally unlikely that they systematically ignore them. Indeed, specific evidence is now accumulating to show that children attend to external models of higher level concepts in a sustained and deliberate manner (Morrison & Kuhn, 1983). The objective, then, must be to understand the specific ways in which the individual's constructive activity utilizes these external data.

Summary: Neoconstructivist Directions

The preceding discussion briefly traces the impact that Piaget's work has had on American developmental psychology from its introduction in the 1950s to the present day. During this period, American researchers collected data suggesting asynchrony in emergence of stage-related competencies, the contribution of heterogeneous skills to performance on assessment tasks, and susceptibility of this performance to environmental influence. All of these kinds of evidence contributed to a disillusionment with stage doctrine in its strong form—the doctrine that all of cognitive development can be accounted for by the evolution of a single, unitary structure. The lesser attention devoted to Piaget's more central constructivist hypothesis also revealed a set of serious problems and limitations, however, centering around the effects of specific forms of experience on the individual's cognitive development.

Faced with the limitations they perceived in Piaget's constructivist formulation, a number of developmentalists concerned with questions of process sought ways to modify or to expand on the Piagetian model to take into greater account the specific influence of the environmental context in which development takes place. Fischer (1980; Fischer & Pipp, 1984), for example, while maintaining many of the central features of Piaget's structuralism, has proposed a model in which new cognitive skills are at least initially wedded to the concrete contexts in which they are acquired; they are not the totally general, content-free acquisitions implied by Piaget's theory. Also, to a large extent in reaction to the neglect of social context in Piaget's constructivism, a renewed interest occurred in developmental theories originating within Soviet pscyhology, notably those of Luria (1976) and Vygotsky (1978). The Soviet perspective has had a substantial impact in recent years with respect to methodology as well as theory, as we discuss later. The attention of a large number of researchers in cognitive development, however, turned in another direction.

THE INFORMATION-PROCESSING APPROACH

The information-processing approach to the study of cognitive development is not as readily classifiable as have been the theoretical perspectives examined up to this point. The major reason is that by the admission of its own adherents, it is not a comprehensive theory of development or even of cognition but rather an approach to the study of cognition and, to a lesser extent, of its development. Thus, it does not take an explicit position on some of the questions a theory of cognitive development must address.

The Computer Metaphor

The origins of the information-processing approach are in cognitive rather than in developmental psychology. A major impetus for its development was the technological innovation of the modern electronic computer. At the heart of the approach is the concept that the human intellect may function as an information-processing system, of which a mechanical information-processing system—that is, the computer—is a fruitful model. How did it happen that this approach so rapidly attracted the attention and enthusiasm of a large number of developmental psychologists? It is not difficult to trace the major reasons.

Recall our earlier example of the transitivity inference. Piaget attributed the child's ability at the level of concrete operations to infer A < C, given the information A < B and B < C, to the underlying thought structure acquiring the characteristic of reversibility: The operation A < B entailed the reverse operation B > A, and B could thus be regarded as simultaneously greater than A and less than C, thereby serving as the mediator linking A and C. This explanation in terms of underlying logical structure, however, does not identify the specific mental processes by which the child produces a judgment of transitivity in a particular instance. And thus critics of Piaget's structural approach complained that there was no way to ever prove or disprove the correctness of such models as explanations of the child's behavior.

Moreover, researchers studying the transitivity inference identified a number of specific processes that must go into its correct performance such as encoding and retention of the initial relations. From such work it is only a short step to the suggestion that performance of a cognitive task is made up entirely of the serial execution of a number of individual processes such as these. The computer-inspired information-processing model from cognitive psychology offered a formal model of just such a possibility, for it is by means of such serial execution of operations that the computer functions. The guiding assumption underlying the model is that human cognitive functioning is composed of a set of individual processes that operate sequentially and that are not necessarily governed by the same principles of operation. The information-processing approach can be characterized, then, as one that focuses on these individual processes and the manner in which they operate individually and combine serially to produce the subject's performance.

What are these individual processes? The major source of influence in defining them has been the information-processing operations executed by a computer. Thus, it is assumed that information from the environment must be encoded and stored in symbolic representational form. Various processes then operate on the contents of this representation, manipulating and transforming it in ways that create new representations. These processes may be constrained by the fixed processing capacity of the system, and representations may be constrained by a fixed storage capacity. When processing is completed, output is generated in the form of a final performance, or solution to the problem.

A few information-processing psychologists have taken the computer metaphor quite literally, and have attempted to describe the cognitive operations generating a performance by means of a very exact and detailed model that could actually serve as a program enabling a computer to produce the performance. This approach has the attractive feature of containing a ready test of the model's sufficiency: Does the program successfully simulate performance on a computer? Klahr and Wallace (1976), for example, modeled performance of a number of the Piagetian concrete operational tasks, using as the basic elements of their models a collection of "condition–action" links termed "productions." In sharp contrast, however, to the study of "condition–action" (or stimulus–response) links by behaviorists of the 1950s, the work of information-processing psychologists like Klahr and Wallace is focused squarely on modeling those processes inside the "black box" that behaviorists sought to bypass. An example of the production system proposed by Klahr and Wallace to produce a transitivity judgment is shown in Fig. 5.4, which illustrates the extremely precise, detailed nature of such a model. Every minute aspect of the process must be represented explicitly or the model will fail to meet the sufficiency criterion. The computer cannot make any decisions itself that the program has left unspecified.

Klahr and Wallace's models were criticized by some as substituting one formalism (i.e., Piaget's models employing symbolic logic) with another; and indeed, following Klahr and Wallace's pioneering effort, only a few attempts to construct similar models appeared. A good deal of work followed, however, by researchers who endorsed the general spirit of Klahr and Wallace's approach without casting their models in the form of explicit computer simulations. Interestingly, these researchers continued to employ Piagetian tasks in their work,

```
03000   QUANTIFIER:(CLASS SUBIT COUNT ESTIMATE)
03100
03600   APPQUANT:(OPR CALL) simulate quant opr selection
03700            results in (GOAL * QQQQ(X)) where QQQQ
03800            is SUBIT, COUNT or EST
03900
04200   REL.WORD:(CLASS MORE LESS LONGER SHORTER BIGGER SMALLER EQUAL SAME)
07900
08000            transitivity rules
08100   PTRAN:((* GOAL TRAN(X QREL Y QREL Z) --> SAT (X ===> OLD X) SEREAD)
08200   PTR789:((* GOAL TRAN(X QREL Z)(X QREL Y)(Y QREL Z) --> MARKREL (X QREL Y QREL Z))
08300   PTR1:((* GOAL TRAN) (X QGT Y)(Y QGT Z) --> (X QGT Z))
08400   PTR2:((* GOAL TRAN) (X QLT Y)(Y QLT Z) --> (X QLT Z))
08500   PTR3:((* GOAL TRAN) (X QEQ Y)(Y QEQ Z) --> (X QEQ Z))
08600   PTR.RE:((* GOAL TRAN(X QREL Y)(Z QREL X) --> (NTC (Z QREL X)))
08700   PTR4:((* GOAL TRAN(X QGT Y) --> (X ===> OLD X)(Y Q< X))
08800   PTR5:((* GOAL TRAN(X QLT Y) --> (X ===> OLD X)(Y Q> X))
08900   PTR6:((* GOAL TRAN(X QEQ Y) --> (X ===> OLD X)(Y Q= X))
09000   PTRAN.FAIL:((* GOAL TRAN) --> (* ==> -))
09100
09200   MARKREL:(ACTION (NTC (X Y)(OLD **)(NTC (Y Z)(OLD **)
09300            (NTC (X Z)(OLD **))
09400   SEREAD:(OPR CALL) read series for desired relation
11400
11600            main productions
11700   P1A:((* GOAL GET.REL X Y)(X QREL Y) --> SAT (NTC (X QREL)(OLD **) SAY.IT)
11900   P1B:((* GOAL GET.REL Y X)(X QREL Y) --> SAT (NTC (X QREL)(OLD **) SAY.IT)
12100   P2:((* GOAL GET.REL(TS)X- GOAL CON) ABS --> (* GOAL CON))
12200   P3:((* GOAL GET.REL)X- GOAL TRAN) ABS --> (* GOAL TRAN))
12300   P4:((* GOAL GET.REL X Y) --> (* GOAL COMPARE X Y))
12600   P6A:((* GOAL COMPARE X Y) (X QREL Y) --> SAT)
12700   P6B:((* GOAL COMPARE X Y) (X QREL Y) --> SAT)
12800   P7:((* GOAL COMPARE X Y) (QS (X)) (QS (Y))   --> RELATE)
13100   P9A:((* GOAL COMPARE X Y)(VALUE X) -->(VALUE ===> OLD VALUE) (* GOAL QUANTIFY (X)))
13300   P9B:((* GOAL COMPARE X Y)(VALUE Y) --> (VALUE ===> OLD VALUE)(* GOAL QUANTIFY (Y)))
13500   P10:((* GOAL QUANTIFY (X)) (GOAL + QUANTIFIER (X)) --> SAT)
13600   P11:((* GOAL QUANTIFY (X)) --> APPQUANT )
14500
14700   PS.TRAN:(PTRAN PTR789 PTR1 PTR2 PTR3 PTR.RE PTR4 PTR5 PTR6 PTRAN.FAIL)
14800   PSM2:(P1A P1B P2 P3 P4 P6A P6B P7 P9A P9B P10 P11)
14900   PSEXEC:(PA PZ PSVERB PSVS PS.TRAN PS.CON PSM2 PQ)
```

FIG. 5.4.   PS.QC6, a model for quantitative comparison, including conservation and transitivity rules (from Klahr & Wallace, 1976).

and they began to include tasks from Piaget's formal operational stage as well as the concrete operational stage.

In an approach advocated by Siegler (1983), for example, the child's performance on a task is described by the "rule" to which that performance conforms. The rule specifies a sequence of acts that are performed in order to execute the task. A test of the adequacy of the rule in characterizing the child's behavior is the extent to which it predicts performance over a variety of specific task items. The most widely cited example is Siegler's (1976) rule-based model of performance on Piaget's balance scale task. The subject is shown a balance scale on which weights are placed at various distances from the center, and the subject must predict whether one or the other (or neither) side of the scale will go down following the removal of a supporting block. Siegler showed that the performance of 5- and 6-year-old children on such problems conformed to what he termed Rule I, in which only the number of weights is considered: Predict that the side with more weights will go down; if the weights are equal, predict balance. Older children's performance conformed better to Rule II—identical to Rule I except that in the case of equal weights, predict the side with weights at a greater distance from the fulcrum will go down—or to Rule III, which includes processing of both weight and distance information but lacks a consistent rule for integrating them. Not until mid- to late adolescence did a fully correct rule (Rule IV) begin to characterize some subjects' performance (consistent with Piaget's findings on this task). The major virtue of this kind of rule-based model of performance on a cognitive task is its explicit characterization of the sequence of mental operations the individual allegedly utilizes to execute the task.

A somewhat different approach originated with Pascual-Leone (1970) and later Case (1978a, 1978b, 1985). At the heart of their work is what they term "task analysis" of the operations a subject would have to perform in order to execute a cognitive task. An example is their task analysis of Piaget's isolation-of-variables task. In one form of the task, Piaget asked children and adolescents to experiment with a set of rods that differed on several dimensions (e.g., length, thickness, material) to discover what determined their flexibility. Not until early adolescence, Piaget found, do subjects employ an isolation-of-variables strategy: to hold the level on all other variables constant while systematically varying the level of one variable to assess its effect. Piaget linked this development to emergence of the cognitive structure of formal operations.

Based on his task analysis, Case (1978b) argued that what the subject needs in order to perform this task is very simple:

> All the subject must do is to identify an object with an extreme position value on the dimension to be tested (e.g., a long stick), then identify an object with an extreme negative value (e.g., a short stick), and then check to see if there is any *other* difference between these two objects that might affect the result of interest (e.g., bending). (p. 199)

Portrayed more formally, the subject must execute the set of procedures shown in Table 5.1 (from Case, 1978b).

The virtues of the information-processing approach to analyzing performance on cognitive tasks are readily apparent, and it is easy to see why the approach was particularly attractive to those developmentalists who had become disillusioned with Piagetian stage theory. In contrast to Piagetian models of cognitive competence—which seemed vague, abstract, removed from specific behavior, and unverifiable—information-processing analyses offered explicit, precisely articulated models of the series of cognitive operations a subject actually executes in performing a cognitive task. Less readily apparent, however, were several of the strengths of the constructivist approach that one sacrificed in adopting the information-processing approach. The reason this loss was less apparent has to do with what we have already noted with respect to the way American psychologists interpreted Piaget; that is, their focus on the theory of stages at the expense of the theory of constructivism.

A Return to Reductionism

The constructivist and information-processing perspectives differ radically in two respects. One is the information-processing perspective's explicit commitment to reductionism, in contrast to the constructivist perspective's explicit commitment to antireductionism, or holism. The other is the focus within the constructivist perspective on reflective aspects of cognition, in contrast to their de-emphasis within the information-processing perspective. Consider the issue of reductionism first.

The dual respects in which the modern-day information-processing approach is committed to reductionism closely parallel the respects in which the behaviorist approach of the 1950s and 1960s was described as committed to reductionism. First, in a theoretical vein, molar behavior is regarded as composed of a number of smaller, individually controlled elements. Second, in a methodological vein, the most fruitful research strategy is considered to be focused on a particular, well-specified task domain (such as our earlier example of paired-associate learning), which, once well understood, will permit generalization to broader (and more significant) domains of behavior. Piagetian theory and research strategy, of course, are notable, in contrast, as nonreductionistic—individual elements can be properly interpreted only in relation to the whole.

Methodologically, the result has been a series of exceptionally meticulous, detailed models of the procedures subjects employ in performing a particular task, ones that serve as pioneering examples in some sense of the precision to which psychological models might aspire. One of the major criticisms, however, that has been leveled against these task analyses of specific cognitive tasks pertains to their verifiability. Although closer to observable performance than Piaget's logical models, task analyses by no means constitute a magical key that

TABLE 5.1
Detailed Model for Control of Variables[a] (from Case, 1978)

Step or Operation	Specific Schemes	Symbol[b]
1. Identify the object with extreme positive value on the dimension to be tested (e.g., long).	(1) Operative scheme corresponding to the working definition of the positive pole of the dimension to be tested (e.g., for length, if the object sticks out the most, call it the longest).	ψ Dimension to be tested $(+)$
	(2)[c] Figurative scheme representing the array of the objects in the visual field.	ϕ Array
2. Identify the object with value at the other extreme of dimension to be tested.	(1) Operative scheme corresponding to the working definition of the other pole of dimension to be tested (e.g., for length, if the object is recessed the most, call it the shortest).	ψ Dimension to be tested $(-)$
	(2)[c] Figurative scheme representing the array of the objects in the visual field.	ϕ Array
3. Check to see if there is any difference between the two objects, other than the one to be tested.	(1) Figurative scheme representing the dimension to be tested.	ϕ Dimension to be tested.
	(2) Operative scheme representing the routine for scanning back and forth between the two objects and isolating any salient difference between them.	ψ Find difference
	(3) Figurative scheme representing object A.	ϕ Object A
	(4)[c] Figurative scheme representing object B.	ϕ Object B
4. If a difference is found recycle to Step 2.		
5. If no difference is found, conduct the test for property (i.e., see if object A > B on property of interest, e.g., bending).		

Note: Adapted from "Structures and Structures: Some Functional Limitations on the Course of Cognitive Growth" by R. Case, *Cognitive Psychology,* 1974, *6,* 544–573. Copyright 1974 by Academic Press. Reprinted by permission.

[a]Problem Question: Given a set of multidimensional objects with property X (e.g., bending), does dimension Y effect magnitude of X?

[b]ψ = operative scheme; ϕ = figurative scheme.

[c]Scheme activated by perceptual field. No M-power necessary.

unlocks the secret of how a correct (or incorrect) performance is produced. How do we know that a particular task analysis is correct? Researchers might collect converging behavioral evidence, such as eye movement patterns or reaction times, that are in accordance with what would be predicted by a given task analysis, but alternative hypotheses always remain possible. Indeed, researchers engaged in task analysis of cognitive tasks have tended to produce as many different analyses of a given task as there are analyzers of it. Empirical data have not as yet served in the role of *disconfirming* a task analysis that has been proposed.

Another criticism of task analysis and the information-processing approach more generally has been that it limits itself to proposing models of performance on specific tasks, and has not undertaken to integrate those models into a broader theory of human cognitive performance. Adherents of the information-processing approach, on the other hand, have defended this omission as a matter of appropriate sequence: Precise models of performance in very specific, restricted domains are alleged to be prerequisites for the formulation of broader, more comprehensive theories. Stated differently, the information-processing psychologist justifies, in the short term at least, sacrificing explanatory breadth for explanatory precision. Here again, the parallel to the historically earlier reductionist research strategy adhered to by behaviorists is clear. And so the debate over reductionism continues, with the information-processing approach assuming the proreductionist role.

Theoretically, the concept promoted by the information-processing approach—that multiple, largely independent processes are likely to be involved in performance of a cognitive task—has contributed valuably to thinking about cognitive development; it has served in particular, as an antidote to Piagetian stage doctrine, which treated performance as the manifestation of a single underlying stage structure. But the problem, and the reductionism debate, arises in deciding whether it is justified to go on to maintain that the performance is *nothing but* the serial execution of a specified set of individual processes, or whether some higher order organizing entity must be invoked. This brings us to the second major way in which the constructivist and information-processing perspectives differ.

The most serious criticism that has been lodged against the information-processing approach is that it has concerned itself predominantly with "strategy execution," and scarcely at all with "strategy selection." Consider for example Case's analysis of the isolation-of-variables strategy portrayed in Table 5.1. One can agree with Case that the sequence of strategies he specifies is not difficult to execute, and it is not surprising to learn that he was successful in teaching 8-year-olds to execute it (Case, 1974). But if not specifically directed to do so, how would an individual know that this set of strategies *ought* to be applied to such a problem? Without such knowledge, knowledge of how to execute the strategies is of limited value.

In comparison to knowledge of the first type—that is, knowledge of how to execute strategies, which is to a considerable extent ascertainable from the surface features of performance—knowledge of this second type is subtle and complex (Kuhn, 1983). In order to select a strategy as the appropriate one to apply in solving a problem, the individual must understand the strategy, understand the problem, and understand how the strategy and problem intersect or map onto one another, which entails understanding the range and limits of the strategy's appropriate application. In the case of the isolation-of-variables strategy represented in Table 5.1, such knowledge includes an understanding of (a) why the isolation or "all other things equal" method is the only means of achieving the task objective; (b) how and why each component of the strategy (such as ". . . check to see if there is any *other* difference between these two objects that might affect the result") constitutes an essential step in correct application; and (c) why any other strategy would not yield a correct solution.

To be convinced of the importance of this second kind of knowledge, one need only note that it is this knowledge that will determine whether or not an individual utilizes the strategy when an appropriate occasion arises in other situations, in the absence of direct instruction. It is the absence of such knowledge that is responsible for the common failures of generalization following training interventions: The subject learns the strategy in the particular context in which it is taught, but fails to apply it subsequently in other contexts in which it is equally appropriate. This problem of transfer of training, or more precisely failure of transfer, is one that has occupied psychologists from early (James, 1890) to modern times (Ferrara, Brown, & Campione, 1986).

Knowledge of one's own cognitive strategy as it applies to a task implies a *reflection on* the strategy that clearly differentiates it from *execution of* the strategy. The reader may recognize such a developing reflection on one's actions as at the heart of the constructivist account of cognitive development, originating with Baldwin and Piaget. It is just such reflection that is involved in strategy selection, to use the language of information-processing, but is difficult to incorporate into the information-processing model. Another way to characterize the distinction between execution of and reflection on a strategy is as a distinction between implicit and explicit knowledge of the strategy (Gelman, 1985; Kuhn, Amsel, & O'Loughlin, in press). A subject may be regarded as having implicit knowledge of a strategy if his or her performance reflects the use of that strategy or rule (e.g., the subject always predicts that the side with more weights will go down, in the balance scale example considered earlier). Implicit knowledge may exist only from the third-party perspective of an observer. Subjects whose performance reflects implicit knowledge of a strategy may or may not have explicit knowledge of it, as indicated both by their awareness that this is the strategy they are applying and by their ability to articulate this fact.

A slightly different aspect of this reflection on a strategy is implicated in another concept central to Piagetian theory, that of logical necessity. Consider once again the example of the transitivity inference. In the research by Trabasso and his colleagues described earlier, young children who did not show the transitivity concept were trained with respect to each of a set of individual relations, that is $A < B, B < C, C < D, D < E$, using a set of sticks of graduated lengths. It was hypothesized that subjects encoded and represented the set of relations as a visual image, that is, $A < B < C < D < E$. If so, this would explain how a child was able to answer questions about the relation between nonadjacent elements, for example, A and C, correctly: The child could simply refer to the internal pictorial array that had been formed, and produce the information $A < C$. These findings have prompted an extended debate as to whether such children had indeed been shown to have mastered the concept of transitivity (Breslow, 1981); and Piagetians were quick to make the distinction between an "empirical" judgment of transitivity and a judgment of transitivity that had the characteristic of logical necessity. In other words, the child just indicated might "read off" from her mental representation the fact that $A < C$; but it does not follow that she sees the relation $A < C$ as an inevitable logical necessity following from the relations $A < B$ and $B < C$, rather than as an empirical fact that happened to be true but could have been otherwise. The distinction is a difficult one to assess empirically, yet it is this logical necessity of the transitivity judgment that was the heart of the matter for Piaget. And such concepts of logical necessity can only come about as a product of reflection on one's own mental actions—in this case the mental actions of relating A to B and B to C.

Why is it that those utilizing an information-processing approach have tended not to focus on the processes of reflection on one's own cognition, processes that are the core of the constructivist perspective and that are implicated in the concept of logical necessity or the exercise of strategy selection? This neglect is most likely ascribable not to accident but to the fact that the information-processing perspective does not lend itself readily to the incorporation of this aspect of cognition, precisely because its underlying metaphor, the information-processing computer, does not—indeed cannot—reflect on what it is doing at a level differentiated from the "doing" itself. Unlike humans, computers do not "know" what they are doing. The computer can contemplate or evaluate its own actions only in the limited sense represented by the programmer specifying the operations that will constitute such an "evaluation;" for example, a condition—action link directing that processing be terminated once a certain set of conditions is met. But, again, such "evaluating" operations are not at a level distinct from the processing operations themselves.

Summary: Toward a Developmental Information-Processing Model

There are both strengths and limitations of the currently popular information-processing approach to the study of cognitive development. The major strength is the explicitness and precision with which it attempts to model specific kinds of cognitive performances. In addition, the information-processing approach is responsible for the concept that such performance is composed of a set of sequentially operating individual processes. This specificity and precision, however, are tied closely to a significant limitation—the scant attention that has been paid to integrating specific models into a broader theory of cognition and, particularly, cognitive development.

The major limitation that has been focused on is the lack of attention to what we have referred to as *reflective cognition*. If the information-processing approach is not to restrict itself unduly in explaining cognitive development, it can be argued that it will eventually have to go beyond a literal model of the computer to incorporate the reflective, or evaluative components of cognition and cognitive development. One indication of its need to do so is the frequent finding that subjects are able to execute all of the component strategies that a task analysis requires for performance, and yet the subjects do not assemble those components to produce the performance. Something else appears necessary for success.

This "something else" is often referred to as *metacognition,* that is, cognition about cognition. The term *metacognition* has been employed in such broad and diverse ways, however, that its usefulness as a scientific construct has been jeopardized (Forrest-Pressley, MacKinnon, & Waller, 1985). In its most general sense, the term metacognition has been used to refer to an "executive" function that selects, controls, and monitors the use of cognitive strategies, but it is often left unclear as to whether this function entails conscious awareness. Theorists who have an information-processing perspective and have concerned themselves with metacognition (e.g., Sternberg, 1984, this volume; Sternberg & Powell, 1983) have tended to regard metacognitive processes as functioning in an unconscious, automatic manner. This approach to metacognition thus does not incorporate the reflective aspects of metacognition—that is, individuals' reflective awareness of the cognitive operations they perform. The much earlier view expressed in Vygotsky's (1962) writing, in contrast, regards reflective awareness and deliberate control as the dual aspects of metacognition. The two can be regarded as describing the subjective (or *phenomenological*) and the objective (or *behavioral*) aspects of the same phenomenon: Someone aware of his or her own mental acts is able to reflect on those acts as objects of cognition, and is also likely to be able to access and apply them in a manner under voluntary control.

The rapidly increasing attention that is being addressed to metacognition and specifically to strategy selection (Paris & Oka, 1986; Pressley, Borkowski, & O'Sullivan, 1984; Siegler, in press; Siegler & Shrager, 1984; Sternberg, 1984) suggests a growing belief in the significant role it is likely to play in understanding cognitive development. What is necessary, however, is a fruitful conceptual and methodological framework in terms of which metacognitive processes can be studied, one that can accommodate the reflective as well as the control aspects of metacognition. Despite its centrality to his theory, Piaget's treatment of the topic has proven too abstract and divorced from specific contexts to be useful in generating much empirical research. At the same time, the computer model that underlies the information-processing approach, as we have noted, is not well-suited to capture the reflective aspects of metacognition.

One further limitation of the information-processing approach, that has only been alluded to until now, is one that has been widely noted and acknowledged by both adherents and critics of the approach—information-processing models offer no explanation of change. This limitation is obviously crucial if the approach is to provide an account of development. Why and how is the information-processing system modified over the course of development? However, information-processing is in good company here, for it is the mechanism of change that has proved the most difficult and formidable problem for all theories of cognitive development. Let us turn, then, to the more general question of mechanisms of developmental change.

MECHANISMS OF DEVELOPMENTAL CHANGE

Only a decade or two ago, it appeared that the question of mechanism in cognitive development was a clear-cut one. There were only two possibilities, and it seemed, moreover, that the data from a set of critical experiments would make it easy to choose between the two. Either the learning theorists were right, and the same basic processes of learning could account for development as well; or Piaget was right, and a small number of reorganizations of the cognitive system as a whole that occurred only a few times during the course of the individual's development were sufficient to account for all developmental change.

To decide between these two alternatives, it was thought, one needed only to conduct some so-called "training" studies. In the training study the investigator attempts to induce, via simple learning mechanisms, competencies held by Piaget to be manifestations of a global stage structure. If such studies were successful, the developmental process could be explained by simple learning mechanisms. If they were unsuccessful, Piaget's concept of global stage transformation would be implicated.

Remarkably, several hundred such training studies were carried out in the decade from the early 1960s to the early 1970s. Even more striking, the vast majority of these studies was devoted to inducing a single Piagetian competency, the conservation of quantity. The one thing that can be concluded about these studies is that they did not clearly decide the issue, and "the issue" indeed is now recognized to be much more complex than just portrayed. Many of the studies showed significant changes in children's performance on conservation tasks following training of a variety of different kinds, ranging from telling the children the correct answer ("The amount doesn't change") and rewarding them for making it, to more cognitively oriented attempts to get children to appreciate the logic that dictates the invariance. However, exactly what these results implied about how and why children shift during the natural course of development from believing that quantity varies with perceptual rearrangement to believing that it is invariant, is far from clear.

In what is perhaps the most widely cited conservation training study, one often praised as a model of elegant experimental design, Gelman (1969) claimed that young children fail to conserve because they do not attend to the relevant attribute—for example, to the number of elements rather than the length of the row in the case of number conservation. She demonstrated that by reinforcing children over many trials for choosing as "same" (as a standard) the row with the same number of items but different length (rather than the row of the same length by a different number of items), she could induce many of them to subsequently respond correctly in the standard conservation task; that is, to respond that the number of items in two rows remained the same after one of them was spread out so as to be of greater length than the other. In the terms used by Gelman, she taught such children to discriminate which of two possibilities (spatial magnitide or number) the term "same" refers to. Gelman, however, quite pointedly did not go on to draw from her findings the conclusion that natural attainment of the conservation concept involves "nothing but" (i.e., is reducible to) simple processes of discrimination learning and reinforcement. Nor have the many others who have cited her study seemed prepared to draw such a conclusion.

Exactly what conclusions are to be drawn from such studies, then, is far from clear. Much of the uncertainty can be traced to two major sources of ambiguity surrounding experiments that have utilized the training study methodology. First, many observers questioned the authenticity of the experimentally induced attainments: Had the child merely acquired the surface behaviors indicative of an understanding of conservation, or had some genuine change in understanding—that is, cognitive reorganization—taken place? Although much debate ensued, the matter was largely unresolvable inasmuch as opinion differed widely as to what conservation attainment in fact consists of: Is some underlying cognitive reorganization involved or merely the acquisition of a simple empirical fact or rule (e.g., quantity doesn't change through perceptual rearrangement)? In others words, what is it that is developing?

Even if these fundamental issues were agreed upon, however, and the experimentally-induced changes were accepted as genuine, a second and even more fundamental and troubling issue remains with respect to the method itself: the issue of *can* versus *does*. If a particular treatment is sufficient to produce a behavior in an experimental laboratory situation, it does not follow that the salient features of such a treatment are always, or ever, involved in the emergence of that behavior during the natural course of development. It is this second issue that is probably most responsible for the disillusionment with the training study as a tool for investigating mechanisms of developmental change. Perhaps the most striking testimony to its limitations is the fact that despite the 200 or more training studies of conservation conducted in the last three decades, there continues to exist a remarkably wide variety of theories regarding the process by which conservation is attained (Acredolo, 1981; Anderson & Cuneo, 1978; Brainerd, 1979; Pinard, 1981; Shultz, Dover, & Amsel, 1979; Siegler, 1981). Thus, the vast conservation training study literature has not significantly constrained our theories of the developmental process that underlies the attainment of conservation.

Multiple Dimensions and Mechanisms of Change

Along with abandoning the idea of training studies as providing a critical test of empiricist versus constructivist explanations of change, there came a gradual abandonment of the idea that either explanation could provide a comprehensive theoretical account of developmental change in cognitive functioning. One reason is that, following in part from work done within the information-processing approach, a considerably more complex picture of what it is that is developing has emerged—a ''what'' that encompasses a diverse set of competencies, rather than only a single entity. As a result, it is likely to require a more complex process, or set of processes, to explain that development. A range of possibilities exists with respect to what it is that may develop, including basic processing capacity, processing efficiency, processes of encoding and representation, knowledge, strategies, and metacognitive processes of strategy selection and regulation. Developmental changes in each of these conceivably could be governed by different mechanisms; moreover, changes in some (for example, processing capacity) might be invoked to account for changes in others (for example, strategy usage).

Processing Capacity. A possibility that is very attractive because of its simplicity is that the change responsible for most if not all advances in cognitive functioning with age is an increase in basic processing capacity, presumably as the result of neurological development. Thus, this alternative attributes cognitive development most directly to an underlying biological process of maturation. Pascual-Leone (1970) and Case (1985) have advanced separate versions of an elaborate ''neo-Piagetian'' theory of cognitive development founded on the assumption of age-linked increase in absolute processing capacity. The fact that performance increases with age on tests of basic processing such as digit span appears to support such a view. A 3-year-old can repeat an average of only three digits, where a 10-year-old can repeat an average of six digits.

That such improvements in performance are attributable to increases in processing capacity, however, is extremely difficult, if not impossible, to prove since a number of hard-to-discount alternative explanations exist. In the instance of digit span, for example, the older child may be employing some strategic device, such as rehearsal or chunking, that the younger child is not. In other words, it is difficult to prove that children of the two ages are executing the task in exactly the same way, the only difference being that the older children have a quantitatively greater capacity. Furthermore, as discussed earlier, capacity is highly influenced by familiarity with the material: If the domain is one in which a particular child is highly experienced (e.g., chess boards), that child's recall performance may exceed that of much older children less familiar with the domain. Similarly, Case and his colleagues demonstrated that the capacity of adults drops to that of 6-year-olds if the adults are required to execute a digit memory task using a newly learned set of digit symbols (Case, Kurland, & Goldberg, 1982).

Processing Efficiency.   Case (1985) has argued, in opposition to Pascual-Leone, that improvements with age in performance on tests such as digit span only appear to be the result of an absolute capacity increase. Actually, he claims, improved performance is ascribable to an increase in the efficiency with which basic operations, such as encoding, are executed; accordingly, less capacity is required for their execution. This leaves the individual with a greater remaining "functional" capacity for holding the products of those operations in memory, even though total capacity remains unchanged. In support of his view, Case cites recent evidence that performance on measures of basic operations—for example, counting an array of objects—becomes faster and more efficient with age, making plausible his view that such increases in efficiency are at least in part responsible for increases in functional capacity and hence in performance on processing tests such as digit span. Whether the fundamental change is one of processing efficiency, as Case claims, or of total processing capacity, as Pascual-Leone claims, both argue that such change itself is a function of underlying neurological development; Case raises the possibility, however, that experience of a very broad general sort may also contribute to increased efficiency.

An issue even more crucial to debate, however, is the extent to which age-related increases in processing capacity (whether absolute or only "functional") underlie all forms of developmental change in cognitive functioning, as both Case and Pascual-Leone claim. The fact that performance on measures of basic processing improves with age has been established, as previously indicated. But we also know that cognitive functioning changes developmentally in many other ways. Children acquire new, qualitatively different strategies they did not have previously: they integrate existing strategies in new ways, they encode new and different kinds of information and represent it in new and different ways, and they develop new forms of executive, or metacognitive, control over their cognitive functioning. Most developmentalists today would agree with the view that increases in basic processing efficiency and/or capacity are implicated at most as necessary conditions for many of these other kinds of changes. But they fall far short of being by themselves sufficient to explain how these changes come about.

Let us turn then to these other kinds of changes and the mechanisms that may underlie them.

Encoding and Representation.   Another factor that undergoes developmental change, and might account for improvements in performance on many kinds of cognitive tasks, is improved encoding and representation of information essential to successful execution of the task. No matter how efficiently they are developed, operations cannot be performed on material that has not been attended to, encoded, and in some manner represented within the cognitive system. Siegler (1976; Siegler & Klahr, 1982) demonstrates this point nicely in the case of the balance beam task described earlier: At a certain level children encode information about weight but do not encode information about distance of the weight from the fulcrum, as evidenced by their ability to reproduce weight but not distance information in tests of recall. The encoding of distance information is an obvious prerequisite to the execution of the more advanced strategies in which distance is taken into account, although Siegler's work does not prove that it is a change in encoding behavior that causes the change in strategy. Conceivably, the causal relation is the reverse: The child's intent to use a new strategy leads the child to encode new kinds of information.

Knowledge.   Still another factor that clearly undergoes developmental change is the particular knowledge the child possesses within specific content domains. The growth of domain-specific knowledge was long ignored by developmental researchers, or considered incidental to, or a by-product of, what were presumed to be more fundamental changes in modes of cognitive processing and strategy use. Yet older children have acquired a much larger knowledge base than have younger children, with respect to virtually any content domain in which we might examine their cognitive functioning. Is it not likely that these variations in knowledge play a role in the difference in performance observed across age groups? Keil (1981, 1984) has argued that the acquisition of domain-specific knowledge in fact plays the major role in developmental change, and that more general changes in process or strategy play a lesser role. In research on the ability to understand metaphors (Keil, 1986), for example, he notes that very young children are able to understand metaphorical relations between certain domains (e.g., animal terms and automobiles, as in "The car is thirsty"), but that relations between other domains are comprehended only at a much later age (e.g., human food consumption and reading, as in "She gobbled up the book"). Based on such evidence, Keil argues that what is most significant developmentally is not the ability to understand metaphor—that is, the juxtaposition of semantic fields—itself, but the gradual extension of this ability to new semantic fields, in a sequence that Keil argues is predictable from an analysis of the structure of those fields. Consistent with his emphasis on domain-specific knowledge, Keil (1984) advocates a research approach in which the investigator focuses attention on the structure of the knowledge that is acquired, and from this analysis makes inferences about how transitions in cognitive development occur, rather than searching for general mechanisms of change. The approach taken by Chi (1978) in her research on memory for chess boards, described earlier, is similar in its emphasis to Keil's, as is the view expressed by Glaser (1984). Carey (1985) makes an argument for the even stronger position that all of cognitive development is reducible to changes in domain-specific knowledge. Critics of the domain-specific view, such as Sternberg (1984, 1985), claim that proponents of this view—in their zeal to correct what they see as the neglect of domain-specific knowledge and overemphasis on general strategies in prior work—are guilty of the reverse overemphasis. What produces variations in the knowledge base individuals have acquired? Or, to put the question in its most fundamental form, what are the *processes* by means of which knowledge is acquired? This question leads inevitably to a consideration of strategy.

Strategy Execution.   How does an individual come to use new or modified strategies in performing a cognitive task? Constructivist accounts traditionally have emphasized the role of self-regulatory mechanisms within the individual: The individual gradually constructs a more adequate, comprehensive, and better equilibrated set of cognitive operations to be applied to the external world. But, as noted, such accounts have tended to minimize the role of the external environment. Within some versions of the constructivist account, exposure to material reflecting the higher level structure toward which the individual is developing is a necessary condition for change; other theories within the constructivist framework hold to the more radical position (reflected in Piaget's writings) that the individual literally constructs anew each more advanced mode of cognitive functioning based on the discrepant feedback produced by actions executed at the existing level. According to this formulation, then, simply the functioning of the cognitive system leads to its modification, a view endorsed by theorists operating from such disparate frameworks as Piaget (1971) and Klahr and Wallace (1976).

This stronger version of constructivism ignores the fact that models of the more advanced concepts or strategies the individual will acquire are often prevalent in the individual's environment, as emphasized by the Soviet theories of Luria and Vygotsky mentioned earlier. Case's (1978b) work on the isolation-of-variables strategy suggests that an individual can be taught to execute this strategy through social facilitation, at least in a laboratory context. The role of social influence in its acquisition in natural contexts is another question. But the role of both these processes (individual construction and social facilitation) must be considered in positing an explanation of how an individual masters execution of a new strategy. Even though external models are not directly or automatically internalized, it is most unlikely that they are systematically ignored.

Strategy Selection and Regulation.   With respect to one final factor, the individual's metacognitive decision to utilize particular strategies, the power of social facilitation is less clear. An individual might be instructed successfully in exactly how to execute a particular strategy and even be instructed regarding the conditions under which it is appropriate to apply the strategy, provided these conditions can be well specified. But whether the individual will choose to use the strategy in contexts that are not identical to the instructed one is more problematic. For example, children might be taught to use rehearsal to facilitate memory and yet not employ the strategy in their own activities, a finding that has, in fact, been reported by Paris and Lindauer (1982). As was suggested earlier, whether or not a strategy is selected in noninstructed, natural contexts is likely to depend on individuals' metacognitive understanding of the strategy itself; that is, their understanding of their own actions. In other words, the individual must understand the value and significance of the strategy as well as how to execute it, and the acquisition of this appreciation, or metacognitive understanding, is likely to be the more difficult, complex attainment of the two.

Piaget proposed that the mechanism underlying the development and application of new strategies was *equilibration,* the functioning of which he described only in rather general and formal terms. Strategies become consolidated and coordinated with one another through exercise. The feedback from this exercise, however, causes the individual to perceive the limitations of these strategies; and it provides the impetus, or *disequilibrium,* necessary for the construction of new strategies that will be more adequate for dealing with the tasks encountered and so leave the organism in a state of improved equilibrium with its environment. Several information-processing theorists have undertaken to introduce a developmental mechanism into their models by describing such a process in the language of information-processing (Klahr, Langley, & Neches, 1986), although this language, as we noted earlier, is constrained by the fact that it does not readily incorporate the reflective aspects of cognition that are very likely to be involved in developmental change. Klahr and Wallace (1976) were the first to attempt such a model. They described a self-modifying production system with features such as consistency detectors, which lead strategies to become more efficient. Case (1984, 1985) likewise has described a process whereby a set of strategies becomes modified during the course of their own functioning. Such efforts, however, have tended only to describe such a process, in a language very different from Piaget's. What is most important now are models that can generate new, testable hypotheses about how the process operates.

Summary: New Approaches to Studying Change

Two major factors have been discussed that have limited progress in understanding the mechanisms of developmental change. One is the lack of satisfactory methods of empirical investigation. The other is the scarcity of specific hypotheses amenable to empirical testing. On the positive side is the fact that we now have a considerably more sophisticated conception of what it is that is developing and, as a result, of the mechanism—or, more likely, *mechanisms*—that will be necessary to account for this development.

Also on the positive side is the fact that in recent years, after being diverted by a number of subsidiary issues such as the existence of stages, current developmentalists of virtually every theoretical orientation have identified a better understanding of the process of change as their primary objective; and a great many of them have begun to focus their research efforts on investigating the mechanisms of developmental change. In particular, researchers interested in both learning and development have begun to explore the use of new "microgenetic" methods as means of obtaining detailed observations of the process as it occurs. These methods differ markedly from the classical training study methodology discussed earlier in that the focus is on the change process itself, rather than on pretest and post-test performance.

Microgenetic methods show promise in affording insight into the change process, although the approaches used do not fit into traditional categories of research methods. Lawler (1985), for example, observed a single subject over several months during the course of which the child mastered some elementary mathematical concepts. His observations led him to emphasize as a central feature of the process the integration of strategic knowledge that initially functions within isolated, unintegrated domains. Similarly, Kuhn and Phelps (1982) observed preadolescent subjects in repeated encounters with a problem-solving task over a period of months. Most subjects' progress, they found, occurred only very gradually and involved prolonged use of both less and more advanced strategies in conjunction with one another. It was during this period of observation, Kuhn and Phelps proposed, that the subject was gaining metacognitive understanding of which strategies were effective and why, as well as gaining practice in the execution of the more advanced strategies. Their observations also pointed to an aspect of the change process that has been largely ignored. The most formidable problem for subjects appeared to be not the acquisition and consolidation of new strategies but rather the ability to abandon old, less adequate strategies, which is a reversal of the way development has typically been conceived. Other current approaches to the microgenetic study of developmental change are reflected in work by Karmiloff-Smith (1984) within a constructivist framework, and in work by Paris and his colleagues (Paris, Newman, & McVey, 1982) within an information-processing framework; the work by Paris also points to the importance of metacognitive regulation of strategy usage.

COGNITIVE DEVELOPMENT IN CONTEXT

The evolution in methods for studying mechanisms of change that has been described arose out of recognition of the need to study processes of development in contexts as similar as possible to those contexts in which they occur naturally, if the inferences made on the basis of such study are to be valid. In a similar way, the field of cognitive development regarded more broadly has in the last few years moved in a direction that reflects this concern.

In part this movement reflects a reaction to the shortcomings that have been perceived in theories and methods that have not concerned themselves with context. These shortcomings have been noted in the preceding sections of this chapter—the futility of the search for context-free processes of learning and memory; the vulnerability of assessments of Piagetian stage level to task effects; the indifference of constructivist accounts of development to children's specific experiences; and the task-boundedness of information-processing models of cognitive performance. In a more positive vein, however, the increasing attention given to context is attributable as well to the influence of two disparate schools of thought and research, one focused on the relation of culture and cognition and the other on cognitive development across the life span. Although the two can be regarded as possessing common roots in the philosophical school of contextualism (Dixon & Lerner this volume), they are both relatively new to developmental psychology and thus far have existed largely independent of one another. They both, however, have contributed to what has been termed the new functionalism in cognitive development theory and research (Beilin, 1984).

Culture and Cognition

Populations containing large numbers of unschooled children, adolescents, and adults seemed to provide an ideal means for investigating the effects of schooling on cognitive development. A number of large-scale cross-cultural studies of cognition that were undertaken had as their major purpose the identification of these effects. These studies, however, turned out to be much less decisive than had been hoped. Sharp, Cole, and Lave (1979) reported the inferior performance of unschooled subjects from a non-Western culture on a wide range of cognitive tasks. These authors, however, were quick to realize the limited interpretability of their findings. The kinds of tasks administered to their unschooled subjects were by and large identical or related to the kinds of tasks and activities that schooled individuals engage in at school (activities such as categorization and memorization). Little could be inferred on the basis of such findings, then, beyond the conclusion that experience in performing school-related skills enhances the performance of those skills. The nature of cognition among unschooled individuals remained an embarrassingly open question.

Exactly the same dilemma was recognized as applying within as well as across cultures (Rogoff, 1982). A Soviet study by Istomina (1977), for example, has been widely cited as demonstrating the critical importance of assessing cognitive performance in contexts that are familiar and meaningful to the subjects being assessed. In Istomina's study, preschoolers asked to memorize a list of items remembered, on the average, only half as many items as they remembered when asked to retrieve the same set of items from a make-believe grocery store. Istomina's study has subsequently been criticized as reflecting an over-simplified conception of the role of context and as being perhaps itself only replicable under a limited range of cultural and contextual conditions (Weissberg & Paris, 1986). A number of different contextual and motivational features of the two conditions no doubt influence subjects' performance in each of these conditions. The important point remains, however, that cognition and cognitive development must be examined in the context of cognitive activities that are meaningful and salient in the lives of the individuals being investigated, if valid conclusions are to be drawn. The appropriate unit of investigation, it has been suggested, should become cultural (and subcultural) practices, not psychological tests and experiments (Laboratory of Comparative Human Cognition, 1983).

Researchers working within this contextualist perspective have been attracted to the theories of the Soviet psychologists Vygotsky (1962, 1978) and Luria (1976) because of their emphasis on the effects of the culture on the individual. It is the child's first social relations, and in particular the resulting exposure to a language system, that give rise to mental development, according to the Soviet view. The mode of such transmission is social interaction: What starts out as interpersonal regulation—for example, a mother guiding her child in performing a task the child is unable to do alone—gradually becomes intrapersonal regulation: The child becomes capable of regulating his or her own actions to produce the performance, without external guidance. Wertsch (1979, 1984) has conducted interesting observational studies of this process as it occurs during the course of a mother assisting her child in a task. The influence of the Vygotsky/Luria perspective in recent developmental work has been an important one, as it balances Piaget's emphasis on the role of individuals in producing their own development. In emphasizing the external influences stemming from social interaction, however, the Soviet view neglects the complementary part of the individual–environment interaction; that is, the role of the individual. Little attention is given to how children attribute meaning to the social interactions they are involved in, and how this attributed meaning mediates the process by which society affects mind. Descriptions of the shift from interpersonal to intrapersonal regulation in parent–child interaction provide an insightful conceptualization of how parents structure their behavior in efforts to aid the child, but they provide less insight into the cognitive processes that enable the child to make use of the adult's input.

Cognition and Adulthood

The situation confronting the researcher interested in cognitive development during the 80% of the life span that remains after childhood is in many ways similar to that of the cross-cultural researcher. For a number of converging reasons, studies of cognitive development have traditionally stopped at roughly the point in the life cycle when both biological maturation and universal schooling cease. For most individuals beyond this point, school-related tasks are no longer a significant part of their everyday activities, yet such tasks are the only tools researchers have to assess their cognitive functioning. In contrast to the study of child development, studies of adult cognition and cognitive development lack the advantage of a meaningful anchor in either biology or the cultural universal of schooling. Nor is there any other readily apparent anchor or unifying concept with respect to the intellectual life of adults that could serve as a point of departure for such studies.

Developmentalists who first undertook to study the course of cognitive functioning across the life span understandably did not wish to add the burden of new, unvalidated measures to the already considerable set of methodological challenges they faced. As a result, the bulk of our present knowledge about cognitive development in adulthood is based on adult performance on the measures of cognitive functioning that have received the most extensive examination by psychologists, those associated with the psychometric assessment of intelligence. These also, of course, happen to be measures whose origins lie in the prediction of school performance. Some of the findings from these developmental studies have led to increasing uneasiness about the measures themselves.

Life-span developmental psychology (Baltes, Reese, & Lipsitt, 1980; Dixon, Kramer, & Baltes, 1985) undertook as one of its initial missions the seemingly straightforward task of assessing whether, during the course of adulthood, normative age-related changes in intellectual performance occur that are not attributable to sampling, testing, or historical (cohort) factors. Not only does this seemingly fundamental question remain unanswered but most life-span developmental psychologists have come to the view that it is not the right question to ask. Several consistent findings from the life-span study of performance on psychometric tasks have led to this conclusion. The major such finding is one regarding the substantial effects of cohort. In other words, the accumulated historical experience common to members of a particular cohort makes that cohort membership an equally or more powerful predictor of performance than is the predictor of chronological age. These results have led theorists in the life-span movement to postulate a model that includes several sources of influence on life-span development, age-graded influences, history-graded influences (unique to cohorts), and nonnormative influences (unique to individuals).

A second major finding has been that of substantial plasticity in the performance of adults, especially older adults, on psychometric tasks. Simple practice over an interval of time is often sufficient to improve the performance of older adults dramatically (Blieszner, Willis, & Baltes, 1981; Schaie & Willis, in press). This finding has led to serious questioning of the validity of these measures in providing accurate or meaningful assessments of normative intellectual functioning across the adult years of the life span. Specifically, psychometric assessment measures have been criticized as youth-centered (Baltes & Willis, 1979; Schaie, 1978)—that is, developed for the purpose of measuring intelligence in the early part of the life cycle and, subsequently, applied to the testing of intellectual functioning in older persons regardless of their appropriateness for those age groups.

These two major findings from life span research on intellectual functioning have led to two related developments in the life-span research program. One development is a recognition of the need to base assessment instruments for adult populations on the kinds of intellectual tasks that are salient in adult life (Willis & Schaie, 1986). In reality we have very little knowledge of the cognitive activities that are part of the everyday lives of the majority of adults who do not pursue scholarly careers. What are these activities and how well or poorly do average adults carry them out? Without such an "ecology of adulthood cognition," we do not have the knowledge that would allow us to evaluate the appropriateness of traditional laboratory tasks in the assessment of adult cognition across the life span.

The second development is a shift away from questions of normative age-graded intellectual functioning toward questions of range, modifiability, plasticity, and process with respect to intellectual functioning during the adult years (Dixon & Baltes, 1986). This shift reflects an acknowledgment of the substantial role of specific experiential factors (in contrast to inevitable, biologically governed aging) in intellectual functioning during the adult years of the life span. It is also closely linked to the shift toward more ecologically relevant measures. If specific experiences particular to individuals are accorded a major role, it becomes more essential than ever to attempt to assess their impact with respect to specific intellectual activities and functions that are significant in these individuals' lives.

Other psychologists not associated with the life-span group turned initially to Piaget—in particular to his stage of formal operations—as the most promising gateway to the study of adult cognitive development. Formal operations held the promise of a qualitative rather than quantitative approach to the assessment of cognitive functioning, and the reasoning strategies described by Inhelder and Piaget (1958) as reflecting formal operations appeared to possess the broad generality that made it likely they would be successful in characterizing an individual's reasoning across a wide range of everyday contexts. Moreover, all of the available data pointed to the conclusion that the stage of formal operations, unlike the earlier Piagetian stages, is not attained universally. This finding suggested both that significant variability in the use of formal operational reasoning exists within adult populations, and that a developmental perspective may be useful in understanding adult cognition. It seemed a simple matter to remedy the problem that Inhelder and Piaget's assessment tasks were drawn largely from the domain of physics, unfamiliar to most adolescents and adults. Familiar, everyday content could easily be substituted without altering the more general forms of the problems posed to subjects.

It soon became apparent, however, that the problem was a deeper one that would not be solved simply by recasting Piaget's tasks into "everyday" content

(Kuhn, Pennington, & Leadbeater, 1983). Doing so still leaves painfully open the question of the extent to which the *form* of reasoning that subjects are asked to engage in (irrespective of the content) is anything like the forms of reasoning they normally have occasion to engage in. To the extent this question remains unresolved, so does the significance of subjects' proficient or inferior performance. Thus we remain unable to say whether poor performance on such tasks reflects important deficits in adult reasoning, or whether it reflects the inappropriateness of the measures used to evaluate the cognitive competence that subjects possess. More broadly, it has come to be recognized that, both theoretically and methodologically, it is important to look beyond competence in formal logic to understand cognitive functioning in adulthood. Logic may play a quite different role in adult thinking than it plays in the thought of adolescents. As one researcher has put it, "Playful exercise of cognitive schemes, endless generating of 'ifs' and 'whens', no longer may be adaptive; the task becomes instead to attempt to utilize best one's knowledge toward the management of concrete life situations" (Labouvie-Vief, 1980, p. 153).

A case can be made for the value of a developmental framework in investigating the ecology of adult cognition. Some of the most interesting recent work that undertakes to examine the cognitive functioning of adults in ecologically valid contexts (Scribner, 1986; Wagner & Sternberg, 1986) has not been undertaken explicitly within a developmental framework. If a major goal is to understand the range, the modifiability, the plasticity of adult cognitive functioning, a developmental framework may be, if not essential, at least extremely illuminating: In what directions and toward what ends might adults' cognitive functioning be modified? The age relations in youthful samples can serve as a basis for ordering response patterns into an ordinal hierarchy of developmental levels. Often, a second criterion for such ordinal ranking exists: the adequacy, power, or validity of the reasoning reflected by different response patterns, on logical/rational grounds. To the extent the two orderings match, they reinforce one another in a bootstrapping fashion, even though neither one alone nor even both together "prove" the correctness or the validity of the ordering. A third is longitudinal data indicating sequential order of attainment. A fourth form of evidence is the predictive power of the ordered levels—that is, the extent to which knowledge of an individual's position in the ordering can predict performance in some external criterion domain—in the way, for example, that aptitude test scores predict school performance.

To the extent a particular sequential ordering receives validation by any combination of these means, it then can serve as a framework in terms of which performance variability in adult samples (which typically is not age-linked to any appreciable extent) can be conceptualized. In other words, administering the same set of measures to a combination of youthful and mature samples of subjects provides a framework for interpreting the performance of the latter. To be sure, such an approach provides not a set of answers with respect to understanding adult cognition but rather a set of questions—an investigative frame-work—in terms of which the cognitive functioning of adults can be examined.

PAST PROGRESS AND FUTURE DIRECTIONS

In this chapter I have described how the study of cognitive development has been conceived and conducted in American psychology over a period of almost half a century, culminating in the current emphasis on studying cognitive development and the mechanisms underlying it in ways that are sensitive to the contexts in which this development occurs, and to their effects on the developmental process. How might we summarize the progress that the evolution we have described reflects?

Evolution in Theory

One way to summarize this evolution is as the successive rejection of a series of explanatory mechanisms on the grounds of their being too simple to explain what a theory of cognitive development must account for—in other words, too simple to answer the question posed at the outset as underlying the study of cognitive development: How do mind and reality come to be coordinated with one another?

A biologically governed unfolding of developmental forms without regard to environmental influence is no longer taken seriously as a model of psychological development. The more recent hypothesis of a biologically governed, quantitatively increasing processing capacity has similarly been criticized as inadequate by itself to explain how and why cognition develops.

Similarly rejected as too simple to account for the complexity of cognitive functioning and its development are explanatory mechanisms that bypass the internal functioning that takes place within the organism. Influences of external variables on the developmental process are now widely accepted as mediated by characteristics internal to the individual.

Likewise rejected are simple acquisition mechanisms purported to function in an identical manner irrespective of the material being acquired and its relation to what is already known by the acquirer, and to the capabilities of his or her cognitive system. Put another way, it is now widely accepted that mechanisms of learning and retention do not function independently of the individual's intellect as a whole.

While the individual's intelligence, or active structuring of experience, is thus recognized, there also have been criticism and widespread rejection of explanatory mechanisms that attribute cognitive development to the progressive restructuring of this intelligence, as an activity of the individual that takes place isolated from social contexts that might influence it. Individuals develop in a social context of other individuals, and the interdependence of cognitive and social processes must therefore be acknowledged and investigated.

Parallel with this evolution in concepts of an adequate explanation of developmental process has been an evolution in concepts of what it is that is developing. The concept of isolated competencies that accumulate independently has been rejected as ignoring the crucial organizational features of behavior and knowledge. But likewise largely rejected has been the concept of a single structured whole that develops as an integrated entity and mediates all more specific components of cognitive functioning. A major contribution of the information-processing approach has been to highlight the fact that there exist a number of distinct cognitive functions each of which may undergo developmental change. A unique contribution of the constructivist perspective, on the other hand, and one difficult for the information-processing approach to encompass, is its focus on the reflective aspects of cognition and its development—and the "meaning-making" endeavor that such reflection is a part of.

The preceding summary conversely serves to prescribe the features a fully satisfactory explanatory account of cognitive development would need to possess:

1. It would need to refer to mental processes that take place within the organism, including those aspects of such processes referred to as reflective, or metacognitive.
2. It would need to characterize development as a gradual coordination of individual mind and external physical and social reality, in which neither internal nor external forces predominate over the other.
3. It would need to address the social contexts in which development occurs and the ways in which those contexts relate to individual development.
4. It would need to account for context specificity of cognitive attainments as well as trans-situational commonalities in cognitive functioning.
5. It would need to specify mechanisms by means of which developmental change occurs.

During the next several decades, theories that are proposed to account for cognitive development are likely to possess at least the preceding characteristics, as well as others not yet clear. That this is so serves as an indication that the field has progressed, despite the absence of an accumulation of the "hard facts" a reader of this chapter might have anticipated.

Evolution in Method

Not surprisingly, as the field of cognitive development has evolved in its theoretical sophistication, so has it evolved with respect to its methods, and this latter evolution also gives reason for optimism regarding the field's future. Just a decade or so ago researchers in the field of cognitive development could be portrayed, with some justification, as preoccupied with a narrow range of cognitive phenomena investigated in experimental laboratory contexts, where both phenomenon and context were of uncertain relevance to children's cognitive functioning and development in natural settings. Meanwhile, crucial practical decisions as to how children might be reared and educated so as to maximize their cognitive potential, and their productivity and fulfillment as adults, were left to others outside the academic enterprise.

Today such characterizations of the field of cognitive development are much less accurate than they were. As we have indicated, recognition has grown that context and meaning have a profound effect on performance, and increasingly researchers are undertaking to examine cognitive functioning within the natural contexts of meaningful activities engaged in by children—in school as well as in nonschool environments. Cognitive abilities such as reading are currently of great interest to cognitive and developmental psychologists to a large extent because of, rather than despite, their practical importance. The study of cognitive development in contexts not clearly linked to contexts in which that cognitive development occurs naturally constrains significantly the insight such study can yield. There are signs that developmentalists are beginning to take this admonition seriously and that the academic study of cognitive development in the future will not be as divorced from practical or "applied" concerns as it has been.

This issue of ecological validity has been highlighted even further by another trend of the last decade: The study of cognitive development is no longer limited to an exclusive focus on the childhood years. There are indications that it may be fruitful to conceptualize cognitive functioning in adulthood, and particularly the substantial individual variation in cognitive functioning among adults, from a developmental perspective. Parallel to what has been recognized to be the case in cross-cultural work, however, it has been apparent that it will be essential to study cognitive functioning among subjects other than children and in contexts that are meaningful and salient to the individuals studied, if our interpretations are to be valid.

This expansion of the traditional child-focused study of cognitive development to encompass the latter 80% of the life span promises benefits not only for our understanding of adult cognition but for our understanding of cognition and cognitive development during childhood as well. The process of cognitive development during childhood can be fully appreciated only to the extent that we understand the end points toward which it is evolving. The study of cognitive development as a process that takes place throughout life, then, will most likely enrich the conceptual perspectives that over the next several decades will succeed those that have been described in this chapter.

ACKNOWLEDGMENT

Preparation of this chapter was supported by the Redward Foundation.

REFERENCES

Acredolo, C. (1981). Acquisition of conservation. A clarification of Piagetian terminology, some recent findings, and an alternative formulation. *Human Development, 24,* 120–137.

Anderson, N., & Cuneo, D. (1978). The height and width rule in children's judgments of quantity. *Journal of Experimental Psychology: General, 107,* 335–378.

Baltes, P. B., Reese, H. W., & Lipsitt, L. P. (1980). Life-span developmental psychology. *Annual Review of Psychology, 31,* 65–110.

Baltes, P. B., & Willis, S. L. (1979). The critical importance of appropriate methodology in the study of aging: The same case of psychometric intelligence. In F. Hoffmeister & C. Muller (Eds.), *Brain function in old age.* Heidelberg: Springer.

Beilin, H. (1984). Functionalist and structuralist research program in developmental psychology: Incommensurability or synthesis? In H. W. Reese (Ed.), *Advances in child development & behavior* (Vol. 18). New York: Academic Press.

Bijou, S. (1976). *Child development: The basic stage of early childhood.* Englewood Cliffs, NJ: Prentice-Hall.

Bijou, S., & Baer, D. (1961). *Child development: A systematic and empirical theory.* New York: Appleton-Century-Crofts.

Blieszner, R., Willis, S. L., & Baltes, P. B. (1981). Training research in aging on the fluid ability of inductive reasoning. *Journal of Applied Developmental Psychology, 2,* 247–266.

Brainerd, C. (1978). The stage question in cognitive-developmental theory. *Behavioral and Brain Sciences, 1,* 173–213.

Brainerd, C. (1979). Markovian interpretations of conservation learning. *Psychological Review, 86,* 181–213.

Breslow, L. (1981). Reevaluation of the literature on the development of transitive inferences. *Psychological Bulletin, 89,* 325–351.

Brown, A., Bransford, J., Ferrara, R., & Campione, J. (1983). Learning, remembering, and understanding. In P. Mussen (Ed.), *Carmichael's manual of child psychology* (4th ed.). New York: Wiley.

Brown, A., & DeLoache, J. (1978). Skills, plans, and self-regulation. In R. Siegler (Ed.), *Children's thinking: What develops?* Hillsdale, NJ: Lawrence Erlbaum Associates.

Bryant, P., & Trabasso, T. (1971). Transitive inference and memory in young children. *Nature, 232,* 456–458.

Carey, S. (1985). Are children fundamentally different kinds of thinkers and learners than adults? In S. Chipman, J. Segal, & R. Glaser (Eds.), *Thinking and learning skills* (Vol. 2). Hillsdale, NJ: Lawrence Erlbaum Associates.

Case, R. (1974). Structures and strictures: Some functional limitations on the course of cognitive growth. *Cognitive Psychology, 6,* 544–573.

Case, R. (1978a). Intellectual development from birth to adulthood: A neo-Piagetian interpretation. In R. Siegler (Ed.), *Children's thinking: What develops?* Hillsdale, NJ: Lawrence Erlbaum Associates.

Case, R. (1978b). Piaget and beyond: Toward a developmentally based theory and technology of instruction. In R. Glaser (Ed.), *Advances in instructional psychology* (Vol. 1). Hillsdale, NJ: Lawrence Erlbaum Associates.

Case, R. (1984). The process of stage transition: A neo-Piagetian view. In R. Sternberg (Ed.), *Mechanisms of cognitive development.* New York: Freeman.

Case, R. (1985). *Intellectual development: Birth to adulthood.* New York: Academic.

Case, R., Kurland, D. M., & Goldberg, J. (1982). Operational efficiency and the growth of short-term memory span. *Journal of Experimental Child Psychology, 33,* 386–404.

Chi, M. 1978). Knowledge structures and memory development. In R. Siegler (Ed.), *Children's thinking: What develops?* Hillsdale, NJ: Lawrence Erlbaum Associates.

Chi, M. (1985). Interactive roles of knowledge and strategies in the development of organized sorting and recall. In S. Chipman, J. Segal, & R. Glaser (Eds.), *Thinking and learning skills* (Vol. 2). Hillsdale, NJ: Lawrence Erlbaum Associates.

Chi, M. (in press). Representing knowledge and metaknowledge: Implications for interpreting metamemory research. In R. Kluwe & F. Weinert (Eds.), *Metacognition, motivation, and understanding*. Hillsdale, NJ: Lawrence Erlbaum Associates.

Chi, M., & Koeske, R. (1983). Network representation of a child's dinosaur knowledge. *Developmental Psychology, 19*, 29–39.

Dixon, R., & Baltes, P. (1986). Toward life-span research on the functions and pragmatics of intelligence. In R. Sternberg & R. Wagner (Eds.), *Practical intelligence*. Cambridge: Cambridge University Press.

Dixon, R., Kramer, D., & Baltes, P. (1985). Intelligence: A life-span developmental perspective. In B. Wolman (Ed.), *Handbook of intelligence: Theories, measurements, and applications*. New York: Wiley.

Ferrara, R., Brown, A., & Campione, J. (1986). Children's learning and transfer of inductive reasoning rules: Studies of proximal development. *Child Development, 57*, 1087–1099.

Fischer, K. (1980). A theory of cognitive development: The control and construction of hierarchies of skills. *Psychological Review, 87*, 477–531.

Fischer, K., & Pipp, S. (1984). Processes of cognitive development: Optimal level and skill acquisition. In R. Sternberg (Ed.), *Mechanisms of cognitive development*. New York: Freeman.

Flavell, J. (1982). On cognitive development. *Child Development, 53*, 1–10.

Flavell, J., Beach, D., & Chinsky, J. (1966). Spontaneous verbal rehearsal in a memory task as a function of age. *Child Development, 37*, 283–299.

Forrest-Pressley, D., MacKinnon, G., & Waller, T. G. (1985). *Metacognition, cognition, and human performance*. Orlando, FL: Academic.

Gagné, R. (1978). Contributions of learning to human development. *Psychological Review, 75*, 177–191.

Gelman, R. (1969). Conservation acquisition: A problem of learning to attend to relevant attributes. *Journal of Experimental Child Psychology, 7*, 167–187.

Gelman, R. (1985). The developmental perspective on the problem of knowledge acquisition: A discussion. In S. Chipman, J. Segal, & R. Glaser (Eds.), *Thinking and learning skills* (Vol. 2). Hillsdale, NJ: Lawrence Erlbaum Associates.

Gesell, A. (1929). Maturation and infant behavior pattern. *Psychological Review, 36*, 307–319.

Gholson, B. (1980). *The cognitive-developmental basis of human learning: Studies in hypothesis testing*. New York: Academic.

Glaser, R. (1984). Education and thinking. *American Psychologist, 39*, 93–104.

Inhelder, B. (1969). Memory and intelligence in the child. In D. Elkind & J. Flavell (Eds.), *Studies in cognitive development*. London: Oxford.

Inhelder, B., & Piaget, J. (1958). *The growth of logical thinking from childhood to adolescence*. New York: Basic.

Istomina, Z. (1977). The development of voluntary memory in preschool-age children. In M. Cole (Ed.), *Soviet developmental psychology*. White Plains, NY: Sharpe.

James, W. (1890). *The principles of psychology* (Vol. 1). New York: Dover.

Karmiloff-Smith, A. (1984). Children's problem solving. In A. Brown & B. Rogoff (Eds.), *Advances in developmental psychology* (Vol. 3). Hillsdale, NJ: Lawrence Erlbaum Associates.

Keil, F. (1981). Constraints on knowledge and cognitive development. *Psychological Review, 88*, 197–227.

Keil, F. (1984). Mechanisms in cognitive development and the structure of knowledge. In R. Sternberg (Ed.), *Mechanisms of cognitive development*. New York: Freeman.

Keil, F. (1986). Conceptual domains and the acquisition of metaphor. *Cognitive Development, 1*, 73–96.

Kendler, H., & Kendler, T. (1975). From discrimination learning to cognitive development: A neobehavioristic odyssey. In W. K. Estes (Ed.), *Handbook of learning and cognitive processes* (Vol. 1). Hillsdale, NJ: Lawrence Erlbaum Associates.

Klahr, D., & Wallace, J. (1976). *Cognitive development: An information-processing view.* Hillsdale, NJ: Lawrence Erlbaum Associates.

Klahr, D., Langley, P., & Neches, R. (Eds.) (1986). *Production system models of learning and development.* Cambridge, MA: MIT Press.

Kuhn, D., Amsel, E., & O'Loughlin, M. (in press). *The development of scientific thinking skills.* Orlando, FL: Academic.

Kuhn, D. (1983). On the dual executive and its significance in the development of developmental psychology. In D. Kuhn & J. Meacham (Eds.), *On the development of developmental psychology.* Basel: Karger.

Kuhn, D., Pennington, N., & Leadbeater, B. (1983). Adult thinking in developmental perspective. In P. Baltes & O. Brim (Eds.), *Life-span development and behavior* (Vol. 5). New York: Academic.

Kuhn, D., & Phelps, E. (1982). The development of problem-solving strategies. In H. Reese (Ed.), *Advances in child development and behavior* (Vol. 17). New York: Academic.

Laboratory of Comparative Human Cognition. (1983). Culture and cognitive development. In P. Mussen (Ed.), *Carmichael's manual of child psychology* (4th ed.). New York: Wiley.

Labouvie-Vief, G. (1980). Beyond formal operations: Uses and limits of pure logic in life-span development. *Human Development, 23,* 141–161.

Lawler, R. (1985). *Computer experience and cognitive development: A child's learning in a computer culture.* New York: Halsted.

Lerner, R. (1982). Children and adolescents as producers of their own development. *Developmental Review, 2,* 342–370.

Levin, I. (1986). *Stage and structure: Reopening the debate.* Norwood, NJ: Ablex.

Liben, L. (1977). Memory in the context of cognitive development: The Piagetian approach. In R. Kail and J. Hagen (Eds.), *Perspective on the development of memory and cognition.* Hillsdale, NJ: Lawrence Erlbaum Associates.

Luria, A. (1976). *Cognitive development: Its cultural and social foundations.* Cambridge, MA: Harvard University Press.

Martin, S. (1959/60). Rediscovering the mind of the child. *Merrill-Palmer Quarterly, 6,* 67–76.

Morrison, H., & Kuhn, D. (1983). Cognitive aspects of preschoolers' peer imitation in a play situation. *Child Development, 54,* 1041–1053.

Newman, D., Riel, M., Martin, L. (1983). Cultural practices and Piagetian theory: The impact of a cross-cultural research program. In D. Kuhn & J. Meachum (Eds.), *On the development of developmental psychology.* Basel: Karger.

Paris, S., & Carter, A. (1973). Semantic and constructive aspects of sentence memory in children. *Developmental Psychology, 9,* 109–113.

Paris, S., & Lindauer, B. (1976). The role of inference in children's comprehension and memory for sentences. *Cognitive Psychology, 8,* 217–227.

Paris, S., & Lindauer, B. (1982). The development of cognitive skills during childhood. In B. Wolman (Ed.), *Handbook of developmental psychology.* Englewood Cliffs, NJ: Prentice-Hall.

Paris, S., Newman, D., & Jacobs, J. (1985). Social contexts and functions of children's remembering. In C. Brainerd & M. Pressley (Eds.), *The cognitive side of memory development.* New York: Springer-Verlag.

Paris, S., Newman, R., & McVey, K. (1982). Learning the functional significance of mnemonic actions: A microgenetic study of strategic acquisition. *Journal of Experimental Child Psychology, 34,* 490–509.

Paris, S., & Oka, E. (1986). Children's reading strategies, metacognition, and motivation. *Developmental Review, 6,* 25–56.

5. COGNITIVE DEVELOPMENT **259**

Pascual-Leone, J. (1970). A mathematical model for transition in Piaget's developmental stages. *Acta Psychologica, 32,* 301–345.

Piaget, J. (1970). Piaget's theory. In P. Mussen (Ed.), *Carmichael's manual of child psychology* (3rd ed.). New York: Wiley.

Piaget, J. (1971). *Biology and knowledge.* Chicago: University of Chicago Press.

Pinard, A. (1981). *The conservation of conservation: The child's acquisition of a fundamental concept.* Chicago: University of Chicago Press.

Pressley, M., Borkowski, J., & O'Sullivan, J. (1984). Memory strategy instruction is made of this: Metamemory and durable strategy use. *Educational Psychologist, 19,* 94–107.

Riegel, K. (1978). *Psychology Mon Amour: A countertext.* Boston: Houghton Mifflin.

Rogoff, B. (1982). Integrating context and cognitive development. In M. Lamb & A. Brown (Eds.), *Advances in developmental psychology* (Vol. 2). Hillsdale, NJ: Lawrence Erlbaum Associates.

Rosenthal, T., & Zimmerman, B. (1978). *Social learning and cognition.* New York: Academic.

Schaie, K. W. (1978). External validity in the assessment of intellectual performance in adulthood. *Journal of Geronotology, 33,* 695–701.

Schaie, K. W., & Willis, S. (in press). Can decline in adult intellectual functioning be reversed? *Developmental Psychology.*

Scribner, S. (1986). Thinking in action: Some characteristics of practical thought. In R. Sternberg & R. Wagner (Eds.), *Practical intelligence.* Cambridge: Cambridge University Press.

Sharp, D., Cole, M., & Lave, J. (1979). Education and cognitive development: The evidence from experimental research. *Monographs of the Society for Research in Child Development, 44* (Serial No. 178).

Shultz, T., Dover, A., & Amsel, E. (1979). The logical and empirical bases of conservation judgments. *Cognition, 7,* 99–123.

Siegler, R. (1976). Three aspects of cognitive development. *Cognitive Psychology, 4,* 481–520.

Siegler, R. (1983). Information processing approaches to development. In P. Mussen (Ed.), *Carmichael's manual of child psychology* (4th ed.). New York: Wiley.

Siegler, R. (1981). Developmental sequences within and between concepts. *Monographs of the Society for Research in Child Development, 46* (Serial No. 189).

Siegler, R. (in press). Unities in strategy choice across domains. In M. Perlmutter (Ed.), *Minnesota symposium on child psychology* (Vol. 21). Minneapolis: University of Minnesota Press.

Siegler, R., & Klahr, D. (1982). When do children learn? The relationship between existing knowledge and the acquisition of new knowledge. In R. Glaser (Ed.), *Advances in instructional psychology* (Vol. 2). Hillsdale, NJ: Lawrence Erlbaum Associates.

Siegler, R., & Shrager, J. (1984). A model of strategy choice. In C. Sophian (Ed.), *Origins of cognitive skills.* Hillsdale, NJ: Lawrence Erlbaum Associates.

Sternberg, R. (1984). Mechanisms of cognitive development: A componential approach. In R. Sternberg (Ed.), *Mechanisms of cognitive development.* New York: Freeman.

Sternberg, R. (1985). All's well that ends well, but it's a sad tale that begins at the end: A reply to Glaser. *American Psychologist, 40,* 571–573.

Sternberg, R., & Powell, J. (1983). The development of intelligence. In P. Mussen (Ed.), *Carmichael's manual of child psychology* (4th ed.). New York: Wiley.

Trabasso, T. (1975). Representation, memory, and reasoning: How do we make transitive inferences? In A. D. Pick (Ed.), *Minnesota symposia on child psychology* (Vol. 9). Minneapolis: University of Minnesota Press.

Trabasso, T., Isen, A., Dolecki, P., McLanahan, A., Riley, C., & Tucker, T. (1978). How do children solve class-inclusion problems? In R. Siegler (Ed.), *Children's thinking: What develops?* Hillsdale, NJ: Lawrence Erlbaum Associates.

Vygotsky, L. (1962). *Thought and language.* Cambridge, MA: MIT Press.

Vygotsky, L. (1978). *Mind in society: The development of higher psychological processes.* Cambridge, MA: Harvard University Press.

Wagner, R., & Sternberg, R. (1986). Tacit knowledge and intelligence in the everyday world. In R. Sternberg & R. Wagner (Eds.), *Practical intelligence*. Cambridge: Cambridge University Press.

Weissberg, J., & Paris, S. (1986). Young children's remembering in different contexts: A reinterpretation of Istomina's study. *Child Development, 57,* 1123–1129.

Werner, H. (1948). *Comparative psychology of mental development*. New York: International Universities Press.

Wertsch, J. (1979). From social interaction to higher psychological processes. *Human Development, 22,* 1–22.

Wertsch, J. (1984). The zone of proximal development: Some conceptual issues. In B. Rogoff & J. Wertsch (Eds.), *Children's learning in the "zone of proximal development."* San Francisco: Jossey-Bass.

Willis, S., & Schaie, K. W. (1986). Practical intelligence in later adulthood. In R. Sternberg & R. Wagner (Eds.), *Practical intelligence*. Cambridge: Cambridge University Press.

Wozniak, R. (1982). Metaphysics and science, reason and reality: The intellectual origins of genetic epistemology. In J. Broughton & D. J. Freeman-Moir (Eds.), *The cognitive-developmental psychology of James Mark Baldwin: Current theory and research in genetic epistemology*. Norwood, NJ: Ablex.

6

Intellectual Development: Psychometric and Information-Processing Approaches

Robert J. Sternberg
Yale University

What is intelligence and how does it develop? As shown by Deanna Kuhn in the previous chapter, psychologists have tried to answer this question in many different ways. In this chapter, the focus narrows to a special concern for psychometric and information-processing approaches to intellectual development. The goal of this chapter is to describe these approaches and to summarize what we have learned from them.

THE PSYCHOMETRIC APPROACH

Psychometric conceptions of intelligence and its development have in common their reliance upon individual-differences data as a means of testing theories, and, in some cases, as a heuristic aiding the formulation of the theories. Psychometric researchers use techniques of data analysis to discover common patterns of individual differences across tests. These patterns are then hypothesized to emanate from latent sources of individual differences, namely, mental abilities.

Psychometric theory and research seem to have evolved along three interrelated but, nevertheless, distinguishable lines. These traditions have conveyed rather different impressions of what aspects of intelligence develop. The three traditions can be traced back to Sir Francis Galton, Alfred Binet, and Charles Spearman.

In his theory of the human faculty and its development, Galton (1883) proposed two general qualities that distinguished the more from the less gifted. The first was energy or the *capacity for labor*. The second was *sensitivity to physical stimuli*. James McKean Cattell brought many of Galton's ideas from England to the United States. Cattell (1890) proposed a series of 50 psychophysical tests, such as dynamometer pressure (the greatest possible squeeze of one's hand), rate of arm movement over a distance of 50 cm, the distance on the skin by which two points need to be separated for them to be felt separately, and letter span in memory. Underlying all of these tests was the assumption that physical tests measure mental ability.

Binet's conception of intelligence and of how to measure it differed substantially from that of Galton and Cattell, whose tests he referred to as "wasted time." To Binet, the core of intelligence was *judgment* (Binet & Simon, 1916a, 1916b). Binet and Simon measured judgment by tasks such as recognizing (a) verbal and pictorial absurdities; (b) similarities and differences; and (c) analogies and other inductive relations. Binet cited the example of Helen Keller as someone of known extraordinary intelligence whose scores on psychophysical tests would be notably inferior, yet who could nonetheless be expected to perform at a very high level on tests of judgment.

An alternative psychometric tradition—a more statistically based one—originated with Charles Spearman. Substance and method have rarely been as closely intertwined as in the investigation of intelligence in the tradition of Spearman. Indeed, use of the most widely accepted method of data analysis in differential psychology, factor analysis, has become almost synonymous with use of the psychometric (or differential) approach to intelligence. In factor analysis, one starts with a correlation matrix, and seeks to discover the latent structure underlying the matrix. The end products are factors. Factors are "categories for classifying mental or behavioral performances" (Vernon, 1971, p. 8). Factors provide one of a number of alternative descriptive systems for understanding the structure of mental abilities (R.J. Sternberg, 1980b). They give us a useful way of identifying constellations of individual differences that in some sense go together, whether because of commonalities in process, structure, content, or whatever.

Spearman's (1904) mislabeled psychometric theory of intelligence—the *two-factor theory*—proposes two kinds of factors of human intelligence (not just two factors). According to this theory, there are (a) a general factor, which pervades all intellectual performances; and (b) a set of specific factors, each of which is relevant to one particular task. Spearman believed the general factor arose from individual differences in levels of mental energy.

Louis L. Thurstone (1938), unlike Spearman, eschewed the notion of a general factor. He proposed a theory that tentatively included seven primary mental abilities. The abilities were verbal comprehension, number facility, memory, perceptual speed, spatial visualization, verbal fluency, and inductive reasoning.

J.P. Guilford proposed an extension of Thurstone's theory that incorporates Thurstone's factors (Guilford, 1967; Guilford & Hoepfner, 1971). It splits the primary mental abilities, however, and adds new abilities so that the number of factors is increased from 7 to 120. According to Guilford, every mental task requires three elements: an operation, a content, and a product. Guilford pictured the relation among these three elements as that of a cube, with each of the elements—operations, contents, and products—representing a dimension of the cube. There are five kinds of operations: cognition, memory, divergent production, convergent production, and evaluation. There are six kinds of product: units, classes, relations, systems, transformations, and implications. And there are four kinds of content: figural, symbolic, semantic, and behavioral. Because the subcategories are independently defined, they are multiplicative, yielding 5 × 6 × 4 = 120 different mental abilities. Each of these 120 abilities is represented by Guilford as a small cube embedded in the larger cube. The theory of 120 independent factors might seem implausible to some; indeed, the methodology Guilford (1967) has used to confirm his theory has been shown to be problematical in many respects when used in the way that Guilford used it (see Horn, 1967; Horn & Knapp, 1973).

A hierarchical model has been proposed by Vernon (1971). At the top of the hierarchy is g or general ability. At the second level are two major group factors, verbal–educational ability and practical–mechanical ability; at the third level are minor group factors; and at the fourth level are specific factors.

Psychometric Conceptions and Intellectual Development

Substantial literatures exist regarding the nature of intelligence and the development of intelligence as perceived from a psychometric point of view. Yet the two literatures are surprisingly autonomous: On the one hand, few of the major factor theorists of intelligence have given serious and detailed consideration to the place of intellectual development in their theories. On the other hand, few of the major developmental students of intelligence have given serious and detailed consideration, in their research, to the place of theories of the nature of intelligence. Despite notable exceptions (e.g., Horn, 1970; Stott & Ball, 1965), the literature on the development of intelligence has been very largely empirical in its orientation (see, for example, Bayley's 1970 review of the literature on the development of mental abilities); and some of the work has been almost entirely atheoretical (see, for example, Broman, Nichols, & Kennedy, 1975). Theory and data have thus been separated in the developmental literature, and the goal here is to provide a framework for interrelating work on the nature of intelligence with work on the development of intelligence. The basis for this integration is an enumeration of some of the possible loci of intellectual development in the factorial theories. The various loci are not mutually exclusive: To the contrary, it seems highly likely that multiple loci exist.

Changes in Number of Factors with Age.   One possible locus of intellectual development is in the number of abilities and, hence, of factors that constitute measured intelligence at different ages. Arguments in favor of change in number of factors as a locus of intellectual development usually take the form of differentiation theories. Although it is conceivable that intelligence could become either more or less differentiated with advancing age, the former position has been by far the more popular, and certainly more plausible, one. Perhaps the most noted proponent of this point of view has been Henry E. Garrett (1938, 1946). Garrett (1946) defined intelligence as comprising the abilities demanded in the solution of problems that require the comprehension and use of symbols. According to his developmental theory of intelligence, "abstract or symbol intelligence changes in its organization as age increases from a fairly unified and general ability to a loosely organized group of abilities or factors" (Garrett, 1946, p. 373). This theory has obvious implications for how various psychometric theories of intelligence might be interrelated. Again, according to Garret (1946):

> It seems to effect a rapprochement between the Spearman General Factor and the Group Factor theories [e.g., that of Thurstone, 1938]. Over the elementary school years we find a functional generality among tests at the symbol level. Later on this general factor of "g" breaks down into the quasi-independent factors reported by many investigators. (p. 376)

Several sources of evidence provide at least tentative support for the differentiation theory. Garrett, Bryan, and Perl (1935), for example, administered 10 tests of memory, verbal ability, and number ability to children of ages 9, 12, and 15 years. With one exception, intercorrelations among the three kinds of tests showed a monotone decrease between the ages of 9 and 12, and between 12 and 15, suggesting increasing independence of the abilities with age. A factor analysis of the correlations showed a decrease in the proportion of variance accounted for by a general factor with increasing age. Similar results were found by Asch (1936), who discovered a decrease in the correlation between verbal and numerical tests from age 9 to age 12. M. P. Clark (1944) administered an early version of the Primary Mental Abilities Test to boys of ages 11, 13, and 15 years and found that scores on tests of verbal, number, spatial, memory, and reasoning abilities showed decreasing correlations with increasing age. Other studies considered together (e.g., Schiller, 1934) also tend to support the hypothesis of a decrease in correlations with age. Reviewing the literature on changes in the organization of mental abilities with age, Bayley (1955) concluded that there was fairly substantial support for the differentiation notion.

In summary, one possible reconciliation among the various theories of the nature of intelligence is in terms of increasing differentiation of abilities with age. Theories postulating small numbers of important factors, such as Spearman's, may be relevant for younger children; theories postulating large numbers of factors, such as Thurstone's or conceivably Guilford's, may be relevant for older children and adults.

Changes in the Relevance or Weights of Factors with Age. A second possible locus of intellectual development is in the relevance or weights of factors as contributors to individual-differences variance in intelligence at different age levels. For example, a perceptual–motor factor may decrease in weight with age, whereas a verbal factor may increase in weight. Thus, it is not the total number of factors, but the importance of individual factors that changes with age. From this perspective, what makes one person more intelligent than another can be quite different across ages because the abilities that constitute intelligence can shift dramatically in their importance. Variants of this viewpoint have been very popular in the literature on the development of intelligence (e.g., Hofstaetter, 1954). Despite their differences, these variants have virtually all been consistent with the notion that abilities of the kind proposed by Galton, and by successors in his tradition, to constitute intelligence seem most relevant for infants and very young children; abilities of the kind proposed by Binet and successors in his tradition seem most relevant for older children and adults. These views, then, like the differentiation views, seem to point the way toward a developmental reconciliation of the theoretical positions. An interesting ramification of these views is that developmental theorizing becomes essential rather than adjunct to understanding theories of intelligence originally proposed for adults.

One of the most well-known data sets supporting the notion that factors change in relevance with age is that of Hofstaetter (1954). Hofstaetter factor-analyzed data from Bayley's (1933, 1943, 1949, 1951) Berkeley Growth Study, which assessed intellectual performance from infancy through adulthood. Hofstaetter found that up to 20 months of age, a first factor, which he named sensorimotor alertness, accounted for most of the individual-differences variance in children's performance on intelligence tests. From the age of 40 months onward, this factor accounted for practically none of the variance in mental-age scores. Between 20 and 40 months, the dominant source of individual-differences variance could be accounted for by a third factor that tapped manipulation of symbols or simply abstract behavior. Hofstaetter suggested that this factor corresponds to Spearman's (1927) *g*, but he further noted that it was only because of limitations in the data that the factor appeared to be unitary in nature. Hofstaetter concluded from his data that the nature of intelligence changes somewhat from one age to another. Semantic use of the term *intelligence* thus reflects the factors that show the highest weights at a given age level.

Bayley's own view of her data is very similar to that of Hofstaetter (1954). Like Piaget (1972), however, Bayley (1955) has emphasized how the abilities of greater importance in later life build upon the abilities of greater importance in earlier life:

Intelligence appears to me . . . to be a dynamic succession of developing functions, with the more advanced and complex functions in the hierarchy depending on the prior maturing of earlier simpler ones (given, of course, normal conditions of care). (p. 807)

For example, verbal tasks require perceptual processing for their completion.

Bayley (1933) identified six factors in the correlational data from her First-Year Scale, and six factors in the data from her Preschool Scale. Like Hofstaetter (1954), she found that the factors that contributed substantially to individual differences in measured intelligence varied with age (see, especially, Bayley, 1970, Fig. 4). She found a general tendency for the more complex factors of thought to become of greater importance to individual differences in intelligence with increasing age.

Stott and Ball (1965) factor-analyzed data from intelligence tests administered to children in the age range from 3 to 60 months. They used Guilford's (1956, 1957) structure-of-intellect model as the theoretical framework within which to interpret their results. Although they found significant loadings for 31 of Guilford's factors at one age or another, and although many factors appeared at multiple age levels, results for the younger age levels (especially below 1 year) included important other factors—such as gross psychomotor skills, locomotor skills, and hand dexterity—that did not fit into the Guilford model and that did not apply at the upper age levels. Thus, the Guilford factors appeared not to be relevant at all ages.

Changes in the Content (Names) of Factors Within a Given Factor Structure. Whereas the point of view discussed above suggests that the structure of mental abilities (or at least the factor structure important for generating individual differences) changes with age, the point of view considered here suggests that, for a given theory, structure stays essentially the same across age groups but the content that fills in this structure changes. For example, g, or general ability, might be conceived as perceptual–motor in nature at the infant level but as cognitive in nature later on. In each case, the factorial structure could be the same; that is, there is a single general factor, but the content of that factor differs across ages. The difference between structure and content is not always clear-cut, and we doubt that theorists propounding each of these positions differ; support for the preceding position requires a different factor structure at each age level, whereas support for the present position requires a different content filling in the structure at each level. Historically, proponents of this present position have tended to be most interested in the changing composition of Spearman's general factor at each level, but have found that what is general changes with age.

McCall, Hogarty, and Hurlburt (1972) factor-analyzed data from the Gesell Developmental Schedule administered to children participating in the Fels Longitudinal Study. Children were studied at 6, 12, 18, and 24 months of age. The authors were interested primarily in the first principal component (general factor) at each age level. They found that, at 6 months of age, items loading on this factor tended to measure visually guided exploration of perceptual contingencies. At 12 months, the factor reflected a mixture of sensorimotor and social imitation as well as rudimentary vocal–verbal behavior. The joint presence of sensorimotor and social imitation was interpreted as consistent with Piaget's (1972) notion that imitation mediates the transition between egocentric sensorimotor behaviors, on the one hand, and more decentered verbal and social behaviors, on the other hand. At 18 months, items loading on the first principal component reflected verbal and motor imitation, verbal production, and verbal comprehension. By 24 months, highly loading items measured verbal labeling, comprehension, fluency, and grammatical maturity. Again we see a transition between the types of behaviors studied by Galton (1883) at the lower levels and the types of behaviors studied by Binet and Simon (1916a, 1916b) at the upper levels. It is important to note that the items loading on the first principal component are factorially but not behaviorally unitary: Multiple behaviors are general across the tests that McCall et al. (1972) studied at each age level. Thus, they load on a single general factor. The authors interpreted their data as supporting what they and Kagan (1971) before them had called a "heterotypic" model of mental development. In such a model, there is a discontinuity in the overt developmental function (i.e., in people's rank orders at different ages, despite the differences in the behaviors of consequence). This model was contrasted with five other models that were not as well supported. One such model, for example, was a "homotypic" model, in which individual differences are purported to remain stable, as are the behaviors that generate the individual differences.

McCall, Eichorn, and Hogarty (1977) studied "transitions in early mental development" in much the same ways as had McCall and his colleagues in an earlier study (1972). In this study, however, the investigators used the developmental data from the Berkeley Growth Study, as had Hofstaetter before them. Whereas Hofstaetter factor-analyzed data across age levels, McCall et al. factor-analyzed data within age levels. The investigators interpreted their data (for infants) as supporting a five-stage model of intellectual development: During Stage 1 (birth to 2 months), the infant is responsive primarily to selected stimulus dimensions that in some sense match the structural predispositions of the infant's sensory–perceptual systems. Stage 2 (3 to 7 months) is characterized by more active exploration of the environment, although the infant's view of the world is alleged still to be completely subjective. At Stage 3 (8 to 13 months), means for doing things begin to be differentiated from ends. The separation is complete by Stage 4 (14 to 18 months), by which time the child is able to associate two objects in the environment without acting on either of them. Symbolic relationships emerge during Stage 5 (21+ months).

Changes in Factor Scores of Fixed Factors with Age.   The views expressed in the previous discussions are all ones of qualitative changes in the nature of intelligence with age. However, most of the voluminous literature reflecting the psychometric approach to the development of intelligence has dealt with quantitative changes and how to account for them. The preponderance of studies has been atheoretical, although the emphasis here is on theoretically motivated research.

Two basic findings in the literature that have needed to be accounted for are, first, that absolute level of intelligence (as measured, say, by mental age or a comparable construct) increases with age; and, second, that correlations between measurements of intelligence decrease with increasing intervals of time between measurements (see, e.g., Bayley, 1933, 1970; Dearborn & Rothney, 1941; Honzik, 1938; Sontag, Baker, & Nelson, 1958). An elegant attempt to account for these findings was made by J.E. Anderson (1940), who proposed that correlations of IQ at various ages with terminal IQ (perhaps at about the age of 16) increase because "the prediction of final status is based upon a larger proportion of that which is included in the total: that is, scores at 10 years include more of that which is present at 16 years than do scores at 3 years" (p. 388). Anderson suggested that the increase in overlap between final scores and successively later scores would be predicted by a model in which increments to intelligence are additive over the age span, and uncorrelated (or only modestly correlated) with each other and with the current level of intelligence. Anderson tested this simple model by reanalyzing data from the Harvard Growth Study (Dearborn, Rothney, & Shuttleworth, 1938) and the Honzik (1938) study. He compared mental growth curves from these data to Monte Carlo curves generated by cumulating the first to the sixteenth random numbers (where each number represented a "year" of mental growth) in a table of random numbers of 300 artificial subjects. In the random-number table, of course, successive increments in the accumulated sum are uncorrelated both with each other and with the current value of the sum. According to Anderson's model, the closer in time two measurements are made, the less time there has been for intervening changes to take place and, hence, the more highly related those two measurements will be. Fits of the data to the model were quite good, providing at least tentative support for the model.

Most of the research that has been conducted on quantitative development of intelligence has been consistent with Anderson's assumption that intelligence increases in absolute amount over age, and that one's goal should be to plot the form of this function and to account in some way for why the function takes this form. Bayley (1966, 1968), for example, plotted mental growth curves from infancy to 36 years on the basis of her data from the Berkeley Growth Study. Her findings were typical of this literature: Absolute level of intelligence increased fairly rapidly until early adolescence, showed some decrease in the rate of increase from early to middle adolescence, and then pretty much leveled off in middle to late adolescence. However, the assumption of a monotonic growth curve throughout the life span has been challenged as representing a composite of two different component functions, each of which is purported to show a different pattern of growth throughout the life span. The two component functions, in this view, represent what R. B. Cattell (1963, 1971) and Horn (1968) have referred to as *fluid* and *crystallized intelligence*.

Fluid and crystallized intelligence are proposed by R. B. Cattell (1963, 1971) and Horn (1968) to be subfactors of general intelligence (*g*). Fluid ability is best measured by tests that require mental manipulation of abstract symbols such as, for example, figural analogies, series completions, and classification problems. Crystallized ability is best measured by tests that require knowledge of the cultural milieu in which one lives such as, for example, vocabulary, general information, and reading comprehension. Horn and Cattell (1966) reported that although the mean level of fluid intelligence was systematically higher for younger adults than for older adults, the mean level of crystallized intelligence was systematically higher for older than for younger adults. In general, crystallized ability seemed to increase throughout the life span, whereas fluid intelligence seemed to increase up until the 20s and to decrease slowly thereafter.

Schaie (1974) questioned what he called the myth of intellectual decline, namely, that some or all intellectual functions decline after some point in adulthood. Schaie noted that the evidence on the question of decline is mixed. Cross-sectional studies have tended to support the notion of a decline (e.g., Jones & Conrad, 1933; Wechsler, 1939), whereas longitudinal studies have not (e.g., Bayley & Oden, 1955; Owens, 1953). Mixed designs suggest that the decline may be relatively small, on the average, with significant individual differences in just how large it is.

Conclusions

To conclude, developmental theories are of particular interest because they provide one kind of reconciliation between alternative psychometric theories of intelligence. For example, some abilities theorized by Galton to be important in intelligence do indeed appear to be so in infancy and perhaps for a few years thereafter. As infancy draws to a close, however, these abilities seem to become less important, and the abilities theorized by Binet and Simon (1916a) to be of consequence in intelligence seem to acquire greater importance. By adulthood, the latter kinds of abilities seem to be of much greater importance in measured intelligence, and probably in general adaptation to most adult environments, than do the former kinds of abilities. A reconciliation of sorts among some of the factor theories is also possible on the differentiation view, according to which the number and fineness of factors increase with age. The information-processing work described here elaborates on and provides a more complete account of just what aspects of intelligence develop.

THE INFORMATION-PROCESSING APPROACH

Information-processing conceptions of intelligence and its development have in common their reliance on stimulus (rather than subject) variation as their primary means for testing theories of intelligent functioning. Underlying all of these conceptions is a view of intelligence as deriving from the ways in which people mentally represent and process information. Information-processing researchers use techniques of data analysis, such as computer simulation and mathematical modeling, to discover patterns of stimulus variation that suggest strategies of information processing in tasks requiring the exercise of one's intelligence.

Information-processing research has used the computer program as a metaphor and a heuristic for understanding how humans process information. The major distinguishing feature of the approach, however, is not its reliance on computational notions but rather its concern with how information is processed during the performance of various kinds of tasks.

One of the earliest and most important articles propounding the information-processing approach was that of Donders (1868). Donders proposed that the time between a stimulus and a response can be decomposed into a sequence of successive processes, with each process beginning as soon as the previous one ends. The durations of these processes can be ascertained through the use of a subtraction method; that is, subjects solve each of two tasks proposed by the experimenter to differ only in that the more difficult task requires one more component process for its solution than does the simpler task. The duration of this process can then be computed by subtracting the time taken to solve the easier task from the time taken to solve the harder task. The subtraction method was popular for several decades (Jastrow, 1892) but then came into disfavor (Kulpe, 1895) because of the method's assumption of strict additivity: One had to assume that one could insert into, or delete from, a task a given process without somehow affecting the execution of other processes. This assumption seemed so unreasonable at the time (and still does to many people) that the method went into hibernation for about a century, until it was reactivated in modified form.

Almost 100 years later, two works (Miller, Galanter, & Pribram, 1960; Newell, Shaw, & Simon, 1960) appeared in a single year that revived the information-processing approach. The goal of both programs of research was, as Miller et al. put it, "to discover whether the cybernetic [computer-based] ideas have any relevance for psychology" (p. 3). Both groups of investigators concluded that they did have relevance, and, moreover, that the computer could be a highly useful tool in psychological theorizing. Miller et al. sought to understand human behavior in terms of Plans, wherein a Plan was defined as "any hierarchical process in the organism that can control the order in which a sequence of operations is to be performed" (p. 16). Critical for the information-processing approach was the authors' view that "a Plan is, for an organism, essentially the same as a program for a computer" (p. 16). The authors did not wish to confuse matters, however, by failing to distinguish altogether between computer and human information processing:

> We are reasonably confident that "program" could be substituted everywhere for "Plan" in the following pages. However, the reduction of Plans to nothing but programs is still a scientific hypothesis and is still in need of further validation. For

the present, therefore, it should be less confusing if we regard a computer program that simulates certain features of an organism's behavior as a theory about the organismic Plan that generated the behavior. (p. 16)

The Miller et al. (1960) and Newell et al. (1960) works proposed both theories of information processing and a methodology (computer simulation) for implementing and testing information-processing theories. Newell et al. (1960) proposed a General Problem Solver (GPS) computer program that could actually solve complex problems of the sort that give people considerable diffculty. Subsequent versions of the program (e.g., Ernst & Newell, 1969) could solve large numbers of problems (e.g., Missionaries and Cannibals, Tower of Hanoi, Water Jugs) by using just a small set of routines that were applicable across the entire range of problems. In summary, the computer simulation method allowed experimental psychologists to test theories of human information-processing by comparing predictions generated by computer simulation to actual data collected from human subjects. Some investigators have preferred to test their theories by using quantitative models with parameters estimated directly from the human data.

The Unit of Behavior

Whereas many psychometric theorists of intelligence have agreed on the factor as the fundamental unit in terms of which intellectual behavior should be analyzed, many information-processing theorists have agreed on the elementary information process as the fundamental unit of behavior (Newell & Simon, 1972). It is assumed that all behavior of a human information-processing system is the result of combinations of these elementary processes. The processes are elementary in the sense that they are not further broken down into simpler processes by the theory under consideration. The level of analysis that is considered to be "elementary" will depend on the type of behavior under consideration and the level at which the theory attempts to account for the behavior. The processes must be well defined, and the collection of them must be sufficiently general and powerful to compose all macroscopic performances of the human information-processing system (Newell & Simon, 1972).

R. J. Sternberg (1979, 1980b) has expanded the notion of the elementary information process by proposing that elementary information processes, or what he calls components, can be subdivided by function. Components can be distinguished on the basis of function into two basic and different kinds: *metacomponents* and *performance components*. Metacomponents are higher order control processes that are used for executive planning and decision making in problem solving. Metacomponents (a) decide just what the problem is that needs to be solved; (b) select lower order components to effect solution of the problem; (c) select a strategy for combining lower order components; (d) select one or more representations or organizations of information upon which the lower order components and strategies can act; (e) decide upon a rate of problem solving that will permit the desired level of accuracy or solution quality; and (f) monitor progress toward a solution. Performance components may be viewed as executing the plans and implementing the decisions laid down by the metacomponents. Performance components in a variety of tasks tend to organize themselves into four stages of strategy execution (R. J. Sternberg, 1981). One or more of these components are usually needed to (a) encode the elements of a problem; (b) combine these elements in the execution of a working strategy; (c) compare the solution obtained to available answer options; and (d) respond.

Intellectual development occurs through interactions of the components. The various kinds of components are thought to be interrelated in four basic ways. First, one kind of component can directly activate another. Second, one kind of component can indirectly activate another. Third, one kind of component can provide direct feedback to another kind of component. Fourth, one kind of component can provide indirect feedback to another kind of component. Direct activation (feedback) refers to the immediate passage of control or information from one kind of component to another kind. Indirect activation (feedback) refers to the passage of control or information from one kind of component to another via a third kind of component.

In the proposed system of interrelations, only metacomponents can directly activate and receive feedback from each other kind of component. Thus, all control *to* the system passes directly from the metacomponents, and all information *from* the system passes directly to the metacomponents. The other kinds of components can activate each other only directly, and they receive information from each other only indirectly; in each case, mediation must be supplied by the metacomponents. For example, acquisition of information affects retention of information, as well as various kinds of transformations (performances) on that information, but only via the link of the three kinds of components to the metacomponents. Feedback from the acquisition components can be passed to any other kind of component but only through the filter of the metacomponents.

Consider a typical empirical study of the components of information processing. Keating and Bobbitt (1978) took tasks studied by Hunt, Frost, and Lunneborg (1973) and Hunt, Lunneborg, and Lewis (1975) and studied them in the context of a developmental paradigm. Their self-stated major goal was to "discover whether reliable individual differences in cognitive processing exist in children and, if so, whether these differences are systematically related to age and ability" (Keating & Bobbitt, 1978, p. 157). Like Hunt and his colleagues, their primary interest was in individual differences in the component processes of information-processing activities, rather than in global response times or error rates reflecting a conglomeration of processes.

Keating and Bobbitt's experiments used 20 subjects in each of grades three (average age, 9), seven (average age, 13), and eleven (average age, 17). Half of the subjects at each age level were characterized as being of high mental ability (scores in roughly the 90th to 95th percentile of the Raven Progressive Matrices), and half were characterized as being of average mental ability (scores in roughly the 40th to 45th percentile of the Raven Progressive Matrices).

The authors were interested in the children's performance on three basic sets of information-processing tasks. The first set included simple reaction-time and choice reaction-time tasks. In the simple reaction-time task, subjects were instructed to press a button as soon as a red light appeared; in the choice reaction-time task, subjects were instructed to press a green button whenever a green light appeared or a red button whenever a red light appeared. Subjects did not know, of course, which color of light would appear on a given trial. The second set of tasks involved retrieval and comparison of information in memory. This set included two letter-matching tasks, a physical-match task, and a name-match task, based upon the tasks adopted by Hunt et al. (1975) from Posner, Boies, Eichelman, and Taylor (1969). In the physical-match task, subjects were asked to sort cards that had pairs of letters printed on them that either were or were not physical matches. Examples of the former would be "AA" and "bb"; examples of the latter would be "Aa" and "Ba." In the name-match task, subjects were presented with cards to sort that had pairs of letters printed on them that either were or were not name matches. Examples of the former would be "Aa," "BB," and "bB"; examples of the latter would be "Ab," "ba," and "bA." In the first task, the subject had to sort the cards by the physical appearance of the stimuli; in the second task, the subject had to sort by the names of the stimuli. The third set of tasks involved scanning sets of either one, three, or five digits held in working memory. In this task, which Hunt et al. (1973) adopted from the varied-set procedure of S. Sternberg (1969b), subjects are asked to store the short list of items in memory. This list thus becomes a memory set. Subjects are then presented with a target item and are asked to indicate as quickly as possible whether the target is one of the items in the memory set. For example, if the memory set were "3, 9, 6," an affirmative response would be required for "9," but a negative response would be required for "2."

The results of the experiments on the three sets of tasks generally confirmed Keating and Bobbitt's (1978) hypothesis of developmental differences. In the simple reaction-time and choice reaction-time tasks, the investigators found significant main effects of age, ability level, and task (simple or choice reaction time). In each case, means were in the expected direction, with older and brighter children performing the tasks more rapidly and with simple reaction time faster than choice reaction time. Of somewhat greater interest was a significant age-by-task interaction, whereby the difference between choice reaction time and simple reaction time was greater for younger children than for older children. The ability level by task interaction was nonsignificant, but in the expected direction, with lesser ability children showing a greater increment in choice relative to simple reaction time than was shown by higher ability children. Thus, increased task complexity affected the response times of children who were less able (at least as measured by age and possibly as measured by Raven score) more than it affected the response times of those who were more able.

In the letter-retrieval and comparison task, there were significant main effects of age, ability, and task (physical or name match). Again, the results were as expected; older and brighter children were faster in card sorting, and the name-match condition took longer than the physical-match condition. Again, there were significant age-by-task and ability-by-task interactions, with older and brighter children less differentially affected by the added demands of the name-match task than were younger and duller children.

In the memory-scanning task, significant main effects were found for age, ability level, and set size, with all effects in the expected directions. There was also a significant interaction between set size and ability, with children who were less able showing a greater effect of set size than was shown by those who were more able. To understand this interaction and the main effects fully, subjects' performance on this task was decomposed into two parameters, a *slope* and an *intercept*. The former parameter estimated the duration of the comparison process thought to be performed between the target item and each member of the memory set; the latter parameter estimated the duration of all processes that were constant in duration across set sizes, such as target encoding time and time to respond. The linear model used to estimate these parameters accounted for over 98% of the variance in the latency data and, hence, could be expected to yield meaningful parameter estimates. The authors found in the analysis of slopes that only the main effect of ability was significant, although the age by ability interaction approached significance. In contrast, the intercept was only marginally related to ability level, but strongly related to age. The reason for this particular pattern of findings was not clear.

In an effort to put together the results of the various experiments, correlations were computed between component processes from different tasks. These processes were hypothesized either to be highly related psychologically (e.g., intercept from the memory-scanning task and choice reaction time) or to be only poorly related (e.g., intercept from the memory-scanning task and difference between name and physical match times). In general, the parameters hypothesized to be highly related showed higher intercorrelations (median = .72) than did the parameters hypothesized to be only poorly related (median = .28). An attempt was also made to predict Raven Progressive Matrix scores from three hypothesized components of information processing—choice reaction time minus simple reaction time, name minus physical match time, and memory-scanning slope. These three parameters accounted for 62% of the variance in the Raven Progressive Matrix scores across all ages combined. Age alone accounted for 47% of the variance, however, leaving 15% explained by the central-processing variables.

A useful elaboration of the original Newell–Simon view is the production. A production is a condition–action sequence (Newell & Simon, 1972). If a certain condition is met, then a certain action is performed. Sequences of ordered productions are called *production systems*. The executive for a production system is expected to make its way down the ordered list of productions until one of the conditions is met. The action corresponding to that condition is executed and control is returned to the top of the list. The executive then makes its way down the list again, trying to satisfy a condition. When it does so, an action is executed, control returns to the top, and so on. Hunt and Poltrock (1974) have suggested that the productions may be probabilistically ordered so that the exact order in which the list is scanned may differ across subsequent scannings of the list.

Cognitive development is assumed by some to occur through the operation of self-modifying production systems (see Klahr, 1979, 1984, for reviews of the literature on such production systems). The basic idea is that the action in a condition–action sequence is to build a new production. Anderson, Kline, and Beasley (1979) have proposed four transition mechanisms by which modification could occur. A designation production is one that simply has as its action the instructions to build a new production of a certain kind. A strengthening mechanism increases the probability that a production will be activated. A generalization mechanism weakens the specific conditions that activate a production so that the production is more likely to be executed under a broader variety of circumstances. Finally, a discrimination mechanism strengthens the specifications for activation of a production so that the production will be activated only when more specific conditions are met than was originally the case. Notice that a critical assumption underlying the last three mechanisms is that productions have differential strengths that affect the likelihood of being executed if they are reached. A rough analogy would be to the eliciting conditions necessary to fire a neuron in the nervous system. Intellectual development, thus, continues throughout one's lifetime and is largely a matter of learning, which can alter the productions constituting a production system and, as a result, the person's way of going about problem solving of various kinds.

Siegler (1981) has suggested that an important aspect of information processing is adherence to mental *rules*. Rules can be considered to be mini-Plans or ministrategies for solving problems of various kinds. As the child grows older, the complexity of rules increases, generally because earlier rules fail to take into account all of the relevant information in a given problem. Siegler has used rules most often to translate Piaget's stages of performance on various tasks into information-processing terms (Siegler, 1976, 1977, 1978, 1981; Siegler & Vago, 1978). He has carried this form of analysis further, however, in devising Piagetian types of tasks that are also susceptible to analysis by the rule-assessment approach.[1] Consider, as Siegler (1981) does, Piaget's (1952) description of

---

[1] See also the chapter by Kuhn (this volume) for further information on Siegler's use of Piagetian tasks.

the developmental sequence of the conservation of liquid quantity. In this task, typically, subjects are shown water being poured from a tall thin jar (or beaker) into a short thick jar (or beaker), or vice versa, and they are asked which jar (or beaker) is holding more water; nonconservers will state that the tall thin jar is holding more water. The rule-assessment approach seeks to explain the difference in the ways information is processed by conservers and nonconservers, as well as to explain intermediate stages of processing.

In Piaget's Stage 1, a child is said to be "unable to reckon simultaneously with the height and cross-section of the liquids . . . he takes into account only the heights" (Piaget, 1952, p. 12). Siegler's Rule I, corresponding to Piaget's Stage 1, begins with the child asking him or herself whether the values of the dominant dimension (usually the height of a column of water in each of two jars) are equal. If the heights (or values on some other dominant dimension) are judged to be equal, the child responds that the alternatives are equal (even though the widths of the jars may be grossly unequal). If the heights (or other dominant values) are judged to be unequal, the child responds that the jar or beaker with the water at greater height (or other dominant dimension) has more water in it. Thus, Piaget's concept of nonconservation has been translated into information-processing terms as a rule (or Plan) actualized through self-interrogation.

In Piaget's Stage 2, "a second relation, that of the width, is explicitly brought into the picture . . . [but] when he is concerned with the unequal levels he forgets the width, and when he notices the difference in width he forgets what he has just said about the relation between the levels" (Piaget, 1952, p. 16). In Siegler's Rule II, the child asks himself or herself whether the values of the dominant dimension are equal. If they are, the child asks whether the values of the subordinate dimension are equal. If so, the child responds that the alternatives are equal; if not, the child responds that the jar or beaker with the greater value on the subordinate dimension has more water in it. Suppose, though, that the values of the dominant dimension are perceived as unequal. In this case, the subject responds that the jar or beaker with the greater value on the dominant dimension has more water in it. Note that, in using this rule, the child will respond correctly if the values of the dominant dimension are equal (say, two beakers of equal height). In this case, the child attends to both the dominant and subordinate dimensions (usually height and width). The child will respond incorrectly, however, if the values on the dominant dimension are unequal, unless the values on the subordinate dimension are equal. When the values on the dominant dimension are unequal, the child ignores the subordinate dimension and gets the problem correct only if it so happens that for the particular problem, the value of the subordinate dimension does not affect the answer to the problem (as when the widths of the two jars are equal). Siegler has proposed a Rule III (not considered here) that corresponds to a slightly more advanced substage of Piaget's Stage 2.

In Piaget's Stage 3, "children state immediately, or almost immediately that the quantities of liquid are conserved, and this irrespective of the number and nature of the changes made'' (Piaget, 1952, p. 17). In Siegler's Rule IV, corresponding to Piaget's Stage 3, all information about both dimensions is taken into account. The child first asks whether the values of the dominant dimension are equal. If they are, the child asks whether the values of the subordinate dimension are equal. If so, the alternatives are judged to be equal; if not, the jar with the greater value of the subordinate dimension is said to hold more water. Suppose the values of the dominant dimension are unequal: The child still asks whether the values of the subordinate dimension are equal (unlike in Rule II, where this question was not asked in this case). If the answer is yes, the jar with the greater value of the dominant dimension is judged to hold more water; if the answer is no, the values of the dominant and subordinate dimensions are appropriately combined.

Gelman and Gallistel (1978), like Siegler, have used rules—or, as they have called them, *principles*—as units of cognitive development. They have proposed five principles that they believe govern and define the act of counting. Three of these principles deal with how to count, one with what to count, and a final one with a combination of both. These principles seem roughly analogous in the domain of number to Siegler's rules in the domain of problem solving. There are two important differences, however. First, in Siegler's (1981) formulation, more sophisticated rules are believed to replace simpler rules; in Gelman and Gallistel's (1978) formulation, later principles are added onto (rather than replacing) earlier ones. Second, Gelman and Gallistel's rules are more content-based than are Siegler's, dwelling as they do on counting in particular rather than on cognitive processing in general.

Conclusions

From an information-processing point of view, there are a number of different loci of intellectual development. Some of the most important ones include:

1. *Knowledge base.* Obviously, the knowledge base on which one operates increases in extent with age. The knowledge base includes the external world as well as one's internal cognitions. Metacognitive theorists. in particular, have claimed (although the evidence is still weak) that the latter kind of knowledge plays a major role in one's ability to acquire knowledge about the world.

To understand how the knowledge base increases in extent, one has to understand the processes that operate on it; however, the highly process-oriented approach to research during the early and mid-1970s sometimes failed to take into account the bidirectionality of spheres of influence. Processes need a knowledge base on which to operate, and the extent of the knowledge base in large part determines what processes can operate under which circumstances, as well as how effectively they can operate. Sometimes the distinction between knowledge and process is not clear. In part, this reflects semantic confusions. In the literature on metacognition, for example, the term metacognition has sometimes been used to refer to a kind of *knowledge* (knowledge about cognition) and other times to a kind of *process* (control processes, i.e., processes that control other processes). The understandable tendency to blame metacognitive theorists for this and other semantic confusions has sometimes obscured the more important issue—namely, the presumably close but poorly understood relation between knowledge and processes. This lack of understanding has often led to a tendency to attempt to study knowledge in isolation from process, or vice versa. This tendency has been unfortunate because the close relation between the two means that one cannot be fully understood without a full understanding of the other (see J. R. Anderson, 1976).

Some of the most interesting research in contemporary cognitive developmental psychology has looked at the development of level and structure of knowledge (see R. J. Sternberg, 1984). For example, Keil (1979, 1984) has shown that conceptual development can be understood in part in terms of the growth of knowledge about the structure of ontological catagories—that is, knowledge about what can be predicated of what. Chi and Koeske (1983) showed that young dinosaur experts can show better recall than adult nonexperts when the topic is dinosaurs, but not otherwise (see also Chi, 1978).

2. *Processes.* An important source of intellectual development resides in the new availability and increased accessibility of processes with increasing age. The early and mid-1970s saw a perhaps necessary initial tendency to undertake task analyses that isolated processes involved in particular tasks, but that did not attempt to relate these processes either to each other (within and across tasks) or to external referents. Now that we know how to decompose performance on a fairly large class of tasks, as well as what the outcomes of these task analyses look like, researchers must attempt to understand the interrelations of processes and the relations of processes to other variables. This understanding would permit them to start with cognitive theories that specify processes used in the solution of fairly large numbers of tasks, rather than to start with tasks, specify the processes used in their solution, and then trace the development of what may in many cases be task-specific processes (e.g., R. J. Sternberg, 1980a, 1981, 1985).

3. *Memory.* Despite the enormous amount of research that has been conducted on memory development (see, e.g., Kail & Hagen, 1977), our understanding of exactly what develops in memory is still surprisingly meager. Psychologists still do not even agree with the theory that memory capacity (expressed in terms of some kind of slot notion) increases with age, as demonstrated by Osherson (1974) and by Case (1978, 1984). The importance of studying memory development is illustrated by the finding of Trabasso et al. that what had seemed to be a process limitation of sorts, in the ability of preoperational children to perform transitive inferences, is actually a memory limitation which can be overcome with appropriate training (e.g., Bryant & Trabasso, 1971).

4. *Strategies.* Many tasks (e.g., analogies and balance-scale problems) show changes in the strategies applied to them with increased intellectual development. Moreover, these strategy changes reflect increasingly intelligent ways of solving problems. Indeed, it is not the strategy change per se that is of interest, but what it tells us about the developing mind. For example, in both analogy and balance-scale problems, as children grow older they have an increased tendency to use more of the information given in the problem in a more integrative way. In the study of strategies as in the study of processes, investigators should not become bogged down in task-specific aspects of strategy development, but rather focus on what it is about strategy development that reflects generally increasing cognitive competence. Researchers should also continue to study strategy formation and implementation in real-world as well as in laboratory tasks.

5. *Representations of information.* Processes and strategies act on a knowledge base, and this knowledge base must be represented in some form. One thing that may develop with age is the ability to represent information in a way that renders the information easily accessible and highly relatable to other kinds of information. In pictorial analogies, for example, a tendency was observed on the part of children to move from more separable to more integral representations of attribute information; and Kail, Pellegrino, and Carter (1980) suggested the possibility that in spatial tasks also, older subjects may represent forms to be rotated mentally in a more holistic way. On the other hand, the developmental trend sometimes involves moving from more integral to more separable representations of information (see van Daalen-Kapteijns & Elshout-Moher, 1981; Shepp, 1978; Smith & Kemler, 1978; Werner & Kaplan, 1952). Thus, we need to learn a lot more about the circumstances under which children of different ages represent information in different ways. It appears that changes in representation can be understood only in terms of the sense they make in the context of particular task environments or, at least, classes of task environments.

6. *Process latencies, difficulties, and probabilities.* Many recent studies, such as those of analogical and linear syllogistic reasoning as well as of spatial visualization, have sought to isolate component processes and to assign values of some kind (e.g., duration) to these processes. This is a necessary ingredient in information-processing research, although process values (such as latencies or difficulties) are not so much of interest in their own right as they are of interest in comparison to other process values. Thus, it is important to know what it is, for example, that makes one analogy more difficult than another, one kind of balance-scale problem more difficult than another, or one addition problem more difficult than another. Moreover, it is essential to be able to isolate these values at the level of individual as well as group data because sources of difficulty in intelligent performance may differ widely across different individuals. In order eventually to attempt remediation, we need to know what it is that needs remediation in each individual rather than what it is that needs remediation on the average.

7. *Executive control.* Although this item could be incorporated as a kind of process, I separate it here from processes to distinguish it from the kinds of processes that are used merely in the execution of one kind of problem or another. During the past several years, there has been an increasing tendency to study the executive in human functioning (e.g., Brown, 1982; Brown & De-Loache, 1978; R. J. Sternberg, 1985; Sternberg & Ketron, 1982). The core of intelligence is in the allocation and adaptation of one's mental resources to a given task environment: Future research on intellectual development should give high priority to this aspect of functioning.

TRANSPARADIGMATIC PRINCIPLES OF INTELLECTUAL DEVELOPMENT

In this review of two approaches often found in the study of intellectual development, certain prospective loci of intellectual development emerge. These loci are of particular interest because they suggest that it is possible to pose a fairly small set of transparadigmatic principles of intellectual development that emerge from research almost without regard to the kind of research (see Sternberg & Powell, 1983). Some significant ones are described in the following pages.

More Sophisticated Control Strategies (Metacomponents) Develop with Age

Traditional psychometric analyses of intelligence and its development have, largely for historical reasons, tended not to emphasize *executive processes:* Most factor-analytic investigations of intelligence were done at a time when concern with executive processes had not yet arisen. Some more recent factor-analytic work reflects developing emphases in psychological theorizing on executive functions. Das, Kirby, and Jarman (1975), for example, sought to confirm and extend factor-analytically Luria's (1966a, 1966b, 1973) theory of cognitive information processing. In this theory, information may be processed as some kind of unitary or holistic composite that is primarily spatial in character; or it may be processed in a way that is primarily sequential in nature, following a set temporal order. Das et al. refer to the two kinds of processing as *simultaneous* and *successive syntheses.* Each kind of synthesis may be viewed as representing a different mode of executive decision making, as well as action upon the information about which decisions have been made (see Jarman & Das, 1977). Carroll (1980) has conducted the largest scale set of factor analyses on information-processing tasks ever to be undertaken. He has used this set of factor analyses to provide guidance in proposing a set of basic processes used in information-processing tasks. One of the processes Carroll identified is the Monitor process, whereby subjects utilize instructions, rules, and guidelines for task performance.

"Usually, the process has a hierarchical structure in the sense that it has one or a very small number of major goals, each of these having one or a small number of minor goals or 'subgoals' " (Carroll, 1980, p. 34), and so on, down to the finest possible level of analysis. Development of the Monitor process occurs as the quantity and quality of instructions, rules, and guidelines increase.

All of the information-processing units—components, productions, and rules—make allowances for executive processing in development and for the development of executive processing. Executive processing is handled by higher order metacomponents, productions that drive productions, or high-level rules. R. J. Sternberg's (1985) analysis of the development of intellect has led to the postulation of six metacomponential loci of intellectual development. Brown's (1978, 1982) analysis of memory and metamemory development has led to four metacognitive operations driving cognitive processing. Flavell (1981) has proposed a model of cognitive monitoring that includes four basic components. Markman (1981) has also proposed four signals that people use in monitoring their comprehension. Butterfield and Belmont (1977) have shown that a key aspect of developmentally advanced functioning is the ability to select and apply optimal mnemonic strategies in learning. Almost no matter where one looks in the information-processing literature, executive processes (by whatever name) are seen as critical to intellectual development. R. J. Sternberg's (1980b) list of metacomponents is fairly typical of the kinds of executive processes believed by information-processing researchers to develop with age.

Information Processing Becomes More Nearly Exhaustive with Increasing Age

The psychometric tradition has generally not emphasized process modeling so that there are not many places to look for discussions of how information is encoded. Guilford's (1967) factor-analytically based theory is probably the most exhaustive collection of abilities that has been compiled, and it also takes the greatest account of information-processing abilities. Tests used to measure Guilford's factor of cognition—"immediate discovery, awareness, rediscovery, or recognition of information in its various forms; comprehension or understanding" (Guilford & Hoepfner, 1971, p. 20)—measure, in part, thoroughness with which information is encoded and processed. This is also true of some of the tests measuring Guilford's evaluation ability—"comparison of items of information in terms of variables and making judgments concerning criterion satisfaction (correctness, identity, consistency, etc.)" (Guilford & Hoepfner, 1971, p. 20). In one of Guilford's cognition tests (measuring cognition of symbolic units), for example, subjects must identify words with their vowels replaced by blanks, such as *m g c*. Obviously, one skill that will improve performance on this task is the ability and willingness to try out large numbers of vowel combinations. In solving syllogisms (an evaluation test), performance will be improved to the extent that subjects can generate all possible set relations that derive from the encoding and combination of the two syllogistic premises. Some of the Binet and Wechsler tests that measure recognition of absurdities and incongruities in pictures also test in part the subject's ability to encode the pictures fully enough to detect what is wrong with them. Performance on a number of Carroll's (1980) factor-analytically derived components can also be improved by more thorough processing—apprehension, perceptual integration, encoding, and comparison.

Brown and DeLoache (1978) reviewed the information-processing literatures on extracting the main idea of a passage, visual scanning, and retrieval processes, and they concluded that in all of these kinds of tasks a characteristic of intellectual development was the *increase in the number of exhaustive attempts at information processing* that were made. In visual scanning, for example, Vurpillot (1968) found that young children (e.g., age 4) almost never exhaustively scanned pictures of two houses to determine whether they were identical, whereas older children (e.g., age 9) frequently did. In retrieval, Kobasigawa (1974) found that in recalling categories of words, first graders who spontaneously used an available category cue recalled fewer items than did third graders—the younger children failed to scan exhaustively and, hence, to recall the items listed under each category in their memories. Istomina (1948/1975) also noted the tendency of younger children not to scan their memories exhaustively—when trying to recall a list of words from memory, 4- and 5-year-olds rarely tried to retrieve words not immediately recalled. Siegler (1978) found that a major cause of failure of younger children to solve balance-scale problems was in their failure to encode information relevant to all of the dimensions that affected the way in which the scale balanced. Kogan, Connor, Gross, and Fava (1980) found that younger children's failure to pair pictures metaphorically was due in part to their failure to make all possible comparisons between pictures. Both Siegler (1978) and Kogan et al. (1980) found that training of children to use exhaustive information processing could improve their performance on the tasks investigated. Sternberg and Nigro (1980) and Sternberg and Rifkin (1979) found that in analogical reasoning, there was a tendency for information processing to become more nearly exhaustive with age, both in encoding of stimuli and in comparisons made on the stimuli that have been encoded. In summary, the information processing of children seems to become more nearly complete with increasing age.

The Ability to Comprehend Relations of Successively Higher Orders Develops with Age

We have essentially no idea of when the ability to comprehend first-order relations between given terms of a problem initially develops. Evidence suggests (a) that the ability to comprehend second-order relations, at least of the kind used in analogical reasoning (as in the connections between two halves of an analogy), develops around the age of 12 years (Sternberg & Rifkin, 1979; see also Fischer

& Pipp, 1984); and (b) that the ability to comprehend third-order relations (as in analogies between analogies) develops during adolescence (Sternberg & Downing, 1982). The ability to use these kinds of relations may develop before the ability to discover them.

One of the most explicit statements of the role of *higher order relations* in intelligent performance was made by Raymond B. Cattell, the noted psychometrician. Cattell, like Terman, viewed intelligence as comprising in part the ability to think abstractly (R. B. Cattell, 1971; Cattell & Cattell, 1963). In particular, R. B. Cattell saw abstract thinking as critical to "fluid intelligence," which he and others identified in numerous factor-analytic investigations of intelligence. Because for Cattell (1971), "abstraction . . . is intrinsically a building up of relations among relations" (pp. 185–186), he would presumably be sympathetic to the notion that part of what develops in intelligence is the ability to perceive relations of a successively higher order. Indeed, in his and others' intelligence tests, difficulty of abstract-reasoning items is largely a function of the order of relations one needs to perceive. In the most difficult items in the Cattell Culture Fair Scale (Level 3) and in the Raven Progressive Matrices, it is necessary to see higher order relations to be able to solve the problems. For example, in a series problem, one may not only have a change in the angular rotation of a series of figures but also a change in the rate at which the degree of angular rotation changes.

Spearman's (1927) theory of general intelligence posited eduction of relations as one of three qualitative principles that constituted intelligent cognition. Eduction of relations is inference of the relation between two terms, such as the first two terms of the analogy A:B::C:D. Spearman (1927) showed how the difficulty of transitive-inference problems could be understood in terms of the order of relations necessary in order to comprehend them. Consider, for example, the problem "A is larger than B, B is larger than C, and C is larger than D." On Spearman's (1927) analysis (which is probably not wholly correct), one can educe the relation between A and D by comprehending first the first-order relations between A-B, B-C, and C-D; then the second-order relation (not given explicitly in the problem) between A-B and B-C; and so on. Thus, the fact that A is larger than D is recognized by hierarchical solution of the problem.

In the information-processing domain, Case (1978) has proposed that "the search for 'development beyond formal operations' should . . . concentrate on clarifying the nature of second-order intellectual operations and on searching for third-order operations" (p. 63); and a number of information-processing investigations of analogical reasoning have discovered that the ability to map second-order relations appears around the transition between childhood and adolescence (e.g., Gallagher & Wright, 1979; Levinson & Carpenter, 1974; Lunzer, 1965; Piaget with Montangero & Billeter, 1977; Sternberg & Rifkin, 1979). None of these investigations has found further strategy development during adolescence, however, perhaps because by this time the most conceptually difficult aspect of analogical reasoning, mapping of second-order relations, is already expeditiously accomplished. Sternberg and Downing (1982) tested students of junior high school, high school, and college levels in their ability to perceive analogies between analogies—subjects would be presented with two analogies of the form A:B::C:D and asked how analogous they were. We were particularly interested in the degree to which higher order mapping between the domain (first analogy) and range (second analogy) of this higher order analogy problem would affect judgments of higher order analogy. Analogies were rated by other subjects not involved in the primary task for a number of attributes, including goodness of the higher order mapping. We discovered that there was a monotonic increase in the use of higher order mapping with increasing age. Thus, older children seemed better able than younger children to comprehend relations of a third order, a finding consistent with the principle of intellectual development proposed here.

Flexibility in Use of Strategy or Information Develops with Age

Flexibility in strategy or information utilization means that an individual knows when to change strategy or transfer information and when not to do so. One often associates intellectual immaturity with inflexibility in strategy change and in information transfer. But changing strategy when it is unnecessary or harmful to do so, or transferring information when the information is inappropriate to the use to which one puts it, can be just as dangerous as failing to change or transfer. The locus of development, then, is not so much the ability to change as the ability to know when to change.

Flexible thinking is measured in a number of different ways by a number of different psychometric tests of intellectual ability. In the Guilford (1967) tests of divergent thinking, it is measured by items such as those requiring subjects to think of unusual uses for ordinary objects, like coat hangers or fishing rods. In some forms of the Miller Analogies Test, flexibility is measured by set-breaker items that require the test taker to perceive nonsemantic analogical relations: for example, relations based on the sounds rather than on the meanings of the words constituting the analogy item. Even in less exotic types of test items, flexibility may be measured by one's ability to perceive relations that are out of the ordinary or to solve what seem to be difficult problems in simple ways. On the mathematical aptitude section of the Scholastic Aptitude Test, for example, so-called insight problems are ones that can be solved laboriously by a time-consuming algorithm that is usually immediately obvious, or that can be solved simply and quickly by a shortcut procedure whose applicability will generally not be immediately obvious. One of the more interesting, if indirect, measurements of flexibility is provided by tests such as the *in-basket* (Frederiksen, Saunders, & Ward, 1957), which requires an individual to stimulate important functions of the job of a person in some occupation, usually a business executive. The individual is presented with more tasks to accomplish than can possibly be accomplished in the time allotted, and the individual must allocate the time flexibly to fulfill as well as possible the most important tasks. The importance of flexibility in psychometric thinking about intelligence can be seen in theoretical as well as in practical work. R. B. Cattell's (1935a, 1935b) research led him to believe that flexibility is defined as a switch-over from some old, accustomed, over-learned activity to a new way of effecting the same end. R. B. Cattell contrasted this view of flexibility with Spearman's (1927) notion as the degree of impedance from interference in switching from one mental process to another. Thurstone (1944) also believed flexibility to be an important aspect of the perceptual aspects of intelligence. Flexibility in various forms thus seems to enter into a large number of psychometric conceptions of intellectual functioning and its development.

Flexible thinking of various kinds has played an important role in information-processing investigations of intelligence and their antecedents. The importance of flexibility as a psychological construct in such investigations can be traced back at least to Luchins' (1942) famous water jug problems. In these problems, subjects solved a number of items requiring them to state an algorithm by which water could be poured from one jug to another via a third jug. A number of problems were presented that could be solved by one formula; then, problems were presented that could be solved by this formula or a much simpler one. Strong effects of "set" were found whereby subjects failed to recognize that they could change their strategy to the much simpler one. Later, Atwood and Polson (1976) proposed an information-processing model of performance on this task. In literature on loci of deficiency in the retarded, the ability to transfer information flexibly has been identified by a number of investigators as a major source of difference in performance with normals (see, for example, Butterfield & Belmont, 1977; Campione & Brown, 1974; Feuerstein, 1979, 1980). Recently, Brown and Campione (1982) have proposed that inducing flexible thinking is one of the major needs of any program for training intelligent performance, whether in retarded or normal individuals. It was stated earlier that flexible thinking includes knowing when not to change strategy or transfer information as well as knowing when to do so—a consistent characteristic of more intelligent people both within and between age levels is their ability to settle on a strategy that is generalizable across a large class of problems, rather than to settle on very specific strategies that need to be changed as a result of slight variations in problem type (Bloom & Broder, 1950; Jensen, 1982; Sternberg & Nigro, 1980; Sternberg & Rifkin, 1979). Flexibility in a variety of forms seems to be an essential ingredient of intelligent behavior.

CONTINUITY OF INTELLECTUAL DEVELOPMENT

One of the fundamental questions in the study of intellectual development is whether such development is continuous or discontinuous, and—if it is either fully or partly continuous—in what ways it is so. This question has become a particularly "hot" one in recent years because of a changing perspective on the question's answer.

For most of this century, the accepted view was that intellectual development was discontinuous. Intelligence in infancy—inclusive of at least the first two years of life—seemed to be an entity differing in kind from intelligence in the subsequent years of life. What kinds of evidence led to this conclusion?

First, the nature of the developmental tasks for infants has seemed different from the nature of developmental tasks for older children and adults. For the most part, the infant's tasks seem to be perceptual–motor ones—grasping, crawling, walking, and so on. In Piaget's (1972) theory, these tasks are mastered as part of the "sensorimotor" period, a period that differs greatly from the subsequent ones in terms of the lesser cognitive load, compared with that required in other periods, that seems to be required for task performance.

Second, individual differences in these perceptual–motor tasks seem to be qualitatively different from individual differences in later periods. The crucial difference is perhaps that the perceptual–motor tasks are all mastered by almost all children, with the main source of difference among children residing in when the tasks are mastered. Thus, differences are not so much in degree as in age of mastery: Almost all children (except the physically handicapped and the profoundly retarded) eventually walk, for example. But not all children become, say, adept analogical reasoners or spatial visualizers.

Third, correlations of traditional infant intelligence test scores with later intelligence test scores are usually close to negligible (Bayley, 1970). Of course, such trivial correlations may seem unsurprising in view of the differences in task content between the earlier and the later tests. Nevertheless, the data suggest that the perceptual–motor program that unfolds during the first couple of years of life is truly different in kind from the type of cognitive program that unfolds later.

In the face of what seemed to be overwhelming statistical as well as conceptual evidence, researchers generally concluded that earlier and later intelligence had little, if any, overlap. More recent evidence suggests that such a conclusion was wrong, however. Evidence reviewed by Berg and Sternberg (1985a) and by Bornstein and Sigman (1986) suggests one and possibly two or more sources of continuity in intelligence over the life span (see also Fagan & McGrath, 1981; Lewis & Brooks-Gunn, 1981; McCall, 1979; Sternberg, 1981). One source of continuity is in what might be called "coping with novelty."

Coping with novelty refers to a person's ability to adjust to relatively unfamiliar tasks and situations in life. According to Berg and Sternberg (1985a), at least two constellations of attributes underlie this set of skills: *cognitive* and *motivational*. The former refer to information-processing components used to explore and solve novel kinds of problem domains; the latter refer to relative preferences for dealing with relatively novel as opposed to non-novel domains. Both constellations of attributes are important in coping with novelty, as an individual with the cognitive ability but not the motivation to cope with novel situations may simply confront few such situations in which to exercise cognitive abilities, whereas an individual with the motivation but not the cognition may seek out novelty and then be frustrated by an inability to cope with it.

How are abilities to cope with novelty measured? Several paradigms have been used, but for infants, two stand out: decrement of attention to familiar stimuli and recovery of attention to unfamiliar stimuli.

In the "decrement of attention" paradigm, a stimulus is presented to an infant either for a fixed number of trials (in one variant), or for a variable number of trials, until the infant reaches some predetermined level of habituation (i.e., until the infant is looking at the stimulus for only a proportion of the original time). Amount of decrement of attention to the stimulus can be measured in several ways, such as slope of the decay function for looking at the stimulus, or relative amount of time spent looking at the stimulus on later trials versus amount of time spent looking on earlier trials. The basic finding in study after study is that amount (or rapidity) of habituation is moderately correlated with later intelligence test scores. Typical correlations are in the .40s to .60s, which represents a relatively high level of prediction for this kind of task.

In the "recovery of attention" paradigm, subjects are measured in terms of their preference for looking at novel versus familiar stimuli. Typically, an infant is first familiarized with one particular stimulus. The infant is then given the option to look at a new stimulus or the old one. Greater recovery of attention is a function of the relative amount of time spent looking at the new versus the old stimulus. Correlations between performance on this task and later IQ are typically in the .50–.70 range. Performance on the recovery task correlates only moderately with performance on the decrement task, suggesting that the two tasks measure related but nonidentical abilities. Of course, motivational factors are confounded with cognitive ones on both these tasks, in that later preference and cognitive ability can come into play. It is not clear at present whether these two attributes of performance can ever be fully unconfounded.

In sum, there is now evidence suggesting that coping with novelty, an important part of intelligence (see Sternberg, 1985), shows some degree of continuity from infancy through later childhood. An important lesson from this research is that whether or not we discover continuity depends at least as much on what we measure as on anything else. The work also shows the need for a developmentally based theory of intellectual development that recognizes the importance of coping with novelty in the growth of intellectual skill.

Coping with novelty may not be the only source of lifelong continuity in intellectual development, although it is the best documented. Berg and Sternberg (1985b) have applied Sternberg's (1985) "triarchic" theory of intelligence to the question of continuity over the life span, and have suggested at least two other possible sources of continuity, neither of which has yet been fully operationalized for all points in the life span.

A second source of continuity is in certain of the information-processing components of intelligence. Virtually from the day of birth, children have to define problems, set up strategies for coping with those problems, monitor their solutions to these problems, and so on. The need for these skills persists throughout the life span.

There is a growing body of evidence to suggest some decline in these componential abilities in some older adults. In a review of the literature, Papalia and Bielby (1974) concluded that, on the average, older adults conserve substance, weight, and volume less well than do younger adults. Perlmutter (1979) found that in recall tasks, older adults do not encode information as effectively as do younger adults, unless explicitly encouraged to do so. Cerella, Poon, and Williams (1980) reviewed the available literature and concluded that older adults are substantially slower than younger adults in most cognitive as well as motor tasks. However, reviews by Botwinick (1977) and Horn (1970) suggest that whereas decline in performance is evident for "fluid" information-processing tasks, no such decline appears for most verbal, or "crystallized" tasks. To the extent that there is a decline in old age in cognitive task performance, then, it appears to be selective.

The selectivity of the decline in performance with age becomes all the more apparent when one examines a third source of continuity in intellectual development, namely, adaptation to the environment. Individuals of all ages somehow have to adapt to their circumstances in life. A general finding in the research literature is that older adults perform substantially better on tasks that have some contextual relevance to their lives than on tasks that are abstract and essentially meaningless to them (see Baltes, Dittmann-Kohli, & Dixon, 1984; Berg & Sternberg, 1985b; Labouvie-Vief & Chandler, 1978). Moreover, several contemporary theories of intelligence across the adult life span suggest the importance of contextual relevance in assessing intelligence in older adults (Baltes et al., 1984; Berg & Sternberg, 1985b; Pascual-Leone, 1983). Thus, when viewed in terms of adaptation, intelligence probably shows little or no decline for most people in later life.

CONCLUSION

Two conceptions of intelligence and its development have been described and compared in this chapter. The first, a psychometric approach, emphasizes individual differences among children of the same age and of differing ages to specify what it is that develops with time. The second, an information-processing approach, stresses the mental processes and representations that underlie various kinds of cognition, such as perception, learning, and problem solving. Users of this second approach seek to understand how children of differing ages are similar and dissimilar in terms of the information processing the children do when performing various kinds of cognitive tasks. The two approaches are complementary, the first stressing variation among people and the second variation among tasks. Combining the two approaches results in a richer and more integrated understanding of intellectual development than could be had by using either approach in the absence of the other.

REFERENCES

Anderson, J. E. (1940). The prediction of terminal intelligence from infant and preschool tests. In G. M. Whipple (Ed.), *Intelligence: Its nature and nurture* (Thirty-Ninth Yearbook, National Society for the Study of Education). Bloomington, IL: Public School Publishing Co.

Anderson, J. R. (1976). *Language, memory, and thought*. Hillsdale, NJ: Lawrence Erlbaum Associates.

Anderson, J. R., Kline, P. J., & Beasley, C. M., Jr. (1979). A general learning theory and its application to schema abstraction. In G. Bower (Ed.), *The psychology of learning and motivation* (Vol. 13). New York: Academic Press.

Asch, S. (1936). A study of change in mental organization. *Archives of Psychology,* Whole No. 195.

Atwood, M. E., & Polson, P. G. (1976). A process model for water-jug problems. *Cognitive Psychology, 8,* 191–216.

Baltes, P. B., Dittmann-Kohli, F., & Dixon, R. A. (1984). New perspectives on the development of intelligence in adulthood: Toward a dual-process conception and a model of selective optimization with compensation. In P. B. Baltes & O. G. Brim, Jr. (Eds.), *Life-span development and behavior* (Vol. 6, pp. 33–76). New York: Academic Press.

Bayley, N. (1933). Mental growth during the first three years: A developmental study of 61 children by repeated tests. *Genetic Psychology Monographs, 14,* 1–92.

Bayley, N. (1943). Mental growth during the first three years. In R. G. Barker, J. S. Kounin, & H. F. Wright (Eds.), *Child behaviour and development.* New York: McGraw-Hill.

Bayley, N. (1949). Consistency and variability in the growth of intelligence from birth to eighteen years. *Journal of Genetic Psychology, 75,* 165–196.

Bayley, N. (1951). Development and maturation. In H. Helson (Ed.), *Theoretical foundations of psychology.* New York: Van Nostrand.

Bayley, N. (1955). On the growth of intelligence. *American Psychologist, 10,* 805–818.

Bayley, N. (1966). Learning in adulthood: The role of intelligence. In H. J. Klausmeier & C. W. Harris (Eds.), *Analysis of concept learning.* New York: Academic Press.

Bayley, N. (1968). Behavioral correlates of mental growth: Birth to thirty-six years. *American Psychologist, 23,* 1–17.

Bayley, N. (1970). Development of mental abilities. In P. H. Mussen (Ed.), *Carmichael's manual of child psychology* (3rd ed., Vol. 1). New York: Wiley.

Bayley, N., & Oden, M. H. (1955). The maintenance of intellectual ability in gifted adults. *Journal of Gerontology, 10,* 91–107.

Berg, C. A., & Sternberg, R. J. (1985a). Response to novelty: Continuity versus discontinuity in the developmental course of intelligence. In H. Reese (Ed.), *Advances in child development and behavior* (Vol. 19, pp. 2–47). New York: Academic Press.

Berg, C. A., & Sternberg, R. J. (1985b). A triarchic theory of intellectual development during adulthood. *Developmental Review, 5,* 334–370.

Binet, A., & Simon, T. (1916a). *The development of intelligence in children* (E. S. Kite, Trans.). Baltimore: William & Wilkins.

Binet, A., & Simon, T. (1916b). *The intelligence of the feeble-minded* (E. S. Kite, Trans.). Baltimore: Williams & Wilkins.

Bloom, B. S., & Broder, L. (1950). *Problem-solving processes of college students.* Chicago: University of Chicago Press.

Bornstein, M. H., & Sigman, M. D. (1986). Continuity in mental development from infancy. *Child Development, 57,* 251–274.

Botwinick, J. (1977). Intellectual abilities. In J. E. Birren & K. W. Schaie (Eds.), *Handbook of the psychology of aging* (pp. 580–605). New York: Van Nostrand Reinhold.

Broman, S. H., Nichols, P. L., & Kennedy, W. A. (1975). *Preschool IQ: Prenatal and early developmental correlates.* Hillsdale, NJ: Lawrence Erlbaum Associates.

Brown, A. L. (1978). Knowing when, where, and how to remember: A problem of metacognition. In R. Glaser (Ed.), *Advances in instructional psychology* (Vol. 1). Hillsdale, NJ: Lawrence Erlbaum Associates.

Brown, A. L. (1982). Learning and development: The problem of compatability, access and induction. *Human Development, 25,* 89–115.

Brown, A. L., & Campione, J. C. (1982). Discussion: How, and how much, can intelligence be modified? In D. K. Detterman & R. J. Sternberg (Eds.), *How and how much can intelligence be increased?* Norwood, NJ: Ablex.

Brown, A. L., & DeLoache, J. S. (1978). Skills, plans and self-regulation. In R. S. Siegler (Ed.), *Children's thinking: What develops?* Hillsdale, NJ: Lawrence Erlbaum Associates.

Bryant, P. E., & Trabasso, T. (1971). Transitive inferences and memory in young children. *Nature, 232,* 456–458.

Butterfield, E. C., & Belmont, J. M. (1977). Assessing and improving the executive cognitive functions of mentally retarded people. In I. Bialer & M. Sternlicht (Eds.), *Psychological issues in mental retardation.* New York: Psychological Dimensions.

Campione, J. C., & Brown, A. L. (1974). The effects of contextual changes and degree of component mastery on transfer of training. In H. W. Reese (Ed.), *Advances in child development and behavior* (Vol. 9). New York: Academic Press.

Carroll, J. B. (1980). *Individual difference relations in psychometric and experimental cognitive tasks* (NR150-406 ONR Final Report). Chapel Hill, NC: L. L. Thurstone Psychometric Laboratory.

Case, R. (1978). Intellectual development from birth to adolescence: A neo-Piagetian interpretation. In R. Siegler (Ed.), *Children's thinking: What develops?* Hillsdale, NJ: Lawrence Erlbaum Associates.

Case, R. (1984). The process of stage transition: A neo-Piagetian view. In R. J. Sternberg (Ed.), *Mechanisms of cognitive development.* New York: Freeman.

Cattell, J. McK. (1890). Mental tests and measurements. *Mind, 15,* 373.

Cattell, R. B. (1935a). On the measurement of "perseveration." *British Journal of Educational Psychology, 5,* 76–92.

Cattell, R. B. (1935b). Perseveration and personality: Some experiments and a hypothesis. *Journal of Mental Science, 61,* 151–167.

Cattell, R. B. (1963). Theory of fluid and crystallized intelligence: An initial experiment. *Journal of Educational Psychology, 54,* 105–111.

Cattell, R. B. (1971). *Abilities: Their structure, growth, and action.* Boston, MA: Houghton-Mifflin.

Cattell, R. B., & Cattell, A. K. S. (1963). *Test of g: Culture Fair, Scale 3.* Champaign, IL: Institute for Personality and Ability Testing.

Cerella, J., Poon, L. W., & Williams, D. M. (1980). Age and the complexity hypothesis. In L. Poon (Ed.), *Aging in the 1980s: Psychological issues* (pp. 332–340). Washington, DC: American Psychological Association.

Chi, M. T. H. (1978). Konwledge structures and memory development. In R. S. Siegler (Ed.), *Children's thinking: What develops?* Hillsdale, NJ: Lawrence Erlbaum Associates.

Chi, M. T. H., & Koeske, R. D. (1983). Network representations of a child's dinosaur knowledge. *Developmental Psychology, 19,* 29–39.

Clark, M. P. (1944). Changes in primary mental abilities with age. *Archives of Psychology, 291,* 30.

Daalen-Kapteijns, M. M., van, & Elshout-Mohr, M. (1981). The acquisition of word meanings as a cognitive learning process. *Journal of Verbal Learning and Verbal Behavior, 20,* 386–399.

Das, J. P., Kirby, J., & Jarman, R. F. (1975). Simultaneous and successive syntheses: An alternative model for cognitive abilities. *Psychological Bulletin, 82,* 87–103.

Dearborn, W. F., & Rothney, J. W. M. (1941). *Predicting the child's development.* Cambridge, MA: Science-Art Publishing.

Dearborn, W. F., Rothney J. W. M., & Shuttleworth, F. K. (1938). Data on the growth of public-school children (from the materials of the Harvard Growth Study). *Monographs of the Society for Research in Child Development, 3,* 1(Serial No. 14).

Donders, F. C. (1868–1869). Over de snelheid van psychoische processen. Onderzoekingen gedaan in het Physiologisch Laboratorium der Utrechtsche Hoogeschool. *Tweede reeks,* II, 92–120.

Ernst, G. W., & Newell, A. (1969). *GPS: A case study in generality and problem-solving.* New York: Academic Press.

Fagan, J. F., III, & McGrath, S. K. (1981). Infant recognition memory and later intelligence. *Intelligence, 5,* 121–130.

Feuerstein, R. (1979). *The dynamic assessment of retarded performers: The learning potential assessment device, theory, instruments, and techniques.* Baltimore, MD: University Park Press.

Feuerstein, R. (1980). *Instrumental enrichment: An intervention program for cognitive modifiability.* Baltimore, MD: University Park Press.

Fischer, K. W., & Pipp, S. L. (1984). Processes of cognitive development: Optimal level and skill acquisition. In R. J. Sternberg (Ed.), *Mechanisms of cognitive development.* New York: Freeman.

Flavell, J. H. (1981). Cognitive monitoring. In W. P. Dickson (Ed.), *Children's oral communication skills.* New York: Academic Press.

Frederiksen, J. R., Saunders, D. R., & Ward, B. (1957). The in-basket test. *Psychological Monographs, 71*(9), Whole No. 438.

Gallagher, J. M., & Wright, R. J. (1979). Piaget and the study of analogy: Structural analysis of items. In J. Magary (Ed.), *Piaget and the helping professions* (Vol. 8). Los Angeles, CA: University of Southern California.

Galton, F. (1983). *Inquiries into human faculty.* London: Macmillan.

Garrett, H. E. (1938). Differentiable mental traits. *Psychological Record, 2,* 259–298.

Garrett, H. E. (1946). A developmental theory of intelligence. *American Psychologist, 1,* 372–378.

Garrett, H. E., Bryan, A. I., & Perl R. (1935). The age factor in mental organization. *Archives of Psychology, 176,* 1–31.

Gelman, R., & Gallistel, C. R. (1978). *The child's understanding of number.* Cambridge, MA: Harvard University Press.

Guilford, J. P. (1956). The structure of intellect. *Psychological Bulletin, 53,* 267–293.

Guilford, J. P. (1957). A revised structure of intellect (Reprint No. 19). Los Angeles, CA: University of Southern California, Psychological Laboratory.

Guilford, J. P. (1967). *The nature of human intelligence.* New York: McGraw-Hill.

Guilford, J. P., & Hoepfner, R. (1971). *The analysis of intelligence.* New York: McGraw-Hill.

Hofstaetter, P. R. (1954). The changing composition of intelligence: A study of the t-technique. *Journal of Genetic Psychology, 85,* 159–164.

Honzik, M. P. (1938). The constancy of mental test performance during the preschool period. *Journal of Genetic Psychology, 52,* 285–302.

Horn, J. L. (1967). On subjectivity in factor analysis. *Educational and Psychological Measurement, 27,* 811–820.

Horn, J. L. (1968). Organization of abilities and the development of intelligence. *Psychological Review, 75,* 242–259.

Horn, J. L. (1970). Organization of data on life-span development of human abilities. In L. R. Goulet & P. B. Baltes (Eds.), *Life-span developmental psychology: Research and theory.* New York: Academic Press.

Horn, J. L., & Cattell, R. B. (1966). Refinement and test of the theory of fluid and crystallized general intelligences. *Journal of Educational Psychology, 51,* 253–270.

Horn, J. L., & Knapp, J. R. (1973). On the subjective character of the empirical base of Guilford's structure-of-intellect model. *Psychological Bulletin, 80,* 33–43.

Hunt, E. B., Frost, N., & Lunneborg, C. (1973). Individual differences in cognition. In G. Bower (Ed.), *The psychology of learning and motivation* (Vol. 7). New York: Academic Press.

Hunt, E. B., Lunneborg, C., & Lewis, J. (1975). What does it mean to be high verbal? *Cognitive Psychology, 7,* 194–227.

Hunt, E. B., & Poltrock, S. (1974). Mechanics of thought. In B. Kantowitz (Ed.), *Human information processing: Tutorials in performance and cognition.* Hillsdale, NJ: Lawrence Erlbaum Associates.

Istomina, Z. M. (1975). (Originally published, 1948). The development of voluntary memory in preschool-age children. *Soviet Psychology, 13,* 5–64.

Jarman, R. F., & Das, J. P. (1977). Simultaneous and successive syntheses and intelligence. *Intelligence, 1,* 151–169.

Jastrow, J. (1892). Some anthropological and psychological tests on college students—a preliminary survey. *American Journal of Psychology, 4,* 420.

Jensen, A. R. (1982). The chronometry of intelligence. In R. J. Sternberg (Ed.), *Advances in the psychology of human intelligence* (Vol. 1). Hillsdale, NJ: Lawrence Erlbaum Associates.

Jones, H. E., & Conrad, H. S. (1933). The growth and decline of intelligence: A study of a homogeneous group between the ages of ten and sixty. *Genetic Psychology Monographs, 13,* 223–298.

Kagan, J. (1971). *Change and continuity in infancy.* New York: Wiley.

Kail, R. V., & Hagen, J. W. (Eds.). (1977). *Perspectives on the development of memory and cognition.* Hillsdale, NJ: Lawrence Erlbaum Associates.

Kail, R. V., Pellegrino, J., & Carter, P. (1980). Developmental changes in mental rotation. *Journal of Experimental Child Psychology, 29,* 102–116.

Keating, D. P., & Bobbitt, B. L. (1978). Individual and developmental differences in cognitive-processing components of mental ability. *Child Development, 49* 155–167.

Keil, F. G. (1979). *Semantic and conceptual development: An ontological perspective.* Cambridge, MA: Harvard University Press.

Keil, F. G. (1984). Mechanisms in cognitive development and the structure of knowledge. In R. J. Sternberg (Ed.), *Mechanisms of cognitive development.* New York: Freeman.

Klahr, D. (1979). *Self-modifying production systems as models of cognitive development.* Unpublished manuscript.

Klahr, D. (1984). Transition processes in quantitative development. In R. J. Sternberg (Ed.), *Mechanisms of cognitive development.* New York: Freeman.

Kobasigawa, A. (1974). Utilization of retrieval cues by children in recall. *Child Development, 45,* 127–134.

Kogan, N., Connor, K., Gross, A., & Fava. D. (1980). Understanding visual metaphor: Developmental and individual differences. *Monographs of the Society for Research in Child Development, 45*(1), Whole No. 183.

Kulpe, O. (1895). *Outlines of psychology.* New York: Macmillan.

Labouvie-Vief, G., & Chandler, M. (1978). Cognitive development and life-span developmental theories: Idealistic vs. contextual perspectives. In P. B. Baltes (Ed.), *Life-span development and behavior* (Vol. 1). New York: Academic Press.

Levinson, P. J., & Carpenter, R. L. (1974). An analysis of analogical reasoning in children. *Child Development, 45,* 857–861.

Lewis, M., & Brooks-Gunn, J. (1981). Visual attention at three months as a predictor of cognitive functioning at two years of age. *Intelligence, 5,* 131–140.

Luchins, A. S. (1942). Mechanization in problem solving. *Psychological Monographs, 54* (6), Whole No. 248.

Lunzer, E. A. (1965). Problems of formal reasoning in test situations. In P. H. Mussen (Ed.), European research in cognitive development. *Monographs of the Society for Research in Child Development, 30* (2, Serial No. 100).

Luria, A. R. (1966a). *Higher cortical functions in man.* New York: Basic Books.

Luria, A. R. (1966b). *Human brain and psychological processes.* New York: Harper & Row.

Luria, A. R. (1973). *The working brain.* London: Penguin.

Markman, E. M. (1981). Comprehension monitoring. In W. P. Dickson (Ed.), *Children's oral communication skills.* New York: Academic Press.

McCall, R. B. (1979). Qualitative transitions in behavioral development in the first two years of life. In M. H. Bornstein & W. Kessen (Eds.), *Psychological development from infancy: Image to intention* (pp. 183–224). Hillsdale, NJ: Lawrence Erlbaum Associates.

McCall, R. B., Eichorn, D. J., & Hogarty, P. S. (1977). Transitions in early mental development. *Monographs of the Society for Research in Child Development,* Whole No. 171.

McCall, R. B., Hogarty, P. S., & Hurlburt, N. (1972). Transitions in infant sensorimotor development and the prediction of childhood IQ. *American Psychologist, 27,* 728–748.

Miller, G. A., Galanter, E., & Pribram, K. H. (1960). *Plans and the structure of behavior.* New York: Holt, Rinehart & Winston.

Newell, A., Shaw, J., & Simon, H. A. (1960). Report on a general problem-solving program. In *Proceedings of the international conference on information processing.* Paris: UNESCO.

Newell, A., & Simon, H. A. (1972). *Human problem solving.* Englewood Cliffs, NJ: Prentice-Hall.

Osherson, D. N. (1974). *Logical abilities in children:* Vol. 2. *Logical inference: Underlying operations.* Hillsdale, NJ: Lawrence Erlbaum Associates.

Owens, W. A., Jr. (1953). Age and mental abilities: A longitudinal study. *Genetic Psychology Monographs, 48,* 3–54.

Papalia, D. E., & Bielby, D. (1974). Cognitive functioning in middle and old age adults: A review of research based on Piaget's theory. *Human Development, 17,* 424–443.

Pascual-Leone, J. (1983). Growing into human maturity: Toward a metasubjective theory of adulthood stages. In P. B. Baltes & O. G. Brim (Eds.), *Life-span development and behavior* (Vol. 5, pp. 118–156). New York: Academic Press.

Perlmutter, M. (1979). Age differences in adults' free recall, cued recall, and recognition. *Journal of Gerontology, 34,* 533–539.

Piaget, J. (1952). *The child's conception of number.* New York: W. W. Norton.

Piaget, J. (1972). *The psychology of intelligence.* Totowa, NJ: Littlefield, Adams.

Piaget, J. (with Montangero, J., & Billeter, J.). (1977). Les correlats. *L'Abstraction reflechissante.* Paris: Presses Universitaires de France.

Posner, M., Boies, S., Eichelman, W., & Taylor, R. (1969). Retention of visual and name codes of single letters. *Journal of Experimental Psychology Monograph, 79* (1, Pt. 2).

Schaie, K. W. (1974). Translations in gerontology—from lab to life. *American Psychologist, 29,* 802–807.

Schiller, B. (1934). Verbal, numerical and spatial abilities of young children. *Archives of Psychology, 161,* 1–69.

Shepp, B. (1978). From perceived similarity to dimensional structure: A new hypothesis about perspective development. In E. Rosch & B. B. Lloyd (Eds.), *Cognition and categorization.* Hillsdale, NJ: Lawrence Erlbaum Associates.

Siegler, R. S. (1976). Three aspects of cognitive development. *Cognitive Psychology, 4,* 481–520.

Siegler, R. S. (1977). The 20-question game as a form of problem-solving. *Child Development. 48*, 395–403.

Siegler, R. S. (1978). The origins of scientific reasoning. In R. S. Siegler (Ed.), *Children's thinking: What develops?* Hillsdale, NJ: Lawrence Erlbaum Associates.

Siegler, R. S. (1981). Developmental sequences within and between concepts. *Monographs of the Society for Research in Child Development, 46* (2), Whole No. 189.

Siegler, R. S., & Vago, S. (1978). The development of a proportionality concept: Judging relative fullness. *Journal of Experimental Child Psychology, 25*, 371–395.

Smith, L. B., & Kemler, D. G. (1978). Levels of experienced dimensionality in children and adults. *Cognitive Psychology, 10*, 502–537.

Sontag, L. W., Baker, C. T., & Nelson, V. L. (1958). Mental growth and personality development: A longitudinal study. *Monographs of the Society for Research in Child Development, 23*, (2), Whole No. 68.

Spearman, C. (1904). "General intelligence," objectively determined and measured. *American Journal of Psychology, 15*, 201–293.

Spearman, C. (1927). *The abilities of man.* New York: Macmillan.

Sternberg, R. J. (1979). The nature of mental abilities. *American Psychologist, 34*, 214–230.

Sternberg, R. J. (1980a). Componentman as vice-president: A reply to Pellegrino and Lyon's analysis of "The components of a componential analysis." *Intelligence, 4*, 83–95.

Sternberg, R. J. (1980b). Sketch of a componential subtheory of human intelligence. *Behavioral and Brain Sciences, 3*, 573–584.

Sternberg, R. J. (1981). Toward a unified componential theory of human intelligence: I. Fluid abilities. In M. Friedman, J. P. Das, & N. O'Connor (Eds.), *Intelligence and learning.* New York: Plenum.

Sternberg, R. J. (Ed.). (1984). *Mechanisms of cognitive development.* New York: W. H. Freeman.

Sternberg, R. J. (1985). *Beyond IQ: A triarchic theory of human intelligence.* New York: Cambridge University Press.

Sternberg, R. J., & Downing, C. (1982). The development of higher order reasoning in adolescence. *Child Development, 53*, 209–221.

Sternberg, R. J., & Ketron, J. L. (1982). Selection and implementation of strategies in reasoning by analogy. *Journal of Educational Psychology, 74*, 399–413.

Sternberg, R. J., & Nigro, G. (1980). Developmental patterns in the solution of verbal analogies. *Child Development, 51*, 27–38.

Sternberg, R. J., & Powell, J. S. (1983). The development of intelligence. In P. H. Mussen (Series Ed.) & J. Flavell & E. Markman (Volume Eds.), *Handbook of child psychology* (Vol. 3, 3rd ed.). New York: Wiley.

Sternberg, R. J., & Rifkin, B. (1979). The development of analogical reasoning processes. *Journal of Experimental Child Psychology, 27*, 195–232.

Sternberg, S. (1969a). The discovery of processing stages: Extensions of Donder's method. *Acta Psychologica, 30*, 276–315.

Sternberg, S. (1969b). Memory-scanning: Mental processes revealed by reaction-time experiments. *American Scientist, 4*, 421–457.

Stott, L. H., & Ball, R. S. (1965). Infant and preschool mental tests. *Monographs of the Society for Research in Child Development, 30*, (3), Whole No. 101.

Terman, L. M., & Merrill, M. A. (1973). *Stanford-Binet intelligence scale: Manual for the third revision, Form L-M.* Boston, MA: Houghton-Mifflin.

Thurstone, L. L. (1938). *Primary mental abilities.* Chicago, IL: University of Chicago Press.

Thurstone, L. L. (1944). *A factorial study of perception.* Chicago, IL: University of Chicago Press.

Vernon, P. E. (1971). *The structure of human abilities.* London: Methuen.

Vurpillot, E. (1968). The development of scanning strategies and their relation to visual differentiation. *Journal of Experimental Child Psychology, 6*, 632–650.

Wechsler, D. (1939). *The measurement of adult intelligence.* Baltimore, MD: Williams & Wilkins.

Werner, H. (1948). *Comparative psychology of mental development* (Rev. ed.). New York: International Universities Press.

Werner, H., & Kaplan, E. (1952). The acquisition of word meanings: A developmental study. *Monographs of the Society for Research in Child Development, 15* (1, Serial No. 51).

7 Current Issues in Language Learning

Lila R. Gleitman
University of Pennsylvania

Eric Wanner
Alfred P. Sloan Foundation

INTRODUCTION

Language is learned, in the normal course of events, by children bright or dull, pampered or neglected, exposed to Tlingit or to English. In Leonard Bloomfield's words, "This is doubtless the greatest intellectual feat any one of us is ever required to perform" (1933, p. 29). Appreciation of the enormity of this human capacity, given the intricacy and variety of the languages of the world, has motivated an intense exploration of language learning by linguists and psychologists alike. Both in topic and in theoretical orientation, these approaches vary marvelously. If there is an anchoring point for the disparate efforts, it is Chomsky's break with the Bloomfieldian tradition of language study and, as a particular consequence, his analysis of the logic of language learning. In this chapter, we first review this paradigmatic change in the theory of language learning. Thereafter, we organize current findings in the field as they bear on these two opposing theoretical positions.

BLOOMFIELD AND CHOMSKY ON LANGUAGE LEARNING

Leonard Bloomfield and Noam Chomsky, in succession, utterly dominated the field of linguistics for periods extending over three decades. Within these time periods it is small overstatement that investigating language was a matter of agreeing or disagreeing in detail with the programs developed by these thinkers. Such a history is commonplace in science; for example, the study of learning in

297

American psychology, for five decades, was a series of responses pro and con to a general problem as framed by Thorndike. For language, it is of some interest that Bloomfield and Chomsky appear to have been in close agreement on the essential nature of the problem. Both their most influential works (Bloomfield, 1933; Chomsky, 1965) open with an analysis of language acquisition, supposing that the problem of learning a first language and the problem of language description are at bottom one and the same.

According to both these accounts, language is a pairing of forms to meanings. These pairings differ from language to language, e.g., in English the sound /si/ is paired to the meaning "gaze at with the eyes" while in Spanish the sound /si/ is paired to the meaning "yes." This variability implies that learning must take place by direct exposure to some particular language. But if there were nothing more to language than such associative pairings between sounds and meanings, learning would probably not be hard to describe. For both Bloomfield and Chomsky, the mystery of the learning feat derives from two further crucial facts about the human use of language: It is rule governed, and it is creative. Bloomfield (1933) wrote:

> It is obvious that most speech forms are regular, in the sense that the speaker who knows the constituents and the grammatical patterns can utter them without having heard them; moreover, the observer cannot hope to list them since the possibilities of combination are practically infinite. For instance, the classes of nominative expressions in English are so large that many possible actor–action forms—say, *a red-headed plumber bought six oranges*—may never have been uttered. (p. 275)

Bloomfield's learner came into the world scantily endowed. He could hear. And he had a single principle of data manipulation that allowed him to classify together materials that occurred in the same positions within utterances. For example, the fact that *the* and *a* both occur sentence-initially, before adjectives and nouns, etc., would be the basis for assigning them to the same class. Bloomfield's learning device could also draw inductive generalizations from the distributional properties of the grammatical classes so formed, and so be able to utter new sentences that exhibited the same regularities: "A grammatical pattern (sentence type, construction, or substitution) is often called *an analogy*. A regular analogy permits the speaker to utter speech-forms which he has not heard; we say that he utters them *on the analogy* of similar forms which he has heard" (1933, p. 275).

For Bloomfield, then, a grammar is a description of the analogies that hold for a language, and learning is the set of discovery procedures (the data manipulations) by which the child forms these analogies. The learner first discovers that the continuously varying sound wave can be analyzed into discrete segments (the *phones*), which appear in discoverable recurrent patterns (the *words*), which appear in yet larger recurrent patterns (the *phrases* and *sentences*), all discovered by extracting generalizations about their relative distribution in the corpus presented to the ear (see Harris, 1951, for detailed proposals about discovery procedures at each of these linguistic levels). The child learns to use each sentence appropriately by connecting the learned situation of its use (the stimulus) with its form (the response).[1]

In all fairness to history, Bloomfield was not as explicit as Chomsky in identifying linguistic theory with the problem of language learning, but his position ("The only useful generalizations about language are inductive generalizations," 1933, p. 29) derives coherently from the assumption that child and linguist are in the same position, each required to identify from scratch a linguistic system that potentially might be anything at all: "Features which we think ought to be universal may be absent from the very next language that becomes accessible" (1933, p. 20). If there are no constraints on the form of a natural language, then each child must be endowed with a set of discovery procedures of an entirely unbiased sort to guarantee equally facile learning of any language.

Chomsky's analysis of the learner's problem began in much the same way, with the joint assumptions that the input data are heard sentences (in context) and that the learning procedure must be some sort of inductive generalization from such a corpus. But Chomsky asserted that these assumptions answer the questions about learning only by begging them. After all, how does the child manage to generalize (learn by analogy) always and only from old grammatical sentences to new grammatical sentences? How is the learner to avoid wrong analogies and seize on the right ones? For example, consider a child who has been exposed to the following sentences:

---

[1]Bloomfield (1933) emphasized that the pairing between speech and event must be complex: "Even if we know a great deal about a speaker and about the immediate stimuli which are acting upon him, we usually cannot predict whether he will speak or what he will say." He put this problem down to

> the fact that the human body is a very complex system . . . so that a very slight difference in the state of the body may result in a great difference in its response . . . [we could predict] whether a certain stimulus will lead someone to speak, and, if so, the exact words he will utter . . . if we knew the exact structure of his body at the moment or, what comes to the same thing, if we knew the exact makeup of his organism at some early stage—say, at birth or before—and then had a record of every change in that organism including every stimulus that had ever affected the organism. (p. 33)

Thus, Bloomfield had the courage of his materialist convictions. (See Skinner, 1957, for a modern variant of the same position, but keep in mind that Bloomfield was a professional linguist and made a series of exquisite technical contributions to the study of language structure and history.) Probably no avowed mentalist would disagree with this global claim that speech events are ultimately "caused" by a combination of internal structures and states and the external events they confront. But a large disagreement is whether the description of such speech-to-event relations would constitute an appropriate theory of language knowledge or performance. The problem is that only certain states, events, etc., are relevant to language organization. That is, the relations between sentences and events are mediated by the relations between sentences and their meanings. Presumably, the latter relations constitute a theory of language. (For further discussion, see the final section of this chapter.)

1. John painted the barn red.
2. John painted the barn blue.
3. John painted the red barn.
4. John saw the red barn.

By an analogy based on shared relative position, *blue* and *red* can be substituted for one another in Sentences 1 and 2. The child can therefore try the same substitution in Sentences 3 and 4, correctly inducing new sentences such as:

5. John painted the blue barn.
6. John saw the blue barn.

By similar analogy, the child can substitute *saw* for *painted* in Sentences 3 and 4. However, if the child tries this same substitution for Sentences 1 and 2, he or she will make the *false* induction that

7. John saw the barn red.
8. John saw the barn blue.

are acceptable sentences of English. The problem is that some analogies are the right ones and others the wrong ones, but Bloomfield's learner has no means for making these decisions and hence—according to Chomsky—no sure means for acquiring his native tongue.

Chomsky therefore reasoned that the natural languages could not vary arbitrarily from each other, else Bloomfield's claims must hold and language learning would be impossible. Rather, Chomsky argued that the natural languages must share universal properties, and human infants must be biologically disposed to consider only languages embodying these properties. In sum, the problem now becomes one of clothing Bloomfield's learner with a variety of presuppositions about the system to which it is being exposed, narrowing the hypothesis space on which inductions are performed. At the same time, these predispositions must be cast in some very abstract form so as to accommodate the detailed differences among the real languages:

> The real problem is that of developing a hypothesis about initial structure that is sufficiently rich to account for the acquisition of language, yet not so rich as to be inconsistent with the known diversity of language. (Chomsky, 1965, p. 58)

The focal supposition here is that an unbiased problem-solving device, guessing inductively at a grammar from a finite corpus of instances, cannot be guaranteed to arrive at the correct solution. As one more demonstration of this impasse, consider the question of how the learner is to know whether the sample of sentences heard so far come from the language consisting of exactly those sentences, or from some larger corpus. How could the learner know from a sample of English sentences that the correct grammar is not the union of English grammar and Bantu grammar—although, so far, no Bantu sentences are in the corpus (for a discussion, see Fodor, Bever, & Garrett, 1974)? To the retort "Such hypotheses are mad!" comes the counter-retort "But that is the point!" The problem of explaining language learning is essentially the problem of stating which hypotheses are mad and therefore never to be entertained, and which are sane, for a human learner.

One might, of course, propose that children do launch mad hypotheses in the course of learning their native tongues, only to be reined in by parents who correct them. This proposal faces severe problems. The first comes from examining the real interactions of caretakers with young children: Adults rarely correct their fledglings' syntax (Brown & Hanlon, 1970) and even when they do, children rarely pay attention (McNeill, 1966). Still, one could object that negative information might be available to the child in subtle form. A blatantly ungrammatical utterance by the child may fail to elicit the desired response from an adult who might misunderstand it, and this mismatch between childish expectation and adult reaction may be enough to signal the child that something is amiss.

But true as it may be that negative information of this subtle sort could be available to the child, the objection misses two points. One has to do with the complexities in the child's social environment, an environment in which many things other than language learning and teaching are going on. Owing to this complexity, many of the child's utterances are objected to by caretakers on grounds that have nothing to do with syntax, but instead pertain to the truth or social acceptability of what the child says (Brown & Hanlon, 1970). For example, the perfectly grammatical sentence "I'll color the wall red" may be rejected by the mother. How is the child to know that this is a correction of action, not grammar, while the (much rarer) rejection of sentences such as "Me wuvs yer, Mom" is in aid of grammaticality, not social correctness? Woe to the child—both as social being and as speaker of English—who guesses wrong about the basis for these two rejections of what she has said.

Beyond this practical difficulty, the theory that children learn by correction misses a logically prior point: Children hardly ever *require* correction of either direct or subtle varieties. For the overwhelming number of linguistic generalizations the child never errs at all, and therefore no opportunity to correct him or her ever arises. To be sure, as we shall detail later on, children do make some errors, such as saying "foots" for "feet" or "Mail come" instead of "The mail comes." In such cases, it is possible to believe that children acquire the right forms because they are corrected when they say the wrong forms. But such cases of overt error, while very noticeable to parents and to investigators of child language, are really the exception when compared to the huge number of semantic and syntactic generalizations each child learns without committing any overt errors along the way. To continue with an example mentioned earlier, children learning English do sometimes hear noun-phrases in which an adjective follows a noun, as in "I painted the town red" or "That ice is paper thin" or "Her cheeks were rose red" or "I'm dog tired." But they never overgeneralize, e.g., to "I saw the house red." This failure to make a mistake means that the parent never gets the chance to correct such attempts, either overtly or tacitly.

Thus by and large, it is necessary to assume that the child learns from the "good" sentences he or she hears, i.e., learning from *positive examples,* rather than from being corrected for the "bad" sentences he or she utters, i.e., learning from *negative examples.* Thus the job for investigators of language learning is to explain how, among the myriad grammatical generalizations that children might draw from their limited experience with language, somehow they seem to draw the right ones or very nearly the right ones from the start. That they do so is evident even from examples that are sometimes marshaled to argue just the reverse.

For instance, Ervin (1964) has shown that children are good—all too good— at forming inductive generalizations. Children who at two and three years of age spontaneously and appropriately produce both weak (*talked, pushed*) and strong (*brought, sang*) past-tense endings for English verbs, frequently around age four produce weak endings almost exclusively; that is, they now say "*bringed*" and "*singed*" in systematic violation of the input corpus. For the stock of most frequent English verbs (the ones children are likely to hear), the weak tense ending occurs far less than half the time on types and still less on tokens. This is no formal proof, but it is a clear suggestion that young children are inclined to draw grand inductive generalizations even over noisy data. The corpus violates the generalization the majority of the time; still, the learner evidently prefers a bad generalization to none at all. But now the question must be just how many false generalizations are true of English sentences 30 or 40 percent of the time. For example, it has been noted that substantives preceding -*hood* are very predominantly kinship terms (*childhood, motherhood, neighborhood*) and yet no child supposes that *robin* is a kinship term.

To approach these issues, Chomsky (1965) designed a hypothetical language learner who would be spared these never-ending inductive pitfalls. In some ways, Chomsky's model is an odd candidate for the attention it has received in developmental psycholinguistics, since it was never offered as a serious empirical account of how a child acquires a language. In fact, Chomsky's model is really no more (or less!) than a description of the problem of language acquisition, and it is a description framed from a particular point of view—namely, that in acquiring language the child must master the rules of a generative grammar. However, Chomsky was able to develop a number of very strong claims about acquisition simply by stating the problem in this way, and much of the empirical work in the field can be seen as an effort to develop these claims, to test them, or to reject them outright.

Chomsky's analysis begins with the unarguable claim that children receive little or no formal instruction about the rules that presumably underlie adult performance. Rather, or so it would seem, the child is exposed only to some finite sample of utterances, different for each child, in the presence of certain events and circumstances in the world. Sometimes, though surely not always, these utterances will be appropriate to the circumstances in some way. For instance, a lucky learner may hear "A rabbit is running by" as a rabbit runs by. From such exposure to utterance/situation pairs, the learner must induce a finite representation of the language that projects to an infinite set of sound/meaning pairs.[2]

According to Chomsky's idealization, the child has the internal wherewithal to assign a "partial and tentative" structural description to the input utterance, aided by its context (Chomsky, 1965, p. 32). The child is also armed with an innate linguistic theory that includes all the logical apparatus necessary to construct candidate transformational grammars. An innate learning theory tests these grammars against the input, by matching the structural descriptions generated by the candidate grammar with those given in the primary linguistic data. In case more than one grammar survives this test, Chomsky endowed his hypothetical child with an evaluation measure that provides a way of ranking all the empirically successful grammars. If correct, such a ranking would favor just the grammar that the real child actually emerges with from his encounter with the primary linguistic data.

According to Chomsky's idealization, this process of grammar acquisition takes place instantaneously; that is, grammar construction occurs in the presence of a large body of primary linguistic data, and the evaluation procedure will immediately choose the most highly valued grammar appropriate to these data. Although this is clearly counterfactual, it has never been the source of much controversy because Chomsky was more interested in demonstrating the logical prerequisites to language learning than in making claims about the details of the process. In general, those who have accepted Chomsky's instantaneous model have assumed that it could be "slowed down" without changing any of its essential properties (see, e.g., Roeper, 1982). Those who have rejected this model have objected on other grounds.

We organize our discussion of language learning against the backdrop of Bloomfield's and Chomsky's formulations of the task. Such an organization leaks, in part, for some work in this field verges on issues outside these idealizations. Granting this, we adopt a historical method that is unblushingly Thucydidean, interpreting the varying research efforts in a way that maximizes their joint

---

[2]Note that, although the environment could pair only utterances to situations, the character of learning must be more general than this: To a remarkable degree, adults can assign a compositional meaning to sentences on request, in the absence of external context. And they can comprehend books about ancient history. The theoretical task then becomes: asking how the child recruits information of a certain sort (primary linguistic data, or utterance/situation pairs) and constructs a system of a different sort (sound/meaning, or deep-structure/surface-structure pairs).

coherence. This coherence resides, we believe, in their relation to the logic expressed by these two great linguists, even though some investigators will deny, quite correctly, that they were explicitly influenced by them.

THE CONTENT AND FORM OF THE PRIMARY LINGUISTIC DATA

As Bloomfield and Chomsky would agree, the nature of learning crucially depends on how the learner naturally organizes what he hears; how he represents the input to himself. On Bloomfield's story, the organizing principles must be very general and subject to revision all along the line, for what is to be learned varies arbitrarily. On Chomsky's story, the languages "out there" are of an antecedently well-defined type, so innate knowledge about them is useful; in fact, to the extent that the forms and categories of language are distinct from the forms and categories of cognition in general, innate knowledge of the language principles is the requirement for learning. In detail, the specification of a learning procedure requires the answer to two prior questions having to do with the state of the organism as learning begins: (a) How does the child make a relevant semantic analysis of the situation while listening to adults talk about it; and (b) How does the child analyze the sound wave that results from the adult talk? We address these two issues here. Afterward, in the presence of a tentative specification of the initial state, we address the learning problem: How does the child develop a system that maps between the sounds and the meanings?

Extracting Meaning from the Situation

On Chomsky's formulation, the child is assumed to hear utterances in situations from which she can recover partial and tentative structural descriptions including, of course, some characterization of meaning. No matter the theoretical stance, the same assumption seems to be made by all investigators. For Bloomfield, each "situation" was that extralinguistic event (stimulus) connected by temporal contiguity to a particular linguistic event (response). That all parties agree to the requirement for extralinguistic sources of information is not surprising, for this follows from prior agreement about the analysis of the task: Since a language is a pairing of sounds (linguistic forms) to meanings, and since languages *vary* in these pairings, learning logically requires that samples of the forms be presented, paired with samples of the meanings; the main source for discovering these meanings seems to be in the situations accompanying the speech events. It follows that the prerequisite ability to interpret the real world in a linguistically relevant fashion must exist *ab initio*, if the child is to acquire her native tongue (for an informative discussion, see Wexler, 1982).

It is sometimes assumed that these claims for a learner are quite innocent, that language learning is easy to explain because the child can "rely on meaning from the context." However, it is hard to conceive how such claims could be brought to ground at all. The difficulty is that neither words nor sentences, nor even propositions, are in any direct way encodings of scenes or situations in the world.

As a simplest instance of problems here, consider the fact that a child observing a cat is observing, *a fortiori*, an animal, an object, the nose of a cat, Felix the cat, and the nose-plus-ear of a cat at the same time. Should someone now say "cat," this is presumably the situational context from which the child is to learn that "cat" means 'cat.' But what is to prevent the child from assuming that the meaning is *nose-ear-complex of a cat*, instead? If a (currently unknown) representational principle of mind automatically excludes this as a possible human concept, it is still the case that the child must learn *nose* and *Felix*, as well as *cat*, under these frightful circumstances (Quine, 1960).

These problems re-arise at every level of the linguistic hierarchy, reaching their ultimate exacerbation for the case of the sentence unit. A child who observes a cat sitting on a mat also observes, *a fortiori*, a mat supporting a cat, a mat under a cat, a floor supporting a cat and a mat, and so on. If the adult now says, "The cat is on the mat," even while pointing to the cat on the mat, how is the child to choose among these interpretations of the situation? Especially as the less probable (whatever this means) choices are sometimes made: The adult sometimes does say "What a good bed that mat makes for the cat." Such problems are materially worsened by the fact that the adult may speak of one thing while the child attends to another. The adult may say "Time for your nap" as the child regards the cat on the mat. Worst of all, certain structures in a language, among them those most frequently used with children, are specifically reserved for mismatches with the world: The felicitous occasion for positive imperatives such as "Eat your peas!" or "Go next door to Granny and borrow an egg!" is the absence of pea eating, Grannys, and eggs.

In sum, there is no innocence to the claim that the child learns language by relying on "meaning" or "the world." Nevertheless, it seems impossible to avoid the posit that the child will, in some crucially exploited cases, feel justified in assuming that a sound wave that enters his ear refers in some particular way, from some particular point of view, to a situation he is currently observing, as, for example, cat-on-mat rather than mat-under-cat. Three kinds of evidence bear on (though they do not explain) ways children solve this puzzle: As learning begins, children naturally represent concepts (1) lexically and (2) propositionally; and (3) caretaker and child conspire to converse in ways that map as transparently as possible from these initial lexical and propositional representations to the contexts in which they occur.

The Word Is the Natural Domain of Simple Concepts

Theories of the Lexicon. The classical view of word meaning (Locke, 1690/1965) holds that most words are not simple, but rather are cover labels for a bundle of simpler meaning-atoms, usually called elements, features, or attributes. These basic elements are taken to be those that sensory (or low-level perceptual) experience yields *directly*. Consider a hue experience such as 'red,' assumed (at least for present expository purposes) to be an automatic neural response to specifiable light stimulation. According to the classical theory of word meaning, when a child hears the speech sound "red" while having this experience, he associates the sound with that experience; that association is the meaning of the word *red*.

But on the classical view, the number of basic elements (such as *red*) is rather small, certainly much smaller than the number of words eventually acquired by children. The complex words are built up by combining the simple elements. The basis for combination is generally taken to be the co-occurrence of more than one of the simple elements in experience, and the mechanism for combination is again taken to be association. For example, suppose that *round* and *object*, like *red*, are among the basic elements of experience. If some object that is red and round is usually seen while hearing some speech sound, say, "blitso," then the child will *compose* a new category: the category *blitso* with the meaning 'red round object.' To repeat, the category is constructed because of the co-occurrence of simple elements in experience with each other and with that word.

Compositional theories usually invoke the simple elements for more than learning: The basic elements are taken to be involved in comprehension performances, even those of adults. Pursuing the example above, the learner stores with the sound *blitso*, as its meaning, the list of its elements; i.e., the meaning entry for *blitso* is 'red and round and object.' To speak, the user pulls out *blitso* whenever he wishes to mean 'red and round and object.' To understand the heard word "blitso," the listener looks up this word in his mental dictionary, but does not understand this word directly. Rather, he pulls out its components (red, round, object) and understands these instead. In short, to comprehend words, the listener *de*composes them into their primitive atoms.

A potential problem for such theories is that not all associates of a word, say, *ball*, could be permanently stored in the head as parts of the meaning of that word. This would be an embarrassment of representational riches, and would sometimes do more harm than good for speaking and understanding. For example, sometimes *ball* is heard in the presence of a red thing, and sometimes in the presence of a green thing. Presumably the learner could not and would not want to store all these color associates as part of the meaning of *ball*. On the contrary: English speakers come to know that *ball* can be used appropriately in total disregard of the color of the object observed. To model this fact, compositional theories of meaning limit the number of elements stored as a word's meaning. In the best-known variant, words are semantically represented by their *definitions*, a smallish subset of the basic elements: just those that are individually necessary and jointly sufficient to determine category membership (Locke, 1690/1965; for recent discussions see, e.g., Katz, 1972). The color of a ball is irrelevant to its category membership and so is not chosen as one of the elements stored as its meaning.[3]

In some more recent variants of compositional semantic theory, the necessary and sufficient conditions of the classical view are dropped, and instead the words are semantically represented as a cluster of elements (Wittgenstein, 1953; for recent discussions, see Rosch, 1975; Rosch & Mervis, 1975). In this variant, there is no criterial (necessary and sufficient) list of the features. Rather, there is a set of features associated with each lexical concept, but an individual falls into the class by partaking of some of them. For example, perhaps a bird is characterizable in terms of such attributes as flying, having feathers, being two-legged, and laying eggs. If these features were jointly necessary for 'birdness,' then neither an ostrich nor a bird amputee could be considered a bird. But according to the cluster theories, it will often be sufficient, for an entity to be identified properly as a bird, simply to have feathers and to lay eggs.

Details aside, the two positions just sketched agree in supposing that most words do not represent elementary concepts, but represent certain combinations of those elementary concepts. Whenever the listener hears a word spoken, she identifies it by the sound of its cover label (e.g., "blitso," in our example) but then extracts its meaning elements (*red, round, object*) as a step in the comprehension process.

A radically different position denies the compositional character of word meaning (for discussion, see Fodor, 1975; Fodor, Garrett, Walker, & Parkes, 1980; Armstrong, Gleitman, & Gleitman, 1983). According to this third kind of theory, both the learning and use of words is *holistic*. The bulk of vocabulary items in a language directly encode the elementary categories of experience rather than being constructs out of some very limited, covert, mental vocabulary of "features." To understand the implications of this view, it is easiest to consider a concrete example of how compositional and holistic theories would describe early word learning.

Consider how the word *cat* is to be acquired. Both approaches agree in assuming that the required condition for learning is that someone says "cat" in

---

[3]The machinery by which these choices are to be made is not easy to describe. Presumably, successive exposures will reveal to the learner that balls are not limited to any particular color. Yet it is logically possible to envisage a machine that would represent such facts by adding to a disjunctive definition, i.e., "a ball is a round thing that is red, or green, or violet, or blue and red striped, or . . ." Further machinery would be necessary to conclude that "any color" is closer to the facts about items standardly called balls. But a further problem is that "any color" is sensibly excluded from the definition too, despite the fact that each observed ball is some color. Redundancy rules are often invoked to handle this problem. All physical objects must be some color—whether they be balls, giraffes, pebbles, or sofas. An efficient dictionary would filter the specification *colored* up to the highest level at which it obtains. That is, balls would be described as colored only insofar as balls are described as being physical objects. Since physical objects are described as colored, balls would inherit this property, but *colored* would not be among the necessary and sufficient features specified for *ball*.

the presence of a cat. But the compositional learner has no way of *directly* perceiving 'catness.' Rather, she is able to experience (out there in the world), say, a shape, whiskers, fur, movement, a sinuous tail (or whatever the elementary experiences really are). Her entry for *cat* is a list of such features—and that list may be modified by subsequent events in which someone says "cat" in the presence of some new cat, e.g., a tailless cat. In contrast, the holistic learner is postulated to be able to observe a cat out in the world, under the same conditions, so he directly learns that "cat" means 'cat.' This means that, in advance of any learning, the holistic learner is assumed to have the internal (innate) wherewithal sufficient to represent 'catness' and to recognize an instance of that category in the world. Of course this learner, just like the compositional learner, may make errors during learning. Since by hypothesis he can experience animals, giraffes, statues, etc., as well as cats, he may on occasion misidentify and form a wrong meaning for *cat*. Subsequent exposures may cause him to change his entry for the sound "cat," therefore, but that change is not an addition or subtraction of more elementary features.

Lexical Concept Attainment by the Young Child.   Empirical study of the child word learner has some relevance to the issues just addressed. According to the compositional views, it would be reasonable to suppose that the child's innate equipment, that allows him to interpret the world, consists of the elementary features. Moreover, learning word meanings would consist of learning feature by feature. It has been demonstrated that this position can make sense of some of the child's early word use. Specifically, the young child often overgeneralizes the use of a word; for example, he or she may use the word *ball* to refer to all round things, including faces and the moon as well as balls (things perceptually close to balls, see Clark; 1973), or all things she plays with, including dolls and blocks (things functionally close to balls; see Nelson, 1973).

A number of further investigations appeared to offer more detailed support for the compositional approach to lexical learning. For example, one set of experiments seemed to show that children first learned only one or two features of the meaning of *more* and *less,* those sufficient to establish that these words are *comparative* and have to do with *numerosity* (Donaldson & Balfour, 1968; Palermo, 1973): Two- and three-year-old children will change the number of apples on a magnetic tree if told either to "Make it so there are *more* apples" or "Make it so there are *less* apples." But to perform this task correctly, i.e., to *add* apples in response to *more* and to *subtract* apples in response to *less,* the children would also have to know that *more* represents the positive pole (greater than some standard numerosity) and that *less* represents the negative pole (smaller than the standard numerosity). The investigators showed that the children did not seem to have this additional information. When asked to "Make it so there are less apples," they *added* apples, just as they did for "Make it so there are more apples." The compositional theory of meaning handles this outcome by claiming that the young learners had acquired the features *comparative* and *numerosity,* that these words share, but not the features that distinguish them from each other, *positive pole* and *negative pole.*

Unfortunately, this apparent success of compositional theories in describing word learning has turned out to be largely illusory. Carey (1977) asked young children who made the errors on *less* one more question, involving a nonsense syllable: "Make it so there are *tiv* apples on the tree." The children who had added apples for *less* added them for *tiv* as well. This begins to suggest that a partial meaning for *less* is not what led the children astray in the original demonstrations. They stray in just the same way when they have no lexical entry at all. The simplest answer seems to be that children err on *less* (and *tiv!*) just when they have no idea of what the word means. Given the situation of movable apples, their response bias is to add apples rather than to remove them, but this does not imply that they have "partial knowledge" of words like *less.* Thus the original findings cannot be interpreted as supporting a compositional theory any more than they support a holistic theory.

Carey and Bartlett (1978) subsequently studied word learning in a more direct way, by introducing new words to young children in settings that seem natural. For example, they introduced the unknown word *chromium* (to be assigned the meaning 'olive green') to two- and three-year-olds during play in the following way: Interrupting the ongoing activity, the experimenter pointed toward two trays (one red, one olive green) and said to the child "Get me the chromium tray; not the red one, the chromium one." The contrast color (here, *red*) was always one that pretests had established was known to the child. The children were tested about a week later for what they had learned from this single introducing circumstance. That half the children failed to remember anything about *chromium* is no surprise. But fully half of them had made an initial mapping between *chromium* and color concepts. To be sure, they differed in what they had learned; some children knew that *chromium* meant 'olive green,' others knew only that it was a color word, others that it was a synonym for *green,* and so on. Two properties of this learning are of special interest for evaluating the feature-by-feature learning hypothesis. The first is the rapidity of mapping—learning a meaning from a single introducing event. This is inconsistent with the idea that word meaning always is built up through repeated exposures, that dissociate necessary features from adventitious properties of a single event. The second is that the children's entries for *chromium,* while sometimes "wrong," could rarely be characterized as wrong in the sense of being incomplete. The results seem best characterized by saying the children learned a whole word concept, sometimes the one intended by the experimenter ('olive green') and sometimes some other one (e.g., 'green').

The Carey and Bartlett experiments thus provide a first evidentiary basis for a holistic theory of early word learning. Examination of the lexicons of very young children gives further support to this position, though only in a negative way: by displaying more of the difficulties of the feature-by-feature view. If children were initially sensitive to a very small set of properties that were constitutive of word meanings, it is plausible to suppose that the (relatively few) words that encoded only these elementary properties would be among the first vocabulary items acquired. For example, if a bird is, notionally, a two-legged, feathered, flying, animal, we would expect items such as *feather(ed)*, *fly(ing)* and *animal* to appear earlier than *bird* in the child's lexicon. But the facts seem to be otherwise, with these terms usually appearing in just the opposite order to that predicted: Property terms and superordinate terms are late, compared to basic object terms, in the vocabularies of child learners (cf., Nelson, 1973; Rosch, 1973; Rosch, Mervis, Gray, Johnson, & Boyes-Braem, 1976). Similarly, children learn verbs with many features (if they have features) as easily as verbs with few (if they have features). *Walk* and *run* must have *move* as one of their features; and yet the former words are usually learned before *move*, and there is no obvious stage of learning at which *run* means only *move* (Gentner, 1978, 1982; see Carey, 1982, for an important general discussion of lexical concept attainment).

Despite the descriptive difficulties of compositional theories that we just reviewed, there is good reason to be cautious about accepting the holistic theory of lexical concept attainment as the correct position. For one thing, componential theories of word meaning and word learning are hardly dead in the water. Various rescue operations are very much alive, often proceeding by increasing the power of the logical combinatorial machinery that organizes featural descriptions (Katz, 1972). Moreover, the underlying implications of the holistic view are so awesome as to dictate a wary stance. To embrace it, one must be prepared to suppose that there are as many *simple* categories of experience as there are, say, easy vocabulary items in a language, i.e., that the learner's innate conceptual furnishings are much more extensive and various than are supposed by compositional theories (Fodor, 1975, 1983). In the light of this implication and the fragmentary nature of currently available evidence, a certain agnosticism on these matters may be the best stance to adopt. We do accept as a tentative state-of-the-art generalization that the child selects the linguistic formative *word* as the repository for his elementary experiences with the world. This is the framework principle according to the holistic approach, but at present it is best interpreted more as a program for research than as a theoretical conclusion. Appropriately, Carey's and related early work just cited have been the basis for a burgeoning exploration designed to discover the conditions of learning, the kinds of words learned under varying exposure conditions, the organization of words in the lexicon as a whole, and so on (for further discussion, see Keil, 1979; Markman, Horton, & McLanahan, 1980; Waxman & Gelman, unpublished manuscript).

Before leaving this topic, it is important to note that in present guises neither of the approaches just discussed really touches the problem with which we began: How, when, and why does the learner who can putatively observe Felix, a cat, an animal, a thing (or elements constituative of these), decide which such representation of the world is apposite to a particular external event? This problem area is certainly being addressed, e.g., in the work of Eleanor Rosch and her collaborators on the child's bias toward so-called "basic-level" concepts (Rosch et al., 1976). But general solutions are not likely to be just around the corner.

The Three Bears Description: Formatives Higher and Lower Than the Word Are Learned Late

Details aside, we have organized the literature as suggesting that single words encode single concepts for very young children. But many words are morphologically complex and encode more than one concept at a time. One case is the word *walked*, which encodes tense as well as the lexical content 'walk.' How is the child to treat such items, if he or she associates the linguistic notion *word* with a single conceptual notion? We believe that early speech is consistent with the idea that the child rejects such complexity within the word. Moreover, the child seems to take a very strict view of the way words function as components of propositions; namely, that *each word must code exactly one of the arguments of a predicate, the predicate itself, or a logical word* (such as *and* or *or*). Let us term this The Three Bears description of the roles words play in earliest sentences: To the extent a received word codes more than one of the countenanced functions, it is too big; less than one, it is too small; exactly one, and it is just right. It is because this equation of propositional functions with single words is untrue of the adult language that the child's interpretation of the scope of a word will often differ from the adult's.

One line of evidence comes from the acquisition of American Sign Language (ASL). This manual communication system has by now been studied sufficiently to determine that it is formally and substantively equivalent to other natural languages, differing from these mainly in the modality (eye and hand, rather than ear and mouth) that carries the information (Klima and Bellugi, 1979). Therefore, the case of ASL is not too far afield to consider here, and for the present issue it is particularly informative. Newport and Ashbrook (1977) have shown an early tendency to map each relational element of this system as a separate lexical (sign) item. Certain ASL predicates morphologically incorporate some of their arguments. For example, the actor of *give* is uniformly expressed in the mature language as a modulation of the *give* sign, not as an independent sign. But child learners, systematically violating these input data, express the agent of *give* as a separate sign. The generalization is to the effect that each argument and the predicate ought to be carried by a separate wordlike item. No single word can be both predicate and argument (that would be "too big"), so *give* is first interpreted as carrying only one of these functions.

Even more common is the young learner's indifference to further meanings and functions (other than predicate, argument, logical vocabulary) coded inside the word unit; for example, tense or number. (They are "too small".) Evidence suggests that complex words such as *knew* (*know* + *ed*) and *don't* (*do* + *not*) are treated as unanalyzed wholes by the youngest learners, and only much later unpacked. Errors such as *knowed* developmentally succeed instances of *knew*, as we mentioned earlier (also see Klima & Bellugi, 1966, for this treatment of first negative words). Newport (1981, 1982) has demonstrated for a range of items that young ASL users acquire holistic "frozen signs," only later analyzing these into a root form with associated derivational and inflectional modulations; Gleitman and Gleitman (1970) offer a similar discussion of children's holistic treatment of English compound nouns. The appropriate generalization seems to be that semantic information within the word (e.g., tense) that is neither argument, predicate, nor logical word simply goes unanalyzed at earliest stages, as our Three Bears description predicts.

Morphological analysis of the word item is not only late: it is variable in the linguistic population. Gleitman and Gleitman (1970) have shown that the bulk of mature speakers have difficulty analyzing the internal morphology of English compound nouns. Freyd and Baron (1982) have shown that vocabulary size for academically average eighth-graders and for precocious fifth-graders is about the same for morphologically simple items, but the talented fifth-grade youngsters have a massive advantage for morphologically complex items. Indeed, certain kinds of creative activities involving productive morphological analysis do eventually appear in the repertory of the developing child. For one such process, see Clark (1982) on the creation of denominative verbs by young speakers of English, French, and German. For another, see Bowerman (1982) on the emerging understanding of English lexical causatives. Although such analyses do take place, the authors just cited agree that these are not among the first developments. In fact, Bowerman tenders the same interpretation of her findings as do we: Each early word is an unopened package; only much later does productive lexical analysis begin to appear.

This formulation of early lexical concept attainment allows us to reapproach a famous incident recorded by McNeill (1966) and to interpret it further. McNeill's 2-year-old subject remarks "Nobody don't like me." His mother corrects him: "No, say 'Nobody likes me'." The child mulishly repeats himself. The mother stubbornly recorrects. This interchange repeats itself seven times. On the eighth correction, the child says "Oh: Nobody don't likes me." McNeill takes this as a very strong indication that overt corrections do not very much affect language learning, and we concur. But perhaps we can say more about what the child is willing to revise (adding the *s*) and what he is not (omitting the negative). He is indifferent to the *s* on the grounds just stated—it is not a predicate, an argument, or a logical word—so he can take it as well as leave it. But he cannot apparently conceive that the logical notion *negative* does not have its own separable lexical reflex. He cannot accept that, in a cranky rule of English, the negative can be incorporated into the subject nominal (and, what is more, still have the verb phrase in its semantic scope).

Summarizing, children seem to approach language learning equipped with conceptual interpretive abilities for categorizing the world. As Slobin (1973) has proposed, learners are biased to map each elementary semantic idea (concept) onto the linguistic unit *word*. We have interpreted Carey's findings of holistic word learning as one explication of this proposal: Internal analysis of the word unit is a late and variable step in cognitive–linguistic development. We have also just examined the word as a functional unit in the sentence, concluding that the lexical items are at first stages the linguistic expressions of predicates, their arguments, and logical items.

The Sentence is the Natural Domain of Propositions

A fascinating line of research, beginning with Bloom's (1970) groundbreaking work on children's spontaneous speech, provides evidence at another level about how children meaningfully interpret the world. From the earliest two-word utterances, the ordering of the component words interpreted against their context of use suggests that they are conceived as playing certain thematic roles, such as *agent, instrument,* and the like, within a predicate–argument (propositional) structure (Bloom, Lightbown, & Hood, 1975; Bowerman, 1973; Braine, 1976; Brown, 1973). Greenfield and Smith (1976) have maintained that even isolated first words betray, by their relation to events, rudiments of this propositional conception. Feldman, Goldin-Meadow and Gleitman (1978) have shown that a similar componential analysis describes a manual system of communication developing in isolated deaf children who received no specifically linguistic input, who neither heard speech nor saw formal signing (for further discussion, see Goldin-Meadow, 1982).

To be sure, as Braine (1976) has pointed out, it is by no means clear precisely what these first relational categories are, whether terms such as *agent* are appropriate in scope and content to describe them (see, for example, Braine & Hardy, 1982, for experimental manipulations designed to extract the detailed content of these categories in young children). But whatever the initial categories, there seems to be little doubt that the child approaches language learning equipped with a propositional interpretation of the scenes and events in the world around him. This is not particularly surprising. After a modest number of observations, Premack's chimpanzee, Sarah, can learn to put a sticky star on the agent and a sticky circle on the patient, as shown in brief video movies (Premack, forthcoming). If Sarah, why not human children?

The question remains how much this tells about learning a language. This depends on whether the categories and forms of natural language sentences are simple with respect to the preexisting meaning structures. From varying perspectives, a number of authors have assumed that linguistic categories and forms map transparently from the meaning structures, and hence that the bulk of explanatory apparatus—for child learner and for developmental psycholinguist—exists when these categories are isolated and described (e.g., Bates & MacWhinney, 1982; Braine & Hardy, 1982; Bloom, 1973, 1983). This view is not unreasonable on the face of it. After all, we previously subscribed to the view that the mapping between words and concepts may be quite direct. The question now on the table is whether the relation between sentences and propositional thought is as straightforward as the relation between words and concepts may be (see also Section 3.1 for further discussion of this issue).

A singularly interesting source for understanding this issue is Slobin (1982). Using evidence from a variety of natural languages, he argues that an explanation of language learning from the cognitive–interpretive basis is strictly limited by the real variation among languages. Partly different aspects of meaning are coded in the syntax of different languages. As one of many examples, the child will have to discover whether his language codes tense or aspect, or both, in the syntax. Moreover, even within a single language, it is obvious that there are many ways to say the same thing. So in this sense, too, it is massively overexuberant to hope that knowing meaning is tantamount to knowing language. As Bowerman (1982) has argued, the learner must eventually transcend his initial semantic-categorial organization of language to acquire certain grammatical categories and functions that crosscut these.

Motherese: Saying the Obvious

It is possible to suppose that caretakers' speech to young children has properties that respond to the problems we have been discussing, properties that enhance the probability that learner and teacher will be referring to the same matters from the same perspectives (for the clearest statement of this hypothesis, see Bruner, 1974/75). When speaking to the youngest learners, mothers use language that is propositionally simple, limited in vocabulary, slowly and carefully enunciated, repetitive, deictic, and usually referring to the here and now (Broen, 1972; Cross, 1977; Newport, 1977; Phillips, 1970; Snow, 1977). These same properties of speech to young children have been reported in various language communities (Blount, 1970; Schieffelin, 1979) and social classes (Snow et al., 1976) and among various caretaker types, even including the 4-year-old playmates of 2-year-old learners (Sachs & Devin, 1976; Shatz & Gelman, 1973). Although the syntactic forms vary considerably both within and across caretakers, topics to the youngest listeners are interestingly narrow in range. They are mostly a matter of focusing the listener's attention on a present scene or thing and getting him or her to act upon, or at least gaze upon, that thing: *action directives* (Newport, Gleitman & Gleitman, 1977; Shatz, 1978).

These descriptive facts about maternal speech cohere on the view that it is a matter of getting together with the young listener on what is meant. The motivation for the caretakers is not hard to find, nor need it be explicitly linguistic-tutorial. We need only suppose that the mother wishes to be understood and obeyed, and these properties will fall out.[4]

---

[4]These properties fall out because, apparently, no matter what you say to a young child, it responds by acting, if it responds at all. Shatz (1978) has shown that there is a good match between what mothers say (mothers' speech consists largely of *action directives;* whatever the syntactic form,

But one's enthusiasm for the explanatory potential of these findings requires a good deal of tempering. They suggest only *that* mother and child endeavor to represent the ongoing scene ''in the same way'' but do not suggest *how* they manage to do so. The explanation rests on the (unknown) cognitive system that learner and teacher share, such that in some critically exploited cases they will interpret the same scene in the same way. To be sure, contributions to the solution of such problems are currently appearing; an exemplary discussion, based on syntactic analyses, of bridges between linguistic and conceptual categories has been provided by Jackendoff (1983; see also Landau & Gleitman, in press), and we have also mentioned such experimental work as Keil's (1979), which attempts to describe the child's ontological categories. But the question here is how the *caretaker,* by special manipulations, may be helping the child understand the words and sentences she hears. Contributors to the literature on maternal speech assert—both innocuously and probably truly—that mothers say ''what is obvious'' or ''what is salient'' to children, but this terminological fiat does not seem to resolve anything. The question is why is what's obvious or salient as obvious or salient as it is. If the caretaker's special manipulations help the child understand what is obvious to the caretaker, what is it that allows the child to understand the special significance of these manipulations?

As an instance of the underlying problems here, it is instructive that children blind from birth learn the same lexical items and thematic relations in about the same order as do sighted children (Landau, 1982; Landau & Gleitman, 1984), though clearly what is ''here'' or ''now'' must differ for the blind and the sighted listener. A blind 3-year-old knows, for example, that she is to perform different acts if told to *show* an object or to *give* it to a sighted listener. It is not at all obvious how the mothers of blind children differentially model the here and now so as to secure these surprising competencies.[5] Such findings of course

---

the intent is to get the child to act) and what children are inclined to do. Children ''behave'' in response to speech acts they even partly understand. They are likely to pick up the blocks if you say ''Pick up your blocks'' or ''Could you pick up your blocks?'' but they are just as likely to act even if your intent is merely to get information. For example, if you ask, ''Can you jump to the moon?'' you are liable to get a little jump from the child listener. If the mother is implicitly aware that this is the child's bias, and her motive is to be obeyed—or, what comes to the same thing, to display for herself and others the child's competence—she will select action directives when she speaks to the child. All descriptive evidence supports the view that action directives occur far more often (proportionally) in speech to younger children than in speech to older children and adults. These joint motivations in tutor and learner probabilistically increase the likelihood that the child's interpretation of the meaning of the maternal speech act will be correct.

[5]The finding here is that the blind child holds up an object for the sighted listener to perceive at a distance when told to ''show'' but delivers it to that listener when told to ''give.'' Moreover, the child evidently adapts perceptual-cognitive terms to her own requirements, again in ways that are hard to explain as effects of maternal modeling. She distinguishes *touch* (contact manually) from *look* as used of herself (apprehend manually). For example, she touches her back to ''Touch behind you''

cannot vitiate the claim that children learn language by "relying on meaning in the world." Rather they suggest that—since language clearly *is* learned by relying on meaning in the world—explaining language learning is more mysterious than ever.

Extracting Form from the Sound Wave

Though children may have their own devices for extracting meaning from situations, they will need other kinds of devices for extracting linguistically functioning units from the sound wave. Recall that Bloomfield's learner (and hence structural linguistics [cf. Bloch, 1941; Harris, 1951]) approached the gloriously confusing, continuously varying sound wave in a spirit of complete open-mindedness. This learner, like any objective physicist, would have no excuse to chop the complex and continuous wave form into discrete, linguistically functioning units, and even less excuse to classify these units as real speakers–listeners do. The problem of discovering the language forms from the sound waves, then, is directly comparable to the problem of discovering the meanings from the situations: What makes the learner digitalize the wave, break it into whole phones rather than halves of phones, whole words and phrases rather than nonintegral sequences of these, and so on? The analyses chosen are not inevitable inductions from the wave forms. We ask here what kinds of evidence are available to a listener with the right capacities and inclinations, to determine the forms of particular languages.

The Unit "Phone"

Chao (1934) demonstrated in a brilliant analysis of Chinese that no unified discovery procedure for a classificational scheme for sound-segments was likely to be discovered, because the criteria sufficient to isolate the phones of a particular language could not simultaneously be met (i.e., they were mutually contradictory). Classical phonemics nevertheless continued for some twenty years more to try, apparently on the plausible assumption that, if babies can do it, why not linguists? But babies could not. Therefore, language learners all over the world must be grateful to the Haskins Laboratory group of researchers who have

---

but feels in the space behind her for "Look behind you," without turning her head. She taps a cup when told to touch it, but explores it all over, manually, when told to look at it. She happily stabs at the air above in response to "Touch up" but is angry (when there's nothing to be found there) when responding to "Look up." She responds by touching when told "Touch it but don't look at it" but with confusion when told "Look at it but don't touch it." What claims about the natural categorial representations of humans account for the fact that blind and sighted children represent perceptual exploration so similarly, despite different sources of exposure to the world? It seems that the developmental literature substitutes semantic categories for syntactic ones successfully only by failing to define the former. For the present instance, we will require a semantic description of a term like *look* that subsumes the blind experience.

saved them the bother: The children need never learn to segment the acoustic wave phonetically just because they perceive such a segmentation "automatically" (see particularly Liberman, 1970; Liberman, Cooper, Shankweiler, & Studdert-Kennedy, 1967; for studies of infant phonetic perception, see Eimas, Siqueland, Jusczyk, & Vigorito, 1971; Jusczyk, 1980).

There is much controversy about the size and specific nature of the phonetic segments (for a summary discussion, see Foss & Hakes, 1978)—about whether they are the unique property of human organisms or belong to chinchillas and macaques as well (Kuhl & Miller, 1975), and about whether they derive from properties of speech perception in particular or auditory perception in general (Cutting & Rosner, 1974; Liberman & Pisoni, 1977; Newport, 1982). But these problems do not mitigate the case for rejoicing among the aspiring language learners. For them, it is enough to note that no learning apparatus is required for an initial segmentation of the acoustic wave into discrete phones. This segmentation has already been provided in the nervous system.

At this level, then, an objective, highly instrumented sequence of empirical investigations shows that the language learner has relevant information in advance about the inventory of possible phonetic elements (see Jakobson, 1941, for a seminal discussion in this context). It is interesting that in light of these findings from the acoustics laboratory, American psychology has felt entirely comfortable in adjusting to the fact of innate prespecification at this level. The curiosity is that findings of this sort seem not at all to suggest to many psychologists that higher-level language units may be prespecified in the same or a related sense. However, further findings from language learning suggest that the child has more in his bag of tricks than the phones, as learning begins.

The Unit "Word"

The learner must recover words, word classes, and phrases from their encoding in the wave form. Distributional properties of the phonetic sequences are inadequate bases for these further discoveries, for the phonetic sequences woefully underdetermine the identification of words (is it *an adult* or *a nuhdult?*), word classes (is *yellow* a noun, verb, or adjective?), and phrase boundaries (e.g., *I saw a man eating fish*). Our question, then, is whether there are units—above and beyond the phonetic distinctive features—that physically are manifest in the wave form and operative in the child's induction of language structure.

In an earlier discussion we claimed that the child selects the word unit and identifies it as the linguistic repository of simple concepts. But how does the child extract this linguistic unit from the utterance-context in which it is embedded? The child is rarely offered single words, so this problem is real. Slobin (1973) rightly conjectured that there must be some "acoustically salient" and "isolable" property of words that children can discover prelinguistically, else these claims about word and concept learning beg the question that is at issue. Here, we organize the known facts about the emergence of speech in a way we believe bears on this problem. We will try to demonstrate that there *is* an acoustically salient property well correlated with the linguistic unit *word*. This property, we argue, is an abstract characterization of the sound wave whose surface manifestation in English and other stress–accent languages is the *stressed syllable*. And we will try to show that early speech is consistent with our claim that the child is especially sensitive to this feature of the incoming property of the wave forms.[6]

The most striking fact about the English speaker's first utterances is that the little "functor" words are approximately absent; hence, the speech sounds "telegraphic" (Brown & Bellugi, 1964). To this extent, the child's early linguistic behavior again deviates systematically from the environmental model. Children have their own ideas about the forms, just as they have their own ideas about the meanings. It is particularly interesting that youngsters learning Russian omit the inflectional affixes that are the main device for marking the thematic roles in that language, adopting instead a word order strategy that has poor support in the input data (i.e., the speech of their Russian mothers; see Slobin, 1966). In light of this finding, it is impossible to suppose that the functors are omitted on the grounds that they are not semantically important. Surely it is important to distinguish between the do-er and the done-to and, as just stated, the youngest Russian learners do make this distinction, but by means of word ordering, not inflections. Given these findings, it is not surprising that some investigators have supposed that word order is easy and inflection is hard for the youngest learners. That is to say, they have described these findings as facts about earliest *syntax* (see, e.g., Feldman et al., 1978). Note, however, that it is not easy to bring this syntactic claim to bear on all the little words that are missing from earliest speech. The personal pronouns, the prepositions, the specifiers, are approximately as absent as the inflectionally functioning auxiliaries (e.g., *will*) and affixes (e.g., *-ed*). A bias toward word ordering rather than inflection does not describe these facts very satisfactorily. But if we claim instead that *the unstressed items* are what are missing, we approximate the real facts about early speech very well (see Kean, 1977, for a related hypothesis and the argument that it is relevant to describing aphasic speech).

One immediate objection to this proposed generalization is that, if the child learner is differentially sensitive to stress in the speech signal, he should not be able to tell—for a language such as English—the difference between an un-

---

[6]The specific acoustic correlates of primary stress in English include longer duration, higher fundamental frequency, and intensity (see Lehiste, 1970, for general discussion and the evidence from analysis of the speech wave and its perception). For the following argument to hold, it would be necessary to show that the same, or definably analogous, acoustic properties are available and exploited to mark phrase boundaries in the nonstress-accent languages, and that these are the properties reproduced in early child utterances. This prediction seems plausible enough, e.g., features such as rhythmicity and prepausal lengthening seem to be universal properties of speech, differing only in the details of how they map onto the phrasal units.

stressed morpheme and the unstressed syllables of monomorphemic words. However, there is good evidence, widely known but rarely mentioned, that young speakers cannot make this distinction very well. For example, it is striking that words are often first pronounced as their stressed syllables, e.g., "raff" for *giraffe* and "e-fant" for *elephant*. Moreover, when the unstressed syllables begin to be uttered, it is often in undifferentiated form (as the syllable schwa, /ə/, for all instances), for example "əportcard" for *report card*, "tape-ə-cor-də" for *tape recorder*.[7] Particularly interesting at this stage is the frequent misanalysis of clitic pronouns as the unstressed syllables of preceding words, e.g., "read-it" and "have-it," yielding such utterances as "Readit ə book, Mommie?" and "Have-it ə cookie." These properties of earliest speech suggest that the child analyzes stressed syllables reasonably well, but is less successful in rendering the unstressed syllables and in segmenting the wave form into words on this basis (see also Blasdell & Jensen, 1970, who have shown that young children are better at repeating stressed syllables than unstressed syllables in words presented for imitation; Spring & Dale, 1977, who demonstrated that young infants can discriminate the acoustic correlates of stress location in di-syllables; and Fernald, 1982, 1983, who has shown that infants prefer to listen to speech with the exaggerated prosodic properties of "motherese" even when this speech is filtered to remove all of its segmental content).

Later stages of speech development lend weight to the same generalization. Bellugi (1967) has demonstrated that when the elements of the English verbal auxiliary make their first appearance in children's speech, the items are in their full, rather than their contracted, form—e.g., "I will go" rather than "I'll go"—for some developmental time. This is in contrast to the input corpus (mothers' speech) in which, as Bellugi has shown, these items are contracted in the overwhelming majority (over 90%) of instances. Evidently, the contracted version of a word fails to be the acoustically salient element the child requires, if we take *stressed syllable* to be the appropriate specification of "salience."

Further evidence comes from investigations of input effects on learning. Newport, Gleitman, and Gleitman (1977) provided correlational evidence that the rate of learning of English verbal auxiliary elements is accelerated for children whose mothers used them proportionally most often in the noncontractable, stressed, sentence-initial position (by asking many yes/no questions, such as "Will you pick up the blocks?"). In contrast, the sheer frequency of auxiliary use (ignoring stress and position) is uncorrelated with learning rate. These results are very reliable. The correlations between yes/no questions and the child's rate

---

[7]These phenomena have not been closely studied, to our knowledge, doubtless because their theoretical interest has not been very clear. Hence, we can give no quantitative evidence about how often errors of this kind occur, though surely they are not rare. Anecdotal evidence favoring the view that the unstressed items are at first undifferentiated is quite persuasive. For example, the child of our acquaintance who said "əportcard" at an early stage of development said "Can we go to grandma's repartment house?" just as she switched to "report card."

of auxiliary growth are in the range of .80 even after partialing to correct for baseline differences among the children studied (see Furrow, Nelson, & Benedict, 1979, for a replication of this effect; and Gleitman, Newport, & Gleitman, 1984, for further discussion). It is reasonable to hypothesize either that initial position favors learning (a prediction that would follow from any theory of learning in which memory is a factor) or that the noncontracted, stressed form favors learning. We consider it likely that both these properties are relevant to the observed learning effects.

Intriguing new evidence for the same generalization comes from Slobin (1982), who has studied comprehension among 2- to 4-year-old learners of English, Italian, Serbo-Croatian, and Turkish. The Turkish children comprehended Turkish inflectional cues to thematic roles earlier in life than the learners of Serbo-Croatian comprehended Serbo-Croatian inflectional cues to thematic roles. This is exactly the prediction we would have to make on the supposition that stressed items are available earlier in development than are unstressed items: According to Slobin, the relevant inflectional items in Turkish are a full syllable long, are stressed, do not deform the surrounding words phonetically, and do not contract or cliticize. In Kean's (1979) terms, these items are phonologically *open class*. The late-comprehended Serbo-Croatian inflectional items are subsyllabic, stressless, and phonetically deformed by adjacent material (phonologically *closed class*). In sum, these two languages differ according to whether the inflectional cues to the thematic roles are encoded onto isolable stressed syllables, or not. This distinction predicts the differences in learning rate.

In the other two languages investigated by Slobin, English and Italian, the thematic roles are cued primarily by word order, not inflection. Thus, as with Turkish, they do not require the young learner to notice stressless grammatical items in order to recover the relational roles. Accordingly, there are no main-effect differences in the rate of the relevant comprehension development between Turkish and these two other languages. Only Serbo-Croatian stands apart, showing a clear delay at each point in development.

Our position is that a single principle, the advantage of stressed materials over unstressed materials, accounts for Slobin's main finding: The one language among the four investigated that requires attention to stressless materials for recovering thematic roles is the one for which comprehension is delayed. Inflection itself poses no severe problem for the learner when it is encoded on stressed materials, as in Turkish, nor does sequence pose a severe problem under the same circumstances. Recent evidence from the acquisition of Quiche Mayan (Pye, 1983) is particularly informative. For many verbs in certain syntactic environments, this language stresses inflectional suffixes, while the verb root is unstressed. Young learners often pronounce only one of these two syllables; that is, they are forced to make the choice between the semantically salient root and the perceptually salient suffix. They very consistently choose perceptual salien-

cy, pronouncing the inflection and omitting the root. In fact, morpheme boundary and syllable boundary often do not coincide in this language, providing a
good testing ground for what it is the child is actually picking up and reproducing
of the verb that he or she hears. According to Pye, these children reproduce the
syllable unit rather than the morpheme unit: Often, they pronounce the whole
syllable consisting of the final consonant of the unstressed verb root and the
whole terminus, the inflectional suffix.

Summarizing, the cross-linguistic evidence strongly supports the view that the
unit *stressed syllable* is highly salient perceptually and organizes early speech.
Stressed verb roots are pronounced early (English, Turkish, Italian, and Serbo-
Croatian) and unstressed verb roots are often omitted (Mayan); symmetrically,
stressed inflections are pronounced early (Turkish, Mayan) and unstressed inflections are often omitted (English, Serbo-Croatian). Insofar as attention to
unstressed inflections is crucial to recovering the argument structure, the child
will show some delay in comprehension (Serbo-Croatian). Insofar as the pronun-
ciation of the verb roots is obviously necessary to the adult's comprehension of
the child's message, child messages in those languages that contain unstressed
roots will be hard to understand (Mayan, as noted by Pye, 1983).[8]

The generalizations we have been considering are perforce limited to the
stress–accent languages. As Chomsky has pointed out (see Section 1), the trick
is not to make the learning of some languages easy to describe, if the cost is
rendering the learning of others forever mysterious. That is, something more
abstract than the notion *stress* in the sound wave may be required to account for

---

[8]Notice that Mayan is the only one of the languages just discussed that does not usually confound
inflection with stress. This confound is what makes the extraction of the currect learning variables so
difficult. The same confound between inflectional items and unstressed items complicates interpretation of the many studies of related distinctions in adult performance. Thus there is controversy as to
whether the phonological or syntactic properties of the closed class account for their different
patterning in various tasks with various populations. For example, Kean (1979) has explained certain
speech and comprehension impairments in Broca's aphasics on the phonological hypothesis, while
Marin, Saffran, and Schwartz (1976) emphasize the syntactic distinctiveness of the items these
aphasics cannot manage. Current evidence, for the various task domains, is insufficient to give
overwhelming support to one or the other hypothesis, though only the phonological hypothesis can
serve as part of the explanation—rather than mere description—of language learning. But for the
learning hypothesis to do work, it must be that the acoustic facts correlate with the syntactic facts to
be learned, and so either or both properties could account for distinctive adult performance with open
and closed class. Whatever the correct analysis, it has recently become clear that the open-
class/closed-class distinction has highly reliable effects in a broad range of adult linguistic performances. For example, speech errors differ for the two classes (Fromkin, 1973; Garrett, 1975); lexical
access differs for the two in normals but not in Broca's aphasics (Bradley, Garrett, & Zurif, 1979);
intrasentential code-switching constrains the two classes distinctively (Joshi, 1983); and forgetting
differs in language death (Dorian, 1978). Reading acquisition also differs for the two classes (Labov,
1970; Rozin & Gleitman, 1977), as does the historical development of writing systems (Gleitman &
Rozin, 1977) and the reliability and patterning of judgments of anomaly and paraphrase (Gleitman &
Gleitman, 1979).

this aspect of learning, given the real diversity among the natural languages (see fn. 6 to this chapter). The only well studied case we know of, apart from stress–accent languages, are studies of ASL by Newport and her colleagues (Newport & Ashbrook, 1977; Newport, 1981, 1982). We have noted that learners of ASL first treat each sequentially produced sign as an unanalyzed whole, a "frozen form." The extraction of derivational and inflectional substructures within these signs appears only in later developmental steps (see also Klima and Bellugi, 1979). The question is how to describe the physical, visually observable, manifestation called a separable *sign*.

The linguistic analyses by this group seem to us to suggest physically based distinctions between the frozen-form morphological means of ASL (e.g., handshapes) and the inflectionally and derivationally functioning morphology (e.g., certain movement types that modulate form and meaning). The latter, specially formed and specially functioning properties of manual language, are acquired later. That is to say, there seems to be evidence here for "visually salient," "isolable" properties of visible signs that are analogous to the "acoustically salient" isolable properties of speech signals. Whether there is a substantive principle of similarity underlying this analogy remains, of course, a matter for further investigation.

Whatever the ultimate description of the child's predispositions toward linguistic forms, when framed broadly enough to encompass the real languages and narrowly enough to tame induction so that language can be learned, it will almost certainly show that the child does not approach the speech wave or the visible stream of sign like an objective physicist or structural linguist. To the extent that the child must learn language by discovering the distributional properties of the input corpus (as Bloomfield stipulated), the inductive machinery appears to be constrained by the way the organism represents the materials on which induction operates (as Chomsky stipulated). In addition to discrete, featural descriptions at the phonetic level, we have argued that the child has at his or her disposal another analysis of the input. For certain well-studied languages, a physical distinction between stress and nonstress is an interim characterization. For ASL, there seems to be a related physical distinction. Appropriate characterization of the unit awaits investigation of the acquisition of nonstress–accent languages.

Sequence

We have so far determined that the child is sensitive, from earliest developmental moments, to (1) phonetic segments and (2) stressed syllables. There is clear evidence, again from early points in language learning, that the child is sensitive to the ordering both of the phonetic segments and of the stressed syllables. For the phonetic segments, it is enough to say that children seem to know *tap* from *pat* from *apt*. Errors that can be characterized as phone-order confusions are rare (though not altogether absent, e.g., transpositions such as "pǝ-sketti" for *spaghetti*). There is also very good evidence that sensitivity to the order of words in sentences emerges early.

During the period when the unstressed syllables are mostly missing and ill-analyzed, the child starts uttering more than one word at a time. There is massive evidence that at this point the words are sequenced in the rudimentary sentence. To be sure, the child's observance of ordering constraints are less exact than the adult's; moreover, there is controversy about the nature of the units so sequenced. That is, these might be grammatical units such as *subject,* thematic units such as *agent,* discourse units such as *topic,* or *old information:* All of these postulated units make much the same predictions about which noun-phrase (NP) the child will utter first, and which second, in declarative sentences. This overlap, taken together with the fact of the child's inexactness in honoring these ordering constraints, makes it difficult to identify the psychologically functioning units among these choices (see Section 3). But whatever their correct description, these units are sequenced fairly reliably from the first two-word utterances (for analyses of English, see, e.g., Bloom, 1970; Bowerman, 1973; Brown, 1973). As we have seen, sequencing is common even where the data base provides little support for it, as in the Russian cases reported by Slobin. Most remarkably, the sequencing of signs according to their thematic roles arises without any input support among the deaf isolates studied by Goldin-Meadow and her colleagues.

Given these strong and stable findings, it is surprising that some authors, particularly Slobin (1982), seek to discount sequential ordering in children's speech as theoretically uninteresting. Slobin adopts this stance because of his cross-linguistic finding that competence with inflection precedes competence with word order in certain comprehension tasks (encoding of the thematic roles in Turkish seems to be understood earlier than it is for English). However, as Slobin also acknowledges, attention to word order is clear from the earliest moments in speech—an inconvenient fact for the developmental generalization "inflection first, word order second." We have argued that the facts about what comes first, inflection or word order, are artifacts of phonological properties of the particular languages studied (see also Gleitman & Wanner, 1982): Unstressed material is the hardest to learn; hence, if the inflectional resources of a language are unstressed, they will appear relatively late in the child's speech; if they are stressed, they appear earlier. If we are correct, there seems little reason to take comprehension performances more seriously than speech performances—or the reverse—as indicants of the child's language organization. Findings in both domains are adequately handled by acknowledging that the child is first sensitive to stressed syllables, interpreted as words, and to orderings of these.

Nonetheless, it is important to note that a characterization of the child's word order is not really simple with respect to the adult's word order (the real utterances the learner hears from his caretakers). Only a small proportion of the sentences a child hears, in English, are subject first, because well over half the input sentences are questions and imperatives (Newport, 1977). Moreover, there is suggestive evidence that children do not reproduce the subject-first property of the heard language; rather, they may produce something of their own, perhaps agent first (see Section 3). We have already noted that the noncanonical position of the verbal auxiliary (stressed initial position, as in "Could you jump to the moon?") favors the *learning* of these auxiliaries. Still, the child first *utters* auxiliaries in declarative sentences, where they appear medially ("I could jump to the moon"). The learner, then, seems biased toward a notion of canonical word order, a notion that can arise only very abstractly from properties of the input. This is most striking for instances in which the input language *demands* noncanonical order for certain functions: Young English speakers sometimes express questions by intonation ("I could jump to the moon?") but do not invert the order of subject and auxiliary; this phenomenon is very frequent for wh-questions ("Where I could jump?"), although the inversion appears in just about every yes/no and wh-question that children hear (see Slobin & Bever, 1982, for a detailed discussion of the canonical form bias in young learners).

In summary, we must believe that the child learner is sensitive to sequence, for she orders the words in her utterances from the time there are two words to order, and the orderings she chooses conform in general to canonical or preferred orderings in the language to which she is being exposed. But learners preserve this canonical ordering even if it is not present in the input speech (as in English interrogatives); or if the ordering of the input speech is only a nonsyntactic statistical preference (as in Russian); or if there is no input at all (as in the home sign of the deaf isolates studied by Feldman et al., 1978). Hence, though sequence is a property of the wave form that the learner clearly notes and exploits, this property does not explain the character of what is learned.

The Unstressed Subcomponent of the Lexicon

As we will see in the discussion of inductive processes in language learning, the distinction between open and closed class may play a role in the child's discovery of linguistic structure. This is because, though this distinction may be discovered through a physical property (i.e., stress, in the languages we have discussed), it is well correlated with syntactic analyses that the child will have to recognize in order to recover the structure of sentences. We have seen that the closed class is acquired late. The pattern of development within this class is also distinctive. For example, Brown (1973) has shown that the closed class is learned in an item-by-item fashion over a lengthy developmental period, and in a very regular sequence (for instance, *-ing* is almost always learned before *-ed*). Moreover, learning rate is dependent on properties of the input corpus much more clearly for closed class than for open class (Landau & Gleitman, 1984; Newport et al., 1977). In certain cases of linguistic isolation, the closed class may not emerge (Bickerton, 1975; Feldman et al., 1978; Goldin-Meadow, 1982; Newport & Supalla, 1980).

Slobin (1973, 1977, 1982), citing evidence from language learning, language change, and creolization processes, has conjectured that the closed class arises through the fluent user's need to be quick and efficient in language use. In homely terms, the phonological squeezing of closed class items (e.g., in English, the fact that *will* becomes '*ll* and *him* becomes '*əm*) may be an inevitable concomitant of rapid, fluent communication among linguistic experts. There is good evidence in favor of this hypothesis: The phonologically short, stressless forms of closed-class items make their appearance at late stages of acquisition, in the presence of increasing fluency. An independently interesting fact is that these distinctive properties of the closed class are fully achieved only as they are filtered through the learning process by children who are native speakers. Learning a language later in life, even in the presence of adequate fluency and habitual use, does not yield these same properties (Bickerton, 1975; Newport, 1982).

One sample case has been discussed by Sankoff & Laberge (1973). They have made extensive studies of Tok Pisin, an English-based pidgin developed and acquired by linguistically heterogeneous adults in Papua New Guinea. They have shown that, in its historically earliest forms, this language had only impoverished inflectional resources. Notions such as *future* were expressed by optional, sentence-initial adverbs (such as *baimbai,* from the English *by and by*). In a second stage of evolution—a stage at which the learners were still adults acquiring Tok Pisin as a second language—this item moved into the verb-phrase (VP) and became syntactically obligatory as the marker of the future tense. In fluent usage, the item is often shortened to *bai,* thus erasing the residue of its original semantic content. This seems to show that adults are quite capable of expanding the syntactic resources of their language, as it comes into broad use as the ordinary means of communication. But at this point the new inflectionally functioning item (either *baimbai* or *bai*) is still a word with regular stress, not a clitic; that is, it is phonologically open class, even though it performs a syntactic role—tense marking—that is often reserved for the closed class in fully elaborated languages.

Recently, the use of Tok Pisin has become so general that children are acquiring it as their native language. However, the language they are hearing has little closed-class morphology, so there is little for them to omit in the so-called telegraphic stage; in short, as Bickerton has argued, pidgins share interesting properties with early child speech. These learners, approximately in the period from 5 to 8 years of age, make a further move: *Baimbai* or *bai* is shortened and destressed to /bə/, becoming an obligatory verb prefix. This is an intriguing suggestion that, at a late stage of the learning process, the (phonological) closed class makes its appearance even though it is absent from the input language (see also concordant findings from Bickerton for Hawaiian creoles).

Newport (1982) has provided related evidence from the acquisition of ASL. Very often ASL is learned relatively late in life, either because it is not used by the deaf child's hearing parents (in which case ASL may still be the learner's first language, though exposure begins only when she comes into contact with other deaf individuals) or because deafness is acquired (in which case ASL is acquired as a second language). Newport has demonstrated that learners first exposed to

ASL after the age of about 7 years fail to acquire fully the inflectionally and derivationally functioning substructure of the signs (the gestural equivalents of the closed class). Again, the product of late learning is much like the utterances of native speakers at first stages.

In sum, young learners are biased to notice phonetic features, stressed syllables, and the sequences in which these are ordered. Learning a language later in life seems to show sensitivity to these same properties of the wave form. Unlike adults, children in the later stages of language acquisition become sensitive to the unstressed subcomponent of the language. At the limit (i.e., in the absence of such features in the speech heard), children can add to the stock of language resources by inventing the closed class.

The Unit "Phrase"

If we are right, the stressed syllable stands out from the rest of the wave form approximately as figure stands out from ground in the child's innate visual analysis of space (cf., Spelke, 1982). Although the stressed syllable is by no means equivalent to the mature word form, the evidence strongly suggests that its acoustic correlates (i.e., fundamental frequency, intensity, and duration) are available to the child as a bootstrap into the morphological scheme of the language. Evidence from recent studies of adult speech production and perception shows that potential bootstraps exist in the wave form for other linguistic units. For example, speech timing is affected by major syntactic boundaries, by deletion sites, and by lexical category assignment (cf., Klatt, 1975, 1976; Nakatani & Dukes, 1977; Nakatani & Schaffer, 1978; Sorensen, Cooper, & Paccia, 1978; Streeter, 1978; and many other sources). Whether learners exploit these additional acoustic cues is an open question, but recent work in infant speech perception makes this appear likely (for an informative study, see Fernald & Simon, 1984). We discuss here some ingenious advice, from older children, that suggests a continuing reliance on prosodic cues for phrasal classification.

Read and Schreiber (1982) taught 7-year-olds to play a game in which the children must listen to a sentence and then repeat some portion of it that corresponds to one of its major constituents. Children are remarkably successful at this task, learning to pick out such constituents as surface subject NP with impressive accuracy. However, they show one curious weakness: If the subject NP is only a single word (e.g., a pronoun or a generic nominal), children are regularly unable to disentangle it from the rest of the sentence. Read and Schreiber track this clue to its source, showing that, of all the many properties of single word NP's, it seems to be their intonational contour (or lack of one) that accounts for the difficulty that children experience. Unlike longer NP's, single word phrases are not rendered with falling fundamental frequency and lengthened final vowel at the close of the phrase. It is this phonological merging of the single word NP with the following VP that throws the children for a loop. Apparently phrase boundaries are largely a matter of intonation for these children. They do not appear to be able to locate these boundaries by syntax alone.

It would be perilous to reason in a straight line from 7-year-olds to 1-year olds. Simply because a second-grader shows heavy reliance upon the intonational correlates of phrases, it does not necessarily follow that he or she began learning phrases as an infant through their intonational correlates. Neither do the studies of infant sensitivity to these properties settle the case for whether these perceptions play a causal role in the discovery of syntax. Bever (1970) has argued that the mastery of an abstract syntactic rule can precede the development of heuristic perceptual strategies that come to replace the rule in practice, because they are easier to apply in the rapid-fire business of understanding or producing speech. It is not impossible that phrase-structure learning conforms to Bever's developmental sequence. Read and Schreiber's seven-year-olds may have learned the syntactic structure of phrases first and only then have come to appreciate the intonational correlates of phrases—and even if, as is likely, the discrimination of intonation patterns came well before. It is also possible that Read and Schreiber's judgmental task captures metalinguistic knowledge, or "accessible" knowledge that is partly at variance with linguistic knowledge (Gleitman & Gleitman, 1979). But it is also possible that the seven-year-old's heavy reliance on intonation is a remnant of a dependency formed at the earliest stages of acquisition. If this is the case, it would have important consequences for the way we think about the acquisition of syntax. For, as we argue later, an infant who is innately biased to treat intonationally circumscribed utterance segments as potential syntactic constituents would be at considerable advantage in learning the syntactic rules of his or her language.

Before closing, it is worth mentioning one more (indirect) source of evidence that strengthens the case for the prosodic guidance of syntax acquisition. Morgan and Newport (1981) have shown in an artificial language learning task that different physical cues to phrase grouping, such as intonation contour (when "sentences" from the language are presented orally) or physical closeness of within-phrase items (when sentences are presented visually) are sufficient for an adult subject to induce rather complex phrase-structure grammars, whose elements are nonsense phrases comprised of nonsense syllables. When sentences are presented without these phrasal cues (and without alternative semantic cues to the phrases), adults generally fail to learn the language. Again, this is no guarantee that infants are equally disposed to exploit intonational clues. But the Morgan and Newport result adds one more reasonable basis for entertaining this possibility.

Motherese: Saying it Obviously

We have expressed considerable caution about how caretakers could make special adjustments to render "meanings" easier for children to acquire. This is largely because meanings are not the sort of things that are out there in the world, available to be emphasized to one who (presumably) is not in control of the linguistic–semantic facts of the matter in advance. Barring language knowledge itself, there is no obvious way to remove the multiple possibilities of 'animalness' or 'Felixness' from cat-situations. However, we have just implicitly accepted an opposing position about the role caretakers may well play in revealing the language *forms* to their infants, for the sounds of speech *are* out there in the world, and are, in principle, available for exaggeration (of the "important" properties) and suppression (of the less important properties) so as to help the novice learn. Briefly, we now make this hypothesis more explicit.

As Newport and her colleagues (1977) have shown (see pp. 228–231 of the current chapter for further discussion), it is difficult in the extreme to show specific syntactic and semantic adjustments that mothers make, or to show effects on acquisition predicted by those adjustments that seem relatively stable (e.g., the relative shortness of maternal utterances, or their very heavy use of the imperative structure). The few adjustments that seem to work to aid the learner are largely restricted to rate-effects on closed class acquisition, e.g., of the English verbal auxiliary. In contrast, it is easy to point to universal properties that are specific to "motherese," if attention is restricted to prosody. These have been noted by many investigators, but have been systematically investigated by Fernald and her collaborators (Fernald, 1983), who have shown that motherese is special in having higher pitch, wider pitch excursions, shorter utterances, and longer pauses than speech between adults. These prosodic adjustments occur in all language communities that have been studied and, according to Fernald, they may represent a complementary adaptation by mother and child. Adapting remarks from Darwin, Fernald holds that maternal vocalizations are "sweet to the ears of the species," and so facilitate the mother–infant interaction. Specifically, Fernald and other investigators we have cited have demonstrated that infants are sensitive to the prosodic features characteristic of motherese, and prefer hearing motherese to hearing adult-to-adult speech. As stated earlier, such demonstrations do not constitute a knockdown causal argument, but they do lend persuasiveness to the view that prosodic cues help in the discovery of syntactic form. As we will now argue, the wise child should accept such available bootstraps with some alacrity, for the acquisition of syntax is no mean trick. In short, because help is clearly available in the sound wave, the best guess is that the learner is prepared to recruit it.

THE PROJECTION PROBLEM: PAIRING THE MEANINGS AND THE FORMS

In the preceding discussion, we have summarized the information available about the state of the child requisite to language learning; namely, some means for representing input speech signals and some means for representing the real-world context that co-occurs with the signals. We have asserted that input signals are interpreted as ordered phonetic strings bracketed by stress into words and bracketed by intonation into phrases. Acknowledging that some input may be physically too imperfect or indistinct to allow these analyses, we took the findings from the maternal speech literature to suggest that this problem is not greatly damaging to the position; that is, the mother's speech is generally slow, intonationally exaggerated, and almost always grammatical. As for the meaning representations, we have stated that information about these is currently orders of magnitude more fragmentary. The literature does suggest that the child assumes that words represent concepts and function as the markers of predicates and thematic roles in a propositional structure, carried by the sentence. What the concepts are and just how the sentence heard relates to a particular proposition (the cat-on-mat/mat-under-cat problem) is unknown, but we interpreted the maternal speech literature to suggest a caretaker–child conspiracy designed to respond to these problems. Just as for the speech signals, we assume that the child will have to filter out, as unusable data, those utterances whose interpretation is particularly ambiguous or murky. Granting that almost everything is unresolved here, all parties seem to agree that the preconditions for learning are that the child be able to interpret and represent the sound wave to himself in linguistically relevant ways, and also interpret and represent real-world events to himself in linguistically relevant ways. Having granted these prerequisites, we now raise the question: How does a child learn a language? That is, how does the child project from these data a general system that pairs each possible meaning with each possible form?

Directions for an answer proposed by contributors to the field differ radically. Not only do investigators disagree, they do not even seem to be addressing the same topics. Some investigators (e.g., Braine & Hardy, 1982; Schlesinger, 1971) seek to explain how the child connects semantic-relational (thematic) roles to positions in surface strings. Other investigators (e.g., Maratsos & Chalkley, 1980) ask how the child discovers such syntactic categories as noun and verb. Still others (e.g., Roeper, 1982; Wexler & Culicover, 1980) ask how an abstract learning device might acquire transformational rules. Partly, it is possible to understand all these undertakings as attempts to resolve different subparts of the syntax acquisition question. But we believe that in large part the disparity of topics investigated arises from a much deeper disagreement among these investigators about the complexity of the mapping between form and meaning. Believing this mapping to be essentially simple, some authors propose that it can be learned as a direct projection from thematic roles to the surface string. Others view the relation between form and meaning as more complex, but still believe that it can be learned by a direct projection, albeit in quite the opposite direction: from form to meaning. Still other theorists have held that no such direct projection is possible. For them, the relation between form and meaning is so complex that it must be learned through the mediation of another level of representation.

As a result of their differing beliefs about the complexity of the mapping between sound and meaning, child language investigators have offered an embarrassing variety of hypotheses about what is to be learned: case grammar, constituent structure grammar, and transformational (or lexical-functional) grammar, among others. We take up these hypotheses in turn, concentrating discussion on some current major proponents of each view. In each case, the authors are asking about the discovery of sentence structure—the main battleground of linguistic and psycholinguistic theorizing over the last two decades.

Learning a Case Grammar

In 1966, McNeill put forward the claim that children essentially "talk deep structure" at earliest developmental moments. That is, the ordering of words looks much like the left-to-right sequence of terminal nodes in deep-structure descriptions of the Chomsky (1965) variety. The retort from developmental psycholinguists (e.g., Bowerman, 1973; Braine & Hardy, 1982; Schlesinger, 1971) has been that the child's categories are semantic-relational ones, e.g., *theme, source, goal,* or *agent, instrument, patient* (depending on the particular account). It is these categories that explain the patterning of young children's speech, rather than categories such as *subject noun-phrase.*

Although this view seems plausible, the evidence in its favor is not overwhelming. One problem has to do with the analysis itself. It is not easy to define "semantic roles" nor to assign such roles to the nominals in child sentences, so as to determine whether these categories actually organize the facts about early grammars (see Braine, 1976, for a discussion of these issues). As Wexler & Culicover (1980) have pointed out, the lists of children's productions, so analyzed, themselves seem to contain counterexamples, if the definitions of the semantic roles are accepted literally. For instance, among the examples Schlesinger (1971) gives of agent + action constructions is the child utterance "Mail come"; *mail* cannot be an agent according to accepted definitions for it is not the *animate instigator* of an action. Another difficulty is that the semantic-relational analyses of children's speech may be artifacts of another variable. For a large class of English action verbs of special interest to toddlers, the subject is the agent. If the tots are really biased to use action verbs, for cognitive and motivational reasons, then a coding of the child utterances will pretty well identify subjects with agents. But, especially in light of the occasional counterexamples, it does not follow that the children believe *in principle* that subjects must be agents. A final problem with these analyses is their failure to cover the full range of phenomena observed early in the acquisition period. Young children do acquire certain linguistic subsystems that are known not to be semantically organized. For example, in the earliest learning period, German children acquire gender systems in which *masculine, feminine,* and *neuter* as conceptual categories map only very inexactly onto inflectional categories; similar effects have been reported for young Hebrew speakers (Levy, 1980, 1983; Maratsos & Chalkley, 1980).

Despite all these provisos, there is some intuitive appeal and correlational evidence supporting the semantics-based categorial view. Our question is how this supposition helps to explain language learning. It is our impression that many investigators believe they are making this problem easier by pointing to these functional semantic categories as the ones that operate in early child speech, and by supposing that these categories map onto the child's word orderings or inflectional markings in a *simple* and *direct* way. But to the extent that the child really makes these suppositions of simplicity in the mapping of form to meaning, they can only complicate the problem of learning a language. The reason is that the supposition is false for any adult language. And the reason for *that* (among many others) is that so many subtle semantic dimensions are encoded syntactically that it is literally impossible to find a single linearization for them all.

One outcome of this complexity is that the position of semantically definable propositional components (thematic roles) varies with the predicate. John's role, but not his sentential position, differs in *John is easy to please* and *John is eager to please*, as well as in *John sold a book to Mary* (where he is *source*) and *John bought a book from Mary* (where he is *goal*). John's sentential position, but not his role, differs in *John received a tie from Mary* and *Mary gave a tie to John*; in *John collided with Bill* and *Bill collided with John*; and in *Bill resembles John*, *John resembles Bill*, and *Bill and John resemble each other*. These old saws are no less problematical for being old saws. Moreover, the phenomenon of constructional ambiguity is understandable only if we acknowledge the complexity of relations between surface and logical forms, e.g., *These missionaries are ready to eat* allows two interpretations of the relational role of the missionaries, at least if the listeners are cannibals. Note that none of these examples, nor all of them taken together, argue that the relation between phrase order and sentential meaning is arbitrary—maybe it is arbitrary and then again maybe it is not. The examples show only that these relations cannot be simple or direct; rather, they must be mediated through, and derived from, the interaction of a number of distinct linguistic organizing principles (for discussion, see Chomsky, 1981).

A related problem is that, beyond the puerile sayings of the first 3 years of life, it is difficult indeed to describe sentences as syntactically organized by known or even stateable semantic functions. To understand the descriptive problems here, consider the following first sentence from a recent Letter to the Editor appearing in *TV Guide:*

How Ann Salisbury can suggest that Pam Dauber's anger at not receiving her fair share of acclaim for *Mork and Mindy's* success derives from a fragile ego escapes me.

This writer, whatever his odd preoccupations, displays some formidible syntactic skills. It is hard to state that the first 27 words of his sentence represent some semantic role. What role would that be? Still, the 27 words function together as a linguistic unit; namely, the unit that determines that word 28 is to end with an *s*. Mature language knowledge involves, in addition to many semantically coherent classes, knowledge of such incoherent surface categories as noun-phrase, subject of the clause, and so forth, as the domains of these categorial contingencies. Moreover, if there is anything like an agent or do-er in the sentence above, it would have to be *me*. For its predicate (*escape*), this do-er is the second noun-phrase. But for predicates of quite similar meaning, the do-er is the first noun-phrase. That is, the sentence could be recast:

> I fail to understand how Ann Salisbury can suggest that Pam Dauber's anger at not receiving her fair share of acclaim for *Mork and Mindy's* success derives from a fragile ego.

The point, an old point, is that the grammatical notion *subject* (the NP immediately dominated by S, the NP that agrees in number with the verb) is only complexly related to semantic notions such as the agent or experiencer. Thus, if we claim the child is preprogrammed to construct a semantic representation to match each sentence that he hears, we have arrived only at the beginning of the language learning problem. The rest of the problem involves acquiring the system of rules that relates surface forms to their underlying meanings. Recapitulating, we do not deny the relations between form and meaning, for learner or for user. We only deny that these relations are simple and direct.

Many developmental psycholinguists reject the standard arguments we have just given. Certain investigators suppose, to the contrary, that a grammar based simply on semantic-relational categories can describe the facts about natural language, as used both by children and adults. Such *case grammars* are described below. Another group of investigators accept a more abstract grammar for adults, but postulate that case grammar is the appropriate description for young learners. This latter description implies that the language organization of the child undergoes reorganization sometime during the learning process. We discuss this position in the following section.

Case Grammar as the Outcome of Learning

Some investigators have proposed that case grammar (of roughly the type envisaged by Fillmore, 1968) is the appropriate "psychologically real" descriptive mechanism for human language. In Fillmore's proposal, the combining categories are semantic-relational. The surface configurations of sentences arise by rule from these semantic-categorial (deep case) representations; hence, no separate interpretive device would be required for the semantic interpretation of the syntactic configurations. It has sometimes gone unnoticed that Fillmore postulated a mediating system of rules operating on the initial case representations to account for the complex relations between surface orderings and semantic roles. To our knowledge, Fillmore never argued that these relations would be simple—that is, immediate. In addition, a number of questions have been raised about the descriptive adequacy of this approach. For instance, Chomsky (1972) has pointed out that the same case descriptions would apply to *pinch* and *pull,* accounting for the surface manifestations *John pulled Mary's nose* and *John pinched Mary's nose.* But then it is hard to explain why *John pinched Mary on the nose* is acceptable but *John pulled Mary on the nose* is anomalous, on the relevant reading. Chomsky's approach has been to state the syntactic-categorial facts and, separately, an interpretive system that carries the grammatical structures to the logical structures. Another approach is to list the case relations for each predicate, and surface specifications for that predicate, as lexical information (Bresnan, 1978, 1982). Yet another approach seeks to discover certain limited semantic domains or fields and study the syntactic encodings that apply to predicates within the domain but not to predicates that fall outside it (e.g., Gruber, 1968; Jackendoff, 1983; Landau & Gleitman, 1984). It remains for extensive further research to discover the extent to which semantic fields may constrain syntactic formats. However, in our opinion it is hopeless to suppose that there are a very few semantic-functional categories that transparently determine phrase orders and other syntactic properties. In general, although linguists disagree on *how* to state the relations between semantic roles and grammatical dependencies, none (to our knowledge) assert that these relations will turn out to be simple.

Nevertheless, many developmental psycholinguists have argued for such a view. For example, Braine & Hardy (1982) have conjectured that a sane creator who had the language learning problem in mind would write a case grammar that mapped semantic-relational roles onto surface structures in simple ways. We do not disagree with these directions to a good God, but we have just argued that the real deity has not been so benevolent (probably this is only one of many grounds for questioning the goodness of God). That is, the evidence of natural language design fails to suggest a transparent mapping between meanings and sentence forms. Rather, successful descriptions have had to postulate transformational rules, or lexical rules of a complexity just as great, or rules of like complexity that generate phrase-structure rules recursively, and so on. Though the complexity can be moved, then, from component to component of a grammar, it evidently cannot be *re*moved.

Case Grammar as a Stage in Learning: The Problem of Reorganization

We have argued that the relationships between form and meaning are not simple in adult grammars, i.e., that a very simple case grammar is inadequate to describe the final outcome of learning. Many investigators hold, however, that the youngest learners' grammars are organized by semantic categories, but later change (e.g., Bowerman, 1973). They reject the supposition that the child's early language is just like the adult's—but somewhat less complete—arguing instead that it is different in kind. These differences may be of units (e.g., agents but not subjects) and of combinatorial rules (e.g., serial orderings but not hierarchical arrangements or transformational rules).

The question, then, is whether language acquisition is a relatively seamless progression, characterizable in terms of the steady accretion of knowledge, or whether it involves qualitative changes in organization during the course of growth. Recent investigations seem to support the latter view: Although acquiring more information is surely a part of the learning process, the reorganization of previously acquired information is also a part of the story of language acquisition.

Some of the most interesting empirical investigations of such postulated reorganizations have been carried out by Bowerman (1982). Her primary method is to look at the "errors" a child makes during language learning. With a variety of contents and structures, she has shown that the child uses certain accepted language forms at early stages without error. For example, children will use such known lexical causatives as "I broke the window" (causative of "The window broke") or "I melted the wax." Presumably what is going on here is an item-by-item adoption of heard forms. At a later stage, errors suddenly make their appearance. The child says "Don't eat the baby—she's dirty" (presumably, this is an invented lexical causative corresponding to "The baby eats," i.e., the child means "Don't feed the baby"). As Bowerman argues, through the internal analysis of these late-appearing errors, the novel usages imply that the learner has seen through to a new organization that relates the items that were previously learned separately. This new organization allows the child to project beyond the heard instances in various ways, some of them wrong. (For a related and very interesting example, see Clark, 1982, and Clark & Clark, 1978, on the emergence of denominative verbs in speakers of English, French, and German. And see also Bever, 1970, for an interesting account of reorganization, based on the learning curves for comprehension of English passive voice constructions).

Apparently, there is a significant reorganization of knowledge during the learning period. At the extreme, this makes it reasonable to describe "stages" of language learning that are quite distinct from each other. In particular, an early stage of learning may be well characterized as a simple case grammar. However, if the concept of reorganization is adopted in the language acquisition theory, a new question immediately arises: What causes the child to reorganize his or her grammar—especially to reorganize it in a way that increases the abstractness of the relations between forms and meanings?

One kind of answer is strictly maturational: There may be relevant biological changes in the learner that cause her to revist old linguistic evidence and interpret it differently. Put another way, it could be that there is a succession of learners, each of whom organizes the linguistic data as befits her current mental state. If these learners are really quite separate—if they literally dismantle the old system and substitute a new one—then it becomes quite reasonable to do as many developmental psycholinguists have done: write a (case) grammar for the 2-year-old, and assume no responsibility for that description as a basis for describing the 3-year-old (for discussion, see Gleitman, 1981). But notice that this is a kind of metamorphosis, or tadpole-to-frog, hypothesis. It is not easy to defend, for there is no evidence that we know of to suggest that old principles and categories are literally discarded during the learning period.

The opposing view is that language learning is continuous. One version of this position is that reorganization is motivated by a data-driven process. The learner is presumed first to acquire information about the language essentially one piece at a time, e.g., generalizations that are applicable only to one or a few verbs or nouns (Bowerman, 1982; Braine, 1976). This relatively unorganized method eventually leads to an unmanageable clutter of facts. Organization into general rule systems will both simplify the storage of information and, sometimes, vastly increase the generative capacity of the system.

Another explanation of apparent reorganization has to do with the modular nature of the language system itself. It is possible that language consists of a number of distinct processes and principles that are at least partly autonomous (Chomsky, 1981). The acquisition of some of these modules may be logically contingent on the acquisition of others. If this is the correct view, then the child's usage may look radically different from an adult's, while in reality the underlying knowledge is of a proper subpart of the adult language. For example, suppose that the learner has control of the thematic-role system and some version of a phrase-structure hierarchy (or even a linearization of phrases), but lacks knowledge of a syntactic module that in the adult language stands between these and mediates their relations. By default, the learner may map one-to-one between the modules that he currently controls.

Summary

We have argued against the view that semantic roles in a language map one-to-one onto syntactic configurations. Nonetheless, case grammar may be a useful device for describing the linguistic organization of very young learners. Even if so, as usually stated this hypothesis is at best a data summary for the speech of the youngest learners, giving no hint as to how learning could progress toward the real complexities of the adult language. We have suggested two main ways out of this pickle. The first is biological: The 2-year-old molts linguistically and becomes a 3-year-old, discarding virtually all principles of the prior system. The second also acknowledges that the character of early and late stages of acquisition look very different from each other, but holds that the learning process is at bottom continuous. In one variant, the learner is motivated by the accumulation of information: Groaning under the burden of storing myriad separate facts, he or she tries some higher-order generalizations that subsume more instances. In another variant, the child maintains the original system essentially without change, but adds semiautonomous new modules at the interface between old ones, radically changing the linguistic outcomes at the surface.

Learning a Bloomfieldian Grammar

The case grammar approach to language learning takes as certain the child's mastery of a small set of semantic distinctions (agent–patient, possessor–possessed, etc.) and attempts to build the rest of syntax acquisition on this base. In contrast, the neo-Bloomfieldian position, to the extent that one exists, builds in an altogether different direction and begins with an entirely contrary certainty; namely, the unarguable fact that adults control some syntactic categories that have little if any direct correlation with matters semantic. More than anyone else, Maratsos and his colleagues (Maratsos, 1979, 1982; Maratsos & Chalkley, 1980; Maratsos, Kuczaj, Fox, & Chalkley, 1979) have been identified with the renovation of Bloomfieldian ideas. Chief among their labors has been the simple but essential reminder that adult grammatical categories, such as *noun, verb,* and *adjective,* cannot summarily be reduced to the semantic definitions of grade school. It follows that such categories must be acquired on some basis that is at least partly independent of semantics, a fact that is something of a conundrum for any theory of acquisition run exclusively on semantic machinery.

In his most recent paper, Maratsos (1982) makes a new and interesting pass at this argument. He begins with the fact that there are some syntactic distinctions, such as the German gender distinction, that are notorious for their failure to show any semantic correlation. For these categories, there is no alternative but to learn category members word-by-word on the basis of the syntactic contexts in which they appear. For example, upon hearing "das machen," one can unequivocally assign *machen* to the neuter gender (semantics be damned) and predict that *machen* will pronominalize via *es,* take *das* in the accusative, and so forth. It is this correlated set of syntactic effects that, according to Maratsos, makes up the German neuter gender. To learn the neuter gender is to learn that these syntactic phenomena predict each other, and nothing more.

From here, the argument moves to interesting ground. In effect, Maratsos argues, if *some* syntactic categories must be learned as clusters of distributional facts, then why not *all* syntactic categories, including the major grammatical categories such as noun and verb, as well as the major constituent categories, such as noun-phrase and verb-phrase? Why postulate more than one sort of language acquisition unless forced to it? A very good question, one worth some pursuit.

Maratsos' learning device is basically an inductive scheme that is capable, in principle, of classifying words together on the basis of shared contexts. We have argued from the beginning the failure of unbiased induction to account for the fact of language learning. Nonetheless, learning must ultimately be by inductive generalization. This follows from the fact that languages differ from one another and hence must be learned, in the classical sense of the term (just Bloomfield's point, as we stated in our introductory remarks). The problem is to isolate units on which induction takes place, given the capacities and inclinations of a human language learner. Maratsos explicit proposal seems to be for a general distributional analyzer that recognizes associations among *any* morphemes. We believe, however, that to the extent this proposal seems plausible, it is because it really (albeit implicitly) builds upon a quite narrow and interesting hypothesis about the nature of these units; specifically, the distributional analyzer Maratsos sketches seems to be particularly sensitive to the open-class/closed-class distinction that we described earlier. The bulk of Maratsos' *co-predictors* (correlations exploited to determine word-class membership) turn out to be associations between a closed-class item and an open-class position. For instance, "takes plural *-s*" predicts noun status for a stress-bearing word; "takes *-ed* and *will*" predicts verb status for other words. Note that a blind inductive device might focus on quite different, and ultimately useless, potential correlations, such as the correlation of *black* with *coal, night,* and *ink* vs. the correlation of *white* with *swan, milk,* and *snow;* no syntactically functioning units are picked out by these latter correlations. To the extent that Maratsos' distributional analyzer is plausible, then, it is because it has eyes for something like an open-class/closed-class distinction. These eyes rescue Maratsos' analyzer from contemplating the limitless false analogies it might otherwise be forced to consider as potential bases for grammatical categories. But this rescue raises problems of its own.

First, there is serious empirical doubt as to whether the closed-class items are generally available to children to support the initial construction of grammatical categories. The evidence we have presented thus far suggests that the closed-class and relevant distinctions among the closed-class items are beyond the grasp of the youngest learners. If this is so, these items would not be available to the inductive device at the stage—a very early stage, as the literature tells us—when the initial distinction between noun and verb is acquired (as evidenced by ordering). Moreover, nouns and verbs apparently emerge without difficulty in early stages of Turkish, which has few closed-class resources, according to Slobin's analysis, and in the historically early version of Tok Pisin which, according to Sankoff, has virtually no inflectional resources. Hence, whatever the facts for normally circumstanced English speaking learners, it cannot be maintained that the distinction between noun and verb, in general, arises from a distributional analysis of open-class/closed-class relations.

Maratsos tries to resolve these problems, but succeeds only by means of weakening the pure Bloomfieldian strain of his proposal. Following Braine (1976), he acknowledges that in the initial stages of language acquisition, grammatical categories (perhaps they should be called pregrammatical categories) are probably formed on semantic grounds. Subsequently, when the closed-class distinctions have been mastered (at about age three), the child is in a position to renovate these categories on the basis of distributional properties. Postulating such a renovation is necessary to account for the fact that children make so few category errors based on semantic uniformities. Thus the verb *like* and the adjective *fond (of)* mean much the same thing. Yet children are not heard to invent *John was fonded of by Mary* on the analogy of *John was liked by Mary* (note that this is just the kind of issue that case grammars have difficulty explaining). Presumably, it is the child's growing appreciation of the ways in which verbs and adjectives co-vary with closed-class items that prevents over-generalizations of this sort.

All this seems plausible enough, but it leaves rather mysterious the acquisition of the closed class itself. Notice that this is not simply a problem of picking out phonetic segments that seem to have low initial salience in the wave form. The child must also learn the grammatical significance of these phonetic elements. It is not, for instance, the location of a word just prior to the appropriate sounds for an *-ed* ending that predicts verb status. Consider, as evidence, that there are no verbs *to lightheart, to lighthead,* or *to lightfinger,* corresponding to the adjectives *lighthearted, lightheaded,* and *lightfingered.* There *is* a distributional regularity here characteristic of verbs, but it holds only when the *-ed* form has been assigned the morphemic value, *past tense.* It follows that if the child learns the verb category partly by learning about its deployment with respect to *-ed* as a marker of past tense, then she first must have learned that *-ed* marks past tense. This much Maratsos specifically acknowledges. But the unanswered question is just how the child manages to accomplish this crucial prior feat. Put generally, the child's move from categories based on semantic properties to categories based on the syntactic distribution of grammatical morphemes is not just a matter of changing the basis of induction. The child's new syntactic base *presupposes* the analysis of grammatical morphemes, and this analysis requires an explanation of its own.

We have left the child with a problem that neither Maratsos nor Bloomfield has solved: to induce the morphemic values of the closed-class items. We will now try to show that, armed with tentative semantic heuristics and exploiting phonological properties of the input strings, the child can in principle bootstrap from partial information to converge on the correct solution. This involves a bottom-up attempt to parse the string from its physical form, combined with a top-down attempt to establish its semantically functioning lexical and phrasal categories.

So far we have granted the learner the open-class/closed-class distinction, at least roughly (that is, as picked out by associated phonological properties). We have also adduced some of the evidence demonstrating that the child is sensitive to the sequencing of open-class elements from the earliest stages. From this it is reasonable to conclude that the learner has established rough precursors to these basic open-class categories, perhaps partly on primitive semantic grounds, as Maratsos and Braine both suppose (see also Pinker, 1982). Perhaps the child is willing to guess, based on preliminary correlational evidence, that concrete objects are encoded by nouns and actions and states are encoded by verbs, a few counterexamples notwithstanding.

However, even more detailed information about strings is required to solve the problem we have just raised: particularly, to find out that *-ed* in *lighthearted* is participial, but might be a finite verb ending in, say, *hotfooted.* The problem still exists because neither the meaning nor the morphology of *hotfooted* renders it more or less verb-like than *lightfingered* or *lighthearted;* that is, there is no semantic heuristic basis in the contrast between action and thing for establishing the open-class categories of these particular words. And then there is no basis for establishing the closed-class morphemic value either, as we have already shown. To repeat, this is because the value of *-ed* can be assigned as *past* only if the learner has secure knowledge that it is bound to a verb.

It is now clear that knowing something approximate about semantic correlates of open-class lexical categories is not enough information for resolving the *-ed* discovery problem. Most generally, this is because not every verb is an action and not every noun is a person, place, or thing. Thus the discovery procedure cannot be reduced to the class definitions of grade-school grammar courses (ask yourself on what semantic basis, for example, *thunder* is both a noun and a verb, while *lightning* is a noun only). As we will show, further analysis of the global phrase structure of the sentence is required.

As we have already described, there are a variety of cooperating cues in the sound wave—stress, rhythm, prepausal lengthening, etc.—to help the learner group formatives into phrases, and we have presented evidence (Read & Schrei-ber, 1982; Morgan & Newport, 1981) that learners are probably disposed to exploit these cues. Moreover, recent formal demonstrations suggest that phrase labeling can be derived from the bracketings (Levy and Joshi, 1978). If a child has such a phrase structural analysis in hand, based on such cues, we can at least in principle describe how she or he learns the facts about *ed.*

One traditional way in which the syntactic values of grammatical morphemes have been determined in linguistics is by means of their relative position in the phrase structure of the sentences in which they appear. The advantage of the phrase-structure representation is that it permits global description of the sentence, as divided into an integral sequence of phrases, hierarchically organized together. At the point at which we are now engaging the learner, he or she is in possession of a partial open-class parse, but (a) one that specifically identifies only open-class elements, and among these (b) only items that conform to the semantic heuristic for identifying nouns with objects and verbs with actions. For example, we now are assuming that the child possesses the mental equivalent of grammatical rules that allow her to construct a parse tree like this:

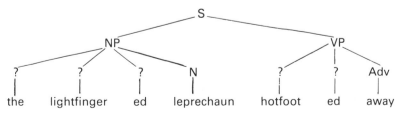

The categorial assignment of *leprechaun* is presumed to be established based on the semantic heuristic, because it is a concrete noun ("a thing"); and differential labeling of the phrasal categories is established by the procedure described by Levy and Joshi (1978). What remain to be specified are the values for *lightfinger* and *hotfoot,* as well as those for the closed-class elements: *the* (determiner), *ed* (participle), and *ed* (finite verb ending). For present purposes, we ignore the solution for *the.* Given the parse tree above, there can be little, if any, uncertainty about the appropriate syntactic categorization of *lightfinger* and *hotfoot,* or the correct assignment of the morphemic value *past* in the second case but not the first. The reasons are straightforward: *Lightfinger* occurs cophrasally before the noun and within the noun-phrase, and hence in a position appropriate to an adjective; that is, before a noun. *Hotfoot* occurs in a verb-phrase, in the position appropriate to the verb. As the first *ed* is bound to an adjective, it cannot be assigned a finite verb interpretation. In contrast, the second *ed* occurs within the verb-phrase and postposed to the verb. Thus, *past* is a possible analysis of *ed.*[9] Assuming that a similar analysis deals with the *the* case, the learner can now construct the final labelings for the parse tree:

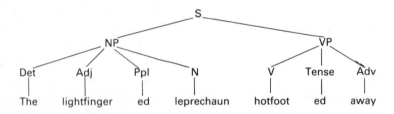

If we accept the moral of this story, the child must learn to parse (though tacitly and unconsciously) and must acquire the syntactic rules on which parsing

---

[9]The fact remains that, given our own prior discussion, the charge can be laid that we have been highhanded (if not lightfingered) in assuming that the learner is disposed to believe properties (adjectives) are of nouns, and times (tenses) are of actions (verbs). We acknowledge that we are assigning such meaningful interpretations of the world, as coded by language, to the child *ab initio,* even though the extent and usefulness of this knowledge is sharply limited by issues mentioned earlier: The interpretation of sentences by reference to scenes is a tricky business; languages vary in the properties of the world that they encode syntactically; and in any case the correlation between form-class and meaning is quite loose. Following Pinker, we here grant only a rough and tentative bias to associate whole concrete objects with the nouns and whole activities with the verbs. Even this, presumably, can be accomplished only in particularly dramatic or compelling circumstances. However the issues here may work out in detail, we submit, without such a rough ability to interpret the world in terms of forms and structures not too distant from the ones used by natural languages, there is simply no account for the acquisition of language (for discussion, see Wexler & Culicover, 1980). As for evidence, it is at least relevant that the creolizing languages we have mentioned (Bickerton, 1975; Sankoff & Laberge, 1973), developed by preliterate societies, move time markers into verb-phrases. And we have mentioned the evidence that even 18-month-olds distinguish actions from objects in their utterances by the order of the words.

depends, to determine the placement and syntactic class values of the closed class. Neither unabetted semantic learning (that *ed* means *past*) nor induction over surface regularities (that *ed* often follows verbs) escapes this conclusion. As we have mentioned in connection with the *thunder/lightning* example, this problem is not specific to such rare items as *hotfooted*, but is a general consequence of the fact that semantic properties are only loosely correlated with the formal lexical classes. To converge on the real richness of the lexical and phrasal properties of any real language, then, the child is forced to consider a deeper and more formal analysis. Detectable clues to the correct analysis can be found in the wave form, by an organism so constructed as to seek them out.

Learning a Transformational Grammar

The question of how syntactic rules are acquired returns us to the first principles of the debate between Chomsky and Bloomfield. Now, however, we can restate the issues in terms of the territory since covered:

1. Given that the child is innately able to "hear" the wave form of parental speech as an ordered string of words, intonationally bracketed into major phrases (possibly, labeled phrases); and

2. Given that the child can, by dint of his own conceptual abilities and through parental efforts to direct his attention (for which, see Bruner 1974/75), achieve an accurate interpretation of some of the sentences he encounters—even before achieving a full grasp of the language he is learning; and

3. Given that the mapping between the semantic interpretation and the surface string is not sufficiently simple to be learned either as a direct projection from semantic representation to the surface string (Braine & Hardy) or vice versa (Maratsos); it follows that

4. We must provide some independent account of how the rules that map between the semantic interpretation and the surface string are acquired.

This task is severely complicated by the fact that there is no single grammatical system now known to be the one psychologically valid statement of these mapping rules. Among the best studied of the alternative grammatical systems are transformational grammar in its several incarnations (Chomsky, 1965, 1975, 1981; Fiengo, 1980); lexical functional grammar (Bresnan, 1982); arc pair grammar (Johnson & Postal, 1980); and relational grammar (Perlmutter, 1980). Given the uncertain choice among these and other alternative descriptions of the adult system, it is difficult to achieve definite results about the process of acquisition. However, it is possible to study some of the boundary conditions under which this acquisition could conceivably take place. It is noteworthy that the study of such conditions can place constraints on the choice among possible grammatical systems because, whatever else is true of adult grammar, it must be learnable by the child. Kenneth Wexler and several colleagues have carried out an extended study of such constraints (see Wexler, 1982, for an overview). Put very simply, Wexler's work is an examination of the compatibility of holding two assumptions: (1) that children learn a mapping between form and meaning (equivalent to our assumption *1* in the preceding list); and (2) that the mapping they learn is, at least in part, a transformational grammar of the so-called "Standard Theory" vintage.

Wexler examined the consistency of these two claims by designing a hypothetical learning device for transformational grammars and determining under what conditions it will converge on the correct transformational grammar for a given language. His earliest result (Wexler & Hamburger, 1973) showed that no such convergence is possible so long as the learner has access only to positive examples of sentences in the target language. This negative result motivated Wexler and his colleagues to examine an altered scenario in which the child is considered able to derive the meaning of adult utterances from extralinguistic circumstances (our assumption *2* in the preceding list) and is also able to derive the deep structures of a transformational grammar from these meanings. On these assumptions, the child is confronted with data consisting of a word string paired with a deep structure for every sentence he or she can interpret in this fashion. Wexler's learning device is extremely simple. Whenever a string/deep-structure pair arrives, it attempts to find a set of transformations in its current grammar that will map from the deep structure to the string. If it is successful, it makes no change in its grammar. If it is unsuccessful, it either deletes one of its current rules at random or attempts to formulate a new transformation (given only its knowledge of elementary transformational operations) that will permit a successful mapping of the current input pair. If such a new rule can be found, it is added to the current grammar.

Hamburger and Wexler (1975) were able to prove that, with this kind of a learning device of this simple type can successfully converge in the limit on the target transformational grammar, but only if the grammar includes certain *new* constraints on the operation of transformational rules. These constraints (for which, see Wexler & Culicover, 1980) are necessary to insure that if the learner makes an error (i.e., infers an incorrect transformation), it will not require a sample sentence of unbounded complexity to reveal that error. A learner requiring examples of unbounded complexity might have to wait an unbounded amount of time to stumble onto even one such example. Hence, convergence could not be guaranteed.

One of the chief thrusts of Wexler's work is linguistic. In collaboration with Culicover, he has attempted to show that the constraints required to guarantee learnability have independent linguistic motivation. Very roughly, the theory imposes constraints on the application of transformational rules under general conditions that would lead to undetectable (from information available in the surface string) errors when deriving a phrase-structure analysis of the sentence derived by the transformation. Wexler and Culicover (1980) have shown that these constraints, put forward to guarantee learning, offer an explanation for certain otherwise mysterious constraints on the applicability of rules that have had to be proposed simply on descriptive grounds: to explain away some nonoccurring structures in adult languages. To the extent that the learnable grammar is also the most successful description of the adult language, it becomes possible to offer learnability as an explanation of descriptive success: The language is as it is just because it must be learned.

No one, incuding Wexler, would propose that his learning device is a full model of how children acquire syntax. It may be that Wexler's current scenario assumes both too much and too little about the input to the child: Too much because it is not known how the child gets from meaning to deep structure without additional learning to supply this mapping, as Wexler acknowledges; too little because, as we have suggested, the child may have intonational access to major phrase boundaries, while Wexler has worked from the assumption that the learner begins by recognizing only the linear string of words. If even partial phrase structure is available to the learning device, certain "undetectable" errors in Wexler's system would become "detectable." Whether the prelinguistic availability of approximate phrase bracketing might have a sufficiently general effect on detectability to render unnecessary any of Wexler and Culicover's transformational constraints is a question that may be worth attention.

Whatever the final details, Wexler's study of learnability is an important move in developmental psycholinguistics. Where much work in the field seems aimed at description for its own sake, Wexler's program serves to refocus attention on explanatory goals. Moreover, it sets exacting standards for the acceptability of explanatory proposals that are a model for future work. How many current notions about how language is learned can offer hard proof that language is, even in principle, learnable in the proposed way? Many arguments in developmental psycholinguistics rest upon unexamined assumptions about learnability that prove to be false once their consequences are examined by more formal techniques. An example of just this sort, and further discussion of Wexler's formal results, will concern us in the following section, describing the "Motherese Hypothesis."

Although the Wexler group's work is surely the most extensive effort to examine the conditions under which a transformational grammar might be acquired, several investigators have taken up the formal approach to studying language learning, sometimes from quite different perspectives about the nature of the learning device and the grammar that is being learned (for further discussion, see Pinker, 1979, 1982, and the collection of learnability studies in Baker & McCarthy, 1981). In fact, as transformational grammar has evolved away from the so-called standard theory, and as the complexity and variety of the transformational rules has steadily diminished, it has become increasingly clear that the learning of transformations is only a small part of the task of learning a generative grammar. Moreover, the very difficulty of establishing rapid convergence for a learning system that proceeds by enumerating grammars has led Chomsky (1981) and others to consider a more restrictive framework in which the child's innate knowledge of universal grammar hypothetically goes well beyond the elementary transformational operations countenanced by Wexler, including instead a rich knowledge of universal rule schemata. In theory, these schemata contain empty slots (where languages vary) that the child needs only to fill in to learn his or her own language. Under this idealization, which is often called "parameter setting" to distinguish it from the hypothesis-testing framework, the child might come pre-armed with schema for core grammar rules informing him that (say) an NP is composed of a head noun plus specifier, but leaving open the problems of determining what order these elements appear in, how specification is marked in this language, and so on. Although some empirical work has recently appeared within this framework (see Roeper, 1982), it is still too early to estimate reliably the value of this alternative way of looking at grammar acquisition.

Saying It Won't Make It So: Caretakers' Role in the Learning Process

As we mentioned earlier, a number of investigators have suggested that the properties of caretaker speech can, in addition to easing the utterance-meaning inductions, contribute causally to solution of the projection problem: relating the forms to the meanings; that is, acquisition of grammar. The idea behind this approach is that the caretaker could order the presentation of syntactic types, so as to narrow the candidate generalizations the child would be in a position to entertain, consistent with his or her data. Certain properties of caretakers' speech to young children give some support to this claim. The caretakers' earliest utterances to children are short and propositionally simple; hence, they are uniclausal. Possibly, mothers say easiest sentences first to littlest ears, successively adding the complications as learning proceeds, and so being responsive at all times to the requirements of an environmentally dependent learning device. This has been called the "fine tuning" hypothesis. (See Cross (1977) and Gleitman et al. (1984) for arguments pro and con.)

There are a number of problems in making good this claim. First, if it is intended to remove requirements for endowments supporting language learning, it could succeed only by transferring this claim from learner to tutor; that is, by placing apparatus in the mother so that she could effectively determine (a) the syntactic simplicity of her potential utterances and (b) the current grammar of the child, plus (c) machinery for rapid implementation of these ideas during her speech planning, so that she could monitor her performance to the child on line, in order to carry out her tutorial aims. It is not obvious why "endowment with linguistic tutorial skills" of this sort should be any more palatable than "endowment with linguistic-learning skills.'' At the very least, this is an empirical question.

Apart from this problem, the evidence of maternal speech does not add plausibility to the view that it would materially aid the acquisition of syntax. For example, the earliest utterances to children are by and large not canonical sentences of the language, and a sizable percentage are not full sentences at all, but are isolated (but well-formed) NP's and interjections. The majority of the full sentences are imperatives and questions. If a transformational grammar is the envisioned end point of learning, it is clear that the child is not selectively receiving simple syntactic structures (i.e., the straightforward, least transformationally deformed outputs of base rules and the obligatory transformations). More generally, it would seem that *any* syntactic theory would have to regard the active, declarative sentences as simplest, but these are not the forms favored by caretakers in their speech to the youngest learners. Moreover, as the child grows older, the percentage of canonical declaratives said to him increases rather than decreases, while the noncanonical forms decrease in proportion. Reliable predictions of the child's growth rate from properties of the maternal speech style that vary among mothers are also limited. In fact, they are limited to the acquisition of the closed-class morphology. Many correlations of other kinds between child's linguistic stage and mother's current usage disappear once these are corrected for baseline differences among child learners. These empirical outcomes limit the extent to which the child's learning of syntax can be assigned to the effects of ''intelligent text presentation'' by the mother (for discussion, see Gleitman et al., 1984; Wexler & Culicover, 1980, ch. 2).

Other problems with this hypothesis are logical. Chomsky (1975) and Wexler (1982) have pointed out that narrowing the learner's data base, although it might do no harm, certainly cannot do good if the outcome of learning is to be a grammar covering the full range of the language. The narrower the range of data, the more hypotheses can describe them. In fact, the difficulty of proving the learnability of language formally would be considerably reduced if it were plausible to suppose that the learner received and could analyze complex input data. This is because the trans-clausal relations within sentences (the transformations, on one formulation) are revealed only in complex sentences, quite obviously.

The major result achieved by the Wexler group thus far has been to devise a set of constraints on transformational operations such that learning is demonstrable from ''degree 2'' input (sentences that are constituted, at maximum, of a clause within a clause within a clause). If the child were assumed able to deal with yet more complex input than this—thus deriving further information about the character of derived phrase structures—fewer constraints (i.e., *less* innate apparatus) would be required, as Wexler and Culicover have shown in detail. To summarize their position, the formal description of learning is *complicated* by the plausible assumption that mothers speak *simply* to their young offspring. Constraints on transformations are required just so that learning can take place, even though the real data are simple (of no more than degree 2 complexity). Why this point has been so hard for developmental psycholinguists to grasp is itself hard to grasp. It seems reasonably obvious that learning should be more difficult from limited and biased ("degenerate," in Chomsky's wording) data than from rich and unbiased data. The degree 2 result, along with the constraints on transformations required to make it work, provides a formal demonstration that would seem to render unassailable the logical point that partial ("simplified") input does not ease the problem of acquiring complex systems.

Despite the logical and empirical difficulties just described, the Motherese Hypothesis continues to be pursued in the developmental psycholinguistic literature (see, for example, the collection of essays in Snow & Ferguson, 1977). This is usually done by claiming that maternal speech aids the young learner in some other and more subtle ways: Perhaps it is the gestures accompanying maternal speech that secure learning; perhaps the mother limits herself, in using a certain form, to a single semantic function for that form. Shatz (1982) has delivered the *coup de grace* to many of these fallback positions by submitting them to a series of observational and experimental tests. She has found that the form–function relations are not materially simplified in maternal speech to young learners, and that these children are quite insensitive to whatever gestural supports to comprehension their parents might be giving (see also Landau, 1982, on language learning in blind children for another kind of support for Shatz's position). It should go almost without saying that the Goldin-Meadow group's demonstrations of the survival of syntax in the absence of formal linguistic input similarly diminish hope that the environment of the learner straightforwardly determines the character of what he or she learns.

There are counterattacks, however, that were not considered by Shatz. One is the conjecture that pragmatics-based theories of language can capture the real richness of human language organization, swallowing what have usually been conceived as syntactic theories (for interesting general discussions, see Clark & Clark, 1978; Searle, 1975; and for a description that specifically attempts to account for the child's acquisition of denominal verbs, see Clark, 1982). How far these approaches, that attempt to incorporate general inferential capacities and richer analyses of situations into the description of language structure, can go is an open question, for understandably there are as yet no well-specified theories of appropriate scope within this framework (at least to our knowledge).

It is worth mentioning that at least one group of investigators has claimed that general social-interactive properties of the mother-child discourse will causally determine the actual form-meaning pairings the child learns. This position has been explicated by Bates and MacWhinney (1982). Their discussion is important, for it recognizes the essentially social nature of language and tries to bring this to bear on the problem of acquisition (see also Fernald & Simon, 1984, for related arguments). This *functionalist* approach to language and its learning is in its infancy, and to this extent the discussion by Bates and MacWhinney is programmatic. At present, it is difficult to say whether social properties of conversations that differ in England and in Germany will account for the fact that English babies put the verb in the middle while German babies put it at the end; that English babies learn to say "I won't put up with that" but not "I won't tolerate with that," and "I painted the wall blue" but not "I painted the wall beautiful"; that they can interpret the *he* in "When he sang, John entranced the audience" anaphorically, but not the one in "He sang, when John entranced the audience"; and all the myriad other facts about how to interpret English sentences meaningfully. On functional grounds, so far as we can see, these issues threaten to require independent explanations, yielding an infinite variety of things that must, and therefore cannot, be learned. Perhaps a functionalist grammar can be written for adults and for children that will bring this approach under control, but for the reasons just stated we must remain pessimistic. However, the descriptive apparatus does not now exist on which to support or falsify the various detailed suggestions about learning that Bates and MacWhinney have proposed.

FINAL THOUGHTS

At the bottom of any scientific paradigm lies a set of beliefs that are usually called metaphysical. It is sometimes claimed that these deep beliefs about the nature of theories and the things they describe cannot be confirmed or disconfirmed by empirical means. It is, however, quite possible to compare different metaphysical beliefs according to the degree of success of the scientific programs they support. Moreover, substantive arguments for one set of metaphysical assumptions over others can be constructed on this basis.

At its deepest level, Chomsky's break with Bloomfield is just this sort of argument. If a grammar can be construed, not as a physical description of linguistic behavior a la Bloomfield, but instead as a description of the linguistic knowledge represented in the human mind, then—so Chomsky argued—it will be possible to construct a more successful and interesting theory of language. Chomsky's familiar commitment to linguistic competence as an object of study is at once a metaphysical decision as to what sort of thing a theory of language is about, and a very practical decision as to what sorts of data the theory will be responsible for and what sorts of constraints on the theory will prove most fruitful. If a grammar describes the speaker's linguistic knowledge, then it is only indirectly revealed in linguistic behavior, and it is not to be held accountable for the physical facts about linguistic behavior for which Bloomfield's grammar must take responsibility. There is a basis (in linguistic judgments) for making an empirical distinction between acceptable and unacceptable sentences, and grammars that aim at describing linguistic knowledge can reasonably restrict themselves to sentences that speakers know to be acceptable. In contrast, attempts, such as Bloomfield's, to construct a grammar that describes behavior directly can at best account for unacceptable sentences (such as slips of the tongue) as improbable utterances, no different qualitatively from the mass of other linguistic-behavioral data.

Although Chomsky's move allows the grammar to escape responsibility for accounting in detail for linguistic behavior, it also imposes a heavy explanatory burden on linguistic theory, and on the theory of language learning in particular. For if a grammar is to be interpreted as a psychological description of human knowledge, then it necessarily raises questions about how this knowledge is acquired. Much of our discussion has attempted to summarize just how well these questions have been answered.

Recently, however, Katz (1981) has mounted an argument against Chomsky's psychologistic interpretation of grammar, one that formally parallels Chomsky's argument against Bloomfield's physicalistic interpretation of grammar. In effect, Katz argues that it is possible to achieve a better theory of language if we drop both the idea that grammar describes human knowledge and the attendant responsibility for showing how such grammatical knowledge is learnable. This can be achieved in Katz's view only if we adopt a Platonic (or realistic) interpretation of the grammar, in which grammatical principles are supposed to describe an abstract reality entirely independent of human knowledge of it, much as the reality of a mathematical relationship (e.g., the Pythagorean Theorem) is sometimes held to be true independent of human appreciation of that truth. According to Katz, this metaphysical interpretation is to be preferred because it permits a full-blooded account of necessary linguistic truths (such as lexical entailments of the "vixen is a fox" variety), which would otherwise have to be held contingent on the nature of the human mind. Moreover, Katz holds that Platonist metaphysics permits simpler solutions to certain thorny problems of grammatical description once the grammar is freed of the requirement that it be rendered in a form learnable by human beings. It may be worth noting that this is exactly the opposite of the views advanced by certain other authors we have discussed (e.g., Wexler, 1982; Newport, 1982), who take the position that the requirement of learnability and its incorporation into linguistic theory explain otherwise mysterious grammatical facts.

Bever (1982) has explored the possible consequences of the Platonist challenge to the Chomskian paradigm for theories of language acquisition. First among these consequences would be the unhooking of linguistic theory and acquisition theory. Linguistic theory describes the set of possible natural languages, and acquisition theory describes the set of languages learnable by humans. According to Platonist assumptions, there is no theoretical reason to expect these two sets to be identical. Thus, Bever argues, the Platonist paradigm remains unembarassed when it turns out that certain cognitive operations never show up in language, just as certain linguistic operations never appear elsewhere in cognition. The Chomskian paradigm can handle such facts by postulating the mental segregation of the linguistic faculty: Language is as it is because of the structure of the human mind, but language is unlike the rest of mind in some respects because the mental organ devoted to language is unlike the rest of mind (in just those respects necessary to explain the difference). Bever claims there is circularity in this formulation: "It is not a literal contradiction to maintain . . . that the essence of language is caused by an organ of the mind. But it does present a picture of language as resulting from a capacity that is mentally isolated in sporadic ways. That is, many aspects of cognition as a whole are reflected in language use and structure; why are the specific exclusions the way they are?" (1982, p. 436). By this route, Bever rejects what he takes to be Chomsky's claim that the essence of language is necessarily caused by the structure of the mind: If there is no independent evidence (independent, that is, of the evidence provided by language itself) for the shape of the mental organ devoted to language, then the claim that the essential structure of language is caused by that mental organ is only a hypothesis, no more certain—although certainly more testable—than the Platonist claim that language is independent of mind.

But once Chomsky's claim has been shown to be hypothetical, one must ask whether the Katz–Bever revelation really changes the empirical problem of explaining language acquisition. Bever argues that one consequence of Platonist assumptions is that it becomes *unnecessary* to hold that language is acquired by a mental organ specifically designed for the task. Fair enough. But it does not follow from this that language acquisition can have a *sufficient* explanation in terms of general learning mechanisms. Even if *language* is caused by the exigencies of some abstract, Platonic reality as Bever suggests, human beings' *knowledge of language* must be psychologically caused. Children must come to know their native tongue. And, as we have been at pains to argue, this knowledge cannot be acquired through unconstrained induction. Exactly what these constraints are and just how they relate to linguistic theory and to general cognition are, we take it, open empirical questions. Indeed, they are the central questions that motivate investigation, and shape our current theories of language and its learning.

ACKNOWLEDGMENTS

This chapter is a revised version of an earlier work (Gleitman & Wanner, 1982), and we thank the Cambridge University Press for allowing us to reprint highly overlapping materials here. The original chapter was constructed as the introduction to a volume of essays from a small group of investigators of child language, and hence organizes the field around these individuals' particular contributions. Although a variety of other sources were cited and discussed, certainly a chapter so constructed will distort credit that is due to many important investigators, by emphasizing particular works and passing too lightly over cognate information contributed by others. Exigencies of time constraints for the present volume prohibited large-scale revision for the current version, which exhibits various technomorphic traces of the prior work. We therefore apologize to contributors to the literature whose work has been inadvertently omitted from this discussion. However, individuals aside, the present chapter does succeed in reviewing our own current vision of the field of language learning and does state our own—to some extent idiosyncratic—beliefs and views about the generalizations to be drawn from currently available data and discussion. We thank The National Foundation for the March of Dimes and the Alfred P. Sloan Foundation, whose continuing support of our work made possible the writing of this paper. And we thank our colleagues, Henry Gleitman, Barbara Landau, and Elissa Newport, whose criticisms of prior drafts materially improved what we have been able to say.

REFERENCES

Armstrong, S. L., Gleitman, L. R., & Gleitman, H. (1983). What some concepts might not be. *Cognition, 13,* 263–308.

Baker, C. L., & McCarthy, J. J. (Eds.). (1981). *The logical problem of language acquisition.* Cambridge, MA: MIT Press.

Bates, E., & MacWhinney, B. (1982). Functionalist approaches to grammar. In E. Wanner & L. R. Gleitman (Eds.), *Language acquisition: State of the art.* New York: Cambridge University Press.

Bellugi, U. (1967). *The acquisition of negation.* Unpublished doctoral dissertation, Harvard University.

Bever, T. G. (1970). The cognitive basis for linguistic structures. In J. Hayes (Ed.), *Cognition and the development of language.* New York: Wiley.

Bever, T. G. (1982). Some implications of the nonspecific bases of language. In E. Wanner & L. R. Gleitman (Eds.), *Language acquisition: State of the art.* New York: Cambridge University Press.

Bickerton, D. (1975). *Dynamics of a creole system.* New York: Cambridge University Press.

Blasdell, R., & Jensen, P. (1970). Stress and word position as determinants of imitation in first language learners. *Journal of Speech and Hearing Research, 13,* 193–202.

Bloch, B. (1941). Phonemic overlapping. *American Speech, 16,* 278–284.

Bloom, L. (1970). *Language development: Form and function in emerging grammars.* Cambridge, MA: MIT Press.

Bloom, L. (1973). *One word at a time.* The Hague: Mouton.

Bloom, L., Lightbown, P., & Hood, L. (1975). Structure and variation in child language. *Monographs of the Society for Research in Child Development, 40* (Serial No. 160).

Bloomfield, L. (1933). *Language.* New York: Henry Holt.

Blount, B. G. (1972). Parental speech and language acquisition: Some Luo and Samoan examples. *Anthropological Linguistics, 14,* 119–30.

Bowerman, M. (1973). Structural relationships in children's utterances: Syntactic or semantic? In T. Moore (Ed.), *Cognitive development and the acquisition of language.* New York: Academic Press.

Bowerman, M. (1982). Reorganizational processes in lexical and syntactic development. In E. Wanner & L. R. Gleitman (Eds.), *Language acquisition: The state of the art.* New York: Cambridge University Press.

Bradley, D. C., Garrett, M. F., & Zurif, E. G. (1979). Syntactic deficits in Broca's aphasia. In D. Caplan, (Ed.), *Biological studies of mental processes.* Cambridge, MA: MIT Press.

Braine, M. D. S. (1976). Children's first word combinations. *Monographs of the Society for Research in Child Development, 41,* (Serial No. 164).

Braine, M. D. S., & Hardy, J. A. (1982). On what case categories there are, why they are, and how they develop: An amalgam of *a priori* considerations, speculation, and evidence from children. In E. Wanner & L. R. Gleitman (Eds.), *Language acquisition: State of the art.* New York: Cambridge University Press.

Bresnan, J. (1978). A realistic transformational grammar. In M. Halle, J. Bresnan, & G. A. Miller (Eds.), *Linguistic theory and psychological reality.* Cambridge, MA: MIT Press.

Bresnan, J. (Ed.). (1982). *The mental representation of grammatical relations*. Cambridge, MA: MIT Press.

Broen, P. A. (1972). The verbal environment of the language learning child. *Monograph of American Speech and Hearing Association, 17*.

Brown, R. (1973). *A first language: The early stages*. Cambridge, MA: Harvard University Press.

Brown, R., & Hanlon, C. (1970). Derivational complexity and order of acquisition in child speech. In J. Hayes (Ed.), *Cognition and the development of language*. New York: Wiley.

Brown, R., & Bellugi, U. (1964). Three processes in the child's acquisition of syntax. *Harvard Educational Review, 34*, 133–151.

Bruner, J. S. (1974/75). From communication to language: A psychological perspective, *Cognition, 3*, 255–287.

Carey, S. (1977). Less may never mean more. In R. Campbell & P. Smith (Eds.), *Recent advances in the psychology of language*. New York: Plenum.

Carey, S. (1982). Semantic development: The state of the art. In E. Wanner & L. R. Gleitman (Eds.), *Language acquisition: The state of the art*. New York: Cambridge University Press.

Carey, S., & Bartlett, E. (1978). Acquiring a single new word. *Papers and reports on child language development*. Department of Linguistics, Stanford University, *15*, 17–29.

Chao, Y-R. (1934). The non-uniqueness of phonemic solutions of phonetic systems. *Bulletin of the Institute of History and Philology, Academia Sinica, 4*, 363–397.

Chomsky, N. (1965). *Aspects of the theory of syntax*. Cambridge, MA: MIT Press.

Chomsky, N. (1972). Some empirical issues in the theory of transformational grammar. In S. Peters (Ed.), *Goals of linguistic theory*. Englewood Cliffs, NJ: Prentice-Hall.

Chomsky, N. (1975). *Reflections on language*. New York: Random House.

Chomsky, N. (1981). *Lectures on government and binding*. Dordrecht: Foris Publications.

Clark, E. V. (1973). What's in a word? On the child's acquisition of semantics in his first language. In T. Moore (Ed.), *Cognitive development and the acquisition of language*. New York: Academic Press.

Clark, E. V. (1982). The young word maker: A case study of innovation in the child's lexicon. In E. Wanner & L. R. Gleitman (Eds.), *Language acquisition: State of the art*. New York: Cambridge University Press.

Clark, E. V., & Clark, H. H. (1978). When nouns surface as verbs. *Language, 55*, 767–811.

Cross, T. G. (1977). Mothers' speech adjustments: The contribution of selected listener variables. In C. E. Snow & C. A. Ferguson (Eds.), *Talking to children*. Cambridge, MA: Cambridge University Press.

Cutting, J., & Rosner, B. (1974). Categories and boundaries in speech and music. *Perception and Psychophysics, 16*, 564–570.

Donaldson, M., & Balfour, G. (1968). Less is more: A study of language comprehension in children. *British Journal of Psychology, 59*, 461–471.

Dorian, N. (1978). The fate of morphological complexity in language death. *Language, 54(3)*, 590–609.

Eimas, P., Siqueland, E. R., Jusczyk, P., & Vigorito, J. (1971). Speech perception in infants. *Science, 171*, 303–306.

Ervin, S. (1964). Imitation and structural change in children's language. In E. Lenneberg (Ed.), *New directions in the study of language*. Cambridge, MA: MIT Press.

Feldman, H., Goldin-Meadow, S., & Gleitman, L. (1978). Beyond Herodotus: The creation of language by linguistically deprived deaf children. *In A. Lock (Ed.), Action, symbol, and gesture: The emergence of language*. New York: Academic Press.

Fernald, A. (1982). *Acoustic determinants of infant preference for "motherese."* Unpublished Ph.D. dissertation, University of Oregon.

Fernald, A. (1983). The perceptual and affective salience of mothers' speech to infants. In C. Feagans, C. Garvey, & R. Golinkoff (Eds.), *The origins and growth of communication*. Norwood, NJ: Ablex.

Fernald, A., & Simon, T. (1984). Expanded intonation contours in mothers' speech to newborns. *Developmental Psychology, 20*, 104–113.

Fiengo, R. (1980). *Surface structure: The interface of autonomous components.* Cambridge, MA: Harvard University Press.

Fillmore, C. J. (1968). The case for case. In E. Bach & R. J. Harms (Eds.), *Universals in linguistic theory.* New York: Holt, Rinehart & Winston.

Fodor, J. A. (1975). *The language of thought.* New York: Crowell.

Fodor, J. A. (1983). *The modularity of mind.* Cambridge, MA: MIT Press, Bradford Books.

Fodor, J. A., Bever, T. G., & Garrett, M. F. (1974). *The psychology of language: An introduction to psycholinguistics and generative grammar.* New York: McGraw-Hill.

Fodor, J. A., Garrett, M. F., Walker, E. C., & Parkes, C. H. (1980). Against definitions. *Cognition, 8*, 263–367.

Foss, D. J., & Hakes, D. T. (1978). *Psycholinguistics: An introduction to the psychology of language.* Englewood Cliffs, NJ: Prentice-Hall.

Freyd, P., & Baron, J. (1982). Individual differences in the acquisition of derivational morphology. *Journal of verbal learning and verbal behavior.*

Fromkin, V. A. (1973). *Speech errors as linguistic evidence.* The Hague: Mouton.

Furrow, D., Nelson, K., & Benedict, H. (1979). Mothers' speech to children and syntactic development: Some simple relationships. *Journal of Child Language, 6*, 423–442.

Garrett, M. F. (1975). The analysis of sentence production. In G. H. Bower (Ed.), *The psychology of learning and motivation* (Vol. 9). New York: Academic Press.

Gentner, D. (1978). On relational meaning: The acquisition of verb meaning. *Child Development, 49*, 988–998.

Gentner, D. (1982). Why nouns are learned before verbs: Linguistic relativity vs. natural partitioning. In S. Kuczaj (Ed.), *Language development: Language, culture, and cognition.* Hillsdale, NJ: Lawrence Erlbaum Associates.

Gleitman, H., & Gleitman, L. R. (1979). Language use and language judgment. In C. J. Fillmore, D. Kempler, & W. S-Y. Wang (Eds.), *Individual differences in language ability and language behavior.* New York: Academic Press.

Gleitman, L. R. (1981). Maturational determinants of language growth. *Cognition, 10*, 103–114.

Gleitman, L. R., & Gleitman, H. (1970). *Phrase and paraphrase.* New York: Norton.

Gleitman, L. R., Newport, E. L., & Gleitman, H. (1984). The current status of the Motherese hypothesis. *Journal of Child Language, 11*.

Gleitman, L. R., & Rozin, P. (1977). The structure and acquisition of reading I: Relations between orthographies and the structure of language. In A. Reber & D. Scarborough (Eds.), *Toward a psychology of reading.* Hillsdale, NJ: Lawrence Erlbaum Associates.

Gleitman, L. R., & Wanner, E. (1982). Language acquisition: The state of the state of the art. In E. Wanner & L. R. Gleitman (Eds.), *Language acquisition: The state of the art.* New York: Cambridge University Press.

Goldin-Meadow, S. (1982). The resilience of recursion: A study of a communication system developed without a conventional language model. In E. Wanner & L. R. Gleitman (Eds.), *Language acquisition: The state of the art.* New York: Cambridge University Press.

Greenfield, P., & Smith, J. (1976). *The structure of communication in early language development.* New York: Academic Press.

Gruber, J. (1968). Look and see. *Language, 43*, 937–947.

Hamburger, H., & Wexler, K. (1975). A mathematical theory of learning transformational grammar. *Journal of Mathematical Psychology, 12*, 137–177.

Harris, Z. S. (1951). *Methods in structural linguistics.* Chicago: University of Chicago Press.

Jackendoff, R. (1983). *Semantics and cognition.* Cambridge: MA: MIT Press.

Jakobson, R. (1941). *Kindersprache, Aphasie, und alllgemeine Lautgesetze.* Stockholm: Almqvist & Wiksell.

Johnson, D. E., & Postal, P. (1980). *Arc-pair grammar.* Princeton, NJ: Princeton University Press.

Joshi, A. K. (1983). Processing of sentences with intra-sentential code-switching. In D. Dowty, L. Kartunnen, & A. Zwicky (Eds.), *Syntactic theory and how people parse sentences.* New York: Cambridge University Press.

Jusczyk, P. W. (1980). Auditory versus phonetic coding of speech signals during infancy. *Proceedings of the CNRS Conference.*

Katz, J. J. *(1972). Semantic theory.* New York: Harper & Row.

Katz, J. J. (1981). *Language and other abstract objects.* Totowa, NJ: Rowman & Littlefield.

Kean, M. L. (1979). Agrammatism: A phonological deficit? *Cognition, 7*(1), 69–84.

Keil, F. C. (1979). *Semantic and conceptual development.* Cambridge, MA: Harvard University Press.

Klatt, D. H. (1975). Vowel lengthening is syntactically determined in a connected discourse. *Journal of Phonetics, 3,* 129–140.

Klatt, D. H. (1976). Linguistic uses of segmental duration in English: acoustic and perceptual evidence. *Journal of the Acoustic Society of America, 59,* 1208–1221.

Klima, E., & Bellugi, U. (1966). Syntactic regularities in the speech of children. In J. Lyons & R. Wales (Eds.), *Psycholinguistics papers.* Edinburgh: Edinburgh University Press.

Klima, E., & Bellugi, U. (1979). *The signs of language.* Cambridge, MA: Harvard University Press.

Kuhl, P. K., & Miller, J. D. (1975). Speech perception by the chinchilla, Voiced-voiceless distinction in alveolar plosive consonants. *Science, 190,* 69–72.

Labov, W. (1970). The reading of the -ed suffix. In H. Levin & J. P. Williams (Eds.), *Basic studies on reading.* New York: Basic Books.

Landau, B. (1982). *Language learning in blind children.* Unpublished Ph.D. dissertation, University of Pennsylvania.

Landau, B., & Gleitman, L. R. (1984). *The language of perception in blind children.* Cambridge, MA: Harvard University Press.

Lehiste, I. (1970). Suprasegmentals. Cambridge, MA: MIT Press.

Levy. L. S., & Joshi, A. K. (1978). Skeletal structural descriptions. *Information and Control, 5*(39), No. 2.

Levy, Y. (1980). *Gender in children's language: A study of first language acquisition.* Unpublished doctoral dissertation. Hebrew University.

Levy, Y. (1983). The acquisition of Hebrew plurals. The case of the missing gender category. *Journal of Child Language, 10*(1), 107–122.

Liberman, A. M. (1970). The grammars of speech and language. *Cognitive Psychology, 1,* 301–323.

Liberman, A. M., Cooper, F. S., Shankweiler, D. P., & Studdert-Kennedy, M. (1967). Perception of the speech code. *Psychological Review, 74,* 431–461.

Liberman, A. M., & Pisoni, D. B. (1977). Evidence for a special speech-perceiving subsystem in the human. In T. H. Bullock (Ed.), *Recognition of complex acoustic signals.* Berlin: Dahlem Konferenzen.

Locke, J. (1965). *An essay concerning human understanding.* New York: Macmillan. (Originally published 1690)

Maratsos, M. (1979). How to get from words to sentences. In D. Aaronson & R. Reiber (Eds.), *Perspectives in psycholinguistics.* Hillsdale, NJ: Lawrence Erlbaum Associates.

Maratsos, M. (1982). The child's construction of grammatical categories. In E. Wanner & L. R. Gleitman (Eds.), *Language acquisition: State of the art.* New York: Cambridge University Press.

Maratsos, M., & Chalkley, M. A. (1980). The internal language of children's syntax: The ontogenesis and representation of syntactic categories. In K. Nelson (Ed.), *Children's language* (Vol. 2). New York: Gardner Press.

Maratsos, M., Kuczaj, S. A., Fox, D.E., & Chalkley, M. A. (1979). Some empirical findings in the acquisition of transformational relations. In W. A. Collins (Ed.), *Minnesota symposia on child psychology* (Vol. 12). Hillsdale, NJ: Lawrence Erlbaum Associates.

Marin, O., Saffran, E., & Schwartz, M. (1976). Dissociations of language in aphasia: Implications for normal function. *Annals of the New York Academy of Sciences, 280,* 868–884.

Markman, E. M., Horton, M. S., & McLanahan, A. G. (1980). Classes and collections: Principle of organization in the learning of hierarchical relations. *Cognition, 8,* 227–241.

McNeill, D. (1966). The creation of language by children. In J. Lyons & R. Wales (Eds.), *Psycholinguistics papers.* Edinburgh: Edinburgh University Press.

Morgan, J., & Newport, E. L. (1981). The role of constituent structure in the induction of an artificial language. *Journal of Verbal Learning and Verbal Behavior, 20,* 67–85.

Nakatani, L. H., & Dukes, K. D. (1977). Locus of segmental cues for word juncture. *Journal of the Acoustic Society of America, 62*(3), 714–724.

Nakatani, L. H., & Schaffer, J. A. (1978). Hearing "words" without words: Prosodic cues for word perception. *Journal of the Acoustic Society of America, 63*(1), 234–245.

Nelson, K. (1973). Structure and strategy in learning to talk. *Monographs of the Society for Research in Child Development, 38,* 1–2.

Nelson, K. (1974). Concept, word, and sentence: Interrelations in acquisition and development. *Psychological Review, 81,* 267–285.

Newport, E. L. (1977). Motherese: The speech of mothers to young children. In N. J. Castellan, D. B. Pisoni, & G. Potts (Eds.), *Cognitive theory* (Vol. 2). Hillsdale, NJ: Lawrence Erlbaum Associates.

Newport, E. L. (1981). Constraints on structure: Evidence from American sign language and language learning. In W. A. Collins (Ed.), *Aspects of the development of competence: Minnesota symposia on child psychology* (Vol. 14). Hillsdale, NJ: Lawrence Erlbaum Associates.

Newport, E. L. (1982). Task specificity in language learning? Evidence from speech perception and American Sign Language. In E. Wanner & L. R. Gleitman (Eds.), *Language acquisition: The state of the art.* New York: Cambridge University Press.

Newport, E. L., & Ashbrook, E. F. (1977). The emergence of semantic relations in American sign language. *Papers and Reports on Child Language Development* (Dept. of Linguistics, Stanford University), *13,* 16–21.

Newport, E. L., Gleitman, H., & Gleitman, L. R. (1977). Mother, I'd rather do it myself: Some effects and noneffects of maternal speech style. In C. E. Snow & C. A. Ferguson (Eds.), *Talking to children: Language input and acquisition.* Cambridge: Cambridge University Press.

Newport, E. L., & Supalla, T. (1980). The structuring of language: Clues from the acquisition of signed and spoken language. In U. Bellugi & M. Studdert-Kennedy (Eds.), *Signed and spoken language: Biological constraints on linguistic form.* Dahlem Konferenzen. Weinheim/Deerfield Beach, Fl./Basel: Verlag Chemie.

Palermo, D. S. (1973). More about less: A study of language comprehension. *Journal of Verbal Learning and Verbal Behavior, 12,* 211–221.

Perlmutter, D. M. (1980). Relational grammar. In E. Moravcsik & J. Wirth (Eds.), *Syntax and semantics* (Vol. 13). New York: Academic Press.

Phillips, J. (1970). *Formal characteristics of speech which mothers address to their young children.* Unpublished doctoral dissertation, Johns Hopkins University.

Pinker, S. (1979). Formal models of language learning. *Cognition, 7,* 217–283.

Pinker, S. (1982). A theory of the acquisition of lexical interpretive grammars. In J. Bresnan (Ed.), *The mental representation of grammatical relations.* Cambridge, MA: MIT Press.

Pye, C. (1983). Mayan telegraphese. *Language, 59*(3), 583–604.

Quine, W. V. (1960). *Word and object.* Cambridge, MA: MIT Press.

Read, C., & Schreiber, P. (1982). Why short subjects are harder to find than long ones. In E. Wanner & L. R. Gleitman (Eds.), *Language acquisition: State of the art.* New York: Cambridge University Press.

Roeper, T. (1982). The role of universals in the acquisition of gerunds. In E. Wanner & L. R. Gleitman (Eds.), *Language acquisition: State of the art*. New York: Cambridge University Press.

Rosch, E. (1973). On the internal structure of perceptual and semantic categories. In T. Moore (Ed.), *Cognitive development and the acquisition of language*. New York: Academic Press.

Rosch, E. (1975). Cognitive representation of semantic categories. *Journal of Experimental Psychology: General, 104*, 192–233.

Rosch, E., & Mervis, C. B. (1975). Family resemblances: Studies in the internal structure of categories. *Cognitive Psychology, 7*, 573–605.

Rosch, E., Mervis, C. B., Gray, W. D., Johnson, D. M., & Boyes-Braem, P. (1976). Basic objects in natural categories. *Cognitive Psychology, 8*, 382–439.

Rozin, P., & Gleitman, L. R. (1977). The structure and acquisition of reading II: The reading process and the acquisition of the alphabetic principle. In A. Reber & D. Scarborough (Eds.), *Toward a psychology of reading*. Hillsdale, NJ: Lawrence Erlbaum Associates.

Sachs, J., & Devin, J. (1976). Young children's use of appropriate speech styles in social interaction and role-playing. *Journal of Child Language, 3*, 81–98.

Sankoff, G., & Laberge, S. (1973). On the acquisition of native speakers by a language. *Kivung, 6*, 32–47.

Schieffelin, B. B. (1979). Getting it together: An ethnographic approach to the study of the development of communicative competence. In E. Ochs & B. B. Schieffelin (Eds.), *Developmental pragmatics*. New York: Academic Press.

Schlesinger, I. M. (1971). The production of utterances and language acquisition. In D. I. Slobin (Ed.). *The ontogenesis of grammar: A theoretical symposium*. New York: Academic Press.

Searle, J. R. (1975). Indirect speech acts. In P. Cole & J. Morgan (Eds.), *Syntax and semantics: Vol. 3: Speech acts*. New York: Academic Press.

Shatz, M. (1978). Children's comprehension of question-directives. *Journal of Child Language, 5*, 39–46.

Shatz, M. (1982). On mechanisms of language acquisition: Can features of the communicative environment account for development? In E. Wanner & L. R. Gleitman (Eds.), *Language acquisition: State of the art*. New York: Cambridge University Press.

Shatz, M., & Gelman, R. (1973). The development of communication skills: Modifications in the speech of young children as a function of listener. *Monographs of the Society for Research in Child Development, 38*(5), (whole No. 152).

Skinner, B. F. (1957). *Verbal behavior*. New York: Appleton-Century Crofts.

Slobin, D. I. (1966). The acquisition of Russian as a native language. In F. Smith & C. A. Miller (Eds.), *The genesis of language: A psycholinguistic approach*. Cambridge, MA: MIT Press.

Slobin, D. I. (1973). Cognitive prerequisites for the development of grammar. In C. A. Ferguson & D. I. Slobin (Eds.) *Studies of child language development*. New York: Holt, Rinehart & Winston.

Slobin, D. I. (1977). Language change in childhood and in history. In J. Macnamara (Ed.), *Language learning and thought*. New York: Academic Press.

Slobin, D. I. (1982). Universal and particular in the acquisition of language. In E. Wanner & L. R. Gleitman (Eds.), *Language acquisition: State of the art*. New York: Cambridge University Press.

Slobin, D. I., & Bever, T. G. (1982). Children use canonical sentence schemas: A crosslinguistic study of word order and inflections. *Cognition, 12*(3), 229–266.

Snow, C. E. (1977). Mothers' speech research: From input to interaction. In C. E. Snow & C. A. Ferguson (Eds.), *Talking to children: Language input and acquisition*. New York: Cambridge University Press.

Snow, C., Arlman-Rupp, A., Hassing, Y., Jobse, J., Joosten, J., & Vorster, J. (1976). Mothers' speech in three social classes. *Journal of Psycholinguistic Research, 5*, 1–20.

Snow, C. E., & Ferguson, C. A. (Eds.). (1977). *Talking to children*. Cambridge: Cambridge University Press.

Sorenson, J. M., Cooper, W. E., & Paccia, J. M. (1978). Speech timing of grammatical categories. *Cognition, 6*(2), 135–154.

Spelke, E. S. (1982). Perceptual knowledge of objects in infancy. In J. Mehler, M. F. Garrett, & E. C. Walker (Eds.), *Perspectives in mental representation.* Hillsdale, NJ: Lawrence Erlbaum Associates.

Spring, D. R., & Dale, P. S. (1977). Discrimination of linguistic stress in early infancy. *Journal of Speech and Hearing Research, 20,* 224–231.

Streeter, L. A. (1978). Acoustic determinants of phrase boundary perception. *Journal of the Acoustic Society of America, 64,* 1582–92.

Waxman, S., & Gelman, R. *Preschoolers' use of superordinate relations in classification.* Unpublished manuscript, University of Pennsylvania.

Wexler, K. (1982). A principle theory for language acquisition. In E. Wanner & L. R. Gleitman (Eds.), *Language acquisition: State of the art.* New York: Cambridge University Press.

Wexler, K., & Culicover, P. (1980). *Formal principles of language acquisition.* Cambridge, MA: MIT Press.

Wexler, K., & Hamburger, H. (1973). On the insufficiency of surface data for the learning of transformational languages. In K. Hintikka, J. Moravcsik, & P. Suppes (Eds.), *Approaches to natural languages.* Dordrecht: Reidel.

Wittgenstein, L. (1953). *Philosophical investigations.* New York: Macmillan.

III SOCIAL, EMOTIONAL, AND PERSONALITY DEVELOPMENT

Language permits abstract thought; it also allows interpersonal communication, which is a basis of social interaction. As Michael Lamb points out in Chapter 8, early social development does not involve language: The first enduring social relationships—infant-parent attachments—develop over the first few months. In these preverbal months, communication proceeds via nonverbal emotional signals. The development and function of these signals are reviewed in this chapter, as are the social relationships established with parents, siblings, and persons beyond the family.

Through their emotional expressions, parents convey love as well as messages of conditional approval and disapproval that reinforce the early but important messages of early socialization. Nowhere is this more apparent than when instilling knowledge of societal norms about acceptable and unacceptable behavior, the focus of Chapters 9, 10, and 11. In Chapter 9, Diane Ruble discusses the development of sex roles and sex differences. As in the case of perceptual and language development, the nature–nurture debate resurfaces with renewed urgency in attempts to explain the processes by which the characteristics of maleness and femaleness emerge. There certainly exist biological differences between the sexes, but the roles they play in the emergence of psychological sex differences remain open to dispute. Few doubt that the messages of approval and disapproval conveyed by parents, peers, teachers, and the media are important: What is debated is the extent to which the ultimate success of psychological forces depends on complementary biologically driven processes.

At least some aspects of conventional sex roles are simply matters of social convention, reflecting as they do societal standards and expectations. Other social expectations and standards attend prosocial and aggressive behavior, which are the focus of Nancy Eisenberg's contribution in Chapter 10. Although sociobiologists and ethologists have discussed the evolutionary bases of both aggressive and altruistic behavior, proximate mechanisms studied by psychologists tend to involve social learning. There is some agreement that hormonal factors may influence the display of aggressive behavior.

Expectations regarding altruism and aggression form part of a larger system of standards comprising morality, and moral development is at the center of Chapter 11 by Martin Hoffman. Underscoring the convergence of altruism and moral development, Hoffman argues that the development of empathy is at the heart of moral development. Empathy is an aspect of interpersonal consideration that emerges in primitive form in infancy and is elaborated and extended over time. Morality, as Hoffman argues, is in large measure a matter of considering the effects of one's actions on others and of avoiding conduct that will deleteriously affect the well-being of others.

Finally, this section ends with a discussion of personality development gone awry. Thomas Achenbach in Chapter 12 recounts the history of attempts to identify the disturbed behavior of children and to develop a common language to be used when describing pathological behavior. Only now, he shows, are we becoming more adept at the description of developmental psychopathology and at the differentiation of disorders. Reliable and widely applied systems of description and classification are, of course, essential to developing and evaluating differentiated, appropriate, and successful modes of treatment.

8 Social and Emotional Development in Infancy

Michael E. Lamb
National Institute of Child Health and Human Development

INTRODUCTION

Over the last century, the amount of attention paid to emotional phenomena and to social and emotional development in infancy has waxed and waned. These increases and decreases in the popularity of social and emotional issues among researchers and theorists have coincided respectively with optimism, occasioned by the emergence of new theoretical perspectives, and with pessimism, attributable to the apparent empirical intractibility of emotions and emotional phenomena. Until recently, empirical advances were also hampered by the absence of a clear, consensually acceptable definition of the "emotions." Until the last few years, each investigator or theorist appeared to have an idiosyncratic definition and focus (see, for example, the anthology edited by Plutchik, 1980), and each thus pursued her or his unique questions in near-isolation. Today, however, there is widespread agreement about what emotions are and how they are elicited (Campos, 1986). Further, where differences remain, they arise because many competing theories address different questions and are thus not necessarily inconsistent with one another. Thus a synthesis of the most useful contributions of each approach is both possible and necessary.

According to Campos (1986), emotions are the consequences of the significance of events—they represent the individual's evaluation of the personal significance of events. Lewis and Michalson (1983) proceed to describe five defining characteristics of emotions. First, there are emotion *elicitors,* endogenous and exogenous stimulus events that trigger biological changes. Second, there are emotion *receptors* that facilitate the encoding of emotional events. Third, are emotional *states* that involve changes in somatic and psychophysiological activity when emotional receptors are activated. Fourth, there are emotional *expressions,* including observable and potentially communicative behaviors and muscle movements. Last, there is emotional *experience,* "the interpretation and evaluation by individuals of their perceived emotional state and expression."

Without contesting these distinctions, Campos and his colleagues (e.g., Campos, Barrett, Lamb, Stenberg, & Goldsmith, 1983; Campos & Stenberg, 1981; Klinnert, Campos, Sorce, Emde, & Svejda, 1983) have emphasized two major *functions* or *purposes* of emotions. First, emotional states or affects *facilitate behavioral reactions* to external events. Second, emotional expressions serve a *communicative* function, alerting others to the emotional state and thus to the behavioral predisposition of the individual. As shown in the following pages, most theorists have focused on one or another of these functions. The psychoanalysts and cognitive developmentalists, for example, have emphasized the covert associations between emotional states and behavior, whereas the ethological-adaptational and social-cognitive theorists have focused on the communicative functions of emotional expressions. Here we detail the contrasting positions of the theorists who dominated work on emotional development for so long, and then we describe the novel integrative approach that now dominates the field.

Four issues have dominated the literature on emotional development—chronology (when do the basic affects and emotions emerge?), explanation, intrapersonal regulation, and interpersonal regulation. With respect to social development, the principal concerns have always been with the mechanisms underlying the formation of enduring emotional bonds or relationships to specific people, notably parents, and with the effects of varying social experiences on later personality. In this chapter, I review the ontogeny and explanations of five milestones in socioemotional development, before describing research on the origins of individual differences and on the development of social relationships with peers and siblings. The contents of this chapter complement those of the next four chapters, in which aspects of social and emotional development are also explored. Because the authors of these chapters emphasize events and developments that occur after infancy, however, the focus here is on infancy. In the next section of this chapter, the five major perspectives on social and emotional development—psychoanalysis, learning theory, ethological-adaptational theory, cognitive-developmental theory, and social cognition—are reviewed roughly in the order in which they attained prominence. Then in the third section, the five best-studied milestones of social and emotional development are described: the emergence of social smiling, stranger anxiety or wariness, separation anxiety, social attachment to parents, and the fear of heights. The explanations provided by the major theories for each of these "milestones" are discussed and evaluated in the fourth section. Each approach is able to explain some but not all of the developments discussed; in several cases different theorists have identified different issues to "explain." In the fifth section, we present Campos' integrative approach, one designed to incorporate the best features of the older competing theories. This approach has achieved a measure of consensual acceptance, and currently dominates research and theorizing on emotional development. The origins and nature of individual differences in socioemotional development are described and discussed in the final substantive section. Most of the research described emphasizes endogenous (i.e., temperamental) bases or experiential histories as the bases of individual differences with most discussions of interaction focused nearly exclusively on infant–mother interaction.[1] Recognizing that attachments to parents and negative responses to strangers do not fully represent the infant's social experiences, we also describe social relationships with peers and siblings.

MAJOR THEORIES AND APPROACHES

Although many theorists have discussed the nature of socioemotional development, most have provided explanations that can be placed into one of five major categories: Psychoanalysis, learning theory, ethological-adaptational theory, cognitive-developmental theory, and social-cognitive theory.

Psychoanalysis and Its Derivatives

Systematic attention to social and emotional development began with psychoanalytic theory in the first decade of the twentieth century. Freud was the first theorist to speculate about the formative significance of early experiences such as feeding, infantile sexuality, and toilet training, which had formerly been considered relatively unimportant. In addition, Freud was perhaps the first theorist to pose questions about the development of emotions, rather than only about their nature and significance in adults.

Freud (1923/1962) proposed that the human mind was organized into three mental systems—the id, ego, and superego. He viewed the id, which strives for immediate gratification by any available means, as the source of all human motivation. Unlike the id, which is present at birth, the ego develops slowly and attempts to establish control over the id by ensuring that gratification is obtained only by appropriate means and at appropriate times and places. Among the crucial psychological functions of the ego are: the delay of gratification; perception, thought, and language; and the experience and expression of emotions

---

[1]In order to reflect accurately the writings of the theorists discussed here, I too refer most often to *mothers* and infants, recognizing that the role rather than the gender or even biological relatedness of the parent is likely to be most important. *Parent* is often not an appropriate substitute, given both the intentions of the theorists and the differential formative roles assumed by parents simply by virtue of vastly differing degrees of involvement.

(external expressions) and affects (internal feeling states). The development of the ego can thus be assessed by observing the emergence of these three general functions. The superego, which governs the moral and ethical conduct of the individual, was believed to develop in early to middle childhood. By definition, the superego has most to do with the topics discussed by Hoffman in his chapter on moral development, later in this book.

Because Freud focused on the development of the superego, most psycho-analytic theory concerning early social and emotional development is attributable to Anna Freud (his daughter) and Rene Spitz. It was Spitz (e.g., 1965) who proposed that ego development is not simply a function of biological maturation; instead, he argued, the emergence of ego processes is primarily determined by the quality of mother–child interaction. In Spitz's view, the major milestones of socioemotional development identified earlier in this chapter were "organizers" which reflected the attainment of new stages of ego development. When mater-nal care—like other theorists, he actually meant care by the primary care-pro-vider, who is usually the mother—was adequate, biological maturation ensured that these milestones occurred at predictable times; but when the child's care was deficient, ego development was retarded and thus the milestones were attained more slowly, if at all. According to psychoanalysts, parent–child interaction affects development by producing both gratification and frustration (e.g., sched-ule feeding); this means that parents are thus responsible for both increases and decreases in drive. Because drive increases produce "unpleasure," whereas drive reductions produce quiescence (absence of unpleasure) or pleasure, the care-provider is inextricably tied into the child's affective life.

The affects that result from need gratification help to "organize" the ego processes of perception, cognition, and memory. They facilitate perception by giving salience to stimuli in the environment that coincide with need and need reduction. When the interaction is generally gratifying, the stimuli that become salient are likely to be those that relate to the care-providers, particularly their faces.

Learning Theory

Behaviorism was founded by John Watson, who was frustrated by the tendency, especially on the part of European theorists, to speculate about the effects of unobservable events or unobservable mental structures and processes. If it were to be a science, argued Watson (1913), psychology must limit itself to phe-nomena that are empirically verifiable. He proposed that emotional development proceeded as a result of learned associations with or modifications of one of the three basic (i.e., unlearned or innate) emotions he posited: fear (elicited by loud noises or the loss of support); rage (elicited by the restriction of bodily move-ments); and love (elicited by stroking, patting, or stimulating an erogenous zone). For Watson and the learning theorists who followed him, only emotional expressions were of interest; internal affective states were not independently explorable or verifiable and were thus ignored.

Whereas classical conditioning aims to account for the transfer of an existing response to new stimuli that did not initially elicit the reaction, operant conditioning is useful for explaining increases or decreases in the frequency of emotional reactions that occur spontaneously. The operant conditioning of emotional reactions only became the focus of attention in the 1950s. A further development took place a decade later, when Bandura and Walters (1959, 1963) reintroduced the notion of learning through mere observation, which they called "observational learning." They argued that many behavior patterns, including emotional expressions, could be learned simply by seeing them displayed by other people who were attractive models for the child.

Ethological-Adaptational Theory

Unlike psychoanalysts and learning theorists, ethological-adaptational theorists such as Bowlby (1969) consider the communicative functions of emotions to be of paramount importance. During infancy, they argue, emotional expressions such as smiles and cries affect the behavior of parents and caretakers by promoting proximity to protective adults, and thus play a special role in regulating social relationships. Further, Bowlby suggested, the repeated association of proximity-promoting signals with appropriate (i.e., proximity-promoting) responses on the part of adults underlies the formation of attachment bonds between infants and adults. In so doing, Bowlby not only provided an answer to questions about why emotions and social relationships exist in infancy (they exist because they have survival value), but also proposed a mechanism whereby social bonding might proceed.

Cognitive-Developmental Approaches

Another group of theorists concern themselves with the cognitive processes that are the proximate causes of emotions or affects. Seeking to explain how fear came to be elicited by the appearance of a totally novel stimulus, Hebb (1946, 1949) provided a physiological explanation in terms of the discrepancy between the pattern of stimulation occasioned by previous encounters with familiar stimuli, and the pattern of stimulation produced by the novel stimulus. This discrepancy produces the distress which we call fear, Hebb argued, because it is adaptive to be fearful of the unknown. Modifying Hebb's formulation, developmental psychologists such as Kagan (e.g., 1971, 1974) and McCall (e.g., McCall & McGhee, 1977) provided an explanation of the same sort, in which they attributed fear or distress to the discrepancy between memories (or *schemata*) and the features of novel objects. When there is great similarity, there is little discrepancy, and thus little distress is occasioned. As the magnitude of the discrepancy increases, the amount of distress increases up to the point at which discrepancy becomes so great that the stimulus cannot be assimilated. The amount of distress thereupon starts to decrease—producing an inverted U-shaped curve relating distress to degree of discrepancy. Kagan (1971, 1974; Kagan, Kearsley & Zelazo, 1978) has argued that the discrepancy model can account for emotional phenomena such as smiling, separation anxiety, and stranger anxiety or wariness.

Social Cognition

Despite similarities with the cognitive developmentalists—notably an emphasis on the child's attempts to interpret his or her experiences and on the maturational emergence of certain crucial abilities—those who have proposed a social-cognitive approach differ in some important ways from cognitive developmentalists. Where the cognitive developmentalists focus on *discrepancy,* one group of social-cognitive theorists has emphasized *ambiguity* and the *communicative* function of emotional expressions. For example, Campos and his colleagues (e.g., Klinnert et al., 1983) have shown that when in ambiguous situations, infants of 10 months of age or older will examine their parents' faces for emotional cues—presumably because this information may help them to disambiguate the situation. The child then modifies emotion and behavior in accordance with the parent's emotional expression.

The propensity to both seek and utilize the information thus obtained may vary, depending on the degree of trust the infants have in their parents (Dickstein, Thompson, Estes, Malkin, & Lamb, 1984). The development of trustful relationships has itself been an issue of concern to social-cognitive theorists. Following Ainsworth (1973, 1979), for example, Lamb (1981a, 1981b) suggested that variations in the responsiveness and sensitivity of parents to their children's signals may produce differences in the extent to which children come to count on their parents' reliability, consistency, and behavioral appropriateness.

Summary

Although each group of theorists has attempted to explain central aspects of socioemotional development, each has addressed a slightly different question. Psychoanalysts have focused on the way in which social experiences retard or accelerate the endogenous processes underlying development. Learning theorists have focused on the way in which social experiences affect the emergence or later development of certain emotional reactions in the absence of any underlying endogenous developmental process. The ethological-adaptational theorists have asked what purpose these emotional reactions might currently serve, or might have served during the evolutionary history of the species. The cognitive-developmental theorists have asked what basic cognitive processes underlie changes in social and emotional behavior, whereas those who adopt a social-cognitive perspective propose that we may obtain a broader view of socioemotional development if we assume that children actively try to make sense of their social and nonsocial experiences. Thus we find both differences in basic assumptions and differences in focus. The joint insights may be more useful than those provided by any one approach on its own.

MILESTONES IN SOCIOEMOTIONAL DEVELOPMENT

Despite great differences in approach and emphasis, all of the theories just described have attempted to explain a narrow set of social and emotional phenomena: the emergence of social smiling, fearful reactions to strangers and heights, distressed reactions to separation from parents, and the formation of discriminating social attachments. The onset and nature of these five milestones, and then explanations of them, are described in this section and the next.

Social Smiling

Although newborns produce facial expressions that resemble smiling, these expressions usually occur when the infant is either drowsy or sleeping, and seem to represent involuntary physiological reactions. Voluntary smiling in a waking state usually does not occur until the infant is 4 to 6 weeks of age. Initially, smiles are elicited by a variety of stimuli, including faces, bells, and bull's-eyes (Emde & Harmon, 1972); but gradually they are limited to social stimuli and contexts, with the human face, viewed full-on, becoming the most effective stimulus for eliciting smiles (Ahrens, 1954). From the second and third months, the infant appears capable of recognizing specific faces, and thereafter the faces of familiar people elicit smiles most readily.

Stranger Anxiety or Wariness

Although positive reactions to strange adults are somewhat muted from late in the first quarter-year (Bronson, 1972), frankly negative reactions typically do not occur until the third quarter-year of life. The intensity of these reactions varies from infant to infant as does the age of onset, although most infants seem to pass through a phase of adverse responses to strangers that usually begins between 6 and 15 months of age (Emde, Gaensbauer, & Harmon, 1976). Scarr and Salapatek (1970) reported a second peak around 18 months, but this is not well established. In many cases, signs of wariness, distress, or avoidance alternate with indices of positive affiliation, indicating that infants are often attracted to strangers as well as alarmed by them (Bretherton, 1978; Bretherton & Ainsworth, 1974; Nash & Lamb, in prep.).

Separation Anxiety

Beginning around 6 to 8 months of age (and perhaps even earlier: Stayton, Ainsworth, and Main, 1973), infants begin to protest separation from specific people, not simply the termination of enjoyable activities. If the separation is prolonged, the reaction changes from distress, agitation, and anger (termed "protest"), to despondency and apparent depression (called "despair"), to apparent recovery (otherwise known as "detachment") as the child regains responsiveness to social overtures (Bowlby, 1973, 1980; Robertson & Bowlby, 1952). Long-term separations that take place prior to the onset of separation anxiety (as, for example, when a 4-month-old child is moved from a foster home to an adoptive home) may produce temporary disequilibrium as the child adjusts to new routines and styles; but there is no comparison between this and the intensity of protest and despair observed when older infants experience similar separations (e.g., Yarrow & Goodwin, 1973).

Social Attachments

Most theorists believe that the emergence of separation protest signals a major qualitative change in the nature of social relationships indicative of a change in the child's cognitive capacity—perhaps the onset of recall memory or object permanence (Piaget, 1936/1952)—which allows the child to remember and therefore miss the parent when he or she is not present. This qualitative change, manifested behaviorally by the emergence of separation anxiety, is often viewed as a sign that true social attachments to specific individuals have been formed (Ainsworth, 1973; Bowlby, 1969). Other indices of these bonds include: use of the adult as a secure base whose presence facilitates exploration; selective use of the adult for comfort or protection in the event of distress or fear; and a preferential desire for proximity to or contact with the adult.

Fear of Heights

The second half-year of life is also a time when several nonsocial emotional changes take place. Because some animals appear fearful on the deep side of the visual cliff (see Chapter 4) from birth, for example, it had often been speculated that the fear of heights was innate (e.g., Walk, 1978). This does not appear to be the case in humans. As described by Bornstein in Chapter 4, the first crucial study was one by Campos, Langer, and Krowitz (1970) who showed that by 2 to 3 months of age infants could distinguish between deep and shallow drops-off when suspended over them: their heart rate decreased when they viewed depth, indicating attention and interest. Later Fox, Aslin, Shea, and Dumais (1980) used a more complex procedure to show that stereoptic perception of depth emerges around 3 to 4 months. Interestingly, however, infants of this age do not show any signs of fear when suspended over a deep "cliff." Fearful reactions—

including heart rate acceleration, distress, and refusal to cross the deep side of the visual cliff, despite the support provided by clear perspex—typically do not emerge until around 8 months of age (Campos, Hiatt, Ramsay, Henderson, & Svejda, 1978). Thus the *fear* of depth emerges several months after the capacity to *perceive* depth, presumably because the sensation of depth does not initially have any fearful meaning. Once the infant is able to locomote and fall, however, depth becomes a very meaningful clue to danger, and thus begins to elicit fear.

Summary

Social smiling usually begins in the second month, and becomes common and reliable within a few weeks. After an initial period of promiscuous sociability, infants come to reserve their broadest and readiest smiles for familiar people. Five or six months later, several new emotional reactions—including stranger anxiety, separation anxiety, the fear of heights, and social attachment—all emerge at roughly the same time. Despite these somewhat coincident developmental schedules, these milestones do not appear to be causally related to one another. Their disparate origins are explored further in the next section, where the focus is on explanations and interpretations of these milestones of socioemotional development.

EXPLANATIONS AND INTERPRETATIONS OF SOCIOEMOTIONAL MILESTONES

Social Smiling

Psychoanalytic Theory. As mentioned earlier, the pleasurable sensation of need gratification helps to organize perception by making certain stimuli salient. When parent–infant interaction develops favorably, the stimuli that become salient are likely to be features of the care-provider, especially of his or her face. Need and need reduction also help organize memory: The child learns that the appearance of the facial stimuli means that drive reduction is about to take place. Hence, Spitz (1965) uses the term "sign gestalt" to refer to the facial features that elicit social smiles.

According to Spitz, infants do not learn to smile; they learn to notice the features of the face which *automatically* elicit smiling. Of course if there was no consistent care-provider, or no regular coincidence of certain stimuli and certain drive states, the face gestalt would not be noticed until later, if at all. Ambrose (1961) found that social smiles occurred earlier in family-reared than institutionally-reared infants, while Spitz and Wolf (1946) found that social smiling was delayed by cold or hostile mother–infant interaction.

The onset of social smiling heralds what Spitz called the stage of the preobject, during which the child does not yet understand the identity of the care-provider. During this stage, many facelike stimuli elicit smiling, whereas familiar faces in profile do not. Continued interaction promotes further perceptual refinements until, with time, recognition of the parent becomes so affectively laden that an important new set of cognitive and emotional processes emerge, including evocative (recall) memory, separation anxiety, and stranger anxiety.

Unfortunately, 6- to 12-week-old infants smile not only at faces, but also at a wide range of nonsocial stimuli, such as bells and bull's-eye patterns (Emde & Harmon, 1972). Psychoanalytic theory cannot explain such smiling, and we must thus doubt the veracity of its explanation regarding the onset of social smiles.

Learning Theory.   Learning theorists explain the emergence of social smiling by proposing that the features of the face are associated, through a process of classical conditioning, with the pleasurable state that was brought about by drive reduction or need gratification (resulting from feeding, drinking, keeping warm). Later increases in the frequency of social smiling can be affected by operant contingencies: Parents respond enthusiastically when the infant smiles and thus reward or reinforce smiling. Two crucial studies have demonstrated the classical conditioning and deconditioning of emotions (albeit fear rather than smiling: Watson & Rayner, 1920; Jones, 1924), while others have demonstrated that the frequency of smiling (and crying) can indeed be increased by reinforcement (e.g., Schwartz & Rosenberg, 1968; Etzel & Gewirtz, 1967). Thus there appears to be some empirical support for this theory's predictions.

Unfortunately, learning theory appears better able to explain the transfer of emotional reactions from one stimulus to another, and variations in the frequency of smiling and other emotional expressions, than to explain the initial emergence of emotional reactions. In the case of social smiling, for example, we know that—contrary to Watson's predictions—feeding, holding, or stroking babies does not consistently elicit smiling. Nor does any other form of drive reduction (Spitz, 1965). No unconditional stimulus initially and innately elicits smiles, which is crucially important if conditional stimuli (like faces or voices) are later to become effective elicitors of smiles through conditioning. Imitation and observational learning likewise cannot explain the onset of social smiling, because blind babies begin smiling to their parents' voices at the same age as sighted infants (Fraiberg, 1977). And although the frequency of smiling can be shaped through operant conditioning, it is not plausible to suggest that infants' mouth movements are shaped in successive approximations until recognizable smiles are evident.

Ethological-Adaptational Theory.   Evidence concerning maturational and biogenetic influences on emotional development led psychologists to turn toward evolutionary biology, in the form of the ethological-adaptational theory, for insight into the communicative nature of socioemotional development. There is a clear developmental—presumably maturational—progression from an internal to an external elicitation of smiles. Newborns smile quite readily, but only in rapid-eye-movement states (Emde & Harmon, 1972). For a few weeks after birth, they also smile when they are drowsy but not when they are awake. Only after 4 to 6 weeks of age do infants smile in response to environmental stimulation. This developmental sequence appears to be under maturational control, because premature infants begin to smile at environmental stimuli at the same conceptional age as full-term infants (Dittrichova, as cited by Bower, 1977). Twin studies show that monozygotic twins are more alike than dizygotic twins in their tendencies to smile during the first four months of life, suggesting that genetic factors influence individual differences in emotional reactions (Freedman, 1974). From the ethological-adaptational perspective, social smiles are viewed as signals indicating that stimulation should be maintained or increased (Emde, Kligman, Reich, & Wade, 1978; Frodi, Lamb, Leavitt, & Donovan, 1978). As predicted, furthermore, interaction is adversely affected when emotional signals deviate from the species-specific norm. Thus mothers are disappointed by the muted facial expressions of blind and Down's syndrome babies (Emde & Brown, 1978; Fraiberg, 1974), while infants are upset when adults sit impassively in front of them (Fogel, Diamond, Langhorst, & Demo, 1979; Lamb, Morrison, & Malkin, 1987; Tronick, Als, Adamson, Wise, & Brazelton, 1978).

Ethological theorists believe that the emergence of social smiling is maturationally determined, and that the emergence of social smiling marks the beginning of a sensitive period for the development of social attachments—a period that is said to end with the emergence of stranger anxiety or wariness. This "explanation" only tells us *why* infants smile—focusing on the hypothetical adaptive value of the behavior; but it tells us nothing about *how*—by what psychological, cognitive, or neurophysiological mechanisms the behavior is elicited. Thus the ethological-adaptational theory provides a different sort of explanation than do the psychoanalytic, learning, or cognitive theories, albeit one that is not open to conclusive verification or refutation.

Cognitive-Developmental Theory. Kagan (1971) proposed that smiling occurs when an environmental event is assimilated to (i.e., fitted into) a central schema. Smiling to faces thus reflects the emergence of recognition memory and mastery of the task of recognizing, first, faces in general, and later the face of the primary care-provider. Smiling at nonsocial stimuli, such as bells and bull's-eyes, is explained by hypothesizing that a new perceptual skill—the ability to perceive curvilinear stimuli—emerges in the third month. Before then, infants do not perceive curvilinearity, hence pay little attention to such stimuli, and thus do not smile at them. When the skill first emerges, however, it permits the successful but effortful processing of information, and smiling is thus elicited. After three months, sounds are also processed differently: Earlier, they were only listened to whereas now they can also be looked at. Practicing this new schema results in smiling. The U-shaped functions relating emotional responses to the amount of experience were indeed found, albeit in a study concerned with the elicitation of smiles caused by success in nonsocial tasks varying in the degree of difficulty (Zelazo, 1972).

Not all cognitive theorists emphasize discrepancy between stimuli and memory schemas as much as Kagan and Hebb do. Sroufe, for example, has shown that degree of discrepancy can account for the *intensity,* but not for the *hedonic quality,* of an emotional reaction. As a result, the same stimulus can elicit very different emotional responses depending on the context in which testing takes place (Sroufe, Waters, & Matas, 1974; Sroufe & Wunsch, 1972). For instance, when mothers wear a mask, 9- to 12-month-old infants will tend to smile or laugh; whereas if it is worn by unfamiliar adults, infants may cringe, turn away, or cry. These findings suggest that infants are capable of much more complex cognitive activities than memory and the perception of discrepancy. Following Bowlby (1969), Sroufe (1977, 1979) interprets these findings to mean that infants (like adults) are capable of rudimentary cognitive inferences or appraisals designed to determine whether stimuli are potentially pleasurable or harmful. Kagan (1974) denies the existence of such abilities in the first year of life. On the other hand, Kagan's model depends on the development (presumably by maturation) of the capacity to perceive and attend to curvilinear stimuli. There is little independent evidence that such a development takes place. Without this new perceptual skill, Kagan is unable to explain the onset of smiling, not only to faces, but also to bells and bull's-eyes. Sroufe similarly proposes the existence of cognitive mechanisms (appraisal processes) for which there has yet to be independent verification.

Social-Cognitive Theory. There have been no attempts by social-cognitive theorists to explain the emergence of social smiling.

Stranger Anxiety or Wariness

Psychoanalytic Theory. According to Spitz (1965), the onset of stranger anxiety is predicated on ego development sufficient to permit evocative (i.e., recall) memory. Spitz believed that stranger anxiety results from a rudimentary inference process in which the child compares the stranger to an internal representation of the mother. If the mother is absent, the child anticipates that she will not be available to meet his or her needs. As a result, distress occurs. Spitz felt that—as in the case of smiling—the quality of adult–infant interaction affects the expression of stranger anxiety; and, as predicted, studies show that negative reactions to strangers are either absent or mild among infants reared in institutions (e.g., Rheingold, 1961).

One problem with this explanation is that the emergence of stranger anxiety around 6 to 9 months of age coincides with the emergence of fear in response to a variety of events or stimuli—such as heights, looming stimuli, masks, and Jack-in-the-boxes (Campos, 1976; Scarr & Salapatek, 1970; Sroufe, 1979). It seems unlikely that these emotional changes result from ego development mediated by parent–infant interaction, and thus one wonders whether this explanation of stranger anxiety is correct.

Learning Theory. Learning theory is similarly unable to explain the emergence of stranger anxiety. Strangers generally do not hurt or discomfort infants, rendering a conditioning explanation unlikely. Furthermore, parents are not usually afraid of strangers (especially when the stranger is a relative), so observational learning is clearly not involved. Operant contingencies do not plausibly explain the phenomenon.

Ethological-Adaptational Theory. Ethological-adaptational theorists hold that stranger anxiety occurs because it is adaptive for infants to avoid potential dangers, just as it is adaptive for them to seek the proximity of protective adults, especially when distressed or frightened. The purpose of stranger distress, from this point of view, is to summon the protective parent (Bowlby, 1969). Because fear mediates flight, ethologists argue that the fear of strangers should not emerge until the onset of independent locomotion (by crawling), which allows infants to wander unsupervised into contact with strange adults, as well as to flee from danger. Ethological theorists also propose that infants may be biologically prepared to respond to certain cues to danger. Among these are individuals who loom large over infants: strangers who tower over infants are feared more than persons at the infants' level (Weinraub & Putney, 1978). Likewise, unfamiliar full-sized adults are feared more than midgets, and both are feared more than strange children (Brooks & Lewis, 1976). Individual variability is of central concern to evolutionary biologists, and proponents of the evolutionary/adaptational view are readily able to incorporate findings from behavior genetics research. Twin studies show genetic influences on individual differences in reactions to strangers (Buss & Plomin, 1984; Freedman, 1974; Lamb, 1982; Plomin & DeFries, 1985; Plomin & Rowe, 1979), and adopted children resemble their biological mothers with respect to shyness (Daniels & Plomin, 1985). Generally, however, the ethological theory attempts to explain only the "*whys*" of stranger anxiety; it does not attempt to explain *how*—by what psychological and physiological mechanisms—negative stranger reactions are mediated.

Cognitive-Developmental Theory. Cognitive theorists initially proposed that discrepancies between the features of the stranger and some internal memory explain the occurrence of stranger anxiety, because the child is unable to assimilate the stranger's features to any existing schema. One major problem with this explanation, however, was that infants can visually discriminate between parents and strangers by 3 months of age whereas they do not show fear or distress until four or five months later (Bronson, 1972; Haith & Campos, 1977). Consequently, Kagan et al. (1978) amended Hebb's basic notions quite substantially, adding the proposition that in the third quarter-year infants develop the capacity to generate hypotheses and thereafter actively attempt to understand how the environment operates, instead of merely registering sensory inputs passively. Before this capacity develops, a discrepancy between environmental stimulation and a schema yielded interest rather than fear; after 8 months, however, fear or distress results when children attempt to understand environmental events and their hypotheses fail. Kagan thus portrays wariness of unfamiliar stimuli, as well as separation distress, as the predictable results of failures to understand the environment: If the child knew where the parent went, when she or he would return, or what the stranger would do, no negative reactions would result.

Because the quality of parent–infant interaction is not viewed as a determinant of stranger anxiety, Kagan would expect distress or wariness to emerge according to a normative timetable, regardless of differences in prior social experiences. Substantiating this prediction, he has argued that stranger anxiety emerges at about the same time in infants from Israeli kibbutzim, the Kalahari desert, Greek orphanages, Guatemalan Indian groups, and middle-class American families (Kagan 1974; Kagan et al., 1978).

Sroufe (1977, 1979), however, believes that discrepancy can account for the intensity of emotional reactions to strange people or objects but that hedonic quality is determined by the context as well as by the child's past experiences. For example, the stranger's approach is more likely to elicit cardiac acceleration and fussing in an unfamiliar setting than in the home (Sroufe et al., 1974). The parents' proximity, as well as their perceived accessibility, also affect reactions to strangers. Thus when the mother is close by, and the infant is familiarized with the stranger, and the stranger does not behave intrusively, stranger distress has often been found to be weak, subtle, and intermixed with positive, affiliative behaviors (Rheingold & Eckerman, 1973). According to Sroufe, these effects occur because infants have the capacity to *appraise* both stimuli and their contexts in order to determine whether there is reason for fear. Unfortunately, the appraisal process is a hypothetical construct that cannot be observed or studied directly.

Social Cognitive Theory.   Instead of proposing that unfamiliar stimuli are inherently fearsome because their behavioral dispositions are unknown, theorists such as Campos (Campos et al., 1983; Campos & Stenberg, 1981) propose that such stimuli may sometimes be *ambiguous*. In an attempt to resolve the ambiguity, infants look at adults' faces for cues about how to respond. If its mother looks relaxed and happy, the infant concludes that there is nothing to fear and that the stranger may be fun; if its mother looks fearful or unhappy, however, the infant concludes that there is reason to fear or avoid the individual. Consistent with this notion, studies showed that a mother's expressions have a remarkable effect on her child's willingness to play with novel attractive toys (Klinnert, 1984; Sorce, Emde, Campos, & Klinnert, 1985). Researchers have also shown that a 1-year-old's response to a stranger is more positive when the stranger interacts positively with the child's parents before interacting with the child (Boccia & Campos, 1983; Feiring, Lewis, & Starr, 1984), and even when the stranger interacts positively with another stranger (Feiring et al., 1984). This explanation does not of course preclude situations in which the stranger's behavior is sufficiently bizarre and the context so threatening that fear is elicited immediately; it deals only with the situation in which ambiguity exists. Campos and Stenberg (1981) propose that infants begin to seek information from their parents' emotional expressions by 5 months of age, by which time they clearly seem capable of discriminating among various expressions (Oster, 1981). Kuchuk, Vibbert, and Bornstein (1986), however, reported that infants could discriminate some emotions much earlier—by 3 months of age.

Separation Anxiety

Psychoanalytic Theory. Each of the major theories proposes an explanation of separation anxiety very similar to its explanation of stranger anxiety. In the case of psychoanalytic theory, Spitz (1965) proposed that "stranger anxiety" actually occurred because the infant feared separation from the mother. In his view, the development of evocative memory between 6 and 8 months of age allows the infant to remember its mother even in her absence; this permits the baby to feel threatened, and this threat is signaled by anxiety. The hypothesis that recall memory is available by 6 to 8 months contradicted Piaget's belief that this is not possible until the second year; but Spitz argued that, thanks to the organizing influence of affect on cognitive growth (described earlier), the ability to understand the permanence of persons develops before the ability to understand the permanence of objects because an infant's mother is more affectively salient than an inanimate object is. This crucial assumption has not been empirically supported (Jackson, Campos, & Fischer, 1978), however; this lack of substantiation constitutes a fatal flaw in the psychoanalytic explanations of separation anxiety and stranger anxiety.

Learning Theory. Learning theorists explain separation anxiety by suggesting that it represents the withdrawal of a source of both positive gratification and contingent responding (Gewirtz, 1972). This explanation can satisfactorily explain the onset of distress when the separation occurs, but it cannot explain the later emergence of a qualitatively different reaction, that of despair, and the subsequent emergence of detachment (Rajecki, Lamb, & Obmascher, 1978). Qualitative changes in the reaction to prolonged separation suggest that something more complex occurs than is proposed by learning theorists.

Ethological-Adaptational Theory.   Theorists such as Bowlby (1969) perceive separation distress as a signal by the infant designed to summon the absent parent back into proximity. Attachment behaviors like separation protest are said to emerge around 7 to 8 months of age because this is the age at which infants first appreciate person permanence and can thus be said to have established social relationships. This assumption is the same as that made by Spitz and is similarly unsupported by the empirical evidence. A better explanation consistent with the ethological perspective might be that separation protest does not emerge until the onset of locomotor capacities makes it possible for the child to wander off and thus become separated from an attachment figure.

Cognitive-Developmental Theory.   To theorists like Kagan, separation produces a discrepancy from the familiar schema in which mother is present. The child thus generates hypotheses in an attempt to explain what happened to its mother. Not knowing what happened to her or when she will return, the child's hypotheses fail and distress results. Separation protest does not occur before 6 to 8 months because younger infants are not capable of generating hypotheses. The viability of this explanation thus depends on the assumption that the capacity to generate hypotheses emerges around 6 to 8 months of age. No evidence of this sort has yet been presented.

Social Cognitive Theory.   Proponents of a social-cognitive approach have not attempted to explain the onset of separation protest. However, researchers such as Lamb (1981a) have used this perspective to help understand individual differences in infants' behavior upon reunion after brief separations. These explanations are discussed in the section on Emergent Consensus.

Social Attachment

There is considerable overlap between the predictions and assumptions regarding social attachment and those concerning separation anxiety, stranger anxiety, and (to a lesser extent) social smiling. This is because some theorists view "social attachment" simply as a summary term referring to all discriminating social behaviors, whereas others believe that such behaviors mediate and manifest an underlying social bond which continues to exist even at times when no attachment behaviors are occurring. To psychoanalysts, for example, the onset of separation and stranger anxiety is determined by ego development bringing about the capacity for evocative memory. Separation and stranger anxiety are thus viewed as behavioral manifestations of a change in the child's inner socioemotional world.

Psychoanalytic Theory.   Psychoanalytic theorists have, since the time of Freud (1940), emphasized the crucial importance of the infant–mother relationship. Bonds were deemed most likely to form with those who satisfied the infant's hunger, on the grounds that drive reduction was gratifying and that bonds formed to those consistently responsible for this gratification.

Learning Theory.   The psychoanalysts' secondary drive interpretation was adopted nearly intact by learning theorists like Hull, who attempted a reinterpretation in learning terms of central psychoanalytic mechanisms and processes (Dollard & Miller, 1950). Later learning theorists also emphasized the association between features of the care-provider and the gratification implicit in feeding. In the most popular interpretations of early attachment in the context of learning theory, Gewirtz (1972) and Bijou and Baer (1961, 1965) provided operant conditioning models in which the mother became a discriminant reinforcer.

Both the psychoanalytic and learning theory explanations were fatally compromised by research showing that feeding does not play a crucial role in attachment. In one famous study, Harlow and Zimmerman (1959) showed that infant monkeys sought comfort from and preferred to cling to a terrycloth mother surrogate rather than to a wire surrogate which fed them. Such studies, coupled with the general fall from favor of drive reduction theories, led developmental psychologists to abandon both psychoanalytic and learning theory accounts of social attachment, and paved the way for Bowlby's new ethological-adaptational theory. Gewirtz's theory also cannot explain why abused infants cling to rather than flee abusive parents; why infants first protest and then grieve over the loss of parents; and why infants use attachment figures as "secure bases" from which to explore (Rajecki et al., 1978). All of these behavior patterns are consistent with the ethological-adaptational model which links the formation of attachments to the infant's need for protection by more powerful and competent adults.

Ethological-Adaptational Theory.   Like the psychoanalysts, Bowlby (1969) believed that separation anxiety reflected the establishment of a bond between infant and mother. However, he attempted to replace the secondary drive explanation implicit in psychoanalytic theory with an explanation that was more consistent with the postulates of contemporary biology. As mentioned earlier, he believed that infants were equipped with a repertoire of proximity-promoting behaviors. Initially, signals (such as smiles and cries) were effective in achieving proximity or contact by eliciting the responses with which adults were preprogrammed to respond. The fact that proximity depended on the association of infant behaviors and complementary adult responses is important because attachments apparently form to those individuals who are consistently available and respond in appropriate fashion to the infant's signals.

Initially, Bowlby proposed, children are promiscuously sociable, not caring who responds to their proximity-promoting signals (birth to 6 weeks). Once they achieve the capacity to distinguish among individuals, they begin to demonstrate preferences, which become increasingly marked over the ensuing months. However, attachments are said not to form until the appreciation of person permanence around 7 to 8 months of age makes it possible for the child to remain aware of the adult's existence even when she or he is not audible or visible. At this point, an attachment bond is said to exist. The bond can be identified by seeing to whom the infant directs its proximity-promoting signals, but (and this is a crucial assumption) these behaviors only mediate the bond—they are not equivalent to the bond. Among the attachment behaviors are separation protest, locomotor approach, clinging, asking to be held, staying close, directed crying, and use of the adult as a "secure base" from which to explore.

Cognitive-Developmental Theory.   Cognitive theorists like Kagan do not attempt to explain the development of attachment bonds. They believe that the "bond" is really a composite of behavioral changes which can be attributed to emergent cognitive capacities. Others, such as Sroufe, accept Bowlby's explanation of the development of attachment. However, Sroufe has emphasized the appraisal process, described by Bowlby, which allows infants to determine how much proximity/contact they need (the set goal) given the existing circumstances and their locomotor capacities, and to compare that with the degree of proximity/contact currently being enjoyed. Any discrepancy between the present status and the set goal sets in motion behaviors designed to restore the balance. The emphasis is thus on the behavioral adjustments made by infants to remain "close enough" to attachment figures. Much interest has been excited by evidence that there are marked individual differences among infants with respect to their set goals. These differences are believed to underlie individual differences in the "security of attachment," which are discussed more fully later in this chapter.

Social Cognitive Theory.   Finally, social cognitive theorists focus not on the formation of social bonds, but on the way in which differences in parental behavior styles presage the development of distinctive social expectations of those adults' future behavior (e.g., Lamb, 1981a, 1981b). These differences are the same as those discussed by Sroufe, and in this respect there are few differences between cognitive-developmental and social-cognitive theorists. Their contributions are discussed more fully later in this chapter.

Fear of Heights

The a) *psychoanalysts* and b) *learning theorists* have not attempted to explain the emergence of the fear of heights, not considering this to be a central aspect of socioemotional development.

Ethological-Adaptational Theory.   From this point of view, the fear of heights is an adaptive emotion which mediates avoidance of heights and in so doing protects the infant from the danger of falling. As mentioned earlier, theorists such as Izard (1977) believe that emotions emerge when they are adaptive, and thus it is not surprising that the fear of heights emerges when the child acquires the ability to locomote independently (by crawling) and is thus exposed for the first time to the danger of falling (Campos et al., 1978). Age is not the critical variable, because the emergence of fear can be accelerated by giving infants the opportunity for independent locomotion using walkers before they are able to crawl (Bertenthal, Campos, & Barrett, 1984). It is not yet clear, however, whether the experience of falling is also crucial.

Cognitive-Developmental Theory.   Theorists such as Kagan (1974) propose that the fear of heights can be explained in the same way as the fear of strangers. In each case, there is a discrepancy between the current percept and the child's mental schemata, which are based on past experiences. Discrepancy is perceived by 2 to 3 months, but it elicits interest rather than distress prior to the emergence, purportedly around 8 months of age, of the capacity to generate hypotheses. The failure of these hypotheses is said to underlie the emergence of frank distress. As before, a crucial problem with this explanation is the lack of independent evidence that the capacity to generate hypotheses indeed emerges at this time.

Social Cognitive Theory.   Campos and his colleagues (Sorce et al., 1985; Svejda, 1981; Svejda & Campos, 1982) have also shown that the magnitude of fear can be manipulated by varying the emotional cues provided by the child's parent in ambiguous situations. For example, when the child is uncertain whether the depth is sufficient to elicit fear, he or she looks to the parent's face for disambiguating information. If the mother smiles and talks in a positive tone, the infant is likely to cross the "deep" cliff toward her, whereas if the mother produces a fearful face and talks in a negative or fearful tone, the infant is very unlikely to cross the same cliff. Of course if there was no depth or the "cliff" was clearly very deep, the parent's cues would be less influential because there would be little ambiguity in the child's mind, and thus little reason to seek disambiguating information.

Summary

With the exception of the ethological-adaptational theory, all the theories reviewed here attempt to explain the proximal mechanisms whereby emotional reactions are mediated. Learning theory does a poor job of explaining the discrete and abrupt emergence of emotional milestones, whereas the psychoanalytic theory is flawed by the unwarranted linking of stranger and separation anxiety, and by the recourse to unobservable and unverifiable aspects of ego development. Kagan's cognitive developmental theory has uncertain status until it is possible to demonstrate that the ability to generate hypotheses indeed emerges around 8 months of age. Sroufe's cognitive-developmental theory is more successful in explaining both the intensity and hedonic quality of emotional reactions, and is most readily integrated with Bowlby's ethological-adaptational theory. The ethological-adaptational theory has been extremely influential because it has provided a way of explaining why we should expect to see certain emotions developing, and why they should emerge when they do. However, only in the case of social attachments have theorists like Bowlby attempted to explain the proximate mechanisms involved.

Most researchers and theorists agree that a major change in the nature of the infant's social world takes place around 6 to 8 months of age, although (ironically) the empirical evidence shows that this change cannot be attributed to the emergence of person permanence. Bowlby's emphasis on the survival functions of infant behavior has allowed researchers to perceive organization and purpose in infant behavior that formerly appeared merely disorganized and incompetent. On the other hand, Bowlby's belief that infants are limited to forming one initial attachment has been disproved by evidence that infants generally form attachments to both parents at the same time (Lamb, 1976b, 1977), even though most seem to establish preferential relationships with their primary care-providers (Lamb, 1976a, 1976c). These preferences are evident in times of stress, when the infant's need for proximity to trusted protective adults is at its greatest. In the case of traditional fathers who spend relatively little time interacting with their infants, a propensity for exciting playful stimulation seems to increase the salience of their interactions and permit infants to establish attachment relationships to their fathers (Clarke-Stewart, 1978; Lamb, 1977; Lamb, Frodi, Hwang, Frodi, & Steinberg, 1982; Lamb, Frodi, Hwang, & Frodi, 1983).

THE EMERGENT CONSENSUS

The diverse theories discussed in the previous pages are characterized by a unique set of strengths and weaknesses. In an attempt to develop a novel integration, Campos and Barrett (1984; Campos, 1986; Campos et al., 1983) offered an "organizational approach" that rested heavily on, but added to, some of the assumptions of the ethological theorists. Like the ethologists, Campos and his colleagues proposed that the eight "basic" emotions—which they identified as joy, anger, disgust, fear, surprise, sadness, sexual ardor, and affection—depend on a prewired process for which neither social input nor experience are required. Further, they emphasized the functions or purposes of emotions, defined in terms of the personal significance of events and experiences. Campos and his associates view emotions as specific patterns of reaction to events that have personal significance. Personal significance is determined in any or all of three ways. First, some stimuli (e.g., sweet or sour flavors) have specific hedonic characteristics. Second, some events gain significance through the reactions of others. Third, some events gain significance and emotional valence by virtue of the relation between the event and the goals and efforts of the organizer. According to Campos and his colleagues, this mechanism is perhaps the most powerful, potentially able to overcome the effects of the other two processes.

In the view of Campos and his colleagues, emotions serve an important organizational role, determining and regulating intra- and interpersonal behavior while serving an adaptive (i.e., survival) function. Emotions and emotional terms help individuals to structure events and behaviors conceptually, providing coherent summaries for multiple functional relations. The same input to an individual can result in multiple different outputs, and reciprocally, very different inputs can result in similar outputs. For example, many situations may make us angry, and we manifest our anger in a variety of ways. Only by introducing anger as an intervening construct can we make sense of relations between those particular eliciting events and behavioral reactions.

Emotions also serve to organize cognitive processes: For example, Campos et al. (1983) hypothesized that infants come to fear heights by associating heights with their parents' emotional reactions to near falls and precarious situations. In addition, Campos and his colleagues (1983) argued that both cognitions and emotions reflect the organism's strivings for desired goals, to the extent that "emotion elicitation reflects an organism's coordination of events with his own active strivings" (p. 804). For example, joy is expressed when an organism concludes that a significant objective or goal has been attained. The experience of joy energizes the organism, reinforces the activity, encourages others to maintain the pleasurable interaction, and stimulates the organism to attempt new challenges. The integrative and organizational function of emotions is well illustrated by this example and the others provided by Campos et al. In each case, it is clear how important a role is played by the individual's goals; they assure personal significance and thus ensure "emotional" reaction patterns.

Not long ago, researchers thought that neonates could exhibit only an undifferentiated emotion—general excitement—and that discrete emotions subsequently emerged from this substrate as a result of experience, maturation, and cognitive development: distress at 3 weeks, delight at 3 months, anger at 4 months, disgust at 5 months, and fear at 7 months, for example (e.g., Bridges, 1930, 1932). According to Campos et al., this view has been rendered obsolete. At least some specific (as distinct from undifferentiated) emotions are expressed by newborns, while others emerge surprisingly early (Sroufe, 1979). Izard (1978; Izard & Buechler, 1986) believes that interest, disgust, distress, and a precursor of surprise (startle) are expressed by newborns; that anger, surprise, and joy emerge in the next 4 months; and that fear and shyness emerge in the second half-year of life.

Criticizing Izard for confusing the first *expression* of an emotion with the first *experience* of the emotion, Campos et al. (1983) suggested that all of the basic emotional states are present throughout the life span, even in newborns. What occurs over time, they contend, are changes in the expressive capacities and, most important, developmental changes in the eliciting circumstances. In fact, untrained observers readily identify the emotions displayed in photographs of infants (Emde, Izard, Huebner, Sorce, & Klinnert, 1985; Emde, Kligman, Reich, & Wade, 1978; Izard, Huebner, Risser, McGinness, & Dougherty, 1980); and by the time their infants reach 1 month of age, 84% of mothers believe that their babies express anger, 58% fear, 75% surprise, 95% joy, 99% interest, and 34% sadness (Johnson, Emde, Pannabecker, Stenberg & Davis, 1982). The mothers described vocal and facial expressions, along with gestures and arm movements, as the bases for their judgments (Johnson et al., 1982; Klinnert, Sorce, Emde, Stenberg, & Gaensbauer, 1984). These maternal reports suggest that at least some differentiated emotions can be expressed from the time of birth and that infants display most (if not all) of the basic or core emotions surprisingly early. It is not clear, of course, whether the mothers' inferences reflect the babies' actual expressive capacities, as distinguished from their mothers' subjective interpretations based on contextual cues. Nevertheless, the different emotions result in different patterns of caretaker response (Sorce & Emde, 1982). By 3 to 6 months of age, infants also use varying expressions quite frequently in everyday interactions (Malatesta & Haviland, 1982).

Basic emotions do not emerge in the course of development, Campos et al. argue; rather, complex intercoordinated emotions emerge, while change occurs in the effectiveness of different eliciting circumstances, the relation between emotional expressions and emotional experience, and the ability to cope with emotions. In the case of anger, for example, Stenberg, Campos, and Emde (1983) reported that the target of the emotion changed with age. When 4-month-olds are frustrated, they direct their anger at the immediate cause (i.e., the experimenter's hand). At 7 months of age, however, infants direct their anger at the experimenter. One implication of this emphasis on eliciting circumstances is an awareness of domain or context specificity. In consequence, instead of asking when "anger" emerges, for example, researchers can at best specify when anger becomes apparent in a specific set of circumstances.

Recognition of Emotions

According to Klinnert et al. (1983) there are several stages in the development of infants' receptivity to facial expressions of emotion. During the first stage (birth to $1\frac{1}{2}$ months) infants pay nominal attention to the internal features of faces (Hainline, 1978; Haith, Bergman, & Moore, 1977; Maurer & Salapatek, 1976). As a result, neonates probably do not discriminate consistently—if at all— among facial expressions. At around $1\frac{1}{2}$ to 2 months of age, however, infants begin to attend to the internal features of faces. They discriminate among facial expressions (Barrera & Maurer, 1981a, 1981b; LaBarbera, Izard, Vietze, & Parisi, 1976; Oster, 1981; Young-Browne, Rosenfeld, & Horowtiz, 1977) and can even discriminate variations of a single expression at 3 months of age (Kuchuk, Vibbert, & Bornstein, 1986). Schwartz, Izard, and Ansul (1985) showed that 5-month-olds could discriminate between the facial expressions of anger, fear, and sadness, although in the paired-comparison procedure employed, infants of this age could not discriminate between joy, anger, and interest. Because of their newly acquired sensitivity to internal facial features, infants begin in the second trimester to respond discriminatively when their mothers adopt unresponsive "stillfaces," whereas they had previously not appeared to "expect" adults to respond at all (Cohn & Tronick, 1983a, 1983b; Lamb et al., 1987).

The ability to discriminate among facial expressions does not mean that the emotional meaning of the expression is understood by the child (Lamb & Bornstein, 1987; Nelson, 1987). Only in the third stage (4 or 5 to 8 or 9 months), according to Klinnert, is there clear evidence that emotional expressions are distinguished and also meaningful. Infants now display emotional resonance, reacting with appropriate emotion to the emotional displays of others. The emergence of this capacity probably reflects the newfound ability to appreciate the face as a whole, rather than simply parts of it (Bushnell, 1982; Caron, Caron, & Myers, 1982). Infants are also better able to interpret emotional expression conveyed by moving displays than by stationary faces (Walker, 1982). The development of empathy, one form of sensitivity to the emotions of others, has become chronicled in detail by Radke-Yarrow, Zahn-Waxler, and Chapman (1983), whose work is discussed at greater length by Hoffman in Chapter 11.

After 8 to 9 months of age, infants begin to appreciate that others' messages pertain to specific objects or events: They can now understand the referent of a communication, for example (Leung & Rheingold, 1981; Scaife & Bruner, 1975). It is at this point, according to Klinnert, that "social referencing"—the deliberate search for information to help disambiguate uncertain events—begins.

Summary

Previous disagreement and incoherence in the study of emotions have given way in recent years to an integrative consensus regarding the functions and nature of emotions and emotional expressions. In part, the emergent consensus developed from awareness of the complementary strengths and weaknesses of earlier theories, and in part it was promoted by research progress made possible by the development of objective techniques for studying emotional expressions (e.g., Ekman 1982; Oster, 1982; Izard, 1979; Scherer, 1982). The availability of these techniques has obviously facilitated research on individual differences, which we discuss in the next section.

INDIVIDUAL DIFFERENCES IN SOCIOEMOTIONAL DEVELOPMENT

Both the psychoanalytic and learning theory approaches to the study of social development deal with individual differences in socioemotional development, to the extent that variations in the quality of parent–infant interaction may retard development. However, most of the relevant empirical work undertaken by psychoanalytic theorists involved comparing children reared in home settings with those raised in institutions, such as orphanages, where care by a succession of shift nurses replaced normal parent–infant interaction (e.g., Spitz, 1950; Spitz & Wolf, 1946). Learning theorists, by contrast, seemed able to explain the effects of a wide variety of parent–child interaction patterns, until it was demonstrated that individual differences, as assessed by discrete behavioral measures, were highly unstable even over short periods of time (Coates, Anderson, & Hartup, 1972; Masters & Wellman, 1974; Waters, 1978). Cognitive theorists like Kagan, meanwhile, have emphasized normative maturational events rather than individual differences: Several reports focused on the absence of developmental variation despite vast differences in rearing environments (e.g., Fox, 1977; Kagan et al., 1978; Kotelchuck, 1976; Lester, Kotelchuck, Spelke, Sellers, & Klein 1974). The ethological-adaptational theorists seem to have been most successful in their efforts to explore the origins, characteristics, and consequences of individual differences in infant–parent attachment (e.g., Ainsworth, Blehar, Waters, & Wall, 1978; Lamb, Thompson, Gardner, Charnov, & Estes, 1984; Lamb, Thompson, Gardner, & Charnov, 1985). Perhaps the major reason for the apparent success of these theorists is their focus, which is not on discrete behaviors but on the patterned organization of behavior, as discussed in this section.

Operationally, individual differences in social attachments are usually assessed using a procedure called the *Strange Situation* that was developed by Ainsworth and Wittig (1969; Ainsworth et al., 1978). The procedure (see Table 8.1) is designed to subject 10- to 24-month-old infants to gradually increasing amounts of stress, induced by the strange setting, the entrance of a strange female, and two brief separations from the parent. According to Ainsworth,

TABLE 8.1
The Strange Situation

Episode	Persons Present	Change
1	Parent, Infant	Enter room
2	Parent, Infant, Stranger	Unfamiliar adult joins the dyad
3	Infant, Stranger	Parent leaves
4	Parent, Infant	Parent returns
		Stranger leaves
5	Infant	Parent leaves
6	Infant, Stranger	Stranger returns
7	Parent, Infant	Parent returns
		Stranger leaves

After Ainsworth and Wittig (1969).

All episodes are usually three minutes long, but episodes 3, 5, and 6 can be curtailed if the infant becomes too distressed, and episodes 4 and 7 are sometimes extended.

stress should increase the infant's desire for proximity to and/or contact with the protective parent or attachment figure, thus leading to the intensification of the attachment behaviors (e.g., crying, approaching, and clinging) which help infants attain or maintain proximity/contact. Thus, as the stress increases, infants should reduce their exploration and affiliation (for example, with strangers) and increasingly organize their behavior around their parents. Specifically, they should evince distress when separated from their parents, attempt to search for them, and greet them with bids for renewed interaction either in the form of proximity/contact or in the form of distance interaction.

When American infants and parents are observed in the Strange Situation, about 65–70% behave in the pattern just described, which is termed the secure (or "B") pattern because the infant seems to gain security and comfort from the parent to whom it turns in times of stress or alarm. The remainder display one of two types of "insecure" reactions. Typically, 20–25% behave in an avoidant ("A") fashion—turning away from rather than toward the adult, especially upon reunion, when one would expect proximity-seeking behaviors to be at their most intense. Another group, the resistant or "C" group comprising 10–15% of most samples, consists of infants who are unable to use the adult as a base for exploration even in the preseparation episodes. These infants behave in an ambivalent fashion upon reunion—both seeking contact and angrily rejecting it when offered. Ainsworth has argued that the A-, B-, and C-patterns of attachment behavior in the Strange Situation indeed reflect individual differences in attachment security, and she has developed hypotheses concerning the ontogeny of these individual differences.

Determinants of Strange Situation Behavior

Almost from birth, infants learn about people from their interactions with them (Watson, 1985). When care-providers respond promptly and appropriately, according to ethological theorists, infants develop confidence in their own *effectance* (ability to act upon the environment successfully), and *trust* in the reliability or predictability of the persons concerned. Since adults differ in their sensitivity, there should be differences among infants in the extent to which infants have confidence in their own effectance and in the reliability of others. Sensitive parents should have babies who behave in the B-type pattern, described above, whereas A- and C-type attachments would develop when parents were insensitive (Ainsworth, Bell, & Stayton, 1974).

Since Ainsworth's hypotheses were proposed, many other researchers have attempted to test them in independent longitudinal studies (e.g., Bates, Maslin, & Frankel, 1985; Belsky, Rovine, & Taylor, 1984; Egeland & Farber, 1984; Erickson, Sroufe, & Egeland, 1985; Grossmann, Grossmann, Spangler, Suess, & Unzner, 1985; Miyake, Chen, & Campos, 1985; Sagi, Lamb, Lewkowicz, Shoham, Dvir, & Estes, 1985). After reviewing the complicated results of these many studies, Lamb, Thompson, Gardner, and Charnov (1985) concluded that there was general support for the notion that sensitive parenting—that is, nurturant, attentive, nonrestrictive parental care—was associated with Type-B infant behavior in the Strange Situation, at least when studies were conducted in the United States. The mothers of infants who behave in Type-A or Type-C fashion (often called "insecurely attached") manifest less socially desirable patterns of behavior: They may over- or understimulate, fail to make their behaviors contingent on infant behavior, appear cold or rejecting, and sometimes appear inept. Unfortunately, there is too much variability in the results to identify precisely what aspects of parental behavior are formatively important. Some studies identify warmth but not sensitivity, some level of stimulation, some patterning of stimulation but not warmth or amount of stimulation, and so forth.

Stability and Prediction

Stability.   The notion that Strange Situation behavior reflects something that is intrinsic to the relationship was initially supported by indications of remarkable stability over time in patterns of infant behavior (Connell, 1976; Waters, 1978). According to Waters (1978), 48 out of 50 infants obtained the same classification at 12 and 18 months of age. However, test–retest reliability is not always so high. Vaughn, Egeland, Sroufe, and Waters (1979) showed that, in an economically disadvantaged sample, many infants changed from one mode of behavior to another between 12 and 18 months of age. Later, Thompson, Lamb, and Estes (1982) reported instability in a middle-class sample. In both studies, major changes in family circumstances or caretaking arrangements led to changes in Strange Situation behavior. Since parental sensitivity appears to influence Strange Situation behavior, these data might mean that changes in the amount of stress to which the mothers were subjected affected the manner in which they interacted with their infants (Thompson & Lamb, 1986).

Predictive Validity.   Another reason why attachment classifications intrigue developmental psychologists is that they are thought to predict aspects of the child's future behavior. For example, babies who have Type-B attachments to their mothers are more cooperatively playful and sociable when interacting with friendly strangers than are Type-A or -C infants (Main, 1983; Main & Weston, 1981; Thompson & Lamb, 1983c). Similarly, Strange Situation behavior is related to social behavior with peers (Easterbrooks & Lamb, 1979; Pastor, 1981; Sroufe, 1983; Waters, Wippman, & Sroufe, 1979). Type-B infants engage in more frequent and more mature forms of interaction with their peers—sharing more and showing a greater capacity to initiate and maintain interactions, for example. For reasons that are not clear, however, Jacobson, Wille, Tianen, and Aytch (1983; Jacobson & Wille, 1984, 1986) have reported different results, suggesting that the relation between attachment classification and peer competence is neither direct nor powerful.

Other researchers have addressed the relation between Strange Situation classifications and aspects of achievement motivation, reporting that Strange Situation behavior at 12 or 18 months predicts cognitive performance in problem-solving situations and in a variety of stressful and challenging contexts at least until kindergarten age (Arend, Gove & Sroufe, 1979; Matas, Arend, & Sroufe, 1978; Sroufe, 1983). Placed in cognitively challenging situations, children who showed Type-B attachments to their mothers as infants persisted longer and more enthusiastically than did children who showed Type-A or -C attachments. Type-B infants also seem to be more resilient and robust when stressed or challenged (Block & Block, 1980). In addition, Type-B infants appear more socially competent and independent when they later enter preschool (Sroufe, 1983; Sroufe, Schork, Motti, Lawroski, & LaFreniere, 1984), and they also show fewer behavior problems (Bates et al., 1985; Erickson et al., 1985; Lewis et al., 1984).

Evidence concerning the temporal stability of Strange Situation behavior, and its relation to measures of earlier infant–adult interaction and to the child's later achievement and personality, suggests that the Strange Situation measures some meaningful aspect of mother–infant attachment and has important implications for understanding and predicting development. Presumably, Strange Situation behavior with fathers also affects development in analogous ways, although the child's relationships with primary attachment figures, be they mothers or fathers, are likely to be more significant than other attachment relationships.

The predictive validity of longitudinal associations is far from perfect, however (Lamb et al., 1984, 1985). Rather, the relation between Strange Situation behavior in infancy and subsequent child behavior is found only when there is stability in caretaking arrangements and family circumstances, which seem to maintain stability in the patterns of parent–child interaction correlated with patterns of Strange Situation behavior. This raises an interesting question: *Is the prediction over time attributable to individual differences in the quality of early parent–child interaction that shape the child's development, or is it attributable to the continuing quality of parent–child interactions?* Researchers often assume that Strange Situation behavior reflects a part of the child's personality, but the quality of early relationships may be predictively valuable not because it *causes* later differences directly, but because it presages later differences in the quality of relationships which in turn support differences in the child's behavior. Such a pattern of findings would place the locus of stability in continuing parent–child interactions rather than in some aspect of the child's personality.

Cross-Cultural Research

Some of the most provocatively informative work on Strange Situation behavior has been conducted outside the United States. As Table 8.2 shows, the distribution of infants across the A-B-C categories in many other countries differs from that typically found in American samples. These results may demonstrate the importance of factors *other than* or in addition to the quality of parental behavior in explaining Strange Situation behavior (Campos et al., 1983; Lamb et al., 1985). For example, the high degrees of stress manifested by Japanese and

TABLE 8.2
Distribution of Infants across Attachment Types (in Percentages)

Country	Reference	A	B	C
USA	Ainsworth et al. (1978)	20	65	13
Japan	Miyake et al. (1985) and unpublished data	0	77	23
W. Germany	Grossmann et al. (1981) and unpublished data	46	43	8
Israel	Sagi et al. (1985)	8	55	33
The Netherlands	van IJzendoorn et al. (1984)	24	72	4
Sweden	Lamb et al. (1982)	22	76	4

Table based on Table 11.1 in Lamb et al. (1985). Row totals do not always sum to 100 because "unclassifiable" infants are excluded and numbers are rounded off.

Israeli babies in the Strange Situation may have led to increases in the proportion of infants classified as Type-C. The Japanese infants appeared inordinately distressed because they had much less experience with separations from their mothers than American infants typically have. For infants growing up on Israeli kibbutzim, encounters with strangers are unusual and thus elicited great distress in the Strange Situation. Thus, even though the procedure was structurally the same for Japanese, Israeli, and American infants, the psychological meaning for infants from each culture seems to have been very different. In addition, Miyake et al. (1985) reported that the Japanese infants who were classified as Type-C were temperamentally more irritable than Type-B infants from birth. Thus, it appears that culture-specific rearing practices and/or temperamental differences account for at least some of the variance in Strange Situation classifications across cultures.

Summary

The picture emerging from the many studies in which Strange Situation behavior was assessed is a complicated one. Strange Situation behavior appears to reflect individual differences in patterns of infant-parent interaction with Type-B attachments potentiated by warm, sensitive, and supportive parental behavior in the West. However, other factors seem to be important as well—notably culture-specific rearing practices and (perhaps) infant temperament. To understand the formative importance of infant-parent attachment, we need to obtain multiple convergent measures of attachment, rather than rely exclusively on the observation of Strange Situation behavior, which is undoubtedly influenced by factors other than attachment security.

Emotional Development

In the late 1940s and early 1950s, theorists became interested in individual differences in emotional development, prompted by evidence that children who had grown up in institutions frequently seemed listless and affectless, showed no interest in social interaction, and failed to display appropriate emotions in situations that should have elicited either pleasure or distress (Bowlby, 1951).

Interest in the origins of individual differences in emotional development was rekindled in the last few years by evidence that: (a) patterns of emotional expression had similar communicative meanings around the world (Ekman, 1973; Izard, 1971); and (b) emotional expressions were "appropriately" displayed by young infants in affect-eliciting contexts (e.g., Hiatt, Campos, & Emde, 1979; Stenberg et al., 1983). Once researchers knew that they could code and interpret infant expressions, they began to study a variety of experiential influences on emotionality. For example, Gaensbauer (Gaensbauer & Harmon, 1982; Gaensbauer & Hiatt, 1984; Gaensbauer & Sands, 1979) reported that abused and neglected infants evinced a flattening of emotional expressiveness reminiscent of the emotional blunting observed in institutionalized infants. In a detailed case study, Stern (1974) showed that intrusive maternal overstimulation led an infant to become avoidant of eye contact, whereas mothers who were sensitive to their infants' readiness for stimulation had infants who were more sociable and expressive.

Another strategy has involved comparing the emotional expressiveness of infants who behave differently in the Strange Situation. Thompson and Lamb (1983a, 1984, 1986) found that securely attached infants were more emotionally modulated in the Strange Situation than either avoidant or resistant infants were. They speculated that these differences could be attributed to differences in the patterns of early interaction, if sensitively responsive mothers were more likely to (a) provide emotionally arousing stimuli at times when their infants were best able to appreciate them; (b) reinforce and encourage emotional displays; and (c) be more sensitive to subtle variations in infant expressions. Those infants who were highly expressive facially were also most expressive vocally, suggesting that a general cross-modal dimension of expressiveness exists. This dimension is probably not of direct temperamental origin, because there is little relation between parental reports of infant temperament and measures of facial or vocal expressiveness (Thompson & Lamb, 1982, 1983b).

The effects of experience on expressiveness have been documented by Malatesta (e.g., 1985; Malatesta & Haviland, 1982, 1985) and Lewis (e.g., Lewis & Saarni, 1985; Lewis & Michalson, 1982, 1983; Michalson & Lewis, 1985). Malatesta and Haviland (1982, 1985) reported that during face-to-face play, mothers changed their facial expressions nine times a minute for 3-month-olds and seven times a minute for 6-month-olds. Roughly 25% of the time, the mothers responded contingently to their infants' expressions. Typically, this involved responding positively or imitatively to positive expressions, especially those of younger infants, and ignoring their negative expressions. Such interaction would have the effect of reinforcing the display of positive emotions and muting the expression of negative emotions.

The reduction over time in the mothers' tendencies to respond even to their infants' positive emotions might reflect a cultural presumption that the overt display of emotion should be muted. Malatesta (1985; Malatesta, Grigoryev, Lamb, Albin, & Culver, 1986) subsequently reported that, as their infants grew older ($2\frac{1}{2}$ to 5 and $7\frac{1}{2}$ months), mothers became increasingly responsive to expressions of interest and decreasingly responsive to expressions of pain. Developmental changes in maternal behavior appeared to be causally related to the developmental changes observed in infant behavior—increases in positive and decreases in negative affect. Interestingly, Malatesta and Haviland (1982) and Kuchuk et al. (1986) reported dyadic similarities between mothers and infants with respect to expressiveness, suggesting that mothers may effectively socialize their infants' expressive styles from the first months of life. (Of course, it is also possible that these familial similarities in expressiveness reflect a temperamental dimension of genetic origin.) Harkness and Super (1985; see also Super & Harkness, 1982) have described several ways in which adults from different cultural backgrounds socialize their infants by responding in accordance with culture-specific interpretations of the infants' expressions and emotions.

Lewis and Michalson (1984, p. 132) attribute the emergence of some emotional pathology in infancy to misinterpretation of the child's feelings by parents and caretakers. Kaye (1979) has also described the socialization of affect, noting three types of parental imitation: *minimizing* imitation (when the mother imitates a negative expression briefly, before switching to a positive expression); *modulating* imitation (when she imitates the expression but tempers its intensity); and *maximizing* imitation (when she exaggerates her infant's expression). In addition, Malatesta and Haviland (1982) reported that mothers responded differently to the display of anger by sons and by daughters. With sons, mothers knitted their brows, as if showing sympathy for their babies' emotions. With daughters, mothers evinced angry facial expressions, perhaps discouraging (or modeling?) such displays of emotion by girls.

Another aspect of emotional expressiveness is "sociability," the infant's social attractiveness, friendliness, and willingness to respond positively to social bids by others. Individual differences in sociability appear to be consistent across contexts (Stevenson & Lamb, 1979) and moderately stable over a period of several months provided there is stability in attachment patterns (Thompson & Lamb, 1983c). This suggests that individual differences in sociability are affected by prior social experiences. However, although there is a modest relation between Strange Situation behavior and sociability with unfamiliar adults and peers (discussed earlier), there is no significant relation between sociability and amount of experience with adults (Clarke-Stewart, Umeh, Snow, & Pederson, 1980; Stevenson, 1983), maternal employment (Thompson & Lamb, 1983a) or the amount of nonmaternal care (Thompson & Lamb, 1982). Infants appear to be modestly more sociable when their fathers are highly involved in child care (Lamb, Hwang, Frodi, & Frodi, 1982).

Whereas the experiential determinants of individual differences in sociability remain largely unknown, there is mounting evidence of biogenetic influences (Goldsmith & Campos, 1986; Lamb, 1982). The fact that the similarities between monozygotic twins are greater than those between dizygotic twins (Freedman & Keller, 1964; Goldsmith & Campos, 1986; Goldsmith & Gottesman, 1981; Matheny 1980; Plomin & Rowe, 1979; Plomin & deFries, 1985) suggests that sociability is at least somewhat heritable.

Temperament[2]

Research on the heritability of sociability is related to research on temperament, which has intensified in the 1980s (Bates, 1987). Temperament is typically defined as a constitutionally determined behavioral style which is somewhat stable over time (Goldsmith & Campos, 1982; Rothbart & Derryberry, 1981); but its constitutional base does not dictate that temperament be genetically fixed or temporally stable, or that experience need have a minimal impact on temperament. Researchers agree that an adequate model of temperamental variation must acknowledge the reciprocal influences of environment and organism (e.g., Bornstein, Gaughran, & Homel, 1986; Campos et al., 1983; Derryberry & Rothbart, 1984; Lerner & Lerner, 1983; Sameroff & Chandler, 1975; Thomas & Chess, 1977).

The study of temperament has been concerned with two significant questions. First, *What dimensions of behavior comprise temperament?* Different investigators have advocated different dimensions, although *affect, attention,* and *motor activity* are almost universally recognized, with emphasis on the behaviors' temporal and intensive characteristics. Second, *Is temperament stable across time and place?* At first, stability was seen as a necessary component of models of temperament, but three counterarguments have emerged. One is that researchers now expect that aspects of temperament vary somewhat with age and with demands made on the person; temperamental propensities must reflect children's rapidly changing abilities and skills as well as changing environmental constraints (Bornstein et al., 1986; Campos et al., 1983; Lerner & Lerner, 1983; Lerner, Palermo, Spiro, & Nesselroade, 1982; Sameroff & Chandler, 1975). A second argument is that, insofar as temperament is thought to have a genetic component, discontinuous gene action may prompt developmental patterns of "acceleration" and "lag", although such patterns should be more synchronous in monozygotic (MZ) twins than dizygotic (DZ) twins (Matheny, 1980, 1983; Plomin, 1983; Scarr & McCartney, 1983; Wilson, 1983, 1984). The third argument is that some children may be constitutionally *in*consistent; their genetic makeup will "program" changes over time. Moreover, individual differences once believed to be relatively constant across situations, because stability resided

---

[2]This section is based on a chapter in Lamb and Bornstein's (1987) *Development in Infancy;* the chapter was principally written by Marc Bornstein.

in the individual rather than in the physical or social environment, are now thought to evince greater or lesser degrees of sensitivity and susceptibility to environmental influences and contexts (Campos et al., 1983; Goldsmith & Campos, 1984, 1986).

Because temperament is commonly viewed as an hereditary aspect of personality, albeit one certainly influenced by experience, many investigators have adopted a behavior genetics model to explain observed variations in infant temperament (Buss & Plomin, 1984; Goldsmith, 1983; Plomin & DeFries, 1985; Scarr & Kidd, 1983; Scarr & McCartney, 1983; Wilson, 1983, 1984). To evaluate this model, researchers have pursued three lines of investigation: twin and adoption research, cross-cultural research, and gender difference research.

Twin and Adoption Studies.   Researchers have often turned to infant twins in attempts to sort out the degree to which behaviors have identifiable genetic components. Monozygotic (MZ) twins share 100% of their genes, whereas dizygotic (DZ) twins share only 50% on the average. If a behavior has a genetic component, therefore, MZ twins ought to behave more alike than DZ twins, barring more similar treatment of MZ twins. Goldsmith and Campos (1984), for example, found that MZ correlations are significantly greater than DZ correlations for three of six dimensions of Rothbart's (1981) IBQ temperament questionnaire. Plomin and Rowe (1979) also found evidence for differential heritability of social behavior occurring during structured home observations. Dimensions of "activity," "attention span," and "persistence" yielded moderate heritability estimates, whereas individual differences in infants' responses to mothers appeared to be mediated not by heritability but by infants' differential experiences. Most recently, Goldsmith and Campos (1986) have presented twin concordance estimates for an objective laboratory measure of "negative vs. positive affect on the visual cliff," a fear-eliciting situation for which it is possible to measure latency, duration, and intensity of crying and negative vocalizing. Again consistent with a genetic model, MZ correlations for these fear behaviors were moderately greater than DZ correlations.

As part of the Colorado Adoption Project, Plomin and DeFries (1985) measured "affect–extraversion," "activity," and "task orientation" in 12-month-old infants, and both biological and adoptive parents' scores on extraversion, neuroticism, emotionality, sociability, and activity. If these characteristics were heritable, biological parent–offspring correlations ought to be higher than adoptive parent–offspring correlations. In the main, however, biological parental personality predicted infant temperament only moderately.

Cross-Cultural Studies of Infant Temperament.   Cross-cultural studies of temperamental variation among neonates have almost uniformly employed Brazelton's Neonatal Behavioral Assessment Scale, and consistently reveal ethnic differences in temperamental behaviors among neonates. Freedman (1974;

Freedman & Freedman, 1969), for example, found that Chinese-American and Japanese-American neonates were less perturbable, better able to soothe themselves, quicker to habituate, and less labile in terms of states of arousal than their European-American counterparts (see also Callaghan, 1981). Likewise, Keefer, Tronick, Dixon, and Brazelton (1982) found that Gusii (Kenyan) neonates had more labile states of arousal and were more irritable than European-American babies. The Gusii infants also demonstrated an enhanced capacity for self-soothing by sucking their hands. With an expanded sample, Keefer and her associates found other significant group differences: Gusii neonates habituated more rapidly to tactile stimulation, whereas European-American newborns oriented better and habituated more quickly to visual and auditory stimuli. Like Freedman, Keefer and her coauthors attributed the neonatal group differences in part to genetic differences between the Gusii and European-American samples, although the history of pre- and perinatal experiences might also be important.

Gender Studies of Infant Temperament.   If temperament comprises an inherited set of early-appearing behavioral characteristics, infant boys and girls might differ in temperament as well. To date, few formal studies of gender differences in infant temperament have been undertaken, but in those that have, consistent and strong gender differences have not been discovered (Bates, 1986), with a single exception. Boys and girls seem to differ with respect to activity level. Although there is significant overlap between the groups, boys tend to engage in more rough-and-tumble play than do girls, and similar differences exist among nonhuman primates as well (Diamond, 1957).

As far as implications for later development are concerned, Thomas and Chess (1977) argued that the "goodness of fit" between the child's temperament and the demands of the environment determined whether outcomes would be favorable or unfavorable (see also Lerner & Lerner, 1983, 1986). They pointed out that, in the "right" environment, the temperament of a difficult child need not result in subsequent behavior disorders. A benign outcome might occur if the parents of such a child were, for example, careful not to blame themselves for the child's impulsiveness, high activity level, or states of irregularity; if they were tolerant of the child's temperament, and provided activities (such as sports) in which the child's traits were channeled and valued. By contrast, even easy children could develop problems if parents placed excessive demands on them or ignored their legitimate needs because these children were not as demanding as other children. This "goodness-of-fit" notion represents an early expression of the transactional model of development advocated by Sameroff (1975). Constitutionally based individual differences among infants also play a formative role in shaping social interactions (Bell, 1968, 1971; Thomas & Chess, 1977). Difficult babies demand and receive more attention than easy babies in the United States (Bates, Olson, Pettit, & Bayles, 1982; Petit & Bates, 1984), in Israel (Klein, 1984), and in Kenya (DeVries, 1984), for example; and the perception of difficultness in early infancy (along with other factors, to be sure) increases the likelihood of later maltreatment (Sherrod, Altemeier, O'Connor, & Vietze, 1984; Vietze, Falsey, Sandler, O'Connor, & Altemeier, 1980). Thus temperament may have immediate effects on infants' social interactions and thereby cumulative effects on their development.

Summary

Theorists concerned with the origins of individual differences in social and emotional behavior have generally assumed that these differences are determined by differences in the child's early social experiences. Major focus has fallen on the concept of parental sensitivity, which is rather loosely defined and operationalized. This has made it difficult to identify which aspects of parental behavior are especially important, and whether "security of attachment" is influenced by the same aspects of parental behavior as are emotional expressiveness or sociability. More recently, researchers have recognized that at least some aspects of socioemotional development and temperament are affected by heredity. Future work is likely to focus on the ways in which inherent differences interact with aspects of the child's environment to determine individual differences. In studying the child's environment when attempting to elucidate interactions between endogenous and exogenous forces, however, researchers will have to change their focus to include interactions with persons other than parents. Researchers have become increasingly aware of the importance of peer and sibling relationships in this regard, and we now turn our attention to a review of research on siblings and peers.

SIBLINGS AND PEERS

We know relatively little about the formative significance of infants' interactions with other children, even though many infants grow up with older siblings. In rhesus monkeys, however, peer interactions are critical: Infant monkeys learn how to play, how to fight, how to relate to members of the opposite sex, and how to communicate with other monkeys by playing with their peers; when deprived of these interactions, monkeys become socially incompetent adults, even when they have experienced good quality care from their mothers (Harlow, 1969; Suomi & Harlow, 1978). These findings have led developmental psychologists to ask how important peer and sibling relationships are for social and emotional development in human infants.

Sibling Relationships

Siblings in many nonindustrialized countries assume a major responsibility for infant care (Weisner, 1982; Weisner & Gallimore, 1977; Werner, 1984). These siblings spend relatively little time playing with the infants; most of their interactions, like those of Western parents, involve protection or caretaking. In our society, by contrast, siblings seldom assume any responsibility for caretaking, and sibling relationships appear to incorporate features of both the infant–adult and infant–peer systems (Pepler, Corter, & Abramovitch, 1982). On the one hand, sibling dyads often share common interests and have more similar behavioral repertoires than do infant–adult dyads. On the other hand, sibling pairs resemble infant–adult pairs to the extent that they differ (usually according to age) with respect to amount of experience and levels of both cognitive and social ability. These discrepancies often lead to differences in the ways younger and older siblings relate to each other, differences which by and large distinguish them from the infant–peer system (described in the next section). In two observational studies of sibling interaction in a laboratory playroom, Lamb (1978a, 1978b) found consistent asymmetries between the roles assumed by older and younger children. Older siblings "led" the interaction: They engaged in more dominant, assertive, and directing behaviors than their younger siblings did. The infants, meanwhile, appeared inordinately interested in what their siblings were doing; they followed them around, attempting to imitate the older children or at least explore the toys just abandoned by them. This is, of course, a strategy that maximizes the amount the baby can learn about the environment from the older child (Zajonc, 1983). In a home observational study, Abramovitch, Carter, and Lando (1979) reported patterns of interaction similar to those reported by Lamb (1978b), although siblings at home engaged in much more interaction than in the laboratory. And in a longitudinal study, Lamb (1978a) found remarkable stability across time in the amount of interaction engaged in by siblings. The pattern of correlations, furthermore, suggested that the sociability of the younger babies determined the amount of attention they later received from their siblings, rather than that the attention of older siblings helped babies become more sociable.

Individual differences in the quality of sibling relationships were also the focus of a longitudinal study conducted in England by Dunn and Kendrick (1980, 1981, 1982a, 1982b), who found that same-sex siblings got along better than different-sex siblings. In addition, siblings interacted more poorly when mothers and firstborn girls had very positive relationships before and immediately after the birth of the second child, and when there was frequent interaction and play between the siblings and their mothers. These findings suggest that parents exert an important influence on the mutual affective involvement of siblings, who may compete for parental attention. Nadelman and Begun (1982) also found that the quality of interaction between siblings varies depending on the quality of the firstborns' relationships with their mothers. Teti and Lamb (1986) reported that infants who were avoidant of their mothers appeared most likely to establish positive attachments to their preschool-aged siblings. Clearly, competitiveness is not all-consuming: Dunn and Munn (1986) reported that cooperative behavior was frequently observed in interactions between 18- to 24-month-olds and their older siblings.

Older siblings spend at least some of their time teaching object-related and social skills to their younger siblings (including infants), with the amount of teaching increasing with the age of the older child (Cicirelli, 1973, 1974; Minnett, Vandell, & Santrock, 1983; Pepler, 1981; Stewart, 1983). These studies, along with the finding that infants monitor and imitate their older siblings (e.g., Lamb, 1978a, 1978b), confirm that older siblings may influence the cognitive and social skills of infants through some combination of teaching and modeling (Zajonc, 1983).

The effects of age-spacing on the patterns of interaction between infants and their preschool-aged older siblings are unclear; Abramovitch et al. (1979), like Dunn and Kendrick (1981, 1982a), found no age-spacing differences in amounts of positive, negative, and imitative sibling behaviors. Suggesting that broad summary measures may not have been sensitive enough to detect actual differences, Teti, Bond, and Gibbs (1986, in press) used a more fine-grained coding scheme and found that older preschool-aged firstborns indeed created more "intellectual" (e.g., language mastery) and "social" (e.g., game) experiences for their infant siblings than did younger preschool-aged firstborns. In addition, Gibbs, Teti, and Bond (1985) found widely spaced siblings to be more interac- and responsive to each other than closely spaced siblings were. In neither of these investigations, however, did the researchers uncover relations between measures of infant cognitive or linguistic level and either sibling age or measures of sibling interaction.

Developing Relations With Other Children

For babies who do not have siblings, interaction with other children usually does not begin until the child is enrolled in an alternative care setting, an informal play group, or a nursery-school program. Research on these interactions has blossomed in the last decade, however, largely because societal changes have produced a situation in which increasing numbers of children spend much of their time with peers. This propinquity may have increased the formative importance of peer relationships, and also increased the availability of peer groups for study.

According to Hartup (1983), young infants lack the social skills required to sustain social interaction. Mueller and Lucas (1975) described a series of stages in the development of peer relationships in infants who regularly attended a play group from the first year of life. In their view, peer interaction has its roots in patterns of interaction with objects: Late in the first year of life (Stage 1), children treat one another in much the way they treat toys. Over time, however, pairs of children begin (Stage 2) to pay attention to the same object simultaneously, and then (Stage 3) to interact directly with one another. Relatively complex and elaborate interaction with peers is uncommon before the end of the second year, at which time the study was concluded.

Other investigators, however, have cast doubt on the notion that peer interaction emerges from interaction with objects. For example, Hay (Hay, Pedersen, &

Nash, 1982; Hay, Nash, & Pedersen, 1981a, 1981b, 1983), like Vandell, Wilson, and Buchanan (1980), demonstrated that infants can engage in limited— but harmonious—social interaction with other infants as early as 6 months of age, and that the social interactions of younger infants appear to be *less* reliant on object mediation than the play of toddlers. By 12 months of age, reported Zahn-Waxler and Radke-Yarrow (1982), *all* children show prosocial behavior, although there are substantial individual differences. Moreover, as early as 3 months of age, infants' peer-directed reactions are distinguishable from those directed to mothers (Fogel, 1979) and to the infants' own mirror images (Field, 1979). The stages described by Mueller and Lucas (1975) may depend on a coding scheme that fails to detect some subtle aspects of early peer responsiveness.

As might be expected, Becker (1977) and Mueller and Brenner (1977) showed that experience with peers facilitates the growth of interaction skills in infants and toddlers, presumably by allowing interaction with many individuals who have various social styles. Children who are in regular play groups or in preschool or day care settings appear more socially competent with peers than do their age-mates who are cared for at home (Field & Roopnarine, 1982; Finkelstein, Dent, Gallagher, & Ramey, 1978; Harper & Huie, 1985, Roopnarine, 1985). Children in play groups also interact with their parents at a higher rate than do infants and toddlers raised exclusively at home (Vandell, 1979).

Of course, the infant's social life is a coherent whole, which means that there are likely to be similarities between an infant's interactive styles with adults and with peers. As described above, many researchers have examined the relation between patterns of infant–mother attachment in the Strange Situation and their social competence in interaction with peers. Vandell and Wilson (1987) found that 6- and 9-month-old infants who were highly sociable with their mothers were also highly sociable with their siblings and with same-age, same-sex peers. Such studies suggest that, from interactions with their parents, infants develop characteristic social styles and orientations toward people. These styles affect the willingness to engage in interactions with persons other than parents, as well as the likelihood that infants will benefit from those interactions. As we noted earlier, these dispositions are also subject to change if the quality of the child's experiences at home changes (Lamb et al., 1984; Lamb et al., 1985).

GENERAL CONCLUSION

With regard to social and emotional development in infancy, as in most other areas of developmental psychology, controversy has raged concerning continuity and discontinuity—that is, the relation or lack of relation between and among similar activities in different phases of the life cycle. Proponents of one view—

like Kagan et al. (1978) and Kagan (1980)—believe that infancy is not particularly important because there is almost complete discontinuity between infancy and later life. Others—like the psychoanalysts and ethologists—argue that the experiences and behavior patterns developed in infancy are of crucial importance to later life because social orientations and motivations established in infancy set lifelong patterns. In fact, the truth probably lies somewhere between these two extreme positions.

Sameroff (1975; Sameroff & Chandler, 1975) proposed a *transactional* model of development in terms of which both child and parent are believed to bring distinctive characteristics to every interaction. The child's characteristics affect how the child behaves, how parents treat the child, and how the parents' behaviors affect the child. The parents' characteristics have the same consequences during each interaction, both parent and child are psychologically changed, and so they enter the next round of interaction as psychologically different individuals. From this perspective, it is naive to expect any single experience to have direct long-term effects. Nevertheless, events in infancy are deemed important because they initiate multiple processes of development. One implication of this is that continuity may be carried indirectly, through continuity in the supporting environment, or directly through continuity in the child.

Consider the following example drawn from Grossmann, Schwan, and Grossmann's (1986) longitudinal study. During the first two weeks after birth, the infants were tested three times using the NBAS (Brazelton, 1973). Using this, it was possible to divide the sample into "good" and "bad" orienters, that is, babies who were either attentive or nonattentive to social and physical stimuli. Subsequent home observations allowed the Grossmanns to assess the quality of maternal behavior. All six of the babies who were good orienters and had "tender-talking" sensitive mothers developed "secure" attachments by 1 year of age, whereas poor orienters with tender, sensitive mothers did so only one third of the time. Good orienters with less sensitive mothers had a 38% chance of being "securely attached," whereas only one of the eight babies who were poor orienters and had less sensitive mothers developed "secure" attachments. These data suggest that the characteristics of the child and the characteristics of the mother jointly determine the type of attachment they will develop, thus providing an elegant illustration of transactional processes. Research on social and emotional development is likely to retain an emphasis on issues of continuity and discontinuity in the years ahead.

This chapter attests to the diversity of approaches characterizing the study of social and emotional development and to the amount of attention currently being paid to this area. On the basis of evidence now available, it seems that the understanding of socioemotional development—and of infancy in general—is considerably advanced by the perspective of evolutionary biology, which has provided a way of making sense of infant behavior simply by proposing that we consider the adaptive significance and function of infant behavior. This has provided answers to questions about *why* social smiling, stranger anxiety, separation anxiety, social attachment, and the fear of heights occur at all, and why they emerge when they do. This perspective, however, tells us little about the mechanisms whereby these phenomena are mediated and nothing about the way in which individual differences in social and emotional development are to be explained. With respect to the *hows* of development, the most useful answers have come from the cognitive developmental theorists, especially those like Sroufe who have attempted to make their propositions consistent with the ethological-adaptational theory. Biogenetic approaches emphasizing heritability, the analysis of social interaction, and social-cognitive perspectives seem most likely to contribute to our understanding of individual differences in socioemotional development.

ACKNOWLEDGMENTS

I am grateful to Drs. Marc Bornstein, Joseph J. Campos, and Ross Thompson for helpful comments on earlier drafts of this chapter, which was completed while I was at the University of Utah.

REFERENCES

Abramovitch, R., Corter, C., & Lando, B. (1979). Sibling interaction in the home. *Child Development, 50,* 997–1003.

Ahrens, R. (1954). Beitrag zur Entwicklung des Physiognomie—und Mimskerkennens. *Zeitschrift fur exporimentelle und angewandte Psychologie, 2,* 412–454.

Ainsworth, M. D. S. (1973). The development of infant–mother attachment. In B. M. Caldwell & H. N. Ricciuti (Eds.), *Review of child development research* (Vol. 3). Chicago: University of Chicago Press.

Ainsworth, M. D. S. (1979). Attachment as related to mother–infant interaction. In J. S. Rosenblatt, R. A. Hinde, C. Beer, & M. Busnel (Eds.), *Advances in the study of behavior* (Vol. 9). New York: Academic Press.

Ainsworth, M. D. S., Bell, S. M., & Stayton, D. J. (1974). Infant mother attachment and social development: "Socialization" as a product of reciprocal responsiveness to signals. In M. P. M. Richards (Ed.), *The integration of a child into a social world.* Cambridge, England: Cambridge University Press.

Ainsworth, M. D. S., Blehar, M. C., Waters, E., & Wall, S. (1978). *Patterns of attachment.* Hillsdale, NJ: Lawrence Erlbaum Associates.

Ainsworth, M. D. S., & Wittig, B. A. (1969). Attachment and exploratory behavior of one-year-olds in a strange situation. In B. M. Foss (Ed.), *Determinants of infant behaviour* (Vol. 4). London: Methuen.

Ambrose, J. (1961). The development of the smiling response in early infancy. In B. Foss (Ed.), *Determinants of infant behavior* (Vol. 1). London: Methuen.

Arend, R., Gove, F. L., & Sroufe, L. A. (1979). Continuity of individual adaptation from infancy to kindergarten: A predictive study of ego-resiliency and curiosity in preschoolers. *Child Development, 50,* 950–959.

Bandura, A., & Walters, R. H. (1959). *Adolescent aggression: A study of the influence of child-rearing practices and family interrelationships.* New York: Ronald.

Bandura, A., & Walters, R. H. (1963). *Social learning and personality development.* New York: Holt, Rinehart & Winston.

Barrera, M. E., & Maurer, D. (1981a). The perception of facial expressions by the three-month-old. *Child Development, 52,* 203–206.

Barrera, M. E., & Maurer, D. (1981b). Recognition of mother's photographed face by the three-month-old infant. *Child Development, 52,* 714–716.

Bates, J. E. (1986). The measurement of temperament. In R. Plomin & J. Dunn (Eds.), *The study of temperament: Changes, continuities, and challenges.* Hillsdale, NJ: Lawrence Erlbaum Associates.

Bates, J. E. (1987). Temperament in infancy. In J. D. Osofsky (Ed.), *Handbook of infant development.* New York: Wiley.

Bates, J. E., Maslin, C. A., & Frankel, K. A. (1985). Attachment security, mother–child interaction, and temperament as predictors of behavior problem ratings at age three years. In I. Bretherton & E. Waters (Eds.), *Growing points of attachment theory and research. Monographs of the Society for Research in Child Development, 50* (Serial No. 209).

Bates, J. E., Olson, S. L., Pettit, G. S., & Bayles, K. (1982). Dimensions of individuality in the mother–infant relationship at six months of age. *Child Development, 53,* 446–461.

Becker, J. N. T. (1977). A learning analysis of the development of peer-oriented behavior in nine-month-old infants. *Developmental Psychology, 13,* 481–491.

Belsky, J., Rovine, M., Taylor, D. (1984). The Pennsylvania Infant and Family Development Project, III: The origins of individual differences in infant–mother attachment: Maternal and infant contributions. *Child Development, 55,* 718–728.

Bertenthal, B. I., Campos, J. J., & Barrett, K. (1984). Self-produced locomotion: An organizer of emotional, cognitive, and social development in infancy. In R. N. Emde & R. J. Harmon (Eds.), *Continuities and discontinuities in development.* New York: Plenum.

Bertenthal, B. I., Campos, J. J., & Haith, M. (1980). Development of visual organization: Perception of subjective contours. *Child Development, 51,* 1072–1080.

Bijou, S. W., & Baer, D. M. (1961). *Child development I: A systematic and empirical theory.* New York: Appleton-Century-Crofts.

Bijou, S. W., & Baer, D. M. (1965). *Child development II: Universal stage of infancy.* New York: Appleton-Century-Crofts.

Block, J. H., & Block, J. (1980). The role of ego-control and ego-resiliency in the organization of behavior. In W. A. Collins (Ed.), *Minnesota symposium on child psychology* (Vol. 13). Hillsdale, NJ: Lawrence Erlbaum Associates.

Boccia, M., & Campos, J. (1983, April). *Maternal emotional signalling: Its effect on infants' reactions to strangers.* Paper presented at the meeting of the Society for Research in Child Development, Detroit.

Bornstein, M. H., Gaughran, J., & Homel, P. (1986). Infant temperament: Theory, tradition, critique, and new assessments. In C. E. Izard & P. B. Read (Eds.), *Measurement of emotions in infants and children* (Vol. 2). New York: Cambridge University Press.

Bower, T. G. R. (1977). *A primer of infant development.* San Francisco: Freeman.

Bowlby, J. (1944). Forty-four juvenile thieves: Their characters and home life. *International Journal of Psychoanalysis, 25,* 107–128.

Bowlby, J. (1951). *Maternal care and mental health.* Geneva: World Health Organization.

Bowlby, J. (1969). *Attachment and Loss:* Vol. 1. *Attachment.* New York: Basic Books.

Bowlby, J. (1973). *Attachment and Loss:* Vol. 2. *Separation: Anxiety and anger.* New York: Basic Books.

Bowlby, J. (1980). *Attachment and loss:* Vol. 3. *Loss.* New York: Basic Books.

Brackbill, Y. (1958). Extinction of the smiling response in infants as a function of reinforcement schedule. *Child Development, 29,* 115–124.

Brazelton, T. B. (1973). *Neonatal behavioral assessment scale (Clinics in Developmental Medicine, 50.).* Philadelphia, PA: Lippincott.

Bretherton, I. (1978). Making friends with one-year-olds: An experimental study of infant–stranger interaction. *Merrill-Palmer Quarterly, 24,* 29–52.

Bretherton, I., & Ainsworth, M. D. S. (1974). Responses of one-year-olds to a stranger in a strange situation. In M. Lewis & L. Rosenblum (Eds.), *The origins of fear.* New York: Wiley.

Bridges, K. M. (1930). A genetic theory of the emotions. *Journal of Genetic Psychology, 37,* 514–527.

Bridges, K. M. (1932). Emotional development in early infancy. *Child Development, 3,* 324–341.

Bronson, G. (1972). Infants' reactions to unfamiliar persons and novel objects. *Monographs of the Society for Research in Child Development, 32* (4, Serial No. 112).

Brooks, J., & Lewis, M. (1976). Infants' responses to strangers: Midget, adult, and child. *Child Development, 47,* 323–332.

Bushnell, I. W. R. (1982). Discriminations of faces by young infants. *Journal of Experimental Child Psychology, 33,* 298–308.

Buss, A. H., & Plomin, R. (1984). *Temperament: Early developing personality traits.* Hillsdale, NJ: Lawrence Erlbaum Associates.

Callaghan, J. W. (1981). A comparison of Anglo, Hopi, and Navajo mothers and infants. In T. M. Field, A. M. Sostek, P. Vietze, & P. H. Leiderman (Eds.), *Culture and early interactions.* Hillsdale, NJ: Lawrence Erlbaum Associates.

Campos, J. (1976). Heart rate: A sensitive tool for the study of emotional development in the infant. In L. Lipsitt (Ed.), *Developmental psychobiology: The significance of infancy.* Hillsdale, NJ: Lawrence Erlbaum Associates.

Campos, J. J. (April 1986). *Contemporary issues in the study of infant emotion.* Invited address to the International Conference on Infant Studies, Los Angeles.

Campos, J. J., & Barrett, K. C. (1984). Toward a new understanding of emotions and their development. In C. E. Izard, J. Kagan, & R. B. Zajonc (Eds.), *Emotion, cognition, and behavior* (pp. 229–263). Cambridge, England: Cambridge University Press.

Campos, J. J., Barrett, K. G., Lamb, M. E., Stenberg, C., & Goldsmith, H. H. (1983). Socioemotional development. In M. M. Haith & J. J. Campos (Eds.), *Infancy and developmental psychobiology* (Vol. 2). In P. H. Mussen (Gen. Ed.), *Handbook of child psychology.* New York: Wiley.

Campos, J., Hiatt, S., Ramsay, D., Henderson, C., & Svejda, M. (1978). The emergence of fear on the visual cliff. In M. Lewis & L. Rosenblum (Eds.), *The origins of affect.* New York: Plenum.

Campos, J., Langer, A., & Krowitz, A. (1970). Cardiac responses on the visual cliff in pre-motor human infants. *Science, 170,* 195–196.

Campos, J., & Stenberg, C. (1981). Perception, appraisal, and emotion: The onset of social referencing. In M. E. Lamb & L. Sherrod (Eds.), *Infant social cognition.* Hillsdale, NJ: Lawrence Erlbaum Associates.

Caron, R. F., Caron, A. J., & Myers, R. S. (1982). Abstraction of invariant face expressions in infancy. *Child Development, 53,* 1008–1015.

Cicirelli, V. G. (1973). Effects of sibling structure and interaction on children's categorization style. *Developmental Psychology, 9,* 132–139.

Cicirelli, V. G. (1974). Relationship of sibling structuring and interaction on younger sib's conceptual style. *Journal of Genetic Psychology, 125,* 36–49.

Clarke-Stewart, K. A. (1978). And daddy makes three: The father's impact on mother and young child. *Child Development, 49,* 466–478.

Clarke-Stewart, K. A., Umeh, B. J., Snow, M. E., & Pederson, J. A. (1980). Development and prediction of children's sociability from 1 to 2½ years. *Developmental Psychology, 16,* 290–302.

Coates, B., Anderson, E. P., & Hartup, W. W. (1972). Interrelations in the attachment behavior of human infants. *Developmental Psychology, 6,* 218–230.

Cohn, J. E., & Tronick, E. Z. (1983a). Communicative rules and the sequential structure of infant behavior during normal and depressed interaction. In E. Tronick (Ed.), *The development of human communication and the joint regulation of behavior.* Baltimore, MD: University Park Press.

Cohn, J. E., & Tronick, E. Z. (1983b). Three-month-old infants' reactions to simulated maternal depression. *Child Development, 54,* 185–193.

Connell, D. B. (1976). *Individual differences in attachment: An investigation into stability, implications, and relationships to structure of early language development.* Unpublished doctoral dissertation, Syracuse University.

Daniels, D., & Plomin, R. (1985). Origins of individual differences in infant shyness. *Developmental Psychology, 21,* 118–121.

DeVries, M. W. (1984). Temperament and infant mortality among the Masai of East Africa. *American Journal of Psychiatry, 141,* 1189–1194.

Derryberry, D., & Rothbart, M. K. (1984). Emotion, attention, and temperament. In C. E. Izard, J. Kagan, & R. B. Zajonc (Eds.), *Emotions, cognition, and behavior.* Cambridge, England: Cambridge University Press.

Diamond, S. (1957). *Personality and temperament.* New York: Harper.

Dickstein, S., Thompson, R. A., Estes, D., Malkin, C. M., & Lamb, M. E. (1984). Social referencing and the security of attachment. *Infant Behavior and Development, 7,* 507–516.

Dollard, J., & Miller, M. E. (1950). *Personality and psychotherapy.* New York: McGraw-Hill.

Dunn, J., & Kendrick, C. (1980). The arrival of a sibling: Changes in patterns of interaction between mother and first-born child. *Journal of Child Psychology and Psychiatry, 21,* 119–132.

Dunn, J., & Kendrick, C. (1981). Interaction between young siblings: Associations with the interactions between mothers and first-born. *Developmental Psychology, 17,* 336–343.

Dunn, J., & Kendrick, C. (1982a). *Siblings: Love, envy, and understanding.* Cambridge, MA: Harvard University Press.

Dunn, J., & Kendrick, C. (1982b). Siblings and their mothers: Developing relationships within the family. In M. E. Lamb & B. Sutton-Smith (Eds.), *Sibling relationships: Their nature and significance across the life span.* Hillsdale, NJ: Lawrence Erlbaum Associates.

Dunn, J., & Munn, P. (1986). Siblings and the development of prosocial behavior. *International Journal of Behavioral Development, 9,* 265–284.

Easterbrooks, M. A., & Lamb, M. E. (1979). The relationship between quality of infant–mother attachment and infant competence in initial encounters with peers. *Child Development, 50,* 380–387.

Egeland, B., & Farber, E. A. (1984). Infant–mother attachment: Factors related to its development and changes over time. Child Development, 55, 753–771.

Egeland, B., & Farber, E. A. (1984). Infant–mother attachment: Factors related to its development and changes over time. *Child Development, 55,* 753–771.

Ekman, P. (1973). Cross-cultural studies of facial expression. In P. Ekman (Ed.), *Darwin and facial expression: A century of research in review.* New York: Academic Press.

Ekman, P. (1982). Methods for measuring facial action. In K. Scherer & P. Ekman (Eds.), *Handbook on methods in research on nonverbal communication.* New York: Cambridge University Press.

Emde, R. N., & Brown, C. (1978). Adaptation to the birth of a Down's syndrome infant. *Journal of the American Academy of Child Psychiatry, 17,* 299–323.

Emde, R. N., Gaensbauer, T. J., & Harmon, R. J. (1976). Emotional expression in infancy: A biobehavioral study. *Psychological Issues,* Vol. 10 (Whole No. 1).

Emde, R. N., & Harmon, R. J. (1972). Endogenous and exogenous smiling systems in early infancy. *Journal of the American Academy of Child Psychiatry, 11,* 177–200.

Emde, R., Kligman, D., Reich, J., & Wade, T. (1978). Emotional expression in infancy: I. Initial studies of social signaling and an emergent model. In M. Lewis and L. Rosenblum (Eds.), *The development of affect.* New York: Plenum.

Emde, R. N., Izard, C., Huebner, R., Sorce, J. F., & Klinnert, M. (1985). Adult judgements of infant emotions: Replication studies within and across laboratories. *Infant Behavior and Development, 8,* 79–88.

Erickson, M. F., Sroufe, L. A., & Egeland, B. (1985). The relationship between quality of attachment and behavior problems in preschool in a high-risk sample. In I. Bretherton & E. Waters (Eds.), Growing points of attachment theory and research. *Monographs of the Society for Research in Child Development, 50* (Serial No. 209).

Etzel, B., & Gewirtz, J. (1967). Experimental modification of caretaker-maintained high rate operant crying in a 6- and a 20-week-old infant (*Infans tyrannotearus*): Extinction of crying with reinforcement of eye contact and smiling. *Journal of Experimental Child Psychology, 5,* 303–317.

Feiring, C., Lewis, M., & Starr, M. D. (1984). Indirect effects and infants' reactions to strangers. *Developmental Psychology, 20,* 485–491.

Field, T. M. (1979). Infant behaviors directed toward peers and adults in the presence and absence of mother. *Infant Behavior and Development, 2,* 47–54.

Field, T. M., & Roopnarine, J. L. (1982). Infant–peer interactions. In T. M. Field, A. Huston, H. C. Quay, L. Troll, & G. E. Finley (Eds.), *Review of human development.* New York: John Wiley.

Finkelstein, N. W., Dent, C., Gallagher, K., & Ramey. C. T. (1978). Social behavior of infants and toddlers in a day care environment. *Developmental Psychology, 14,* 257–262.

Fogel, A. (1979). Peer vs. mother directed behavior in 1- to 3-month-old infants. *Infant Behavior and Development, 2,* 215–226.

Fogel, A., Diamond, G. R., Langhorst, B. H., & Demos, V. (April 1979). *Alteration of infant behavior as a result of "still-face" perturbation of maternal behavior.* Paper presented to a meeting of the Society for Research in Child Development, San Francisco.

Fox, N. (1977). Attachment of kibbutz infants to mother and metapelet. *Child Development, 48,* 1228–1239.

Fox, R., Aslin, R.. Shea, S., & Dumais, S. (1980). Stereopsis in human infants. *Science, 207,* 323–324.

Fraiberg, S. (1974). Blind infants and their mothers: An examination of the sign system. In M. Lewis and L. Rosenblum (Eds.), *The effect of the infant on the caregiver.* New York: Wiley.

Fraiberg, S. (1977). *Insights from the blind.* New York: Basic Books.

Freedman, D. (1974). *Human infancy: An evolutionary perspective.* Hillsdale, NJ: Lawrence Erlbaum Associates.

Freedman, D. G., & Freedman, N. C. (1969). Behavioral differences between Chinese-American and European-American newborns. *Nature, 244,* 1227.

Freedman, D. G., & Keller, B. (1964). Inheritance of behavior in infants. *Science, 140,* 196–198.

Freud, S. (1923/1962). *The ego and the id.* New York: Norton.

Freud, S. (1940). *An outline of psychoanalysis.* New York: Norton.

Frodi, A. M., Lamb, M. E., Leavitt, L. A., & Donovan, W. L. (1978). Fathers' and mothers' responses to infant smiles and cries. *Infant Behavior and Development, 1,* 187–198.

Gaensbauer, T. J., & Harmon, R. J. (1982). Attachment and affiliative systems under conditions of extreme environmental stress. In R. N. Emde & R. J. Harmon (Eds.), *Development of attachment and affiliative systems.* New York: Plenum.

Gaensbauer, T. J., & Hiatt, S. (1984). Facial communication of emotion in early infancy. In N. A. Fox & R. J. Davidson (Eds.), *The psychobiology of affective development.* Hillsdale, NJ: Lawrence Erlbaum Associates.

Gaensbauer, T. J., & Sands, K. (1979). Distorted affective communications in abused/neglected infants and their potential impact on caretakers. *Journal of the American Academy of Child Psychiatry, 18,* 238–250.

Gewirtz, J. L. (1972). Attachment, dependency, and a distinction in terms of stimulus control. In J. L. Gewirtz (Ed.), *Attachment and dependency.* Washington, DC: Winston.

Gibbs, E. D., Teti, D. M., & Bond, L. A. (April 1985). *Infant–sibling communication as a function of age-spacing.* Paper presented at the Biennial Meeting of the Society for Research in Child Development, Toronto, Canada.

Goldsmith, H. H. (1983). Genetic influences on personality from infancy to childhood. *Child Development, 54,* 331–335.

Goldsmith, H. H., & Campos, J. J. (1984). The concept of temperament in human development. In R. N. Emde & R. J. Harmon (Eds.), *Development of attachment and affiliative systems.* New York: Plenum.

Goldsmith, H. H., & Campos, J. J. (1986). Fundamental issues in the study of temperament: The Denver Twin Temperament Study. In M. E. Lamb, A. L. Brown, & B. Rogoff (Eds.), *Advances in developmental psychology* (Vol. 4). Hillsdale, NJ: Lawrence Erlbaum Associates.

Goldsmith, H. H., & Gottesman, I. I. (1981). Origins of variation in behavioral style: A longitudinal study of temperament in young twins. *Child Development, 52,* 91–103.

Grossmann, K. E., Grossmann, K., Huber, F., & Wartner, U. (1981). German children's behavior towards their mothers at 12 months and their fathers at 18 months in Ainsworth's Strange Situation. *International Journal of Behavioral Development, 4,* 157–181.

Grossmann, K., Grossmann, K. E., Spangler, G., Suess, G., & Unzner, L. (1985). Maternal sensitivity and newborns' orientation responses as related to quality of attachment in northern Germany. In I. Bretherton & E. Waters (Eds.), Growing points of attachment theory and research. *Monographs of the Society for Research in Child Development, 50* (Serial No. 209).

Grossmann, K. E., Schwan, Z., & Grossmann, K. (1986). Infants' communications after brief separation: A reanalysis of Ainsworth's Strange Situation. In B. Read & C. E. Izard (Eds.), *Measuring emotions in infants and children* (Vol. 3). Cambridge, England: Cambridge University Press.

Hainline, L. (1978). Developmental changes in visual scanning of face and nonface patterns by infants. *Journal of Experimental Child Psychology, 25,* 90–115.

Haith, M. M., Bergman, T., & Moore, M. (1977). Eye contact and face scanning in early infancy. *Science, 198,* 853–855.

Haith, M., & Campos, J. (1977). Human infancy. *Annual Review of Psychology, 28,* 251–294.

Harkness, S., & Super, C. M. (1985). Child–environment interactions in the socialization of affect. In M. Lewis & C. Saarni (Eds.), *The socialization of emotions.* New York: Plenum.

Harlow, H. F. (1969). Age-mate or peer affectional system. In D. S. Lehrman, R. A. Hinde, & E. Shaw (Eds.), *Advances in the study of behavior* (Vol. 2). New York: Academic.

Harlow, H. F., & Zimmerman, R. R. (1959). Affectional responses in the infant monkey. *Science, 130,* 421.

Harper, L. V., & Huie, K. S. (1985). The effects of prior group experience, age, and familiarity on the quality and organization of preschoolers' social relationships. *Child Development, 56,* 704–717.

Hartup, W. W. (1983). Peer relations. In E. M. Hetherington (Ed.), *Socialization, personality, and social structure* (Vol. 4). In P. H. Mussen (Gen. Ed.), *Handbook of child psychology.* New York: Wiley.

Hay, D. F., Nash, A., & Pedersen, J. (March, 1981a). *Reciprocal contact between six-month-old peers.* Paper presented at the International Conference on Infant Studies, Austin, Texas.

Hay, D. F., Nash, A., & Pedersen, J. (1981b). Responses of six-month-olds to the distress of their peers. *Child Development, 52,* 1071–1075.

Hay, D. F., Nash, A., & Pedersen, J. (1983). Interaction between six-month-old peers. *Child Development, 54,* 557–562.

Hay, D. F., Pedersen, J., & Nash, A. (1982). Dyadic interactions in the first years of life. In R. H. Rubin & H. S. Ross (Eds.), *Peer relationships and social skills in childhood.* New York: Springer-Verlag.

Hebb, D. O. (1946). On the nature of fear. *Psychological Review, 53,* 259–276.

Hebb, D. O. (1949). *The organization of behavior.* New York: Wiley.

Hiatt, S., Campos, J., & Emde, R. (1979). Facial patterning and infant emotional expression: Happiness, surprise, and fear. *Child Development, 50,* 1020–1035.

Izard, C. E. (1971). *The face of emotion.* New York: Appleton-Century-Crofts.

Izard, C. E. (1977). *Human emotions.* New York: Plenum Press.

Izard, C. E. (1978). On the ontogenesis of emotions and emotion–cognition relationships in infancy. In M. Lewis & L. Rosenblum (Eds.), *The development of affect.* New York: Planum.

Izard, C. E. (1979). *The maximally discriminative facial movement scoring system.* Unpublished manuscript, University of Delaware.

Izard, C. E., & Buechler, S. (1986). Theoretical perspectives on emotions in developmental disabilities. In M. Lewis & L. Taft (Eds.), *Development disabilities: Theory, assessment, and intervention.* New York: Medical and Scientific Books.

Izard, C. E., Huebner, R., Risser, D., McGinness, G., & Dougherty, L. (1980). The young infant's ability to produce discrete emotion expressions. *Developmental Psychology, 16,* 132–140.

Jackson, E., Campos, J., & Fischer, K. (1978). The question of décalage between object permanence and person permanence. *Developmental Psychology, 14,* 1–10.

Jacobson, J. L., & Wille, D. E. (1984, April). *The influence of attachment pattern on peer interaction at 2 and 3 years.* Paper presented to the International Conference on Infants Studies, New York.

Jacobson, J. L., & Wille, D. E. (1986). The influence of attachment pattern on developmental changes in peer interaction from the toddler to the preschool period. *Child Development, 57,* 338–347.

Jacobson, J. L., Wille, D. E., Tianen, R. L., & Aytch, D. M. (April 1983). *The influence of infant–mother attachment on toddler sociability with peers.* Paper presented to the Society for Research in Child Development, Detroit.

Johnson, W., Emde, R. N., Pannabecker, B., Stenberg, C., & Davis, M. (1982). Maternal perception of infant emotion from birth through 18 months. *Infant Behavior and Development, 5,* 313–322.

Jones, M. C. (1924). The elimination of children's fears. *Journal of Experimental Psychology, 7,* 382–390.

Kagan, J. (1971). *Change and continuity in infancy.* New York: Wiley.

Kagan, J. (1974). Discrepancy, temperament and infant distress. In M. Lewis and L. Rosenblum (Eds.), *The origins of fear.* New York: Wiley.

Kagan, J. (1980). Perspectives on continuity. In O. F. Brim, Jr. & J. Kagan (Eds.), *Continuity and change in human development.* Cambridge, MA: Harvard University Press.

Kagan, J., Kearsley, P., & Zelazo, P. (1978). *Infancy: Its place in human development.* Cambridge, MA: Harvard University Press.

Kaye, K. (1979). Thickening thin data: The maternal role in developing communication with language. In M. Bullowa (Ed.), *Before speech.* Cambridge, England: Cambridge University Press.

Keefer, C. H., Tronick, E., Dixon, J., & Brazelton, T. B. (1982). Specific differences in motor performance between Gusii and American newborns and a modification of the Neonatal Behavioral Assessment Scale. *Child Development, 53,* 754–759.

Klein, P. S. (1984). Behavior of Israeli mothers toward infants in relation to infants' perceived temperament. *Child Development, 55,* 1212–1218.

Klinnert, M. D. (1981). *The regulation of infant behavior by maternal facial expression.* Unpublished doctoral dissertation, University of Denver.

Klinnert, M. (1984). The regulation of infant behavior by maternal facial expression. *Infant Behavior and Development, 7,* 447–465.

Klinnert, M., Campos, J., Sorce, J., Emde, R., & Svejda, M. (1983). Emotions as behavior regulators: Social referencing in infancy. In R. Plutchik and H. Kellerman (Eds.), *Emotions in early development*. New York: Academic Press.

Klinnert, M., Sorce, J., Emde, R. N., Stenberg, C., & Gaensbauer, T. (1984). Continuities and change in early affective life: Maternal perceptions of surprise, fear, and anger. In R. N. Emde & R. J. Harmon (Eds.), *Continuities and discontinuities in development*. New York: Plenum.

Kotelchuck, M. (1976). The infant's relationship to the father: Experimental evidence. In M. E. Lamb (Ed.), *The role of the father in child development*. New York: Wiley.

Kuchuk, A., Vibbert, M., & Bornstein, M. H. (1986). The perception of smiling and its experiential correlates in 3-month-old infants. *Child Development, 57,* 1054–1061.

LaBarbera, J. D., Izard, C. E., Vietze, P., and Parisi, S. A. (1976). Four- and six-month-old infants' visual responses to joy, anger, and neutral expressions. *Child Development, 47,* 535–538.

Lamb, M. E. (1976a). Effects of stress and cohort on mother– and father–infant interaction. *Developmental Psychology, 12,* 435–443.

Lamb, M. E. (1976b). Interactions between eight-month-old children and their fathers and mothers. In M. E. Lamb (Ed.), *The role of the father in child development*. New York: Wiley.

Lamb, M. E. (1976c). Twelve-month-olds and their parents: Interaction in a laboratory playroom. *Developmental Psychology, 12,* 237–244.

Lamb, M. E. (1977). Father–infant and mother–infant interaction in the first year of life. *Child Development, 48,* 167–181.

Lamb, M. E. (1978a). The development of sibling relationships in infancy: A short-term longitudinal study. *Child Development, 49,* 1189–1196.

Lamb, M. E. (1978b). Interactions between 18-month-olds and their preschool-aged siblings. *Child Development, 49,* 51–59.

Lamb, M. E. (1978). Qualitative aspects of mother– and father–infant attachments. *Infant Behavior and Development, 1,* 265–275.

Lamb, M. E. (1981a). Developing trust and perceived effectance in infancy. In L. P. Lipsitt (Ed.), *Advances in infancy research* (Vol. 1). Norwood, NJ: Ablex.

Lamb, M. E. (1981b). The development of social expectations in the first year of life. In M. E. Lamb & L. R. Sherrod (Eds.), *Infant social cognition: Empirical and theoretical considerations*. Hillsdale, NJ: Lawrence Erlbaum Associates.

Lamb, M. E. (1982). Individual differences in infant sociability: Their origins and implications for cognitive development. In H. W. Reese & L. P. Lipsitt (Eds.), *Advances in child development and behavior* (Vol. 16). New York: Academic.

Lamb, M. E., & Bornstein, M. H. (1987). *Development in infancy* (2nd ed.). New York: Random House.

Lamb, M. E., Frodi, A. M., Hwang, C.-P., Frodi, M., & Steinberg, J. (1982). Mother– and father–infant interaction involving play and holding in traditional and nontraditional Swedish families. *Developmental Psychology, 18,* 215–221.

Lamb, M. E., Frodi, M., Hwang, C.-P.. & Frodi, A. M. (1983). Effects of paternal involvement on infant preferences for mothers and fathers. *Child Development, 54,* 450–458.

Lamb, M. E., Gaensbauer, T. J., Malkin, C. M., & Schultz, L. (1985). The effects of abuse and neglect on security of infant–adult attachment. *Infant Behavior and Development, 8,* 35–45.

Lamb, M. E., Hwang, C.-P., Frodi, A. M., & Frodi, M. (1982). Security of mother– and father–infant attachment and its relation to sociability with strangers in traditional and nontraditional Swedish families. *Infant Behavior and Development, 5,* 355–367.

Lamb, M. E., Morrison, D. C., & Malkin, C. M. (1987). The development of infant social expectations in face-to-face interaction: A longitudinal study. *Merrill-Palmer Quarterly, 33,* 241–254.

Lamb, M. E., Thompson, R. A., Gardner, W., & Charnov, E. L. (1985). *Infant–mother attachment: The origins and developmental significance of individual differences in Strange Situation behavior*. Hillsdale, NJ: Lawrence Erlbaum Associates.

Lamb, M. E., Thompson, R. A., Gardner, W., Charnov, E. L., & Estes, D. (1984). Security of infantile attachment as assessed in the "Strange Situation": Its study and biological interpretation. *Behavioral and Brain Sciences, 7,* 127–171.

Lerner, J. V., & Lerner, R. M. (1983). Temperament and adaptation across life: Theoretical and empirical issues. In P. B. Baltes & O. G. Brim, Jr. (Eds.), *Lifespan development and behavior* (Vol. 5). New York: Academic.

Lerner, J. V., & Lerner, R. M. (1986). *Temperament and social interaction in infants and children.* San Francisco: Jossey-Bass.

Lerner, R. M., & Lerner, J. V. (1983). Temperament–intelligence reciprocities in early childhood: A contextual model. In M. Lewis (Ed.), *Origins of intelligence* (2nd ed.). New York: Plenum.

Lerner, R. M., Palermo, M., Spiro, A., & Nesselroade, J. R. (1982). Assessing the dimensions of temperamental individuality across the life span: The dimensions of temperament survey (DOTS). *Child Development, 53,* 149–159.

Lester, B. M., Kotelchuck, M., Spelke, E., Sellers, M. J., & Klein, R. E. (1974). Separation protest in Guatemalan infants: Cross-cultural and cognitive findings. *Developmental Psychology, 10,* 79–85.

Leung, E., & Rheingold, H. (1981). Development of pointing as a social gesture. *Developmental Psychology, 17,* 215–220.

Lewis, M., & Michalson, L. (1982). The socialization of emotions. In T. Field & A. Fogel (Eds.), *Emotion and early interaction.* Hillsdale, NJ: Lawrence Erlbaum Associates.

Lewis, M., & Michalson, L. (19S3). *Children's emotions and moods: Developmental theory and measurement.* New York: Plenum.

Lewis, M., & Michalson, L. (1984). The socialization of emotional pathology in infancy. *Infant Mental Health Journal, 5,* 125–134.

Lewis, M., & Saarni, C. (Eds.), (1985). *The socialization of emotions.* New York: Plenum.

Lewis, M., Feiring, C., McGuffog, C., & Jaskir, J. (1984). Predicting psychopathology in six-year-olds from early social relations. *Child Development, 55,* 123–136.

Lieberman, A. F. (1977). Preschoolers' competence with a peer: Relations with attachment and peer experience. *Child Development, 48,* 1277–1287.

Main, M. (1983). Exploration, play, and cognitive functioning related to infant–mother attachment. *Infant Behavior and Development, 6,* 167–174.

Main, M. B., & Weston, D. R. (1981). Security of attachment to mother and father: Related to conflict behavior and the readiness to establish new relationships. *Child Development, 52,* 932–940.

Malatesta, C. Z. (1985, April). *Facial expressions of infants and mothers during early interaction.* Paper presented to the Society for Research in Child Development, Toronto.

Malatesta, C. Z., Grigoryev, P., Lamb, C., Albin, M., & Culver, C. (1986). Emotion socialization and expressive development in preterm and full-term infants. *Child Development, 57,* 316–330.

Malatesta, C. Z., & Haviland, J. M. (1982). Learning display rules: The socialization of emotion expression in infancy. *Child Development, 53,* 991–1003.

Malatesta, C. Z., & Haviland, J. M. (1985). Signals, symbols, and socialization: The modification of emotional expression in human development. In M. Lewis & C. Saarni (Eds.), *The socialization of emotions.* New York: Plenum.

Masters, J. C., & Wellman, H. M. (1974). The study of human infant attachment: A procedural critique. *Psychological Bulletin, 81,* 213–237.

Matas, L., Arend, R. A., & Sroufe, L. A. (1978). Continuity of adaptation in the second year: The relationship between quality of attachment and later competence. *Child Development, 49,* 547–556.

Matheny, A. P. (1980). Bayley's Infant Behavior Record: Behavioral components and twin analyses. *Child Development, 51,* 1157–1167.

Matheny, A. P. (1983). A longitudinal twin study of stability of components from Bayley's Infant Behavior Record. *Child Development, 84,* 356–360.

Maurer, D., & Salapatek, P. (1976). Developmental changes in the scanning of faces by young infants. *Child Development, 47,* 523–527.

McCall, R., & McGhee, P. (1977).The discrepancy hypothesis of attention and affect. In F. Weizmann & I. Užgiris (Eds.), *The structuring of experience.* New York: Plenum.

Michalson, L., & Lewis, M. (1985). What do children know about emotions and when do they know it? In M. Lewis & C. Saarni (Eds.), *The socialization of emotions.* New York:Plenum.

Minnett, A. M., Vandell, D. L., & Santrock, J. W. (1983). The effects of sibling status on sibling interaction: Influence of birth order, age spacing, sex of child, and sex of sibling. *Child Development, 54,* 1064–1072.

Miyake, K., Chen, S.-J., & Campos, J. J. (1985). Infant temperament, mother's mode of interaction, and attachment in Japan: An interim report. In I. Bretherton & E. Waters (Eds.), *Growing points in attachment theory and research. Monographs of the Society for Research in Child Development, 50* (Serial No. 209).

Mueller, E., & Brenner, J. (1977). The origins of social skills and interaction among playgroup toddlers. *Child Development, 48,* 854–861.

Mueller, E., & Lucas, T. (1975). A developmental analysis of peer interaction among toddlers. In M. Lewis & L. Rosenblum (Eds.), *Friendship and peer relations.* New York: Wiley.

Nadelman, L., & Begun, A. (1982). The effect of the newborn on the older sibling: Mothers' questionnaires. In M. E. Lamb & B. Sutton-Smith (Eds.), *Sibling relationships: Their nature and significance across the lifespan.* Hillsdale, NJ: Lawrence Erlbaum Associates.

Nash, A., & Lamb, M. E. (in preparation). *Becoming acquainted with unfamiliar adults and peers in infancy.* Unpublished manuscript, University of Utah.

Nelson, C. A.(1987). The recognition of facial expressions in the first two years of life: Mechanisms of development. *Child Development, 58,* 889–909.

Oster, H. (1981). ''Recognition'' of emotional expression in infancy? In M. Lamb & L. Sherrod (Eds.), *Infant social cognition: Empirical and theoretical considerations.* Hillsdale, NJ: Lawrence Erlbaum Associates.

Oster, H. (1982). Measuring facial movement in infants. In P. Ekman & W. Friesen (Eds.), *Analyzing facial action.* New York: Plenum.

Pastor, D. L. (1981). The quality of mother–infant attachment and its relationship to toddlers' initial sociability with peers. *Developmental Psychology, 17,* 326–335.

Pepler, D. (1981, April). *Naturalistic observations of teaching and modeling between siblings.* Paper presented at the Biennial Meeting of the Society for Research in Child Development, Boston.

Pepler, D., Corter, C., & Abramovitch, R. (1982). Social relations among children: Comparison of sibling and peer interaction. In K. H. Rubin & H. S. Ross (Eds.), *Peer relationships and social skills in childhood.* New York: Springer-Verlag.

Petit, G. S., & Bates, J. E. (1984). Continuity of individual differences in the mother–infant relationship from 6 to 13 months. *Child Development, 55,* 729–739.

Piaget, J. (1936/1952). *The origins of intelligence in children.* New York: International Universities Press.

Plomin, R. (1983). Developmental behavioral genetics. *Child Development, 54,* 253–254.

Plomin, R., & DeFries, J. C. (1985). *The origins of individual differences in infancy: The Colorado Adoption Project.* New York: Academic.

Plomin, R., & Rowe, D. (1979). Genetic and environmental etiology of social behavior in infancy. *Developmental Psychology, 15,* 62–72.

Plutchik, R. (1980). *Emotion: A psychoevolutionary synthesis.* New York: Harper & Row.

Radke-Yarrow, M., Zahn-Waxler, C., & Chapman, M. (1983). Children's prosocial dispositions and behavior. In E. M. Hetherington (Ed.), *Socialization, personality, and social structure* (Vol. 4). In P. H. Mussen (Gen. Ed.), *Handbook of child psychology.* New York: Wiley.

Rajecki, D. W., Lamb, M. E., & Obmascher, P. (1978). Toward a general theory of infantile attachment: A comparative review of aspects of the social bond. *Behavioral and Brain Sciences, 1*, 417–463.

Rheingold, H. (1961). The effect of environmental stimulation upon social and exploratory behavior in the human infant. In B. Foss (Ed.), *Determinants of infant behavior* (Vol. 1). London: Methuen.

Rheingold, H., & Eckerman, C. (1973). Fear of the stranger: A critical examination. In H. Reese (Ed.), *Advances in child development and behavior* (Vol. 8). New York: Academic Press.

Rheingold, H., Gewirtz, J., & Ross, H. (1959). Social conditioning of vocalizations in the infant. *Journal of Comparative and Physiological Psychology, 52*, 68–73.

Robertson, J., & Bowlby, J. (1952). Responses of young children to separation from their mothers. *Courier, 2*, 131–142.

Roopnarine, J. L. (1985). Changes in peer-directed behaviors following preschool experience. *Journal of Personality and Social Psychology, 48*, 740–745.

Rothbart, M. K. (1981). Measurement of temperament in infancy. *Child Development, 52*, 569–578.

Rothbart, M. K., & Derryberry, D. (1981). Development of individual differences in temperament. In M. E. Lamb & A. L. Brown (Eds.), *Advances in developmental psychology* (Vol. 1). Hillsdale, NJ: Lawrence Erlbaum Associates.

Sagi, A., Lamb, M. E., Lewkowicz, K., Shoham, R., Dvir, R., & Estes, D. (1985). Security of infant–mother, –father, and –metapelet attachments among kibbutz-reared Israeli children. In I. Bretherton & E. Waters (Eds.), Growing points of attachment theory and research. *Monographs of the Society for Research in Child Development, 50* (Serial No. 209).

Sameroff, A. J. (1975). Early influences on development: Fact or fancy? *Merrill-Palmer Quarterly, 21*, 267–294.

Sameroff, A., & Chandler, M. J. (1975). Reproductive risk and the continuum of caretaking casualty. In F. D. Horowitz (Ed.), *Review of child development research* (Vol. 4). Chicago, IL: University of Chicago Press.

Scaife, M., & Bruner, J. (1975). The capacity for joint visual attention in the infant. *Nature, 253*, 265–266.

Scarr, S., & Kidd, K. K. (1983). Developmental behavior genetics. In M. M. Haith & J. J. Campos (Eds.), *Infancy and developmental psychobiology* (Vol. 2). In P. H. Mussen (Gen. Ed.), *Handbook of child psychology.* New York: Wiley.

Scarr, S., & McCartney, K. (1983). How people make their own environments: A theory of genotype–environment effects. *Child Development, 54*, 424–435.

Scarr, S., & Salapatek, P. (1970). Patterns of fear development during infancy. *Merrill-Palmer Quarterly, 16*, 53–90.

Scherer, K. (1982). The assessment of vocal expression in infants and children. In C. E. Izard (Ed.), *Measuring emotion in infants and children.* New York: Cambridge University Press.

Schwartz, A. N., & Rosenberg, D. (1968). *An analysis of the components of social reinforcement of infant vocalization.* Masters Thesis, University of Denver.

Schwartz, G. M., Izard, C. E., & Ansul, S. E. (1985). The 5-month-old's ability to discriminate facial expressions of emotion. *Infant Behavior and Development, 8*, 65–77.

Sherrod, K. B., Altemeier, W. A., O'Connor, L., & Vietze, P. M. (1984). Early prediction of child maltreatment. *Early Child Development and Care, 13*, 335–350.

Sorce, J. F., & Emde, R. N. (1982). The meaning of infant emotional expressions: Regularities in caregiving responses in normal and Down's Syndrome infants. *Journal of Child Psychology and Psychiatry, 23*, 145–158.

Sorce, J. F., Emde, R. N., Campos, J. J., & Klinnert, M. D. (1985). Maternal emotional signaling: Its effect on the visual cliff behavior of 1-year-olds. *Developmental Psychology, 21*, 195–200.

Spitz, R. A. (1950). Possible infantile precursors of psychopathology. *American Journal of Orthopsychiatry, 20*, 240–248.

Spitz, R. A. (1965). *The first year of life.* New York: International Universities Press.

Spitz, R. A., & Wolf, K. M. (1946). Anaclitic depression. *Psychoanalytic Study of the Child, 2,* 313–342.

Sroufe, L. A. (1977). Wariness of strangers and the study of infant development. *Child Development, 48,* 731–746.

Sroufe, L. A. (1979). The coherence of individual development. *American Psychologist, 34,* 834–841.

Sroufe, L. A. (1983). Individual patterns of adaptation from infancy to preschool. In M. Perlmutter (Ed.), *Minnesota symposium in child psychology* (Vol. 16). Hillsdale, NJ: Lawrence Erlbaum Associates.

Sroufe, L. A., Schork, E., Motti, F., Lawroski, N., & LaFreniere, P. (1984). The role of affect in social competence. In C. E. Izard, J. Kagan, & R. Zajonc (Eds.), *Affect, cognition, and behavior.* New York: Plenum.

Sroufe, L. A., Waters, E., & Matas, L. (1974). Contextual determinants of infant affective response. In M. Lewis & L. Rosenblum (Eds.), *The origins of fear.* New York: Wiley.

Sroufe, L. A., & Wunsch, J. (1972). The development of laughter in the first year of life. *Child Development, 43,* 1326–1344.

Stayton, D. J., Ainsworth, M. D. S., & Main, M. B. (1973). The development of separation behavior in the first year of life: Protest, following and greeting. *Developmental Psychology, 9,* 213–225.

Stenberg, C., Campos, J., & Emde, R. (1983). The facial expression of anger in seven-month-old infants. *Child Development, 54,* 178–184.

Stern, D. (1974). Mother and infant at play: The dyadic interaction involving facial, vocal, and gaze behaviors. In M. Lewis & L. A. Rosenblum (Eds.), *The effect of the infant on its caregiver.* New York: Wiley.

Stevenson, M. B. (1983, May). *A longitudinal study of sociability and cognitive performance.* Paper presented to the International Workshop on the "At Risk" Infant, Jerusalem.

Stevenson, M. B., & Lamb, M. E. (1979). The effects of sociability and the caretaking environment on infant cognitive performance. *Child Development, 50,* 340–349.

Stewart, R. B. (1983). Sibling interaction: The role of the older child as teacher for the younger. *Merrill-Palmer Quarterly, 29,* 47–68.

Suomi, S. J., & Harlow, H. F. (1978). Early experience and social development in rhesus monkeys. In M. E. Lamb (Ed.), *Social and personality development.* New York: Holt, Rinehart, & Winston.

Super, C. M., & Harkness, S. (1982). The development of affect in infancy and early childhood. In D. A. Wagner & H. W. Stevenson (Eds.), *Cultural perspectives on child development.* San Francisco: Freeman.

Svejda, M. (1981). *The development of infant sensitivity to affective measures in the mother's voice.* Unpublished doctoral dissertation, University of Denver.

Svejda, M., & Campos, J. J. (1982, March). *The mother's voice as a regulator of the infant's behavior.* Paper presented to the International Conference on Infant Studies, Austin, Texas.

Teti, D. M., Bond, L. A., & Gibbs, E. D. (1986). Sibling-created experiences: Relationships to birth-spacing and infant cognitive development. *Infant Behavior and Development, 9,* 27–42.

Teti, D. M., Bond, L. A., & Gibbs, E. D. (in press). Sibling effects in the context of family relationships. In P. Zukow (Ed.), *Sibling interactions across cultures.* New York: Springer-Verlag.

Teti, D. M., & Lamb, M. E. (1986, April). *Attachment and caregiving between infants and older siblings.* Paper presented at the International Conference on Infant Studies, Los Angeles.

Thomas, A., & Chess, S. (1977). *Temperament and development.* New York: Brunner-Mazel.

Thomas, A., Chess, S., Birch, H. G., Hertzig, M. E.. & Korn, S. (1963). *Behavioral individuality in early childhood.* New York: New York University Press.

Thompson, R. A., & Lamb, M. E. (1982). Stranger sociability and its relationship to temperament and social experiences during the second year. *Infant Behavior and Development, 5,* 277–288.

Thompson, R. A., & Lamb, M. E. (1983a). Continuity and change in socioemotional development during the second year. In R. Emde & R. Harmon (Eds.), *Continuity and discontinuity in development.* New York: Plenum.

Thompson, R. A., & Lamb, M. E. (1983b). Individual differences in dimensions of socioemotional development in infancy. In R. Plutchik & H. Kellerman (Eds.), *Emotions in early development.* New York: Academic.

Thompson, R. A., & Lamb, M. E. (1983c). Security of attachment and stranger sociability in infancy. *Developmental Psychology, 19,* 184–191.

Thompson, R. A., & Lamb, M. E. (1984). Assessing qualitative dimensions of emotional responsiveness in infants: Separation reactions in the Strange Situation. *Infant Behavior and Development, 7,* 423–445.

Thompson, R. A., & Lamb, M. E. (1986). Infant–mother attachment: New directions for theory and research. In P. Baltes, D. Featherman, & R. M. Lerner (Eds.), *Lifespan development and behavior* (Vol. 7). Hillsdale, NJ: Lawrence Erlbaum Associates.

Thompson, R. A., Lamb, M. E., & Estes, D. (1982). Stability of infant–mother attachment and its relationship to changing life circumstances in an unselected middle-class sample. *Child Development, 53,* 144–148.

Tronick, E., Als, H., Adamson, L., Wise, S., & Brazelton, T. B. (1978). The infant's response to entrapment between contradictory messages in face-to-face interaction. *Journal of the American Academy of Child Psychiatry, 17,* 1–13.

Vandell, D. L. (1979). A microanalysis of toddlers' social interaction with mothers and fathers. *Journal of Genetic Psychology, 134,* 299–312.

Vandell, D. L. (1979). The effect of a playgroup experience on mother–son and father–son interaction. *Developmental Psychology, 15,* 379–385.

Vandell, D. L., & Wilson, K. S. (in press). Infant's interactions with mother, sibling, and peer: Contrasts and relationships between interaction systems. *Child Development, 58.*

Vandell, D. L., Wilson, K. S., & Buchanan, N. R. (1980). Peer interaction in the first year of life: An examination of its structure, content, and sensitivity to toys. *Child Development, 51,* 481–488.

Vaughn, B., Egeland, B., Sroufe, L. A., & Waters, E. (1979). Individual differences in infant–mother attachment at twelve and eighteen months: Stability and change in families under stress. *Child Development, 50,* 971–975.

Vietze, P., Falsey, S., Sandler, H., O'Connor, S., & Altemeier, W. A. (1980). Transactional approach to prediction of child maltreatment. *Infant Mental Health Journal, 1,* 248–261.

Walk, R. (1978). Depth perception and experience. In R. Walk & H. Pick (Eds.), *Perception and experience.* New York: Plenum.

Walker, A. (1982). Intermodal perception of expressive behaviors by human infants. *Journal of Experimental Child Psychology, 33,* 514–535.

Waters, E. (1978). The reliability and stability of individual differences in infant–mother attachment. *Child Development, 49,* 483–494.

Waters, E., Wippman, J., & Sroufe, L. A. (1979). Attachment, positive affect, and competence in the peer group: Two studies in construct validation. *Child Development, 50,* 821–829.

Watson, J. B. (1913). Psychology as the behaviorist views it. *Psychological Review, 20,* 158–177.

Watson, J. B., & Rayner, R. (1920). Conditioned emotional reactions. *Journal of Experimental Psychology, 3,* 1–14.

Watson, J. S. (1985). Contingency perception in early social development. In T. M. Field & N. A. Fox (Eds.), *Social perception in infants.* Norwood, NJ: Ablex.

Weinraub, M., & Putney, E. (1978). The effects of height on infants' social responses to unfamiliar persons. *Child Development, 49,* 598–605.

Weisner, T. (1982). Sibling interdependence and child caretaking: A cross-cultural view. In M. E. Lamb & B. Sutton-Smith (Eds.), *Sibling relationships: Their nature and significance across the lifespan*. Hillsdale, NJ: Lawrence Erlbaum Associates.

Weisner, T., & Gallimore, R. (1977). My brother's keeper: Child and sibling caretaking. *Current Anthropology, 18*, 169–181.

Werner, E. E. (1984). *Kith, kin, and hired hands*. Baltimore: University Park Press.

Wilson, R. S. (1983). The Louisville twin study: Developmental synchronies in behavior. *Child Development, 54*, 298–316.

Wilson, R. S. (1984). Twins and chronogenetics: Correlated pathways of development. *Acta Genetica Gemellologica, 33*, 149–157.

Yarrow, L., & Goodwin, M. (1973). The immediate impact of separation: Reaction of infants to change in mother figures. In L. J. Stone, H. T. Smith, & L. B. Murphy (Eds.), *The competent infant*. New York: Basic Books.

Young-Browne, G., Rosenfeld, H. M., & Horowitz, F. D. (1977). Infant discrimination of facial expressions. *Child Development, 48*, 555–562.

Zahn-Waxler, C., & Radke-Yarrow, M. (1982). The development of altruism: Alternative research strategies. In N. Eisenberg (Ed.), *The development of prosocial behavior*. New York: Academic.

Zajonc, R. B. (1983). Validating the confluence model. *Psychological Bulletin, 93*, 457–480.

Zelazo, P. (1972). Smiling and vocalizing: A cognitive emphasis. *Merrill-Palmer Quarterly, 18*, 349–365.

9 Sex-Role Development

Diane N. Ruble
New York University

INTRODUCTION

The study of sex-role acquisition has been of central concern to developmental psychologists for many years. Sex roles influence choices, values, and behaviors throughout the life span. As Mussen (1969) suggests, "No other social role directs more of an individual's overt behavior, emotional reactions, cognitive functioning, covert attitudes, and general psychological and social adjustment" (p. 707). Furthermore, sex-role demands have been implicated in physical health and life expectancy differences, favoring women, and mental health problems, especially depression, favoring men (Frieze, Parsons, Johnson, Ruble, & Zellman, 1978; Pleck, 1981; Ramey, 1982). Sex-role development also has been a primary focus of debate among the major theories of social-personality development, and is a frequent target of the nature–nurture controversy (Lamb & Urberg, 1978). Finally, sex-role development also has a political flavor because of its implications for gender equality, such as equal pay, political representation, and so on.

Like the study of most aspects of development, the study of sex-role development has seen a number of shifts in methodological approaches and conceptual emphases (Wittig, 1985). Unlike most areas of development, however, there has been a shift in value placed on the final outcome of this developmental process. Early literature contained an implicit assumption that adopting sex-typed standards and behaviors was good—that it was, in fact, necessary for psychological adjustment. Thus, understanding the antecedents of sex-typing was viewed as providing information necessary for optimal socialization of appropriately sex-typed individuals. In contrast, current research appears to be guided by an

411

implicit assumption that sex-role differentiation may be bad—that it places limits on individual growth and flexibility (Bem, 1983; Huston, 1985; Lamb & Urburg, 1978; Pleck, 1981). Thus, understanding the antecedents of sex-typing may be viewed, alternatively, as providing information necessary for raising children with sexually egalitarian beliefs and behaviors.

Along with shifts in approaches and emphases in the literature there has been a proliferation of terms associated with the study of sex-role development. Although most of the terms appear quite similar on the surface, many of the distinctions have become important conceptually. Thus, it is neccessary to provide a brief guide to terminology. (Huston, 1983, 1985, and Rosen & Rekers, 1980, provide a more detailed discussion of sex-role taxonomies and definitions.)

A very basic distinction is between the terms "sex" and "gender." These terms are commonly used as synonyms and many dictionaries define them as such. Because the term "sex" has multiple meanings, there has been a trend toward using "gender" to refer to the various dimensions of maleness and femaleness (Rosen & Rekers, 1980). Because both terms have become associated with certain concepts and certain sets of literature, however, we will use them interchangeably. Their intended meanings, then, will be linked to the terms they precede—terms like *stereotype, identity, role,* and so on. The most common of such distinctions is between gender "role" and gender "identity" or "orientation" (e.g., Kagan, 1964; Money & Ehrhardt, 1972). Although there is debate about the exact nature of the distinction (Rosen & Rekers, 1980), "role" typically refers to cultural expectation of behaviors, characteristics, and social status of males versus females. It is the "public face" of gender. In contrast, "identity" or "orientation" typically refers to the individual's perception of his or her own consistency with these cultural expectations. Thus, it has a more "private" connotation. Other terms and distinctions are defined as they become relevant to the discussions.

We begin our consideration of sex-role development with a discussion of the different ways males and females have been perceived, beginning in ancient times. These beliefs about the dimensions of masculinity and femininity indicate the social standards or conventions that individuals must conform to if they desire to be perceived as appropriately sex-typed. Thus, in addition to general cultural beliefs we will examine individual self-perceptions—how well they conform to sex-role norms, and the implications of perceiving oneself as relatively masculine and/or feminine.

In the next section, we examine whether men and women are, in reality, as different in *personality* as they are believed to be. There are a number of methodological and interpretational problems in the literature on sex differences in personality and, as a result, there is controversy about how prevalent and extensive such differences are. There is little debate, however, about differences in male and female *roles*—differences that have implications for status and value.

Thus, both of the first two sections are concerned with ''end-points'' of sex-role development—what people believe about sex differences and how the two sexes behave after experiencing various developmental influences.

The remainder of the chapter examines what these influences are and how powerful they appear to be. Three types of developmental influences are considered: (a) biological factors (b) external socialization pressures; and (c) cognitive developmental structures and self-generated motivation. First, we consider how one might distinguish biological bases of sex-typing from cultural influences. We then discuss various possible biological mechanisms, using two types of sex-typed behavior as exemplars. The first example concerns how hormones may influence sex differences in social behaviors, with reference to both animal and human studies. The second example concerns how genetics, brain organization, and hormonal changes at puberty may influence sex differences in intellectual functioning.

Next, we begin the question of sociocultural bases of sex-typing with a discussion of the distinction between the two major theories of sex-role development. Evidence relevant to *social-learning theory* is considered. We ask whether or not boys and girls are treated differently by socializing agents. Are children encouraged by the culture to engage in sex-appropriate activities? Is aggression or physical activity reinforced in boys, and dependence reinforced in girls? We also ask whether boys and girls may become sex-typed by means of observational learning, and we consider what children might learn from models when, for example, they watch television.

Finally, evidence relevant to *cognitive-developmental theories* of sex-typing is discussed. Two general questions are considered. The first concerns when knowledge about sex roles develops. When does basic gender labeling of oneself and others, as well as the recognition of sex stereotypes, occur? The second question concerns which ways this knowledge structures children's sex-role choices and behavior. Do changes in children's concepts about gender affect what information they attend to, imitate, and remember? Such evidence is pertinent to possible variations across the life span in flexibility versus rigidity, in adherence to sex roles, and in the possibility of change.

DIMENSIONS OF BEING MALE OR FEMALE

Historical Perspective

What is the ''true'' nature of the sexes? Interest in this question dates back to ancient times. According to Aristotle (Book IX of *The History of Animals,* Chapter 1; cited in Miles, 1935, p.700), for example, women are ''. . . more compassionate . . . more envious, more querulous, more slanderous, and more contentious . . .''; while men are ''. . . more disposed to give assistance in danger'' and ''. . . more courageous . . .'' Recent reviews of such historical beliefs and myths have identified several central themes or images (Bullough, 1973; Gould, 1976; Hunter, 1976; Hyde & Rosenberg, 1976; Tavris & Wade, 1984; Whitbeck, 1976; Williams, 1983); but, interestingly, they have tended to focus on the nature of women rather than of men. This one-sided view may have evolved because most records were kept by men (Bullough, 1973), and a male perspective is likely to be on how the other group (women) is different.

Although there are many different labels and connotations attached to images of women, depending on the writer and the period of history being examined, the themes can be categorized into two extreme views. These range from the positive pole, in which women are regarded as love goddesses and wholesome mother figures, to the extreme negative view of women as inferior and evil (Bullough, 1973; D.N. Ruble & T. Ruble, 1982).

The negative pole is represented by several images, with beliefs in womens' inferiority at the core. Woman is viewed as a partial man, deficient in both sexual capacity and quality of mind (Whitbeck, 1976). With Eve as her representative, she is both an afterthought (an inferior being) and an evil seductress (Hunter, 1976; Tavris & Wade, 1984). The story of Samson and Delilah represents the common theme that being seduced by a woman drains a man of his strength (Williams, 1983). The contrasting view of woman portrays her as worthy of worship. She has been viewed as the fertility goddess, the mother of all, and as virtue incarnate (Bullough, 1973; Gould, 1976; Hyde & Rosenberg, 1976; Williams, 1983). The tradition of chivalry, placing women "on a pedestal," epitomizes this image (Hunter, 1976; Yorburg, 1974). There is ambivalence, however, about the side of woman's nature that is worshipped. Placing woman on a pedestal confined her to an essentially passive and powerless and thus subordinate role (Bullough, 1973; Hunter, 1976; Williams, 1977).

Of course, beliefs about the sexes have varied considerably throughout time just as they continue to vary cross-culturally (see Tavris & Wade, 1984). Nevertheless, throughout history women and men have been perceived as different in fundamental and important ways; these differences have often been viewed as "natural," intrinsically linked to the roles of the sexes in society (Shields, 1975).

Empirical research on sex differences and sex roles has been conducted for decades (see Miles, 1935), and interest in these topics has continued to grow. In the late 1960s, after the rise of the women's liberation movement, much of this research raised questions about the inferior nature of women and about why women's roles and achievements are typically of lower status. More recently, questions about men, masculinity, and restrictions associated with male roles have also appeared in the literature (Doyle, 1983; Lamb, 1976; Pleck, 1981; Pleck & Brannon, 1978). In spite of this new level of awareness, however, strong beliefs about differences between males and females remain. Before discussing these differences and how they develop, we examine what these common *beliefs* are.

Dimensions of Masculinity and Femininity

Two types of questions have characterized the research on masculinity and femininity. The first concerns beliefs about people in general—social norms concerning what the typical male and female are like and how they differ. The second concerns self-perceptions and individual differences. How masculine or feminine is a particular man or woman? In some respects, these two types of questions are very different. The first deals with *stereotypes*—beliefs about the personal attributes of men and women and the likelihood that an unknown male or female will possess a given trait. The second deals with sex-role *orientation*—the extent to which men and women perceive themselves in reality to possess the characteristics associated with maleness or femaleness. These two issues are clearly related, however. Individuals may perceive themselves as possessing a certain set of attributes because of cultural sex stereotypes; and, reciprocally, cultural stereotypes may reflect the conglomerate reality of individual sex-role orientations. Moreover, when dealing with both stereotypes and personal orientations, there is a common set of problems in conceptualizing and measuring masculinity and femininity.

Sex Stereotypes. Numerous modern studies have identified characteristics that may be considered stereotypes of men and women (e.g., Bem, 1974; Broverman, Vogel, Broverman, Clarkson, & Rosenkrantz, 1972; Heilbrun, 1976; Rosenkrantz, Vogel, Bee, Broverman, & Broverman, 1968; Spence, Helmreich, & Stapp, 1974, 1975). Despite the considerable conceptual and methodological inconsistencies that characterize this literature, there is some degree of consensus concerning the types of characteristics associated with one sex versus the other (D.N. Ruble & T. Ruble, 1982). These stereotypes have remained relatively stable from the 1960s to the 1980s, at least among college students, despite the increased concern with equality between the sexes (T. L. Ruble, 1983).

Instead of trying to compile an extensive list of the characteristics that have been identified as stereotypic, we describe briefly a few studies to illustrate both typical methods and conclusions. In one study, the investigators developed a questionnaire to assess stereotypes by starting with a list of 122 bipolar items (e.g., Not at all Aggressive–Very Aggressive), and asked 74 college men and 80 college women to rate the extent to which each item was characteristic of an adult male and an adult female (Rosenkrantz et al., 1968). An item was considered "stereotypic" if at least 75% of the students rated one pole as more typical of one sex than the other. Thus, the definition of stereotypic was based on an arbitrary criterion.

The results of several studies based on the 1968 questionnaire were summarized a few years later (Broverman et al., 1972). It was concluded that there is a strong consensus about the differing characteristics of men and women across widely divergent groups within the culture. The positively valued masculine traits formed a cluster of behaviors reflecting competence, rationality, and assertion; the positively valued feminine traits formed a cluster reflecting warmth and expressiveness, consistent with historical images of maternal love and virtue.

Spence, Helmreich, and Stapp (1974,1975) refined the 1968 questionnaire to produce a new instrument, called the Personal Attributes Questionnaire (PAQ). Similar to the procedure used by Rosenkrantz et al. (1968), 248 college men and 282 college women rated the *typical* adult male and female on 138 bipolar items (the original 122 items plus 16 extra ones). Another group rated the *ideal* male and female. Items this time were identified as "stereotypic" on the basis of statistically significant differences in the ratings. The ratings of the ideal male and female were used to determine whether the "masculine" pole (e.g., Aggressive) was valued more or less than the "feminine" pole (e.g., Not at all Aggressive). Based on this analysis, three types of characteristics were identified, as shown in Table 9.1. Male-valued items are those for which ratings for *both* ideal males and ideal females were higher on the masculine side of the scale. Female-valued items are those for which ratings for *both* ideal males and ideal females were higher on the feminine side of the scale. Finally, sex-specific items are those for which ratings for the ideal male were higher on the masculine side and ratings for the ideal female were higher on the feminine side. Inspection of Table 9.1 indicates that positively valued male and female traits identified in this study are consistent with the conclusions of Broverman et al. (1972), in spite of different criteria used to identify these traits.

Sex-Role Orientation.   The study of self-perceptions along sex-typed dimensions has been a central and longstanding issue in sex-role development research. In early research masculinity and femininity were viewed as representing a bipolar continuum on a single scale, and it was assumed that a person could be either masculine or feminine, but not both. Implicit in the approach was a positive value placed on a high degree of sex typing; and, thus, a major question was how to promote healthy males and females by helping them acquire appropriately sex-typed attitudes, interests, and traits (e.g., Biller, 1971; Brown, 1957; Kagan, 1964).

More recently, the bipolar assumption has been criticized on the grounds that individuals can possess characteristics that are *both* masculine and feminine (Bem, 1974; Constantinople, 1973; Heilbrun, 1976; Spence & Helmreich, 1978). Bem has applied the term *androgynous* to people who possess both masculine and feminine characteristics. Spence and Helmreich prefer the term *dualistic* to refer to the idea that masculinity and femininity are independent dimensions of personality that may develop in the same individual. Thus, in contrast to early work on sex-role development, these new formulations assume that an individual may possess both qualities associated with masculinity (e.g., assertive) and qualities associated with femininity (e.g. sensitive to the needs of others), and still function effectively. Several self-report instruments have been

TABLE 9.1
Personal Attributes Questionnaire Items Classified as to
Male Valued, Female Valued, and Sex Specific

Male-Valued

Independent	Adventurous	Self-confident
Not easily influenced	Outspoken	Feels superior
Good at sports	Interested in sex	Takes a stand
Not excitable, minor crisis	Makes decisions easily	Ambitious
Active	Does not give up easily	Stands up under pressure
Competitive	Outgoing	Forward
Skilled in business	Acts as leader	Not timid
Knows ways of world	Intellectual	

Female-Valued

Emotional	Strong conscience	Creative
Does not hide emotions	Gentle	Understanding
Considerate	Helpful to others	Warm to others
Grateful	Kind	Likes children
Devotes self to others	Aware of others' feelings	Enjoys art and music
Tactful	Neat	Expresses tender feelings

Sex-Specific

Male	Female
Aggressive	Cries easily
Dominant	Excitable, major crisis
Likes math and science	Feelings easily hurt
Loud	Home-oriented
Mechanical aptitude	Needs approval
Sees self running show	Needs security
	Religious

Source: Spence, Helmreich, and Stapp (1975), Table 1, p. 31.

developed to study the effects of individual differences in sex-role orientations. Individuals indicate the extent to which they personally exhibit each of a series of characteristics. (See, for example, the traits used in the Spence and Helmreich, 1978, Personal Attributes Questionnaire [PAQ] presented in Table 9.1.) Individuals can then be grouped according to their self-ratings into different categories. Bem (1977) and Spence, Helmreich, and Stapp (1975), for example, used four categories: feminine (high feminine–low masculine); masculine (low feminine–high masculine); androgynous (both high); and undifferentiated (both low).

The underlying question of the research based on these new formulations of sex-role identity is whether androgynous individuals are more behaviorally adaptive and psychologically healthy than individuals who are rigidly sex-typed. Although there have been some inconsistencies across studies, the answer to this question has often been affirmative. Several researchers have reported, for example, that androgynous individuals score higher on measures of self-esteem and other measures of psychological or social well-being than sex-typed or undifferentiated subjects (Bem, 1975, 1977; Ickes & Barnes, 1978; Orlofsky & Windle, 1978; Spence, Helmreich, & Stapp, 1975; Whitley, 1983,1985).

There is, however, a noteworthy limitation to the conclusion that androgyny represents the preferred orientation. Several studies have reported weak or no differences between androgynous- and masculine-typed individuals. Most studies of self-esteem, for example, have found that both androgynous and masculine groups were higher than feminine-typed and/or undifferentiated groups (e.g., Bem, 1977; Heilbrun, 1976). Furthermore, some research has suggested that flexibility and adjustment are *more* strongly associated with masculinity than with androgyny (Jones, Chernovetz, & Hansson, 1978). These findings have led some to question the meaning of positive correlations between an androgynous orientation and socially valued behaviors. Kelly and Worell (1977), for example, suggest that it may be primarily the masculine aspects of an androgynous orientation (e.g., instrumentality) that lead to social reinforcements in our society, a conclusion supported by a recent review (Taylor & Hall, 1982).

Additional Dimensions of Masculinity and Femininity

The view of masculinity and femininity as separate and relatively independent dimensions represents an important conceptual distinction. But this dualistic model may itself constitute a limited reflection of reality, because neither masculinity nor femininity is likely to be unidimensional. Thus, in measuring either stereotypes or self-perceptions, a single summary score of masculinity or femininity that ignores variations in the subtraits may be inappropriate (Brannon, 1978; Constantinople, 1973). Assume, for example, that the stereotype of "masculinity" is composed of two relatively independent factors: achievement and assertiveness. Further, assume that we have two instruments that attempt to measure "masculinity." One instrument has 10 items related to achievement and 5 items related to assertiveness. The other instrument has 5 achievement items and 10 assertiveness items. If overall scores are obtained by simply summing items, then we essentially have an achievement-dominated instrument versus an assertiveness-dominated instrument. It is obviously misleading to assume that equal scores on the two instruments represent equivalent measures of "masculinity." Recent research, therefore, has incorporated a multidimensional view of the traits associated with men and women and attempted to identify "core concepts" of masculinity and femininity (e.g., Ashmore & Del Boca, 1979; Cicone & Ruble, 1978; Deaux & Lewis 1984; Deaux, Winton, Crowley, & Lewis, 1985; Pleck, 1981).

Summary

Beliefs about differences between men and women have existed throughout history and remain strong today. Empirical research on these beliefs takes two forms. The first concerns sex *stereotypes*—what people think the typical man and woman are like. The second concerns sex-role *orientation*—what people think they themselves are like. A major conceptual and methodological issue in measuring these beliefs is whether sex-typed traits represent a bipolar continuum on a single scale, or whether individuals can possess characteristics that are both masculine and feminine. Recent research has adopted the latter assumption, and people are viewed as having the capacity to be androgynous or dualistic. It is further assumed that an androgynous orientation is healthier than a sex-typed orientation, but empirical research has provided mixed support for this hypothesis. Current research is moving beyond dualistic conceptions of masculinity and femininity to consider the multiple dimensions that comprise these constructs.

SEX DIFFERENCES: DO BELIEFS REFLECT REALITY?

Summarizing the Results

Are commonly held beliefs about the characteristics of males and females supported by data about how people actually behave? Is it true that the average man is relatively aggressive, independent, and good at mathematical tasks—whereas the average woman is relatively passive, dependent, and good at verbal tasks? There are no simple answers to these questions. Such characteristics are difficult to define and to observe, and there are many inconsistencies in the conclusions drawn by different studies.

The most comprehensive review of the sex differences literature appears in a book published in 1974 by Eleanor Maccoby and Carol Jacklin. They compiled over 2,000 studies, published mainly after 1966, that examined sex differences in personality and in intellectual abilities. They then tabulated the number of studies reporting statistically significant sex differences and compared them to the number of studies in that domain that did not find statistically significant differences. On the basis of these "box score" tabulations, Maccoby and Jacklin (1974) suggested that empirical data supported the existence of sex differences in only four areas: aggressive behavior, and mathematical, spatial, and verbal skills. According to their data: (a) boys are more physically aggressive at all ages (through college age) and across cultures; (b) beginning around puberty, boys' mathematical skills increase faster than girls'; (c) males tend to perform better on tasks involving spatial skills than do girls; and (d) from middle elementary school through high school, girls tend to perform better than boys on tasks involving verbal skills. In other domains in which sex differences might be expected, Maccoby and Jacklin felt either that the question was still open (e.g., activity level, compliance, nurturance) or that the evidence did *not* support sex differences (sociability, analytic skills).

The Maccoby and Jacklin conclusions have generated a fair amount of controversy (e.g., Block, 1976a, 1976b, 1983). The controversy centers primarily around the "box score" approach that Maccoby and Jacklin used and the possibility that this approach may have led to erroneous conclusions. Two main problems have been noted. First, some studies are stronger methodologically than others. Giving each study equal weight, therefore, may be misleading. particularly if methodological weakness leads to a particular type of finding, such as no sex difference. Indeed, failure to find a "true" difference is more likely for studies which lack statistical power because of small sample sizes. Thus, there may be validity to the suggestion that Maccoby and Jacklin underrepresented the number of true sex differences. On the other hand, studies finding sex differences are more likely to be catalogued in terms of sex differences, and thus more accessible for review, than are studies that do not. Thus, there are biases in both directions affecting the Maccoby and Jacklin conclusions.

A second problem with the box score approach is deciding how to categorize the studies. For example, social sensitivity may be defined in several ways including role taking, nurturance, or empathy. If males and females differ consistently in only one of these behaviors, such as empathy, then an analysis of a category which includes all of the above indices of social sensitivity may be misleading. That is, the category may be too broad, and a large number of "no-difference" results for role-taking would obscure actual sex differences in empathy (M. L. Hoffman, 1977).

A few recent reviews of sex differences have been able to avoid some of the problems associated with a box score approach by using a technique called meta analysis. Briefly, meta analysis is a way to aggregate the results of multiple independent studies relevant to a single hypothesis. Statistical procedures can be applied to the combined data sets in order to assess, for example, overall effect sizes (Cohen, 1977). These analyses have revealed reliable sex differences in activity level (Eaton & Enns, 1986), aggression (Hyde 1984), influenceability (Eagly & Carli, 1981), empathy (Eisenberg & Lennon, 1983), mathematical reasoning (Rossi, 1983), proportional reasoning (Meehan, 1984), and spatial ability (Horan & Rosser, 1984; Hyde, 1981; Linn & Petersen, 1985). In general, such reviews have concluded that differences between the sexes are small, accounting for less than 5% of the variance; or that they are restricted to studies using particular methods, even for presumably well-established differences such as verbal, spatial, and quantitative skills (Eagly & Carli, 1981; Eisenberg & Lennon, 1983; Hyde, 1981; Linn & Peterson, 1985). Even small differences, however, often have important practical implications for such things as job selection (Burnett, 1986; Eaton & Enns, 1986). Interestingly, meta analyses of cognitive sex differences have further suggested that the extent of sex differences has changed over time; more recent articles show females performing better relative to males than earlier articles (Becker & Hedges, 1984; Rosenthal & Rubin, 1982).

Interpreting the Results

An additional problem involved in answering the question, "Do beliefs reflect reality?" concerns the interpretation of results of sex differences studies. What, for example, does it mean to report findings that women conformed more than men? Does it reflect a long-term characteristic of men and women, built-in and stable, or does it reflect a short-term behavioral response to the experimental situation? What the lay public and most researchers want to know, presumably, concerns the former interpretation. Yet there are many features of a study that may elicit differential reactions of males and females, reactions which are irrelevant to the focus of the study but which nevertheless contaminate the findings. Sex of experimenter, familiarity with the situation, or interest in the topic of the experiment are all aspects of the methods of a study that may interact with the sex of the subject to influence the results (Eagly & Carli, 1981; Karabenick, 1983; Pedersen, Shinedling, & Johnson, 1968; Sistrunk & McDavid, 1971; Spence, Deaux, & Helmreich, 1985). Thus, in some cases, apparent sex differences in personality or abilities may represent little more than artifacts of the situation.

Situational determinants of sex differences are particularly problematic for interpreting a research finding because they may be quite subtle. Subjects can present themselves as behaving more or less consistently with prevailing sex stereotypes on the basis of seemingly incidental aspects of the situation, such as the relative number of males and females in the room (D.N. Ruble & Higgins, 1976), the attractiveness of the subject's partner in the study (Zanna & Pack, 1975), or the topic described as the focus of the study (Signorella & Vegega, 1984). To the extent that studies sample situations eliciting stereotypic rather than nonstereotypic responding, the research literature may have overrepresented the extent to which stable sex differences exist. If, for example, a woman is dependent in some situations and independent in others, the research literature is biased if studies are more likely to examine situations eliciting the woman's dependent behavior.

Although it is difficult to examine directly how prevalent this bias might be, there are several reasons to believe it is a problem. First, hypotheses tend to be formulated in terms of prior beliefs, such as stereotypes. Thus, in designing the study, the experimenter may be predisposed to select a situation or set of measures likely to elicit stereotyped responding, not because of overt bias but rather because the hypothesis makes such situations more accessible in memory. In this context, it is interesting to note that studies of conformity conducted by women are less likely to find sex differences than those conducted by men (Eagly & Carli, 1981). Second, in strange situations, such as experiments, people may tend to present themselves relatively conservatively and to behave more consistently with cultural beliefs than they do in familiar situations. Certainly knowledge of a cultural belief system may influence subjects' self-reports of their own characteristics, particularly if they believe this is what the experimenter is looking for. It is not surprising, therefore, that sex differences are more likely to be found when self-report measures are used as opposed to actual behavior (e.g., Eisenberg & Lennon, 1983). Moreover, many types of sex differences are positively related to developmental level (Eaton & Enns, 1986; Frieze et al., 1978). Since knowledge of gender-related cultural beliefs increases with age, such developmental trends also support the present assertion that sex differences reflect, in part, situational demands or expectations. Thus, not only is there a lack of empirical support for most differences believed to exist between the sexes, but also those differences that *are* found may represent something other than dispositional qualities of males and females.

Implications for the Study of Sex-Role Development

If sex differences are not as prevalent or strong as commonly believed, what, then, is the study of sex-role development concerned with? Why has there been so much theoretical and empirical attention devoted to the development of sex-typing and gender-related socialization processes? One answer is that although basic temperamental characteristics may be relatively similar for the two sexes, their roles in society are not. As adults, men and women have very different functions and responsibilities in the home and in the work place (Eccles & Hoffman, 1985; Frieze et al., 1978; T. L. Ruble, Cohen, & D. N. Ruble, 1984; Spence, Deaux, & Helmreich, 1985). Although over half of all women are now in the labor force, they continue in disproportionate numbers to work in the lowest paying industries. Women account for almost all nurses and secretaries while men represent almost all engineers, carpenters, and mechanics. Overall, women earn only 59% of what men earn; and major wage differentials exist even when comparisons are made within occupational types, such as farm laborers or food service workers (Norwood, 1982; Rytina, 1982). Thus, not only do men and women have different roles but they also appear to have different intrinsic worth, at least as measured by financial compensation.

Precursors of such role differences begin quite early: Young boys and girls exhibit distinctive tastes in toys, books, sports, and other kinds of recreational activities. By adolescence, distinctive roles are evident in dating behavior and occupational choices. Moreover, at all age levels, males and females differ in more subtle aspects of roles, such as dress and mannerisms. Sex-role differentiation, then, is pervasive; and the study of developmental processes can help us understand why. Such knowledge is important for reasons other than to satisfy basic scientific curiosity. On the one hand, gender differentiation may be viewed as a normal, natural outcome of development; and, indeed, much early research was oriented toward the value of helping promote normal masculine and feminine identification and roles (e.g., Kagan, 1964). A related concern is understanding the processes leading to atypical sex-role development, such as transsexualism, and making decisions about if and when to try clinical intervention in such cases (Green, 1975; Zucker, 1982). On the other hand, sex-role differentiation may be viewed as an undesirable outcome because it limits the options available to individual men and women. Social penalties are imposed on males who want to stay home and care for their children and on females who do not. Discriminatory processes operate on women who seek positions of power and prestige, and on men who seek to pursue traditionally female occupations, such as nursing. Thus, understanding developmental processes is also relevant to promoting gender equality and to reducing the limiting aspects of sex roles.

Summary

In spite of the large number of studies examining sex differences, the results remain inconclusive. Maccoby and Jacklin's (1974) extensive review suggested that on the basis of sheer numbers of positive results alone, reasonably strong support exists for only four differences: aggression, spatial skills, mathematical skills, and verbal abilities. These conclusions may be challenged, however, in two very different ways. First, they may *underrepresent* the number of sex differences because of inadequacies in the box score approach. Indeed, the results of meta-analyses conducted after Maccoby and Jacklin (1974) completed their review suggest that there are a number of other small but reliable differences between the sexes. Second, the Maccoby and Jacklin conclusions, as well as the meta-analytic studies, may *overrepresent* the differences because subjects and/or observers are affected by sex-stereotypic beliefs. Nevertheless, in spite of problems of interpretation, it is clear that the available evidence does *not* justify existing stereotypes. The research has failed to show that the characteristics of males and females are as different as we believe them to be. Yet men and women do play very different social roles; and such differences begin early, as reflected in boys' and girls' different interests and activities. The study of sex-role development is concerned with the antecedents of these sex-differentiated roles and values.

SEX-ROLE DEVELOPMENT: BIOLOGICAL FACTORS

For some people, the reasons for a sex-typed division of labor are no mystery. Asking them why men do not stay home to raise children is like asking them why humans do not flap their arms and fly. They believe that men and women are ordained, by their biological predispositions and limitations, to fulfill certain roles; that women care for children because they have a maternal instinct and men do not; that men are the providers and the protectors because they have greater strength and because women must be left free to care for children. Although this extreme form of Freud's "Anatomy is Destiny" argument is no longer accepted as legitimate by most researchers, questions about the influence of biological factors on sex-role development remain. One question concerns which aspects of sex-role development are influenced by biological factors. A second question concerns the mechanisms by which biology exerts its influence.

The Search for Biological Influences

The fact that biology is involved in sexual dimorphism is indisputable. The presence of a Y chromosome leads the undifferentiated gonads in the embryo to become testes. The absence of the Y chromosome turns the gonads into ovaries. Genetic factors are also involved in the greater vulnerability of males to problems during pregnancy and birth (Maccoby, 1980). Hormones have a direct effect on prenatal anatomical and brain differentiation (McEwen, 1981; Money & Ehrhardt, 1972); and during puberty hormones lead to further physical differentiation of the sexes, such as breast development and beard growth. But do these obvious biological differences carry over to psychological development and role differentiation? This is not an easy question to answer. How is it possible to determine whether or not biological factors are involved in these processes? Which kinds of data provide the best clues?

Sex Differences in Infants.   One possible approach is to study sex differences in infants. The basic logic of this approach is that socialization will have relatively little effect on behavior during the first weeks and months after birth, and thus observed differences must reflect biological influences. One problem with this approach is that it is difficult to identify those behaviors of babies that might be precursors of later sex-role differences: Which infant behaviors reflect dominance or nurturance? A second problem is that socialization may begin at birth, at the moment babies are wrapped in either pink or blue blankets. Thus, any differences that are found are difficult to attribute exclusively to biological influences.

Few consistent differences between infant girls and boys have been found, however. Males appear to be somewhat physically stronger (Maccoby, 1980) and more active (Eaton & Enns, 1986). Some early studies suggested other differences, such as greater attachment to parents by girls than by boys, but subsequent research has yielded inconsistent results (Frieze et al. 1978; Maccoby & Jacklin, 1974). Thus, studies of infant sex differences provide little insight into possible biological bases of sex roles.

Cross-Cultural Universals.   A second possible approach is cross-cultural analysis. According to the logic of this approach, sex differences that are relatively consistent across cultures are thought to imply some biological basis. There are, in fact, several behaviors that show a relatively high degree of cross-cultural consistency. In virtually all cultures, women are the primary caretakers and men are the protectors during war. Furthermore, there is evidence of some consistency in related characteristics—interest in infants, dominance, and aggression (Frieze et al., 1978; Maccoby, 1980; Rohner, 1976).

Although such findings are suggestive of biological influences, their implications must be considered with caution. Cross-cultural universals may be explained by similarities in sex-role socialization across cultures (Barry, Bacon, & Child, 1957). Also, there are ample indications of cultural diversity even within the relatively consistent behaviors. Perhaps the best known example is Margaret Mead's study of three primitive tribes in New Guinea (Mead, 1935). Among the Arapesh, both men and women acted as women are generally expected to act— gentle and nurturant. Among the Mundugamor, both men and women acted as men are generally expected to act—aggressive, with little indication of parental orientation. Among the Tchambuli, stereotypic roles were reversed. There is also cultural diversity in the magnitude of sex differences, even when the direction of the difference is consistent across cultures. Sex-typed division of labor, for example, is affected by variations in economic and familial structure across cultures (Rosaldo, 1974). Finally, cultural variation in some sex-related behaviors may be so extreme that the magnitude of sex differences pales by comparison. In one study, levels of aggression in several cultures were rated on a 12-point scale. Males were found to be more aggressive in 10 of 14 cultures but the differences were slight (one or two points along the scale). The most and least aggressive cultures, however, differed by 8 points along the scale (Rohner, 1976). Such cultural diversity leads us to question how much importance to attach to biological influences in the development of sex-role behaviors. Cultural range appears much greater than sex differences within any given culture. Nevertheless, cultural universals in the direction of sex differences in, for example, aggression and parenting, are suggestive of biological influences operating directly or in interaction with socialization.

Examining Biological Mechanisms.   A third approach to the study of biological bases of sex roles involves a more direct examination of possible biological mechanisms. The issue is whether or not variations in certain biological factors are associated with variations in sex-role behaviors. This question has been addressed in two ways. First, the hypothesized biological mechanisms (e.g., hormone levels) can be manipulated in an experiment. This approach has the advantage of being able to infer that behavior variations (e.g., level of aggression) were *caused* by the manipulation. It has the disadvantage, though, that such studies are obviously restricted to animals. Since the effects of any given manipulations may vary greatly from species to species, it is difficult to know to what extent the results of animal studies are applicable to humans. Second, naturally occurring variations in hypothesized biological mechanisms, such as the timing of maturation or hormone levels, can be related to behaviors. Although this kind of analysis can be applied to humans, it has the problem—intrinsic to a correlational study—of inferring causality.

In order to illustrate these approaches to studying biological mechanisms, we describe in the following pages how they apply in two frequently researched questions about the biological bases of sex differences. The first concerns the influence of hormones, particularly during perinatal periods. The second concerns the biological bases of intellectual functioning, such as mathematical or spatial abilities. This review is not intended to be exhaustive; there are many other sex-role behaviors that may have a biological basis. It is intended instead to illustrate some possible approaches and necessary cautions.

Biological Mechanisms—Social Behavior

Animal Studies.   A remarkable change occurs in the behavior of a normal adult female rodent several times a month. She displays a variety of sexual enticement behaviors, such as small hopping movements or wiggling her ears, and she is responsive to the sexual advances of a nearby male. As he mounts her, she raises her rump and her head, assuming the "lordosis" posture. If, however, the same male made advances a day later, the same female would either run away or face the male in an aggressive posture and, if necessary, kick or bite him in order to repel the advance (Kimble, 1973; McEwen 1976).

How can we account for these extraordinary changes in behavior in such a short period of time? Fulfilling the sexual sequence depends on the hormonal state of the animal. For the female, there are cyclic variations in the levels of two hormones, estrogen and progesterone, circulating in the bloodstream. Only when she is in a state of estrus, a peak in hormonal levels occurring every fourth or fifth day, will she be sexually receptive. If these hormonal surges are stopped by the removal of her ovaries, sexual receptivity ceases, though it can be restored by hormone injections. The male's mounting behavior is governed by the hormone testosterone, a type of androgen, which, in contrast to the female hormones, does not show major variations. If the level of testosterone is reduced by means of castration, however, the frequency of mounting is correspondingly reduced.

These data provide clear evidence of hormonal effects on social behavior. Experimental manipulation of hormone levels has a direct effect on sexual behavior in rodents. But to further understand the mechanisms involved in hormone–behavior relationships, an additional question must be addressed. What would happen if our two normal adult male and female rodents were injected with hormones characteristic of the other sex? If the male was injected with estrogen and progesterone, would he assume the lordosis posture? Perhaps surprisingly, the answer is no. Adult rodents show little or no behavioral response to injections of the "wrong" hormones.

Hormones have two types of effects on behavior. One is an "excitatory" or "activating" influence, in which the presence of a hormone triggers a particular behavior. This is the kind of influence we have just described; estrogen and progesterone activate the adult female's lordosis response. The other effect is an "organizational" influence that occurs during development. Sexual differentiation is dependent on whether or not gonadal hormones (estrogen and testosterone) are present during a sensitive period early in development. The timing of the sensitive period varies across species: In humans it occurs prenatally; in rats it occurs during the early postnatal period.

Numerous experiments in which hormone levels have been experimentally manipulated during this sensitive period have shown that low levels of gonadal hormones lead to the development of female characteristics, whereas high levels lead to the development of male characteristics (Hines, 1982). A genetically female rat injected with testosterone within a week after birth, for example, develops masculinized genitalia; and, as an adult, her sexual behavior is responsive to the excitatory influence of testosterone but not of estrogen and progesterone. That is, given testosterone, she will exhibit more mounting behavior than a normal adult female. When given estrogen and progesterone, she will exhibit fewer lordosis responses than a normal adult female. Thus, hormones present around the time of birth have an organizational influence on the brain, through the development of neurons and the formation of synaptic contacts, that is irreversible (McEwen, 1976). Subsequently, the animal is sensitive only to particular hormones and insensitive to others, and the sexual behavior of the adult shows a clear and lasting influence of this developmental event.

The organizational influence of hormones has been linked in many nonhuman mammals to nonsexual behaviors as well (Eccles-Parsons, 1982; Hines, 1982; Lamb, 1975; Moore, 1985; Quadagno, Briscoe, & Quadagno, 1977). These include parenting behaviors, aggression, rough-and-tumble play, open-field exploration, and running patterns on an activity wheel. Increased aggression often results, for example, when animals exposed to testosterone during the sensitive period are injected with testosterone after puberty (e.g., McEwen, 1981). These data suggest that nonhuman mammals are predisposed to act in a masculine and feminine way depending on the hormonal environment present at early points during development, though many explanations other than masculine versus feminine brain organization remain plausible (Moore, 1985). The question of whether such findings are relevant to understanding sex-role differentiation in humans is considered next.

Human Studies.   During normal human development, males are exposed to higher levels of testosterone prior to and shortly after birth than females (Maccoby, 1980). Is this difference reflected in later behavior? This question cannot be answered easily. For obvious ethical reasons, it is not possible to manipulate experimentally the hormonal environment of humans. Thus, conclusive evidence about causal relationships between hormones and behavior cannot be gathered. There are, however, individuals who develop in abnormal hormonal conditions for one reason or another. Genetic defects can change normal hormone secretions, and a fetus can be exposed to abnormal hormone levels when a pregnant woman receives hormone treatments for medical reasons. Several such syndromes are possible, and these provide a kind of natural set of experiments for examining the effects of hormones on human behavior.

A number of different abnormal genetic/hormonal combinations have been identified. One frequently studied syndrome is when the fetus, either male or female, is exposed to abnormally high levels of androgens. Another syndrome is when a genetic male is insensitive to androgen because of a genetic defect. The basic question underlying such studies is whether individuals exposed prenatally to hormone environments that deviate from normal male or female levels exhibit concomitant masculine or feminine behavioral differences from normal controls. Do, for example, genetic females exposed prenatally to androgens exhibit more masculine behavior as young girls or women than their normally developing counterparts?

Many different aspects of femininity and masculinity have been examined. These can be grouped into three categories: (a) *gender roles*—for example, in personality, play behavior, interest in marriage and children; (b) *sexual preference*—heterosexual, homosexual, or bisexual; and (c) *gender identity*—degree of knowledge about and satisfaction with being a male or a female. Few, if any, clear-cut conclusions have emerged from this research, in part because of numerous null effects and inconsistencies across studies and in part because of inherent methodological and interpretational problems in this type of research.

Some very intriguing findings have emerged, however. The most consistent result, and probably the best-known, is that prenatal exposure to androgens is related to more masculine gender-role behavior in females (Baker, 1980; Eccles-Parsons, 1982; Hines, 1982). In two investigations, for example, girls exposed to androgen showed fewer wedding fantasies, less interest in infant care and dolls, increased incidence of tomboyism, and elevated activity level, as compared either to control girls matched on demographic variables (Ehrhardt, Epstein, & Money, 1968) or to siblings (Ehrhardt & Baker, 1974). Such findings suggest that the hormonal balance during the sensitive period may predispose humans toward masculine or feminine behavior, as in animals. A closer look at the research, however, indicates that a firm conclusion is not yet possible (Moore, 1985). Most important, children exposed to abnormal prenatal hormones typically are born with physical abnormalities, such as ambiguous genitalia. It is thus possible that a girl's "masculine" behavior reflects her own, the interviewers', or socializing agents' reactions to her masculine appearance (Eccles-Parsons, 1982; Quadagno et al., 1977). In fact, most studies of individuals exposed to abnormal prenatal hormones but without physical abnormalities report null effects (see Hines, 1982). Nevertheless, a few studies have reported significant effects, such as higher aggression, on paper-and pencil measures for affected individuals as compared to controls (Reinisch, 1981).

In short, the research on effects of prenatal hormones in humans suggests that even when such effects are found, they tend to be small and within the range of normal behavior. Moreover, in most cases, gender identity and sexual orientation are consistent with the sex of rearing, regardless of genetic sex (Baker, 1980; Money & Ehrhardt, 1972). The most striking example of this sex-of-rearing effect is a case study of monozygotic twin boys, one of whom the family decided to rear as a girl because of an accident during circumcision (Money & Ehrhardt, 1972). At 17 months of age, this child had surgery to create a vagina and was later given steroids. Subsequent interviews with the parents suggested that this sex-reassignment and socialization effort was quite successful. In one interview, for example, the mother compared the daughter to the son as follows:

> She likes for me to wipe her face. She doesn't like to be dirty, and yet my son is quite different. I can't wash his face for anything. . . . She seems to be daintier. Maybe it's because I encourage it. (p. 19)

At age 12, the girl was reported as continuing to do fine (Money & Tucker, 1975).

Such data have been used to support conclusions that the effects of socialization practices are extremely powerful, in some cases even overriding genetic and biological influences (e.g., Frieze et al., 1978). This position, however, is not without controversy. With respect to the twin case study, for example, Diamond (1982) reports that a new set of psychiatrists who first saw this girl at age 13 indicated that she had significant problems with sexual identity. He argues that this follow-up report supports his "strong belief in the force of an inherent male or female nervous system bias for the development of sexual identity and partner choice" (Diamond, 1982, p. 182). It should be noted, however, that the nature of the problems Diamond reported were masculine appearance, statements that being a boy is easier, preference for a masculine occupation, and seeming unhappiness—all of which are not uncommon characteristics of early adolescent girls. Thus, the question of exactly which conclusions to draw from this case study remains unresolved. It does indicate, however, some of the difficulties of identifying appropriate criteria for distinguishing between biological and socialization influences.

Recent data have stimulated another debate relevant to examining the relative influences of socialization and biology. On the basis of various studies of individuals with abnormal prenatal hormones, Money and Ehrhardt (1972) concluded that socialization is the primary determinant of identity and sexual orientation, as long as a clear and consistent gender assignment was made by 3 or 4 years of age. They argued that after this "critical period" gender reassignment cannot be successfully accomplished. This conclusion has been called into question, however, by studies of male pseudohermaphrodites from interrelated families in the Dominican Republic (Imperato-McGinley, Peterson, Gautier, & Sturla, 1979). Because of a genetic disorder, these children were born with ambiguous external genitalia, even though they had normal male hormone levels, and they were reared as females. In contrast to the Money and Ehrhardt (1972) critical period hypothesis, these individuals took on male sexual orientations at puberty when physical virilization occurred. These data suggest that the effects of prenatal hormones may outweigh socialization in determining sexual orientation. Many questions about these findings have been raised, however (Baker, 1980; Rubin, Reinisch, & Haskett, 1981). For example, were the boys truly raised unambiguously as girls, given their ambiguous appearance? Perhaps the culture provided an atmosphere of acceptance that made these transitions possible. Indeed, after a time, the culture developed three gender labels: *Guevedoce* ("eggs at 12"), *guevote* ("penis at 12"), and *machihembra* ("first woman, then man"). This example, then, highlights our need to understand better the delicate and complex balance of biological and cultural influence in gender role development.

Biological Mechanisms—Intellectual Functioning

Recent articles published in the prestigious *Science* magazine and other research journals have re-ignited a major controversy (Benbow & Stanley, 1980, 1983; Raymond & Benbow, 1986). These articles reported the results and interpretation of a mathematical talent search. Seventh- to tenth-grade girls and boys were invited to take the SATs in mathematics, and the top 2–5% of those were invited to take courses at Johns Hopkins University. The article was focused on the observation that every year in which the test was given, more than twice as many boys as girls scored over 500. On the basis of these findings, the authors concluded: "We favor the hypothesis that sex differences in achievement in and attitude toward mathematics result from superior male mathematical ability, which may in turn be related to greater male ability in spatial tasks." With respect to causation, the authors stated that ". . . male superiority is probably an expression of a combination of both endogenous and exogenous variables," but that ". . . environmental influences are more significant for achievement in mathematics than for mathematical aptitude" (Benbow & Stanley, 1980, p. 1264). They also suggested that parental socialization seems unable to account for sex differences in mathematical reasoning (Raymond & Benbow, 1986). This conclusion has been interpreted as an unusually strong statement about the biological bases of sex differences, and has elicited a large number and wide range of responses from the scientific community (See Letters to *Science*, April 10, 1981) and from the popular press (e.g., *New York Times*, Dec. 7, 1980, p. 102; *Newsweek*, Dec. 15, 1980). In this section, we will consider possible biological mechanisms contributing to sex differences in mathematics and other intellectual skills.

Genetic Biases.   Few contemporary researchers suggest that sex differences in intellectual skills are a direct result of genetic transmission. A few years ago. the possibility was considered that spatial skills were influenced by a recessive gene on the X chromosome (e.g., Lehrke, 1972). The basic argument was that the positive influence of this recessive gene was more likely to be expressed in males, because they do not have a second X chromosome (as do females) to offset the effects of this gene. (The principle is the same as for the transmission of color-blindness.)

This hypothesis has been examined by means of intrafamilial correlations of performance. Since sons receive their mothers' X chromosomes, it was expected that higher correlations between sons and mothers would be found than between sons and fathers. Some early research has supported this prediction (see Wittig, 1976); but more recent research with larger samples has not (see Boles, 1980; Vandenberg & Kuse, 1979). Because of these inconsistent findings, and additional conceptual problems in interpreting the reported correlations, the X-linked hypothesis remains open (Caplan, MacPhearson, & Tobin, 1985; Linn & Petersen, 1985; Thomas, 1983).

Brain Organization: Laterality of Function.   The two hemispheres of the brain show different specialization of function in adults; the left hemisphere is specialized for verbal skills and the right for spatial abilities. One possible explanation for sex differences in intellectual skills is that the extent of lateralization of function, or the timing during the process of development when it occurs, may differ for girls and boys. Waber (1977), for example, has reported that late-maturing adolescents do better on tests of spatial skills than early-maturing adolescents. Possible mechanisms underlying sex differences in spatial skills, therefore, may be related to the later maturation of boys as compared to girls (Waber, 1979). In other words, boys' slower maturation may lead to greater lateralization and, in turn, to superior spatial skills. Although there is some support for Levy's (1972) hypothesis that males show greater lateralization of function than females (McGlone, 1980), definitive conclusions are not yet possible (Bryden, 1979). In addition, more recent research has suggested that the effect of maturational timing on spatial skills is very weak, limited to special populations or extreme groups (Linn & Petersen, 1985; Newcombe & Bandura, 1983; Waber, Bauermeister, Cohen, Ferber, & Wolff, 1981). The issue of differential timing of lateralization is even less clear-cut (see Eccles-Parsons, 1982, and Huston, 1983). Finally, although a recent study of the effects of prenatal exposure to DES showed the expected differences in lateralization (i.e., DES-exposed women showed a more masculine pattern of lateralization), there were no corresponding differences between exposed and unexposed women in verbal or visuospatial ability (Hines & Shipley, 1984). Thus, it appears to be premature to draw conclusions about the role of brain lateralization in sex differences in intellectual functioning.

Hormonal Changes at Puberty. The advent of puberty is marked by a number of dramatic biological changes. In terms of hormonal status, there are sharp increases in testosterone levels for boys, and in estrogen and progesterone levels for girls. If sex differences in intellectual functioning are related to hormone levels, such differences should presumably increase or begin during adolescence. Moreover, one might predict that higher levels of testosterone would be associated with greater skill at these kinds of tasks.

Some evidence supports this view. In one study, hormonal status—as inferred from measurements of body shape and genital development—was related to measures of spatial scores. As predicted, masculine body type for girls was associated with better spatial skills. For boys, however, the reverse relationship was found (Petersen, 1979). Thus, spatial abilities did not show a direct relationship to inferred influence of testosterone but instead were related to androgynous body type. A more recent study, however, with a larger sample, failed to find a significant relationship between androgynous body type and intellectual performance, though the trends were in the predicted direction (Berenbaum & Resnick, 1982).

Thus, to date, no direct relationship between hormal changes at puberty and intellectual functioning has been demonstrated. Attempts to demonstrate relations among masculine/feminine sex-role orientation, cognitive performance, and biological factors have been inconclusive (Linn & Petersen, 1985). Moreover, attempts to examine the influence of hormones in terms of changes in intellectual or motor performance across phases of the menstrual cycle have also failed to demonstrate such a relationship (e.g., Ruble & Brooks-Gunn, 1979; Sommer, 1973). The suggestion that spatial skills may be related to androgynous body type is quite intriguing. It is not clear, however, that such effects are necessarily related to hormone levels, since a number of social differences (e.g., self-perceptions, interpersonal relations) are also associated with variations in body type.

Summary

Men and women perform different roles in our society. One obvious question in regard to this observation is whether or not it is "natural." Are men and women biologically predisposed toward different roles, interests, and abilities? There is evidence that would support an affirmative response. Many differences are consistent across cultures, and experimental and correlational studies have identified biological mechanisms that may be related to these differences. On the other hand, none of the findings can be interpreted as conclusive evidence for a biological basis of sex-role behavior. There are problems with applying animal studies to humans, and with demonstrating that a naturally occurring correlation between a biological factor and a sex difference is necessarily due to the biological factor instead of possible socialization alternatives. Thus, to date, we can only describe biological processes that *might* influence sex differences in social behavior and intellectual functioning; more definitive conclusions must await future research.

SOCIAL BASES OF SEX TYPING

Cultural forces exert powerful control over our behavior. Culture dictates how long our skirts are, whether our pants are flared or straight, whether we wear makeup, or even whether we intentionally scar our bodies. Additionally, how and where we deliver our babies, the significance of puberty, and the treatment of women during menstruation all vary dramatically from culture to culture. With respect to gender roles, although biological factors may create predispositions and limitations, most investigators agree that sociocultural factors act as the primary determinants of an individual's gender orientation and behavior. Controversy continues, however, over *how* the child learns gender identity and roles, and *when* in development this learning takes place.

The major current hypotheses about sex-role development are based on two theoretical orientations: *social learning* and *cognitive development*. These two approaches share a number of common features, but they also differ in two fundamental ways. First, they emphasize different sources of influence. Social-learning theories emphasize processes acting on the child from the environment. Children are viewed as being shaped by external forces toward male or female roles. It is assumed that this shaping takes place by the same learning processes involved in the acquisition of all behaviors—reinforcement and modeling. That is, boys and girls learn by being rewarded and punished for exhibiting different behaviors and by imitating the behavior of male and female models, such as parents (Bandura, 1969; Mischel, 1970). In contrast, cognitive-developmental theories emphasize internal rather than external forces. Children are viewed as being motivated to learn social rules because of a basic orientation toward mastering the environment (See Kuhn, this volume). Sex-role learning, therefore, represents children's active construction of rules during interactions with their social world (Kohlberg, 1966; Kohlberg & Ullian, 1974; D. N. Ruble, 1987).

A second distinction between the theories concerns the importance of developmental level. Social-learning theories view sex-role development as a process of cumulative experience. Age or developmental level is unimportant except as it relates to past reinforcement and modeling history. In contrast, developmental timing is a central feature of cognitive-developmental theories. Children's constructions of gender rules are viewed as progressing in a series of stages, and the impact of gender-related information on their stereotypes and behaviors depends on children's level of gender understanding.

Although the two types of theories differ in their assumptions about the mechanisms and timing of sex-role development, they both emphasize the importance of the ready availability of gender information in our culture. Furthermore, the research literature suggests that elements of both theories are necessary for a complete understanding of sex-role development. In this section we focus on the literature most commonly associated with social-learning theories, and in the next section we discuss cognitive-developmental influences on sex-typing.

Socializing Agents and Social Pressure

Basic to social-learning theories is the concept of operant conditioning or reinforcement. Behaviors that are reinforced in some way increase, while those that are not reinforced decrease or become extinguished. The effectiveness of operant conditioning has been shown across a wide range of behaviors. It is an extremely powerful shaping mechanism, and it can sometimes operate in ways that are subtle and not intuitively obvious. To illustrate: Consider the problem of a nursery school teacher desiring to reduce the amount of aggression in his classroom. He begins by punishing every aggressive act—sternly calling to the child by name, asking her to sit in a corner, and so on. What the teacher discovers is that the level of aggression goes up, not down. The teacher was in effect reinforcing the child's aggression by attending to it. When the teacher, instead, attended to the child's cooperation and ignored her aggression, the amount of aggression in the classroom decreased (Brown & Elliott, 1965).

Thus, reinforcement does affect behavior, but it is not always obvious *what* is reinforcing. This kind of problem has made it difficult to determine whether or not socializing agents are shaping behavior by differential reinforcement for boys and for girls. It is possible, for example, that the two sexes respond to different reinforcements. In this case, even a parent who acts exactly the same way toward a son and a daughter may, in fact, be providing differential reinforcement.

Conclusions about whether boys and girls receive differential treatment have been mixed. In 1974, Maccoby and Jacklin concluded that there was little evidence of direct shaping of masculine and feminine behavior. The research showed no evidence, for example, that boys are reinforced for aggression and girls are reinforced for dependency. Thus, it appeared that infant and toddler boys and girls were treated very similarly (Maccoby & Jacklin, 1974).

More recent reviews of the literature, however, suggest that such conclusions may be premature (e.g., Block, 1978, 1983; Huston, 1983). In particular, Maccoby and Jacklin (1974) may have underestimated the importance of subtle differences in treatment and neglected the role of the father, peers, and siblings. In addition, some studies not available at the time of the Maccoby and Jacklin review have employed clever techniques of observing or eliciting differential responses to boys and girls. We turn now to a consideration of the various ways that boys' and girls' sex roles are differentially shaped by the social environment. Our review will emphasize differential treatment by parents, though similar processes operate for teachers, peers, and other socializing agents (Block, 1983; Fagot, 1985a; Lamb, Easterbrooks, & Holden, 1980).

Social Expectations.   From the moment of swaddling a newborn in a pink or blue blanket, different expectations about a girl versus a boy are evident. In one study, for example, within the first 24 hours of their baby's life, parents were asked to describe him or her as they would to a close friend. Even though the boys and girls were objectively very similar in terms of health, size, and weight, they were described very differently. Boys were believed to be better coordinated, more alert, stronger, and bigger than girls. Girls were believed to be smaller, softer, more finely featured, and less attentive than boys (Rubin, Provenzano, & Luria, 1974).

Whether or not expectations are made explicit, there is now considerable evidence that people do respond differently to boys and girls on the basis of gender-related expectations. This phenomenon is shown most clearly in situations in which people's beliefs about the sex of a child is manipulated. In general, adults are more likely to offer a doll to a child they think is a girl and to offer stereotypically male toys, such as trucks, to a child they think is a boy (Huston, 1983). Moreover, a few studies have shown that boys are encouraged in more physical or motor activities than are girls (Frisch, 1977; Smith & Lloyd, 1978). Such findings suggest that young boys and girls do receive differential treatment, in part because of adults' expectations of what boys and girls are like.

Parents' Treatment of Sons and Daughters.   It is possible that such expectation effects disappear when adults know a child well. Thus it is important to ask directly whether parents treat their young sons and daughters differently. There is growing evidence of an affirmative answer to this question; and interestingly, fathers and mothers appear to be differentially affected by their child's gender. Referring back to the expectation studies, men tend to perceive infants in more stereotypic terms than do women (Huston, 1983), and this difference extends to parents' perceptions of their own children (Rubin et al., 1974). Fathers play with sons differently than mothers play with either sons or daughters (Block, 1983; Lamb, 1977). Fathers are rougher and engage in more physical stimulation and gross motor play with their infant or toddler sons (Parke & Suomi, 1980). Fathers are also more likely to offer sex-stereotypic toys to their infants, daughters as well as sons (Jacklin & Maccoby, 1983).

Differential shaping of boys and girls appears stronger during the toddler and preschool years. First, some research has shown that parents interact more with girls and leave boys alone more (e.g., Fagot, 1978). Such differences may be important to the development of a sense of personal control and independence, although these findings are not consistent (Huston, 1983). Second, several studies have suggested that boys receive more physical punishment (Jacklin & Maccoby, 1983; Maccoby & Jacklin, 1974). Third, there is evidence of differential reinforcement of sex-appropriate play. Parents provide different toys for their sons than for their daughters and encourage them to develop sex-typed interests

(Cairns, 1979; Maccoby & Jacklin, 1974; Rheingold & Cook, 1975). In addition, one study (Fagot, 1978) reported that toddlers received more positive reactions when they engaged in sex-appropriate activities than when they engaged in activities appropriate for the other sex. A wide range of activities elicited differential responses, including doll play, asking for help, manipulating objects, and climbing. As with younger children, differential treatment is stronger for fathers than for mothers. Fathers are more likely to initiate rough-and-tumble play with boys than with girls (Jacklin & Maccoby, 1983).

Differences between fathers' and mothers' reactions to play are particularly well illustrated in one clever experimental study. The experimenter asked preschool children to play with a highly sex-typed set of toys—either dollhouse, kitchen play area, and women's dress-up outfits or an army game, highway tollbooth, and cowboy outfits. The children were instructed to play with the toys as boys would or as girls would, depending on which set they were given. The child's mother, father, or a same-sex playmate then entered the room and their responses to the child's sex-appropriate or sex-inappropriate play were observed. Fathers were found to be much more negative (e.g., interfering with play, showing signs of disgust) than were mothers or peers when their children, particularly their sons, were engaged in sex-inappropriate play. Mothers showed relatively little differential reaction, while peers exerted pressure on boys only (Langlois & Downs, 1980). Thus, there is clear evidence that young children are pressured to respond according to sex-role expectations. Boys receive more pressure than girls, and fathers exert more pressure than mothers.

A fourth area of differential treatment of preschoolers concerns teaching behavior and achievement expectations. Parents have lower expectations for and attach less importance to the long-range accomplishments of daughters than of sons (L. W. Hoffman, 1977; Parsons, Ruble, Hodges, & Small, 1976). These differences are particularly pronounced in the area of mathematical achievement (Eccles-Parsons, 1983). Direct observations of interactions between parents and young children show differential behaviors consistent with such expectations. Parents demand more independent performance from boys and are more likely to help girls quickly. Not surprisingly, fathers tend to show more such differences than mothers (Block, 1983), though mothers are more likely to help and correct the mistakes of daughters than of sons (Huston, 1983).

After the preschool years, boys and girls have very different experiences of freedom and restriction. Boys are allowed to investigate wider areas of the community and are expected to run errands at an earlier age (Saegert & Hart, 1976). They are also more likely to be left unsupervised after school, less likely to be picked up at school, and less likely to have restrictive rules imposed on them regarding how far away from home they can go alone (Block, 1983; Huston, 1983). As Huston (1983) notes, this difference is not based on parents having lower evaluations of their daughters' competence or maturity. Rather, it appears to reflect fears of chance encounters with strange males, leading parents to chaperone and protect their daughters from possible danger. Regardless of the reason, the difference may be quite significant for the growth of personal feelings of effectance and free exploration and may lead girls toward greater conformity to cultural norms and values.

One subtle aspect of differential treatment is worth highlighting. Parents' responses to same-sex children are different from their responses to opposite-sex children. Parents seem to feel they play a special socialization role for same-sex children, and this sense seems to be particularly strong for fathers. Parents interact more with same-sex children, and they tend to be somewhat more restrictive and controlling with them (Lamb, 1977; Rothbart & Maccoby, 1966).

The specialness of the same-sex parent–child relationship, taken together with findings of differential play practices of mothers and fathers, suggests that children reared by a single parent may experience a very different kind of sex-role socialization from children raised by both parents. Given that fathers are particularly important in encouraging physical play and discouraging feminine play for boys, the absence of the father would be expected to result in less masculine behavior and orientation for boys. Indeed, the available literature is consistent with this prediction (see Huston, 1983). In one study, for example, boys from two-parent families played more with masculine toys than did boys from father-absent families, though there were no differences in gender identity (Brenes, Eisenberg, & Helmstadter, 1985). Of particular interest are the findings from a longitudinal study of preschool children of divorced parents when the mother had custody (Hetherington, Cox, & Cox, 1979). Two years after the divorce, the boys, then 6 years of age, showed less masculine play preferences and behaviors than matched comparison boys from two-parent homes. Father absence shows less effect on the sex-role development of girls. Such girls do, however, appear to show difficulties in social interactions with males beginning in adolescence (Hetherington et al., 1979). Interestingly, consistent with the apparent special role of the same-sex parent, a study of mother-absent divorced families suggested that girls' sex-role development and general adjustment is more affected in this situation than is that of boys (Santrock & Warshak, 1979).

In sum, parents provide socialization experiences that differ for boys and girls. Boys are encouraged to be physical and allowed to be more independent, while girls are more likely to receive assistance rather than to be encouraged toward independent mastery. Both sexes receive support for engaging in sex-appropriate play. Some effects, however, vary by sex of parent. Fathers are more likely to encourage sex-appropriate activities in their children than mothers are, and both parents tend to be more attentive and controlling toward same-sex children. Such effects suggest that boys and girls may respond differentially to father-absence versus mother-absence, and studies of single-parent families yield results consistent with this pattern of findings.

Observational Learning

As with the acquisition of most complex behaviors, it seems unlikely that differential shaping and reinforcement are sufficient to account for the development of sex roles. Direct tuition of masculine and feminine ''styles'' of dress, play, communication, interests, and so on would seem to require substantially more time and effort than seem available to socializing agents. For this reason, much research on sex-role development has been concerned with how children learn masculine and feminine behavior by observing others. These ''modeling'' processes are central to both social-learning and cognitive-developmental approaches.

Certainly there are a wide variety of sex-stereotypic models available that children may imitate. Consider the fairy tales that children read. In Snow White, for example, the heroine survives because of her great beauty. The huntsman spares her life, the seven dwarfs accept and protect her, and the king's son rescues her from death—all because she is beautiful. This emphasis on appearance and attractiveness for girls and women is pervasive throughout our culture. Beauty contests, the use of the female body in advertising, the emphasis on makeup, and many other aspects of the culture all convey the message that the path to success for women is through their faces and their bodies. This emphasis on beauty may create a double bind for women who want to achieve success through personal competence, since attractiveness and competence are viewed by many people as incompatible in women (Heilman & Saruwatari, 1979). In contrast, boys and men are portrayed as the doers. With respect to television, for example, they represent two-thirds to three-quarters of the major characters in virtually every kind of program (Huston, 1983); and compared to female characters they show more of every kind of social behavior, except deference and passivity (McArthur & Eisen, 1976; Sternglanz & Serbin, 1974). Interestingly, even subtle production features of television support sex stereotyping. There is more variability of scenes, loud music, and sound effects in commercials directed at males than in those directed at females (Welch, Huston-Stein, Wright, & Plehal, 1979).

In brief, it is now well demonstrated that the portrayal of the sexes throughout American society is overwhelmingly consistent with sex stereotypes (Huston, 1983; D. N. Ruble & Ruble, 1982). Thus, models of sex-sterotypic behavior are readily available. The main question of interest thus becomes how influential such models are during sex-role development.

From a social-learning perspective, children acquire appropriate male and female behavior in large part by observing and imitating same-sex models. In their games, for example, children model appearance when they play dress-up and they model roles when they play doctor/nurse. There is considerable debate, however, about the strength of evidence showing early same-sex modeling (Lewis & Weinraub, 1979; Maccoby & Jacklin, 1974). There is little evidence that children are differentially exposed to or selectively attend to same-sex models; and relatively few studies demonstrate that children are more likely to imitate a model of the same sex than of the other sex (Huston, 1983; Maccoby & Jacklin, 1974).

Recent analyses suggest that hypotheses about the role of observational learning in sex-role development may be oversimplified. That is, a large number of variables are likely to affect modeling processes. These include attributes of the child, such as previously learned concepts; importance of gender; perception of the situation; and attributes of the model, such as power, competence, and similarity (Huston, 1983). Thus, it is difficult to understand fully the impact of observational learning independent of the child's emerging constructions of gender. Accordingly, we present the evidence on observational learning along with the discussion of cognitive-developmental processes in the next section.

Summary

There is considerable evidence of external pressures that are different for girls and boys, consistent with the perspective of social-learning theories. First, people's responses to a child depend on their expectations of his or her gender. Second, children are encouraged to engage in conventionally sex-appropriate play. Third, boys receive more physical stimulation and more physical punishment than girls, especially from fathers. There are also differences in expectations for achievement and for acceptance of independence and free exploration. Interestingly, parents' responses to same-sex children are different from their responses to opposite-sex children, and these differences may have implications for the experiences of children reared in single-parent homes. Finally, children are influenced by sex-stereotypic models that are readily available in the society.

COGNITIVE-DEVELOPMENTAL BASES OF SEX TYPING

The influence of external pressures on children's developing sex-role orientation is undeniable. The full impact of such external forces cannot be completely understood, however, without reference to changes within the child. According to the cognitive-developmental position, changes in children's understanding of gender structure their experiences. Emerging cognitive structures may influence both the salience and interpretation of gender information. As a result, both the quantitative and qualitative impact of gender information may vary with developmental level. In this section we consider two questions: (a) When do different kinds of gender knowledge develop? (b) In what ways do they structure sex-role choices and behavior?

The Development of Children's Sex-Role Knowledge and Identity

Knowledge and Awareness of Stereotypes. Numerous studies have examined the development of children's sex stereotypes. Both perceptions about children (their characteristics, playthings, activities) and about adults (their characteristics, activities) have been studied. The major issues are *when* children become aware of sex stereotypes, the *contents* of their perceptions, and age-related differences in the *strength* of stereotypes. It is difficult to draw firm conclusions about these issues because the studies use different sets of stimuli, questions, modes of response, and age ranges of subjects. Nevertheless, a few consistent trends can be identified.

Children's knowledge of sex roles and interests appears to develop at an early age. By 3 to 4 years of age, children are quite accurate in assigning sex-stereotypic labels to *activities, occupations,* and *playthings* (Edelbrock & Sugawara, 1978; Fauls & Smith, 1956; Garrett, Ein, & Tremaine, 1977; Guttentag & Longfellow, 1977; Hartley, 1960; Masters & Wilkinson, 1976; Nadelman, 1970, 1974; Papalia & Tennent, 1975). Stereotyping of objects has even been shown in children as young as two years of age (Thompson, 1975; Weinraub, Clemens, Sockloff, Etheridge, Gracely, & Myers, 1984). In contrast, studies examining sex-typed *traits* suggests that this kind of knowledge develops somewhat later. In one study, for example, children were asked which of two silhouette pictures (male or female) was best characterized by each of several traits (e.g., who gets into fights, who cries a lot). Only fourteen of the sixty 5-year-olds responded above a chance level, as compared with sixty out of eighty 8-year-olds and forty-seven of forty-eight 11-year-olds (Best et al., 1977).

In general, an increase in stereotyping with age would be expected in young children, consistent with increased experience and cognitive skills; and, indeed, young children do seem to demonstrate increasing knowledge of sex stereotypes at least through the kindergarten level (Edelbrock & Sugawara, 1978; Flerx, Fidler, & Rogers, 1976; Reis & Wright, 1982; Thompson, 1975; Vener & Snyder, 1966). After this age, however, there are mixed developmental trends. Many studies show a sharp *increase* in knowledge between 5 and 8 years of age with some leveling off after that (Best et al., 1977; Masters & Wilkinson, 1976; Nadelman, 1974; Williams, Bennett, & Best, 1975). Other research, however, suggests *decreases* (e.g., Garrett et al., 1977) or *curvilinear* relationships of stereotyping with age (e.g., Guttentag & Longfellow, 1977; Ullian, 1976; Urberg, 1979). A similar curvilinear trend was found in a recent study of social judgments. Third-grade children were found to pay more attention to gender stereotypes when predicting an actor's future behavior than were subjects in kindergarten, sixth grade, or college (Berndt & Heller, 1986).

One possible reason for these apparent contradictions is differences across studies in the response measure employed. Measures which require a forced choice between males and females tend to show an increase in stereotyping during the early years of school (Best et al., 1977; Masters & Wilkinson, 1976; Nadelman, 1974; Williams et al., 1975); whereas those that allow for a "both" or "neither" response typically show a decrease during these years (Garrett et al., 1977; Guttentag & Longfellow, 1977; Signorella & Liben, 1985; Urberg, 1982). This pattern of results suggests that, while the older children may have more complete knowledge about what kinds of activities and characteristics are stereotypically associated with males or females, they may also apply such stereotypes more flexibly or with finer discriminations (Masters & Wilkinson, 1976).

The idea of increasing flexibility is supported by the results of recent research (Carter & Patterson, 1982; Damon, 1979; Stoddart & Turiel, 1985). Knowledge about sex stereotypes and sex-inappropriate acts was assessed in children at different ages. Children showed awareness of sex-role violations, such as men wearing dresses, by age 5; and from 5 to 7, they were quite insistent that such acts were wrong. After this age, however, children began to make allowance for individual flexibility in the face of sex-role conventions and cultural relativity, at least until adolescence (Stoddart & Turiel, 1985).

Another possible reason for inconsistent age effects is that the various dimensions of sex-stereotypes may be differentially salient and important according to age level. Clearly, the sex-role related concerns of early elementary school children differ considerably from those of adolescents, and thus one might predict peaks in the strength of stereotyping corresponding to the different interests of children at differing ages. Indeed, it is frequently suggested that the nature of sex-typing changes during adolescence (Hill & Lynch, 1983; Katz, 1979; Mischel, 1970; Newman & Newmann, 1979) in accordance with the child's newly emerging identity as a sexual being and with strong peer pressures (Urberg & Labouvie-Vief, 1976). Lamb and Urberg (1978) have suggested, for example, that the insecurities associated with the sudden changes in and importance of physical appearance during adolescence may lead to a new commitment to traditional sex roles. Indeed, some research has reported a heightened degree of stereotyping in adolescence relative to middle elementary school (Guttentag & Longfellow, 1977; Hill & Lynch, 1983; Urberg, 1979). In addition, the results of a large interview study suggested a pattern of alternating acceptance and rejection of sex-role norms, based on age-related changes in perceiving sex differences as being biologically versus socially caused (Ullian, 1976).

In conclusion, by the age of 5 children have a reasonably well-defined set of stereotypes about the more concrete aspects of sex roles—specific activities, playthings, and occupations. More abstract aspects of sex roles (i.e., traits) are acquired somewhat later. In general, *knowledge* of stereotypes increases to an asymptote with age as shown by studies that require forced-choice responding.

When other response options are provided, however, stereotypic versus equalitarian perceptions show fluctuations with age, depending on the nature of the stereotypes being assessed and the age range of the sample included in the study.

Gender Labeling and Identity. A second issue in the development of sex-role knowledge is when children are able to apply accurate gender labels (e.g., boy or girl) to themselves and to others. Unfortunately, defining and operationalizing this construct is not as straightforward as it might initially appear; and there are wide variations in the age at which this skill is acquired, depending upon which measure is used. One measure consists of categorizing people according to common noun labels (e.g., "boy," "mommy"). Children's ability to distinguish between the sexes is first established on the basis of superficial physical characteristics (hair style, clothing, body type), with genitals acquiring increasing importance with age (Kohlberg, 1966; McConaghy, 1979; Thompson & Bentler, 1971). Early studies indicated that children were able to identify both their own sex and the sex of others by 4 years of age (Brown, 1956; Rabban, 1950). More recent research suggests that this skill emerges at a surprisingly young age; 24-month-olds accurately applied gender labels to pictures of others, and by 30 months of age the children were accurately applying such labels to themselves (Thompson, 1975; Weinraub et al., 1984).

Other research, however, suggests that this simple classification represents only a rudimentary understanding of gender. Specifically, children do not appear to understand that gender is a stable and consistent aspect of identity until several years after they can accurately label males and females (De Vries, 1969; Eaton & Von Bargen, 1981; Emmerich, Goldman, Kirsh, & Sharabany, 1977; Kohlberg, 1966; Marcus & Overton, 1978; Slaby & Frey, 1975), and not until after they are able to infer new properties of a person on the basis of gender category information (Gelman, Collman, & Maccoby, 1986). According to Kohlberg (1966), this concept of gender identity *constancy* is the critical aspect of gender labeling, because it "can provide a stable organizer of the child's psychosexual attitudes only when the child is categorically certain of its unchangeability" (p. 95).

Gender constancy refers to the consistent labeling of oneself and others as male or female in spite of superficial transformations, such as hairstyle, clothing, or changes in toy interest. In one study (Slaby & Frey, 1975), this concept was measured by a series of questions and counterquestions, grouped into three aspects of gender constancy. These were: (a) *identity* (e.g., "Is this a woman or a man? Is this a [opposite sex of subject's first response]?") (b) *stability* (e.g., "When you grow up, will you be a mommy or a daddy?"); and (c) *consistency* (e.g., "If you played [opposite sex of subject] games, would you be a boy or a girl?"). These levels showed the characteristics of developmental stages in that they were sequentially ordered (fitting the response pattern of a Guttman scale) and age-related in the sample of 2- to 5-year-olds. Identity was the easiest and was mastered by 4 years of age; stability and consistency were understood by $4\frac{1}{2}$

to 5 years of age. More recent studies have reported similar results (Fagot, 1985b). Cross-cultural research also suggests that a stagelike developmental sequence holds across cultures, suggesting the importance of cognitive-developmental factors in the growth of gender understanding. Cultural factors did appear to influence, however, the age at which different stages were acquired (Munroe, Shimmin, & Munroe, 1984).

The developmental course of understanding gender constancy has not yet been definitively established, however. Measures of gender constancy have varied across studies, leading to differences in the age at which this kind of knowledge is exhibited. Some measures, for example, involve perceptual transformations, such as depicting male or female clothes or hair on dolls or live models that accompany the questions. These studies suggest that an understanding of gender constancy develops somewhat later and is closely associated with the development of the ability to perform accurately on Piagetian measures of the constancy of physical objects—that is, at approximately 5 to 7 years of age in middle-class children (De Vries, 1969; Kohlberg, 1966; Marcus & Overton, 1978). Research using other criteria for gender understanding has reported that gender constancy was *not* achieved even by most 7-year-olds (Emmerich et al., 1977). A recent review of the literature suggests that the most important distinctions across measures are: (a) the number of consistency items included (the higher the proportion the later the attainment of constancy); and (b) the likelihood of inducing a "pretend" mode of responding in children (Martin & Halverson, 1983a). According to these authors, the literature indicating that gender constancy is attained by age 5 is more accurate than studies suggesting a later development. Thus, there is some debate about when gender constancy develops, though it clearly develops later than simple gender labeling and some aspects of sex-role stereotyping. The developmental timing of this concept is important because it is central to theoretical statements about the acquisition of sex roles, and to understanding the nature of the relationships between different kinds of sex-role knowledge and sex-typed behavior.

The Influence of Sex-Role Knowledge on Behavior

To what extent does children's knowledge of sex stereotypes play a role in producing sex-typed behavior? Is the initial acquisition of sex-role behavior dependent on a prior knowledge of stereotypes or a prior knowledge of gender labeling? Direct evidence on these important questions is scarce. It is possible, however, to begin to examine these issues by means of an analysis of two aspects of the available evidence: (a) comparisons across studies as to kinds of knowledge that developmentally precede different sex-role behaviors; and (b) correlations within single studies among the various components of sex roles.

Gender Constancy and Sex-Role Behavior. According to cognitive-developmental theory (Kohlberg, 1966; Kohlberg & Ullian, 1974), structural cognitive changes that allow children to perceive constancy of gender serve as the organizer of sex-role behaviors. It is hypothesized that children become interested in same-sex models, and perceive sex-appropriate behaviors as reinforcing, *because* of their newly acquired concept of the inevitability of their gender. Thus there should be little evidence of preference for sex-appropriate models and activities until this concept emerges at approximately 5 to 7 years of age (Constantinople, 1979; Lewis & Weinraub, 1979; Maccoby & Jacklin, 1974).

In contrast to this hypothesis, however, the empirical evidence suggests that some aspects of sex-typing are evident by 3 years of age (Brooks-Gunn & Matthews, 1979; Constantinople, 1979; Edelbrock & Sugawara, 1978; Fagot, 1985b; Weinraub et al., 1984). By age 4, children indicate preferences for sex-stereotypic toys (e.g., Emmerich & Shepard, 1984; Fling & Manosevitz, 1972; O'Brien, Huston, & Resley, 1983), there is sex differentiation in play (e.g., Cramer & Hogan, 1975; Fagot, 1984), and boys tend to be somewhat more physically aggressive and active than girls (Maccoby & Jacklin, 1974). Thus, the pattern of data shows clearly that the concept of gender constancy is not a necessary precondition for observing sex-typed behavior. The attainment of gender constancy, however, may have a special impact on sex-role development in other ways. According to Kohlberg (1966), once children develop a conception of a constant, categorical gender identity, they become motivated to learn what behavior is appropriate for their gender and to act accordingly. Thus, it is at this point in development that children should actively begin to seek information about their own gender and to attend to and imitate same-sex models.

Only a few studies are relevant to whether attention to same-sex models varies as a function of gender constancy. In one study, preschool boys at advanced stages of gender constancy spent more time selectively attending to a same-sex model in a movie than did boys at lower stages, consistent with cognitive-developmental theories (Slaby & Frey, 1975). In contrast, Bryan and Luria (1978) failed to find differential attention to slides of males or females in children aged 5 to 6 years and 9 to 10 years. It is not clear, however, that the results of the latter study seriously question the validity of this hypothesis: The stimuli were relatively simple and only a single model was presented at a time. Thus, there was no need for the children to selectively attend as there was in the Slaby and Frey study, in which male and female models were presented simultaneously.

There is also little information directly relevant to the association between gender constancy and sex-specific *behavior*. Only a few of the many studies of modeling show that children differentially imitate same-sex models (Barkley, Ullman, Otto, & Brecht, 1977; Maccoby & Jacklin, 1974). Most of these studies, however, examined preschool children, who presumably had not yet attained gender constancy. Furthermore, in most studies including older children, developmental changes have not been examined. In one study that divided children into age levels, same-sex imitation was found for 7- to 8-year-olds but not for younger children, consistent with the cognitive-developmental hypothesis (Ward, 1969).

A few studies have shown a direct relationship between gender constancy and differential modeling (Frey & Ruble, 1981; Perloff, 1982; D. N. Ruble, Balaban, & Cooper, 1981). In one study, for example, preschool and kindergarten children were shown a toy commercial in which either two boys or two girls played with a toy pretested to be perceived as equally appropriate for girls and boys. The subjects then had an opportunity to play with the target toy and with other toys of interest. An analysis of the time spent playing with the target toy revealed that only children at advanced levels of gender constancy were affected by the conditions portrayed in the commercial. For this group, children who viewed same-sex children in the commercial subsequently played with that toy significantly longer than children who had seen opposite-sex children in the commercial. In contrast, children at low levels of gender constancy showed no effect of the sex of the models (D. N. Ruble et al., 1981). In addition, high gender-constant children's sex stereotyping was more influenced by the sex of the models than were low gender-constant children's, in this study and in other research (DeLisi & Johns, 1984; Frey & Ruble, 1981).

Thus, there is tentative support for the idea that the development of gender constancy is related to children's responsiveness to sex-role models. A somewhat different picture emerges, however, when the measure of sex-role behavior is based on preferences for sex-appropriate activities. According to Kohlberg (1966), children's increasing awareness of the unchangeability of their gender is accompanied by increasing preference for same-sex activities. The evidence is, however, mixed on this point.

One study reported partial support for the hypothesis. When only information about gender appropriateness was available, virtually all children selected a same-sex toy, regardless of their level of gender understanding. In contrast, when the nature of the toy varied on two dimensions—the activity level involved in playing with the toy as well as its sex appropriateness—children who had achieved gender stability were more likely to base their choice on sex appropriateness than those who had not (Eaton, Von Bargen, & Keats, 1981). Other research has reported associations between gender constancy and: (a) same-sex social interaction for preschool girls but not boys (Smetana & Letourneau, 1984); and (b) same-sex playmate and role preferences (Emmerich & Shepart, 1984; Munroe et al., 1984). Most studies, however, find little evidence that gender-constancy development relates to sex-appropriate activities. In one study, for example, kindergartners and first- and second-grade children were asked about their preferences for games, television characters, and peers. Although there were some age-related changes in same-sex preferences, there was no relationship between gender constancy and sex-role preference (Marcus & Overton, 1978). Other research supports this finding (Emmerich & Shepard, 1984; Fagot, 1985b).

One explanation of failures to support the cognitive-developmental predictions is that neutral or opposite-sex activities may be less threatening once children understand that their gender will not change regardless of their sex-role preferences (Marcus & Overton, 1978). Alternatively, current preferences may be relatively insensitive to children's increased interest in gender-related information, because some sex differentiation of activities is readily acknowledged to be present prior to a child's *stable* identification as a boy or girl (Kohlberg, 1966). Behavioral preferences in early childhood are probably multiplied determined by such factors as reinforcement from socializing agents, as well as what playthings are available and the characteristics of those playthings (Eisenberg, Murray, & Hite, 1982). As Fagot (1985a) argues, sex role behaviors early on become overlearned, essentially automatic processes, and as such the relation between cognitive variables and performance is likely to be poor. Thus, the greater attention to gender-related information associated with the attainment of gender constancy may not have much impact on play habits, especially since the information received is not likely to deviate much from stereotypic patterns already formed.

In conclusion, there is some evidence that children's changing awareness of the constancy of their gender is associated with heightened susceptibility to information from sex-role models. From this we can draw the potentially important inference that this stage of development may represent a point at which changes in sex-stereotypic behavior would be possible, if children viewed same-sex models exhibiting nonstereotypic behavior during this time of information seeking. Indeed, greater flexibility of stereotypes has been shown in children at advanced levels of gender constancy (Frey & Ruble, 1981; Urberg, 1982).

Other Gender-Related Cognitions and Sex-Typing.   Although the attainment of gender constancy has been the primary focus of the cognitive-developmental perspective, other kinds of cognitions may influence sex-typing and sex-role development. Consider, for example, the evidence presented in the preceding sections that some aspects of both sex-typed behavior and sex-role knowledge begin to emerge after 2 years of age. Perhaps these early types of knowledge (gender labeling and the stereotyping of objects) exert some organizing influence on children's preferences and activities, which in turn helps lead to progressive cognitive awareness and differentiation. Thus, children's growing knowledge about gender and stereotyping may influence sex-typed behavior prior to their achieving gender constancy.

Indeed, several recent theoretical analyses have suggested that sex-role knowledge probably influences how information is categorized, and that these categorization processes play a role in guiding children's activities both before and after gender constancy is achieved (Bem, 1983, 1984; Constantinople, 1979; Martin & Halverson, 1981; Pleck, 1975). Early sex-role learning may be viewed in terms of the acquisition of a set of rules, similar to language acquisition (e.g., Constantinople, 1979; Pleck, 1975). According to Constantinople (1979), for example, children begin to screen information from the environment in terms of sex-role categories because of the abundance of sex-related cues in the environment and because of their natural inclinations to generalize and form categories. All that is required to set this process in motion is the initial labeling of people, objects, and activities according to gender. There is, in fact, recent evidence that 2-year-olds who answered gender label questions correctly were more likely to play with same-sex children, and—for boys—to participate less in gender-inappropriate activities than 2-year-olds who did not answer gender label questions correctly (Fagot, 1985b; Fagot, Leinbach, & Hagen, 1986). Moreover, girls who knew gender labels were less aggressive than girls who did not (Fagot et al., 1986).

Recently, the term "schema," common in the literatures on cognitive development and information processing, has been applied to the study of sex roles (Bem, 1981, 1984; Martin & Halverson, 1981; Ruble & Stangor, 1986). The content and importance of an individual's gender schemas—naive theories about sex roles—influence what kind of information is encoded and recalled. Thus, once gender schemas are formed, they may help to maintain sex-typed preferences and stereotypes because they contribute to biased information processing. They also should serve as guides to behavior because they provide information about which activities are appropriate and which should be avoided.

Several studies support the prediction that gender schemas direct information processing, such that gender-consistent information is encoded more efficiently and better remembered (Bem, 1981; Martin & Halverson, 1981). Some studies show, for example, that highly stereotyped children remembered more pictures that were consistent with sex stereotypes than pictures that violated sex stereotypes (Liben & Signorella, 1980; Signorella & Liben, 1984). Other research has shown that sex-typed individuals are more likely to encode information in terms of sex-linked associations, and are faster to embrace sex-appropriate attributes as descriptive of themselves, than are non-sex-typed individuals (Bem, 1981).

One phenomenon is a particularly interesting demonstration of the influence of gender schemas or expectations on information processing. In some circumstances, children apparently distort gender-inconsistent information and as a result make surprising errors reporting what they saw only a short time previously. In one study, for example, children viewed films of male and female doctors and nurses. When subsequently asked to identify in photographs what they had seen, children who had seen a male doctor and a female nurse were 100% accurate. In contrast, most of the children who saw a male nurse and a female doctor said they saw a female nurse and a male doctor (Cordua, McGraw, & Drabman, 1979). Other, more recent studies have reported similar effects (Frey & Ruble, 1981; Martin & Halverson, 1983b). It is noteworthy that these studies involved young children (6 years and under). It is possible that extreme distortions of this kind are more likely when children are in the process of constructing gender rules. The greater flexibility in stereotyping that seems to follow gender constancy, for example, may render such distortions less necessary.

One problem with gender schema theories is that the presence of a schema does not necessarily imply that information-processing biases will operate in favor of gender-consistent information. The social psychological literature suggests that under some circumstances subjects may recall schema-*inconsistent* information better than schema-*consistent* information (Crocker, Hannah, & Weber, 1983; Hastie & Kumar, 1979; Ruble & Stangor, 1986). Indeed, a recent review suggests that memory for gender-consistent information varies with age and with individual differences in schema strength: Preschoolers do not show better memory for gender-consistent than gender-inconsistent information; only highly stereotyped 5- to 7-year-olds show this effect; and children older than 8 years show the effect regardless of level of stereotyping (Ruble & Stangor, 1986). Thus, it is necessary to be cautious about conclusions that gender schema act to maintain sex typing.

It is possible to conclude, however, that gender beliefs influence information processing. There are also indications that children's behaviors are influenced by gender beliefs or labels. Children imitate a model selectively, depending on the sex appropriateness of the task (e.g., Barkley et al., 1977; Frey & Ruble, 1981; Masters et al., 1979), and they select toys and activities that are consistent with gender labels (e.g., Schau, Kahn, Diepold, & Cherry, 1980; Thompson, 1975). Furthermore, some research suggests that actual performance is influenced by perceptions of the sex appropriateness of the task (e.g., Montemayor, 1974). In one study, for example, children explored novel objects labeled for their own sex more than similar objects labeled for the other sex, and one week later remembered more detailed information about own-sex than other-sex objects (Bradbard, Martin, Endsley, & Halverson, 1986). Interestingly, the effect of labeling on *exploration* was stronger for older children, whereas the effect of labeling on *memory* was stronger for younger children.

Finally, it has been proposed that self-schemas regarding masculinity/femininity may be related to cognitive performance—that is, that individuals perform better when their sex-role orientation is consistent with the gender stereotyping of the task (Antill & Cunningham, 1982; Nash, 1979). A recent meta-analysis supported this hypothesis for spatial and mathematical tasks; higher masculine and lower feminine sex-role orientation scores were associated with better performance on these tasks, particularly for female subjects (Signorella & Jamison, 1986). These results are consistent with the idea that sex-role orientation influences activity preferences, which, in turn, facilitate the development of different kinds of cognitive skills; and, indeed, preference for spatial activities, which are generally considered masculine, is related to spatial performance (Newcombe, Bandura, & Taylor, 1983). The direction of causality in the relation between sex-role orientation and cognitive performance remains open, however, and biological as well as social explanations must be considered (Baucom, Besch, & Callahan, 1985; Linn & Petersen, 1985). As Signorella and Jamison (1986) note, it seems likely that models incorporating multiple explanatory factors will be necessary to explain patterns of sex differences in cognitive performance (e.g., Eccles [Parsons], Adler, & Meece, 1984).

One central question about gender-schematic processing remains to be addressed: Under what conditions do individuals respond according to gender schemas, and when do they not? One way to address this question is to look at the strength or salience of an individual's gender beliefs with respect to a particular situation. Bem (1981), for example, reports individual differences in gender orientation in adults that influence gender-related information processing. To understand the influence of gender-schematic processing in sex-role development, however, we need to examine relevant socialization and developmental variables. What situations make gender schemas salient in children at different age levels? Evidence presented earlier suggests that gender-schematic processing may be high when children are learning about the constancy of their gender. In addition, several of the studies reviewed earlier indicate that the nature and strength of stereotypes may undergo a fairly dramatic change during adolescence, suggesting that there may be other important developmental shifts in information-processing. Thus, a developmental analysis of the relationship between different kinds of sex-role knowledge and behavior at several key points in the life span would likely provide some important insights concerning the relationship of these two key dimensions of sex-role development (Emmerich, 1973; Huston-Stein & Higgins-Trenk, 1978; Katz, 1979).

Summary

A vast range of studies suggest that children's growing knowledge of gender may influence their sex-role development in a number of ways. Children begin to use gender categories for themselves and others by 2 or 3 years of age and, soon after, they show an understanding of a quite sophisticated range of sex stereotypes. Although cognitive-developmental theories have emphasized the importance of achieving gender constancy at around 5 or 6 years of age, understanding this concept is clearly not requisite to exhibiting sex-typed behavior. Children's changing awareness of the constancy of their gender does, however, seem to be related to their susceptibility to information from sex-role models. In addition, there is growing evidence that earlier forms of gender knowledge help structure children's sex-typed preferences and activities. Gender beliefs can even lead young children to distort information to be consistent with sex stereotypes. Thus, sex-role cognitions influence both the processing and the behavioral response to gender-related information.

CONCLUSION

Males and females are assumed to differ in a number of ways, and for many individuals, these sex stereotypes provide guidelines for self-perceptions and personal standards. Nevertheless, such standards may represent neither the reality nor the ideal. The literature on sex differences in personality traits suggests that males and females are more similar than is commonly believed. Furthermore, there is general consensus among theorists and researchers that individuals may possess both masculine and feminine characteristics. Indeed, it may be maladaptive to be too rigidly sex-typed. Yet, early in development boys and girls begin to show very different interests and activity preferences, and such sex-*role* differentiation remains strong throughout the life span. A long tradition of developmental research has been concerned with how sex-role differentiation occurs.

One approach focuses on biological bases of sex roles. Hormone levels present at sensitive periods during development have been implicated in the emergence of sex-typed sexual and social behavior of animals and, possibly, humans. Some research also suggests that sex differences in intellectual functioning may be influenced by genetic factors, brain lateralization, and hormonal changes at puberty. There is at present, however, no conclusive evidence regarding biological mechanisms in these areas. Findings are inconsistent and often subject to alternative interpretations.

Another approach concerns the shaping of sex roles through social learning processes—reinforcement and observational learning. Boys and girls do seem to be treated differently. They receive differential encouragement to engage in physical activity, to be independent, to play with trucks or dolls, and so on. Social learning may also occur through observation, and there is no question that sex-stereotypic models are readily available to children. Again, however, there is debate about how observational learning leads to sex-typing and how potent a force it is.

A third approach concerns internal motivations to exhibit sex-appropriate behavior because of emerging cognitive structures or sex schemas. Consistent with cognitive-developmental theory, changes in children's understanding of gender appear to structure their experiences. There is evidence, for example, that understanding the constancy of gender at about age 5 is related to the influence of same-sex models. There is debate, however, about the developmental timing of these cognitive structuring processes. Recent theoretical analyses have suggested that sex-categorization processes present by age 3 may influence children's attention to and recall of gender-related information at this young age.

No doubt the development of sex roles, in all of its complexity, is multiply determined. To illustrate: Prenatal hormonal variation and other biological factors may create predispositions in an infant or young child toward masculine or feminine characteristics. At the same time, sex-stereotypic expectations, present from the moment of birth, exert shaping influences. These biological and social forces may even interact at various points in development. Small sex differences in, for example, activity level may be exacerbated by parents' willingness to play roughly with boys but not girls. By age 3, children begin to construct organizing principles and seek to generalize the sex-role rules they are learning. Thus, at this point, children's internal motivations to act appropriately are added to external pressures toward sex-typing. The sex-stereotypical models, available throughout the culture, can then be integrated into children's emerging structures and serve as guidelines for behavior. Although children subsequently become more flexible in the application of sex-role rules learned during childhood, new learning of social norms and new needs for rigid adherence to them probably emerge at adolescence and at later points throughout the life span.

REFERENCES

Antill, J. K., & Cunningham, J. D. (1982). Sex differences in performance on ability tests as a function of masculinity, femininity, and androgyny. *Journal of Personality and Social Psychology, 42,* 178–728.

Ashmore, R. D., & Del Boca, F. K. (1979). Sex stereotypes and implicit personality theory: Toward a cognitive–social psychological conceptualization. *Sex Roles, 5,* 219–248.

Baker, S. W. (1980). Biological influences on human sex and gender. *Signs: Journal of Women in Culture and Society, 6,* 80–96.

Bandura, A. (1969). Social learning theory of identificatory processes. In R. A. Goslin (Ed.), *Handbook of socialization theory and research.* Chicago: Rand McNally.

Barkley, R. A., Ullman, D. G., Otto, L., & Brecht, J. M. (1977). The effects of sex typing and sex appropriateness of modeled behavior on children's imitation. *Child Development, 48,* 721–725.

Barry, H., III, Bacon, M. K., & Child, I. L. (1957). A cross-cultural survey of some differences in socialization. *Journal of Abnormal and Social Psychology, 55,* 327–332.

Baucom, D. H., Besch, P. K., & Callahan, S. (1985). Relation between testosterone concentration, sex role identity, and personality among females. *Journal of Personality and Social Psychology, 48,* 1218–1226.

Becker, B. J., & Hedges, C. V. (1984). Meta-analysis of cognitive gender differences: A comment on an analysis by Rosenthal and Rubin. *Journal of Educational Psychology, 76,* 583–587.

Bem, S. L. (1974). The measurement of psychological androgyny. *Journal of Consulting and Clinical Psychology, 42,* 155–162.

Bem, S. L. (1977). On the utility of alternative procedures for assessing psychological androgyny. *Journal of Consulting and Clinical Psychology, 45,* 196–205.

Bem, S. L. (1975). Sex role adaptability: One consequence of psychological androgyny. *Journal of Personality and Social Psychology, 31,* 634–643.

Bem, S. L. (1981). Gender schema theory: A cognitive account of sex typing. *Psychological Review, 88,* 354–364.

Bem, S. L. (1983). Gender schema theory and its implications for child development: Raising gender-aschematic children in a gender-schematic society. *Signs, 8,* 598–616.

Bem, S. L. (1984). Androgyny and gender schema theory: A conceptual and empirical integration. In T. B. Sondergger (Ed.), *Nebraska Symposium on Motivation* (Vol. 32, pp. 179–226). Lincoln: University of Nebraska Press.

Benbow, C. P., & Stanley, J. C. (1980). Sex differences in mathematical ability: Fact or artifact? *Science, 210,* 1262–1264.

Benbow, C. P., & Stanley, J. C. (1983). Sex differences in mathematical reasoning ability: More facts. *Science, 222,* 1029–1031.

Berenbaum, S. A., & Resnick, S. (1982). Somatic androgyny and cognitive abilities. *Developmental Psychology, 18,* 418–423.

Berndt, T. J., & Heller, K. A. (1986). Gender stereotypes and social inferences: A developmental study. *Journal of Personality and Social Psychology, 50,* 889–898.

Best, D. L., Williams, J. E., Cloud, M. J., Davis, S. W., Robertson, L. S., Edwards, J. R., Giles,

H., & Fowles, J. (1977). Development of sex-trait stereotypes among young children in the United States, England, and Ireland. *Child Development, 48,* 1375–1384.

Biller, H. B. (1971). *Father, child, and sex role: Paternal determinants of personality development.* Lexington, MA: Heath.

Block, J. H. (1976a). Debatable conclusions about sex differences. *Contemporary Psychology, 21,* 517–522.

Block, J. H. (1976b). Issues, problems, and pitfalls in assessing sex differences. *Merrill-Palmer Quarterly, 22,* 283–308.

Block, J. H. (1978). Another look at sex differentiation in the socialization behaviors of mothers and fathers. In J. Sherman & F. L. Denmark (Eds.), *The psychology of women: Future directions of research.* New York: Psychological Dimensions.

Block, J. H. (1983). Differential premises arising from differential socialization of the sexes: Some conjectures. *Child Development, 54,* 1335–1354.

Boles, D. B. (1980). X-linkage of spatial ability: A critical review. *Child Development, 51,* 625–635.

Bradbard, M. R., Martin, C. L., Endsley, R. C., & Halverson, C. F. (1986). Influence of sex stereotypes on children's exploration and memory: A competence versus performance distinction. *Developmental Psychology, 22,* 481–486.

Brannon, R. (1978). Measuring attitudes (toward women, and otherwise): A methodological critique. In J. Sherman & F. Denmark (Eds.), *Psychology of women: Future directions of research.* New York: Psychological Dimensions.

Brenes, M. E., Eisenberg, N., & Helmstadter, G. C. (1985). Sex role development of preschoolers from two-parent and one-parent families. *Merrill-Palmer Quarterly, 31,* 33–46.

Brooks-Gunn, J., & Matthews, W. S. (1979). *He and she.* Englewood Cliffs, NJ: Prentice-Hall.

Broverman, I. K., Vogel, S. R., Broverman, D. M., Clarkson, F. E., & Rosenkrantz, P. S. (1972). Sex role stereotypes: A current appraisal. *Journal of Social Issues, 28*(2), 59–79.

Brown, D. G. (1956). Sex-role preference in young children. *Psychological Monographs, 70*(14), whole issue.

Brown, D. G. (1957). Masculinity–femininity development in children. *Journal of Consulting Psychology, 21,* 197–205.

Brown, P., & Elliott, R. (1965). Control of aggression in a nursery school class. *Journal of Experimental Child Psychology, 2,* 103–107.

Bryan, J. W., & Luria, Z. (1978). Sex-role learning: A test of the selective attention hypothesis. *Child Development, 49,* 13–23.

Bryden, M. P. (1979). Evidence for sex-related differences in cerebral organization. In M. A. Wittig & A. C. Petersen (Eds.), *Sex-related differences in cognitive functioning.* New York: Academic Press.

Bullough, V. L. (1973). *The subordinate sex.* Urbana: University of Illinois Press.

Burnett, S. A. (1986). Sex-related differences in spatial ability: Are they trivial? *American Psychologist, 41,* 1012–1014.

Cairns, R. B. (1979). *Social development: The origins and plasticity of interchanges.* San Francisco: Freeman.

Caplan, P. J., MacPhearson, G. M., & Tobin, P. (1985). Do sex-related differences in spatial abilities exist? *American Psychologist, 40,* 786–799.

Carter, D. B., & Patterson, C. J. (1982). Sex roles as social conventions: The development of children's conceptions of sex-role stereotypes. *Developmental Psychology, 18,* 812–824.

Cicone, M. V., & Ruble, D. N. (1978). Beliefs about males. *Journal of Social Issues, 34,* 5–16.

Cohen, J. (1977). *Statistical power analysis for the behavioral sciences* (2nd ed.). New York: Academic Press.

Constantinople, A. (1973). Masculinity–femininity: An exception to the famous dictum? *Psychological Bulletin, 80,* 389–407.

Constantinople, A. (1979). Sex-role acquisition: In search of the elephant. *Sex Roles, 5,* 121–134.

Cordua, G. D., McGraw, K. O., & Drabman, R. S. (1979). Doctor or nurse: Children's perceptions of sex typed occupations. *Child Development, 50,* 590–593.

Cramer, P., & Hogan, K. (1975). Sex differences in verbal and play fantasy. *Developmental Psychology, 11,* 145–154.

Crocker, J., Hannah, D. B., & Weber, R. (1983). Person memory and causal attributions. *Journal of Personality and Social Psychology, 44,* 55–66.

Damon, W. (1979). *The social world of the child.* San Francisco: Jossey-Bass.

Deaux, K., & Lewis, L. L. (1984). Structure of gender stereotypes: Interrelationships among components and gender label. *Journal of Personality and Social Psychology, 46,* 991–10004.

Deaux, K., Winton, W., Crowley, M., & Lewis, L. L. (1985). Level of categorization and content of gender stereotypes. *Social Cognition, 3,* 145–167.

DeLisi, R., & Johns, M. L. (1984). The effects of books and gender constancy development on kindergarten children's sex-role attitudes. *Journal of Applied Developmental Psychology, 5,* 173–181.

De Vries, R. (1969). Constancy of generic identity in the years three to six. *Monographs of the Society for Research in Child Development, 34*(3), Serial No. 127.

Diamond, M. (1982). Sexual identity: monozygotic twins reared in discordant sex roles and a BBC follow-up. *Archives of Sexual Behavior, 11,* 181–186.

Doyle, J. A. (1983). *The male experience.* Dubuque, IA: Wm. C. Brown.

Eagly, A. H., & Carli, L. L. (1981). Sex of researchers and sex-typed communications as determinants of sex differences in influenceability. A meta-analysis of social influence studies. *Psychological Bulletin, 90,* 1–20.

Eaton, W. O., & Enns, L. R. (1986). Sex differences in human motor activity level. *Psychological Bulletin, 100,* 19–28.

Eaton, W. O., & Von Bargen, D. (1981). Asynchronous development of gender understanding in preschool children. *Child Development, 52,* 1020–1027.

Eaton, W. O., Von Bargen, D., & Keats, J. G. (1981). Gender understanding and dimensions of preschooler toy choice: Sex stereotype versus activity level. *Canadian Journal of Behavioral Science, 13,* 203–209.

Eccles (Parsons), J., Adler, T., & Meece, J. L. (1984). Sex differences in achievement: A test of alternate theories. *Journal of Personality and Social Psychology, 46,* 26–43.

Eccles-Parsons, J. (1982). Biology, experience and sex dimorphic behaviors. In W. Gove & G. R. Carpenter (Eds.), *The fundamental connection between nature and nurture: A review of the evidence.* Lexington, MA: Lexington Books.

Eccles-Parsons, J. (1983). Expectancies, values, and academic behaviors. In J. T. Spence (Ed.), *Achievement and achievement motives.* San Francisco: Freeman.

Edelbrock, C., & Sugawara, A. I. (1978). Acquisition of sex-typed preferences in preschool-aged children. *Developmental Psychology 14,* 614–623.

Ehrhardt, A. A., & Baker, S. W. (1974). Fetal androgens, human central nervous system differentiation, and behavior sex differences. In R. C. Friedman, R. M. Richart, & R. L. Vande Wiele (Eds.), *Sex differences in behavior.* New York: Wiley.

Ehrhardt, A. A., Epstein, R., & Money, J. (1968). Fetal androgens and female gender identity in the early treated adrenogenital syndrome. *Johns Hopkins Medical Journal, 122,* 160–167.

Eisenberg, N., & Lennon, R. (1983). Sex differences in empathy and related capacities. *Psychological Bulletin, 94,* 100–131.

Eisenberg, N., Murray, E., & Hite, T. (1982). Children's reasoning regarding sex-typed toy choices. *Child Development, 53,* 81–86.

Emmerich, W. (1973). Socialization and sex-role development. In P. B. Baltes & K. W. Schaie (Eds.), *Life-span developmental psychology: Personality and socialization.* New York: Academic Press.

Emmerich, W., Goldman, K. S., Kirsh, B., & Sharabany, R. (1977). Evidence for a transitional phase in the development of gender constancy. *Child Development, 48,* 930–936.

Emmerich, W., & Shepard, K. (1984). Cognitive factors in the development of sex-typed preferences. *Sex Roles, 11,* 997–1007.

Fagot, B. I. (1978). The influence of sex of child on parental reactions to toddler children. *Child Development, 49,* 459–465.

Fagot, B. I. (1984). Teacher and peer reactions to boys' and girls' play styles. *Sex Roles, 11,* 691–762.

Fagot, B. I. (1985a). Beyond the reinforcement principle: Another step toward understanding sex role development. *Developmental Psychology, 21,* 1097–1104.

Fagot, B. I. (1985b). Changes in thinking about early sex-role development. *Developmental Review, 5,* 83–98.

Fagot, B. I., Leinbach, M. D., Hagen, R. (1986). Gender labeling and the adoption of sex-typed behaviors. *Developmental Psychology, 22,* 440–443.

Fauls, L., & Smith, W. (1956). Sex-role learning of five-year-olds. *Journal of Genetic Psychology, 89,* 105–117.

Flerx, V. C., Fidler, D. S., & Rogers, R. W. (1976). Sex role stereotypes: Developmental aspects and early intervention. *Child Development, 47,* 998–1007.

Fling, S., & Manosevitz, M. (1972). Sex typing in nursery school children's play interests. *Developmental Psychology, 7,* 146–152.

Frey, K. S., & Ruble, D. N. (1981). *Concepts of gender constancy as mediators of behavior.* Paper presented at the Biennial Meeting of the Society for Research in Child Development, Boston.

Frieze, I. H., Parsons, J. E., Johnson, P. B., Ruble, D. N., & Zellman, G. L. (1978). *Women and sex roles: A social psychological perspective.* New York: W. W. Norton.

Frisch, H. L. (1977). Sex stereotypes in adult–infant play. *Child Development, 48,* 1671–1675.

Garrett, C. S., Ein, P. L., & Tremaine, L. (1977). The development of gender stereotyping of adult occupations in elementary school children. *Child Development, 48,* 507–512.

Gelman, S. A., Collman, P., & Maccoby, E. E. (1986). Inferring properties from categories versus inferring categories from properties: The case of gender. *Child Development, 57,* 396–404.

Gould, C. C. (1976). Philosophy of liberation and the liberation of philosophy. In C. C. Gould & M. W. Wartofsky (Ed.), *Women and philosophy: Toward a theory of liberation.* New York: G. P. Putnam.

Green, R. (1975). The significance of feminine behavior in boys. *Journal of Child Psychology and Psychiatry, 16,* 341–344.

Guttentag, M., & Longfellow, C. (1977). Children's social attributions: Development and change. In C. B. Keasey (Ed.), *Nebraska symposium on motivation.* Lincoln: University of Nebraska Press.

Hartley, R. (1960). Children's concepts of male and female roles. *Merrill-Palmer Quarterly, 6,* 83–91.

Hastie, R., & Kumar, P. A. (1979). Person memory: Personality traits as organizing principles in memory for behavior. *Journal of Personality and Social Psychology, 37,* 25–38.

Heilbrun, A. B., Jr. (1976). Measurement of masculine and feminine sex role identities as independent dimensions. *Journal of Consulting and Clinical Psychology, 44,* 183–190.

Heilman, M. E., Saruwatari, L. (1979). When beauty is beastly: The effect of appearance and sex on evaluations of job applicants for managerial and non-managerial jobs. *Organizational Behavior and Human Performance, 23,* 360–372.

Hetherington, E. M., Cox, M., & Cox, R. (1979). Play and social interaction in children following divorce. *Journal of Social Issues, 35,* 26–49.

Hill, J. P., & Lynch, M. E. (1983). The intensification of gender-related expectations during early adolescence. In J. Brooks-Gunn & A. C. Petersen (Eds.), *Girls at puberty* (pp. 201–228). New York: Plenum Press.

Hines, M. (1982). Prenatal gonadal hormones and sex differences in human behavior. *Psychological Bulletin, 92,* 56–80.

Hines, M., & Shipley, C. (1984). Prenatal exposure to diethylstilbestrol (DES) and the development of sexually dimorphic cognitive abilities and cerebral lateralization. *Developmental Psychology, 20,* 81–94.

Hoffman, L. W. (1977). Changes in family roles, socialization, and sex differences. *American Psychologist, 32,* 644–657.

Hoffman, M. L. (1977). Sex differences in empathy and related behaviors. *Psychological Bulletin, 84,* 712–722.

Horan, P. F., & Rosser, R. A. (1984). A multivariate analysis of spatial abilities by sex. *Developmental Review, 4,* 387–411.

Hunter, J. (1976). Images of woman. *Journal of Social Issues, 32*(3), 7–17.

Huston. A. C. (1983). Sex-typing. In E. M. Hetherington (Ed.), *Social development,* volume in P. H. Mussen (General Ed.), *Carmichael's manual of child psychology* (4th ed.). New York: Wiley.

Huston, A. (1985). The development of sex-typing: Themes from recent research. *Developmental Review, 5,* 1–17.

Huston-Stein, A., & Higgins-Trenk, A. (1978). The development of females: Career and feminine role aspirations. In P. B. Baltes (Ed.), *Life-span development and behavior* (Vol. 1). New York: Academic Press.

Hyde, J. S. *(1981).* How large are cognitive gender differences? *American Psychologist, 36,* 892–901.

Hyde, J. S. (1984). How large are gender differences in aggression? A developmental meta-analysis. *Developmental Psychology, 20,* 722–736.

Hyde, J. S., & Rosenberg, B. G. (1976). *Half the human experience: The psychology of women.* Lexington, MA: D.C. Health.

Ickes, W., & Barnes, R. D. (1978). Boys and girls together—and alienated: On enacting stereotyped sex roles in mixed-sex dyads. *Journal of Personality and Social Psychology, 36,* 669–683.

Imperato-McGinley, J., Peterson, R. E., Gautier, T., & Sturla, E. (1979). Androgens and the evolution of male-gender identity among male pseudohermaphrodites with 5-reductase deficiency. *New England Journal of Medicine, 300,* 1233–1240.

Jacklin, C. N., & Maccoby, E. E. (1983). Issues of gender differentiation in normal development. In M. D. Levine, W. B. Carey, A. C. Crocker, & R. T. Gross (Eds.), *Developmental–Behavioral Pediatrics,* Philadelphia: W. B. Saunders.

Jones, W., Chernovetz, M. E., & Hansson, R. O. (1978). The enigma of androgyny: Differential implications for males and females? *Journal of Consulting and Clinical Psychology, 46,* 298–313.

Kagan, J. (1964). Acquisition and significance of sex typing and sex role identity. In M. L. Hoffman & L. W. Hoffman (Eds.), *Review of child development research* (Vol. 1). New York: Russell Sage.

Karabenick, S. A. (1983). Sex-relevance of content and influenceability: S. Strunk and McDavid revisited. *Personality and Social Psychology Bulletin, 9,* 243–252.

Katz, P. A. (1979). The development of female identity. *Sex Roles, 5,* 155–178.

Kelly, J. A., & Worell, J. (1977). New formulations of sex roles and androgyny: A critical review. *Journal of Consulting and Clinical Psychology, 45,* 1101–1115.

Kimble, D. P. (1973). *Psychology as a biological science.* Pacific Palisades, CA: Goodyear.

Kohlberg, L. (1966). A cognitive-developmental analysis of children's sex-role concepts and attitudes. In E. E. Maccoby (Ed.), *The development of sex differences.* Stanford, CA: Stanford University Press.

Kohlberg, L., & Ullian, D. Z. (1974). Stages in the development of psychosexual concepts and attitudes. In R. C. Friedman, R. M. Richart, & R. L. Vande Wiele (Eds.), *Sex differences in behavior.* New York: Wiley.

Lamb, M. E. (1975). Physiological mechanisms in the control of maternal behavior in rats: A review. *Psychological Bulletin, 82,* 104–119.

Lamb, M. E. (1976). *The role of the father in child development.* New York: Wiley.

Lamb, M. E. (1977). The development of parental preferences in the first two years of life. *Sex Roles, 3,* 495–497.

Lamb, M. E., Easterbrooks, M. A., & Holden, G. A. (1980). Reinforcement and punishment among preschoolers: Characteristics, effects and correlates. *Child Development, 51,* 1230–1236.

Lamb, M. E., & Urberg, K. A. (1978). The development of gender role and gender identity. In M. E. Lamb (Ed.), *Social and personality development.* New York: Holt, Rinehart & Winston.

Langlois, J., & Downs, C. (1980). Mothers, fathers, and peers as socialization agents of sex-typed play behavior in young children. *Child Development, 51,* 1237–1247.

Lehrke, R. (1972). A theory of X-linkage of major intellectual traits. *American Journal of Mental Deficiency, 76,* 611–619.

Levy, J. (1972). Lateral specialization of the human brain: Behavioral manifestations and possible evolutionary basis. In J. A. Kiger (Ed.), *The biology of behavior.* Corvallis, OR: Oregon State University Press.

Lewis, M., & Weinraub, M. (1979). Origins of early sex-role development. *Sex Roles, 5,* 135–154.

Liben, L. S., & Signorella, M. L. (1980). Gender-related schemata and constructive memory in children. *Child Development, 51,* 11–18.

Linn, M. C., & Petersen, A. C. (1985). Emergence and characterization of sex differences in spatial ability: A meta-analysis. *Child Development, 56,* 1479–1498.

Maccoby, E. E. (1980). *Social development.* New York: Harcourt Brace Jovanovich.

Maccoby, E. E., & Jacklin, C. N. (1974). *The psychology of sex differences.* Stanford, CA: Stanford University Press.

Marcus, D. E., & Overton, W. F. (1978). The development of cognitive gender constancy and sex role preferences. *Child Development, 49,* 434–444.

Martin, C. L., & Halverson, C. F. (1981). A schematic processing model of sex typing and stereotyping in children. *Child Development, 52,* 1119–1134.

Martin, C. L., & Halverson, C. F. (1983a). Gender constancy: A methodological and theoretical analysis. *Sex Roles, 9,* 775–790.

Martin, C. L., & Halverson, C. F. (1983b). The effects of sex-typing schemas on young children's memory. *Child Development, 54,* 563–574.

Masters, J., Ford, M., Arend, R., Grotevant, H., & Clark, L. (1979). Modeling and labeling as integrated determinants of children's sex-typed imitative behavior. *Child Development, 50,* 364–371.

Masters, J. C., & Wilkinson, A. (1976). Consensual and discriminative stereotypes of sex-type judgments by parents and children. *Child Development, 47,* 208–217.

McArthur, L. Z., & Eisen, S. V. (1976). Achievements of male and female storybook characters as determinants of achievement behavior by boys and girls. *Journal of Personality and Social Psychology, 33,* 467–473.

McConaghy, M. J. (1979). Gender permanence and the genital basis of gender: Stages in the development of constancy of gender identity. *Child Development, 50,* 1223–1226.

McEwen, B. S. (1976). Interactions between hormones and nerve tissue. *Scientific American, 235,* 48–58.

McEwen, B. S. (1981). Neural gonadal steroid actions. *Science, 24,* 1303–1311.

McGlone, J. (1980). Sex differences in human brain asymmetry: A critical survey. *Behavior and Brain Sciences, 3,* 215–263.

Mead, M. (1935). *Sex and temperament in three primitive societies.* New York: Morrow.

Meehan, A. M. (1984). A meta-analysis of sex differences in formal operational thought. *Child Development, 55,* 1110–1124.

Miles, C. (1935). Sex in social psychology. In C. Murchinson (Ed.), *Handbook of social psychology*. Worcester, MA: Clark University Press.

Mischel, W. (1970). Sex-typing and socialization. In P.H. Mussen (Ed.), *Carmichael's manual of child psychology*. New York: Wiley.

Money, J., & Ehrhardt, A. A. (1972). *Man & woman: Boy & girl*. Baltimore: Johns Hopkins University Press.

Money, J., & Tucker, P. (1975). *Sexual signatures: On being a man or woman*. Boston, MA: Little, Brown.

Montemayor, R. (1974). Children's performance in a game and their attraction to it as a function of sex-typed labels. *Child Development, 45*, 152–156.

Moore, C. L. (1985). Another psychobiological view of sexual differentiation. *Developmental Review, 5*, 18–55.

Munroe, R. H., Shimmin, H. S., & Munroe, R. L. (1984). Gender understanding and sex role preference in four cultures. *Developmental Psychology, 20*, 673–682.

Mussen, P. H. (1969). Early sex-role development. In D. A. Goslin (Ed.), *Handbook of socialization theory and research*. Chicago: Rand McNally.

Nadelman, L. (1970). Sex identity in London children: Memory, knowledge, and preference tests. *Human Development, 13*, 28–42.

Nadelman, L. (1974). Sex identity in American children: Memory, knowledge, and preference tests. *Developmental Psychology, 10*, 413–417.

Nash, S. C. (1979). Sex role as a mediator of intellectual functioning. In M. A. Wittig & A. C. Petersen (Eds.), *Sex-related differences in cognitive functioning* (pp. 263–302). New York: Academic Press.

Newcombe, N., & Bandura, M. M. (1983). The effect of age at puberty on spatial ability in girls: A question of mechanism. *Developmental Psychology, 19*, 215–224.

Newcombe, N., & Bandura, M. M., & Taylor, D. G. (1983). Sex differences in spatial activities. *Sex Roles, 9*, 377–386.

Norwood, J. L. (September 1982). *The male–female earnings gap: A review of employment and earnings issues*. U.S. Department of Labor, Bureau of Labor Statistics, Report 673.

O'Brien, M., Huston, A. C., & Resley, T. (1983). Sex-typed play of toddlers in a day care center. *Journal of Applied Developmental Psychology, 4*, 1–10.

Orlofsky, J. L., & Windle, M. T. (1978). Sex-role orientation, behavioral adaptability, and personal adjustment. *Sex Roles, 4*, 801–811.

Papalia, D. E., & Tennent, S. S. (1975). Vocational aspirations in preschoolers: A manifestation of early sex role stereotyping. *Sex Roles, 1*, 197–199.

Parke, R. D., & Suomi, S. J. (1980). Adult male–infant relationships: Human and non-human evidence. In K. Immelman, G. Barlow, M. Main, & L. Petrinovitch (Eds.), *Behavioral development: The Bielefeld interdisciplinary project*. New York: Cambridge University Press.

Parsons, J. E., Ruble, D. N., Hodges, K. L., & Small, A. W. (1976). Cognitive-developmental factors in emerging sex differences in achievement-related expectancies. *Journal of Social Issues, 32*, 47–62.

Pedersen, D. M., Shinedling, M. M., & Johnson, D. L. (1968). Effects of sex of examiner and subject on children's quantitative test performance. *Journal of Personality and Social Psychology, 10*, 251–254.

Perloff, R. M. (1982). Gender constancy and same-sex imitation: A developmental study. *The Journal of Psychology, 111*, 81–86.

Petersen, A. C. (1979). Hormones and cognitive functioning in normal development. In M. A. Wittig & A. C. Petersen (Eds.), *Sex-related differences in cognitive functioning: Developmental issues*. New York: Academic Press.

Pleck, J. H. (1975). Masculinity–femininity: Current and alternative paradigms. *Sex Roles, 1*, 161–178.

Pleck, J. H. (1981). *The myth of masculinity*. Cambridge, MA: The MIT Press.

Pleck, J. H., & Brannon, R. (Eds.). (1978). Male roles and the male experience. *Journal of Social Issues, 34*, 1–4.

Quadagno, D. M., Briscoe, R., and Quadagno, J. S. (1977). Effect of perinatal gonadal hormones on selected nonsexual behavior patterns: A critical assessment of the non-human and human literature. *Psychological Bulletin, 84*, 62–80.

Rabban, M. (1950). Sex-role identification in young children in two diverse social groups. *Genetic Psychology Monographs, 42*, 81–158.

Ramey, E. R. (1982). The natural capacity for health in women. In P. W. Berman & E. R. Ramey (Eds.), *Women: A developmental perspective* (pp. 3–12). Washington: U.S. Department of Health and Human Services.

Raymond, C. L., & Benbow, C. P. (1986). Gender differences in mathematics: A function of parental support and student sex typing? *Developmental Psychology, 22*, 808–819.

Reinisch, J. M. (1981). Prenatal exposure to synthetic progestins increases potential for aggression in humans. *Science, 211*, 1171–1173.

Reis, H. T., & Wright, S. (1982). Knowledge of sex-role stereotypes in children aged 3 to 5. *Sex Roles, 8*, 1049–1056.

Rheingold, H., & Cook, K. (1975). The content of boys' and girls' rooms as an index of parent behavior. *Child Development, 46*, 459–463.

Rohner, R. P. (1976). Sex differences in aggression: Phylogenetic and enculturation perspectives. *Ethos, 4*, 57–72.

Rosaldo, M. Z. (1974). Women, culture and society: A theoretical overview. In M. Z. Rosaldo & L. Lamphere (Eds.), *Women, culture and society*. Stanford: Stanford University Press.

Rosen, A. C., & Rekers, G. A. (1980). Toward a taxonomic framework for variables of sex and gender. *Genetic Psychology Monographs, 102*, 191–218.

Rosenkrantz, P., Vogel, S., Bee, H., Broverman, I., & Broverman, D. M. (1968). Sex-role stereotypes and self-concepts in college students. *Journal of Consulting and Clinical Psychology, 32*, 287–295.

Rosenthal, R., & Rubin, D. B. (1982). Further meta-analytic procedures for assessing cognitive gender differences. *Journal of Educational Psychology, 74*, 708–712.

Rossi, J. S. (1983). Ratios exaggerate gender differences in mathematical ability. *American Psychologist, 38*, 348.

Rothbart, M. K., & Maccoby, E. E. (1966). Parents' differential reactions to sons and daughters. *Journal of Personality and Social Psychology, 4*, 237–243.

Rubin, J. S., Provenzano, F. J., & Luria, Z. (1974). The eye of the beholder: Parents' views on sex of newborns. *American Journal of Orthopsychiatry, 5*, 353–363.

Rubin, R. T., Reinisch, J. M., & Haskett, R. F. (1981). Postnatal gonadal steroid effects on human behavior. *Science, 211*, 1318–1324.

Ruble, D. N. (1987). The acquisition of self-knowledge: A self-socialization perspective. In N. Eisenberg (Ed.), *Contemporary topics in developmental psychology*. New York: Wiley.

Ruble, D. N., Balaban, T., & Cooper, J. (1981). Gender constancy and the effects of sex-typed televised toy commercials. *Child Development, 52*, 667–673.

Ruble, D. N., & Brooks-Gunn, J. (1979). Menstrual symptoms: A social cognition analysis. *Journal of Behavioral Medicine, 2*, 171–194.

Ruble, D. N., & Higgins, E. T. (1976). Effects of group sex composition on self-presentation and sex-typing. *Journal of Social Issues, 32*, 125–132.

Ruble, D. N., & Ruble, T. (1982). Sex stereotypes. In A. G. Miller (Ed.), *In the eye of the beholder*. New York: Praeger.

Ruble, D. N., & Stangor, C. (1986). Stalking the elusive schema: Insights from developmental and social-psychological analyses of gender schemas. *Social Cognition, 4*, 227–261.

Ruble, T. L. (1983). Sex stereotypes: Issues of change in the 1970's. *Sex Roles, 9*, 397–402.

Ruble, T. L., Cohen, R., & Ruble, D. N. (1984). Sex stereotypes: Occupational barriers for women. *American Behavioral Scientist, 27,* 339–356.

Rytina, N. F. (1982). Earnings of men and women: A look at specific occupations. *Monthly Labor Review,* 25–31.

Saegert, S., & Hart, R. (1976). The development of environmental competence in girls and boys. In P. Burnet (Ed.), *Women and society.* Chicago: Maaroufa Press.

Santrock, J. W., & Warshak, R. A. (1979). Father custody and social development in boys and girls. *Journal of Social Issues, 35,* 112–125.

Schau, C. G., Kahn, L., Diepold, J. H., & Cherry, F. (1980). The relationships of parental expectations and preschool children's verbal sex typing to their sex-typed toy play behavior. *Child Development, 51,* 266–270.

Shields, S. A. (1975). Functionalism, Darwinism and the psychology of women: A study in social myth. *American Psychologist, 30,* 739–754.

Signorella, M. L., & Jamison, W. (1986). Masculinity, femininity, androgyny, and cognitive performance: A meta-analysis. *Psychological Bulletin, 100,* 207–228.

Signorella, M. L., & Liben, L. S. (1984). Recall and reconstruction of gender-related pictures: Effects of attitude, task difficulty, and age. *Child Development, 55,* 393–405.

Signorella, M. L., & Liben, L. S. (1985). *Effects of labels on children's memory of gender-related pictures.* Paper presented at the biennial meeting of the Society for Research in Child Development, Toronto.

Signorella, M. L., & Vegaga, M. E. (1984). A note on gender stereotyping in research topics. *Personality and Social Psychology Bulletin, 10,* 107–109.

Sistrunk, F., & McDavid, J. W. (1971). Sex variable in conforming behavior. *Journal of Personality and Social Psychology, 17,* 200–207.

Slaby, R. G., & Frey, K. S. (1975). Development of gender constancy and selective attention to same-sex models. *Child Development,* 849–856.

Smetana, J. G., & Letourneau, K. J. (1984). Development of gender constancy and children's sex-typed free play behavior. *Developmental Psychology, 20,* 691–696.

Smith, C., & Lloyd, B. (1978). Maternal behavior and perceived sex of infant: Revisited. *Child Development, 49,* 1263–1265.

Sommer, B. (1973). The effect of menstruation on cognitive and perceptual-motor behavior: A review. *Psychosomatic Medicine, 35,* 515–534.

Spence, J. T., Deaux, K., & Helmreich, R. L. (1985). Sex roles in contemporary American society. In G. Lindzey & E. Aronson (Eds.), *Handbook of social psychology* (3rd ed., Vol. 2, pp. 149–178). New York: Random House.

Spence, J. T., & Helmreich, R. L. (1978). *Masculinity and femininity.* Austin: University of Texas Press.

Spence, J. T., Helmreich, R., & Stapp, J. (1974). The personal attributes questionnaire: A measure of sex-role stereotypes and masculinity–femininity. *JSAS Catalog of Selected Documents in Psychology, 4,* 43 (MS No. 617).

Spence, J. T., Helmreich, R., & Stapp, J. (1975). Ratings of self and peers on sex role attributes and their relations to self-esteem and conceptions of masculinity and femininity. *Journal of Personality and Social Psychology, 32,* 29–39.

Sternglanz, S. H., & Serbin, L. A. (1974). Sex role stereotyping in children's television programs. *Developmental Psychology, 10,* 710–715.

Stoddart, T., & Turiel, E. (1985). Children's concepts of cross-gender activities. *Child Development, 56,* 1241–1252.

Tavris, C., & Wade, C. (1984). *The longest war.* New York: Harcourt, Brace, Jovanovich.

Taylor, M. C. & Hall, J. A. (1982). Psychological androgyny: Theories, methods, and conclusions. *Psychological Bulletin, 92,* 347–366.

Thomas, H. (1983). Familial correlational analyses, sex differences, and the X-linked gene hypothesis. *Psychological Bulletin, 93,* 427–440.

Thompson, S. K. (1975). Gender labels and early sex role development. *Child Development, 46,* 339–347.

Thompson, S. K., & Bentler, P. M. (1971). The priority of cues in sex discrimination by children and adults. *Developmental Psychology, 5,* 181–185.

Ullian, D. Z. (1976). The development of conceptions of masculinity and femininity. In B. Lloyd & J. Archer (Eds.), *Exploring sex differences.* London: Academic Press.

Urberg, K. A. (1979). Sex role conceptualization in adolescents and adults. *Developmental Psychology, 15,* 90–92.

Urberg, K. A. (1982). The development of the concepts of masculinity and femininity in young children. *Sex Roles, 8,* 659–668.

Urberg, K. A., & Labouvie-Vief, G. (1976). Conceptualization of sex-roles: A life-span developmental study. *Developmental Psychology, 12,* 15–23.

Vandenberg, S. G., & Kuse, A. R. (1979). Spatial ability: A critical review of the sex-linked major gene hypothesis. In M.A. Wittig & A.C. Petersen (Eds.), *Sex-related differences in cognitive functioning.* New York: Academic Press.

Vener, A., & Snyder, C. A. (1966). The preschool child's awareness and anticipation of adult sex-roles. *Sociometry, 29,* 159–168.

Waber, D. P. (1977). Sex differences in mental abilities, hemispheric lateralization, and rate of physical growth at adolescence. *Developmental Psychology, 13,* 29–38.

Waber, D. P. (1979). Cognitive abilities and sex-related variations in the maturation of cerebral cortical functions. In M. A. Wittig & A. C. Petersen (Eds.), *Sex-related differences in cognitive functioning.* New York: Academic Press.

Waber, D. P., Bauermeister, M., Cohen, C., Ferber, R., & Wolff, P. H. (1981). Behavioral correlates of physical and neuromotor maturity in adolescents from different environments. *Developmental Psychobiology, 14,* 513–522.

Ward, W. D. (1969). Process of sex-role development. *Developmental Psychology, 1,* 163–168.

Weinraub, M., Clemens, L. P., Sockloff, A., Etheridge, T., Gracely, E., & Myers, B. (1984). The development of sex-role stereotypes in the third year: Relationships to gender labeling, gender identity, sex-typed toy preference, and family characteristics. *Child Development, 55,* 1493–1503.

Welch, R. L., Huston-Stein, A., Wright, J. C., & Plehal, R. (1979). Subtle sex-role cues in children's commercials. *Journal of Communication, 29,* 202–209.

Whitbeck, C. (1976). Theories of sex differences. In C.C. Gould & M.W. Wartofsky (Eds.), *Women and philosophy: Toward a theory of liberation.* New York: G.P. Putnam.

Whitley, B. E. (1983). Sex role orientation and self-esteem: A critical meta-analytic review. *Journal of Personality and Social Psychology, 44,* 765–778.

Whitley, B. E. (1985). Sex role orientation and psychological well-being: Two meta-analyses. *Sex Roles, 12,* 207–225.

Williams, J. E., Bennett, S., & Best, D. (1975). Awareness and expression of sex stereotypes in young children. *Developmental Psychology, 11,* 635–642.

Williams, J. H. (1983). *Psychology of women.* New York: Norton.

Wittig, M. A. (1976). Sex differences in intellectual functioning: How much of a difference do genes make? *Sex Roles: A Journal of Research, 2,* 63–74.

Wittig, M. A. (1985). Metatheoretical dilemmas in the psychology of gender. *American Psychologist, 40,* 800–811.

Yorburg, B. (1974). *Sexual identity, sex roles and social change.* New York: Wiley.

Zanna, M. P., & Pack, S. J. (1975). On the self-fulfilling nature of apparent sex differences in behavior. *Journal of Experimental Social Psychology, 11,* 583–591.

Zucker, K. J. (1982). Childhood gender disturbance: Diagnostic issues. *Journal of the American Academy of Child Psychiatry, 21,* 274–280.

10 The Development of Prosocial and Aggressive Behavior

Nancy Eisenberg
Arizona State University

INTRODUCTION

Issues related to altruism and aggression have been of interest to psychologists, philosophers, and laypersons alike because of the impact such behaviors have on social interactions and the quality of human life. Among psychologists, interest in aggression has been more pervasive and consistent (e.g.. Dollard, Doob, Miller, Mowrer, & Sears, 1939) than has interest in altruism, perhaps because the extreme consequences of aggression—crime, war, death, injury, and destruction—are obvious and compelling whereas the consequences of altruism are less salient. However altruism has received considerable attention especially since the brutal stabbing and murder of Kitty Genovese in 1964, which was witnessed by 38 persons, none of whom did anything to assist. The press coverage of this incident shocked people by illustrating public apathy and stimulated prominent psychologists to examine the circumstances under which people assist one another.

In this chapter, the development both of aggression and of such positive behaviors as altruism are examined. Factors that may facilitate or inhibit such behavior, especially socialization and personal characteristics, are emphasized; situational factors (e.g., the cost of a given behavior) are not reviewed as broadly. Comprehensive reviews of relevant theory and research concerning altruism and aggression are available elsewhere (Eisenberg, 1982, 1986; Lefkowitz, Eron, Walder, & Husemann, 1977; Parke & Slaby, 1983; Radke-Yarrow, Zahn-Waxler, & Chapman, 1983; Rushton & Sorrentino, 1981).

The first issue considered in this chapter is developmental change in aggressive and prosocial responding. In recent years, researchers have learned exciting information about the early development of prosocial behavior and have been seeking to chart the course of prosocial and aggressive development throughout childhood. Next, factors that might account for both developmental and individual differences in aggressive and prosocial behavior are discussed. Such variables include biological (genetic) factors, as well as factors such as role-taking, interpersonal problem-solving capabilities, moral reasoning, and emotional responsivity (e.g., empathy). There has been some controversy regarding the degree to which some of these factors (e.g., heredity) affect the development of social behaviors such as those discussed in this chapter. The third topic that is addressed is the role of socialization in the development of prosocial and aggressive tendencies. Finally, an integrative model of moral action is used to illustrate the possible interrelations among the many variables that seem to affect prosocial and aggressive responding. By means of this model I hope to illustrate how cognitive, affective, and socialization variables are all relevant to an understanding of moral and social development.

It is essential to define altruism and aggression before turning to the substance of this chapter, because definitions of these concepts have varied across researchers and theoretical perspectives (see Eisenberg, 1982; Parke & Slaby, 1983). Both altruism and aggression have been defined in terms of their positive and negative consequences for others. In recent years, however, notions regarding *intentions* have been incorporated into many definitions. In specific, altruism frequently has been defined as voluntary behavior that is intended to benefit another and is not motivated by the expectation of external reward (Eisenberg, 1982, 1986; Staub, 1978). Altruism is considered to be a subtype of the larger category of prosocial behavior—that is, voluntary behavior intended to benefit another, regardless of motive. Similarly, recent researchers define aggression not solely in terms of its negative consequences for others, but as behavior "that is aimed at harming or injuring another person or persons" (Parke & Slaby, 1983, p. 550).

Unfortunately, in many situations it is not possible to determine an actor's motives or whether a given act was intentional. Thus, in reviewing relevant research, it is not possible to confine discussion to studies in which it is clear that altruism or aggression, as defined previously, occurred. Rather it is necessary to examine the broader domain of prosocial responding as well as a range of behaviors that appear to be aggressive (i.e., behaviors in which an individual injures another, whether or not the behavior was intentional or motivated by the desire to harm another). This reality unfortunately results in a greater focus on the consequences of individuals' actions than on their motives.

DEVELOPMENTAL TRENDS

Prosocial Behavior

Until relatively recently, many researchers seemed to assume that young children were egoistic until approximately 6 to 7 years of age. This was because Piaget and Inhelder (1956) found that children younger than this were not as capable as children aged 6-7 years at taking another's perspective (which would be expected to relate positively to altruistic behavior; see Underwood & Moore, 1982b). However, it is now clear that young children are capable of both limited perspective-taking (e.g., Shantz, 1983) and other-oriented prosocial behaviors (Radke-Yarrow, Zahn-Waxler, & Chapman, 1983). Although children 6 months of age apparently do not try to help and exhibit little empathy toward distressed peers (Hay, Nash, & Pedersen, 1981), children 12 months of age often react in an agitated manner to another's distress (Radke-Yarrow & Zahn-Waxler, 1984). In the second year of life, children not only respond emotionally to another's distress (e.g., Radke-Yarrow & Zahn-Waxler, 1984; Weston & Main, 1980), but begin to comfort distressed others (Radke-Yarrow & Zahn-Waxler, 1984), help others with tasks and chores (Rheingold, 1979), and share objects (Rheingold, Hay, & West, 1976). Such other-oriented behaviors increase in frequency during the second year of life, and also are likely to become more effective with age (Hoffman, 1984; Radke-Yarrow & Zahn-Waxler, 1984).

There is considerable evidence that preschool and school-aged children frequently behave prosocially (Radke-Yarrow et al., 1983; Underwood & Moore, 1982a). It appears that some types of prosocial actions (such as donating) generally increase in frequency in the school years, whereas others (such as comforting) may not (Radke-Yarrow et al., 1983). Moreover, there is evidence that the ways in which children react to others' distresses (e.g., with emotionality, avoidance, or cognitive evaluation) are stable from age 2 to age 6 or 7 for many children (Radke-Yarrow & Zahn-Waxler, 1984). Little is known about developmental changes in altruistic responding in adulthood (see Eisenberg & Fabes, in press).

There are conceptual reasons to expect some types of prosocial behaviors, especially altruistic behaviors, to increase with age. Some evidence suggests that parents increasingly encourage prosocial behavior in the first two years of life (Power & Parke, 1986). Moreover, some capabilities that have been conceptually linked to altruism and are positively related to prosocial responding (e.g., role-taking and moral reasoning) increase with age during childhood. Some of these, as well as other attributes or capacities that are related to prosocial behavior during childhood, are reviewed later in this chapter.

Aggressive Behavior

Aggressive behavior is evident among humans from an early age. Conflicted or disruptive interactions are quite common among children as young as 1 to 2 years of age. Such interactions appear to decrease somewhat in frequency during the third year of life, particularly in relation to positive behaviors (Holmberg, 1980; Maudry & Nekula, 1939). For example, Hay and Ross (1982), in a study of pairs of unacquainted 21-month-olds, found that most children engaged in at least one conflict during 1 hour of time (split into four 15-minute sessions). These conflicts tended to be brief (22.7 seconds), and most of the time (72%) involved contested objects. Instrumental behaviors (e.g., trying to grab a toy) were more effective than communicative actions such as gesturing or verbally requesting. Moreover, there was stability in children's tendencies to initiate disputes over a period of four days; thus, dispositional factors apparently influenced the children's behavior even at 21 months of age.

In the preschool years, children's physical aggression appears to decrease whereas verbal aggression increases (Goodenough, 1931; Jersild & Markey, 1935). Moreover, Hartup (1974) found that 4- to 6-year-olds exhibited more *instrumental* aggression (aggression aimed at retrieval of an object, privilege, or territory) than did 6- to 7-year-olds; whereas 6- to 7-year-olds exhibited more *hostile* aggression (aggression aimed at hurting another) than did 4- to 6-year-olds.

With increasing age, elementary-school children become more adept at differentiating accidental from intentional provocations (Ferguson & Rule, 1980; Shantz & Voydanoff, 1973; also see Parke & Slaby, 1983). This sociocognitive understanding would be expected to affect the likelihood that children would counteraggress if they were injured by another accidently. However, aggressive elementary-school boys do not seem to be very skilled at discerning the fact that an apparently aggressive act was unintentional when cues regarding the other's motive are ambiguous (Dodge, 1980).

Individual differences in level of aggression appear to be quite stable throughout childhood. Hay and Ross (1982) noted stability in 21-month-olds' behavior over a four-day period. Other researchers have noted high levels of stability in males' aggressiveness throughout childhood (Lefkowitz, Eron, Walder, & Huesmann, 1977; Olweus, 1977, 1979; Parke & Slaby, 1983). Moreover, boys have demonstrated high consistency across different modes of aggressive expression, for example, between verbal attack and engaging in passive yet coercive and manipulative behavior (Deluty, 1985b). Somewhat less stability over time (Kagan & Moss, 1962) and consistency across modes of aggression (Deluty, 1985b) has been noted by some researchers studying girls; however, in a recent review Olweus (1982; cited in Parke & Slaby, 1983) found nearly as high estimates of stability for girls (.44) as for boys (.50). It is possible that aggressiveness is stable for girls during childhood but not from childhood into adolescence (Parke & Slaby, 1983). Clearly, aggressive behavior is considered less acceptable for adolescent and adult females than males and, consequently, older females may be socialized to be less aggressive than males (Parke & Slaby, 1983).

THE ROLE OF BIOLOGICAL FACTORS IN AGGRESSION AND ALTRUISM

Perhaps because of the widespread occurrence of aggression in the animal world as well as in human society, theorists often have suggested that aggressive behavior may be ascribable, at least in part, to biological factors (e.g., Dollard, Doob, Miller, Mowrer, & Sears, 1939; Lorenz, 1966; see Parke & Slaby, 1983, for a review of theories). Moreover, in recent years, sociobiologists like Wilson (1978) have suggested that altruism also has a biological basis. Thus there has been a considerable amount of research concerning the relation of biological factors to aggressive and prosocial behavior.

One common approach to studying the role of biology in aggressive behavior has been to examine the relation of aggressive behavior to hormones, especially masculine hormones such as androgens. In the research on nonhuman subjects, there is fairly reliable evidence that male hormones are positively related to agonistic behavior, at least for some species (Tieger, 1980; also see Ruble, this volume). The data are somewhat less consistent for humans, however (Parke & Slaby, 1983), although there is some evidence of a relation between testosterone levels and some types of male aggression, especially aggressive responses to threat or provocation (e.g., Mattsson, Schalling, Olweus, & Low, 1980; Olweus, Mattsson, Schalling, & Low, 1980).

Another way in which biology may indirectly influence aggressive responding is through temperamental differences. There is clear evidence of individual differences in temperament from early in life (e.g., Korner, Zeanah, Linden, Berkowtiz, Kraemer, & Agras, 1985; St. Clair, 1978). These, and differences in related personality dimensions, likely are due, in part, to genetic factors (Mednick, Gabrielli, & Hutchings, 1984; Rushton, Fulker, Neale, Nias, & Eysenck, 1986; also see Campos, Barrett, Lamb, Goldsmith, & Stenberg, 1983; Goldsmith, 1983; Scarr & Kidd, 1983). Moreover it appears that differences in temperament (real and/or as perceived by parents) are also associated with differential treatment by parents (e.g., more intrusive control factors), as well as with more conflict between mother and child (Bates, Maslin, & Frankel, 1985; Lee & Bates, 1985; see Daniels, Plomin, & Greenhalgh, 1984, however). The results of conflicted interaction may be higher levels of aggression and more behavioral problems (Lee & Bates, 1985; Olweus, 1980). Such an outcome is likely, given that the style of interaction found between mothers and difficult infants resembles the one Patterson (1982) has identified in families with aggressive boys (see pp. 43–44).

In comparison to the work on human aggression, there is far less empirical work related to the biological bases of human altruism. This is despite the fact that some sociobiologists have argued that social behaviors such as altruism have a strong genetic basis because they are adaptive in an evolutionary sense. They have noted the frequent occurrence of altruism among groups of animals who live together (Wilson, 1978). In Wilson's view, altruism has evolved because individuals who assist those around them (who tend to be kin) pass on their genes by preserving those genes in their relatives. Other sociobiologists have argued that other mechanisms such as the return of favors by recipients of aid (Trivers, 1971), or cultural factors (e.g., Campbell, 1975, 1983), affect the transmission of prosocial behavior from one generation to the next.

Research with humans regarding the heritability of altruism is only suggestive. In twin studies adults' self-reports of altruism, nurturance, and empathy have been found to be more similar among monozygotic than dizygotic same-sex pairs of twins (Mathews, Batson, Horn, & Rosenman, 1981; Rushton et al., 1986). Although it is possible that part of the similarity between monozygotic twins is due to genetically-based personality traits that influence how individuals wish to appear to themselves and/or to others (i.e., how they respond to self-report questionnaires), it is likely that genetic factors actually influence prosocial responding. It is not clear whether this effect is mediated by hormonal factors, differences in the brain that affect empathizing (see Hoffman, 1981), or other unknown factors. Nonetheless, it is clear that one cannot ignore the potential heritability of factors related to the performance of prosocial and aggressive acts.

In summary, it appears that genetic factors play a role in individual differences in prosocial and aggressive behavior. However, the ways in which genetic factors actually influence aggressive and prosocial behavior are less clear. Because the role of biology in social behavior has become a popular, albeit controversial issue, it is likely that more will be learned about this issue in the coming years.

CAPABILITIES RELATED TO PROSOCIAL RESPONDING

True altruism generally is believed to be motivated by either empathic or sympathetic responsiveness or the desire to adhere to internalized moral principles (e.g., Batson, in press; Eisenberg, 1986; Hoffman, in press; Staub, 1979). Thus, empathy and the capacities related to empathizing and moral internalization are of central importance in theories and research concerning altruism. Moreover, psychologists frequently have suggested that the ability to empathize with the victim of one's own aggression (e.g., Feshbach, 1978) and to understand another's motives and feelings (e.g., Dodge, 1980) are associated with low levels of aggressive responding. For these reasons, it is necessary to review individual differences in relevant emotional and sociocognitive capabilities in relation to aggressive and prosocial behavior.

Empathy

Altruism.   As was noted previously, philosophers (e.g., Blum, 1980; Hume, 1777/1966) and psychologists (Batson, in press; Eisenberg, 1986; Hoffman, 1984, and Chapter 11 of this volume; Staub, 1979) have often cited empathy (or sympathy) as an important mediator of altruistic responding. The assumption is that people who vicariously experience another's distress, sadness, or other such reactions are motivated to alleviate the other's need.

In general, empirical research supports the assumption that empathy (and sympathetic concern, which is often associated with empathy) tends to be positively related to prosocial responding (see Eisenberg & Miller, 1987). Especially among older children and adults, experiencing another's affect predicts subsequent assisting of that person, and empathic persons seem to assist others more than do less-empathic persons. As was discussed previously, this relation has been noted even among young children, at least in situations involving familiar others (Radke-Yarrow & Zahn-Waxler, 1984; Weston & Main, 1980).

Of course, not all prosocial behavior is motivated by empathic or sympathetic reactions. In many situations people may assist others for nonaltruistic motives, for example to attain rewards or social approval, or they may assist because of the desire to adhere to internalized moral values (Bar-Tal, 1982; Eisenberg, 1986). Moreover, in some situations in which people could assist, there is no reason to feel empathy or sympathy because the potential recipient of aid does not seem distressed and/or there are no cues regarding the other's emotional state.

Alternatively, people often respond to others' distresses by feeling anxiety or other negative emotional reactions that are experienced as self-concern and that result in a self-orientation rather than an other-orientation. Such a reaction has been called *empathic distress* (Hoffman, 1984) or *personal distress* (Batson, in press), and may be especially common among young children because they have greater difficulty than older persons in distinguishing between their own and others' internal states (Hoffman, 1984; Radke-Yarrow & Zahn-Waxler, 1984). When individuals experience predominantly personal distress in reaction to another's situation, they should be expected to act in a manner that will reduce their own distress (see Batson, in press). In many instances, escaping from the situation rather than assisting the other person presents the easiest way to reduce feelings of personal distress; only when escape is difficult might people who are experiencing personal distress be expected to assist a needy other (see Batson, in press). Indeed, Batson and his colleagues have obtained considerable data suggesting that this is the case for adults, and Eisenberg, McCreath, and Ahn (in press) have obtained partial support for it with preschoolers.

There are methodological as well as conceptual reasons for the fact that some researchers have not found a positive relation between empathy or sympathy and prosocial (especially altruistic) responding. One is that different indices of empathy may assess different things. For example, empathy in children frequently has been assessed with what has been called "picture-story" indices. With measures of this sort, individuals are exposed to stories and/or pictures containing information about another's affective state or situation (e.g., a child who lost his dog). Then they are asked to report, either verbally or by means of nonverbal pointing responses, what they themselves are feeling. Empathy is operationalized by self-report of the emotion that the hypothetical other would be expected to feel (Eisenberg & Lennon, 1983; Hoffman, 1982).

Although most other indices of empathy—such as facial expressions, physiological indices, self-report of emotional reactions in experimental situations, and questionnaires—have been positively associated with prosocial behavior, picture-story indices have not (Eisenberg & Miller, 1987). This may be due to a variety of reasons. For example, the stories used to evoke emotion may be too short to elicit an emotional response. Moreover, it is likely that the use of verbal responses and the presence of demand characteristics (the child is repeatedly asked how he or she feels) make the measure vulnerable to the effects of social desirability (Eisenberg, 1986; Eisenberg & Lennon, 1983; Hoffman, 1982). Other problems include the fact that children may not be able to shift their emotions as quickly as they themselves are shifted from scenario to scenario, and the fact that the experimenter's sex interacts with the child's sex in affecting children's responses (i.e., that children give more empathic responses when tested by same-sex experimenters; Eisenberg & Lennon, 1983). Thus, it is quite possible that picture-story indices of empathy have not been positively related to prosocial behavior because they are not valid indices of emotional empathy.

In summary, there is evidence to support the assumption that altruism is sometimes motivated by sympathetic or empathic reactions. The nature of this interrelation probably changes with age, as children become better able to differentiate between their own and others' emotional reactions and become better able to assist appropriately. Moreover, it is likely that the tendency to respond sympathetically (i.e., with other-oriented concern rather than personal distress) increases with age (see Hoffman, 1984), and therefore affects the quality of prosocial responding. Our understanding of empathy and sympathy is likely to increase considerably in the near future as investigators approach its study with multimethod procedures involving somatic (e.g., facial reactions), physiological (e.g., heart rate), and self-report indices (Eisenberg & Strayer, in press).

Aggression. As was mentioned previously, some psychologists have suggested that empathic and sympathetic reactions play an important role in inhibiting or reducing individuals' aggressive tendencies and behaviors (N. Feshbach, 1978, and in press; S. Feshbach, 1971). It is assumed that vicariously experiencing a victim's distress serves to inhibit further aggression by the empathizer toward the victim, and that empathic and aggressive responses are incompatible.

In fact there seems to be a negative relation between an empathic disposition, as assessed with questionnaires, and school-aged children's and adults' aggression. However, this relation is quite modest; moreover, indices of empathy do not seem to be consistently related to young children's aggression (Miller & Eisenberg, 1986). In addition, for highly aggressive boys, perceiving cues related to another's pain may be positively related to aggression (Hartmann, 1969; Perry & Perry, 1974). Thus the relation of empathy to aggression seems to be of lesser strength than the relation of empathy to prosocial behavior. This may be because individuals who wish to injure another sometimes may use the information gained by empathizing to ascertain that they are successful in their aggression. Moreover, in many instances people probably ignore or distort their victims' cues and therefore do not empathize with their victims' experience (Bandura, 1973).

Perspective-Taking and Related Sociocognitive Capabilities

Perspective-Taking. Another factor that has been linked theoretically to altruism and to low levels of aggression is the ability to take the affective or cognitive perspective of another—that is, to understand and infer another's feelings and emotional reactions, thoughts, motives, and intentions (Batson, in press; Eisenberg, 1986; Hoffman, 1984; Parke & Slaby, 1983). The assumption has been that young children or adults with limited perspective-taking tendencies or capacities should be less likely than those with more sophisticated capacities to infer when another is in need or distress. Consequently, such persons should be relatively unlikely to attend to another's need, which should lessen the probability that the individual will empathize with the other, attempt to assist in the other's need, or cease aggression toward the other. Moreover, perspective-taking may facilitate sympathy even when another's need is obvious, or may be a source of knowledge which elicits feelings of social responsibility based on internalized values or norms.

Perspective-taking abilities have been especially important in developmental models of altruism because some aspects of prosocial responding increase with age (Moore & Eisenberg, 1984; Radke-Yarrow et al., 1983). Because perspective-taking skills have been found to improve dramatically with age (e.g., Selman, 1980; Shantz, 1983) and to reflect an understanding of others' feelings, it is logical that perspective-taking capabilities often have been cited as mediating age-related advances in prosocial behavior. Similarly, advances in perspective-taking could be responsible in part for the age-related decrease in some types of aggression (e.g., object-related aggression).

Consistent with theory and logic, there appears to be a significant positive relation between perspective-taking capabilities (as assessed with laboratory tasks) and prosocial behavior (Eisenberg, 1986; Underwood & Moore, 1982). However, this relation has not been found in a number of studies (e.g., Eisenberg-Berg & Lennon, 1980; Rushton & Weiner, 1975; Zahn-Waxler, Radke-Yarrow, & Brady-Smith, 1977). Moreover, although training in role-taking has been positively related to a decrease in delinquent acts for 11- to 13-year-old delinquents (Chandler, 1973), it has not been consistently related to the inhibition of aggression for nondelinquent children (e.g., Iannotti, 1978; see Parke & Slaby, 1983). It is likely that a variety of factors, conceptual and methodological, account for the variation in results across studies.

One important fallacy pervading much of the relevant research is the view that perspective-taking usually or always should relate positively to prosocial behavior and negatively to aggressive behavior. However, a significant relation should occur only if the act in question requires, or would be facilitated or inhibited by, an understanding of the other's feelings or cognitions. Often this simply is not the case. Evidence of the other's need may be clear to nearly all, or the other may not even be in any distress or need. Moreover, performance of a particular prosocial behavior may be relatively unthinking and automatic, either because of its low cost as in the care of helping when one has nothing else to do (Langer, Blank, & Chanowitz, 1978; Eisenberg & Shell, 1986; also see Karniol, 1982) or because of its compelling crisislike quality (Piliavin, Dovidio, Gaertner, & Clark, 1981). Alternatively, a prosocial act may be motivated by a variety of factors other than an understanding of others' feelings and cognitions; for example, the need for approval or the desire to obtain concrete rewards. Similarly, aggressive acts are often performed for reasons that are more related to the aggressor's feelings than to the victim's.

Another possible reason for the relatively weak association between perspective-taking and prosocial or aggressive behavior in some studies is methodological. Perspective-taking is often assessed in one situation, whereas behavior is assessed in another context that does not require perspective-taking skills. Moreover, many instruments used to assess perspective-taking may not be adequate. For some of the instruments, the inferential processing inherent in perspective-taking is not necessary or sufficient for success (Higgins, 1981). For example, in one measure, children are asked to select appropriate gifts for their parents and peers (Zahn-Waxler et al., 1977). To do so, children may access information stored in their memories regarding others' preferences, rather than engage in active perspective-taking (Higgins, Feldman, & Ruble, 1980; Higgins & Parsons, 1983). Moreover, given that perspective-taking skills change dramatically with age, it is important that the appropriate instrument be used with a given age group. If an instrument is too simple or too difficult, children may not vary much in their responses and there may be a ceiling or floor effect, which would reduce the likelihood of finding a significant correlation between perspective-taking and any other variable.

In brief, there is empirical support for the assumption that perspective-taking facilitates prosocial behavior and may sometimes inhibit aggression, although not in all situations. It is likely that this empirical relation would be stronger if appropriate indices of perspective-taking were used in all studies, and if perspective-taking were examined in relation to specific behaviors for which it is likely to be relevant. Nonetheless, it should be noted that perspective-taking is merely an inferential capacity that can be used for a variety of purposes, including Machiavellian purposes. Indeed, a worthy goal for future research would be to delineate further the circumstances in which perspective taking can be expected to relate meaningfully to behavior.

Interpersonal Problem-Solving Skills.   Perspective-taking capabilities represent one set of sociocognitive skills that has been examined in relation to prosocial and aggressive behaviors. A related set of skills, called interpersonal problem-solving skills, has also received considerable attention. Some of these skills tend to be correlated with perspective-taking (Shure, 1982), but they are somewhat different from it. Specifically, interpersonal problem-solving skills include the following: (a) sensitivity to the existence of potential interpersonal problems; (b) alternative-solution thinking (the ability to generate a variety of different solutions to interpersonal problems); (c) means–end thinking (the ability to articulate the steps that may be necessary in order to carry out the solution to an interpersonal problem); (d) consequential thinking (the ability to consider the consequences of social acts for others as well as the self, and to generate alternative consequences to a social action prior to deciding what to do); and (e) causal thinking (an understanding of the fact that how one feels and acts may have been influenced by, and in turn may influence, how others feel and act) (see Shure, 1982; Spivack, Platt, & Shure, 1976).

As for perspective-taking, interpersonal problem-solving skills increase with age (Marsh, 1982). Moreover, these skills have been positively associated with positive peer interactions, helpfulness, and concern for others (Marsh, Serafica, & Barenboim, 1981; Olson, Johnson, Belleau, Parks, & Barrett, 1983; Shure, 1980), and negatively related to aggression (Gouze, Rayias, & Bieber-Schneider, 1983; Marsh et al., 1981). In addition, training in interpersonal problem-solving skills has been associated with increases in children's prosocial behaviors (Spivack & Shure, 1974). These relations sometimes have been positive and significant for one sex but not the other, and for some interpersonal problem-solving skills and not others (Deluty, 1985a; Marsh et al., 1981; Olson et al., 1983; see Eisenberg, 1986). Nonetheless, the data are consistent with the conclusion that aggressive and prosocial actions often are mediated, in part, by individuals' abilities to understand interpersonal situations, the possible alternative solutions to social dilemmas, and the manner in which various solutions can be carried out and can affect outcomes.

Perhaps the most detailed model of how sociocognitive abilities affect behavior is Dodge's (1985) social-information processing model of aggression. He has suggested a five-step sequence of processing; children who do not process cues in the sequence suggested are viewed as more likely to enact aggressive behaviors. Dodge's five steps are as follows: (a) *encoding* (includes the perception of social cues, the search for cues, and attention to cues); (b) *interpretation* (includes integration of memory store, goals, and new data; search for interpretations; match of data to programmed rule structure); (c) *response search* (includes search for responses and generation of potential responses); (d) *response decision* (includes assessment of consequences of potential responses, evaluation of adequacy of potential responses, and decision of optimal response); and (e) *enactment* (includes behavioral repertoire search and emission of behavior). Dodge has suggested that socially competent behavior occurs only when one has successfully completed all five steps.

Dodge found that aggressive boys were especially likely to attribute hostile intentions to others whose actions resulted in negative consequences, but only when the others' intentions were ambiguous (Dodge, 1980). This may be because aggressive boys tend to react more quickly and with less attention to available social cues when making attributions than do less aggressive boys; indeed, aggressive boys overattributed hostility to peers in unwarranted circumstances only when they responded quickly (Dodge & Newman, 1981). Moreover, Dodge and Frame (1982) found that aggressive boys exhibited selective recall of hostile cues, which accounts, in part, for their biased attributions. Thus, it appears that aggressive boys exhibit deficits in encoding in some situations (e.g., ambiguous ones) and may also have problems with interpretation of data. In addition, based on other work (Eisenberg, 1986; Shure, 1982; Spivack et al., 1976), it would appear that impulsive and inhibited children also may have problems generating alternative responses and assessing the adequacy and consequences of alternative modes of action.

In summary, it is clear that sociocognitive and information-processing capabilities are related to the quality of children's social behaviors. When considering such capabilities, however, it is important to note that individuals may differ both in their capacities to process socially relevant information in optimal ways, and in their tendencies to do so.

The Relation of Moral Reasoning to Prosocial and Aggressive Behavior

People act prosocially and aggressively for a variety of reasons. For example, people help others for concrete rewards, for public approval, to improve their relations with others, in response to feelings of sympathy for others, because of the desire to act in a manner consistent with internalized values and norms, and for other reasons. Assisting others for value-based reasons (as well as sympathy) generally has been considered as more moral than assisting for egoistic reasons (although some persons have argued that individuals adhere to internalized values for egoistic reasons—that is, to avoid self-censure; Batson, in press). Similarly, inhibition of aggression due to concern for the other or to one's internalized principles is considered more moral than failing to aggress due to fear of retribution. It is because of the salient role of values in theories of morality that researchers interested in prosocial and aggressive behavior have studied its relation to moral judgment.

Building upon the earlier work of Piaget (1932/1965), Kohlberg (1981, 1984) has delineated a well-known sequence of stages of moral reasoning. These stages, which are believed to develop with age and exposure to social role-taking opportunities (Colby, Kohlberg, Gibbs, & Lieberman, 1983; Kohlberg, 1981), reflect a range of motives from blind obedience to authority and the desire to avoid punishment to a personal commitment to internalized, universal moral principles (see Hoffman, in this volume).

Kohlberg studied the development of moral reasoning by presenting individuals with hypothetical moral dilemmas (e.g., about a man who stole a drug to save his wife's life), and then asking them to resolve the dilemma and explain their reasoning. Most of his dilemmas were concerned with the violation of laws, rules, authorities' dictates, or formal obligations (e.g., in regard to stealing, killing, disobeying parents, breaking promises). Although prosocial action— such as stealing a drug to help one's wife—was a possibility in a few dilemmas, the possibility of such prosocial action was always at the cost of violating a formal prohibition—in this case, breaking the law. In contrast, some researchers recently have examined moral reasoning about dilemmas in which prosocial action and the conflict between one's own and others' needs are salient (e.g., Eisenberg, 1982, 1986; Eisenberg, Lennon, & Roth, 1983; Eisenberg-Berg, 1979; Gilligan, 1977).

In recent years, cognitive-developmental theorists have argued that the level of one's moral reasoning should be positively related to the quality and extent of one's moral behavior, although this relation is not expected to be direct or simple (see Blasi, 1980; Eisenberg, 1986, 1987; Kohlberg & Candee, 1984). One assumption is that people's moral reasoning reflects the general ordering of their values, and the logic used to prioritize their needs, wants, values, and goals when these conflict in a given situation (Berndt, 1981; Eisenberg, 1986; Staub, 1982).

Consistent with this theory, the level of moral reasoning has been found to relate positively to some moral behaviors, including prosocial behaviors (Blasi, 1980; Eisenberg, 1986; Underwood & Moore, 1982b). Children or adults who reason at developmentally advanced levels, which tend to reflect more other-oriented concerns and moral principles, are more likely to help or share than are their counterparts who reason at less-mature levels. Moreover, prosocial behaviors seem to be associated with children's and adolescents' use of other-oriented modes of reasoning (i.e., those reflecting role-taking, empathy, or sympathy) used when responding to prosocial moral dilemmas (Eisenberg, 1986). In addition, children who exhibit a higher quality of prosocial behavior—that is, more altruistic—tend to provide higher level justifications for their prosocial actions than do children who assist in situations requiring less altruism (Bar-Tal, 1982). This latter finding is consistent with the view that individuals' moral reasoning affects their actions, although it is also possible that self-reported motives derive, in part, from a post hoc examination of the quality of one's own prior actions (see Eisenberg, 1986).

Level of moral judgment seems to be associated with aggressive as well as prosocial behavior. In general, delinquent individuals tend to use lower level reasoning than do matched nondelinquents, although there is considerable interindividual variation in the level at which delinquents reason (Blasi, 1980; Jurkovic, 1980). For some delinquents, moral reasoning seems to be retarded due to limited logical and perspective-taking capabilities (e.g., Chandler, 1973; Jurkovic & Prentice, 1977), which may have biological, temperamental, personality, or familial roots (Jurkovic, 1980). However, it is likely that many delinquents are capable of higher level reasoning, which they do not use on account of deficiencies in other cognitive or noncognitive processes that affect evocation or utilization of existing sociocognitive capabilities. For example, Jurkovic (1980) has suggested that delinquent youths may not have developed the ability to consolidate necessary intellectual skills (e.g., memory). Alternatively, affective processes (e.g., anxiety, emotional conflict) may interfere with the delinquent's utilization of higher level moral reasoning processes. Moreover, situational factors such as a negative response from peers may prevent a person from functioning at his or her optimal level. Finally, some children simply may not value higher level moral concepts even if they understand them (Jurkovic, 1980; Lickona, 1976), due to experiences in their families, peer groups, or communities.

Although there appears to be an association between the level of moral judgment and the performance of prosocial and aggressive behaviors, one should not expect a positive relation in all situations. Lower level reasoning may be positively related to prosocial action that is motivated by egoistic concerns (e.g., people may assist because they expect a monetary reward for doing so), whereas aggressive acts are sometimes motivated by higher level moral principles (e.g., support for a "just" war). Moreover, in many circumstances, pro- or antisocial behavior may be enacted without much conscious processing. In such situations, situational cues, habitual patterns of behavior, or a variety of personal preferences may be more relevant than the individual's level of moral reasoning. With regard to prosocial acts, those that are low in cost may be especially likely to be unrelated to moral reasoning because behaviors with little cost to the self are unlikely to evoke moral conflict and are quite likely to be performed without much thought (Eisenberg & Shell, 1986).

In summary, the existing research is consistent with the view that the way people resolve moral dilemmas bears some relation to their social behavior if that behavior involves moral issues. Those who reason in a more mature manner frequently behave in more altruistic and less antisocial ways. However, this relation between reasoning and behavior is only of moderate strength, and many other factors undoubtedly mediate the relation (e.g., costs for helping). Moreover, it is likely that acting in ways that are moral sometimes may facilitate the development of higher level moral judgment. Inconsistency between one's actions and one's cognitions may serve as a stimulus for further development in moral reasoning, due to the need to maintain consistency between one's behaviors and beliefs (i.e., due to the need to reduce cognitive dissonance; see Rholes & Lane, 1985). In addition, engaging in potentially moral behavior may provide the opportunity for learning about others' feelings and perspectives (i.e., may enhance role-taking), which in turn may stimulate the development of moral judgment. In brief, it is likely that the causal relation between moral reasoning and moral behavior is neither direct nor unidirectional.

THE SOCIALIZATION OF PROSOCIAL AND
AGGRESSIVE BEHAVIOR

Prosocial and aggressive behavior may have biological roots and may be a function, in part, of inherent personal characteristics. However, it is also clear that social influences affect the development and maintenance of prosocial and aggressive behavior and that characteristics of the individual and his or her social environment mutually influence one another (e.g., Grusec & Kuczynski, 1980; Keller & Bell, 1979; see Parke & Slaby, 1983).

In most relevant studies, especially of altruism, the effects of a particular child-rearing procedure on children's behavior have been examined, rather than the outcome of the mutual interaction of child and environmental factors. Moreover, investigators have usually examined the influence of a single socialization factor on children's behavior rather than the effect of a configuration of practices (e.g., warmth combined with high standards and the use of reasoning as discipline). Therefore, most of the following review includes the results of studies in which the focus was on the effect of one specific child-rearing practice; however, some relevant research concerning configurations of child-rearing practices also is reviewed.

Among the social factors that influence the development of prosocial and aggressive behavior are both cultural factors and the practices of socializers in the child's everyday world. The literature concerning child-rearing factors in the everyday context is much more abundant and informative than the research concerning cultural factors. Nonetheless, it should be noted that cultural factors such as routine assignment of responsibility for others within the family unit, and the societal emphasis on cooperative, prosocial behavior rather than self-oriented behavior, appear, based on the available research, to enhance positive behavior, including prosocial behavior (e.g., Bronfenbrenner, 1970; Kagan & Madsen, 1972; Whiting & Whiting, 1975; see Mussen & Eisenberg-Berg, 1977; Radke-Yarrow et al., 1983). Unfortunately, however, there is little research concerning cultural influences on the emergence of altruistic or hostile behaviors. Thus it is unclear to which degree, and in which ways, cultural values and practices affect altruistic and aggressive responding.

Discipline

Students of socialization have focused on the relation between children's moral behavior and specific disciplinary practices (i.e., practices used in reaction to sins of omission or commission). This is because disciplinary encounters provide a clear opportunity for socialization agents to instruct, preach, and punish, and in other ways attempt to shape children's behavior. Commonly used modes of discipline include punitive and inductive (i.e., reasoning) approaches.

Punitive approaches. Punitive tactics include physical punishment and the withdrawal of objects or privileges, or the threat thereof. They involve the use of power to impose one's will on another (Hoffman, 1970; and Chapter 11 of this volume).

The literature is inconsistent with regard to the relationship between punitive techniques and both prosocial and aggressive behavior (Moore & Eisenberg, 1984; Parke & Slaby, 1983; Radke-Yarrow et al., 1983). Although punitive procedures infrequently have been positively related to prosocial behavior (as in Hoffman & Saltzstein, 1967, for boys), they have been both negatively related (e.g., Abelson, 1985; Bar-Tal, Nadler, & Blechman, 1980; Dlugokinski & Firestone, 1974) and unrelated (e.g., Feshbach, 1975; Mussen, Rutherford, Harris, & Keasey, 1970; Zahn-Waxler, Radke-Yarrow, & King, 1979) to prosocial outcomes. Similarly, although punitive discipline often has been positively associated with aggression (e.g., Bandura & Walters, 1963; Baumrind, 1971; Hoffman, 1960; see Parke & Slaby, 1983), it is not clear that parental punitiveness has long-term effects on children's aggression (Eron, Walder, & Lefkowitz, 1971; Lefkowitz et al., 1977).

What might explain these inconsistent findings? One possible explanation is that different behaviors are included in researchers' measures of punitive discipline, such as love withdrawal (e.g., Abelson, 1985) or some combination of controlling, demanding, rejection, and/or restrictive reasoning practices (e.g., Feshbach, 1975; Turner & Harris, 1984). More important, the effect of punitive practices appears to be related to the severity of the practices and to the child-rearing context in which it is embedded. For example, Baumrind (1971, 1986) reported that parents who provided a nurturant, responsive child-rearing environment, yet maintained high standards and occasionally used power-assertive techniques, tended to rear socially responsible boys (their girls were neither high nor low in social responsibility). However, when parental demands were enforced in a punitive, authoritarian context, boys exhibited relatively low levels of socially responsive behavior. Similarly, Roe (1980) found that children's prosocial and caring behaviors toward others appeared to be unaffected by their mothers' use of physical punishment if punishment occurred in the context of an overall positive relationship. With regard to aggressiveness, high levels of children's aggression have been positively associated with more severe parental punitiveness such as, for example, parental abuse of their children (George & Main, 1979; see Parke & Slaby, 1983). Thus, it is likely that severe punitive practices, especially when embedded in a nonsupportive environment, enhance the probability of children exhibiting aggressive patterns of behavior.

Negative effects of highly punitive practices may occur for several reasons (see Hoffman, 1970, 1983, and in this volume; Moore & Eisenberg, 1984). First, due to the threat inherent in punitive discipline, children may focus their attention on the impending consequences of their behavior for themselves, rather than on the consequences of their behavior for others. Second, when highly punitive procedures are used, control over the child is exerted by actual or implied force, thus providing an external motivation for compliance. In specific, children may learn to attribute the source of their negative arousal to their parents' punitive behaviors rather than to their own transgressions or internal responses, and consequently may generate external self-attributions for their behavior (Dix & Grusec, 1983; Smith, Gelfand, Hartmann, & Partlow, 1979). Third, the high arousal associated with punitive discipline should make it difficult for the child to attend to any information or teaching provided by the parent. Fourth, by using punitive techniques, the parent may model hostile, punitive, and threatening behavior, and thereby communicate that such behavior is an acceptable mode of response to others. This issue becomes especially important if, as suggested by Wolfe, Katell and Drabman (1982), preschool children choose disciplinary procedures for others that match parental practices.

Inductive Procedures.   The use of inductive or reasoning procedures frequently has been viewed as an effective means of promoting children's moral development (Hoffman, 1970 and in this volume). Evidence regarding the effects of inductive techniques is considerably stronger for prosocial than for aggressive behaviors partly due to the scarcity of research concerning the relation of inductive procedures to children's aggression.

In general there appears to be a positive, but somewhat inconsistent, relationship between inductive discipline and prosocial behavior (see Moore & Eisenberg, 1984; Radke-Yarrow et al., 1983). Moreover, there is limited evidence that inductive procedures are negatively related to aggression (e.g., Abelman, 1985).

Inductions apparently can be effective with children as young as $1\frac{1}{2}$ to 2 years of age (Zahn-Waxler, Radke-Yarrow, & King, 1979). Their effectiveness can be enhanced by several factors, including a nonpunitive family context (Abelman, 1985; Hoffman, 1983), maternal affective intensity while delivering inductions (Zahn-Waxler et al., 1979), and the child's prior exposure to inductive techniques (Dlugokinski & Firestone, 1974). Personal characteristics of children such as general responsivity to adults (Keller & Bell, 1979) and perceived temperament (Simonds & Simonds, 1981) may also influence parental preferences for inductive forms of reasoning, and thereby affect children's opportunities to learn about and acquire appropriate social behaviors.

Theorists have identified several aspects of the inductive rearing context that may promote (or perhaps in their absence hinder) children's acquisition of moral behaviors (Dienstbier, 1983; Hoffman, 1970, 1983; Staub, 1979; Zahn-Waxler et al., 1979). By having his or her attention focused on the consequences that inappropriate behavior has on others' feelings and behavior, the child may learn to take the role of others and to empathize with their feelings and needs. Second, children may learn to make appropriate causal attributions concerning the effect of their behavior on others' needs and feelings. Third, inductive messages often are delivered within a supportive care-taking context (Baumrind, 1971). There-fore, although any given inductive message may be accompanied by a strong expression of parental emotion, such emotion is likely to be interpreted by the child as an indication of the value the parent assigns to the situation, rather than to indicate impending physical punishment or personal threat. Consequently, the child may be able and motivated to attend to information provided by the parent about the situation. Fourth, with inductions, a child should be likely to attribute the cause of his or her own negative arousal to the transgression rather than to the threat of punishment or the socializer, and thus develop internal self-attributions for his or her own behavior. In addition, when inductions are accompanied by statements regarding the socializers' expectations and instructions for reparation, children learn not only that they are responsible for the consequences of their behavior, but also how to act responsibly in social interactions. Finally, socializ-ing agents who use inductive reasoning are likely to model a calm, nonpunitive approach to negotiating social interaction, one which children can initiate in other social situations.

Other Nondisciplinary Socialization Techniques

Modeling.   Due, perhaps, to the importance of modeling in social learning theory (Bandura, 1977; 1986), researchers frequently have examined the role of modeling in the development of prosocial and aggressive behavior (Bandura, 1973; Moore & Eisenberg, 1984; Radke-Yarrow et al., 1983). With regard to behavior, they have generally found that exposure to prosocial models enhances the likelihood of subsequent prosocial action whereas exposure to selfish models appears to disinhibit selfish behavior (e.g., Lipscomb, McAllister, & Bregman, 1985; see Moore & Eisenberg, 1984; Radke-Yarrow et al., 1983). The effects of prosocial modeling have been found to persist over time (e.g., Rice & Grusec, 1975; Rushton, 1975) and to generalize to somewhat different situations (e.g., Elliot & Vasta, 1970; Rushton, 1975; Yarrow, Scott, & Waxler, 1973).

Similarly, exposure to aggressive models has been associated with increases in immediate and subsequent aggressive behaviors, even if the model is on television or videotape (Bandura, 1973; Parke & Slaby, 1983; Rushton, 1979; Stein & Friedrich, 1975). Young children may be more likely than older persons to imitate televised violence, although persons of all age groups are susceptible to the effects of viewing television violence (Parke & Slaby, 1983). Further, the effects of televised violence seem considerably stronger and more consistent than the effects of prosocial television content on behavior, although the latter does have a modest positive effect on children's prosocial behavior (Moore & Eisen-berg, 1984; Stein & Friedrich, 1975).

Despite the strong evidence that individuals often imitate prosocial or ag-gressive models, it is clear that modeling is not always an effective means of influence (e.g., Lipscomb, Larrieu, McAllister, & Bregman, 1982; White, 1972; also see Parke & Slaby, 1983; Radke-Yarrow et al., 1983), and that some types of models are imitated more than others. For example, children are more likely to imitate either powerful and/or competent models (e.g., Eisenberg-Berg & Geisheker, 1979; Grusec, 1971) or nurturant models whose warmth is not unconditional (Weissbrod, 1976; Yarrow, Scott, & Waxler, 1973). In contrast, unconditional or noncontingent warmth seems to communicate permissiveness—that anything the child wants to do is acceptable—and therefore children are likely to do as they please after contact with an unconditionally warm model (e.g., not to help if it is costly; Grusec & Skubiski, 1970; Weissbrod, 1976).

The reasons for the effectiveness of modeling procedures have been debated for years (Bandura, 1969, 1986; Kohlberg, 1981). It is likely that modeling teaches children new behaviors, disinhibits and facilitates (i.e., encourages) the display of behaviors already in their repertoires, and provides cues as to the appropriateness of a given behavior (Bandura, 1977, 1986). The behavior of models also can serve as stimulus enhancers (i.e., can draw observers' attention to particular objects and environmental settings), resulting in greater use of certain objects or environments; or the modeled behavior can serve to elicit emotional arousal in observers which can alter the intensity and form of their own behavior (Bandura, 1986). In addition, the fact that children attribute modeled prosocial behavior to internal motives (e.g., altruism) rather than external pressures (Dix & Grusec, 1983) may account, in part, for the effectiveness of modeling procedures at promoting positive behaviors.

Moral Exhortations (Preachings). Individuals not only physically enact behaviors for others to imitate, but also may symbolically—such as verbally—model a course of behavior (e.g., say they are going to behave in a given manner) or promote a mode of behavior (e.g., discuss the merits of a course of action). Preachings, as defined here, differ from inductions in that they are not used as discipline in response to a specific transgression.

Preachings usually have been studied in relation to prosocial, not aggressive, behavior. Researchers have found that the effectiveness of preachings in promoting prosocial actions varies with their content. Those exhortations that merely refer to prosocial norms (e.g., "We should share our tokens"), or are power-assertive in content (i.e., involve threats of disapproval; Perry, Bussey, & Freiberg, 1981), or refer to self-oriented reasons for sharing (Burleson & Fennelly, 1981), are not very effective for promoting subsequent anonymous prosocial behavior. In contrast, children's sharing seems to be enhanced by preachings that include symbolic modeling (e.g., a description of what the model intends to do; Grusec & Skubiski, 1970; Rice & Grusec, 1975) or include reasons that are likely to evoke a sympathetic response (Burleson & Fennelly, 1981; Dressel & Midlarsky, 1978; Eisenberg-Berg & Geisheker, 1979; Perry et al., 1981). Moreover, the influence of such preachings can be relatively long-lasting (e.g., over a 3- or 8-week period; Grusec, Saas-Kortsaak, & Simutis, 1978; Rushton, 1975).

Direct Instructions and the Assignment of Responsibility

Another type of verbal procedure that can be used to promote a given pattern of behavior is direct instruction (i.e., the use of verbal prompts, commands, or directions to behave in a given manner). This technique has been studied primarily in relation to prosocial behaviors.

Constraining, directive instructions (e.g., "What I'd like you to do is give some of the pennies each time") appear to enhance subsequent public and private sharing significantly more than do permissive instructions (e.g., "You may give some pennies if you like, but you don't have to"; Brown & Israel, 1980; Israel & Brown, 1979; Israel & Raskin, 1979; Weissbrod, 1976) or instructions to behave greedily (i.e., not to share; Dressel & Midlarsky, 1978; Weissbrod, 1980; also see Moore & Eisenberg, 1984). The effectiveness of constraining instructions may decrease with age in the elementary-school years, however, especially with regard to long-term effectiveness (Israel & Raskin, 1979; White & Burnam, 1975).

Provision of opportunities to engage in prosocial behaviors also seems to promote children's prosocial tendencies (see Moore & Eisenberg, 1984; Staub, 1979). Similarly, assigning a child the responsibility for others seems to enhance prosocial responding (Maruyama, Fraser, & Miller, 1982; Peterson, 1983a), as does routine assignment of chores that promote the welfare of the family unit (Whiting & Whiting, 1975).

There are several possible explanations for why prosocial tendencies are enhanced by practices and procedures that require one to assist others. One reason may be that children who engage in prosocial action come to think of themselves as altruistic and, consequently, may engage in more future prosocial behavior in order to be consistent with their self-image (Beaman, Cole, Preston, Klentz, & Steblay, 1983). Especially over time, children may forget that their prosocial behavior was initially involuntary or was externally imposed, and may begin to view themselves as generally helpful (Perry & Perry, 1983). A second reason may be that children often receive reinforcement for required prosocial acts; such rewards could be material, social, or internal, and may include feelings of competence or empathic satisfaction. Third, when children are induced to assist others, they may have opportunities to take the perspective of these others and learn about their feelings and needs. This learning could result in increased prosocial tendencies in the future. Finally, children who are induced to assist others may learn new prosocial behaviors that can be used in future contexts.

Provision of Self-Attributions.   Another way in which socializers can influence children's moral behaviors is by providing information that leads children to revise their self-image. For example, when adults attribute children's prosocial behaviors to internal causes (e.g., kindness), the children are more prosocial on subsequent occasions (Grusec, Kuczynski, Rushton, & Simutis, 1978; Grusec &

Redler, 1980; Holte, Jamruszka, Gustafson, Beaman, & Camp, 1984) than if their behavior were attributed to compliance with an adult's expectations (Grusec et al., 1978) or if no attribution was made by the adult (Grusec & Redler, 1980). Internal attributions have also been found to enhance a variety of potentially moral behaviors, including self-control (Toner, Moore, & Emmons, 1980) and cooperation (Jensen & Moore, 1977). However, the provision of attributions does not seem to be an effective procedure until approximately 7 to 8 years of age (Grusec & Redler, 1980), perhaps because younger children have difficulty understanding the notion of consistency in personality (Rotenberg, 1982; Eisenberg & Cialdini, 1983; Grusec, 1983). Thus, socializers' attributions may not alter young children's enduring views of their own personality, and they should not attempt to motivate them to behave in a manner that is consistent with prior behavior.

Consistency of Discipline. An aspect of discipline that has been positively associated with aggressive behavior is consistency of punishment, both across socialization agents (e.g., mother vs. father) and across incidents for a given socializer (Gleuck & Gleuck, 1950; Parke & Deur, 1972; Sawin & Parke, 1979). Moreover, it appears that previous exposure to intra-agent or interagent inconsistency in punishment (e.g., inconsistent verbal punishment) may increase children's subsequent resistance to control by socializers (Deur & Parke, 1970; Sawin & Parke, 1979; also see Parke & Slaby, 1983). It is likely that children do not take inconsistent punishment seriously; alternatively, inconsistent punishment for aggression may be perceived as partial reinforcement or may result in a confusing communication to the child regarding what is the desirable mode of behavior. Inconsistent punishment also should be expected to have an undesirable effect on the control of selfish behavior; however, little research concerning this issue has been conducted.

Warmth and Nurturance. Socializers' warmth and nurturance have been associated with both the aggressive and the prosocial behavior of children. With regard to the former, maternal rejection or indifference has been positively associated with aggressive behavior (Olweus, 1980; also see Martin, 1975; Parke & Slaby, 1983); however, paternal acceptance has been positively associated with aggression for some boys (Parke & Slaby, 1983). It is likely that parental acceptance is associated with aggression primarily when it is combined with permissiveness regarding aggression and/or parental use of power assertion techniques (Olweus, 1980).

The relation of warmth to prosocial behavior also is complex. As for modeling, noncontingent warmth is not consistently related to prosocial behavior, possibly because such warmth is interpreted as permissiveness (Weissbrod, 1976, 1980; see Moore & Eisenberg, 1984). However, in real life warmth is not usually noncontingent; parents are not always nurturant regardless of their child's actions.

In studies in which warmth was not necessarily noncontingent, there seems to be a modest although not highly consistent positive relation between prosocial behavior and indices of warmth, especially in studies involving observational rather than self- or other-report procedures (e.g., Bryant & Crockenberg, 1980; Hoffman, 1970; Moore & Eisenberg, 1984; Yarrow et al., 1973; Zahn-Waxler et al., 1979). However, it is likely that the effects of parental nurturance are moderated by other socialization practices. For example, Baumrind (1971, 1986) found that parental warmth combined with permissiveness (low control and failure to set high standards) is associated with low social responsibility in sons (but not daughters); whereas warmth combined with high standards and reasonable control was associated with higher social responsibility among boys. As has been suggested by Hoffman (1970), it is likely that nurturance acts as a background or contextual factor that enhances the likelihood that the child will orient positively toward the parent and be receptive to parental influence, including parental modeling and inductions, if such influence is used. If socializers are warm but do not set standards, children do not appear to develop behaviors that involve self-denial.

Familial Patterns of Social Interaction. In most of the studies previously reviewed, one or, at most, several child-rearing factors were examined in relation to prosocial or aggressive behavior. The only exceptions to this rule are Baumrind's (1971, 1986) and Olweus' (1980) work; they have studied the relation of aggression or prosocial responding to various configurations of parental techniques.

In contrast to the bulk of the literature, Patterson (1981, 1982) has examined the role of family interaction patterns in aggression. He and his colleagues have identified a pattern of coercive interactions that serve to elicit, maintain, and promote aggression among family members. This coercive process works as follows. When one family member presents an aversive stimulus, the second is likely to respond with the same if the latter believes that coercion may be effective. Thus, the aversive interchange often escalates and may even engulf more of the family. In addition, the family members who prevail are reinforced for the use of aversive tactics. Through this process, children are socialized into aggressive patterns of behavior and parents may learn to use highly punitive child-rearing tactics in an attempt to control their children's aggression.

According to Patterson (1981, 1982), a pattern of coercive interchanges is most likely to occur in families with an aggressive child. This may be due to an interaction between characteristics of both the aggressive child and the parents in these families. The parents often are ineffective in their use of punishment, and are relatively punitive. Moreover, aggressive children appear to be less responsive to parental punishment. Aggressive children also seem to seek immediate payoffs and ignore long-term costs, frequently use coercive means to obtain goals, and are deficient in the social skills that might be used to obtain goals without the use of aggression.

In summary, Patterson's work is consistent with the view that coercive familial patterns of behavior, often due to characteristics of both parents and children, are likely to result in the escalation of both the parents' and the children's aggression. Thus, parental punitiveness is associated with the child's aggression, but causation may be bidirectional. This work illustrates the point that it is necessary for researchers to consider more than unidirectional parental influences when studying the development of moral behavior.

Summary of the Research Concerning Socialization

The research concerning the role of socializers in the development of children's prosocial and aggressive behavior has been limited in its contribution by the investigators' heavy reliance on unidirectional causal models (from parent to child), and by their tendency to focus on only one aspect of the socialization encounter at a time. Nonetheless, it is clear that the quality of children's interactions with socializers, as well as the nature of the socializers' practices, are important factors affecting children's prosocial and aggressive behavior. Parental warmth combined with other positive practices such as the use of inductions, the modeling of positive behaviors, and the provision of opportunities to assist others seems to be associated with the development of prosocial proclivities. A pattern of coercive family interactions and inconsistent discipline is most clearly related to the development of aggressive behaviors. The ways in which characteristics of the child such as temperament, cognitive capabilities, and social behavior affect socializers' actions merit greater attention, however. Similarly, there is need for further research concerning the role of siblings (e.g., Dunn & Munn, 1986) and extrafamilial influences such as peers, teachers, and socializing institutions (e.g., churches and schools), in the socialization process.

A MULTI-FACTOR MODEL OF MORAL BEHAVIOR

Thus far, a variety of factors that appear to affect prosocial and aggressive responding have been reviewed. These have included biological, social/environmental, and personal (e.g., level of moral judgment and perspective-taking, empathic/sympathetic responding) variables. This review of potential influences on prosocial and aggressive behavior has been far from comprehensive, however. Factors such as the following all should affect whether or not an individual behaves prosocially or aggressively in a given situation: (a) situational factors (e.g., cost of assisting, likelihood of disapproval for aggression); (b) other personal factors (e.g., self-identity with regard to helpfulness or aggressiveness, level of self-esteem and self-focus); (c) cognitive-evaluative processes (e.g., evaluation of the expected utility of a behavior, attributions regarding the cause of another's aggression or need for assistance, beliefs about expectations of one's reference group); and (d) relevant personal competencies (e.g., knowledge of skills or strategies for carrying out a given behavior, sense of self-efficacy).

Eisenberg (1986) has presented a model of the ways in which the various factors may, in combination, affect the enactment of a prosocial behavior (see Fig. 10.1). Although this model was developed as a heuristic for understanding prosocial behavior, it also is useful in considering the enactment of aggressive behaviors. Figure 10.1 illustrates that the relation between behavior and prior socialization and sociocognitive skills (e.g., perspective-taking), both of which may be influenced by the child's biologically based characteristics, is not direct. Characteristics of the specific situation influence the individual's interpretation of it, and whether or not a potential actor responds emotionally (e.g., empathizes). Moreover, depending on the specifics of a given situation, other motivational factors can be activated (e.g., the need to maintain self-esteem; beliefs regarding the cause of another's behavior; personal values, goals, and preferences). In other words, pre-existing characteristics of the individual including his or her hierarchy of goals, preferences, and values (which are reflected in moral reasoning) may become salient in a given situation, and may interact with cognitive appraisals and emotional reactions to affect that individual's intentions with regard to behavior. These characteristics, as well as tendencies to role-take and to empathize, and the quality of evaluative processes, change with development in ways that affect prosocial responding.

In some instances in which a potential action is habitual or there is an overwhelming emotional reaction, an individual may decide what to do in a given situation without much cognitive evaluation. However in many situations a variety of motivational factors are activated, some of which may conflict. For example, the individual's sympathetic reaction to a needy other may coincide with concern regarding the cost of assisting the other. In such a circumstance, the individual's various goals, desires, needs, and so forth must be prioritized. This ordering should reflect not only his or her a priori personal goals and values (which change with age; Eisenberg, 1986), but also affective and cognitive

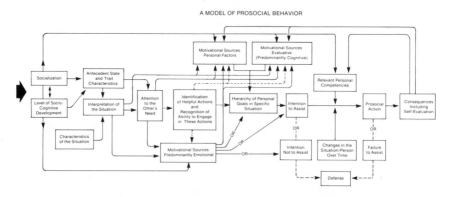

FIG. 10.1. A model of prosocial behavior. Reprinted from Eisenberg (1986) with permission of Lawrence Erlbaum Associates.

reactions elicited by specifics of the particular situation. For example, in some situations the potential actor may feel little affect; thus, goals and values related to helping another in distress may be less easily activated, in a given circumstance, than environmental cues (e.g., the other's facial expression) which are likely to elicit sympathy. Moreover, if factors in the situation are interpreted by the individual to indicate that the needy other is responsible for his or her own distress, a sympathetic reaction may not occur or could be neutralized.

Based upon the individual's hierarchy of personal goals (i.e., motivational preferences for certain end-states; Staub, 1978) in a specific situation, a person may attempt to help or may aggress. If the decision-making process is inconclusive in a situation involving prosocial acts, the individual may defend against feelings of obligation by minimizing the other's need, by derogating the other, or by some other defensive technique (Schwartz & Howard, 1981). Such defensive processes in the case of indecision may be less necessary with regard to aggression, because the intent to aggress often is not the morally or socially desirable response. When the individual defends against indecision, the initial situation may be reinterpreted; for example, the other's need may be viewed as less clear. Defensive reactions can occur not only when the individual cannot make a decision, but also if he or she decides to take a course of action that is not viewed as entirely appropriate by the individual and/or society.

Just because an individual decides to behave in a given manner (e.g., to help or aggress) does not necessarily mean that he or she will do so (Ajzen & Fishbein, 1977). In some circumstances, the situation may change in relevant ways before the individual has an opportunity to act (e.g., the other person who had needed assistance may have been helped by someone else or the individual's own anger toward that person may have dissipated). In other situations, the individual may not have the relevant skills for prosocial or aggressive behavior (e.g., Pomazel & Jaccard, 1976), or may not realize that they have the skills (Peterson, 1983a, 1983b). For example, children are less likely than adults to know how to successfully help or aggress in some situations. Moreover, some persons may not have the social skills or may not be sufficiently extroverted to assist another; similarly, individuals may not be sufficiently assertive to aggress even if they had intended to do so. Finally, carrying out a given course of prosocial action may require knowledge of effective helping strategies, an abiding sense of obligation or responsibility, or sufficient self-control (e.g., delay of gratification; see Kanfer, 1979). Because relevant self-regulatory processes (Kopp, 1982) and judgments of moral responsibility (Eisenberg, 1986) increase with age in both childhood and adolescence, older children and adults should be considerably more likely than young children to have the personal capabilities necessary for enacting intended behaviors—although even adults sometimes lack the self-control or felt responsibility to carry through on their initial intentions.

The final aspect of the model concerns the consequences of prosocial or aggressive behavior. The performance of a given behavior, such as helping, often results in the increased likelihood of enacting a similar behavior at a later time (Beaman et al., 1983). This may be due to changes in one's self-image (e.g., as an altruistic person) or to internal consistency pressures to match prior behavior (Eisenberg, Cialdini, McCreath, & Shell, 1987; Festinger, 1957; Wicklund & Brehm, 1976). Moreover, rewards for the performance of a given behavior may increase the likelihood of the behavior recurring. For example, young children may learn to be aggressive because their initial instances of aggression with peers are successful (Patterson, Littman, & Bricker, 1967).

In summary, altruistic and aggressive behaviors, like most social behaviors, are complex and determined by a variety of factors. Sociocognitive and affective factors, as well as genetic and personal characteristics, and situational variables, all interact in influencing behavior. Moreover, some relevant personal, sociocognitive, and affective factors may change with age, such as the ways in which individuals resolve moral dilemmas and their perspective-taking skills. Consequently, investigators' approach to the study of altruism and aggression (as well as other moral behaviors) must be based on models of human functioning that recognize at least part of the complexity of human behavior and development.

ACKNOWLEDGMENTS

Preparation of this chapter was funded by grants from the National Science Foundation (BNS-8509223) and the National Institute of Child Health and Human Development (1 RO1 HD17909 and K 04 HD00717).

REFERENCES

Abelson, R. (1985). Styles of parental disciplinary practices as a mediator of children's learning from prosocial television portrayals. *Child Study Journal, 15,* 131–145.

Ajzen, I., & Fishbein, M. (1977). Attitude–behavior relations: A theoretical analysis and review of empirical research. *Psychological Bulletin, 84,* 888–918.

Bandura, A. (1969). Social-learning theory of identificatory processes. In D. A. Goslin (Ed.), *Handbook of socialization theory and research* (pp. 213–262). Chicago, IL: Rand-McNally.

Bandura, A. (1973). *Aggression: A social learning analysis.* Englewood Cliffs, NJ: Prentice-Hall.

Bandura, A. (1977). *Social learning theory.* Englewood Cliffs, NJ: Prentice-Hall.

Bandura, A. (1986). *Social foundations of thought and action.* Englewood Cliffs, NJ: Prentice-Hall.

Bandura, A., & Walters, R. H. (1963). *Social learning and personality development.* New York: Holt, Rinehart & Winston.

Bar-Tal, D. (1982). Sequential development of helping behavior: A cognitive-learning approach. *Developmental Review, 2,* 101–124.

Bar-Tal, D., Nadler, A., & Blechman, N. (1980). The relationship between Israeli children's helping behavior and their perception of parents' socialization practices. *Journal of Social Psychology, 111,* 159–167.

Bates, J. E., Maslin, C. A., & Frankel, K. A. (1985). Attachment security, mother–child interaction, and temperament as predictors of behavior-problem ratings at age three years. *Monographs of the Society of Research in Child Development, 50,* 167–193.

Batson, C. D. (in press). Prosocial motivation: Is it ever truly altruistic? In L. Berkowitz (Ed.), *Advances in experimental social psychology.* New York: Academic Press.

Baumrind, D. (1971). Current patterns of parental authority. *Developmental Psychology Monographs, 1,* 1–103.

Baumrind, D. (1986, April). *A developmental perspective on adolescent risk-taking in contemporary America.* Paper presented at the National Invitational Conference on Health Futures of Adolescents, Daytona Beach, FL.

Beaman, A. L., Cole, C., Preston, M., Klentz, B., & Steblay, N. M. (1983). Fifteen years of foot-in-the-door research. *Personality and Social Psychology Bulletin, 9,* 181–196.

Berndt, T. J. (1981). Relations between social cognition, nonsocial cognition, and social behavior: The case of friendship. In J. H. Flavell & L. Ross (Eds.), *Social cognitive development* (pp. 176–199). Cambridge, MA: Cambridge University Press.

Blasi, A. (1980). Bridging moral cognition and moral action: A critical review of the literature. *Psychological Bulletin, 88,* 1–45.

Blum, L. A. (1980). *Friendship, altruism and morality.* London, England: Routledge & Kegan Paul.

Bronfenbrenner, U. (1970). *Two worlds of childhood: U.S. and U.S.S.R.* New York: Russell Sage Foundation.

Brown, M. S., & Israel, A. C. (1980, September). *Effects of instructions, self-instructions and discipline on children's donating.* Paper presented at the American Psychological Association, Montreal.

Bryant, B. K., & Crockenberg, S. B. (1980). Correlates and dimensions of prosocial behavior: A study of female siblings with their mothers. *Child Development, 51,* 529–544.

Burleson, B. R., & Fennelly, D. A. (1981). The effects of persuasive appeal form and cognitive complexity on children's sharing behavior. *Child Study Journal, 11,* 75–90.

Campbell, D. T. (1975). On the conflicts between biological and social evolution and between psychology and moral tradition. *American Psychologist, 30,* 1103–1126.

Campbell, D. T. (1983). The two distinct routes beyond kin selection to ultra sociality: Implications for the social sciences. In D. Bridgeman (Ed.), *The nature of prosocial development: Interdisciplinary theories and strategies* (pp. 11–41). New York: Academic Press.

Campos, J. J., Barrett, K. C., Lamb, M. E., Goldsmith, H. H., & Stenberg, C. (1983). Socioemotional development. In M. M. Haith & J. J. Campos (Eds.), *Infancy and developmental psychobiology* (pp. 783–915). New York: Wiley.

Chandler, M. J. (1973). Egocentrisim and anti-social behavior: The assessment and training of social perspective-taking skills. *Developmental Psychology, 9,* 326–332.

Colby, A., Kohlberg, L., Gibbs, J., & Lieberman, M. (1983). A longitudinal study of moral judgment. *Monographs of the Society for Research in Child Development, 48* (Serial No. 200), 1–124.

Daniels, D., Plomin, R., & Greenhalgh, J. (1984). Correlates of difficult temperament in infancy. *Child Development, 55,* 1184–1194.

Deluty, R. H. (1985a). Cognitive mediation of aggressive, assertive, and submissive behavior in children. *International Journal of Behavioral Development, 8,* 355–369.

Deluty, R. H. (1985b). Consistency of assertive, aggressive, and submissive behavior for children. *Journal of Personality and Social Psychology, 49,* 1054–1065.

Deur, J. L., & Parke, R. D. (1970). The effects of inconsistent punishment on aggression in children. *Developmental Psychology, 2,* 403–411.

Dienstbier, R. A. (1983). The role of emotion in moral socialization. In C. E. Izard, J. Kagan, & R. B. Zajonc (Eds.), *Emotions, cognitions, and behavior* (pp. 484–514). Cambridge, England: Cambridge University Press.

Dix, T., & Grusec, J. E. (1983). Parental influence techniques: An attributional analysis. *Child Development, 54,* 645–652.

Dlugokinski, E. L., & Firestone, I. J. (1974). Other-centeredness and susceptibility to charitable appeals. Effects of perceived discipline. *Developmental Psychology, 10,* 21–28.

Dodge, K. A. (1980). Social cognition and children's aggressive behavior. *Child Development, 51,* 162–170.

Dodge, K. A. (1985). A social information processing model of social competence in children. In M. Perlmutter (Ed.), *Cognitive perspectives on children's social and behavioral development: Minnesota Symposium on Child Psychology* (Vol. 18). Hillsdale, NJ: Lawrence Erlbaum Associates.

Dodge, K. A., & Frame, C. L. (1982). Social cognitive biases and deficits in aggressive boys. *Child Development, 53,* 620–635.

Dodge, K. A., & Newman, J. P. (1981). Biased decision-making processes in aggressive boys. *Journal of Abnormal Psychology, 90,* 375–379.

Dollard, J., Doob, L. W., Miller, N. E., Mowrer, O. H., & Sears, R. R. (1939). *Frustration and aggression.* New Haven, CT: Yale University Press.

Dressel, S., & Midlarsky, E. (1978). The effects of models' exhortations, demands, and practices on children's donation behavior. *Journal of Genetic Psychology, 132,* 211–223.

Dunn, J., & Munn, P. (1986). Siblings and the development of prosocial behavior. *International Journal of Behavioral Development, 9,* 265–284.

Eisenberg, N. (Ed.). (1982). *The development of prosocial behavior.* New York: Academic Press.

Eisenberg, N. (1986). *Altruistic emotion, cognition and behavior.* Hillsdale, NJ: Lawrence Erlbaum Associates.

Eisenberg, N. (1987). The relation of altruism and other moral behaviors to moral cognition: Methodological and conceptual issues. In N. Eisenberg (Ed.), *Contemporary issues in developmental psychology* (pp. 165–189). New York: Wiley.

Eisenberg, N., & Cialdini, R. B. (1984). The role of consistency pressures in behavior: A developmental perspective. *Academic Psychology Bulletin, 6,* 115–126.

Eisenberg, N., Cialdini, R. B., McCreath, H., & Shell, R. (1987). Consistency-based compliance: When and why do children become vulnerable? *Journal of Personality and Social Psychology, 52,* 1174–1181.

Eisenberg, N., & Fabes, R. A. (in press). The development of prosocial behavior from a life-span perspective. In P. B. Baltes, D. L. Featherman, & R. M. Lerner (Eds.), *Life-span development and behavior* (Vol. 9). Hillsdale, NJ: Lawrence Erlbaum Associates.

Eisenberg, N., & Lennon, R. (1983). Sex differences in empathy and related capacities. *Psychological Bulletin, 94,* 100–131.

Eisenberg, N., Lennon, R., & Roth, K. (1983). Prosocial development: A longitudinal study. *Developmental Psychology, 19,* 846–855.

Eisenberg, N., McCreath, J., & Ahn, R. (in press). Vicarious emotional responsiveness and prosocial behavior: Their interrelations in young children. *Personality and Social Psychology Bulletin.*

Eisenberg, N., & Miller, P. (1987). The relation of empathy to prosocial and related behaviors. *Psychological Bulletin, 101,* 91–119.

Eisenberg, N., & Shell, R. (1986). The relation of prosocial moral judgment and behavior in children: The mediating role of cost. *Personality and Social Psychology Bulletin, 12,* 426–433.

Eisenberg, N., & Strayer, J. (in press). *Empathy and its development.* New York: Cambridge University Press.

Eisenberg-Berg, N. (1979). Development of children's prosocial moral judgment. *Developmental Psychology, 15,* 128–137.

Eisenberg-Berg, N., & Geisheker, E. (1979). Content of preachings and power of the model/preacher: The effect on children's generosity. *Developmental Psychology, 15,* 168–175.

Eisenberg-Berg, N., & Lennon, R. (1980). Altruism and the assessment of empathy in the preschool years. *Child Development, 51,* 552–557.

Elliot, R., & Vasta, R. (1970). The modeling of sharing: Effects associated with vicarious reinforcement, symbolization, age, and generalization. *Journal of Experimental Child Psychology, 10,* 8–15.

Eron, L. D., Walder, L. O., & Lefkowitz, M. M. (1971). *Learning of aggression in children.* Boston, MA: Little, Brown.

Ferguson, T. J., & Rule, B. G. (1980). Effects of inferential set, outcome severity, and basis of responsibility on children's evaluations of aggressive acts. *Developmental Psychology, 16,* 141–146.

Feshbach, N. D. (1975). The relationship of child-rearing factors to children's aggression, empathy, and related positive and negative behaviors. In J. deWit & W. W. Hartup (Eds.), *Determinants and origins of aggressive behavior* (pp. 426–436). The Hague, Netherlands, Mouton.

Feshbach, N. D. (1978). Studies of empathic behavior in children. In B. A. Maher (Ed.), *Progress in experimental personality research* (Vol. 8, pp. 1–47). New York: Academic Press.

Feshbach, N. D. (in press). Parental empathy and child adjustment/maladjustment. In N. Eisenberg & J. Strayer (Eds.), *Empathy and its development.* New York: Cambridge University Press.

Feshbach, S. (1971). The dynamics and morality of violence and aggression: Some psychological considerations. *American Psychologist, 26,* 281–292.

Festinger, L. (1957). *A theory of cognitive dissonance.* Stanford, CA: Stanford University Press.

George, C., & Main, M. (1979). Social interactions of young abused children: Approach, avoidance, and aggression. *Child Development, 50,* 306–318.

Gilligan, C. (1977). In a different voice: Women's conceptions of self and morality. *Harvard Educational Review, 47,* 481–517.

Gleuck, S., & Gleuck, E. (1950). *Unraveling juvenile delinquency.* Cambridge, MA: Harvard University Press.

Goldsmith, H. H. (1983). Genetic influences on personality from infancy to adulthood. *Child Development, 54,* 331–355.

Goodenough, F. L. (1931). *Anger in young children.* Minneapolis, MN: University of Minnesota Press.

Gouze, K., Rayias, M., & Bieber-Schneider, R. (1983, August). *Cognitive correlates of aggression in second grade children.* Paper presented at the annual convention of the American Psychological Association, Anaheim, CA.

Grusec, J. E. (1971). Power and the internalization of self-denial. *Child Development, 42,* 93–105.

Grusec, J. E. (1983). The internalization of altruistic dispositions: A cognitive analysis. In E. T. Higgins, D. N. Ruble, & W. W. Hartup (Eds.), *Social cognition and social development: A sociocultural perspective* (pp. 275–293). Cambridge, MA: Cambridge University Press.

Grusec, J. E., & Kuczynski, L. (1980). Directions of effect in socialization: A comparison of the parents' versus the child's behavior as determinants of disciplinary practices. *Developmental Psychology, 16,* 1–9.

Grusec, J. E., Kuczynski, L., Rushton, J. P., & Simutis, Z. M. (1978). Modeling, direction instruction, and attributions: Effects on altruism. *Developmental Psychology, 14,* 51–57.

Grusec, J. E., & Redler, E. (1980). Attribution, reinforcement, and altruism: A developmental analysis. *Developmental Psychology, 16,* 525–534.

Grusec, J. E., Saas-Kortsaak, P., & Simutis, Z. M. (1978). The role of example and moral exhortation in the training of altruism. *Child Development, 49,* 920–923.

Grusec, J. E., & Skubiski, L. (1970). Model nurturance, demand characteristics of the modeling experiment and altruism. *Journal of Personality and Social Psychology, 14,* 352–359.

Hartmann, D. P. (1969). Influence of symbolically modeled instrumental and pain cues on aggressive behaviors. *Journal of Personality and Social Psychology, 11,* 280–288.

Hartup, W. W. (1974). Aggression in childhood: Developmental perspectives. *American Psychologist, 29,* 336–341.

Hay, D. F., Nash, A., & Pedersen, J. (1981). Responses of six-month-olds to the distress of their peers. *Child Development, 52,* 1071–1075.

Hay, D. F., & Ross, H. S. (1982). The social nature of early conflict. *Child Development, 53,* 105–113.

Higgins, E. T. (1981). Role taking and social judgment: Alternative perspectives and processes. In J. H. Flavell & L. Ross (Eds.), *Social cognitive development* (pp. 119–153). Cambridge, MA: Cambridge University Press.

Higgins, E. T., Feldman, N. S., & Ruble, D. N. (1980). Accuracy and differentiation in social prediction: A developmental analysis. *Journal of Personality, 48,* 520–540.

Higgins, E. T., & Parsons, J. E. (1983). Social cognition and the social life of the child: Stages as subcultures. In E. T. Higgins, D. N. Ruble, & W. W. Hartup (Eds.), *Social cognition and social development: A socio-cultural perspective* (pp. 15–62). New York: Cambridge University Press.

Hoffman, M. L. (1960). Power assertion by the parent and its impact on the child. *Child Development, 31,* 129–143.

Hoffman, M. L. (1970). Moral development. In P. H. Mussen (Ed.), *Carmichael's manual of child development* (pp. 261–359). New York: Wiley.

Hoffman, M. L. (1976). Empathy, role-taking, guilt, and development of altruistic motives. In T. Lickona (Ed.), *Moral development and behavior: Theory, research and social issues* (pp. 124–143). New York: Holt, Rinehart & Winston.

Hoffman, M. L. (1981). Is altruism part of human nature? *Journal of Personality and Social Psychology, 40,* 121–137.

Hoffman, M. L. (1982). The measurement of empathy. In C. E. Izard (Ed.), *Measuring emotions in infants and children* (pp. 279–296). Cambridge, MA: Cambridge University Press.

Hoffman, M. L. (1983). Affective and cognitive processes in moral internalization. In E. T. Higgins, D. N. Ruble, & W. W. Hartup (Eds.), *Social cognition and social development: A sociocultural perspective* (pp. 236–274). Cambridge, MA: Cambridge University Press.

Hoffman, M. L. (1984). Interaction of affect and cognition in empathy. In C. E. Izard, J. Kagan, & R. B. Zajonc (Eds.), *Emotions, cognitions, and behavior* (pp. 103–131). Cambridge, MA: Cambridge University Press.

Hoffman, M. L. (in press). The contribution of empathy to justice and moral judgment. In N. Eisenberg & J. Strayer (Eds.), *Empathy and its development.* Cambridge, MA: Cambridge University Press.

Hoffman, M. L., & Saltzstein, H. D. (1967). Parent discipline and the child's moral development. *Journal of Personality and Social Psychology, 5,* 45–57.

Holmberg, M. C. (1980). The development of social interchange patterns from 12 to 42 months. *Child Development, 51,* 448–456.

Holte, C. S., Jamruszka, V., Gustafson, J., Beaman, A. L., & Camp, G. C. (1984). Influence of children's positive self-perceptions on donating behavior in naturalistic settings. *Journal of School Psychology, 22,* 145–153.

Hume, D. (1966). *Enquiries concerning the human understanding and concerning the principles of morals* (2nd ed.). Oxford, England: Clarendon Press. (Original work published 1777).

Iannotti, R. J. (1978). Effect of role-taking experiences on role taking, empathy, altruism, and aggression. *Developmental Psychology, 14,* 119–124.

Israel, A. C., & Brown, M. S. (1979). Effects of directiveness of instructions and surveillance on the production and persistence of children's donations. *Journal of Experimental Child Psychology, 27,* 250–261.

Israel, A. C., & Raskin, P. A. (1979). Directiveness of instructions and modeling: Effects of production and persistence of children's donations. *Journal of Genetic Psychology, 135,* 269–277.

Jensen, A. M., & Moore, S. G. (1977). The effect of attribute statements on cooperativeness and competitiveness in school-age boys. *Child Development, 48,* 305–307.

Jersild, A. T., & Markey, F. O. (1935). Conflicts between preschool children. *Child Development Monographs, 21.*

Jurkovic, G. J. (1980). The juvenile delinquent as a moral philospher: A structural–developmental perspective. *Psychological Bulletin, 88,* 709–727.

Jurkovic, G. J., & Prentice, N. M. (1977). Relation of moral and cognitive development to dimensions of juvenile delinquency. *Journal of Abnormal Psychology, 86,* 414–420.

Kagan, J., & Moss, H. A. (1962). *Birth to maturity.* New York: Wiley.

Kagan, S., & Madsen, M. C. (1972). Experimental analyses of cooperation and competition of Anglo-American and Mexican children. *Developmental Psychology, 6,* 49–59.

Kanfer, F. H. (1979). Personal control, social control, and altruism: Can society survive the age of individualism? *American Psychologist, 34,* 231–239.

Karniol, R. (1982). Settings, scripts, and self-schemata: A cognitive analysis of the development of prosocial behavior. In N. Eisenberg (Ed.), *The development of prosocial behavior* (pp. 251–278). New York: Academic Press.

Keller, B. B., & Bell, R. Q. (1979). Child effects on adult's method of eliciting altruistic behavior. *Child Development, 50,* 1004–1009.

Kohlberg, L. (1981). *The philosophy of moral development: Moral stages and the idea of justice.* San Francisco, CA: Harper & Row.

Kohlberg, L. (1984). *Essays on moral development: Vol. II. The psychology of moral development.* San Francisco: CA: Harper & Row.

Kohlberg, L., & Candee, D. (1984). The relationship of moral judgment to moral action. In W. M. Kurtines & J. L. Gewirtz (Eds.), *Morality, moral behavior, and moral development* (pp. 52–73). New York: Wiley.

Kopp, C. B. (1982). Antecedents of self-regulation: A developmental perspective. *Developmental Psychology, 18,* 199–214.

Korner, A. F., Zeanah, C. H., Linden, J., Berkowitz, R. I., Kraemer, H. C., & Agras, W. S. (1985). The relation between neonatal and later activity and temperament. *Child Development, 56,* 38–42.

Langer, E. J., Blank, A., & Chanowitz, B. (1978). The mindlessness of ostensibly thoughtful action. *Journal of Personality and Social Psychology, 36,* 635–642.

Lee, C. L., & Bates, J. E. (1985). Mother–child interaction at age two years and perceived difficult temperament. *Child Development, 56,* 1314–1325.

Lefkowitz, M. M., Eron, L. D., Walder, L. O., & Huesmann, L. R. (1977). *Growing up to be violent: A longitudinal study of the development of aggression.* New York: Pergamon Press.

Lickona, T. (1976). Research on Piaget's theory on moral development. In T. Lickona (Ed.), *Moral development and behavior: Theory, research, and social issues* (pp. 219–240). New York: Holt, Rinehart & Winston.

Lipscomb, T. J., Larrieu, J. A., McAllister, H. A., & Bregman, N. J. (1982). Modeling and children's generosity: A developmental perspective. *Merrill-Palmer Quarterly, 28,* 275–282.

Lipscomb, T. J., McAllister, H. A., & Bregman, N. J. (1985). A developmental inquiry into the effects of multiple models on children's generosity. *Merrill-Palmer Quarterly, 31,* 335–344.

Lorenz, K. (1966). *On aggression.* New York: Harcourt, Brace, & World.

Marsh, D. T. (1982). The development of interpersonal problem-solving among elementary school children. *Journal of Genetic Psychology, 140,* 107–118.

Marsh, D. T., Serafica, F. C., & Barenboim, C. (1981). Interrelationsbips among perspective taking, interpersonal problem-solving, and interpersonal functioning. *Journal of Genetic Psychology, 138,* 37–48.

Martin, B. (1975). Parent–child relations. In F. D. Horowitz (Ed.), *Review of child development research* (Vol. 4, pp. 463–540). Chicago, IL: University of Chicago Press.

Maruyama, G., Fraser, S. C., & Miller, N. (1982). Personal responsibility and altruism in children. *Journal of Personality and Social Psychology, 42,* 658–664.

Mathews, K. A., Batson, C. D., Horn, J., & Rosenman, R. H. (1981). "Principles in his nature which interest him in the fortune of others . . . '': The heritability of empathic concern for others. *Journal of Personality, 49,* 237–0247.

Mattsson, A., Schalling, D., Olweus, D., & Low, H. (1980). Plasma testosterone, aggressive behavior and personality dimensions in young male delinquents. *Journal of the American Academy of Child Psychiatry, 19,* 476–490.

Maudry, M., & Nekula, M. (1939). Social relations between children of the same age during the first two years. *Journal of Genetic Psychology, 54,* 193–215.

Mednick, S. A., Gabrielli, W. F., & Hutchings, B. (1984). Genetic influences in criminal convictions: Evidence from an adoption cohort. *Science, 224,* 891–894.

Miller, P., & Eisenberg, N. (1986). *The relation of empathy to aggression, psychopathy, and related moral functioning.* Manuscript submitted for publication.

Moore, B. S., & Eisenberg, N. (1984). The development of altruism. In G. Whitehurst (Ed.), *Annuals of child development* (pp. 107–174). Greenwich, CT: JAI Press.

Mussen, P., & Eisenberg-Berg, N. (1977). *The roots of caring, sharing, and helping.* San Francisco, CA: Freeman.

Mussen, P., Rutherford, E., Harris, S., & Keasey, C. (1970). Honesty and altruism among preadolescents. *Developmental Psychology, 3,* 169–194.

Olson, S., Johnson, J., Belleau, K., Parks, J., & Barrett, E. (1983, April). *Social competence in preschool children: Interrelations with sociometric status, social problem-solving, and impulsivity.* Paper presented at the meeting of the Society for Research in Child Development, Detroit, MI.

Olweus, D. (1977). Aggression and peer acceptance in adolescent boys: Two short-term longitudinal studies of ratings. *Child Development, 48,* 1301–1313.

Olweus, D. (1979). Stability and aggressive reaction patterns in males: A review. *Psychological Bulletin, 86,* 852–875.

Olweus, D. (1980). Familial and temperamental determinants of aggressive behavior in adolescent boys: A causal analysis. *Developmental Psychology, 16,* 644–666.

Olweus, D., Mattsson, A., Schalling, D., & Low, H. (1980). Testosterone, aggression, physical and personality dimensions in normal adolescent males. *Psychosomatic Medicine, 42,* 253–269.

Parke, R. D., & Deur, J. L. (1972). Schedule of punishment and inhibition of aggression in children. *Developmental Psychology, 7,* 266–269.

Parke, R. D., & Slaby, R. G. (1983). The development of aggression. In P. H. Mussen (Ed.), *Handbook of child psychology: Vol. 4. Socialization, personality, and social development* (E. M. Hetherington, Ed.) (pp. 547–641). New York: Wiley.

Patterson, G. R. (1981). Mothers: The unacknowledged victims. *Monographs of the Society for Research in Child Development, 45* (5, Serial No. 186).

Patterson, G. R. (1982). *Coercive family processes.* Eugene, OR: Castilla Press.

Patterson, G. R., Littman, R. A., & Bricker, W. (1967). Assertive behavior in children: A step toward a theory of aggression. *Monographs of the Society for Research in Child Development, 32* (Serial No. 113).

Perry, D. G., Bussey, K., & Freiberg, K. (1981). Impact of adults' appeals for sharing on the development of altruistic dispositions in children. *Journal of Experimental Child Psychology, 32,* 127–138.

Perry, D. G., & Perry, L. C. (1974). Denial of differing in the victim as a stimulus to violence in aggressive boys. *Child Development, 45,* 55–62.

Perry, D. G., & Perry, L. C. (1983). Social learning, causal attribution, and moral internalization. In J. Bisanz, G. L. Bisanz, & R. Kail (Eds.), *Learning in children: Progress in cognitive development research* (pp. 105–136). New York: Springer-Verlag.

Peterson, L. (1983a). Influence of age, task competence, and responsibility focus on children's altruism. *Developmental Psychology, 19,* 141–148.

Peterson, L. (1983b). Roles of donor competence, donor age, and peer presence on helping in an emergency. *Developmental Psychology, 19,* 873–880.

Piaget, J. (1965). *The moral judgment of the child.* New York: The Free Press. (Original work published in London: Kegan Paul, 1932).

Piaget, J., & Inhelder, B. (1956). *The child's conception of space.* London: Routledge & Kegan Paul.

Piliavin, J. A., Dovidio, J. F., Gaertner, S. L., & Clark, R. D. III (1981). *Emergency intervention.* New York: Academic Press.

Pomazal, R. J., & Jaccard, J. J. (1976). An informational approach to altruistic behavior. *Journal of Personality and Social Psychology, 33,* 317–326.

Power, T. G., & Parke, R. D. (1986). Patterns of early socialization: Mother– and father–infant interaction in the home. *International Journal of Behavioral Development, 9,* 331–341.

Radke-Yarrow, M., & Zahn-Waxler, C. (1984). Roots, motives, and patterns in children's prosocial behavior. In E. Staub, D. Bar-Tal, J. Karylowski, & J. Reykowski (Eds.), *Development and maintenance of prosocial behavior: International perspectives on positive behavior* (pp. 81–99). New York: Plenum.

Radke-Yarrow, M., Zahn-Waxler, C., & Chapman, M. (1983). Prosocial dispositions and behavior. In P. Mussen (Ed.), *Manual of child psychology: Vol. 4. Socialization, personality, and social development.* (E. M. Hetherington, Ed.) (pp. 469–545). New York: Wiley.

Rheingold, H. (1979, March). *Helping by two-year-old children.* Paper presented at the biennial meeting of the Society for Research in Child Development, San Francisco, CA.

Rheingold, H. L., Hay, D. F., & West, M. J. (1976). Sharing in the second year of life. *Child Development, 47,* 1148–1158.

Rholes, W. S., & Lane, L. W. (1985). Consistency between cognitions and behavior: Cause and consequence of cognitive development. In J. B. Pryor & J. D. Day (Eds.), *The development of social cognition* (pp. 97–114). New York: Springer-Verlag.

Rice, M. E., & Grusec, J. E. (1975). Saying and doing: Effects on observer performance. *Journal of Personality, 32,* 584–593.

Roe, K. V. (1980). Toward a contingency hypothesis of empathy development. *Journal of Personality and Social Psychology, 39,* 991–994.

Rotenberg, K. J. (1982). Development of character constancy of self and other. *Child Development, 53,* 505–515.

Rushton, J. P. (1975). Generosity in children: Immediate and long term effects of modeling, preaching, and moral judgment. *Journal of Personality and Social Psychology, 31,* 459–466.

Rushton, J. P. (1979). Effects of prosocial television and film material on the behavior of viewers. In L. Berkowitz (Ed.), *Advances in experimental social psychology* (Vol. 12, pp. 321–351). New York: Academic Press.

Rushton, J. P., Fulker, D. W., Neale, M. C., Nias, D. K. B., & Eysenck, H. J. (1986). Altruism and aggression. The heritability of individual differences. *Journal of Personality and Social Psychology, 50,* 1192–1198.

Rushton, J. P., & Sorrentino, R. M. (Eds.), (1981). *Altruism and helping behavior: Social, personality, and developmental perspectives.* Hillsdale, NJ: Lawrence Erlbaum Associates.

Rushton, J. P., & Weiner, J. (1975). Altruism and cognitive development in children. *British Journal of Social and Clinical Psychology, 14,* 341–349.

Sawin, D. B., & Parke, R. D. (1979). The effects of interagent inconsistent discipline on children's aggressive behavior. *Journal of Experimental Child Psychology, 28,* 525–538.

Scarr, S., & Kidd, K. K. (1983). Developmental behavioral genetics. In P. Mussen (Ed.), *Handbook of child psychology: Vol. 2. Infancy and developmental psychobiology* (M. M. Haith & J. J. Campos, Eds.) (pp. 344–433). New York: Wiley.

Schwartz, S. J., & Howard, J. A. (1981). In J. P. Rushton & R. M. Sorrentino (Eds.), *Altruism and helping behavior* (pp. 189–211). Hillsdale, NJ: Lawrence Erlbaum Associates.

Selman, R. L. (1980). *The growth of interpersonal understanding: Developmental and clinical analyses.* New York: Academic Press.

Shantz, C. V. (1983). Social cognition. In P. H. Mussen (Ed.), *Handbook of child psychology: Cognitive development* (Vol. 3, pp. 495–555, J. Flavell & E. Markman, Eds.). New York: Wiley.

Shantz, D. W., & Vogdanoff, D. A. (1973). Situational effects on retaliatory aggression at three age levels. *Child Development, 44,* 149–153.

Shure, M. B. (1980). *Interpersonal problem-solving in ten-year-olds.* Final grant report to the National Institute of Mental Health (Grant No. RO1 MH 27741).

Shure, M. B. (1982). Interpersonal problem solving: A cog in the wheel of social cognition. In F. C. Serafica (Eds.), *Social-cognitive development in context* (pp. 133–166). New York: Guilford.

Simonds, M. P., & Simonds, J. F. (1981). Relationship of maternal parenting behaviors to preschool children's temperament. *Child Psychiatry and Human Development, 12,* 19–31.

Smith, C. L., Gelfand, D. M., Hartmann, D. P., & Partlow, M. P. (1979). Children's causal attributions regarding help-giving. *Child Development, 50,* 203–210.

Spivack, G., Platt, J. J., & Shure, M. B. (1976). *The problem-solving approach to adjustment.* San Francisco, CA: Jossey-Bass.

Spivack, G., & Shure, M. B. (1984). *Social adjustment of young children.* San Francisco, CA: Jossey-Bass.

Staub, E. (1978). *Positive social behavior and morality: Social and personal influences* (Vol. 1). New York: Academic Press.

Staub, E. (1979). *Positive social behavior and morality: Vol. 2. Socialization and development.* New York: Academic Press.

Staub, E. (1982, September). *Toward a theory of moral conduct: Goal orientations, moral judgment, and behavior.* Paper presented at the annual meeting of the American Psychological Association, Washington, DC.

St. Clair, K. L. (1978). Neonatal assessment procedures: A historical review. *Child Development, 49,* 280–292.

Stein, A. H., & Friedrich, L. K. (1975). Impact of television on children and youth. In E. M. Hetherington (Ed.), *Review of child development research* (Vol. 5, pp. 183–256). Chicago, IL: University of Chicago Press.

Tieger, T. (1980). On the biological basis of sex differences in aggression. *Child Development, 51,* 943–963.

Toner, I. J., Moore, L. P., & Emmons, B. A. (1980). The effect of being labeled on subsequent self-control in children. *Child Development, 51,* 618–621.

Trivers, R. L. (1971). The evolution of reciprocal altruism. *The Quarterly Review of Biology, 46,* 35–57.

Turner, P. H., & Harris, M. B. (1984). Parental attitudes and preschool children's social competence. *Journal of Genetic Psychology, 144,* 105–113.

Underwood, B., & Moore, B. S. (1982a). The generality of altruism in children. In N. Eisenberg (Ed.), *The development of prosocial behavior* (pp. 25–52). New York: Academic Press.

Underwood, B., & Moore, B. S. (1982b). Perspective-taking and altruism. *Psychological Bulletin, 91,* 143–173.

Weissbrod, C. S. (1976). Noncontingent warmth induction, cognitive style, and children's imitative donation and rescue effort behaviors. *Journal of Personality and Social Psychology, 34,* 274–281.

Weissbrod, C. S. (1980). The impact of warmth and instruction on donation. *Child Development, 51,* 279–281.

Weston, D. R., & Main, M. (1980, April). *Infant responses to the crying of an adult actor in the laboratory: Stability and correlates of "concerned attention."* Paper presented at the Second International Conference on Infant Studies, New Haven, CT.

White, G. M. (1972). Immediate and deferred effects of model observation and guided and unguided rehearsal on donating and stealing. *Journal of Personality and Social Psychology, 21,* 139–148.

White, G. M., & Burnam, M. A. (1975). Socially cured altruism: Effects of modeling, instructions, and age on public and private donations. *Child Development, 46,* 559–563.

Whiting, B. B., & Whiting, J. W. M. (1975). *Children of six cultures: A psychocultural analysis.* Cambridge, MA: Harvard University Press.

Wicklund, R. A., & Brehm, J. W. (1976). *Perspectives on cognitive dissonance.* Hillsdale, NJ: Lawrence Erlbaum Associates.

Wilson, E. O. (1978). *On human nature.* Cambridge, MA: Harvard University Press.

Wolfe, D. A., Katell, A., & Drabman, R. S. (1982). Parents' and preschool children's choices of disciplinary childrearing methods. *Journal of Applied Developmental Psychology, 3,* 167–176.

Yarrow, M. R., Scott, P. M., & Waxler, C. Z. (1973). Learning concern for others. *Developmental Psychology, 8,* 240–260.

Zahn-Waxler, C., Radke-Yarrow, M., & Brady-Smith, J. (1977). Perspective-taking and prosocial behavior. *Developmental Psychology, 13,* 87–88.

Zahn-Waxler, C., Radke-Yarrow, M., & King, R. A. (1979). Child rearing and children's prosocial initiations toward victims of distress. *Child Development, 50,* 319–330.

11 Moral Development

Martin L. Hoffman
New York University

INTRODUCTION

Moral issues have preoccupied students of philosophy from the time of Aristotle. And in the study of psychology, moral development has been a topic of increasing research interest for over six decades. As noted by Gibbs and Schnell (1985), "moral development has ascended from the status of an 'odd' topic in the 1960s to a major theoretical and research area" (p. 1071). The sustained, indeed the increasing, interest in the topic may lie in its importance for the organization of society as well as the fact that it epitomizes the existential human dilemma of how people come to grips with the inevitable conflicts between their personal egoistic needs and their social obligations.

Philosophers have postulated several answers to this dilemma that have parallels in current psychological theory. One answer is the doctrine of original sin, associated with early Christian theology, that states that people are born egoistic and can only acquire a sense of moral obligation through punitive socialization experiences that subordinate their egoistic drives. This doctrine is reflected in Freudian theory and certain social learning theories that stress the importance of punishment in moral development. The doctrine of innate purity, associated with writers like Rousseau, that sees children as inherently good though vulnerable to corruption by society, has its parallel in Piaget's view that adults are constraining and that moral development requires the give-and-take of unsupervised interactions with peers. Philosophers like Kant, who attempted to derive universal moral principles, provided part of the inspiration for Kohlberg's efforts to construct an invariant sequence of moral developmental stages. And the British utilitarian tradition represented by David Hume and Adam Smith, who focused

497

on empathy as a necessary social bond, finds expression in current theory and research on empathic morality (Hume, 1751/1957; Smith, 1759/1965).

The flavor of the moral development literature, which is now quite vast, can best be communicated by organizing it into three broad categories: stage theories of moral development; processes in the internalization of moral standards; and social influences on moral development.

STAGE THEORIES

A major concern of cognitive-developmental research has been the building of a series of stages that depict growth in an individual's moral conceptions. I review the moral-cognitive stage theories of Piaget, whose views are over 50 years old but remain a rich source of research ideas, and of Kohlberg, whose work has dominated research in this area for two decades. The innovations made by Damon and by Turiel are also briefly described. And, finally, Hoffman's stage scheme for moral motivation and affect is reviewed.

Moral-Cognitive Development

Piaget's two stages derived from the attitudes expressed by different-aged children toward the origin, legitimacy, and alterability of rules in the game of marbles; and from children's responses to stories such as the well-known one in which children are asked to judge who is naughtier, a boy who accidentally breaks several cups or a boy who breaks one cup while trying to get jam out of the cupboard (Piaget, 1932). In Piaget's first stage—referred to as moral realism, morality of constraint, or heteronomous morality—children feel an obligation to comply with rules because rules are sacred and unalterable. They tend to view behaviors as totally right or wrong and to think that everyone views them in the same way. They judge the rightness or wrongness of an act on the basis of the magnitude of its consequences, the extent to which it conforms to established rules, and whether or not it is punished. They believe in "imminent justice"— the theory that violations of social norms are followed by physical accidents or misfortunes willed by God or by some inanimate object.

The child in the more advanced stage—called autonomous morality, morality of cooperation, or reciprocity—views rules as established, maintained through reciprocal social agreement, and thus subject to modification in response to human needs. He or she recognizes a possible diversity in views. The child's judgments of right and wrong stress intentions as well as consequences. Punishment, it is believed, should be reciprocally related to the misdeed (e.g., through restitution) rather than arbitrary and administered by authority. Duty and obligation are no longer defined in terms of obedience to authority but in terms of conforming to peer expectations, considering other people's welfare, expressing gratitude for past favors, and, above all, putting oneself in the place of others.

Piaget believes that both cognitive development and social experience play roles in the transformation from one stage to the next. Although he is not clear about how the two interact, one can interpret the threads of his argument as follows. The young child's moral immaturity is based on (a) two cognitive limitations, namely, *egocentrism* (assuming that others view events the same as he or she does) and *realism* (confusing subjective with objective experience—for example, perceiving dreams as external events); and (b) the child's heteronomous respect for adults—a syndrome of feelings including inferiority, dependency, affection, admiration, and fear, which produces feelings of obligation to comply with adult's commands and to view their rules as sacred and unchangeable. Moral growth requires that the child give up egocentrism and realism and develop a concept of self that is distinct from others, who have their own independent perspective about events. This shift occurs in children's interactions with peers in two ways:

1. In growing older, the child attains relative equality with adults and older children, which lessens his or her unilateral respect for them and gives the child confidence to participate with peers in decisions about applying and changing rules on the basis of reciprocity. This new mode of interaction renders the child's initial conception of the rules no longer tenable. These rules are no longer seen as having an infinite past and a divine or adult origin, but as products of cooperation and agreement based on the human goals they serve; and they are seen also as amenable to change by mutual consent.

2. Interacting with peers often requires taking alternate and reciprocal roles with them, which facilitates the awareness that one is coordinated with others— that one reacts to similar situations in similar ways; that the consequences of one's acts for one's peers, and of theirs for oneself, are similar; and that these events seem different when viewed from different vantage points. The child thus becomes sensitized to the internal states that underlie the acts of others, which contributes, among other things, to the tendency to take other people's intentions into account.

Social experience, then, serves to stimulate and challenge children because it contradicts their expectations. The resulting cognitive disequilibrium motivates children to utilize their newly attained cognitive capabilities to resolve the contradiction; it is through this effort that pre-existing patterns of moral thought are reorganized.

Although Piaget's theory appeared in the late 1920s, most of the published research based on it was done in the 1950s and 1960s. The earlier findings, critically reviewed by Hoffman (1970a), provide considerable support for Piaget's postulated age-developmental sequence in Western countries such as

England, Switzerland, and the United States, although adults may sometimes use earlier forms of moral reasoning in certain situations. The data do not indicate that the same sequence occurs in other types of societies. The assumption of consistency across stage attributes (that subjects with high scores on one attribute such as "consequences" also score highly on other attributes such as "imminent justice") is generally not upheld, but the research appears to lack some of the controls needed for a critical test. Nor has a critical test been made of Piaget's central hypothesis that peer interaction is necessary for moral growth. (The influence of peers is discussed in some detail later.) The level of moral judgment has been found to relate positively to the cognitive level displayed in solving mathematics and physics problems, and to the role-taking ability of children at various ages (e.g., Ambron & Irwin, 1975; Damon, 1975).

A series of experiments in the 1960s and 1970s attempted to test Piaget's assumption that progress from one stage to the next requires cognitive diseq-uilibrium, by seeing if one's level of moral reasoning could be changed by simple exposure to models who verbalize moral judgments at higher or lower levels than one's own. The social-learning theorists who did most of this work expected that such exposure would produce changes, whereas cognitive-develop-mentalists would not ordinarily expect social influences to operate in such a direct manner. In general, these experiments showed that the subjects' moral judgments were affected by the model's verbalizations. The earlier experiments (e.g., Bandura & MacDonald, 1963) were criticized for demonstrating nothing more than momentary, specific response shifts rather than actual changes in level of moral reasoning (Turiel, 1966). Later research, however, indicates that children not only shift their verbal responses toward the model but also increase their understanding of the principle that intentions should be taken into account when making moral evaluations of behavior. Furthermore, in some cases the effects appear to last up to a year (e.g., Sternlieb & Youniss, 1975).

That mere exposure to models can produce such shifts has been interpreted as evidence against cognitive-developmental theory (e.g., Kurtines & Greif, 1974). Another interpretation (Hoffman, 1979b) is that the children in these studies did not merely imitate the model. Rather, they knew that acts may or may not be intentional but gave intentions less weight than consequences, perhaps because the stories used, like Piaget's, portrayed more harmful consequences for acciden-tal than for intended acts. This interpretation fits the evidence (e.g., Imamoglu, 1975) that children as young as 5 years consider intentions when the conse-quences of accidental and intended acts are equal (the modeling studies in ques-tion used older children). Repeated exposure to an adult model who consistently assigns greater weight to intentions despite the disparity in consequences might then have produced cognitive disequilibrium, which the subjects could have reduced by reexamining and changing their views. This interpretation is conso-nant with cognitive-developmental theory but it does not make the cognitive-developmental assumption that movement is always progressive, since a model who espouses "consequences"—the less mature response—might also produce cognitive disequilibrium. This interpretation could be tested by having subjects report their thoughts and feelings on hearing the model's expressed views.

Kohlberg's Universal Stage Model

In developing his model, Kohlberg attempted to retain the best of Piaget's analysis and fit it into a more refined, comprehensive, and logically consistent framework. Thus, Kohlberg sees moral development as occurring in a series of six qualitatively distinct stages. The end product of these stages is a sense of justice (rather than other moral principles, such as love for humanity). This sense of justice enables one to determine the legitimate moral claims of people in a situation and to balance these claims in a way that best handles the perspectives of all contending parties. Each stage is a homogeneous type of moral reasoning strategy or conceptual framework designed to answer moral questions and evaluate issues; moral reasoning within a stage is thus consistent across different moral problems and situations. Each stage builds on, reorganizes, and encompasses the preceding one and is therefore more comprehensive, providing new perspectives and criteria for making moral evaluations. The content of moral values does not play a role in defining a stage.

An important feature of Kohlberg's approach is that all individuals, regardless of culture, are viewed as going through the stages in the same order, varying only in how quickly and how far they move through the stage sequence. The stages are held to be constructed by individuals as they try to make sense out of their own experience, rather than implanted by culture through socialization. In addition, progress always moves forward through the stage sequence, never backward.

Kohlberg's six stages are based on extensive case analyses of boys ranging from 10 to 16 years of age (Kohlberg, 1976). The data were obtained from 2-hour interviews that focused on nine hypothetical moral dilemmas in which acts of obedience to laws, rules, or commands of authority conflict with the needs or welfare of other persons. The child was asked to choose whether one should perform the obedience-serving act or the need-serving act and to answer a series of questions probing the thinking underlying his choice. Kohlberg's interest was not in the action alternatives selected by the children, which presumably reflected the content of their moral values, but in the quality of their judgments as indicated by the reasons given for their choices and their ways of defining the conflict situations.

Each stage was initially defined in terms of its position on 30 different moral issues that the children brought into their thinking. The six stages were ordered into three levels of moral orientation, the basic themes and major attributes of which were as follows:[1]

---

[1]I say "were" because certain nuances in the stage descriptions have been altered owing to changes in the scoring system that are mentioned later.

1. In the first, *premoral* level, control of conduct is external in two senses: One's standards consist of external commands or pressures, and one's motive is to avoid external punishment or to obtain rewards. In Stage 1, one's definition of good and bad is based on obedience to rules and authority, but this is not a heteronomous stage in Piaget's sense, because punishment is feared like any other aversive stimulus. In Stage 2, acts that are instrumental in providing satisfaction to the self, and occasionally to others, are defined as "right".

2. The second, *conventional* level defines morality as conforming to the expectations of others and maintaining the social order. Control of conduct is external in that standards consist of rules and expectations held by those who are significant others by virtue of personal attachment or delegated authority. Motivation, however, is largely internal: The child now takes the role of significant others and respects their judgment, although this is based on anticipation of their praise or censure. Thus, the personal reactions of authority now serve as cues to the rightness or wrongness of an act and the moral virtue of the actor.

In Stage 3, the orientation is to gain approval and to please and help others; the morally good person is one who possesses moral virtues, and, when judging others, considers their intentions. Stage 4 is a morality based on maintaining authority and social order, in which the orientation is to "doing one's duty," showing respect for authority, and maintaining the social order for its own sake. People at this stage believe that virtue should be rewarded, and they take the perspective of others who have legitimate rights and expectations in situations.

3. The third, *postconventional* level is that of moral principles. Morality is defined as acting in accord with shared or sharable standards, rights, and duties. The possibility of conflict between two socially accepted standards is acknowledged, and attempts at rational adjudication are made. Control of conduct is internal in two senses: The standards have an internal source, and the decision to act is based on an internal process of thought and judgment concerning right and wrong. In Stage 5, the norms of right and wrong are defined in terms of laws or institutionalized rules that are seen to have a rational base; for example, they express the will of the majority, maximize social utility or welfare, or are necessary for institutional functioning. Although recognized as arbitrary, sometimes unjust, and one of many alternatives, the law is generally the ultimate criterion of what is right. Duty and obligation are defined in terms of contract, not the needs of individuals. When conflict exists between the individual and the law or contract, though there may be sympathy for the former, the latter ordinarily prevails because of its greater functional rationality for society.

Stage 6 is the morality of individual principles of conscience. The orientation is not only to existing rules and standards but also to conscience as a directing agent, to mutual respect and trust, and to those principles of moral choice that involve an appeal to logical universality and consistency. Conduct is controlled by an internalized ideal that exerts pressure toward those actions that seem right, regardless of the reactions of others present. If the individual acts otherwise, self-condemnation and guilt result. Although Stage 6 people are aware of the importance of law and contract, moral conflict is generally resolved in terms of broader moral principles such as the Golden Rule or the greatest good for the greatest number.

Individuals progress through these six stages, according to Kohlberg, primarily because of experiences of cognitive disequilibrium. This is an extension of the concepts of disequilibrium and equilibration in Piaget's theory of intellectual (rather than moral) development (cf. Kuhn, this volume). The hypothesis, developed initially by Turiel (1966), and elaborated more recently by Blasi (1983), is that one's moral growth results from exposure to levels of moral reasoning that are moderately higher than one's own current level. The resulting cognitive conflict or disequilibrium produces tension, which results in the person's attempting to make sense out of the contradiction.

These moral stages, according to Kohlberg, also reflect a sequence of successive changes in role-taking ability. The ability to take another person's perspective is seen as having special significance in the transition from premoral to conventional morality (i.e., from Stage 2 to Stage 3). Indeed, Kohlberg at times seems to imply that role-taking is seen as functioning primarily in the service of cognitive conflict; in other words, that role-taking experiences provide the individual with different perspectives, and so instigate cognitive conflict and its resolution by modifying the existing moral structure. In any case, role-taking ability is fostered by opportunities to discuss other people's points of view with them and to participate in decision making with them, notions that resemble Piaget's.

Kohlberg devised an elaborate Moral Judgment Scale to determine an individual's stage of moral development (Kohlberg, 1958). Subjects make judgments about nine hypothetical moral dilemmas and justify each judgment. The scoring is based primarily on the reasons given to support these judgments. Kohlberg's initial scoring system, on which most of the reported research is based, underwent several drastic revisions in the 1970s. The most recent procedure (Colby, Gibbs, Kohlberg, Speicher-Dubin, Power, & Candee, 1980) is extremely complex, as were its predecessors. It puts emphasis on fewer moral issues than the previous systems, and more weight on the highest stage attained by the subject on each issue. It requires that an idea in the subject's protocol must be explicitly stated to credit the subject with that idea. And finally, in recognition of the paucity of responses fitting Stage 6, this stage is removed as a scoring possibility.

An earlier, relatively minor change in the scoring was prompted by the finding in the Kohlberg and Kramer (1969) longitudinal study that a number of subjects attained higher scores (usually Stage 4) in high school than in their early college years (often Stage 2). This finding initially appeared to challenge the theory, which postulates forward rather than backward movement. For a time it was also viewed as possibly reflecting a kind of temporary disorganization that may characterize movement from conventional to principled morality. Careful examination of the protocols, however, indicated that the Stage 2 responses of the retrogressors did not show the unconcerned, self-centered, hedonistic reasoning characteristic of the "natural" Stage 2 responses of younger subjects. Rather, these subjects appeared to view morality in conventional Stage 4 terms, to have thought about it and questioned its validity. In the revised scoring system these reponses were assigned stage scores of 4.5. It should be noted that by age 25 all of these subjects are reported by Kohlberg as having developed strong, principled reasoning (Stages 5 and/or 6).

Relevant Research.   There have been many studies using various versions of Kohlberg's scale, and Rest's far more practical Defining Issues Test (Rest, Davidson, & Robbins, 1978) that appears to tap similar moral concepts. Much of this research is peripheral to Kohlberg's theory and will not be discussed here; it includes, for example, studies relating moral judgments to IQ, to Piaget's cognitive developmental levels, to ideology, and to political activism. I discuss only those findings that bear on the central tenets of the theory—that the postulated stage sequence is invariant, that moral growth is fostered by cognitive conflict and role-taking opportunities, and that the stages are homogeneous—and those that bear on the relation between Kohlberg's stages and moral behavior. We now turn to those findings:

1. Regarding the assumption of stage sequence invariance, Rest (1983) has reviewed a dozen cross-sectional and longitudinal studies and reports that they show significant developmental changes in the direction postulated by Kohlberg's theory. Rest adds several important qualifications, however: Many subjects show no improvement in moral judgment over time, especially adults who are not in school; about one out of 14 subjects who are in school actually move downward; and there is no clear longitudinal evidence that Stage 6 follows Stage 5. Rest also reviews several short-term intervention studies modeled more or less after Turiel's (1966) experiment, in which subjects were exposed to moral arguments one or more stages above or below their own predominant stage. The invariant sequence assumption predicts that subjects exposed to arguments one stage above their own would show the greatest change on a post-test, because in this condition subjects would be more likely to grasp the significance of the argument and experience the disequilibrium necessary for moral-cognitive growth. Arguments more than a stage above the subjects' would be too far advanced for them to understand, and arguments below the subjects' stage would be seen by them as less adequate than their own and not worthy of consideration. Rest concludes that the findings in these studies are inconclusive. He also discusses the difficulties in using experiments such as these to discover the determinants of development.

2. The studies just discussed also bear on the importance of cognitive disequilibrium, but in view of the inconclusive findings they cannot be seen as providing support for the idea that cognitive disequilibrium promotes moral growth. As for role-taking, a review by Kurdek (1978) shows that it generally relates positively to the level of moral judgment, although only about half the reported associations are significant. In any case, these correlational studies do not address the issue of whether role-taking is an antecedent or a consequence of moral judgment development, or whether moral judgment is a form of role-taking, with development in moral and nonmoral role-taking occurring simultaneously or through mutual influence. In a one-year follow-up of 10 subjects who had initially scored low on both role-taking and moral reasoning. Selman (1971) found that more children advanced in role-taking than in moral reasoning, and the two who did advance in moral reasoning were among those who advanced in role-taking. He interprets this as suggesting that the development of role-taking skills may be a necessary but not sufficient condition for the development of moral thought. This interpretation, however, overlooks the fact that a year earlier a third of the children with high moral reasoning scores in Selman's initial, larger sample had *low* role-taking scores. Thus, although it seems reasonable that cognitive conflict and role-taking could help foster growth in moral thinking, clear empirical evidence is still lacking.

3. Kohlberg assumes that each stage is homogeneous and that there is a high degree of uniformity in a person's moral reasoning level in different situations. The homogeneity assumption cannot be tested in most of the published research because total moral maturity scores or dominant stage scores are given with no indication of the individual moral dilemma scores. The few studies reporting such data do not support the assumption. Thus, not one subject in a sample of 75 college students obtained the same stage score in five Kohlberg dilemmas (Fishkin, Keniston, & MacKinnon, 1973). The scores obtained by adolescent boys and also by their mothers showed considerable "scatter" (Hudgins & Prentice, 1973). And two-thirds of a large college sample used different stages in Kohlberg's dilemmas then in evaluating a social protest movement (Haan, 1975). A small amount of situational variation might be expected due to random errors of measurement and might justify invoking Piaget's concept of "décalage." The high degree of variation obtained in these studies, however, argues against décalage, and therefore perhaps against the assumption that stages are homogeneous.

4. Kohlberg's theory does not predict a direct relation between moral reasoning and behavior. Individuals may exhibit the same behavior for different reasons, or different behaviors for the same reason. There should be some relationship between moral reasoning and behavior, however, and Langer (1969) has suggested a possible mechanism: A discrepancy between one's level of moral reasoning and one's overt behavior creates a state of disequilibrium, and to reduce this the individual is compelled to lessen the discrepancy by bringing

behavior and reasoning closer together. Whatever the mechanism, there is evidence of a generally positive relationship between moral reasoning and moral behavior (reviewed by Rest, 1983). Some interesting anomalies in these findings, due perhaps to variations in testing and scoring procedures, have been pointed out by Kurtines and Greif (1974). Examples are the fact that Stage 3 could characterize both the delinquents in a study by Fodor (1972) and the conformers in a study bv Saltzstein, Diamond, and Belenky (1972); and that Haan, Smith, and Block (1968), in their study of participation in student protests, found many Stage 2s among college students, whereas Schwartz, Feldman, Brown, and Heingartner (1969) found none. In general, there appears to be a positive relationship between moral reasoning scores and moral behavior, but there is no clear evidence that any distinctive pattern of behavior is associated with any particular moral stage.

It is natural to expect a highly cognitive system of increasingly complex types of moral reasoning such as Kohlberg's to show an age-related progression, and the research supports this expectation. It is evident from our review, however, that the research does not support Kohlberg's claim that this age progression reflects stages in moral reasoning that are homogeneous and appear developmentally in a universal invariant order; nor does it support his claim that moral growth results from role-taking opportunities and exposure to moderately higher levels of moral reasoning. Whether the problem lies in the inadequacies of method or in the theory itself remains to be seen.

Aside from the issue of empirical verification, Kohlberg's theory has been taken to task by Gilligan and Murphy (1979) for not taking the social context of moral action into account, and by Simpson (1974) for being a culturally biased approach that claims universality but is actually based on the style of thinking and social organization that is peculiar to Western culture. Stage 5, for example, makes sense only in a constitutional democracy. Simpson's criticism finds support in Snarey's (1985) recent review. The theory has also been criticized for equating moral maturity with a postconventional level in which the person, in Kohlberg's words, "has differentiated his self from the rules and expectations of others and defines his values in terms of self-chosen principles" (Kohlberg, 1976, p. 33). Some writers (Wallach & Wallach, 1983) view this "always giving one's own principles precedence over the laws and agreements of one's group" (pp. 186-187) as socially dangerous. And others view it as reflecting not cognitive structure, as claimed, but the content of Western individualistic philosophy (Hogan, 1975). Finally, several writers (e.g., Emler, 1983) criticize Kohlberg's theory as being inappropriately cold, cognitive, and rationalistic—as leaving the individual lost in abstract thought, with no affective impetus for moral action or commitment. A balanced summary of these and other considerations can be found in Gibbs and Schnell (1985).

Perhaps the most fundamental problem with Kohlberg's theory is that it rests on the assumption that there is a universal principle of justice or fairness. Kohlberg relies heavily on the philosopher Rawls (1971) who proposed an ingeniously simple, seemingly objective analytic device, the "veil of ignorance," for generating universally valid moral principles. That is, if one does not know what one's position in society will be, then a purely rational, egoistic point of view will lead one to prefer a just society—a society that best represents the interests of everyone. It seems clear, however, that any number of competing justice notions that sound like universal principles may be applied in a given situation. For example, some may think it is fair to allocate society's scarce resources according to the individual's need; others may define fairness as equity and advocate the allocation of resources on the basis of one's productivity or effort; and still others may think the only fair way to allocate resources is to give everyone the same amount. Need, equity, and equality may all be advocated from the veil-of-ignorance perspective—though by different people. People who view themselves as more capable than others, for example, may equate fairness with equity, on the expectation that they will do well in an equitable society. Furthermore, even if the veil-of-ignorance paradigm could generate a universal principle of justice, it tells us nothing about what would motivate people to act in accord with this principle once they know their position in society and their relative competence. The principle one chooses, and especially one's actual behavior in life, may then reflect one's personal interests rather than a universal principle. Indeed, one may choose a principle that justifies one's expected actions and rewards, as has long been suggested by certain "emotive theorists" in philosophy (Brandt, 1967).

The lack of a universally accepted justice principle raises serious questions about any theory (like Kohlberg's) that postulates a moral development stage sequence that is invariant, and in which movement through the stages brings one closer to a universal principle of justice. Until a universally accepted justice principle is found, there may be no grounds for assuming that one stage is higher than another.

Domain-Specific Approaches. An important contribution of Kohlberg's work is that it has stimulated others. Most notable among the newer cognitive developmental approaches are those by Turiel (1983) and Damon (1977). Turiel distinguishes between moral and conventional thinking, viewing each as a distinct conceptual domain with its own developmental history. According to Turiel, *moral* rules serve the function of regulating the behavior that affects other people's rights or well-being, whereas the function of *conventional* rules is to promote behavioral uniformities that coordinate interactions within a social group. Supporting this distinction is evidence that children's reasoning is different in the two domains: Weston and Turiel (1980) found that when school-aged children were presented with a hypothetical school that permitted moral infractions, they clearly regarded such practices as wrong, despite the school's policy.

They were, however, much more likely to accept changes in conventional rules. Smetana (1981) obtained similar results with 3-year-olds. To understand why young children are able to discriminate moral rules from conventional ones, Arsenio and Ford (1985) did two studies. The findings were that young school-aged children (a) justified their decision to intervene in moral situations by referring to affect-related considerations (''He made her feel sad''); and (b) recalled moral transgressions better than conventional ones following the induction of negative affect. This suggests that moral rules may be discriminated from conventional rules because affective information is a salient feature of moral events.

Damon makes distinctions within the moral domain and has studied the development of moral concepts in four areas: friendship, justice and fairness, obedience and authority, and social rules and conventions. Damon views moral thinking as task-specific, and he sees the child as having separate, potentially distinct moral concepts that are applied in different arenas, rather than being parts of a homogeneous, unified moral system. The child may, for example, use one kind of concept when dealing with the distribution of rewards and another kind of concept when considering issues involving authority relationships. To study concepts of justice, Damon asked 4- to 8-year-olds what they thought would be a fair way to divide candy, money, or toys in several hypothetical situations (illustrated with pictures). In one story, three children worked together to make bracelets for an adult. One child made the most and the prettiest bracelets; another was the biggest child; and the third, the youngest, could not work as well or as fast as the others. The adult rewarded the group with ten candy bars. The children being studied were asked what they thought would be the fairest way to divide the candy. In the responses to these and other stories Damon found evidence of age progression—from making little or no distinction between what a child would want for himself and what he thought was fair; to favoring an equal division; to recognizing that some children deserve more because they produced more; and finally, to understanding that several valid conflicting claims (e.g., between productivity and need) could exist and that one's task is to strike a proper balance between them.

Damon's work raises questions for further research. The young child's concepts of justice and fairness appear to be more sophisticated than one would expect for this age group, given Piaget's and Kohlberg's depictions of childhood morality. Where do these early moral concepts come from? To what extent do they affect children's actual behavior, especially when the concepts conflict with the children's own self-interests? How do these early conceptions relate to moral thought and action later in life? Do they have any bearing, for example, on a person's later acceptance of the ideologies that they at least superficially resemble (e.g., ideologies involving the distribution of wealth)?

In Damon's as well as Kohlberg's formulations, the development of moral concepts and cognitive structures is paramount. I now turn to a stage scheme for the development of moral affect and motivation.

MORAL MOTIVATION AND AFFECT DEVELOPMENT

Hoffman's Empathy Scheme

Hoffman's empathy scheme highlights motivation and affect in three types of situations: (a) One is an innocent bystander who observes someone in pain, danger, or some other needful state—momentary or chronic—and experiences conflict between the motive to help the victim and the egoistic motive to continue what one is doing and avoid the cost of helping. The conflict becomes more complex when two or more people need help and a choice must be made. (b) One experiences conflict between egoistic motives and one's feelings of obligation to another, or several others, with whom one is in a continuing relationship. (c) One has already acted in a way that has harmful consequences for others.

When moral development is cast in motivational terms, it raises these questions: What prompts people to go to the aid of someone at a cost to themselves? . . . to refrain from doing something they want to do simply because it might have a harmful effect on someone? . . . to feel bad about themselves when they realize that their actions have hurt someone? Hoffman's answer is empathy—especially empathic distress and other empathy-based affects. This is not new. As noted earlier, philosophers have long seen the value of empathy as a socially cohesive, moral force. There are also good evolutionary reasons for expecting empathy to serve as a reliable moral motive (Hoffman, 1981). And there is considerable empirical evidence that empathy and guilt function as moral motives; in other words, that they dispose one toward moral action (Hoffman, 1978, 1982). I now summarize the main concepts in Hoffman's developmental scheme for empathy and point out its limitations.

Development of Empathy. Hoffman defines empathy as a vicarious affective response that is more appropriate to someone else's situation than to one's own. Though an affect, empathy has a fundamental cognitive component: Older children and adults know that they are responding to something happening to someone else, and, based on their knowledge about others and their own past experience, they have an idea of what the other may be feeling; young children who lack the self–other distinction may be empathically aroused without these cognitions. Thus, the level of empathy depends on the level of cognition; and empathy development corresponds, at least partly, to the development of a cognitive sense of others. Hoffman suggests four broad social-cognitive levels (Hoffman, 1975a) that, when combined with empathic affect, result in the following four developmental levels of empathic distress:

1. *Global Empathy.* For most of the first year, witnessing another person in distress may result in a global empathic distress response. Distress cues from the dimly perceived "other" are confounded with unpleasant feelings empathically aroused in the self. Because infants cannot differentiate themselves from the

509

other, they may at times act as though what happened to the other happened to themselves. An 11-month-old girl, on seeing a child fall and cry, looked as if she was about to cry herself, and then put her thumb in her mouth and buried her head in her mother's lap, which is what she would do if she herself were hurt.

2. *"Egocentric" Empathy.*   Hoffman hypothesizes that, with the child's acquisition of "object permanence" including the gradual emergence of a sense of the other as physically distinct from the self, the affective portion of the child's global empathic distress is transferred to the separate image-of-self and image-of-other that emerge. The child can now be aware that another person, and not oneself, is in distress, but the other's internal states are unknown and may be assumed to be the same as one's own. An 18-month-old boy fetched his own mother to comfort a crying friend although the friend's mother was also present—a behavior that, although confused, is not entirely egocentric because it indicates that the child is responding with appropriate empathic affect.

3. *Empathy for Another's Feelings.*   With the beginning of role-taking, at about 2 to 3 years, one becomes aware that other people's feelings may differ from one's own and are based on their own needs and interpretations of events, and so one becomes more responsive to cues about what the other is feeling. Furthermore, with language, children can empathize with a wide range of increasingly complex emotions, and eventually with several conflicting emotions. Empathizing with a victim's distress, they may also empathize with the victim's desire not to feel obligated, hence not to be helped.

4. *Empathy for Another's Life Condition.*   By late childhood, owing to the emerging conception of oneself and others as continuing people with separate histories and identities, one becomes aware that others feel pleasure and pain not only in the immediate situation, but also in their larger life experience. Consequently, though one may still respond empathically to another's immediate distress, one's empathic response is intensified when one realizes the other's distress is not transitory but chronic. Thus, one's empathically aroused affect is combined with a mental representation of another's general level of distress or deprivation. It also seems likely that, along with the ability to form social concepts, one's empathy arousal may be combined with a mental representation of the plight of an entire group or class of people (e.g., the poor, oppressed, outcast, or retarded). This empathic level can provide a motive base, especially in adolescence, for the development of certain moral and political ideologies that are centered around alleviation of the plight of unfortunate groups (Hoffman, 1980, in press b).

When one has advanced through these four levels and encounters someone in pain, danger, or distress, one is exposed to a network of information about the other's affective state. The network may include verbal and nonverbal expressive cues from the victim, situational cues, and one's knowledge about the other's general affective experience that goes beyond the immediate situation. These sources of information are assumed to be processed differently. Empathy aroused by nonverbal and situational cues is mediated by largely involuntary, cognitively "shallow" processing modes. These include: (a) classical conditioning of empathic affect resulting from previous co-occurrences of distress cues from others and one's own experiences of actual distress (Aronfreed & Paskal, 1965), or from similarities between the other's current situation and one's own previous distress experiences (Humphrey, 1922); and (b) a two-step process involving the automatic, involuntary imitation of the victim's facial and postural movements (mimicry) and the resulting afferent feedback that contributes to one's understanding and feeling of the victim's affect (Lipps, 1906). On the other hand, empathy that is aroused by verbal messages from the victim, or by one's knowledge about the victim, requires more complex processing, such as semantic interpretation, or imagining oneself in the other's place (Stotland, 1969).

Hoffman suggests that the various cues, arousal modes, and processing levels usually contribute to the same affect, but that contradictions occur, such as between different expressive cues (e.g., facial expression and tone of voice) or between expressive and situational cues. If one's knowledge of the other's life condition conflicts with the other's immediate expressive cues, the latter may lose much of their force for an observer who knows that they only reflect a transitory state. Imagine someone who does not know that he has a terminal illness, laughing and having a good time. A young child might respond with empathic joy, whereas a mature observer might experience empathic sadness or a mingling of sadness and joy. Similarly, a mature observer's empathic distress (but not a child's) might decrease if the other person is known to have a generally happy life and the immediate distress is therefore known to be a short-lived exception. Clearly, the most advanced empathic level involves some distancing—responding partly to one's overall mental image of the other rather than only to the other's immediate stimulus value. (See Hoffman, 1986, for a more general discussion of the interaction of sensory, perceptual, and higher order cognitive processes in generating affect.) This fits Hoffman's definition of empathy, not as an exact match of another's feelings but as an affective response that is more appropriate to the other's situation than to one's own.

Sympathetic Distress.   The transition from global to "egocentric" empathy can, according to Hoffman, involve an important qualitative shift in feeling: Once children are aware of others as distinct from themselves, their own empathic distress, which is a parallel response—a more or less exact replication of the victim's presumed feeling of distress—may be transformed, at least in part, into reciprocal concern for the victim. That is, they may continue to respond in a purely empathic manner—to feel uncomfortable and highly distressed themselves—but they may also experience a feeling of compassion, or "sympathetic distress," for the victim, along with a conscious desire to help because they feel sorry for the victim rather than just to relieve their own empathic distress.

Hoffman's evidence for this shift comes from observational research (Murphy, 1937; Zahn-Waxler, Radke-Yarrow, & King, 1979) and anecdotes such as those cited earlier, which show that: (a) children progress developmentally from first responding to someone's distress by seeking comfort for the self, to later trying to help the victim rather than the self; and (b) there appears to be an in-between stage, in which children feel sad and comfort both the victim and the self, which occurs at about the same time that they first become aware of others as distinct from themselves.

What developmental processes account for this shift? Hoffman suggests that the unpleasant, vicarious affect that is experienced as part of the child's initial global, undifferentiated self is transferred to the separate image-of-self and image-of-other that emerge as part of the self–other differentiation process; as is the wish, not necessarily conscious, to terminate the unpleasant affect. Consequently, the child's empathic distress response now includes a wish to terminate the other's distress—the sympathetic distress component—and a more ''purely'' empathic wish to terminate distress in the self. The last three empathy development levels therefore apply to sympathetic as well as empathic distress.

Causal Attribution and Empathy.   In Hoffman's view, the partial transformation of empathic into sympathetic distress occurs when the other is clearly perceived as a victim having no control over his or her plight, as in an accident or illness. Other causal attributions are possible, depending mainly on cues that are relevant to causality. If these cues indicate that the victim is responsible for his or her own plight, this may be incompatible with empathic or sympathetic distress because the other may no longer appear as a victim; the observer may feel indifferent or even derogate the victim.

Empathic Anger.   If the cues indicate a third person is to blame, one may feel anger with that person—empathic anger. A simple example of empathic anger is the 17-month-old boy in a doctor's office who responded to another child's being administered an inoculation by hitting the doctor. Empathic anger can interfere with empathic or sympathic distress, or one might alternate among all of these feelings. If one were to discover that the victim had previously harmed the attacker, one might blame the victim and empathize with the attacker's anger. Yet another possibility is that one discovers that the victim has a history of being mistreated in his or her relationship with the attacker. In this case one may assume the victim had a choice (why else would he continue the relationship?), is therefore responsible for his own plight, and is thus not a victim. One's empathic and sympathetic distress for the victim and empathic anger at the attacker may then decrease sharply. Young children's empathic anger is apt to miss these nuances, and if children's perceptions are confined to the immediate situation they may respond in all these cases with simple empathic anger directed at the visible culprit.

Guilt Feelings.   A special case is one in which the cues indicate that the observer is the cause of the other's distress. It seems reasonable to assume that empathic distress occasioned by pain or distress in others that is caused by the observer will be transformed by self-blame into a feeling of guilt. Guilt feelings not only have the same cognitive requisites as empathy but others as well. Included are the awareness that one has choice over one's actions and that one's actions have an impact on others, and the ability to contemplate or imagine an action and its effects on others. These cognitive abilities are necessary for an anticipatory guilt feeling and for a feeling of guilt over omission or inaction.

Hoffman has presented a scheme for guilt, along with modest observational evidence, that highlights the parallel development of guilt and empathy (Hoffman, 1982). The scheme, briefly, is as follows: (a) Before children become aware of others as separate physical entitities they respond to simple expressions of pain in others with empathic distress; they may also at times experience a rudimentary guilt feeling, even though they may lack a keen sense of being the causal agent, simply because of the contiguity of their actions to others in distress, and to distress cues from those others. (b) Once they know that others are separate physical entities, children experience empathic (and sympathetic) distress when observing someone who is physically hurt, but the empathic distress can be transformed into guilt if they perceive that their own actions are responsible for the hurt. (c) Similarly, once aware that others have internal states, the empathic distress experienced in the presence of someone having painful or unhappy feelings can be transformed into guilt if one perceives one's actions as causally related to these unpleasant feelings. Even if one is an innocent bystander but for some reason does not help, one may feel guilty because one blames oneself, not for *causing* the other's plight but for contributing to its continuation by not intervening to help—*guilt over inaction.* (d) Finally, once aware of the identity of others—groups as well as individuals—beyond the immediate situation, one's empathic response to their general plight can be transformed into guilt if one feels responsible for that plight. At this advanced level, one can not only categorize victims but can also categorize oneself as a member of a group. One may then feel guilt by association if one's group is seen as causing the victim's distress or benefiting from the same social system that disadvantages the victim. Furthermore, Hoffman (1980) suggests that one may feel guilty if one simply sees oneself as being in a relatively advantaged position vis-à-vis the victim—*existential guilt.*

"Empathic Injustice".   Other information besides that pertaining to the cause of the victim's distress may shape one's empathic response. The contrast between the victim's plight and one's own good fortune was just mentioned. Another contrast that may shape one's empathic response is between the victim's plight and other people's good fortune: If one observes highly disadvantaged people in a context in which the extravagant life style of others is salient, one's

empathy for the victim may be transformed in part into empathic anger at those who flaunt their affluence. Still another contrast is that between the victim's plight and his own general conduct or character. If the victim is viewed as bad, immoral, or lazy one may conclude that his fate was deserved, and one's empathic and sympathetic distress might decrease. If the victim is viewed as basically good, however, or at least not bad, immoral, or lazy, one might view his fate as undeserved or unfair. One's empathic distress (or sympathetic distress, guilt, or empathic anger—whichever is appropriate) might then be expected to increase. Furthermore, the empathic affect may be transformed in part into a feeling that has elements in common with guilt and empathic anger but appears subtly different enough to be given a new name: a sense of *empathic injustice* (Hoffman, in press a). Empathic injustice may be important for a comprehensive moral theory because it seems closer than other empathic affects to bridging the gap between simple empathic distress and most moral principles.

Complex Combinations.   Complex combinations of empathic affects are possible. A shabbily dressed man, for example, is observed robbing an obviously affluent person on the street. A young child might feel empathic and sympathetic distress for the victim and anger at the immediate, visible culprit. A mature observer might have these same feelings, but a variety of other empathic affects as well. He might feel guilty over not helping the victim. If he is ideologically liberal, he might empathize and sympathize not only with the victim but also with the culprit because of his poverty. The observer might view the culprit as a victim of society, and feel empathic anger toward society. Furthermore, if the observer is affluent as well as liberal, he might feel guilty over being a relatively advantaged person who benefits from the same society. An ideologically conservative observer might not sympathize with the culprit but respond to him with unalloyed empathic anger instead. He might also feel empathic anger toward society, but in this case because he views the victim, not the culprit, as a victim of society (because of its inadequate law enforcement and citizen protection).

A Note on Attribution.   When situational cues are ambiguous, culture or personality factors may determine which attributions are made. Some observers may blame the victim in order to reduce the discomfort of empathic distress. There may also be a general tendency to attribute the cause of another's condition to that person's own disposition (Jones & Nisbett, 1971), or, more specifically, to blame others for their own misfortune in order to support one's assumptions about a "just world" (Lerner & Simmons, 1966). However, research showing a widespread tendency for people to respond empathically to another's distress (Hoffman, 1981) indicates that blaming others is not necessarily incompatible with responding empathically to them.

The Role of Socialization.   The discussion so far has dealt with the natural processes that may occur under ordinary conditions in most cultures due to the human tendency to respond vicariously to others. People also have egoistic needs, however, and socialization, which in part reflects the larger social norms, may build in varying degrees upon the child's empathic or egoistic proclivities. Hoffman (1970b) suggests that there may be little conflict between empathic and egoistic socialization in early childhood, even in individualistic societies. At some point the two may begin to clash as one learns that one's access to society's limited resources depends partly on how well one competes. Parents know this, and it affects their childrearing practices. For this and other reasons—such as parents' personal needs and stresses—wide variations in these practices, and so in children's capacities for empathy and guilt, can be expected. Specific hypotheses about socialization are presented elsewhere (Hoffman, 1982, 1983).

Toward a Comprehensive Moral Theory. Hoffman (in press a) has recently attempted to link his scheme for empathy-based affects to the moral-cognitive domain, especially the two predominant moral principles in Western society: consideration of others' welfare, and justice or fairness. His argument, briefly, is: (a) When one observes another person in distress, one often responds with one or more empathic affects. (b) To respond with empathic affect does not require the victim to be physically present. Because of the human capacity for representation and the power of represented events to evoke affect, one need only imagine the victim, as when reading about someone's plight, arguing over moral issues, or making judgments about hypothetical moral dilemmas. (c) Many, if not most moral encounters involve victims and potential victims and consequently evoke empathic affects. (d) Empathic affects are congruent with the moral principles and therefore capable of activating them in moral encounters. (e) The resulting co-occurrence of empathic affect and moral principle may create a bond between them. (f) In this way, moral principles, even those initially acquired in "cool" didactic contexts, may gain an affective charge and take on the characteristics of "hot cognitions."

Relevant Research. Research bearing on aspects of Hoffman's empathy theory are reviewed elsewhere (Hoffman, 1975a, 1978). Briefly, observations by Murphy (1937) and by Zahn-Waxler et al. (1979) suggest that when children under one year of age witness someone being hurt, they may stare at the victim, appear to be agitated themselves, often cry, and seek comfort for themselves. In the second year, they cry less often under such circumstances but their faces typically show empathic distress; they may do nothing, make tentative approaches, or actively try to comfort the victim—usually inappropriately due to their cognitive limitations. By 3 or 4 years, they show empathic distress but also try to help in more appropriate ways, which is also true of older children and adults. Further, in both children and adults the intensity of empathic affect and the speed of overt helping responses appear to increase as the intensity of distress cues from victims increases (Gaertner & Dovidio, 1977; Geer & Jarmecky, 1973; Murphy, 1937); the intensity of empathic affect appears to drop following acts of helping, and high levels of intensity continue if one does not attempt to help (Darley & Latane, 1968; Murphy, 1937). These findings fit the expected pattern if empathic distress operates as a prosocial moral motive, and they fit with Hoffman's stage scheme. Direct tests of the scheme have not been made, however, although there is experimental evidence for the hypothesis that arousing empathic distress in school-age children intensifies the guilt they feel over harming others (Thompson & Hoffman, 1980). Finally, there is correlational evidence for a relation between empathic affect and moral principles (Montada, Schmitt, & Dalbert, 1986).

Limitations of Empathic Morality.   There are potentially important limitations to empathic morality discussed by Hoffman (in press a). Most noteworthy are empathic bias and empathic overarousal. Regarding empathic bias, observers are more empathic to victims who are familiar and similar to themselves than to victims who are different, although they are also empathic to the latter (Feshbach & Roe, 1968; Klein, 1971; Krebs, 1970). It also seems evident that people are more empathically aroused by someone's distress in the immediate situation than by distress they know is being experienced by someone elsewhere, or distress likely to be experienced in the future, because several empathy-arousing processes (especially the involuntary processes such as conditioning, association, mimicry) are dependent on immediate situational and personal cues. These familiarity and "here-and-now" biases constitute a potential flaw in empathic morality and raise questions about its applicability in situations involving conflicting moral claims.

Hoffman (in press a) argues that the flaw is not fatal. He also suggests that it may be possible to minimize empathic bias by socialization and moral education curricula that highlight the commonalities among human groups, place high value on spatial and temporal impartiality, teach people to look beyond the immediate situation and ask themselves whether persons not present may be affected by their actions, and train them in the techniques of multiple empathizing.

Regarding empathic overarousal, empathic distress has an aversive quality, and we might expect it to be intense enough at times to direct one's attention to one's own distress, with the result that one does not try to help the victim. There is suggestive evidence for such an "overarousal" effect in highly empathic children (Kameya, 1976). In addition, highly empathic student nurses may experience conflict between their desire to help terminally ill patients and their own intense empathic distress that makes them want to leave these patients (Stotland, Mathews, Sherman, Hansson, & Richardson, 1979). Empathic distress usually does lead to helping behavior, however (see review by Hoffman, 1981). This suggests there may be a broad range of empathic arousal—perhaps determined by a person's general level of distress tolerance—within which he or she is most responsive to another's distress. Beyond that range one may be subject to empathic overarousal—hence too preoccupied with one's own aversive state to help another, or too prone to employ perceptual or cognitive strategies that reduce the empathic distress, such as looking away from the victim, thinking distracting thoughts, or making derogatory attributions. The overarousal effect surely limits the effectiveness of empathic morality. The limitation should not be overdrawn in the absence of further research, however, because the overarousal effect may enable humans to preserve their energies in hopeless situations and thus be more readily available to help others in situations where help might be more effective. For example, Stotland's nurses may have spent more time with other patients.

It thus appears that a morality based on empathic affects alone may be limited by familiarity and here-and-now biases, and by the possibility of overarousal. For these limitations to be effectively reduced may require certain moral socialization and education experiences that result in one's empathic affects being combined with moral principles (see Hoffman, in press a).

MORAL INTERNALIZATION THEORIES

Whereas *stage* theories describe moral modes and attempt to delineate qualitative differences in the modes children employ as they grow up, *internalization* theories deal with those experiences and processes that provide people with a moral sense and that motivate them to act morally in situations involving conflict between their own needs and the needs of others, without regard to social approval and other egoistic concerns. Since Freud and Durkheim, social scientists have agreed that most people do not go through life viewing society's moral norms—many of which deal with this conflict—as external, coercively imposed pressures. The norms may be initially external and often conflict with one's desires, but they may eventually become a part of one's motive system to some extent, and may help guide behavior even in the absence of external authority. There is disagreement, however, in the definition of moral internalization. Thus, a given theory of what fosters moral internalization—sometimes called moral autonomy, moral motivation, or introjection—may deal with a particular facet of morality (affective, behavioral, cognitive) and treat a certain aspect of the child's experience that is ignored by other theories.

Psychoanalytic Theory

The first complete theory of moral internalization was Freud's. Although it is not presented in any one place, the theory can be pieced together through two decades of Freud's published work (e.g., Freud, 1925/1961). The central thrust of the theory, which applies mainly to males, is as follows: The young child inevitably suffers many frustrations—some ascribable to parental interventions—that contribute to the development of hostility toward the parents. The child also desires close bodily contact with the mother for erotic pleasure. The main rival is the father, and the child's rivalrous behavior and expressed desires for the mother are often punished. Due to anxiety over the anticipated punishment—especially the loss of parental love, and abandonment—children repress their hostile and erotic feelings. To master the anxiety and maintain repression, as well as to avoid punishment and to elicit continuing affection from their parents, children adopt certain rules and prohibitions emanating from their parents that often reflect society's moral norms. Children also acquire a generalized motive to emulate the behavior and adopt the internal states of their parents, especially fathers. Finally, they adopt the parents' capacity to punish themselves when they violate a prohibition or are tempted to do so—turning inward the hostility they originally directed toward their parents. This self-punishment is experienced as a guilt feeling dreaded for its intensity and its resemblance to earlier anxieties about punishment and abandonment. Children therefore try to avoid guilt by acting in line with incorporated parental prohibitions, and by erecting defense mechanisms against conscious awareness of contrary impulses. These basic conscience-formation processes are accomplished by 5 to 6 years of age, and are worked through and solidified during the remaining, relatively calm years of childhood.

Moral internalization (superego formation) is thus a product of the child's introjection of parental prohibitions, which is motivated largely by the child's fear of losing parental love. The result is a disciplinary agency within the child that can detect transgression and mete out punishment in the form of guilt feelings. This all occurs early in life, before children can process complex information. Consequently these moral norms become part of an inflexible, primarily unconscious, and often strict impulse control system. It is interesting to note that the superego rests on an egoistic motive base (anxiety avoidance), although it presumably results in moral action.

With minor variations this theory of Freud's is widely accepted by psychoanalytic writers, although its main support comes from the scattered observations of adult patients. The hypothesis that anxiety over the loss of parental love contributes to moral internalization finds little support in parental-discipline research (see review by Hoffman, 1970a): Love-withholding discipline does not correlate with moral internalization (although it does correlate with the inhibition of anger); according to this research. The hypothesis that parent identification fosters moral internalization also receives limited support: Identification correlates with some visible moral behaviors, such as helping or making moral judgments about others; it does not correlate with guilt, which is an index of using moral standards for the evaluation of one's own behavior (Hoffman, 1971, 1975d). This makes sense because parents rarely communicate the source of their guilt to young children, who cannot make the necessary inferences about the parent's internal states without this information.

More fundamentally, it is unlikely that a largely unconscious, internalized control system can be adaptive, let alone account for the complexities of moral behavior. That this system is quasi-pathological has long been noted by Freud and other psychoanalytic writers (e.g., Freud, 1930/1955; Lederer, 1964). Some have tried to modify it to account for "positive" aspects of morality, but the processes invoked remain close to Freud's (see reviews by Hoffman 1970b, 1980). Others have suggested that, although the superego persists through childhood, it is disrupted in adolescence owing to hormonal changes, social demands, and new information about the world that may contradict it (e.g., Blos, 1976; Erikson, 1970; Settlage, 1972). Considerable anxiety results from this disruption and from the resulting threat to the close, dependent relation with the parents that supported the superego. The child must therefore find a new, more mature moral basis, or erect defenses to ward off uncontrollable impulses and to maintain the superego intact. These writers suggest mechanisms for a mature morality in adolescence, but the mechanisms are not clearly defined and persuasive data support is not offered (see review by Hoffman, 1980).

Social-Learning Theory

Social-learning theorists typically avoid terms such as *moral internalization* that pertain to internal psychological states that are several steps removed from observable behavior; but they do attempt to explain a similar phenomenon—overt moral action (defined by cultural norms) or the absence of deviant action, under conditions of temptation and nonsurveillance. One social-learning theory states that, owing to a history of experiences in which one has been punished for deviant acts, painful anxiety states may become associated with these acts—that is, with the kinesthetic and perceptual cues produced by the acts and the cognitive cues associated with them (e.g., Aronfreed & Reber, 1965; Mowrer, 1960). This anxiety over deviation may subsequently be experienced when one deviates or contemplates deviating even when no one is present, and it can best be avoided by inhibiting the act. Individuals may thus appear to behave in an internalized manner, although they are actually responding to a subjective fear of external punishment. When deviation anxiety diffuses and detaches from the conscious fear of detection, the inhibition of a deviant act can be seen as a primitive form of internalization that has much in common with the concept of the superego. Indeed, the initial inspiration for this theory was Mowrer's (1960) attempt to translate psychoanalysis into learning terms.

Social-learning theories also address the child's exposure to models who behave in a moral manner or are punished for behaving in a deviant manner. In the former case, it is assumed that children learn by observing and emulating the model in future situations when the model is absent. In the case of punishment to a deviant model, it is assumed that the child is punished vicariously or, anticipating the model's fate. avoids the deviant behavior.

Social-learning theory has inspired much research that, unfortunately, is plagued by serious problems (Hoffman, 1977b). In experimental studies designed to simulate the effects of punishment by parents, the entire socialization process is usually telescoped into a single adult–child interaction; that is, the child's immediate response to a particular punishment by the experimenter is used to indicate the presence or absence of moral behavior. This use of a single instance of compliance as the moral index blurs the distinction between moral action and mere compliance with an arbitrary request by authority; besides, compliance is a questionable moral index to begin with, as is evidenced by Milgram's (1963) finding that compliance can, at times, lead to immoral action. The research on models also has other problems and the findings do not provide clear support for the theory (see review by Hoffman, 1977b). Although observing models who deviate from a moral norm clearly increases the likelihood of deviant behavior in children, observing models who resist temptation and adhere to the norm does not appear to increase the likelihood of moral behavior. This may indicate that simply observing models who act morally does not arouse motives powerful enough to overcome the child's egoistic tendencies. The research also suggests that although observing models who deviate and are not punished fosters deviant behavior in the child, observing models who are punished has relatively little effect. The relevance of the latter research to internalization may be questionable, quite apart from the findings, because the children may be using punishment to the model only as an index of what might happen to them if they were to behave in the deviant manner.

There is another, more subtle social-learning approach that derives from the notion that one may engage in an act in order to gain reward from oneself (Bandura, 1977). It follows that if children are socialized to act morally and to experience self-rewards afterward, they will come to guide their behavior in accord with the moral norms even in the absence of external authority. This conception of internalization seems plausible, although there is as yet no evidence for it, and it does leave certain important questions unanswered. For example, why should self-reward contribute to moral action? People may reward themselves for any behavior, as Bandura states. But the behaviors for which they reward themselves depend on the cultural norms guiding their socialization, and in our highly individualistic society these norms are as apt to include competitive aggressive behavior as they are morally considerate behavior. Self-reward may not be a reliable mediator of moral action, therefore, for most people in individualistic societies. Furthermore, the self-reward concept does not explain how the self that is rewarded develops in the first place and what the mechanisms are by which moral actions come to reward that self.

Hoffman (1981) has suggested a type of self-reward that may meet some of these objections; namely, the self-reward that is inherent in empathy. A person who helps others may experience a decrease in empathic distress, as noted earlier; but beyond that, when the victim shows visible signs of relief or joy after being helped, the helper may also feel empathic relief or empathic joy. Having experienced these pleasurable empathic feelings, one may be subsequently motivated to help others in order to experience those feelings once again. This view of empathic pleasure as a moral motive still lacks empirical evidence: As noted elsewhere (Hoffman, 1982), the available evidence indicates that although people feel good after helping others, they do not necessarily help others in order to feel good.

"Self-awareness" theory should also be mentioned here (Duvall, Duvall, & Nealy, 1979; Duvall & Wicklund, 1972), although it may not properly be classed as a social-learning theory. Self-awareness theory assumes that one's moral norms for correct actions are an intrinsic part of one's "self." Anything in a situation that focuses attention on oneself may therefore activate and make one aware of one's moral norms. According to this theory, if one's behavior deviates from an activated moral norm, a state of tension may result that can be reduced by bringing one's behavior into line with the norm. Focusing people's attention on themselves can therefore lead to moral actions. In one field experiment, trick-or-treating children entering a home were told from another room to take only one piece of candy from a large bowl on a table near the front door (Beaman, Klentz, Diener, & Svanum, 1979). Children were more likely to take only one candy in the self-focus condition (the candy bowl was placed in front of a large mirror) than in the control condition. This theory, as well as the finding, is intriguing and potentially important; but as yet it contributes little toward an understanding of moral internalization because, as with the self-reward conception, it ignores the problem of how the self develops, how a person's moral norms become linked to the self, and why the egoistic aspects of the self are not activated when attention is focused on oneself.

Attribution Theory

The earliest attributional explanation of moral internalization is simply this: If the pressure put on children is just enough to get them to change their behavior and comply with a moral norm but is not enough for them to notice the pressure, they will then attribute their compliance to their own will rather than to the pressure (Festinger & Freedman, 1964). A more elaborate version of this basic theory is Lepper's (1983) "minimal sufficiency principle," which specifies that internalization is facilitated by parental discipline that puts the least amount of pressure on children needed to gain their compliance. According to this principle, when children are induced to behave in a manner that goes against their initial inclination, they seek to explain their resulting compliant behavior to themselves. If the external pressure is clear and unmistakable, the compliance is simply attributed to the external pressure; in future temptation situations in which there is no external pressure, there is no reason to comply. If the pressure by the parent is not salient, it allows children to generate internal explanations for their compliance; for example, they may see their conformity as stemming from their own intrinsic motivation to be good. When confronted with a later temptation to break the rule even in the absence of surveillance, they will not be able to do so without violating their own attitude, or their own self-image of being a good person. However, although these formulations have an elegant simplicity, they bypass the question of why children should subordinate their desires and change their behavior against their will when they are unaware of any pressure to do so.

An attribution theory advanced by Dienstbier (1978, 1984) is unusual in that it attempts to deal with affect and motivation. According to Dienstbier, the child is emotionally aroused when disciplined by the parent. The aroused emotion is at first undefined but is then given meaning as the child attributes it either to the punishment the child expects to receive (if the parent has made punishment salient) or to the deviant act and its harmful effects (if explanation is used and punishment is mild). At a later date, when the temptation to behave in a similar deviant manner occurs again, the emotional discomfort that the child feels when contemplating the deviant act will likewise be attributed either to the anticipated punishment or to the deviant act. If no authority is present and detection is unlikely, attributing the aroused emotion to anticipated punishment—which would have been likely in the child for whom punishment has been made salient—is irrelevant to the situation, and the child has no reason to resist temptation and refrain from the deviant act. Attributing the emotion to the act itself, however—which is likely in the child who is frequently exposed to explanations—is relevant even when no one is present and thus this attribution can be expected to play a role in facilitating the child's resistance to temptation. The use of explanations and mild punishment therefore contributes to moral internalization.

This explanation, which is in keeping with Schachter and Singer's (1962) formulations about the necessity of cognitive appraisal for experiencing specific emotions, is also elegant and simple. But here, too, the elegance may have been gained at the cost of ignoring certain important details. According to Dienstbier's theory, if punishment is salient the child attributes the aroused emotion to punishment; if explanation about the act is salient the child attributes the aroused emotion to the act and to the harm done. That is, the particular attribution made by the child is isomorphic with respect to the aspect of the situation that is made salient by the parent's behavior. The attribution may thus be little more than a labeling of the emotion according to the stimulus highlighted by the parent's behavior. What is lacking is an explanation of why the emotion is aroused in the first place and how it contributes to moral internalization. We may also ask how it is possible for the emotion aroused in discipline encounters to remain in an undefined state until appropriate attributions are made. Is it not likely that the parent's action (e.g., threatening to strike the child) elicits an *immediate* and specific emotional response in the child, such as fear, rather than an undefined feeling that is experienced as fear only after it is attributed to the parent's action? What is gained by introducing the concept of attribution? Another limitation of this and the other attribution approaches is that, like some social-learning para-digms, it seems to view moral internalization as nothing more than compliance without awareness of the external pressure that led to that compliance. Com-pliance without awareness may be part of moral internalization, but it is surely not the whole thing.

Cognitive-Developmental Theory

In contrast to our earlier discussion of cognitive-developmental theory, which focused on the theory's major preoccupation, stages, we here examine how cognitive-developmental theory treats the concept of moral internalization. Cog-nitive developmentalists, like social-learning theorists, tend to avoid terms like moral internalization but for a different reason: Such a term seems to suggest something outside the child that becomes part of his or her internal moral struc-ture. The child thus appears relatively passive in acquiring moral norms, rather than actively constructing them. Although these writers avoid the term, they do appear to have an implicit moral internalization concept that may have been apparent in the earlier description of Kohlberg's stage theory. This cognitive-developmental concept is that: (a) when people are exposed to new and morally relevant information that is more comprehensive and in keeping with a level of moral thought optimally higher than their own, they engage in active mental efforts to process this information and integrate it with their own prior view; (b) the normal human tendency is to move toward the higher level; and (c) the highest levels are autonomous and principled, and one may be said to have internalized them by virtue of having constructed them oneself.

This concept of internalization involves two assumptions. One assumption, implicit in stage theory, is that the new information must be at an optimally higher level than one's own and that one tends to move toward higher, more principled levels. This assumption may be questioned, especially in view of the serious limitations of stage theory summarized earlier. The other assumption, which is implicit in most cognitive theories—including nonstage theories—is that the process of construction is active and involving and that as a result the products of construction, regardless of their domain (e.g., moral, physical), become part of one's system of knowledge structures and it is in that sense that they are internalized. This notion of internalization, which may be divorced from stage theory, remains plausible, and it has a certain appeal because the individual is viewed as capable of thinking matters through and accepting moral and other concepts on more or less rational grounds.

Affective-Cognitive Synthesis

In Hoffman's view of internalization, moral norms are internalized to the degree that one feels an obligation to act in accord with them, and the obligation is no longer based on the fear of punishment or disapproval. The moral norm in question is simply that people should consider the welfare of others as well as themselves. As with other moral norms, it presumably has motivational, affective, and cognitive components. Thus, one is motivated to consider and avoid harming others; one feels good after acting in accord with the norm, and guilty (in the sense discussed earlier) after violating it; and one has cognitive representations of the reasons why certain actions are right or wrong—the prohibitions against acting in various ways that might harm others, and the probable consequences of one's actions for others. When a norm is internalized it is usually experienced as deriving autonomously from within oneself, with little recollection of where it actually originated. The question Hoffman tries to answer is what socialization experiences are necessary for developing such a complex network of moral cognition, affect, and motivation. His answer, the rationale for which is presented elsewhere (Hoffman, 1983), is that the relevant socialization experiences consist primarily of discipline encounters with parents that result in children's feeling empathy and empathy-based guilt over acting in a harmful manner toward others.

The central finding in a rather large body of research (see review by Hoffman, 1977b) indicates that a moral orientation that is characterized by the person's acting morally without regard to external sanctions, as well as by high guilt, is fostered by the frequent use of inductions. These are disciplinary techniques that point up the effects of the child's behavior on others, either directly (''If you keep pushing him, he'll fall down and cry'') or indirectly (''Don't yell at him, he was only trying to help''). They become more complex as the child grows older and may often include suggestions of reparative acts, such as apologies. In contrast, a moral orientation that is based primarily on the fear of punishment is associated with the excessive use of power-assertive discipline—force, deprivation of privileges, threats, or commands. There is evidence, however, that occasional power-assertion—to let children know the parent feels strongly about something, or to control children's unreasonably defiant behavior—when administered by parents who normally employ inductions, contributes positively to moral internalization (e.g., Zahn-Waxler et al., 1979). There is no relation between moral internalization and love-withdrawal techniques, which are direct but nonphysical expressions of the parent's anger or disapproval (e.g., the mother ignores, turns her back on, refuses to speak or listen to, explicitly states dislike for, isolates, or threatens to leave the child). Love-withdrawal, however, does appear to contribute to children's inhibition of anger. Hoffman's explanation of these findings is an information-processing type of theory (Hoffman, 1977b, 1983) that can be summarized as follows:

1. Most disciplinary techniques have a power-assertive or love-withdrawal component that may be needed to get children to stop what they are doing and pay attention to the information contained in the inductive component that may also be present. This inductive component points up the harmful consequences of

the child's action for others. Too little power-assertion or love-withdrawal may result in children ignoring the parent. Too much power-assertion or love-withdrawal may produce fear, anxiety, or resentment in children, which may interfere with the effective processing of the induction; whether the children comply or not, these feelings may direct their attention to the consequences of their actions for themselves. Techniques that include a salient inductive component ordinarily achieve the best balance, and if phrased in terms that the child can comprehend they draw the child's attention to the consequences of his or her action for the victim. This will often engage the child's empathic response system at whatever empathic level the child has attained (see earlier discussion of developmental levels of empathic distress).

2. Inductions help make it clear that the child caused the other's distress. This is especially important for young children who may not spontaneously see causal connections between their acts and other's states because of motivation, cognitive limitations, intense affect, or the ambiguity of the situation. The result of pointing out the connection is that children may then attribute blame to themselves. Self-blame may combine with empathic distress, as discussed earlier, to produce a feeling of guilt. These guilt feelings, aroused in countless discipline encounters over time, may produce a moral motive in children.

3. Inductions also give children information pertaining to the cognitive component of the moral principle of considering others. Aside from indicating the harmful consequences of children's actions, inductions may also communicate a prohibition against harming others, the reasons why particular actions are right or wrong, and the parent's values in regard to considering others. This information may be encoded, stored in memory, and cumulatively organized over time, and the resulting structure may constitute the cognitive component of the child's emerging moral principle. Because guilt feelings have accompanied the initial processing of this information in discipline encounters, the resulting moral-cognitive structure is charged with guilty affect and so acquires the characteristics of a motive. The principle of considering others may thus become a "hot cognition" resulting from the synthesis of affect and cognition in discipline encounters. In future situations, when the child acts or contemplates acting in a harmful manner, cues from the other person or the situation may activate one or another component of the principle; this may then enter into the balance of the forces determining how the child acts, quite apart from any concerns about punishment or disapproval. The principle can then be considered internalized.

4. The child's mental activity in processing inductions—the semantic interpretation of the informational content, and the act of relating it to his or her action and to the victim's condition—makes the child's own internal processes salient. For this reason, and also because of the way information appears to be stored in memory (semantically processed material is cumulatively organized and integrated into one's enduring knowledge structures, whereas situational

details are often processed in a shallower fashion and forgotten relatively quickly), children may come to perceive themselves, rather than their parents, as the source of this information. And they may feel that the guilt feelings originally generated in discipline encounters have come from within themselves.

Although this theory stresses discipline by parents in acquiring an early moral motivational base, the child may be receptive to inductions from other adults as well. Interaction with peers may also contribute under certain conditions, expanding the domain of situations in which the norm may be activated (but see the later discussion of peer influence). This domain is also expanded as children acquire the language and social-cognitive skills that enable them to comprehend the effects of their actions on others beyond the immediate situation, or to anticipate these effects ahead of time.

This theory is consistent with the discipline research that it was designed to explain. It is also in keeping with research that shows that: (a) optimal levels of anxiety foster the semantic processing of verbal messages, whereas intense anxiety fosters attention to the physical details of the message and the relative neglect of its semantic content (Kahneman, 1973; Mueller, 1979); (b) semantic processing by children and adults is cumulatively organized and enduring, whereas processing of situational details is relatively short-lived (Brown, 1975; Craik, 1977; Stein & Glenn, 1979; Tulving, 1972); (c) when people observe someone in distress they typically experience empathic distress, and when they are aware of being the cause of the other's distress they ordinarily feel guilty (Hoffman, 1982; in press a); and (d) guilt feelings function as motives for moral action (Hoffman, 1978, 1982). The theory gains plausibility from its fit with these bodies of research, but research is needed that tests hypotheses that are derived directly from it—for example, that guilt is more often aroused by induction than by other types of discipline; that guilt adds motive force to moral structures resulting from children's processing and integration of the content of inductions; and that the resulting moral motive is activated in later temptation situations and contributes to the balance of forces that determine how a person acts.

The Role of Moral Internalization in Society

Sociologists have long noted that there are not enough overt control forces to keep societies running smoothly, and moral values and norms have emerged to aid in this task. But although society benefits when individuals act in accordance with its moral values, this action does not generally reward the individual actor unless the value has been internalized. Internalization, then, serves the function of integrating the goals of the individual with those of society by translating the "social" into the "moral." As stated by Simmel over 80 years ago, "The tendency of society to satisfy itself as cheaply as possible results in appeals to 'good conscience' through which the individual pays to himself the wages for his righteousness, which otherwise would probably have to be assured to him in some way through law or custom'' (Simmel, 1902, p. 19).

Other sociologists argue against excessive reliance on internalization and draw attention to *external* social controls and the vulnerability of moral standards to external pressure. There is evidence for this contention. Milgram's (1963) experiments have shown that people sometimes obey requests by respectable authority figures to behave in ways that contradict their professed, and presumably internalized, standards. In a survey conducted by Baumhart (1961), most business executives agreed with the statement that "businessmen would violate a code of ethics whenever they thought they could avoid detection." In another survey, Harvard graduate students in political science, presented with details of cases of official duplicity, gave responses indicating "an orientation toward seeing things not in ethical but in cost–benefit terms and whether one might get caught" (reported by Otten, 1974). Ross and DiTecco (1975) cite instances in which morality actually broke down on a large scale when policing agencies were removed. These examples, together with familiar Watergate and corporate bribery revelations, should help us to discard any simplistic notion that a person's internal moral standards persist unchanged through life without environmental support, and to accept the face that internalized standards are vulnerable to external pressure and temptation.

Moral internalization may nevertheless be important for society. As an example, when many members of a society have internalized its moral standards these internalized standards may act as a brake and soften the impact of external (e.g., technical, economic) pressures for social change. The situation is complicated because subgroups—age, socioeconomic, ethnic—vary in the extent to which their members internalize moral standards and are exposed to external pressures against those standards. As a result, conflicts between subgroups, as well as between internalized standards and external pressures within subgroups, are to be expected. All of these conflicts constitute a major dynamic in social change. Moral internalization, then, although it is vulnerable to external pressures, can nevertheless serve a central, primarily stabilizing function in the social process.

THE INFLUENCE OF SOCIALIZATION
ON MORAL DEVELOPMENT

The research on moral socialization, half a century old, has generally been empirical, with little concern for theory. The exception is child-rearing research, which was inspired largely by psychoanalytic notions and eventually provided the basis for many internalization theories. Only recently has the search for socialization influences expanded to include peers, television, and sex roles, although this research remains scanty. The influence of school experiences, possibly very profound, has been totally neglected.

Childrearing Practices and Moral Internalization

The moral principle studied in most childrearing research is simply that people should consider the needs and welfare of others (e.g., they should tell the truth, keep promises, help others; they should not lie, steal, betray a trust, physically attack others, or hurt others' feelings). The focus has been on two aspects of the parents' role: disciplinarian and model.

There is an empirical generalization, noted earlier, that induction relates positively to moral internalization, and power-assertion relates negatively. Most of this research was done with children ranging from 4 to 12 years of age, although there is evidence that the generalization holds up for children as young as 2 years of age (Zahn-Waxler et al., 1979). The generalization is also supported by laboratory research (Kuczynski, 1983; Sawin & Parke, 1980).

One interpretation of this generalization is that because most of the findings are correlational, causal inferences cannot be made (Bell, 1968; Bell & Chapman, 1986). Although the general point about causal inference and correlational research is beyond dispute, it has been argued on theoretical, logical, and empirical grounds that the weight of the evidence in this particular case is far more favorable to one causal inference—that is, that the type of discipline affects moral internalization—than to any other (Hoffman, 1975c); and that it is therefore scientifically indefensible to assume we know nothing about causality in this domain.

The argument, in part, is this. First, parents begin to discipline their children in earnest by the time they are 2 years of age, which is several years before children show the earliest signs of moral internalization. Thus, parents are found to attempt to change children's behavior against their will, by 2 years old, on an average of about once every six to seven minutes (e.g., Minton, Kagan, & Levine, 1971), and they are usually successful. Second, parents exert far more control over children's behavior than the reverse (Lytton, 1979; Schoggen, 1963; Wright, 1967). Third, the internal states presumably elicited for the first time in children in disciplinary encounters (e.g., guilt over harming others, fear of punishment or of loss of love because of a misdeed) resemble the internal states elicited later, in moral encounters or temptation situations, in children who have or have not internalized a particular moral norm. These findings suggest that the effects of parental discipline predate children's moral internalization, and that the primary causal influence is from parental discipline to child morality. The influence may be mutual, of course, once the process is set in motion: When children begin to act in a morally internalized manner, they may elicit more inductions from their parents.

Several findings have been offered in rebuttal. They are: (a) altering children's behavior can affect disciplinelike actions by adult experimenters (Keller & Bell, 1979); (b) if children engage in impulsive, fast-moving play, this is more predictive of their unawareness of rules and conventions than is parent behavior (Johnson & McGillicuddy-Delisi, 1983); and (c) parental discipline is influenced by the nature of the child's deviant act, and by the extent to which the child is distracted (Chapman, 1979; Grusec & Kuczynski, 1980). The first finding is irrelevant because the adult in the study was a stranger with no power over the child. The second finding is irrelevant because unawareness of rules and conventions is not moral internalization. The last two findings miss the point of Hoffman's parent-to-child argument. The argument is not that the child lacks influence on the parent's disciplinary behavior, but that regardless of the child's actions—whether deviant, distracted, or attentive—parents can use whatever discipline technique they choose. The same argument can be made regarding genetic influences: If parents of children who were temperamentally abrasive at birth used few inductions, it might show that temperament affects the use of induction, but it would not be evidence against the contribution of induction to moral internalization. Many factors—possibly including genetics, social class, and IQ—can affect the parents' use of induction, but this does not negate the immediate, "proximal" impact that induction may have on the child's internal states in disciplinary encounters. The immediate impacts, cumulatively integrated over time, are presumably what count in moral internalization. In any case, two of the internalization theories discussed earlier, those of Dienstbier (1978) and of Hoffman (1977b, 1983), represent attempts to explain the ways in which inductions contribute to moral internalization.

It should be noted that the above argument applies to the relation between parental discipline and the child's moral internalization. It may not be applicable to other social influences (television, for example, as we shall see) or to other child behaviors, including empathy. Empathy may have a genetic component (Hoffman, 1981); and furthermore, it does not presuppose the turning against one's own self-interest that moral internalization implies and that presumably requires external intervention to overcome. The importance of parental discipline for empathy is therefore more problematic than it is for moral internalization.

Since the time of Freud, it has generally been assumed that children identify with their parents and adopt their parents' ways of evaluating their own behavior. The motive for identification is to avoid physical attack or the loss of parental love. To nonpsychoanalytic writers, children identify with their parents in order to acquire desired parental characteristics (privileges, control of resources, power over others). As the relevant research has been summarized at different points in this chapter and some of the methods criticized, it is necessary only to review the main findings here. The research (see reviews by Hoffman, 1971, 1975d) suggests that identification may contribute to those aspects of morality that are reflected in parents' words and deeds, though not to feeling guilty over violating moral standards (Hoffman, 1971), perhaps because parents rarely communicate the source of their guilt feelings to children. Children's motivation to identify with their parents may also not be strong enough to overcome the pain of self-criticism that accompanies guilt feelings.

In the early 1960s, Bandura suggested that identification is an unnecessarily complex concept; imitation is simpler, more amenable to research, yet equally powerful as an explanatory concept. Numerous experiments followed. Those that study the effects of adult models on children's moral judgment and resistance to temptation (reviewed by Hoffman, 1977b) are especially pertinent. The results include the following: (a) children readily imitate adult models who yield to temptation (e.g., leave assigned task to watch a movie), as though the model serves to legitimize the deviant behavior, but they are much less likely to imitate a model who resists temptation; and (b) when children who make moral judgments of others on the basis of the *consequences* of their acts are exposed to adult models who judge acts on the basis of *intentions,* those children show an increased understanding of the importance of intentions—and this effect may last for several months. (The theoretical implications of these findings were discussed earlier.)

It seems reasonable to conclude tentatively that identification can contribute to the adoption of visible moral attributes requiring little self-denial, and to the adoption of standards of moral evaluation that are internalized in the sense that children use them as criteria of right and wrong in judging others. However, identification does not—as inductive discipline apparently does—contribute to the use of moral standards as evaluative criteria for examining one's own behavior.

Peer Influences

Despite longstanding interest in the topic, peer interaction and its effects on children have only recently been studied systematically, and much of the research is descriptive. There has been little research on how interaction with peers affects the child's moral development. The dominant theoretical orientation is Piaget's (discussed earlier) in which unsupervised interaction with peers is essential for moral development: The absence of gross differentials of power provides children with the experiences—such as role-taking or decision making—necessary to develop moral norms and belief systems that are based on mutual consent and cooperation among equals. More recently and in a similar vein, Youniss (1980) has suggested that friendship among children is an obvious context in which they begin to understand cooperation and to jointly discover principles that serve mutual ends. An opposite conception is reflected in Golding's (1962) novel *Lord of the Flies,* and may be derived from Freud's view that one's morality may be thrown off in large groups where "all individual moral acquisitions are obliterated and only the most primitive, the oldest, the crudest mental attributes are left" (Freud, 1924, p. 288). This conception leads to the prediction that unsupervised peer interaction may release the child's inhibitions and undermine the effects of previous socialization at home. Which conception is right?

The research provides tentative answers concerning the effects of peer interaction on aggression, as well as suggestive insights about moral development. Before discussing these matters, I should note that there is support for the widespread assumption that peer influence increases as children grow older, with the peak occurring in adolescence (e.g., Berndt, 1979). By early adolescence most children are aware of operating in two separate and sometimes conflicting social tracks—a peer track and an adult track. As for the direction of peer influences—do peer groups support or undermine adult values? The answer is less clear. Most of the research on high school subcultures finds broad areas of agreement with adult values, along with modest differences in emphasis such as greater stress on athletics and popularity rather than on academic achievement (e.g., Coleman, 1961). A significant exception is the use of drugs by adolescents, which was found to be associated with the use of drugs by their friends (Kandel, 1971).

Regarding the role of peer interaction in the socialization of aggression, there is, first of all, an accumulating body of research suggesting that peer groups may not generally play a constructive role in handling aggression and conflict. Studies of free play in preschools show frequent conflict (ranging from two to twenty-four and averaging about nine incidents per hour), usually over possessions (Hay, 1984). The conflicts are usually brief and end without adult interference, but this is because the winner is usually the initiator who uses force, threats, or menacing gestures, and the other child simply gives in. Getting so easily what he or she wants probably reinforces the initiator's dominant behavior. Dominant behavior in the onlooking children may also be reinforced vicariously: Grusec and Abramovitch (1982) found that the peer models children choose to imitate are usually the dominant ones in the group.

Direct aggression, too, seems to be generally reinforced by preschoolers. After nine months of observations in two preschools, Patterson, Littman, and Bricker (1967) state that "the most striking aspects of [the] data are the richness of the schedules of positive reinforcement supplied for all three aggressive responses [bodily attack, attack with an object, invasion of territory]" (p.20). They conclude that the nursery school setting is unlikely to reduce aggression in children who are aggressive when they enter the school, and likely to increase aggression over time in some children who are initially not aggressive. The latter conclusion is consistent with experimental research reviewed by Hoffman (1977b) indicating that if a child observes a peer who behaves aggressively and is not punished, the likelihood of the observing child behaving aggressively is increased.

There is some evidence that older children, too, may reinforce aggression. Graziano, Musser, Rosen, and Shaffer (1982) found that third graders were more generous to altruistic peers than to aggressive peers when they did not expect any further interaction with them. When they expected further interaction—which is of course more likely in naturalistic settings—they were more generous to the aggressive peers. The authors suggest the children had already learned that an aggressive child is more likely to retaliate in the future. They are consequently more generous to such a child and thus end up reinforcing aggression.

Some writers (Hartup, 1983) suggest that peer groups may generate norms that guide individual members' actions and thus contribute to their moral development. In the best-known naturalistic study that provides relevant data (Sherif, Harvex, White, Hood, & Sherif, 1961), norms did emerge among the 11-year-old male groups, and the group's members were expected to follow the norms under threat of sanctions. Included were norms pertaining to dress (number of buttons on one's shirt), emotional expression ("Don't cry if you're hurt"), and readiness to fight outsiders. The closest thing to a moral norm was the norm against "cussing" that developed as a reaction to criticism by outsiders that some of their members cussed too much.

Do peer groups do anything that discourages aggression? Yes. In 45 spontaneous instances of physical attack during free play by 3- to 5-year-old boys, the aggression stopped or was stopped by another in those 27 instances in which the victim engaged in one of these "gestures of appeasement" or submission: bowing the head, kneeling with eyes averted, lying motionless with outstretched limbs (Ginsburg, Pollman, & Wauson, 1977). The only time a bystanding child helped the victim was when the attacker did not stop despite the victim's appeasement gesture. The help usually consisted of jumping on the attacker's back, allowing the victim to escape. Thus, even here, the aggression itself is not punished. Disapproval is expressed, but not so much for the aggression as for not responding to the appeasement gesture.

If peer groups reinforce aggression and dominance we might expect initially aggressive and dominant children to continue that way, and some who initially are not aggressive and dominant to become so over time. Several studies—in nursery schools, summer camps, and adolescent day groups—do indeed show aggression and dominance hierarchies emerging over time, especially in male groups (e.g., Sackin & Thelen, 1984; Savin-Williams, 1979; Strayer & Strayer, 1976). The investigators typically have an ethological orientation that views these hierarchies as functioning to reduce conflict and aggression. The hierarchies accomplish this, as among primates, by enabling each group member to anticipate the negative consequences of his or her resistance to demands by those higher in the hierarchy, and to avoid these consequences by yielding to the demands. The research supports this view: Conflict and aggression typically escalate early in a group's formation, reach a peak, and decline once a dominance hierarchy solidifies. The process of forming the hierarchy may involve many instances of physical attack, but once it is formed it can be maintained by subtle expressions of displeasure and occasional mild threats by dominant members. Researchers often ignore the psychological effects on the participants. An exception is Savin-Williams (1979) who notes the advantages for dominant members ("being the focus of attention may enhance self-esteem"). He also suggests subordinate members may benefit both by gaining group approval and by not having to make decisions or take responsibility for others. This may be much too rosy a picture, considering that many of those who become subordinate were initially compelled by force to give up what they wanted. In any case, this is not the kind of control Piaget had in mind, nor is it obvious how it might contribute positively to development of internal moral control.

Groups are more than dominance hierarchies, of course. Some members exist comfortably and friendship patterns emerge outside the hierarchy, and even within the hierarchy friendly interactions often occur. But there is no evidence that friendly interaction alone contributes to moral development, and, besides, the dominance hierarchy is likely to be activated whenever conflicts of interest arise. All things considered, Piaget's contention that unsupervised peer interaction is conducive to moral development may not be entirely accurate. Certainly with respect to aggression, peers appear to offer little constructive guidance or control. And dominance hierarchies may often preclude the equal, reciprocal interactions among peers that Piaget envisioned as crucial for moral development.

There is suggestive evidence that peer interactions may have a positive effect, but only in the context of appropriate supervision or "coaching" by adults. In the previously mentioned naturalistic study by Sherif et al. (1961), it was found that when two previously unacquainted groups of boys competed in team sports, considerable animosity—to the point of violence—developed. By working together on a superordinate goal, introduced by the camp counselors, they reduced their negative feelings. Similarly, in the preschool studies by Patterson et al. (1967) aggression was reduced by teachers who altered the composition of the group or introduced new activities that stimulated cooperative interaction. In the classic study by Lewin, Lippitt, and White (1938), "democratic" leadership, which included a great deal of adult involvement, had far more constructive effects than a "laissez-faire" approach that involved minimal adult intervention. In very much the same vein, there is a little-known study by Turner (1957) showing the capabilities of 4- to $6\frac{1}{2}$-year-old children for self-government. The children's behavior was truly impressive but it did require the very active, sensitive participation of the teacher. The teacher made numerous suggestions, provided the vocabulary and tools of democratic procedure, determined which matters the children could decide, and handled the inevitable power conflicts. Finally, there is evidence that children imitate a variety of actions by their peers, including moral actions such as helping others. If adults can structure groups so as to induce enough children to act prosocially, other members of the groups may see fit to follow their lead.

More research is needed concerning the role of peers in moral socialization; for example, we need to know whether naturally forming unsupervised peer groups at various ages, in different segments of society and operating in different settings, actually support or contradict prevailing moral norms. What types of peer interaction are most conducive to moral actions? How do children manage the different and sometimes competing messages of peers, parents, and teachers? Do dominance hierarchies control aggression, and if so, at what cost? What is the contribution of childhood friendships to moral socialization?

The Effects of Television

Children of all ages spend many hours watching television, and the trend in the amount of viewing time continues upward. Although wide variations exist depending on the segment of the audience surveyed, the average television set is on for almost seven hours a day, and children are among the most frequent viewers (Roberts & Bachen, 1981). The effect of television viewing on children has been the subject of considerable research, most of it on violence. Some argue that watching filmed violence may *reduce* one's proneness to violent behavior because of the cathartic release it provides (Feshbach & Singer, 1971). Others note that viewers, especially children, learn by observing and imitating television characters. Thus, if a child sees people (especially those presented in a positive light with whom the child might identify) handling social conflict situations in a violent manner, he or she might respond in a similar fashion when placed in a conflict situation. Repeated exposure may also blunt a sensitivity to violence, leading the child to underestimate. or to fail to anticipate, the painful consequences of aggressive acts (Thomas, Horton, Lippincott, & Drabman, 1977).

Laboratory experiments have shown fairly conclusively that children exposed to a live or filmed model behaving aggressively (or helping or sharing) are apt to behave like the model shortly afterward (see review by Hoffman, 1977b). These studies suggest that when children observe a violent television program they are likely to have an immediate tendency toward aggressive behavior. The important social issue is whether television violence has long-term effects. It does, according to researchers employing sample surveys who consistently find positive correlations between children's viewing of violent television programs and such measures of aggression as the amount of conflict with parents, frequency of fighting, and delinquent behavior (see review by Roberts & Bachen, 1981). These correlations do not demonstrate a causal connection, however. They may, for example, reflect a tendency for aggressive children to prefer violent television, as indicated in findings by Atkin, Greenberg, Korzenny, and McDermott (1979) and by Fenigstein (1979). Or there might be a third variable that predicts both aggressive behavior and the preference for violent television. Efforts have been made to overcome this ambiguity. In several studies in which the samples were large enough to control for a variety of third variables, the relationship between the viewing of violence and the tendency toward aggressive behavior remained, although considerably weakened. A more stringent, though possibly flawed (Rogosa, 1980) technique for establishing a causal connection from correlational data is the "time-lagged" design. This method was employed by Eron, Huesmann, Lefkowitz, and Walder (1972), and by Eron (1982), who found that children who preferred violent television were rated as more aggressive in their behavior ten years later.

Perhaps the most convincing way to test for long-term effects is to control the television viewing experience of children and observe their social behavior in a natural setting over an extended period of time. This is difficult, time-consuming, and expensive research. It demands the active cooperation of parents, schools, and other institutions. Control groups that are similar to the group watching the violent program are required, but must either watch a different program or participate in other activities. Children in a control group may resent being deprived of their usual television fare, and their possible anger over this change must be accounted for in analyzing the data. Children must be observed before, during, and shortly after watching the film, as well as some time later. The observers must not know whether they are observing experimental or control subjects.

Few experiments of this type have been attempted. All of them lack at least one of the above requirements, and, as I noted earlier (Hoffman, 1979a), the results are inconclusive. Feshbach and Singer (1971), in two studies in which 625 boys from 9 to 15 years of age in seven residential schools and institutions watched either aggressive programs (e.g., "Gunsmoke") or nonaggressive programs (e.g., "The Dick Van Dyke Show"), found no evidence that the violent programs led to an increase in aggressive behavior. Indeed, *less* aggression was found among lower-class boys, who were highly aggressive to begin with, and among low-intelligence hyperactive boys. who had watched the violent television programs. In a partial replication that eliminated some design flaws, no significant differences in aggressive behavior were found between boys exposed to the aggressive and the nonaggressive television diets (Wells, 1973). Parke, Berkowitz, Leyens, West, and Sebastian (1977) improved the design still further and used it in three studies of adolescent boys living in reformatories. Aggressive behavior was found to increase during and immediately following violent programs, but there were apparently no prolonged effects.

In a study by Friedrich and Stein (1973), children in a summer nursery school watched three 20-minute episodes per week for four weeks of an aggressive ("Batman" or "Superman"), neutral, or prosocial ("Mister Rogers' Neighborhood") program. Measures of interpersonal aggression, which combined physical and verbal responses, were based on observations made for two weeks before, during, and following exposure to the television programs. Overall, there were no significant differences among the three groups—although when the sample was divided on the basis of initial aggression scores, there was a tendency for certain subgroups to become more aggressive if they watched the violent programs. In a re-analysis of these data, Armor (1976) found that the children exposed to the *prosocial* programs actually exhibited the greatest post-treatment rise in aggression. Sawin (1973) also found no evidence for an aggression-increasing effect of viewing television violence.

In short, the data suggest some relationship between television viewing and aggressive behavior, but studies employing the most stringent methods have not been performed. As one moves from the highly controlled but artificial laboratory experiments to controlled interventions in natural settings, the findings become less clear. Both types of research clearly show that televised violence can have immediate aggression-enhancing effects. Correlational research indicates long-term effects but lacks the methodological rigor to support a causal inference. Studies in which television has been introduced into a community for the first time show children behaving more aggressively than they did previously, but appropriate controls are lacking (Joy, Kimball, & Zabrack, 1977). The field intervention studies show that children's aggressive tendencies in natural settings may be elevated while the children are watching television violence and for a short time afterward, but without further research the nature of long-term effects is not certain. These conclusions, drawn previously by Freedman (1984) and Hoffman (1984b), are still applicable and seem to call for more research.[2] It may well be, however, that the subjects' life experiences between the interventions and the observations of their violent behavior will always make the proper determination of the effect of television on violence difficult. And, perhaps more generally, the source of violence in society should not be sought in television's representation of society, but in society itself—for example, the influence of angry interactions among adults on children's aggressive behavior (Cummings, Zahn-Waxler, & Radke-Yarrow, 1981).

Other studies have examined how a child's identification with benign television characters may form a basis for influence. Can this kind of programming encourage in children such prosocial behavior as cooperation, sharing, and giving comfort? In the study by Friedrich and Stein (1973) cited earlier, the findings did not show a consistent pattern. However, when special training was added (e.g., role-taking based on themes in the programs), exposure to prosocial films led to an increase in helping behavior. The results of this and other studies (e.g., Coates, Russer, & Goodman, 1976) suggest that the prosocial behavior of young children can be increased through television when it is supplemented by certain training procedures. The results are thus very promising, but as most television viewing will continue to occur outside of educational contexts, further research is required on the type of programs that can increase children's prosocial behavior without requiring supplementary techniques.

---

[2]See a review by Pearl, Bouthilet, and Lazar (1982) that concludes that this research does provide relatively clear support for the long-term negative effects of television violence.

Sex-Role Socialization and Moral Internalization

About 50 years ago, Freud suggested that, owing to anatomical differences, girls are not compelled to resolve the Oedipus complex quickly and dramatically and therefore do not identify with parents as fully as boys. Consequently, females have less internalized moral structures than males. In Freud's (1925/1961) words:

> For women the level of what is ethically normal is different from what it is in men. Their superego is never so inexorable, so impersonal, so independent of its emotional origins . . . they have less sense of justice, less tendency to submit themselves to the great necessities of life and frequently permit themselves to be guided in their decisions by their affections or emnities. (pp. 257–258)

Freud's followers have differed in the details, but have drawn essentially the same conclusion: Females are more dependent on the moral views of others; males more often internalize moral principles and act autonomously in accord with them. Other developmental theories have ignored sex differences in moral internalization. An exception is Aronfreed's (1961) hypothesis that our society expects males to be self-reliant and to exercise control over their actions and environments, and expects females to be more responsive to directions from without; consequently, the moral orientations of boys rely more on inner resources than do the moral orientations of girls.

The available evidence, contrary to these views, is that females are more morally internalized than males. In a national survey, 14- to 16-year-olds were asked why parents made rules and what would happen if there were none. Boys more often said parents made rules to keep children out of trouble (Douvan & Adelson, 1966), suggesting an external orientation in boys. In an experimental study in the Milgram tradition, females more often resisted instructions to violate a norm against harming others (Kilham & Mann, 1974), which suggests that this norm is more deeply internalized in females. This finding is particularly interesting because females more often conform to instructions in experiments that do not bear on moral issues (e.g., Wallach & Kogan, 1959). In a field experiment, females more often returned valuable items found in the street when no witnesses were present; when others were present, there were no sex differences (Gross, 1972). In an extensive study of hundreds of 10- to 14-year-olds in the Detroit area, females gave strong evidence of having more internalized moral orientations than males: They were more likely to feel guilty after violating a moral norm (as indicated in story completion responses), whereas males showed more fear of external punishment (Hoffman, 1975b). Females also revealed a more humanistic moral orientation, placing a greater value on going out of one's way to help others; males placed a higher value on achievement, but this appeared to reflect an instrumental rather than a moral orientation. And finally, in a review of the research, females were found to be more empathic than males on most empathic indices except physiological, which may reflect male socialization to control the outward expression of affect (Hoffman, 1977a, 1978). A similar pattern of sex differences in moral orientation has been reported by Gilligan (1977).

These sex differences in moral orientation may be due partly to childrearing differences, as parents of girls more often use inductive discipline and express affection (Zussman, 1978). But the same pattern of sex differences in moral orientation has also been found in parents, indicating the need for a broader explanation. One suggestion Hoffman (1975b) has offered is that because females traditionally have been socialized into the ''expressive'' role—to give and receive affection and to be responsive to other people's needs—they are well equipped to acquire humanistic moral concerns. Boys are socialized this way too, but as they approach adolescence they are well equipped to acquire humanistic moral concerns. Boys are socialized this way too, but as they approach adolescence they are increasingly instructed in the ''instrumental'' character traits and skills needed for achievement and occupational success, which may often conflict with humanistic moral concerns. Burton (1972), for example, found that under pressure for high achievement, parents may sometimes communicate that it is more important to succeed than to be honest.

These findings, if substantiated, are potentially important. Because our society still defines masculinity largely in terms of achievement and success, the indoctrination of adolescent boys into the male role may often conflict with the moral norms they may have internalized in childhood. And, because the indoctrination pressures may be powerful, they may often override the moral norms and dull the edges of males' sensitivity to the needs of others. The instrumental world may thus often operate as a corrupting influence on the morality of males. It is important to know if this analysis is correct and whether it will also apply to women, who are taking on the instrumental role in increasing numbers. If it does apply to women, will this have future implications for the moral socialization of children?

CONCLUDING REMARKS

In this chapter, I have critically reviewed the major moral development literature. Rather than present a detailed summary, I shall discuss the major points in the context of suggestions for future research.

1. It seems clear that the search for an invariant developmental sequence in the direction of a universal moral principle has not borne fruit. The problem may be methodological, but it may also be more fundamental: There is no consensus as to whether a universal moral principle exists, let alone what that principle may

be. Investigators like Kohlberg are thus compelled to postulate their own moral principles, construct developmental stages through which individuals advance to attain them, devise measuring instruments, and collect data showing that people do in fact progress through these stages. When research fails to demonstrate invariant sequences, instruments are scrapped, new ones are devised, and the procedure is repeated in the hope that this time the invariant sequences will be revealed. I suggest that it may be better to start out empirically, as Damon has, and search for the actual steps in children's development of moral concepts in different moral domains. The question of whether or not moral structures cut across domains and develop in an invariant order may be left for the future.

2. The evidence that empathy and guilt feelings may provide a basis for moral motivation appears to be strong. Though an empathy- and guilt-based morality thus seems plausible, it may have several built-in limitations: If the empathy aroused is too intense, it may be transformed into an egoistic concern for one's own distress; a similar transformation may occur even with less intensity if the other's distress is communicated only through language (Hoffman, in press a); and an empathy-based morality may be biased in favor of people similar to oneself and people who are present in the immediate situation. It may be possible to overcome these limitations through socialization, and through education that provides connecting links between empathic affects and moral principles. In any case, a human response system like empathy that can transform another's physical or psychological pain into one's own distress deserves continued study and recognition for its importance in moral development.

Hoffman's stage theory of empathy, which highlights the interaction of affect and cognition, gains plausibility from its fit with several domains of research, although more research is needed before the theory can be evaluated. We need research to find out how empathy influences moral judgment and whether it contributes to the internalization of moral principles. We need research on conditions that lead to empathic overarousal, as well as basic research on the empathic process itself. I single out mimicry not only for its possible role in morality but also for its potentially broader contribution to social cognition. Do humans obtain information about others' internal states by unconsciously imitating their facial expressions and posture? How early in life do they begin to do this?

3. It is surprising, given the abundant evidence for guilt feelings as a reliable moral motive, that guilt has been neglected in developmental research. Perhaps guilt is viewed negatively in psychology because of its long association with psychopathology. In any case, there is evidence that a seemingly adaptive type of guilt can be fostered by parental disciplinary techniques that point up the consequences of the child's actions for others. Further work is needed on the socialization practices that contribute to adaptive and maladaptive guilt. As for cognitive prerequisites, it seems reasonable to hypothesize that to feel guilty one must be aware of having choice and control over one's own actions, and must be able to make causal inferences relating one's actions to changes in another's state or

condition. Yet Zahn-Waxler et al. (1979) have found evidence for a rudimentary guilt feeling in 15-month-old infants, who presumably lack most of these cognitive abilities. I have tried to explain this finding elsewhere (Hoffman, 1982). Briefly, the children's behavior illustrates not only guilt but empathic distress, and also confusion about causality (e.g., the child, though innocent, responds to the mother's sad expression by looking sad and saying "I sorry, did I hurt you, mommy?"). I suggest children may feel culpable because of a sense of omnipotence (due to incomplete separation from parents) and because this, together with their confusion about causality, may lead them to view all things associated with their actions as caused by them.

4. The limitations of empathy-based moral systems stem primarily from their motivational properties. Cognitive moral theories escape these criticisms because they postulate no moral motive. But without a motive these theories cannot answer certain questions: What prompts people to subordinate their own interests in the service of helping others, keeping promises, or telling the truth? And what makes them feel bad when they harm someone? Cognitive moral theories deal with principles such as justice and fairness; lacking a motive base, these theories have difficulty explaining how such principles become activated in situations in which one's egoistic motives are also involved, and why people may not only advocate but also act in accordance with these principles even when they are in opposition to their own interests.

5. It follows that a comprehensive moral development theory requires both a motive and a principle component. The motive component is necessary to assure the activation of the principles and thus the enactment of moral behavior even when one's own self-interest is involved. The principle component, although perhaps inevitably lacking universality, may help clarify the objectives of moral behavior, reduce personal bias, and in general transcend many of the limitations inherent in empathy. One step toward a comprehensive theory, implicit in much of the preceding, is to recognize that moral encounters vary in complexity. Perhaps the simplest is the situation of the innocent bystander, in which the basic elements of moral conflict are immediately present—an empathy-based motive to help someone and an egoistic motive to continue what one was doing and avoid the cost of helping. The situation becomes more complex when, in addition to an empathic motive to help, one also feels an *obligation* to do so, the source of which may lie beyond the immediate situation (e.g., activation of the general principle of reciprocity, or social responsibility). Still more complex are situations involving mutual rights and expectations. Moral principles should take on more importance as situations become more complex.

6. A further step toward a comprehensive theory may be to search for developmental connections between empathic distress and the moral principles stressed in our society, such as consideration for others, justice, fairness, and reciprocity. Because empathic distress is a response to another's internal state or condition, it seems reasonable to expect that empathic distress will often evolve

naturally into a motive to consider others. Although an empathic child may consider others without necessarily having a sense of moral obligation, this may change in adolescence when one's self-concept begins to include one's perception of how one relates to others (Damon, in press). Considering others may then acquire an obligatory quality; that is, it may become a principle by which one more or less consciously guides one's actions and evaluates oneself.

There may also be a developmental link, albeit a less direct one, between empathy and the principles of justice, fairness, equity, and reciprocity. This may be obvious when there is a clear victim, perhaps someone treated unfairly. But I have suggested that, even without a clear victim, an empathic observer may construct one. For example, statements of the equity principle that people deserve what they earn often have an empathic ring. Consider this response by a 13-year-old male subject to the question, Why is it wrong to steal from a store? "Because the people who own the store work hard for their money and they deserve to be able to spend it for their family. It's not fair; they sacrifice a lot and they make plans and then they lose it all because somebody who didn't work for it goes in and takes it." Responses like these suggest that empathy may provide a motive base for being receptive to principles of equity and fairness, and for guiding one's actions in accordance with them.

7. I mentioned the self only briefly, but one's moral principles sometimes are an integral part of one's self-concept, and people may be powerfully motivated to act in accordance with those moral principles that are tied to the self. If one's actions depart from these principles, they could produce feelings of shame or guilt. A morality that is closely tied to one's self-concept may not have the limitations of empathic morality. Such a morality may therefore be necessary for making extreme sacrifices for others, and for taking stands against agencies of established moral authority. If so, a comprehensive moral theory requires greater research attention to the relation between moral development and the development of the self.

In conclusion, I suggest three broad directions for future research: The search for developmental links between simple empathy-based moral motives and complex cognitive processes involved in choosing moral principles, building moral ideologies, and establishing moral priorities; the search for other motives that may provide a more direct and certain link than does empathy to the principles and ideologies involving justice, fairness, and reciprocity; and the search for processes in the development of a motivational self-system and its possible link to moral concepts.

REFERENCES

Ambron, S. R., & Irwin, D. M. (1975). Role-taking and moral judgment in five- and seven-year-olds. *Developmental Psychology, 11*, 102–110.

Armor, D. J. (1976). *Measuring the effects of television on aggressive behavior*. Santa Monica: Rand.

Aronfreed, J. (1961). The nature, variety, and social patterning of moral responses to transgression. *Journal of Abnormal and Social Psychology, 63,* 223–240.

Aronfreed, J., & Paskal, V. (1965). *Altruism, empathy, and the conditioning of positive affect.* Unpublished manuscript, University of Pennsylvania.

Aronfreed, J., & Reber, A. (1965). Internalized behavioral suppression and the timing of social punishment. *Journal of Personality and Social Psychology, 1,* 3–16.

Arsenio, W. F., & Ford, M. E. (1985). The role of affective information in social-cognitive development: Children's differentiation of moral and conventional events. *Merrill-Palmer Quarterly, 31,* 1–17.

Atkin, C., Greenberg, B., Korzenny, F., & McDermott, S. (1979). Selective exposure to televised violence. *Journal of Broadcasting, 23,* 5–13.

Bandura, A. (1977). *Social learning theory.* Englewood Cliffs, NJ: Prentice-Hall.

Bandura, A., & MacDonald, F. J. (1963). Influence of social reinforcement and the behavior of models in shaping children's moral judgments. *Journal of Abnormal and Social Psychology, 67,* 274–281.

Baumhart, R. C. (1961). How ethical are businessmen? *Harvard Business Review, 39,* 6–19.

Beaman, A. L., Klentz, B., Diener, E., & Svanum, S. (1979). Self-awareness and transgression in children: Two field studies. *Journal of Personality and Social Psychology, 37,* 1835–1846.

Bell, R. Q. (1968). A reinterpretation of the direction of effects in studies of socialization. *Psychological Review, 75,* 81–95.

Bell, R. Q., & Chapman, M. (1986). Child effects in studies using experimental or brief longitudinal approaches to socialization. *Developmental Psychology, 22,* 595–603.

Berndt, T. (1979). Developmental changes in conformity to peers and parents. *Developmental Psychology, 15,* 608–616.

Blasi, A. (1983). Moral cognition and moral action: A theoretical perspective. *Developmental Review, 3,* 178–210.

Blos, P. (1976). The split parental image in adolescent social relations. *Psychoanalytic Study of the Child, 31,* 7–33.

Brandt, R. B. (1967). Emotive theory of ethics. In P. Edwards (Ed.), *The encyclopedia of philosophy.* New York: Crowell.

Brown, A. L. (1975). The development of memory: Knowing, knowing about knowing, and knowing how to know. In H. W. Reese (Ed.), *Advances in child development and behavior* (Vol. 10). New York: Academic Press.

Burton, R. V. (1972). *Cheating related to maternal pressures for achievement.* Unpublished manuscript, Psychology Department, University of Buffalo.

Chapman, M. (1979). Listening to reason: Children's attentiveness and parental discipline. *Merrill-Palmer Quarterly, 25,* 251–263.

Coates, B., Russel, H. E., & Goodman, I. (1976). The influence of "Sesame Street" and "Mister Rogers' Neighborhood" on children's social behavior in the preschool. *Child Development, 47,* 139–144.

Colby, A., Gibbs, J., Kohlberg, L., Speicher-Dubin, B., & Candee, D. (1980). *Standard Form Scoring Manual.* Center for Moral Education, Harvard University.

Coleman, J. S. (1961). *The adolescent society.* New York: The Free Press.

Conger, J. J., & Miller, W. C. (1966). *Personality, social class, and delinquency.* New York: Wiley.

Craik, F. I. M. (1977). Depth of processing in recall and recognition. In S. Dornic (Ed.), *Attention and performance* (Vol. 6). Hillsdale, NJ: Lawrence Erlbaum Associates.

Cummings, E. M., Zahn-Waxler, & Radke-Yarrow, M. (1981). Young children's responses to expressions of anger and affection by others in the family. *Child Development, 52,* 1274–1282.

Damon, W. (1975). Early conceptions of positive justice as related to the development of logical operations. *Child Development, 46,* 301–312.

Damon, W. (1977). *The social world of the child.* San Francisco: Jossey-Bass.

Damon, W. (in press). Self-understanding and moral development from childhood to adolescence. In J. Gewirtz & W. Kurtines (Eds.), *Morality, moral development, and moral behavior: Basic issues in theory and research.* New York: Wiley.

Darley, J. M., & Latane, B. (1968). Bystander intervention in emergencies: Diffusion of responsibility. *Journal of Personality and Social Psychology, 8,* 377–383.

Dienstbier, R. A. (1978). Attribution, socialization, and moral decision-making. In J. H. Harvey, W. Ickes, & R. F. Kidd (Eds.), *New directions in attribution research* (Vol. 2). Hillsdale, NJ: Lawrence Erlbaum Associates.

Dienstbier, R. A. (1984). The role of emotion in moral socialization. In C. Izard, J. Kagan, & R. B. Zajonc (Eds.), *Emotions, cognitions, and behavior.* New York: Cambridge University Press.

Douvan, E., & Adelson, J. (1966). *The adolescent experience.* New York: Wiley.

Duvall, S., Duvall, V. H., & Nealy, R. (1979). Self-focus, felt response, and helping behavior. *Journal of Personality and Social Psychology, 37,* 1769–1788.

Duvall, S., & Wicklund, R. A. (1972). *A theory of objective self-awareness.* New York: Academic Press.

Emler, N. (1983). Morality and politics: The ideological dimensions of the theory of moral development. In H. Weinreich-Haste & D. Locke (Eds.), *Morality in the making: Thought, affect, and the social context.* Chichester, England: Wiley.

Erikson, E. H. (1970). Reflections on the dissent of contemporary youth. *International Journal of Psychoanalysis, 51,* 11–22.

Eron, L. O. (1982). Parent–child interaction, television violence, and aggression of children. *American Psychologist, 37,* 197–211.

Eron, L. O., Huesmann, L. R., Lefkowitz, M. M., & Walder, L. O. (1972). Does television violence cause aggression? *American Psychologist, 27,* 253–263.

Fenigstein, A. (1979). Does aggression cause a preference for viewing media violence? *Journal of Personality and Social Psychology, 37,* 2307–2317.

Feshbach, N. D., & Roe, K. (1968). Empathy in six- and seven-year-olds. *Child Development, 39.* 133–145.

Feshbach, S., & Singer, R. D. (1971). *Television and aggression.* San Francisco: Jossey-Bass.

Festinger, L., & Freedman, J. L. (1964). Dissonance reduction and moral values. In P. Worchel & D. Byrne (Eds.), *Personality change.* New York: Wiley.

Fishkin, J., Keniston, K., & MacKinnon, C. (1973). Moral reasoning and political ideology. *Journal of Personality and Social Psychology, 27,* 109–119.

Fodor, E. M. (1972). Delinquency and susceptibility to social influence among adolescents as a function of moral development. *Journal of Social Psychology, 86,* 257–260.

Freedman, J. L. (1984). Effect of television violence on aggressiveness. *Psychological Bulletin, 96,* 227–246.

Freud, S. (1924). Thoughts for the time on war and death, in *Collected Papers.* London: The Hogarth Press.

Freud, S. (1925/1961). Some physical consequences of the anatomical distinction between the sexes. In J. Strachey (Ed. and Trans.), *Standard edition of the complete psychological works of Sigmund Freud* (Vol. 19). London: The Hogarth Press.

Freud, S. (1930/1955). *Civilization and its discontents.* London: The Hogarth Press.

Friedrich, L. K., & Stein, A. H. (1973). Aggressive and prosocial television programs and natural behavior of preschool children. *Monographs of the Society for Research in Child Development, 38* (4, Serial. No. 151).

Gaertner, S. L., & Dovidio, J. F. (1977). The subtlety of white racism, arousal, and helping behavior. *Journal of Personality and Social Psychology, 35,* 291–307.

Geer, J. H., & Jarmecky, L. (1973). The effect of being responsible for reducing another's pain on subject's response and arousal. *Journal of Personality and Social Psychology, 26,* 232–237.

Gibbs, J. C., & Schnell, S. V. (1985). Moral development "versus" socialization. *American Psychologist, 40*, 1071–1080.

Gilligan, C. (1977). In a different voice: Women's conceptions of the self and of morality. *Harvard Educational Review, 47*, 481–517.

Gilligan, C., & Murphy, J. M. (1979). Development from adolescence to adulthood. The philosopher and the "dilemma of fact." In D. Kuhn (Ed.), *Intellectual development beyond childhood*. San Francisco: Jossey-Bass.

Ginsburg, H. J., Pollman, V. A., & Wauson, M. S. (1977). An ethological analysis of nonverbal inhibitors of aggressive behavior in male elementary school children. *Developmental Psychology, 13*, 417–418.

Golding, W. G. (1962). *Lord of the flies*. New York: Howard-McCann.

Graziano, W. G., Musser, L. M., Rosen, S., & Shaffer, D. R. (1982). The development of fair-play standards in same-race and mixed-race situations. *Child Development, 53*, 938–947.

Gross, A. E. (1972, September). *Sex and helping; Intrinsic glow and extrinsic show*. Paper presented at the meetings of the American Psychological Association, Honolulu.

Grusec, J. E., & Kuczynski, L. (1980). Directions of effect in socialization: A comparison of the parent's vs. the child's behavior as determinants of disciplinary techniques. *Developmental Psychology, 16*, 1–9.

Grusec, J. E., & Abramovitch, R. (1982). Imitation of peers and adults in a natural setting: A functional analysis. *Child Development, 53*, 636–642.

Haan, N. (1975). Hypothetical and actual moral reasoning in a situation of civil disobedience. *Journal of Personality and Social Psychology, 32*, 255–270.

Haan, N., Smith, M. B., & Block, J. (1968). Moral reasoning of young adults: Political–social behavior, family background, and personality correlates. *Journal of Personality and Social Psychology, 10*, 183–201.

Hartup, W. W. (1983). Peer relations. In E. M. Hetherington (Ed.), *Social development*, in P. Mussen (Ed.), *Carmichael's manual of child psychology* (4th ed.). New York: Wiley.

Hay, D. F. (1984). Social conflict in early childhood. *Annals of Child Development, 1*, 1–44.

Hoffman, M. L. (1970a). Moral development. In P. H. Mussen (Ed.), *Carmichael's manual of child psychology* (Vol. 2). New York: Wiley.

Hoffman, M. L. (1970b). Conscience, personality, and socialization techniques. *Human Development, 13*, 90–126.

Hoffman, M. L. (1971). Identification and conscience development. *Child Development, 42*, 1071–1082.

Hoffman, M. L. (1975a). Developmental synthesis of affect and cognition and its implications for altruistic motivation. *Developmental Psychology, 11*, 607–622.

Hoffman, M. L. (1975b). Sex differences in moral internalization. *Journal of Personality and Social Psychology, 32*, 720–729.

Hoffman, M. L. (1975c). Moral internalization, parental power, and the nature of parent–child interaction. *Developmental Psychology, 11*, 228–239.

Hoffman, M. L. (1975d). Altruistic behavior and the parent–child relationship. *Journal of Personality and Social Psychology, 31*, 937–943.

Hoffman, M. L. (1977a). Sex differences in empathy and related behaviors. *Psychological Bulletin, 84*, 712–722.

Hoffman, M. L. (1977b). Moral internalization: Current theory and research. In L. Berkowitz (Ed.), *Advances in experimental social psychology* (Vol. 10). New York: Academic Press.

Hoffman, M. L. (1978). Empathy, its development and prosocial implications. In C. B. Keasey (Ed.), *Nebraska Symposium on Motivation* (Vol. 25). Lincoln: University of Nebraska Press.

Hoffman, M. L. (1979a). Development of moral thought, feeling, and behavior. *American Psychologist, 34*, 958–966.

Hoffman, M. L. (1979b). Identification and imitation in children. *ERIC Reports, ED 175 537*.

Hoffman, M. L. (1980). Adolescent morality in developmental perspective. In J. Adelson (Ed.), *Handbook of adolescent psychology*. New York: Wiley Interscience.

Hoffman, M. L. (1981). Is altruism part of human nature? *Journal of Personality and Social Psychology, 40*, 121–137.

Hoffman, M. L. (1982). Development of prosocial motivation: Empathy and guilt. In N. Eisenberg (Ed.), *Development of prosocial behavior*. New York: Academic Press.

Hoffman, M. L. (1983). Affective and cognitive processes in moral internalization: An information-processing approach. In E. T. Higgins, D. Ruble, & W. Hartup (Eds.), *Social cognition and social development: A socio-cultural perspective*. New York: Cambridge University Press.

Hoffman, M. L. (1984a). Interaction of affect and cognition in empathy. In C. Izard, J. Kagan, & R. Zajonc (Eds.), *Emotion, cognition, and behavior*. New York: Cambridge University Press.

Hoffman, M. L. (1984b). Moral development. In M. E. Lamb & M. H. Bornstein (Eds.), *Developmental psychology*. Hillsdale, NJ: Lawrence Erlbaum Associates.

Hoffman, M. L. (1986). Affect, motivation, and cognition. In R. M. Sorrentino & E. T. Higgins (Eds.), *Handbook of motivation and cognition: Foundations of social behavior* (pp. 244–280). New York: Guilford.

Hoffman, M. L. (in press a). The contribution of empathy to justice and moral judgment. In N. Eisenberg & J. Strayer (Eds.), *Empathy: A developmental perspective*. New York: Cambridge University Press.

Hoffman, M. L. (in press b). Empathy and prosocial activism. In N. Eisenberg, J. Reykowski, & E. Staub (Eds.), *Individual and societal perspectives*. Hillsdale, NJ: Lawrence Erlbaum Associates.

Hogan, R. (1975). Theoretical egocentrism and the problem of compliance. *American Psychologist, 30*, 533–540.

Hudgins, W., & Prentice, N. (1973). Moral judgment in delinquent and nondelinquent adolescents and their mothers. *Journal of Abnormal Psychology, 82*, 145–152.

Hume, D. (1751/1957). *An inquiry concerning the principle of morals* (Vol. 4). New York: Liberal Arts Press.

Humphrey, G. (1922). The conditioned reflex and the elementary social reaction. *Journal of Abnormal and Social Psychology, 17*, 113–119.

Imamoglu, E. O. (1975). Children's awareness and usage of intention cues. *Child Development, 46*, 39–45.

Johnson, J. E., & McGillicuddy-Delisi, A. (1983). Family environment factors and children's knowledge of rules and conventions. *Child Development, 54*, 218–226.

Jones, E. E., & Nisbett, R. E. (1971). The action and the observer: Divergent perceptions of the causes of behavior. In E. E. Jones, D. E. Kanouse, H. H. Kelley, R. E. Nisbett, S. Valins, & B. Weiner (Eds.), *Attribution: Perceiving the causes of behavior*. Morristown, NJ: General Learning Press.

Joy, L. A., Kimball, M., & Zabrack, M. L. (1977). *Television exposure and children's aggressive behavior*. Presented at Canadian Psychological Association, Vancouver.

Kahneman, D. (1973). *Attention and effort*. Englewood Cliffs, NJ: Prentice-Hall.

Kameya, L. I. (1976). *The effect of empathy level and role-taking training upon prosocial behavior*. Unpublished doctoral dissertation, University of Michigan.

Kandel, D. (1971). Adolescent marijuana use: Role of parents and peers. *Science, 5*, 216–220.

Keller, B. B., & Bell, R. Q. (1979). Child effects on adult's method of eliciting altruistic behavior. *Child Development, 50*, 1004–1009.

Kilham, W., & Mann, L. (1974). Level of destructive obedience as a function of transmitter and executant roles in the Milgram Obedience Paradigm. *Journal of Personality and Social Psychology, 29*, 696–702.

Klein, R. (1971). Some factors influencing empathy in six- and seven-year-old children varying in ethnic background (Doctoral dissertation, University of California, Los Angeles, 1970). *Dissertation Abstracts International, 31*, 3960A. (University Microfilms No. 71-3862)

Kohlberg, L. (1958). *The development of modes of moral thinking and choice in the years 10–16.* Unpublished doctoral dissertation, University of Chicago.

Kohlberg, L. (1976). Moral stage and moralization: The cognitive-developmental approach. In T. Lickona (Ed.), *Moral development and behavior: Theory, research, and social issues* (pp. 31–53). New York: Holt, Rinehart & Winston.

Kohlberg, L., & Kramer, R. (1969). Continuities and discontinuities in childhood and adult moral development. *Human Development, 12,* 93–120.

Kohlberg, L., Levine, C., & Hower, A. (1983). Moral stages: A current formulation and a response to critics. *Contributions to Human Development: Vol. 10.* Basel: Karger.

Krebs, D. L. (1970). Altruism: An examination of the concept and a review of the literature. *Psychological Bulletin, 73,* 258–303.

Kuczynski, L. (1983). Reasoning, prohibitions, and motivations for compliance. *Developmental Psychology, 19,* 126–134.

Kurdek, L. A. (1978). Perspective-taking as the cognitive basis of children's moral development: A review of the literature. *Merrill-Palmer Quarterly, 24,* 3–28.

Kurtines, W., & Greif, E. B. (1974). The development of moral thought: Review and evaluation of Kohlberg's approach. *Psychological Bulletin, 81,* 453–470.

Langer, J. (1969). Disequilibrium as a source of development. In P. H. Mussen, J. Langer, & M. Covington (Eds.), *Trends and issues in developmental psychology.* New York: Holt, Rinehart & Winston.

Lederer, W. (1964). Dragons, delinquents, and destiny. *Psychological Issues, 4.*

Lepper, M. (1983). Social-control processes and the internalization of social values: An attributional perspective. In E. T. Higgins, D. Ruble, & W. Hartup (Eds.), *Social cognition and social development: A socio-cultural perspective.* New York: Cambridge University Press.

Lerner, M. J., & Simmons, C. (1966). Observer's reaction to the innocent victim: Compassion or rejection? *Journal of Personality and Social Psychology, 67,* 371–378.

Lewin, K., Lippitt, R., & White, R. K. (1938). Patterns of aggressive behavior in experimentally created "social climates." *Journal of Social Psychology, 10,* 271–299.

Lipps, T. (1906). Das Wissen von fremden Ichen. *Psychologische Untersuchungen,* 694–722.

Lytton, H. (1979). Disciplinary encounters between young boys and their mothers and fathers: Is there a contingency system? *Developmental Psychology, 15,* 256–268.

Milgram, S. (1963). Behavioral study of obedience. *Journal of Personality and Social Psychology, 67,* 371–378.

Minton, C., Kagan, J., & Levine, J. (1971). Maternal control and obedience in the two-year-old. *Child Development, 42,* 1873–1894.

Montada, L., Schmitt, M., & Dalbert, C. (1986). Thinking about justice and dealing with one's privileges: A study on existential guilt. In H. W. Bierhoff, R. Cohen, & J. Greenberg (Eds.), *Justice in social relations.* New York: Plenum Press.

Mowrer, O. H. (1960). *Learning theory and behavior.* New York: Wiley.

Mueller, J. H. (1979). Anxiety and encoding processing in memory. *Personality and Social Psychology Bulletin, 5,* 288–294.

Murphy, L. B. (1937). *Social behavior and child personality.* New York: Columbia University Press.

Otten, A. L. (1974, April 11). Politics and people. *Wall Street Journal.*

Parke, R. D., Berkowitz, L., Leyens, J. P., West, S. G., & Sebastian, R. J. (1977). Some effects of violent and nonviolent movies on behavior of juvenile delinquents. In L. Berkowitz (Ed.), *Advances in experimental social psychology* (Vol. 10 pp. 136–172). New York: Academic Press.

Patterson, G. R., Littman, R. A., & Bricker, W. (1967). Assertive behavior in young children: A step toward a theory of aggression. *Monographs of the Society for Research in Child Development, 35,* 5.

Pearl, D., Boutheilet, L., & Lazar, J. (1982). *Television and behavior: Ten years of scientific progress and implications for the 1980's.* U. S. Department of Health and Human Services, Public Health Service.

Piaget, J. (1932). *The moral judgment of the child.* New York: Harcourt.

Rawls, J. (1971). *A theory of justice.* Cambridge, MA: Harvard University Press.

Rest, J. R. (1983). Morality. In J. Flavell & E. Markman (Eds.), *Cognitive development.* In P. Mussen (Ed.), *Carmichael's manual of child psychology* (4th ed.). New York: Wiley.

Rest, J., Davidson, M. L., & Robbins, S. (1978). Age trends in judging moral issues: A review of cross-sectional and longitudinal studies of the Defining Issues Test. *Child Development, 49,* 263–279.

Roberts, D. F., & Bachen, C. M. (1981). Mass communications effects. *Annual Review of Psychology, 32,* 307–356.

Rogosa, D. (1980). A critique of cross-lagged correlation. *Psychological Bulletin, 88,* 245–258.

Ross, M., & DiTecco, D. (1975). An attributional analysis of moral judgments. *Journal of Social Issues, 31,* 91–110.

Sackin, S., & Thelen, E. (1984). An ethological study of peaceful associative outcomes to conflict in preschool children. *Child Development, 55,* 1098–1102.

Saltzstein, H. D., Diamond, R. M., & Belenky, M. (1972). Moral judgment level and conformity behavior. *Developmental Psychology, 7* 327–336.

Savin-Williams, R. C. (1979). Dominance hierarchies in groups of early adolescents. *Child Development, 50,* 923–935.

Sawin, D. B. (1973). *Aggressive behavior among children in small playgroup settings with violent television.* Doctoral dissertation, University of Minnesota.

Sawin, D. B., & Parke, R. D. (1980). Empathy and fear as mediators of resistance-to-deviation in children. *Merrill-Palmer Quarterly, 26,* 123–134.

Schachter, S., & Singer, J. E. (1962). Cognitive, social, and physiological determinants of emotional state. *Psychological Review, 69,* 379–399.

Schoggen, P. (1963). Environmental forces in the everyday lives of children. In R. G. Barker (Ed.), *The stream of behavior: Explorations of its structure and content.* New York: Appleton-Century-Crofts.

Schwartz, S. H., Feldman, K. A., Brown, M. E., & Heingartner, A. (1969). Some personality correlates of conduct in two situations of moral conflict. *Journal of Personality, 37,* 41–57.

Selman, R. (1971). The relation of role-taking to the development of moral judgments in children. *Child Development, 42,* 79–91.

Settlage, C. F. (1972). Cultural values and the superego in late adolescence. *Psychoanalytic Study of the Child, 27,* 57–73.

Sherif, M., Harvey, O. J., White, B. J., Hood, W. R., & Sherif, C. (1961). *Intergroup conflict and cooperation: The robbers cave experiment.* Norman, OK: University Book Exchange.

Simmel, G. (1902). The number of members as determining the sociological form of the group. *American Journal of Sociology, 8,* 1–46.

Simpson, E. L. (1974). Moral development research: A case study of scientific culture bias. *Human Development, 17,* 81–106.

Smetana, J. (1981). Preschool children's conceptions of moral and social rules. *Child Development, 52,* 1333–1336.

Smith, A. (1759/1965). The theory of moral sentiments. In A. Selby-Bigge (Ed.), *British moralists.* New York: Dover.

Snarey, J. (1985). The cross-cultural universality of social–moral development: A critical review of Kohlbergian research. *Psychological Bulletin, 97,* 202–232.

Stein, N. A., & Glenn, C. (1979). An analysis of story comprehension. In R. O. Freedle (Ed.), *New directions in discourse processing.* Norwood, NJ: Ablex.

Sternlieb, J. L., & Youniss, J. (1975). Moral judgments one year after intentional or consequence modeling. *Journal of Personality and Social Psychology, 31,* 895–897.

Stotland, E. (1969). Exploratory investigations of empathy. In L. Berkowitz (Ed.), *Advances in experimental social psychology* (Vol. 4). New York: Academic Press.

Stotland, E., Mathews, K. E., Sherman, S. E., Hansson, R., & Richardson, B. Z. (1979). *Empathy, fantasy, and helping*. Beverly Hills, CA: Sage.

Strayer, F. F., & Strayer, J. (1976). An ethological analysis of social agonism and dominance relations among preschool children. *Child Development, 47*, 980–989.

Thomas, M. H., Horton, R. W., Lippincott, E. C., & Drabman, R. S. (1977). Desensitization to portrayals of real-life aggression as a function of exposure to televised violence. *Journal of Personality and Social Psychology, 35*, 450–458.

Thompson, R., & Hoffman, M. L. (1980). Empathy and the arousal of guilt in children. *Developmental Psychology, 15*, 155–156.

Tulving, E. (1972). Episodic and semantic memory. In E. Tulving & W. Donaldson (Eds.), *Organization of memory*. New York: Academic Press.

Turiel, E. (1966). An experimental test of the sequentiality of developmental stages in the child's moral judgments. *Journal of Personality and Social Psychology, 3*, 611–618.

Turiel, E. (1983). *The development of social knowledge: Morality and convention*. New York: Cambridge University Press.

Turner, M. E. (1957). *The child within the group: An experiment in self-government*. Stanford, CA: Stanford University Press.

Wallach, M., & Kogan, N. (1959). Sex differences and judgment processes. *Journal of Personality, 27*, 555–564.

Wallach, M. A., & Wallach, L. (1983). *Psychology's sanction for selfishness: The error of egoism in theory and therapy*. San Francisco: Freeman.

Wells, W. D. (1973). *Television and aggression: Replication of an experimental field study*. Unpublished manuscript, Graduate School of Business, University of Chicago.

Weston, D., & Turiel, E. (1980). Act–rule relations: Children's concepts of social rules. *Developmental Psychology, 16*, 417–424.

Wright, H. F. (1967). *Recording and analyzing child behavior*. New York: Harper & Row.

Youniss, J. E. (1980). *Parents and peers in social development: A Sullivan–Piaget perspective*. Chicago: University of Chicago Press.

Zahn-Waxler, C., Radke-Yarrow, M., & King, R. M. (1979). Childrearing and children's prosocial initiations toward victims of distress. *Child Development, 50*, 319–330.

Zussman, J. U. (1978). Relationship of demographic factors to parental discipline techniques. *Developmental Psychology, 14*, 685–686.

12 Developmental Psychopathology

Thomas M. Achenbach
University of Vermont

INTRODUCTION

Unlike most of the topics of this book, the developmental study of psychopathology is not an established subspeciality of developmental psychology. Instead it draws on many specialties, such as developmental, clinical, and cognitive psychology, as well as genetics, psychiatry, epidemiology, biology, and education. This chapter therefore deals with developmental aspects of psychopathology from diverse perspectives.

For those who are attracted by the challenge of shaping new paradigms, this is an exciting period when a few committed researchers can have a major impact on how troubled children are helped. Yet it will require patience and a tolerance of ambiguity to fashion the disparate pieces into a coherent whole. It will also require a readiness to span the study of academic psychology, psychopathology, and clinical applications.

A Conceptual Framework for Developmental Psychopathology

A developmental approach to psychopathology views maladaptive behavior in relation to developmental tasks, processes, and sequences. It represents a way of looking at maladaptive behavior characterized by the following key features:

1. To judge whether an individual's behavior is "deviant," we need to know *what is typical for comparable individuals* at the same level of development. This requires normative data on large representative samples, stratified by important demographic variables and assessed by methods geared to each developmental level.

549

2. To judge whether an individual's behavior is "pathological," we need to know the *likely outcome* of the behavior in subsequent developmental periods. This requires longitudinal or follow-up studies of behavior to determine which patterns have especially unsatisfactory outcomes.

3. To understand maladaptive behavior, we must view it in relation to the individual's previous developmental history, the developmental tasks the individual faces, and the progress of important adaptive competencies. This requires knowledge of normal development in such areas as biological maturation, cognition, emotional functioning, social competencies, and academic skills.

4. To design appropriate interventions, we need to know how to *facilitate development* rather than merely to reduce discomforts, remove "symptoms," or restore a previous level of functioning. This requires knowledge of developmental processes and the mechanisms of behavioral change.

5. To evaluate the effects of interventions, we need *long-term comparisons of the outcomes* of specific interventions and no-treatment control conditions. Evaluations of outcomes must assess general developmental progress, as well as the problems that initially prompted the interventions.

All of the previous are relevant to the study of psychopathology at all stages of the life cycle. They could well provide guidelines for a life-span developmental psychopathology. It is in the period from birth to maturity, however, that the need for a developmental approach is most compelling, for the following reasons:

1. Conspicuous developmental changes occur much more rapidly in many more areas during this period than during adulthood. For example, 6-month-olds, 4-year-olds, 8-year-olds, and 16-year-olds differ far more dramatically from each other in physical, cognitive, social, emotional, and educational development than do adults who are separated by almost any span of years.

2. The period from birth to maturity is marked by a host of conspicuous developmental milestones, such as walking, talking, bowel control, the onset of schooling, learning to read, involvement in peer groups, puberty, and school graduation. While there are also adult developmental milestones, they are less explicit and more variable in nature and timing, depending heavily on differences in occupation, marriage, parenting, and so on.

3. Children's problems, competencies, and needs must be judged in light of their requirements for further development, whereas most adults reach plateaus in their physical, cognitive, social, and educational development.

4. The judgment that a child needs help is usually made by others, such as parents and teachers, whereas adults often seek help for themselves, formulate their own referral complaints, and spontaneously assume the role of patient.

5. Because children are so dependent on their families, family functioning

has a more decisive impact on children's problems and what is done about them than is true for most adults, who are freer to alter their family circumstances.

6. There are marked differences between children's disorders—which typically involve exaggerations of normal behavior or failures to develop important behaviors—and adult disorders—which more often involve marked declines from attained levels or the emergence of behavior that is clearly pathognomonic (i.e., indicative of pathology).

Many approaches to childhood disorders rest on assumptions derived from adult disorders. Such assumptions may unduly bias the study of psychopathology that characterizes the period of rapid development. We will therefore try to distinguish those aspects of each approach that may facilitate the developmental study of psychopathology from those aspects that may hinder it. After considering the major approaches, we address current challenges for the developmental study of psychopathology.

NOSOLOGICAL APPROACHES

Efforts to construct *nosologies* (classifications of disease) for abnormal behaviors evolved during the nineteenth century as a result of two related factors. One was the movement to provide large-scale institutional care. This necessitated different arrangements for different types of management problems, such as violent versus depressed behavior. A second factor was the growth of research on the organic causes of disease and the extension of organic disease models to mental disorders. This became enshrined in the dogma that "mental diseases are brain diseases," as it was expressed in Wilhelm Griesinger's influential psychiatric textbook of 1845 (translated by Robertson and Rutherford in 1867).

Both the institutional management needs and the organic disease model stimulated efforts to distinguish among types of disorders. It was hoped that descriptions of symptom syndromes would ultimately distinguish among disease entities, which would then be found to have different organic causes.

The most successful prototype of the organic disease model was *general paralysis* (later called *paresis,* or "incomplete paralysis"). Progressively more precise descriptions between 1798 and the 1840s converged on a syndrome defined mainly by mental symptoms, such as memory loss and irrationality, combined with physical symptoms of motor impairment, and usually ending in death. From the 1840s through the 1870s, research revealed inflamed brain tissue in most patients who died of paresis. Syphilitic infection was confirmed as the cause by the end of the nineteenth century.

Organic abnormalities also helped to define certain syndromes of mental retardation. *Downs syndrome,* for example, was first described in 1866 by Langdon Down, an Englishman who thought the "mongoloid" facial features reflected an evolutionary throwback to the "mongol race." In this case, however, it took nearly a hundred years to discover that an extra chromosome was responsible (Lejeune, Gautier, & Turpin. 1963).

Kraepelin's Nosology

Aside from a few clear-cut syndromes characterized by fairly obvious physical abnormalities, efforts to distinguish between types of mental disorders yielded a mélange of conflicting descriptions, based on diverse assumptions and conceptual principles. As it became clear that most disorders were not distinguishable as self-evident syndromes, efforts were made to integrate the descriptions within more general classification systems, or *taxonomies*.

The most influential taxonomy was published by Emil Kraepelin in 1883, who progressively revised and expanded it over the next 40 years. Kraepelin's first edition was based on the assumption that all mental disorders are—like paresis—caused by brain pathology. The goal of taxonomy was to provide descriptive categories for discriminating among disease entities whose different organic etiologies could then be sought. It was a nosology in the sense that each category was assumed to represent a distinctive disease entity.

In later editions, Kraepelin added psychological processes and the course of the disorder to descriptions of symptoms as defining criteria. For example, *dementia praecox* ("insanity of the young," renamed "schizophrenia" by Eugen Bleuler in 1911) was distinguished from manic-depressive psychosis on the basis of psychological differences and of the more favorable outcomes observed in manic-depressive conditions.

By 1915, Kraepelin had also added disorders that were assumed to have psychological rather than organic causes, plus a category of personality disorders bordering between illness and ordinary eccentricity. Despite this broadening to include disorders not assumed to have organic causes, and disorders that deviated in other ways from the disease model, Kraepelin's nineteenth-century nosological paradigm continues to have a major impact on views of psychopathology. In the following sections, we consider contemporary variations on the nosological theme.

The Diagnostic and Statistical Manual of Mental Disorders

The American Psychiatric Association's *Diagnostic and Statistical Manual* (the "DSM") is widely used to classify mental disorders for purposes of medical records and third-party payments. The DSM is a nosology in which each disorder is presented as a separate diagnostic entity. In the first edition of the DSM ("DSM-I," 1952), there were only two main categories for child and adolescent disorders: Adjustment Reaction and Schizophrenic Reaction, Childhood Type. "Adjustment reaction" referred to problems interpreted as relatively transient responses to stress, whereas "schizophrenic reaction" referred to severe psychopathology not likely to be transient. Although adult diagnoses could also be applied to children, 70% of children seen in mental health clinics were either undiagnosed or were diagnosed as having adjustment reactions (Achenbach, 1966; Rosen, Bahn, & Kramer, 1964).

The second edition of the DSM ("DSM-II," 1968) added several behavior disorders of childhood, such as Hyperkinetic Reaction and Withdrawing Reaction, but adjustment reaction remained the most common diagnosis through 1980 (American Academy of Child Psychiatry, 1983).

The third edition of the DSM ("DSM-III," 1980) departed in several ways from the earlier editions, as well as adding many new disorders of infancy, childhood, and adolescence. One major departure was the listing of criteria that have to be met for each diagnosis. These criteria involve yes-or-no judgments as to the presence of each characteristic required for each diagnosis.

Besides specifying criteria for each disorder, DSM-III provided the following five dimensions or "axes":

Axis I: (a) Clinical syndromes (e.g., Conduct Disorder)
           (b) Conditions that are not attributable to a mental disorder but are a focus of attention or treatment (e.g., "parent–child problem," such as child abuse)
Axis II: (a) Personality disorders (e.g., Compulsive Personality)
           (b) Specific Developmental Disorders (e.g., Developmental Reading Disorder)
Axis III: Physical disorders and conditions
Axis IV: A 7-point rating scale for severity of psychosocial stressors (changed in 1987 to a 6-point scale)
Axis V: A 5-point rating scale for highest level of adaptive functioning during the past year (changed in 1987 to separate 90-point ratings for current functioning and highest level in the past year).

DSM-III was designed to make diagnostic criteria more explicit and reliable, and to broaden diagnosis by taking account of medical conditions, life stresses, and adaptive functioning. It reflected efforts to free diagnostic classification from unsubstantiated theoretical inferences, such as psychoanalytic interpretations of neurotic behavior. In effect, DSM-III constituted a return to the ideals of early Kraepelinian nosology in striving for noninferential descriptions of disorders of unknown etiology.

DSM-III also returned to another aspect of nineteenth-century nosological thinking: the medical disease model for psychopathology. Early drafts of DSM-III held that all mental disorders are medical disorders. This claim was moderated in the final version, but DSM-III repeatedly referred to disorders as "illnesses." Based on the nosological concept of categorical disease entities, the architects of DSM-III formulated each category by starting from

> . . . a clinical concept for which there is some degree of face validity. Face validity is the extent to which the description of a particular category seems on the face of it to describe accurately the characteristic features of persons with a particular disorder. It is the result of clinicians agreeing on the identification of a particular syndrome or pattern of clinical features as a mental disorder. Initial criteria are generally developed by asking the clinicians to describe what they consider to be the most characteristic features of the disorder. (Spitzer & Cantwell, 1980, p. 369)

The clinical concepts of most of DSM-III's adult disorders, such as schizophrenia, date from Kraepelin's nosology. In defining their categories, the DSM-III committee was able to draw on existing research diagnostic criteria (RDC) for the major categories of adult disorders. Unlike the adult disorders, however, many of the child and adolescent disorders had *no* counterparts in previous nosologies or research diagnostic criteria. Spitzer and Cantwell's reference to "face validity" therefore concerns the diagnostic concepts held by those who formulated DSM-III's categories of child and adolescent disorders. Their formulations of these disorders were not validated in any other way.

Subsequent research on the DSM-III child and adolescent categories showed that some did, in fact, correspond to empirically derived taxonomic distinctions (see Achenbach, 1985). However, the reliability of the DSM-III child and adolescent diagnoses was too low to inspire much confidence. Two studies showed that DSM-III diagnoses made from standardized case histories were no more reliable than DSM-II diagnoses, which were themselves not very reliable (Mattison, Cantwell, Russell, & Will, 1979; Mezzich, Mezzich, & Coffman, 1985). Furthermore, the DSM-III *Manual* reported lower reliability for diagnoses of children than for those of adults on Axes I, II, IV, and V (Axis III was not reported on).

Although two studies of inpatients obtained overall interjudge kappas of .74 and .71 for child and adolescent diagnoses, both used an early draft of DSM-III (Strober, Green, & Carlson, 1981; Werry, Methven, Fitzpatrick, & Dixon, 1983). The data reported in the DSM-III *Manual* showed that reliability of child and adolescent diagnoses declined from this early draft to a later draft of the DSM, in contrast to the increasing reliability of adult diagnoses on all four axes. The possible benefits of the rejuvenated nosological approach for adult disorders have thus not been evident for children's disorders. A revision of DSM-III (DSM-III-R, American Psychiatric Association, 1987) has reduced the number of categories for childhood disorders and made other changes, but reliability and validity data are not yet available.

Clinically Identified Syndromes

Besides their effects on formal taxonomies, nosological assumptions have affected views of individual syndromes. The following three disorders illustrate contemporary disease entity concepts of child psychopathology.

Early Infantile Autism.   This syndrome was proposed by Leo Kanner in 1943 after he had seen 11 children who shared certain striking peculiarities. Kanner summarized their peculiarities in terms of two cardinal symptoms:

1. Extreme self-isolation, evident from the first years of life.
2. Obsessive insistence on the preservation of sameness (Eisenberg & Kanner, 1956).

The children Kanner diagnosed as autistic also avoided eye contact with others ("gaze aversion") and showed intriguing speech abnormalities; the latter ranged from a complete lack of speech or delayed onset, through *echolalia* (exact repetition or "echoing" of others' speech), reversal of personal pronouns (substitution of "you" for "I"), and metaphorical speech that lacked communicative intent. Long-term follow-ups of 96 of Kanner's cases showed that, despite signs of high intelligence in many, only 11 achieved adequate adjustments. Even these 11 remained severely limited in interpersonal relationships (Eisenberg & Kanner, 1956; Kanner, 1971; Kanner, Rodrigues, & Ashenden, 1972). Other follow-up studies agree with Kanner's finding that very few autistic children achieve even marginal social adjustments in later life (Lotter, 1978).

Kanner's (1943) initial hypothesis was that autistic children have an "innate inability to form the usual, biologically provided affective contact with people" (p. 250). Despite Kanner's careful descriptions and his hypothesis of an organic etiology, however, others quickly extended the concept of autism to children having few of the abnormalities he described. Furthermore, psychoanalytic theorists blamed autism on parental behavior and unconscious attitudes, singling out mothers who were said to be immature, narcissistic, overintellectual, and incapable of mature emotional relationships (Despert, 1947; Rank, 1949). Indictments were also leveled at mothers who "wish that [their] child should not exist" (Bettelheim, 1967, p. 125) and "parents [who] inadvertently hated one another and used the child emotionally" (Wolman, 1970, p. vii).

There has recently been a marked reaction against psychodynamic views and a return to organic hypotheses about autism. Yet even when autism was interpreted in psychoanalytic terms, it was conceived as a generic entity that the sensitive clinician could detect lurking beneath diverse phenotypes. The striking behavior of autistic children, autism's very early onset, and its seeming imperviousness to a variety of environmental regimens certainly argue for a diseaselike condition. Nevertheless, varied interpretations of the putative underlying disease and varied criteria for diagnosing it have continued to limit agreement among diagnosticians (Siegel, Anders, Ciaranello, Bienenstock, & Kraemer, 1986).

Hyperactivity.   Like autism, hyperactivity has become a popular nosological construct. In contrast to the extreme deviance and rarity of autism, however, hyperactivity involves behaviors that nearly all children show occasionally. Furthermore, hyperactivity typically becomes a cause for clinical concern during the elementary school years rather than during the very early years. And, once hyperactivity is evident, it seldom remains such a devastating lifetime affliction as autism. Why, then, has hyperactivity been viewed as a diseaselike condition?

Two early findings helped make hyperactivity an especially tempting candidate for nosological categorization. One was Bradley's (1937) finding that the amphetamine *Benzedrine* seemed to reduce overactivity in disturbed children. This suggested a specific organic defect underlying hyperactivity.

The other finding grew out of efforts by Strauss, Lehtinen, and Werner to develop methods for diagnosing and educating brain-damaged children (Strauss & Lehtinen, 1947). Normal children, retarded children with brain damage, and retarded children without known brain damage were compared on a battery of perceptual and cognitive tasks. Behavioral differences between the brain-damaged and other children were then interpreted as signs of brain damage.

Largely from this research, a picture of the "brain damaged child" emerged that included the following features: hyperactivity, impulsivity, distractibility, short attention span, emotional lability, perceptual–motor deficits, and clumsiness. Children who had these problems but no direct evidence of brain damage were assumed to have subtle brain damage; this was designated as *Strauss syndrome, diffuse brain damage, minimal brain damage, minimal brain dysfunction,* or *minimal cerebral dysfunction.* "MBD" (minimal brain damage or dysfunction) soon became a synonym for "hyperactivity." Some workers not only equated MBD with hyperactivity, but with the terms "LD" (learning disability) and "SLD" (specific learning disability; e.g., Ochroch, 1981).

As with autism, the nosological constructs of MBD and hyperactivity seemed to expand far beyond the observations on which they were based. The absence of operational criteria allowed the diagnosis to be made in idiosyncratic ways. Analysis of clinicians' use of a standardized set of case materials, for example, showed differences in the cues the clinicians used, their weighting of the cues, and their awareness of the diagnostic "policies" guiding their judgments (Ullman, Egan, Fiedler, Jurenec, Pliske, Thompson, & Doherty, 1981).

When psychiatric nosology first became differentiated with respect to childhood disorders (DSM-II, 1968), hyperactivity was represented as "hyperkinetic reaction of childhood (or adolescence)," characterized by "overactivity, restlessness, distractibility, and short attention span" (p. 50). DSM-II made a distinction between the behavioral phenotype and organic brain damage: "If this behavior is caused by organic brain damage, it should be diagnosed under the appropriate non-psychotic *organic brain syndrome*" (DSM-II, 1968, p. 50).

Furthermore, research during the 1970s and 1980s showed that most "hyperactive" children are probably not brain-damaged and that brain damage does not necessarily result in hyperactivity (e.g., Brown, Chadwick, Shaffer, Rutter, & Traub, 1981; Shaffer, McNamara, & Pincus, 1974).

As brain damage became a less viable explanation for hyperactivity, other organic causes were sought. These have included neurotransmitter abnormalities, abnormalities of arousal in the central nervous system, food sensitivities, food allergies, developmental delays, and constitutional patterns of temperament (see Achenbach, 1982, Chapter 11, for a review of these).

In formulating its child categories, the DSM-III committee decided that attention deficits were more primary than overactivity in what DSM-II had called the Hyperkinetic Reaction. DSM-III therefore replaced the category of Hyperkinetic Reaction with that of Attention Deficit Disorders (ADD), divided into two subtypes: (1) ADD *with* hyperactivity, and (2) ADD *without* hyperactivity.

DSM-III-R has replaced these two ADD categories with a single one called Attention–Deficit–Hyperactivity Disorder. Whereas the DSM-III diagnostic criteria required certain numbers of problems from separate lists representing inattention, impulsivity, and hyperactivity, DSM-III-R provides a single list of problems from which a specified number must be present in order to qualify for the diagnosis. The DSM-III-R has thus moved toward a more unidimensional descriptive criterion for this disorder, in which clinical deviance is defined in terms of a specified number of problems on a dimension (American Psychiatric Association, 1987). The wording of each problem also implies a quantitative dimension, as exemplified by the following items: (a) "*often* talks excessively"; (b) "is *easily* distracted by extraneous stimuli"; and (c) "often interrupts or intrudes on others." Yet each problem must be judged as either present or absent, and the overall criterion must be met in a yes-or-no fashion.

Thus, even though the wording of the items and the requirement of a certain number of items from a list imply quantification, the decision rules impose a categorical nosological construct on the diagnostic process: Each child is diagnosed as either having the disorder or not having it, with no provision for gradations in the certainty of the diagnosis, although the qualifiers "mild," "moderate," and "severe" can be added. Later sections deal with the implications of this categorical model for common behaviors that vary in degree like those used to diagnose attention-deficit hyperactivity.

Childhood Depression.   Interest in childhood depression has followed a course quite different from interest in autism and hyperactivity. Despite early reports of manic-depressive disorders in children (Kasanin & Kaufman, 1929), the psychoanalytic theory dominant from the 1930s through the 1960s held that true depressive disorders were impossible before the superego was fully inter-nalized during adolescence (see Kashani, Husain, Shekim, Hodges, Cytryn, & McKnew, 1981). Following the spread of drug therapies and growing enthusi-asm for biological explanations of adult depression in the 1960s, however, the search for childhood depression was renewed.

Since neither DSM-I nor DSM-II included child depression, and children do not spontaneously complain of depression, one approach was to infer depression from a variety of other problems. In arguing for the use of antidepressant drugs with children, Frommer (1967), for example, inferred depression in

> . . . children who complain of non-specific recurrent abdominal pain, headache, sleep difficulties and irrational fears or mood disturbances such as irritability, unaccountable tearfulness, and associated outbursts of temper. Such children often develop sudden difficulty in social adjustments, which previously were normal; they may either withdraw themselves from the family circle and former friends or display outright aggressive and antisocial behavior. (p. 729)

Other advocates of antidepressant medication diagnosed children as depressed if they showed dysphoric (unhappy, irritable, hypersensitive, or negative) moods and self-deprecatory thoughts, plus at least two of the following: aggression, sleep disturbance, change in school performance, diminished socialization, change in attitude toward school, loss of usual energy, unusual change in appe-tite and/or weight (Weinberg, Rutman, Sullivan, Penick, & Dietz, 1973). Based on assessment of these symptoms by a pediatric neurologist who informally interviewed children and their parents, Weinberg et al. diagnosed 63% of chil-dren referred to an educational clinic as suffering from a "depressive illness."

Childhood depression was further broadened by the concept of *masked de-pression*—depression inferred from aggressive, hyperactive, and other trou-blesome behavior used defensively "to ward off the unbearable feelings of despair" (Cytryn & McKnew, 1979, p. 327). Psychophysiological reactions, truancy, running away, sexual promiscuity, and fire-setting were also added as signs of masked depression (see Kovacs & Beck, 1977). The search for depres-sion underlying so many different behaviors, and the resulting reports of epi-demics of previously undiagnosed depressive illness prompted one observer to dub childhood depression "the MBD of the 1980s."

Although the concept of masked depression has since been retracted by its authors (Cytryn, McKnew, & Bunney, 1980), the search for even "unmasked" depression as a generic entity among children is still plagued by a lack of agreement among various categorical criteria. One reason for disagreement is that broad, inferential criteria classify a much larger proportion of children as depressed than do more stringent criteria. Carlson and Cantwell (1982), for example, found that the Weinberg et al. (1973) criteria produced considerably more diagnoses of depression than did the DSM-III criteria for a major depressive disorder in the same children. (The DSM-III criteria were written for adult disorders but include some extrapolations downward to children.) However, since neither set of criteria is quantified, the more stringent criteria cannot be calibrated to the less stringent criteria in any systematic way: Not all children diagnosed by the more stringent criteria are included in the group diagnosed by the less stringent criteria; and the two sets of criteria cannot be made more congruent by adjusting cutoff points on quantitative dimensions, because they do not employ any.

Conclusion

In the nineteenth century, it was assumed that a descriptive nosology would identify diseases whose different organic etiologies could then be found. Current nosological approaches imply that disorders exist as categorical entities, each of which has a specific etiology. Although this view need not imply exclusively organic etiologies, as psychoanalytic interpretations of autism did not, it currently tends to assume organic etiologies.

In considering three popular candidates for the status of nosological entities, we saw that early infantile autism seems most like a disease entity, featuring very early onset and enduring abnormalities that do not appear to be situational or quantitative variations of normal behavior. Nevertheless, different conceptions of this disorder continue to produce diagnostic disagreements.

The second candidate we considered, hyperactivity (now called, in DSM-III-R, Attention–Deficit Hyperactivity Disorder), has been blamed on a variety of organic abnormalities, but involves situational and quantitative variations of behaviors that most children show in some degree. The overt problem behavior is relatively easy to identify, but the imposition of unvalidated categorical constructs on quantitative variations in the behavior provokes continuing diagnostic disagreements.

The third candidate we considered, childhood depression, has been summarily cast into the nosological mold without prior refinement of the phenotypic picture. Whereas the application of the nosological paradigm to hyperactivity raises problems in categorizing quantitative variations of behavior, current nosological constructs of childhood depression still face problems of *which* phenomena to include as criteria and how to tailor the criteria to major developmental differences in expressions of affect.

MULTIVARIATE APPROACHES

Faced with a dearth of well-defined disorders on which to focus their efforts, researchers have turned to statistical methods for empirically identifying syndromes of behavior problems that tend to occur together in children. After some rudimentary efforts in the 1940s and 1950s, the advent of electronic computers spawned a host of multivariate studies in the 1960s and 1970s. In most of these studies, ratings obtained on behavior checklists were factor analyzed to identify syndromes of covarying behavior problems. Despite differences in the rating instruments, raters, samples of children, and methods of analysis, there has been considerable convergence on certain syndromes (see Achenbach & Edelbrock, 1978, and Quay, 1979, for detailed reviews) and good convergence for findings in different cultures (Achenbach, Verhulst, Baron, & Althaus, 1987). High correlations have also been obtained between syndromes scored from different checklists (Achenbach & Edelbrock, 1983, 1986). Some of the empirically identified syndromes resemble those that are evident in the nosological approaches, although there is no clear correspondence between other syndromes identified by the two approaches. When nosological syndromes have been scored in a quantitative fashion, some show a strong association with scores on empirically-derived syndromes, as illustrated in Fig. 12.1.

Contrasts Between Multivariate and Nosological Approaches

Even where there are similarities between the multivariate and nosological syndromes, there are also some important differences:

1. As we saw earlier, existing nosologies represent negotiated formulations of clinicians' concepts of disorders. Multivariate syndromes, by contrast, are derived statistically from covariation among scores on items rated for samples of children.

2. The criterial attributes of the nosological categories must be assessed according to yes-or-no judgments, whereas the criterial attributes of multivariate syndromes are usually assessed in terms of quantitative gradations.

3. Based on yes-or-no judgments of each criterial attribute, a nosological diagnosis culminates in a yes-or-no decision about whether a child has a particular disorder. Multivariate syndromes, on the other hand, are scored in terms of the *degree to which* a child manifests the characteristics of a syndrome. This is because quantitative indices of each criterial attribute are combined into a summary index of how strongly the child manifests the syndrome. However, cutoff points can also be established on the distribution of scores for a syndrome in order to discriminate among particular classes of children, if desired.

4. The criteria for nosological diagnoses imply comparisons with "normal" age-mates, but they specify no operations for determining how a particular child compares with normal age-mates. The quantification of multivariate syndromes, by contrast, provides a *metric* for comparing a child with other children, such as normal age-mates.

5. Because nosological categories are defined in terms of discrete *types* of

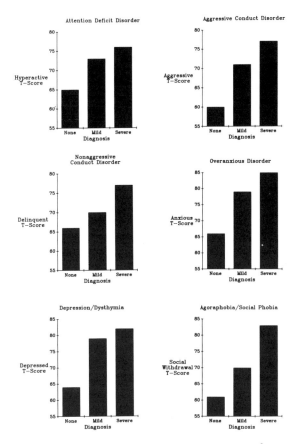

FIG. 12.1. Relations between DSM-III syndrome scores from a structured clinical interview (DISC-P) and T scores on corresponding scales of the Child Behavior Profile. A T score of 70 is the upper limit of the normal range on scales of the Child Behavior Profile. (From Achenbach, 1985, p. 165.)

disorders, children who show characteristics of several types must either get multiple diagnoses or must be placed in a single category according to rules for preempting one diagnosis with another, often with no empirical basis for doing so. The multivariate approach, by contrast, lends itself to a profile format for describing a child in terms of his or her standing on multiple syndromes, without requiring forced choices as to which ones preempt the others.

6. By cluster-analyzing profiles, we can construct a taxonomy of *patterns* of scores obtained on all the syndromes of the profile. We can also *quantify* the degree of a child's resemblance to each profile type, further reducing reliance on categorical forced choices (see Achenbach & Edelbrock, 1983, and Edelbrock & Achenbach, 1980, for detailed examples).

Syndromes Identified Through Multivariate Approaches

Multivariate methods may not contribute much to the initial discovery of rare and extreme abnormalities, such as autism. Once such features have been detected clinically, however, multivariate methods can sharpen the syndromal construct by assessing the discriminative power and covariation of the abnormalities among children having the target disorder and other disorders that must be discriminated from it (e.g., Siegel et al., 1986).

Few children display abnormalities as blatant as autism. Instead, most childhood disorders involve behaviors that most children show to some extent, complicated further by the variability of each child's behavior. Detection of patterns among such behaviors therefore poses a more challenging information-processing task than detection of blatant abnormalities. It is in this information-processing task that multivariate methods can be especially helpful.

What have multivariate analyses of children's behavior problems found? Table 12.1 summarizes the main findings of multivariate studies of behavior problem ratings from case histories, mental health workers, teachers, and parents. The *narrow-band* syndromes listed in Table 12.1 are specific groupings of behavior problems roughly analogous to the syndromes comprising taxonomies like the DSM. The *broad-band* syndromes in the table are more global groupings of behavior that subsume many of the narrow-band syndromes. For example, the broad-band Undercontrolled syndrome includes behaviors such as fighting, destructiveness, disobedience, and impulsivity. Hierarchical analyses of relations between broad- and narrow-band syndromes show that the narrow-band Aggressive, Delinquent, and Hyperactive syndromes group together to form a broad-band Undercontrolled syndrome (e.g., Achenbach & Edelbrock, 1983). It is therefore possible to score children on syndromes at both the narrow- and broad-band levels of the hierarchy. The child's standing on the broad-band syndromes may be useful for general management purposes, whereas the differentiated picture provided by scores on the narrow-band syndromes may facilitate more precise assessment, treatment, and research.

Most multivariate studies have not separated boys and girls of different ages. However, when separate analyses have been done, they have shown sex and age similarities in some syndromes, but important sex and age differences in others. Achenbach and Edelbrock (1983), for example, found a syndrome in parents' ratings of disturbed girls characterized mainly by cruelty toward animals and people, but no clear counterpart of this syndrome among boys. Important age differences were manifest in a syndrome labelled "Depressed"—this syndrome was found in parents' ratings of 6- to 11-year-olds of both sexes but not in parents' ratings of adolescents.

The detection of the Cruel syndrome for girls and the Depressed syndrome for elementary-school-aged children does not mean that the behaviors of these syn-

TABLE 12.1
Number of Studies That Have Identified Syndromes Through
Multivariate Analyses

Syndrome	Case Histories	Mental Health Workers	Teachers	Parents	Total
Broad Band					
Overcontrolled	2	1	6	6	15
Undercontrolled	3	3	6	7	19
Pathological Detachment	3	—	1	—	4
Learning Problems	—	—	1	1	2
Narrow Band					
Academic Disability	—	1	—	3	4
Aggressive	3	4	2	8	17
Anxious	1	2	2	2	7
Delinquent	3	1	1	7	12
Depressed	2	1	1	5	9
Hyperactive	3	2	2	7	14
Immature	—	1	1	3	5
Obsessive–Compulsive	1	—	1	2	4
Schizoid	3	4	—	5	12
Sexual Problems	1	2	—	3	6
Sleep Problems	—	—	—	3	3
Social withdrawal	1	1	2	5	9
Somatic Complaints	1	—	—	7	8
Uncommunicative	—	1	—	2	3

Note: From Achenbach, 1985, p. 92.

dromes were absent from other groups. Cruelty to animals and people was actually reported more often for boys than for girls (Achenbach & Edelbrock, 1981). But the different forms of cruelty did not occur together consistently enough among boys to form a separate syndrome, as they did for girls. Similarly, the depressive behaviors comprising the Depressed syndrome were reported at least as often for adolescents as for younger children. Yet for adolescents they occurred in conjunction with a much greater variety of other behaviors, rather than forming a clear-cut syndrome as they did for younger children.

Profiles of Multivariate Syndromes

Syndromes of covarying behaviors identified through multivariate analyses can be cast into a profile that represents a child's standing on all syndromes simultaneously. To provide a common metric across the syndromes, scores on each syndrome are converted to standard scores based on normative samples or other reference groups.

Whereas syndromes reflect covariation among reported behaviors across samples of children, profiles provide a more comprehensive picture of each child's overall behavior pattern. Cluster analyses of profiles for clinically referred children have revealed some profile types that are elevated only on one syndrome (Achenbach & Edelbrock, 1983). In Fig. 12.2, for example, profile type D found for 12- to 16-year-old boys is elevated mainly on the Hyperactive syndrome. This pattern would be expected for boys diagnosed as having ADD with Hyperactivity. (The Z scores to the left of the profiles indicate standard deviation units from the mean of *clinically-referred* boys. Thus, the mean score for the Hyperactive syndrome in profile type D is one standard deviation above the mean for *clinically-referred* boys; it would be still more deviant from the mean of normal 12- to 16-year-old boys.)

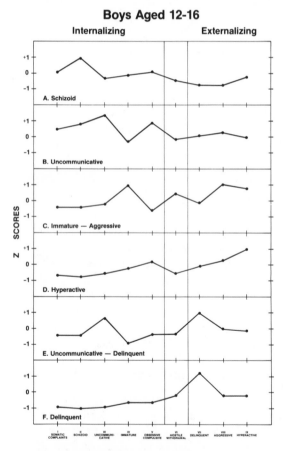

FIG. 12.2.   Behavior profile types identified through cluster analyses. (From Achenbach & Edelbrock, 1983, p. 79.)

Note that the Hyperactive syndrome is just about as elevated in profile type C as it is in type D. If we merely consider the behaviors of the Hyperactive syndrome in isolation, we might lump type C and type D boys together as a categorical nosology would. If we consider the entire profile pattern, however, we would see that, while indeed manifesting high scores on the Hyperactivity syndrome, type C boys are still more deviant on the Immature and Aggressive syndromes of the profile. They also differ from type D boys in being more deviant on the Hostile Withdrawal syndrome, but less deviant on the Obsessive–Compulsive syndrome. Profiles E and F in Fig. 12.2 illustrate a similar contrast between two patterns that each have high scores on the Delinquent syndrome.

A nosology like the DSM takes account of differences in overall patterns by adding each diagnosis for which criteria are met or by preemptively excluding certain diagnoses. This makes sense if each diagnosis has a proven etiology which explains why one diagnosis precludes another. However, in the absence of known etiologies or a litmus test for positively diagnosing each disorder, the multivariate profile approach preserves a more comprehensive basis for a taxonomy of phenotypes than does the categorical nosological approach.

Conclusion

Lacking a differentiated nosology of childhood disorders, researchers have employed multivariate analyses to identify syndromes of covarying behaviors. Despite differences in rating instruments, raters, subject samples, and analytic methods, these analyses show considerable convergence on a few broad-band syndromes and more numerous narrow-band syndromes. Multivariate syndromes utilize quantitative variations in criterial attributes and in aggregates of attributes, rather than yes-or-no judgments of each attribute and of the syndromes themselves.

Besides preserving quantitative variations, multivariate syndromes lend themselves to profile formats that reveal children's *patterns* across all syndromes. These patterns provide a more comprehensive basis for phenotypic taxonomies than categorical nosologies do. By viewing a child's scores across a profile in relation to those of his or her age-mates, we can assess the child's deviance for each syndrome, rather than making categorical judgments of each syndrome in isolation and without an operational basis for comparison with age norms.

GENERAL THEORETICAL APPROACHES TO PSYCHOPATHOLOGY

As we saw in preceding sections, the nosological and the multivariate approaches both identify types of disorders without explaining them according to a single theory. The approaches considered in this section, by contrast, attempt to *explain* psychopathology on the basis of general theories of psychological functioning.

We consider here only the two global theoretical approaches that have had the most impact on views of the development of psychopathology in children—*psychoanalytic theory* and *learning theory*. Because space restrictions preclude comprehensive treatment of these theories, the emphasis here is on the aspects most relevant to developmental psychopathology; however, other aspects of these theories are considered in later sections.

Psychoanalytic Theory

Sigmund Freud's psychoanalytic theory grew out of his attempts to treat hysterical neuroses in the 1880s and the 1890s. His patients displayed dramatic physical symptoms, such as paralyses, that violated the known principles of anatomy. Freud hypothesized that the symptoms were caused by conflicts between forbidden impulses seeking expression and psychological defenses against the impulses. His concept of conflicting psychological forces is the cornerstone of *psychodynamic* theory.

Libido Theory and Psychosexual Development.   In investigating his patients' psychological conflicts, Freud concluded that the forbidden impulses were usually of a sexual nature. By urging patients to relax and say whatever came to mind—a process he called *free association*—Freud found that the patients' thoughts usually led back to childhood sexual experiences, especially seductions by adults. At first, Freud thought that repression of these memories was the basis for adult neurosis. He later concluded, however, that many of the seductions could not actually have occurred, although critics hold that childhood seductions were more common than Freud acknowledged (Masson, 1984).

Why did so many patients "recall" sexual experiences that supposedly did not happen? Freud (1905/1953) inferred that the experiences were childhood fantasies triggered by sexual desires directed toward adults, especially the child's parent of the opposite sex. The desires themselves, he hypothesized, originated in the biologically determined sex drive, which was the source of the affective excitation he termed *libido*. From patients' free associations, Freud inferred that libido was at first centered in the *oral* area, then the *anal* area, and then, between the ages of about 3 and 5, in the *phallic* area—the penis of the boy and the clitoris of the girl.

It was during the *phallic phase* that sexual desires toward the opposite-sex parent became intense, according to this theory. As a result, the child became hostile toward the same-sex parent, who was seen as a competitor. The typical outcome of what Freud called the "Oedipal" situation was that the same-sex parent responded with punitive threats, which caused the child to repress the sexual impulses. Repression was enforced by a process of *identification* with the same-sex parent—that is, by striving to emulate the same-sex parent, the child symbolically "won" the opposite-sex parent while reducing threats from the same sex-parent.

Internalized prohibitions associated with the same-sex parent were thought to hold sexual impulses at bay during the *latency period,* until puberty intensified genital sexual urges, reawakened Oedipal conflicts, and provoked the *Sturm und Drang* of adolescence. Freud's portrayal of this sequence of libidinal phases from birth through adolescence is known as his *theory of psychosexual development.*

Personality Structure and Development.   Also relevant to developmental psychopathology is Freud's theory of personality structure and development. As Freud's concepts of conflicting psychological forces grew more complex, he organized them in terms of three aspects of personality structure: the *id,* encompassing the impulses arising from biological drives; the *ego,* encompassing the executive functions of personality that mediate between id impulses and external reality; and the *superego,* consisting of the ideals and prohibitions internalized via identification with the same-sex parent as a resolution of the Oedipal conflict. These three constructs have retained key roles in psychoanalytic views of development and psychopathology. The ego, in particular, became the centerpiece of later theory, as it was assigned ever-wider functions in construing reality, detecting threats, experiencing anxiety, and activating defenses against anxiety. Anxiety came to be viewed as the *bête noire* of psychopathology, with different disorders being interpreted as reflecting different psychodynamic responses to it.

Implications of Psychoanalytic Theory for Developmental Psychopathology.   Whereas Kraepelin provided the nosology, Freud provided the most popular *explanations* for psychopathology. Like Kraepelin, Freud focused on adult disorder; but his theory dealt with their developmental origins, inferred largely from adult recollections of childhood. Although Anna Freud and others psychoanalyzed children, their reports dealt mainly with elaborations of analytic theory, illustrated with anecdotal observations. Miss Freud's (1965) ''Developmental Profile'' for psychoanalytically assessing children has been illustrated in several case histories, but no reliability or validity data have been published (see Achenbach, 1985, for details).

The nature of psychoanalytic theory makes decisive tests difficult. However, a longitudinal study of the development of children's behavior disorders (Thomas, Chess, & Birch, 1968) suggests that many of Freud's developmental inferences may have mistakenly imputed a causal role to intrapsychic variables that were actually *effects* of other problems:

> . . . in the young child, anxiety has not been evident as an initial factor preceding and determining symptom development. . . . However, intrapsychic conflict and psychodynamic defenses, as well as anxiety, have been evident in older children as later developments in the child's response to the unfavorable and sometimes threatening consequences of an initial maladaptation. . . . The painfulness of severe anxiety . . . makes it a striking symptom which may dominate our perceptions of the clinical picture. The elaborate psychological techniques utilized to minimize or

avoid distress may also contribute dramatically to the elaboration of pathological behavior or thought. It is, therefore, not surprising that in retrospective studies that begin when the child already presents with an elaborated psychological disturbance, the prominent phenomena of anxiety and psychodynamic defenses dominate clinical thinking, and come to be labeled as primary, rather than as secondary, influences on the genesis of behavior disturbance. (pp. 188–189)

Learning Theories

As a major alternative to psychodynamic explanations for the development of child psychopathology, learning theories are distinguished from the psychoanalytic approach by the following features:

1. Learning theories originated with laboratory studies of learning, primarily in animals, rather than with clinical studies of psychopathology.

2. Learning theories focus mainly on observable environmental stimuli and observable responses by the organism, rather than inferred mental events.

3. Learning theories attempt to explain most behavioral change at most ages with a single set of principles, rather than invoking a theory of development per se.

4. Learning theories emphasize environmental rather than biological and intrapsychic causes of psychopathology.

Origins of Learning Theories. Systematic learning theories arose at about the same time as psychoanalytic theory, with laboratory studies by Pavlov, Bekhterev, and Thorndike suggesting general principles that were then extrapolated to a variety of human behavior. John B. Watson (1913, 1919), the "father of behaviorism," became the leading proponent of learning theory explanations for personality and psychopathology. He argued that most fears and other behavior problems resulted from faulty conditioning. Although initially sympathetic to the psychoanalytic advocacy of freer attitudes toward sex and the discussion of personal problems, Watson eventually contended that behaviorist studies of children would replace psychoanalysis, which was "based largely upon religion, introspective psychology, and Voodooism" (1924, p. 18).

Whereas psychoanalysis began as a therapy for adults and was later extended to children, most early applications of learning theory to behavior problems were with children. In a classic case, for example, Mary Cover Jones (1924) applied various conditioning principles to the treatment of a 2-year-old boy's phobia of rabbits. Holmes (1936) reinforced children for coping with their fear of the dark, while Mowrer and Mowrer (1938) used an alarm triggered by urine on a bed pad to cure children of bedwetting. It was not until the 1960s, however, that therapies based on learning theories became widespread.

Subsequent Development of Learning Theories. What happened between the burst of enthusiasm for learning-based therapies in the 1920s and their revival in the 1960s? A great deal of laboratory research and refinement of learning theory was carried out by Clark Hull, B. F. Skinner, Neal Miller, and others. By the 1950s, efforts to apply more sophisticated learning theories to psychopathology became widespread. However, rather than attempting to change problem behavior, these efforts mainly translated the clinical theory and lore of psychoanalysis into learning theory terms.

The most ambitious of the translations was *Personality and Psychotherapy,* by John Dollard and Neal Miller (1950). Dedicating their book to "Freud and Pavlov and their students," Dollard and Miller sought "to combine the vitality of psychoanalysis, the rigor of the natural-science laboratory, and the facts of culture" (p. 3). They called psychotherapy a "window to higher mental life" and "the process by which *normality is created*" (pp. 3, 5). Thus accepting psychoanalytic views of psychopathology and its treatment, Dollard and Miller mainly sought to state these views in more rigorous terms derived from laboratory research on learning. Despite the basic contrasts listed earlier, psychoanalytic and learning theories converged in several ways:

1. Both explained mental processes largely in terms of principles of *association*, whereby sequences of thoughts are governed by previous contiguities among ideas, similarity of content, and other shared features. This associationistic view of mental processes was the basis for the psychoanalytic technique of free association, as well as the psychoanalytic theory of mental symbols.

2. Psychoanalytic theories and most learning theories postulated that reduction of organically based drives promoted the learning of important responses, attitudes, and emotions.

3. Psychoanalytic theory and learning theories made anxiety a central explanatory construct for psychopathology.

4. Psychoanalytic theory and learning theories blamed childhood experiences for most adult psychopathology but did not actually test the relationships that were assumed.

Conclusion

As of the 1950s, laboratory-based learning theories and clinical psychoanalytic theory seemed likely to converge on a sophisticated general theory of psychopathology, its development, and its treatment. This did not happen, however. Instead, the 1960s brought both a flowering of new therapies and an upsurge of developmental theory that took very different directions. In the following sections, we first consider the therapies and then the developmental theory. It should be noted here, however, that learning and psychoanalytic theories both implied developmental etiologies for psychopathology. Yet neither the theories nor their synthesis were based on direct study of human development, nor did they gener-

ACHENBACH

ate therapies whose efficacy was empirically demonstrated. Instead, they were rich heuristic systems whose appeal lay in their apparent capacity for explaining a wide variety of phenomena.

THERAPEUTIC APPROACHES EMERGING SINCE THE ERA OF GRAND THEORIES

Following the era of comprehensive theories of all psychopathology and its treatment, diverse new therapies have emerged that embody specific techniques for dealing with limited classes of problems. Those used most widely with children include behavioral, cognitive, pharmacological, and family therapies.

Behavior Therapies

Despite the efforts of Dollard, Miller, and others to promote a synthesis of learning theory and psychoanalysis, most behavior therapies emerged as reactions against psychodynamic approaches. For example, in *Psychotherapy by Reciprocal Inhibition,* which heralded the renaissance of behavior therapies, Joseph Wolpe (1958) described himself as originally "a staunch follower of Freud." But Wolpe became skeptical of the universality of the Oedipus complex and the efficacy of psychoanalysis beyond the production of comforting insights. Drawing concepts from Pavlov and Hull, Wolpe defined neurotic behavior as ". . . any persistent habit of unadaptive behavior acquired by learning in a physiologically normal organism. Anxiety is usually the central constituent of this behavior, being invariably present in the causal situation. . . . By anxiety is meant the autonomic response pattern or patterns that are characteristically part of the organism's response to noxious stimulation" (pp. 32–34).

Unlike other extrapolations of learning concepts to psychopathology at that time, Wolpe applied his directly to the removal of neurotic symptoms. He did this by training more favorable responses that would "reciprocally inhibit" anxiety responses to particular stimuli. In Wolpe's main method, known as *systematic desensitization,* patients construct *anxiety hierarchies* ranging from the things that make them most anxious down to things that make them minimally anxious. The patient is then taught relaxation responses that Wolpe believes are antagonistic to anxiety. Thereafter, the patient is induced to imagine the anxiety stimuli one by one, starting with the least threatening in the hierarchy. As each stimulus is imagined, the patient is to inhibit his or her anxiety by making relaxation responses. Although young children may not be able to do everything required for this procedure, the same principles have been applied to *in vivo desensitization* of children by presenting the actual feared stimuli in a graded sequence while the child is engaged in pleasurable activities (e.g., Lazarus, Davison, & Polefka, 1965).

Other behavioral methods derive from Skinner's operant conditioning paradigm. Rather than attempting to extinguish anxiety by pairing threatening stimuli with nonfearful responses, operant methods change the reinforcement contingencies of the target behavior. For example, positive reinforcing consequences are made contingent on responses that are to be strengthened, whereas negative consequences are made contingent on responses that are to be weakened.

Behavior therapists at first implied that their techniques were rigorously derived from "modern learning theory." However, paradoxes arose from the apparent success of methods that were theoretically contradictory. A method known as *implosive therapy* or *flooding,* for example, is exactly opposite to Wolpe's systematic desensitization: It presents massive doses of the feared stimuli under the assumption that anxiety responses will be quickly extinguished when no harm results from facing the feared stimuli. And there is evidence that implosive therapy can work with very fearful children (e.g., Ollendick & Gruen, 1972). Many other behavioral techniques likewise have ambiguous ties to general learning theories (see Achenbach, 1982, for further details).

In an article entitled "The End of Ideology in Behavior Modification," London (1972) argued that the ideology of learning theory has been a useful source of metaphors, paradigms, analogies, and a sense of theoretical identity, but that a technological orientation had become more appropriate than an ideological one. By this he meant that the mechanical gadgetry and therapeutic techniques of behavior modification were developing faster than any integrative theory. Proving that each innovation was derived from learning theory was therefore less important than finding useful guides wherever possible. As this view has spread, behavioral techniques have been increasingly combined with other approaches, such as biofeedback, residential treatment, family therapy, group therapy, drug therapy, psychodynamic approaches, and educational approaches (see Achenbach, 1982). The result is that behavioral technology is evident in diverse mental health services to children and adults, but that it is not a direct derivative of any general learning theory. Instead, the technology has a life of its own that generates ad hoc miniature theories and trial-and-error applications to many specific problems.

Cognitive-Behavioral Therapies

Another therapeutic approach emerging in recent years seeks to dispel cognitions that hinder adaptation and to strengthen those that are more adaptive. Although the focus on cognition may seem antithetical to behavioral views, behavior therapies have been a major impetus to certain varieties of cognitive therapy, known as *cognitive-behavioral therapies.*

Some of the most prominent behavior therapies, such as systematic desensitization, make use of imagined stimuli and covert cognitive responses for dealing with such stimuli. Although this was originally viewed as a convenience for manipulating anxiety-evoking stimuli and anxiety responses in the context of therapy, it assumed that behavioral principles derived from overt stimuli and responses were applicable to mental phenomena.

Because particular types of childhood problems—such as impulsivity and poor social skills—imply that the child lacks knowledge about appropriate behavior, these problems have been targeted for some of the most extensive efforts to apply behavioral principles to cognitions. *Self-instructional training,* for example, is designed to teach impulsive children to give themselves verbal instructions while they perform tasks slowly and carefully (Kendall & Braswell, 1985). Through modeling and guidance by the therapist, the making and repetition of overt verbal responses by the child, and reinforcement by the therapist, behavioral principles are used to teach impulsive children more effective strategies for doing schoolwork and similar tasks.

A related approach, called *interpersonal problem-solving training,* is directed at improving social skills. Based largely on Spivack and Shure's (1982) analyses of social cognition, it uses behavioral principles to help children identify interpersonal problems, generate possible solutions, predict the consequences of different actions, and describe the feelings of other people involved in the situation.

Cognitive approaches are especially appealing from a developmental perspective, because they are intended to mesh with a child's current cognitive level and to promote new cognitive skills feasible for children at a particular starting level. Several reviews, however, have concluded that cognitive therapies affect performance on cognitive measures and some aspects of behavior in nonclinical groups, but that they have not yet demonstrated much influence on significant clinical problems (Abikoff, 1985; Beidel & Turner, 1986; Kazdin, 1985). This does not necessarily mean that the approach is wrong, but that much remains to be done in making it powerful enough to help truly troubled children.

Pharmacotherapies

During the 1950s, it was discovered that certain drugs initially developed for other purposes seemed to reduce florid psychotic symptoms in seriously disturbed adults. Further refinement of these drugs led to a revolution in the care of adult mental patients: Major tranquilizers—such as chlorpromazine (Thorazine)—made it possible to reduce physical restraints and to release violent and excited patients from hospitals. Antidepressants—such as imipramine (Tofranil)—stimulated the functioning of severely depressed patients. Milder versions of these drugs, such as Valium, became popular for prescription by physicians and in heavily advertised nonprescription forms. Although the biological mechanisms were not well understood, the apparent benefits of pharmacotherapy spurred psychiatry to turn toward psychopharmacology and away from psychoanalysis.

As discussed earlier, Bradley's (1937) report that amphetamines reduced hyperactivity contributed to the nosological conception of hyperactivity. Few children, however, manifest the florid psychotic or depressive symptoms for which major tranquilizers and antidepressants are prescribed. Despite the occasional use of adult drugs for childhood disorders, there was little evidence for the efficacy of drugs other than stimulants for them (Campbell & Small, 1978).

Even the efficacy of stimulant drugs in reducing overactive behavior has not been followed by long-term improvements in the social and academic functioning of hyperactive children (Weiss & Hechtman, 1986). Nevertheless, as we saw earlier in this chapter, enthusiasm for the psychopharmacological models spawned by adult drug therapies has inspired a hunt for childhood versions of pharmacologically treatable depressive disorders. Whether such disorders exist remains to be seen, but it seems clear that pharmacotherapies, like behavior therapies, now have a life of their own that cannot be credited to any particular theory.

Conjoint Family Therapy

Most therapies for children include work with the child's family, but this usually means that the therapist meets separately with the parents and child. In *conjoint family therapy*, however, all members of the family meet together with one or two therapists. In one of the first published illustrations, Bell (1961) portrayed conjoint family therapy as a way of dealing more quickly and effectively with problems imputed to a child (the "identified patient"). Bell outlined four phases of the therapy:

1. The *child-centered phase*, in which the therapist builds a relationship with the children of a family by being especially attentive to them, supporting their requests for changes in parental behavior, and tending to ignore parental criticism.

2. The *parent–child interaction phase*, in which parents' complaints about the child are prominent and the parents and child tend to talk *about* each other instead of *to* each other.

3. The *father–mother interaction phase*, in which parents express conflicts with each other that are assumed to cause the child's problems.

4. The *termination phase*, in which emphasis on parental interaction and the "identified patient" gives way to an emphasis on the interactions among all family members.

Family therapists view the family as a social system in which each member's behavior is a function of pressures existing in the system as a whole (Goldenberg & Goldenberg, 1980). The problems of the identified patient are viewed as symptoms of family stress. Because these symptoms serve a definite function in the family, removing them without other changes in the family is expected to produce symptoms in other family members or dissolution of the family system.

Despite agreement on the family as a system, family therapists vary widely in their therapeutic philosophies and techniques. Some see the parents alone for a couple of sessions and obtain a family history, whereas others see the parents and the identified patient together from the beginning. Still others insist on seeing all family members together at all times.

Although family therapy has generated a large literature and many schools of thought, controlled research is meager. In one of the few adequately controlled studies, Wellisch, Vincent, and Ro-Trock (1976) found a significantly lower rate of rehospitalization for adolescents who had received family therapy during psychiatric hospitalization than for a control group receiving individual psychotherapy. Yet a comparison of outcomes for adolescent delinquents receiving three types of family therapy or a no-treatment control condition showed that not all forms of family therapy produce the same results (Klein, Barton, & Alexander, 1980). The conditions were:

1. *Behavioral family therapy* (in which family members were prompted and reinforced for clearly communicating their thoughts and for negotiating contractual compromises).
2. *Client-centered family therapy.*
3. *Psychodynamic family therapy.*
4. *No-treatment control.*

Follow-ups showed a recidivism rate of 26% for delinquents receiving behavioral family therapy, which was significantly better than for the client-centered therapy (47%), the psychodynamic therapy (73%), and the no-treatment control condition (50%). Furthermore, significantly fewer siblings of adolescents in the behavioral therapy group later had court contacts (20%) than in the no-treatment (40%), client-centered (59%), or psychodynamic (63%) groups. This suggested that family systems were favorably altered by behavioral methods, but not by the other approaches to family therapy. Within the groups receiving the behavioral approach, however, those having therapists with the best skills in interpersonal relations had the best outcomes of all (Alexander, Barton, Schiavo, & Parsons, 1976). Not only the method of therapy, but the therapists' skills thus played an important role.

Conclusion

After being dominated by psychodynamic approaches, child and adolescent therapies have been augmented by a variety of new techniques. Although behavior therapies were nominally rooted in learning theory, they rapidly assumed diverse forms that were not dictated by any particular learning theory and could not be integrated within a single theory. The serendipitous discovery of the effects of certain drugs on adult psychotic symptoms helped stimulate biological research, but the initial discoveries did not result from theories of psychopathology. Likewise, conjoint family therapy has been a source of miniature theories rather than being itself derived from theory.

Aside from being relatively independent of grand theories, these therapies share another important feature: They are not very developmental, in that they focus neither on the developmental history of disorders, nor on differences in the developmental levels of the children treated, nor on subsequent developmental needs. Instead, they focus on the current status of each disorder and seek to change it by ameliorating environmental contingencies, biochemical variables, or family systems. How can knowledge of development improve our understanding and treatment of psychopathology?

DEVELOPMENTAL APPROACHES

Most of what we have considered so far has concerned psychopathology, rather than development. Where developmental considerations arose, they were secondary to other concerns. For example, the psychoanalytic theory of psychosocial development was constructed from adult recollections in order to explain the origins of neurosis. Likewise, learning theories blamed much of adult psychopathology on childhood learning experiences. Learning principles were assumed to be the same for children and adults, although certain variables, such as verbal labels, were assumed to acquire new roles at certain ages (Dollard & Miller, 1950; Kendler & Kendler, 1970).

Whereas the major therapeutic approaches have not dealt much with development, the major developmental theories have not dealt much with the treatment of psychopathology. We turn now to two developmental theories that are potentially relevant to psychopathology (see Kuhn, this volume, for more on these theories).

Piaget's Theory

Without recounting all the important aspects of Jean Piaget's theory, let us consider some of the features most relevant to the developmental study of psychopathology.

Cognitive Developmental Periods.   The best known feature of Piaget's theory is its sequence of cognitive developmental periods: the *sensorimotor* period, *preoperational* period, *concrete operational* period, and *formal operational* period. The hypothesized characteristics of these periods are familiar to most students of developmental psychology. Whether or not the periods embody precisely the cognitive systems claimed by Piaget, they certainly reflect important differences in the way children process information. Yet none of the major nosological, theoretical, or therapeutic approaches to psychopathology takes account of these differences. For example, although all approaches implicitly recognize differences between infancy and later childhood they do not take account of the differences between the level of language, reasoning powers, logical assumptions, and use of information that distinguish children of different ages, such as 4-year-olds, 8-year-olds, and adolescents.

Figurative versus Operative Aspects of Cognition. Another feature of Piaget's (1977) theory relevant to the developmental study of psychopathology first becomes crucial around the age of 18 months. At this age, Piaget hypothesized, the sensorimotor period is brought to a close by the child's increasing ability to form mental representations. According to Piaget, the process of mental representation has two aspects. The first, which he called the *figurative* aspect, encompasses mental signifiers such as images, symbols, and words, that stand for particular stimuli. These signifiers are roughly analogous to the contents of mental life hypothesized by other theories, such as the mental symbols of psychoanalytic theory and the covert mediating responses of learning theories. Piaget called these mental signifiers *schemas.* He hypothesized that, prior to about 18 months of age, the only schemas a child has are precepts evoked by sensory stimulation. But after about 18 months, according to this theory, mental schemas can be generated with increasing independence of perceptual input. It is this capacity for purposely representing stimuli via mental schemas that marks the transition from sensorimotor to preoperational thought.

Piaget called the second aspect of mental representation the *operative* aspect. In contrast to the mental signifiers of the figurative aspect, the operative aspect refers to organized mental *activities* analogous to behavioral *schemes* evident during the sensorimotor period; in early infancy, for example, the sucking scheme is an organized series of actions encompassing the recognition, grasp, and sucking of suckable objects. Sensorimotor schemes are physical activities, but *mental* schemes are cognitive activities whereby the contents (schemas) of thought are manipulated, according to Piaget. (Translations of Piaget's work often use the terms *schema* and *scheme* interchangeably, but, in the 1960s, Piaget clarified that *schemas* are mental signifiers belonging to the figurative aspect of thought, whereas *schemes* are organized mental activities belonging to the operative aspect.)

Piaget's distinction between operative and figurative aspects of thought has no clear counterpart in other developmental theories. Yet, according to Piaget, cognitive development consists mainly of changes in the operative aspect of thought. He noted that even during the sensorimotor period—from birth to about 18 months—there are significant changes in overt schemes that he divided into six stages. More pervasive changes in operative functioning are marked by the transition to the concrete operational period between the ages of about 5 and 7 years, and the transition to the formal operational period at about the age of 11.

Aside from the advent of mental signifiers at the end of the sensorimotor period, Piaget did not ascribe major developmental changes to the figurative aspect of thought. Nevertheless, the progressive acquisition of new signifiers, such as words, and the growth of operative powers to use signifiers in new ways, both continue to contribute to the development of mental functioning.

The distinction between the figurative and operative aspects of thought enabled Piaget to provide a far more differentiated picture of mental development than did psychoanalytic or learning theorists, whose preoccupation with the *contents* of thought left little room for changes in the *operations* and *structure* of thought. However, despite applications of Piagetian concepts to social thinking under the banner of *social cognition* (e.g., Flavell & Ross, 1981), a large gap remains to be bridged between the differentiated Piagetian picture of cognition and the developmental study of psychopathology.

Causes of Development.   Piaget hypothesized that there are four major sources of development:

1. *Organic maturation.*
2. *Experience* gained through interactions with the physical world, whereby the child observes phenomena and actively experiments to find out how things happen.
3. *Transmission of information* from other people by language, modeling, and teaching.
4. *Equilibration.*

The first three contributors to development—maturation, experience, and social transmission—have counterparts in most theories. But Piaget believed that these three were not enough to explain cognitive development—that, instead, cognitive development involves *construction* of new mental representations when a child's existing concepts prove inadequate. The process of *equilibration* is especially crucial in the major transitions from one period of cognitive development to the next. It brings the other contributors to development together, in the construction of higher order cognitive structures from lower order structures that have reached their limits. To use a computer analogy, cognitive structures resemble computer programs, whereas schemes are like subroutines of these programs, and schemas are like the encoded data that the programs manipulate and transform. Unlike computers, however, living organisms can create for themselves new cognitive challenges to which they respond through the process of equilibration by constructing new representations and operations.

Although Piaget never fully clarified the equilibration process, it represents a crucial aspect of cognition and adaptive activity in general. The essence of this activity is the struggle to overcome gaps and contradictions in our comprehension of the world and ourselves. Such activity is an essential part of healthy development that needs far more attention in the developmental study of psychopathology.

Erikson's Theory

Erik H. Erikson's (1963, 1980) theory of *psychosocial development* is an outgrowth of Freud's theory of psychosexual development. Erikson, however, stresses the social aspects of development rather than the distribution of libido or the origins of adult neurosis. The interface between society and the developing individual is highlighted in his basic assumptions:

> (1) that the human personality in principle develops according to steps predetermined in the growing person's readiness to be driven toward, to be aware of, and to interact with, a widening social radius; and (2) that society, in principle, tends to be so constituted as to meet and invite this succession of potentialities for interaction and attempts to safeguard and to encourage the proper rate and the proper sequence of their unfolding. (Erikson, 1963, p. 270)

Stages of Psychosocial Development. Although Erikson divides childhood development into stages approximating Freud's phases of libidinal development, his stages are defined not only in terms of ascendant erogeneous zones, but also in terms of the *modes of action* employed by the child and the *modalities of social interaction* characterizing interpersonal exchanges at each stage. The initial stage, for example, is dominated by a general incorporative mode that includes incorporation of stimuli through the sense organs, as well as through the mouth. Erikson therefore calls this stage the *oral–sensory stage,* rather than just the oral stage, as Freud called it. The dominant mode of action at this stage is *incorporation* of input from the outside world. Because the infant's social interactions center on getting others to provide for its needs and receiving what they give, the social modality is called *getting.* The four subsequent psychosocial stages are a *second oral–sensory stage* in which more active incorporation is the child's dominant mode and *taking* is the social modality; the *anal-urethral-muscular stage;* the *locomotor and infantile genital stage;* and the *rudimentary genital stage.*

Erikson does not specify *why* development progresses from one stage to the next, but he maintains that failure of the appropriate mode to dominate a stage may disrupt subsequent stages. If a baby repeatedly vomits, for example, this premature dominance of the *eliminative mode* (which normally dominates the anal-urethral-muscular stage) may hinder learning of the social modality of getting. Such disruptions can affect later personality development.

Nuclear Conflicts. Erikson is probably best known for the *developmental crises* or *nuclear conflicts* he ascribes to particular stages. The two oral–sensory stages, for example, raise conflicts over the development of *basic trust versus distrust.* A resolution in favor of basic trust depends on the mother's success in satisfying the child's needs, thereby instilling in the child a sense of trust in the mother and the world she represents. Erikson's conceptions of later conflicts, especially the adolescent conflict over *identity versus role confusion,* have received abundant attention in the developmental and psychodynamic literature and have influenced psychotherapy with children and adolescents.

Although Erikson's theory has not produced a distinctive therapeutic method or testable explanations for psychopathology, several studies have found evidence for sequences of conflictual concerns like those that Erikson hypothesizes (e.g., Ciaccio, 1971; Constantinople, 1969; Waterman, Geary, & Waterman, 1974). Even though the hypothesized conflicts do seem to exist, however, these studies have suggested that some of the conflicts typically remain salient even as later ones rise and fall.

Conclusion

Developmental theories have provided a rich picture of various aspects of development. An interweaving of Piaget's theory and Erikson's theory, in particular, can provide a sense of understanding normal development and its problems. Table 12.2 offers a capsule summary of the relations between these theories and Freud's theory of psychosexual development, as well as of the normal achievements, common behavior problems, and clinical disorders characterizing each period.

Despite the value of comprehensive overviews of development, the sense of understanding bestowed by global theories has not revealed the causes nor provided efficacious methods for the treatment or prevention of most childhood disorders. We therefore turn now to some major problems facing developmental research on psychopathology.

CURRENT PROBLEMS AND ISSUES

As we have seen, there is great diversity among the approaches that touch on the developmental study of psychopathology, but no single approach deals comprehensively with it. Instead, there are nosological approaches to psychopathology in general based largely on medical models for severe adult disorders, but not of much demonstrated value for children's disorders. As an alternative to nosological approaches, there are multivariate approaches for extracting syndromes from the quantitative covariation among reported behaviors. In the absence of known etiologies, multivariate approaches can utilize phenotypic data more efficiently than the arbitrary decision rules imposed by categorical nosological approaches. Multivariate approaches also lend themselves to profile formats for providing comprehensive descriptions of behavior that can serve as a basis for taxonomies of behavior patterns. So far, multivariate behavioral descriptions have been cross-sectional, although comparisons of the syndromes found at different ages suggest developmental differences that are worth testing in longitudinal studies, as discussed later.

TABLE 12.2

Relations Among Developmental Theories, Achievements, Behavior Problems, and Clinical Disorders

Approximate Age	Cognitive Period	Psychosexual Phase	Psychosocial Conflict	Normal Achievements	Common Behavior Problems[a]	Clinical Disorders
0–2	Sensory–Motor	Oral	Basic Trust vs. Mistrust	Eating, digestion, sleeping, social responsiveness, attachment, motility, sensory–motor organization	Stubbornness, temper, toileting	Organically based dysfunctions, anaclitic depression, autism, failure to thrive
2–5	Pre-Operational	Anal	Autonomy vs. Shame and Doubt	Language, toileting, self-care skills, safety rules, self-control, peer relationships	Argues, brags, demands attention, disobedient, jealous, fears,[c] prefers older children, overactive, resists bedtime, shows off, shy,[c] stubborn, talks too much, temper, whines	Speech and hearing problems, phobias, unsocialized behavior
		Phallic-Oedipal	Initiative vs. Guilt			
6–11	Concrete Operational	Latency	Industry vs. Inferiority	Academic skills, school rules, rule-governed games, hobbies, monetary exchange, simple responsibilities	Argues, brags,[b] can't concentrate,[b] self-conscious, shows off, talks too much[c]	Hyperactivity, learning problems, school phobia, aggression, withdrawal
12–20	Formal Operational	Genital	Identity vs. Role Confusion	Relations with opposite sex, vocational preparation, personal identity, separation from family, adult responsibilities	Argues, brags[b]	Anorexia, delinquency, suicide attempts, drug and alcohol abuse, schizophrenia, depression

Note: From Achenbach, 1982, p. 67.
[a]Problems reported for at least 45% of children in nonclinical samples.
[b]Indicates problem reported for ≥45% of boys only.
[c]Indicates ≥45% of girls only.

Aside from the nosological and multivariate approaches to the identification of disorders, we have considered two general theoretical approaches to the understanding of psychopathology: psychoanalytic theory and learning theory, both of which implied developmental origins for psychopathology, but were not based on the study of children's development. Although both had major impacts on views of psychopathology, and efforts were made to join them in a grand synthesis, they gave way to a variety of new therapeutic approaches that have not been dictated by any general theory.

Just as the major approaches to psychopathology have not been based on developmental research, the major approaches to development have not involved much research on child psychopathology. In the case of Piaget's theory, this is understandable, because Piaget sought to construct a genetic epistemology rather than to explain psychopathology. However, Piaget's picture of developmental sequences and processes, and his distinction between operative and figurative aspects of thought, are important for all aspects of development, maladaptive as well as adaptive. Whether we try to determine what has gone wrong when we see a disturbed child or whether we try to help the child, it is always important to know the child's level of cognitive functioning, the limits and misconceptions entailed, and the potential for further growth.

Erikson applied his developmental theory to psychopathology, but mainly in order to illustrate his general developmental principles. Unlike Piaget, he did not provide extensive methodologies for empirically testing his concepts.

In light of where we've been, where should we be going? Although many approaches are pertinent to the development of psychopathology, they do not share a systematic program of research. The following sections highlight issues that must be faced in order to systematize the developmental study of psychopathology.

Operationally Defining Disorders

The lack of accepted operational definitions for disorders of childhood and adolescence has prevented different approaches from converging on a common set of target phenomena. As applied to childhood disorders, the traditional nosological approach has been handicapped by the lack of a taxonomic data base on which to build its categories, and by a precommitment to diagnostic constructs that must be judged as present or absent. Although DSM-III-R provides explicit decision rules for each diagnostic category, these rules are not derived directly from data on the differences among disorders. Furthermore, the decision rules do not constitute *operational* definitions, because no measurement operations are provided for determining whether a child's behavior meets the specified criteria.

Multivariate approaches, by contrast, are designed to derive target disorders from empirical data and to quantify criterial attributes. Because disorders are defined in terms of scores on particular instruments, multivariate approaches also provide operational definitions. However, as with any taxonomic effort, multivariate approaches require decisions about what data to use in formulating taxa, what taxa are useful for what purposes, and what cutting points should be used to discriminate between the normal and "pathological" range, as well as between one taxon and another. These are questions that should be answered through programmatic research. In the absence of known etiologies or clear-cut organic markers, this type of research entails psychometric bootstrapping—that is, trial-and-error revision of measures in order to strengthen their relations both to each other and to admittedly imperfect validity criteria.

In some disorders, such as autism, the age of onset and the clear-cut pathognomonic behavior argue for a taxon of the classical nosological type. Yet even in these disorders, multivariate approaches can help to sharpen the distinctions among children who meet the categorical criteria of the taxon (Siegel et al., 1986). In other disorders, multivariate findings may provide the initial basis for the taxa, but other types of data may then be needed to refine the taxa and to search for etiologies. Whatever approach is taken, however, it should be recognized that the central phenomena must be clarified to permit effective research on most aspects of developmental psychopathology.

Differential Clinical Assessment

Related to the problem of operationally defining disorders is the problem of differential clinical assessment. Although operational definitions specify procedures for determining which taxonomic criteria a child meets, clinical assessment must provide a more comprehensive picture than a taxonomy of disorders can. It is always important to know, for example, the child's family situation, developmental history, medical condition, level of cognitive functioning, school record, peer relations, special competencies, and important life stresses. Some of these may contribute to taxonomic decision, but no taxonomy will ever be comprehensive enough to take detailed account of all of them. Instead, taxonomies overlook many individual characteristics in order to highlight a few that define a class of individuals.

In the assessment of a child, decisions may be needed in relation to several different taxonomies. For example, a boy's behavior may be deviant in a way that meets the criteria for a particular behavior disorder. The boy's IQ may be low enough to classify him as "mildly retarded." This, in turn, may classify him as eligible for special education. He might also have organic problems that classify him as having a perceptual–motor handicap. These multiple classifications serve different purposes and are not mutually contradictory. However, they convey a multifaceted picture of the boy's needs.

In trying to help individual children, we need a comprehensive, idiographic picture of each child that cannot be derived from taxonomic criteria alone. In practice, clinicians have relied much more on idiographic assessment than on linking children to overarching taxonomies. Clinical interviews with children and their parents, a developmental history taken from the parents, comments by teachers, and projective tests are commonly used in deciding what is wrong and what to do about it. Even behaviorally-oriented clinicians rely much more on these procedures than on the direct observations in natural environments that the behavioral literature espouses (Wade, Baker, & Hartmann, 1979). Yet a weakness of all these methods is that the data are obtained in ways that vary from case to case, are of unknown reliability and validity, and cannot be compared with normative baselines for a child's age.

Experimental Intervention and Prevention

The most powerful strategy for testing causal relations is by experimentally manipulating the hypothesized causal variable to see whether it affects the dependent variable of interest. Drug therapies are tested in experimental studies that employ as a control condition inactive placebo drugs identical in appearance to the drug under test. Because the patients and evaluators are kept "blind" as to which is the placebo and which is the active drug, this is known as a "double-blind placebo-controlled" procedure. Experimental studies of this sort have shown that hyperactivity can be reduced with stimulant drugs (Weiss & Hechtman, 1986).

The double-blind placebo-controlled experiment is viewed as an ideal to be emulated in the evaluation of all therapies. Approximations to such experimental evaluations of drug therapies have been carried out with behavior therapies (see Achenbach, 1982), but most nondrug therapies cannot approximate the double-blind placebo-controlled study for several reasons:

1. Placebo conditions cannot be created that are both ethical and convincing alternatives to the active treatment.
2. The differences between experimental and control conditions are too obvious to enable patients and evaluators to remain blind.
3. The onset and offset of the hypothesized therapeutic effects cannot be precisely controlled.
4. Treatments such as psychotherapy and family therapy aim to bring about general changes in functioning that are not assessable via short-term measures of specific behaviors.

Efforts at prevention face even greater obstacles, because the target disorders are not yet evident when the intervention takes place. This means that experimental manipulations must be made with subjects who are not motivated by current distress and may never develop the target disorders. Furthermore, because the target disorders have not yet emerged when the preventive efforts are made, the evaluation of the interventions must last until well into the period at which the disorders would ordinarily emerge.

In light of the foregoing obstacles, it should not be surprising that there are few well-controlled experimental evaluations of interventions for child psychopathology other than drug and behavior therapies. Nevertheless, it is incumbent on advocates of therapeutic and preventive methods to demonstrate that they are safe and effective. How can this be done?

Because experimental studies are so costly, time-consuming, and methodologically difficult, they are likely to be worthwhile only after the tasks outlined in the preceding sections have been accomplished. That is, we should have reliable and valid operational definitions of the disorders, standardized procedures for differential clinical assessment, and longitudinal data on outcomes. If we have a good operational definition of a disorder, if we can reliably differentiate it from other disorders, and if we know that it usually has a poor outcome, then experimental studies of interventions for treating or preventing the disorder may be worthwhile.

The difficulty of creating appropriate placebo control conditions argues for comparing two different treatments in similar groups of children who have the target disorder, rather than a treatment versus a no-treatment group. One treatment might be a new therapy based on close study of children having a particular behavioral pattern found to have poor outcomes in longitudinal follow-ups, whereas the second might be the therapy that such children ordinarily receive.

Let us suppose, for example, that a behavior profile pattern having peaks on depression, social withdrawal, and aggression has especially poor outcomes among 6- to 11-year-old boys. Close study of boys manifesting this pattern indicates that they lack skill in making friends, are often rejected by others, cannot communicate their feelings verbally, and react to frustration with extreme aggression. A possible intervention may be to train them in the skills required for friendship, train them to avoid doing things that precipitate rejection, to communicate their feelings verbally, and to react more constructively to frustration.

After pilot research to perfect a social skills training program, an experimental study can be designed to compare it with one or more treatments ordinarily administered to these boys. For example, it may be possible to compare the new treatment with two commonly used treatments such as individual psychotherapy and family therapy. The candidate subjects would be boys who at the point of admission into a mental health service manifest behavior profiles with peaks on depression, social withdrawal, and aggression. Extensive differential assessment would be used to exclude boys who might be poor subjects because of major problems beyond the reach of the therapies to be tested, such as organic dysfunctions, very low cognitive ability, extreme family instability, or uncooperativeness.

Not only for taxonomic purposes, then, but also for purposes of formulating an idiographic picture of the child which distinguishes that child from other children, we need assessment procedures of proven reliability and validity, based on normative data. Procedures such as interviews, ratings by parents and teachers, self-reports, behavior samples, and tests may all contribute valid assessment data, but research is required to determine what unique contribution each procedure can make and to standardize the best of these procedures for use across diverse settings.

Longitudinal Course of Adaptive and Maladaptive Behavior

The previous two sections dealt with research that is largely cross-sectional— operationally defining disorders and making differential assessments of children at a particular point in time. Although children's *past* histories are always relevant, both to the definitions of disorders and to broader clinical assessment, the main value of these two enterprises lies in their relation to the children's *future* development. In short, the ultimate purpose of operational definitions and differential assessment is to help in facilitating children's development. But this requires knowledge of the typical outcomes of each disorder. And such knowledge, in turn, requires longitudinal research comparing the developmental course of children grouped according to type of disorder and other variables. Although etiological research is also important, the multidetermined nature of most childhood behavior disorders means that longitudinal follow-up studies may yield quicker and surer benefits for troubled children than will etiological research.

As an example, suppose we start with 6- to 11-year-old children for whom parents and teachers have filled out standardized rating forms at the admission into several mental health settings. Forms of this sort for obtaining data on children's problems and competencies are coming into widespread use. They have been subjected to multivariate analyses to produce empirically derived scales for scoring behavioral problems and competencies. The scales have been normed and cast in profile formats. As illustrated in Fig. 12.2, cluster analyses have identified profile patterns shared by substantial subgroups of clinically referred children (see Achenbach & McConaughy, 1987, for practical applications of these procedures).

The profiles derived from parent and teacher ratings of large samples of children provide a good picture of the range of problems for which children are typically referred. The standardization of ratings and classification of children by profile types give us a starting point from which to compare outcomes for children who differ in their initial problems and competencies, as seen by important adults in their natural environments.

If we have parents and teachers fill out the same rating forms again at regular intervals, such as every six months for two years, we can track the course of the child's problems and competencies as judged by these important adults. We can then determine whether the patterns of problems and competencies manifested at the outset of treatment can predict outcomes over the two years. In particular, we can determine whether any patterns have much worse or better outcomes than others. Even if the clinical services are heterogeneous (as they are in most settings), findings of especially poor outcomes for a particular profile pattern would indicate that this was a group in need of close study to find out why their outcomes are so poor and what can be done to help them. Conversely, a group that had exceptionally good outcomes could be examined to identify the factors responsible. For example, were they especially well suited to the services offered? Or might they be especially competent and able to improve regardless of the services? Or might their problems have been specific to a particular developmental period?

Further variables can be readily added to a study of this type. For example, demographic and family data initially obtained (e.g., socioeconomic status, race, rural versus suburban versus urban residence, marital status of parents, number of siblings) may augment the predictive power of profile patterns. Other data, such as IQ and medical conditions, may also be important. However, the more variables included, the larger the samples needed and the greater the risk of chance findings that must be controlled by adjusting significance levels. Furthermore, such studies should also incorporate cross-validation, either in new samples or by splitting samples in half and testing the findings from one half in the other half of the sample.

Studies of this sort can address interesting developmental questions by analyzing changes in reported behavior patterns occurring as children grow older. For example, as shown in Fig. 12.2, cross-sectional research has yielded a profile characterized by exceptional elevations on Uncommunicative and Delinquent syndromes for 12- to 16-year-old boys. Although the Uncommunicative and Delinquent syndromes have also been found among 6- to 11-year-old boys, cluster analyses revealed no profile type characterized by peaks on both these syndromes for this age group. If we follow disturbed 10-year-old boys for three years, would a distinct group show the Uncommunicative–Delinquent profile by the time they are adolescents? If so, what profile patterns did they show before the Uncommunicative–Delinquent pattern emerged?

Or, if we start with 10-year-old boys whose profiles are elevated on Somatic Complaints, will they continue to show a particular pattern in adolescence, when cross-sectional analyses have not revealed a Somatic Complaints profile? Or do they have such good outcomes that the Somatic Complaints profile can be considered a transitory developmental phenomenon that disappears by the time boys reach adolescence?

In summary, it seems clear that even short-term longitudinal studies of the problems and competencies of children already identified as disturbed can be of great value for understanding childhood psychopathology and development. Moreover, such studies can improve services to children by pinpointing groups in need of help not now provided, and by laying the groundwork for devising new ways to help these children. By first identifying those actually having the worst outcomes, we can also concentrate etiological research where it is most needed, instead of initiating etiological studies without knowing the usual outcomes of the disorders we are studying.

If a boy met the criteria for the study and he and his family agreed to participate, a random procedure could be used to assign him to one of the three treatment conditions. Prior to treatment and again at six-month intervals thereafter, behavior ratings by the boys' parents and teachers, self-reports by each boy, and standardized clinical interviews would be used to assess behavioral change. The boys receiving the treatments would ultimately be compared on these variables, plus others such as achievement test performance, friendships, and trouble with the law. Ratings by evaluators such as teachers and clinical interviewers could be blind as to the treatment conditions. Other outcome variables, such as test performance and police records, would not be susceptible to influence by knowledge of treatment conditions.

A single-factor design of this sort could be expanded by comparing two groups who have different initial behavioral patterns across two types of intervention in a two-by-two design. The very few studies reporting adequate subject-by-treatment analyses have revealed unexpected interaction effects that greatly outweighed the main effects of treatment (e.g., Love & Kaswan, 1974; Miller, Barrett, Hampe, & Noble, 1972). Thus, certain treatments may be helpful to some kinds of children but harmful to others. Unless the interactions between child characteristics and treatment effects are assessed, however, we will not know what treatments are optimal for which children.

Conclusion

In this summary of various approaches to development and psychopathology, it seemed clear that no one approach has taken the developmental study of psychopathology as its central objective. We therefore considered several key tasks requiring programmatic research to foster a developmental understanding of psychopathology.

The first task was to construct reliable and valid operational definitions of disorders from empirical data. The second was to establish standardized assessment procedures that can reliably and validly compare each child with other children. The third was to conduct longitudinal follow-ups aimed at determining the characteristic outcomes of particular patterns of adaptive and maladaptive behavior.

Once we have reliable and valid operational definitions of disorders, standardized procedures for differential clinical assessment, and longitudinal data on outcomes, then it may be worth mounting experimental studies of interventions for preventing or treating disorders found to have poor outcomes. These tasks by no means exhaust the possibilities for significant developmental research on psychopathology, but they are of critical importance to almost all theories, disorders, and approaches to treatment.

REFERENCES

Abikoff, H. (1985). Efficacy of cognitive training interventions in hyperactive children: A critical review. *Clinical Psychology Review, 5,* 479–512.

Achenbach, T. M. (1966). The classification of children's psychiatric symptoms: A factor-analytic study. *Psychological Monographs, 80*(7) (Whole No. 615).

Achenbach, T. M. (1982). *Developmental psychopathology* (2nd ed.). New York: Wiley.

Achenbach, T. M. (1985). *Assessment and taxonomy of child and adolescent psychopathology.* Beverly Hills, CA: Sage.

Achenbach, T. M., & Edelbrock, C. S. (1978). The classification of child psychopathology: A review and analysis of empirical efforts. *Psychological Bulletin, 85,* 1275–1301.

Achenbach, T. M., & Edelbrock, C. S. (1981). Behavioral problems and competencies reported by parents of normal and disturbed children aged four to sixteen. *Monographs of the Society for Research in Child Development, 46,* Serial No. 188.

Achenbach, T. M., & Edelbrock, C. S. (1983). *Manual for the Child Behavior Checklist and Revised Child Behavior Profile.* Burlington, VT: University of Vermont Department of Psychiatry.

Achenbach, T. M., & Edelbrock, C. (1986). *Manual for the Teacher's Report Form and Teacher Version of the Child Behavior Profile.* Burlington, VT: University of Vermont Department of Psychiatry.

Achenbach, T. M., & McConaughy, S. H. (1987). *Empirically based assessment of child and adolescent psychopathology: practical applications.* Beverly Hills, CA: Sage.

Achenbach, T. M., Verhulst, F. C., Baron, G. D., & Althaus, M. (1987). A comparison of syndromes derived from the Child Behavior Checklist for American and Dutch boys aged 6–11 and 12–16. *Journal of Child Psychology and Psychiatry, 28,* 437–453.

Alexander, J. F., Barton, C., Schiavo, R. S., & Parsons, B. V. (1976). Systems-behavioral intervention with families of delinquents: Therapist characteristics, family behavior, and outcome. *Journal of Consulting and Clinical Psychology, 44,* 656–644.

American Academy of Child Psychiatry. (1983). *Child psychiatry: A plan for the coming decades.* Washington, DC: Author

American Psychiatric Association. (1st ed., 1952; 2nd ed., 1968; 3rd ed., 1980; 3rd rev. ed., 1987). *Diagnostic and statistical manual of mental disorders.* Washington, DC: Author.

Beidel, D. C., & Turner, S. M. (1986). A critique of the theoretical bases of cognitive–behavioral theories and therapy. *Clinical Psychology Review, 6,* 177–197.

Bell, J. E. (1961). Family group therapy. *Public Health Monograph,* No. 64. Washington, DC: United States Department of Health, Education, and Welfare.

Bettelheim, B. (1967). *The empty fortress.* New York: Free Press.

Bradley, C. (1937). The behavior of children receiving Benzedrine. *American Journal of Psychiatry, 94,* 577–585.

Brown, G., Chadwick, O., Shaffer, D., Rutter, M., & Traub, M. (1981). A prospective study of children with head injuries: III. Psychiatric sequelae. *Psychological Medicine, 11,* 63–78.

Campbell, M., & Small, A. M. (1978). Chemotherapy. In B. B. Wolman, J. Egan, & A. O. Ross (Eds.), *Handbook of treatment of mental disorders in childhood and adolescence.* Englewood Cliffs, NJ: Prentice-Hall.

Carlson, G. A., & Cantwell, D. P. (1982). Diagnosis of childhood depression: A comparison of the Weinberg and DSM-III Criteria, *Journal of the American Academy of Child Psychiatry, 21,* 247–250.

Ciaccio, N. V. (1971). A test of Erikson's theory of ego epigenesis. *Developmental Psychology, 4,* 306–311.

Constantinople, A. (1969). An Eriksonian measure of personality development in college students. *Developmental Psychology, 1,* 357–372.

Cytryn, L., & McKnew, D. H. (1979). Affective disorders. In J. Noshpitz (Ed.), *Basic handbook of child psychology* (Vol. 2). New York: Basic Books.

Cytryn, L., McKnew, D. H, & Bunney, W. E. (1980). Diagnosis of depression in children: Reassessment. *American Journal of Psychiatry, 137,* 22–25.

Despert, L. (1947). Psychotherapy in childhood schizophrenia. *American Journal of Psychiatry, 104,* 36–43.

Dollard, J., & Miller, N. (1950). *Personality and psychotherapy.* New York: McGraw-Hill.

Edelbrock, C., & Achenbach, T. M. (1980). A typology of Child Behavior Profile patterns: Distribution and correlates for disturbed children aged 6–16. *Journal of Abnormal Child Psychology, 8,* 441–470.

Edelbrock, C., Costello, A. J., & Kessler, M. D. (1984). Empirical corroboration of the Attention Deficit Disorder. *Journal of the American Academy of Child Psychiatry, 23,* 285–290.

Eisenberg, L., & Kanner, L. (1956). Early infantile autism, 1943–1955. *American Journal of Orthopsychiatry, 26,* 556–566.

Erikson, E. H. (1963). *Childhood in society* (2nd ed.). New York: Norton.

Erikson, E. H. (1980). Elements of a psychoanalytic theory of psychosocial development. In S. I. Greenspan & G. H. Pollock (Eds.), *The course of life: Psychoanalytic contributions toward understanding personality development: Vol I. Infancy and early childhood.* Adelphi, MD.: NIMH Mental Health Study Center.

Flavell, J. H., & Ross, L. (Eds.) (1981). *Social cognitive development: Frontiers and possible futures.* New York: Cambridge University Press.

Freud, A. (1965). *Normality and pathology in childhood.* New York: International Universities Press.

Freud, S. (1953). Three essays on the theory of sexuality (1905). In *Standard edition of the complete psychological works of Sigmund Freud* (Vol. 7). London: The Hogarth Press.

Frommer, E. A. (1967). Treatment of childhood depression with antidepressant drugs. *British Medical Journal, 1,* 729–732.

Goldenberg, I., & Goldenberg, H. (1980). *Family therapy: An overview.* Monterey, CA: Brookes/Cole.

Griesinger, W. (1867). *Die Pathologie und Therapie der psychischen Krankheiten (Mental pathology and therapeutics)* (C. L. Robertson & J. Rutherford, Trans.). London: New Sydenham Society. (Original work published 1845)

Holmes, F. B. (1936). An experimental investigation of a method of overcoming children's fears. *Child Development, 7,* 6–30.

Jones, M. C. (1924). A laboratory study of fear: The case of Peter. *Pedagogical Seminary, 31,* 308–315.

Kanner, L. (1943). Autistic disturbances of affective contact. *Nervous Child, 2,* 217–250.

Kanner, L. (1971). Childhood psychosis: A historical overview. *Journal of Autism and Childhood Schizophrenia, 1,* 14–19.

Kanner, L., Rodrigues, A., & Ashenden, B. (1972). How far can autistic children go in matters of social adaptation? *Journal of Autism and Childhood Schizophrenia, 2,* 9–33.

Kasanin, J., & Kaufman, M. R. (1929). A study of the functional psychoses in childhood. *American Journal of Psychiatry, 9,* 307–384.

Kashani, J. M., Husain, A., Shekim, W. O., Hodges, K. K., Cytryn, L., & McKnew, D. H. (1981). Current perspectives on childhood depression: An overview. *American Journal of Psychiatry, 138,* 143–153.

Kazdin, A. E. (1985). *Treatment of antisocial behavior in children and adolescents.* Homewood, IL: Dorsey.

Kendall, P. C., & Braswell, L. (1985). *Cognitive–behavioral therapy for impulsive children.* New York: Guilford Press.

Kendler, T. S., & Kendler, H. H. (1970). An ontogeny of optional shift behavior. *Child Development, 41,* 1–27.

Klein, N. C., Barton, C., & Alexander. J. F. (1980). Intervention and evaluation in family settings. In R. H. Price & P. E. Polister (Eds.), *Evaluation and action in the social environment*. New York: Academic Press.

Kovacs, M., & Beck, A. T. (1977). An empirical–clinical approach toward a definition of childhood depression. In J. G. Schulterbrandt & A. Raskin (Eds.), *Depression in childhood: Diagnosis, treatment, and conceptual models*. New York: Raven Press.

Kraepelin, E. (1883). *Compendium der Psychiatrie*. Leipzig: Abel.

Lazarus, A. A., Davison, G. C., & Polefka, D. A. (1965). Classical and operant factors in the treatment of school phobia. *Journal of Abnormal Psychology, 70*, 225–229.

Lejeune, J., Gautier, M., & Turpin, R. (1963). Study of the somatic chromosomes of nine mongoloid idiot children, 1959. In S. H. Boyer (Ed.), *Papers on human genetics*. Englewood Cliffs, NJ: Prentice-Hall.

London, P. (1972). The end of ideology in behavior and modification. *American Psychologist. 27*, 913–920.

Lotter, V. (1978). Follow-up studies. In M. Rutter & E. Schopler (Eds.), *Autism: A reappraisal of concepts and treatment*. New York: Plenum.

Love, L. R., & Kaswan, J. W. (1974). *Troubled children: Their families, schools, and treatments*. New York: Wiley.

Masson, J. M. (1984). *The assault on truth: Freud's suppression of the seduction theory*. New York: Farrar, Straus, & Giroux.

Mattison, R., Cantwell, D. P., Russell, A. T., & Will, L. (1979). A comparison of DSM-II and DSM-III in the diagnosis of childhood psychiatric disorders. *Archives of General Psychiatry, 36*, 1217–1222.

Mezzich, A. C., Mezzich, J. E., & Coffman, G. A. (1985). Reliability of DSM-III vs. DSM-II in child psychopathology. *Journal of the American Academy of Child Psychiatry, 24*, 273–280.

Miller, L. C., Barrett, C. L., Hampe, E., & Noble, H. (1972). Comparison of reciprocal inhibition, psychotherapy, and waiting list control for phobic children. *Journal of Abnormal Psychology, 79*, 269–279.

Mowrer, O. H., & Mowrer, W. M. (1938). Enuresis: A method for its study and treatment. *American Journal of Orthopsychiatry, 8*, 436–459.

Ochroch, R. (1981). *The diagnosis and treatment of minimal brain dysfunction in children. A clinical approach*. New York: Human Sciences Press.

Ollendick, T., & Gruen, G. E. (1972). Treatment of a bodily injury phobia with implosive therapy. *Journal of Consulting and Clinical Psychology, 38*, 389–393.

Piaget, J. (1977). The role of action in the development of thinking. In W. F. Overton & J. M. Gallagher (Eds.), *Knowledge and development* (Vol. I). New York: Plenum.

Quay, H. C. (1979). Classification. In H. C. Quay & J. S. Werry (Eds.), *Psychopathological disorders of childhood* (2nd ed.). New York: Wiley.

Rank, B. (1949). Adaptation of the psychoanalytic technique for the treatment of young children with atypical development. *American Journal of Orthopsychiatry, 19*, 130–139.

Rosen, B. M., Bahn, A. K., & Kramer, M. (1964). Demographic and diagnostic characteristics of psychiatric clinic outpatients in the U.S.A., 1961. *American Journal of Orthopsychiatry, 34*, 455–468.

Shaffer, D., McNamara, N., & Pincus, J. H. (1974). Controlled observations on patterns of activity, attention, and impulsivity in brain-damaged and psychiatrically disturbed boys. *Journal of Psychological Medicine, 4*, 4–18.

Siegel, B., Anders, T. F., Ciaranello, R. D., Bienenstock, B., & Kraemer, H. C. (1986). Empirically derived subclassification of the autistic syndrome. *Journal of Autism and Developmental Disabilities, 16*, 275–293.

Spitzer, R. L., & Cantwell, D. P. (1980). The DSM-III classification of the psychiatric disorders of infancy, childhood, and adolescence. *Journal of the American Academy of Child Psychiatry, 19*, 356–370.

Spivack, G., & Shure, M. B. (1982). The cognition of social adjustment. In B. B. Lahey & A. E. Kazdin (Eds.), *Advances in clinical child psychology*. (Vol 5, pp. 323–372). New York: Plenum.

Strauss, A. A., & Lehtinen, L. E. (1947). *Psychopathology and education of the brain-injured child*. New York: Grune & Stratton.

Strober, M., Green, J.. & Carlson, G. (1981). The reliability of psychiatric diagnosis in hospitalized adolescents: Interrater agreement using the DSM-III. *Archives of General Psychiatry, 38,* 141–145.

Thomas, A., Chess, S., & Birch, H. G. (1968). *Temperament and behavior disorders in children.* New York: New York University Press.

Ullman, D., Egan, D., Fiedler, N., Jurenec, G., Pliske, R., Thompson, P., & Doherty, M. E. (1981). The many faces of hyperactivity: Similarities and differences in diagnostic policies. *Journal of Consulting and Clinical Psychology, 49,* 694–704.

Wade, T. C., Baker, T. B., & Hartmann, D. T. (1979). Behavior therapists' self-reported views and practices. *The Behavior Therapist, 2,* 3–6.

Waterman, A. S., Geary, P. S., & Waterman, C. K. (1974). Longitudinal study of changes in ego identity status from the freshman to the senior year of college. *Developmental Psychology, 10,* 387–392.

Watson, J. B. (1913). Psychology as the behaviorist views it. *Psychological Review, 20,* 158–177.

Watson, J. B. (1919). *Psychology from the standpoint of a behaviorist.* Philadelphia: J.B. Lippincott.

Watson, J. B. (1924). *Behaviorism.* New York: People's Publishing Co.

Weinberg, W. A., Rutman, J., Sullivan, L., Penick, E. C., & Dietz, S. G. (1973). Depression in children referred to an educational diagnostic center: Diagnosis and treatment. *Journal of Pediatrics, 83,* 1065–1072.

Weiss, G., & Hechtman, L. T. (1986). *Hyperactive children grown up: Empirical findings and theoretical considerations.* New York: Guilford Press.

Wellisch, D. K., Vincent, J., & Ro-Trock, G. K. (1976). Family therapy versus individual therapy: A study of adolescents and their parents. In D. H. L. Olson (Ed.), *Treating relationships.* Lake Mills, IO: Graphic Publications.

Werry, J. S., Methven, R. J., Fitzpatrick, J., & Dixon, H. (1983). The interrater reliability of DSM-III in children. *Journal of Abnormal Child Psychology, 11,* 341–354.

Wolman, B. B. (1970). *Children without childhood.* New York: Grune & Stratton.

Wolpe, J. (1958). *Psychotherapy by reciprocal inhibition.* Stanford, CA: Stanford University Press.

IV APPLIED DEVELOPMENTAL PSYCHOLOGY

As hinted in many of the preceding chapters, developmental psychology is not simply a subdiscipline in which scientists seek basic knowledge of developmental processes. The developing individuals at the heart of developmental psychology face real problems and challenges, and the results of empirical research often have implications for the design of educational and socializing regimes and for the development of human social policy. In Chapter 13, Edward Zigler and Matia Finn-Stevenson illustrate the ways in which developmental thinking and research affect social policy, and the ways in which an increasing proportion of developmental research is being oriented to address questions of applied as well as basic science. The old, and often pejorative, distinction between these twin aspects of developmental research is gradually giving way as developmental psychology comes of age as a mature science.

13 Applied Developmental Psychology

Edward F. Zigler and Matia Finn-Stevenson
Yale University

INTRODUCTION

Researchers in developmental psychology have become increasingly appreciative of the close link between basic research in child development and applications of that research. Basic research is generally defined as any research which is motivated by the desire to expand knowledge. Applied research is defined as research which is conducted in an effort to solve a problem or in order to provide information that can be put to some specific use. Although these two types of research are distinct by definition, they actually overlap and contribute to each other to the benefit of both.

Applied research in developmental psychology encompasses a broad array of studies, since the field, which is concerned with the study of children and families, has by its very nature practical applications and relevance. Some of the research conducted on sex-role acquisition, for example, is applied. It is designed to enhance our understanding of how sex roles influence career and other choices, values, and behaviors, and it has implications for current debates about the characteristics and changing social roles of men and women (Eccles & Hoffman, 1984). The research on a number of other developmental topics such as cognition and learning may also be considered applied research, as it is often used in educational settings in efforts to help parents and teachers in their task of educating children, or to enhance children's ability to learn (Dillon & Sternberg, 1986). Since many such developmental topics are covered in other chapters in this book, we have chosen to focus in this chapter on emerging trends in the field of applied developmental psychology—namely, the integration of child development research and social policy, and the increasing recognition among researchers that some of their work should be directed toward the understanding and solution of contemporary problems faced by children and families (Stevenson & Siegel, 1984; Zigler, Kagan, & Klugman, 1983).

Several developments have precipitated these emerging trends in the field. Most notable among these was the implementation during the 1960s and 1970s of federally sponsored social programs. The proliferation of a wide range of these programs, and the funds made available for them, enabled developmental psychologists to apply their knowledge and training to new areas of study such as children's services, which had not previously received attention from the scientific community (Salkind, 1983; Takahishi, DeLeon, & Pallak, 1983; Zigler & Berman, 1983). Other developments which precipitated psychologists' involvement in social policy issues were: (a) the increased recognition among researchers of the reciprocity between basic and applied research (Bryant, 1972; Garner, 1972; Zigler, 1980), and the need to utilize both of these types of research in the study of children (Weisz, 1978; Zigler, 1980); and (b) the realization in recent years that children are influenced not only by the people in their immediate social settings but also by aspects of the larger and more remote social systems such as the school, the workplace, the community, the government, and the mass media over which children and their parents have little, if any, control. As a result of this new understanding, developmental psychologists have broadened their research to include ecological studies which examine development within the wider social context (Bronfenbrenner, 1979). They have also begun to conduct studies that examine the impact of societal changes on the lives of children (Brim & Dustan, 1983).

The latter aspect of the research has important implications. The past thirty years has been a period of vast changes for our society as the result of now-familiar shifts in the economy and employment patterns, in family composition, and in the age structure of the population. In order to assess how these changes are influencing the growth and development of children, a number of developmental psychologists have begun to compile childhood social indicators. These are measures of the constancies and changes in the lives of children and of the health, achievement, behavior, and well-being of children themselves (Parke & Peterson, 1981; Zill, Sigal, & Brim, 1983). The systematic compilation of such indicators provides a knowledge base for understanding the determinants of development, as well as valuable data which facilitates our ability to identify and respond to the needs of children and their families. On the basis of such data, psychologists and others concerned about human welfare note that children face a number of problems in the areas of health and psychological well-being (see Select Committee on Children, Youth, and Families, 1983). Many of these problems stem from stresses on family life and the societal changes described above. They are pervasive and national in scope, requiring that policy efforts toward their solution be made by government as well as by other sectors of society. However, having participated in the policy process, developmental psychologists have come to appreciate that governmental and other kinds of policies, in and of themselves, are limited in what they can accomplish and must be based on scientific knowledge from child development research in order to ensure their effectiveness. Although many developmental psychologists recognize the vital link between scientific research and policy in the design and implementation of social programs, involvement in the policy process is still a relatively new experience for researchers. It is also a major transition from their traditional role as academics confined to university settings. Nevertheless, because their knowledge and expertise are needed in the policy arena, researchers are discovering that they not only contribute to society's ability to enhance the well-being of children and adults, but they themselves benefit from the contact and stimulus of direct experience.

RESEARCH IN APPLIED DEVELOPMENTAL PSYCHOLOGY: CURRENT TRENDS

This point is made in several recent reports (e.g., Task Force on Psychology and Public Policy, 1986; Takanishi, DeLeon, & Pallak, 1983; Brim & Dustan, 1983) which suggest that psychologists' work in applied settings in general and their involvement in the policy arena in particular provide opportunities for research. Such opportunities are exemplified by several areas of study which received their impetus from societal changes that have occurred in recent years. The research on fatherhood (e.g., Lamb, 1981, 1986) is one example. Fathers have always played an important role in children's lives. However, it was not until recently that psychologists began to study the relationship between fathers and children and the ramifications of paternal involvement in the lives of children. Scientific interest in the topic of fatherhood was triggered in part by changes in the traditional roles assumed by men and women. The research on infant day care is another example. Again research on this topic was initiated because of an emerging social issue—namely, the increase in recent years in the number of infants who are cared for by nonrelatives (Klein, 1985). The numerous studies conducted on the effects of the day care experience on infants serve to enrich our understanding of human development and behavior, and they also enable psychologists to analyze this social issue in light of available knowledge and make policy recommendations accordingly (Zigler & Muenchow, 1983).

Changes in Family Life

Several other social changes have occurred in recent years, and these, too, present unique and important opportunities for policy development and often serve as the catalyst for the conduct of research. Notable among these are the transformations in family life. There have been many who have at one time bemoaned these changes as signals of the family's demise. However, by now most developmental psychologists agree that although the family has undergone rapid and radical changes, it remains the most important institution in determining child growth and development. Nevertheless, researchers emphasize the need to acknowledge and study the multiple forms that families may now take. The traditional nuclear family, which includes the husband as the breadwinner, the mother as a housewife, and two or more children living at home, represents fewer than 7% of all families in the United States (Select Committee on Children, Youth, and Families, 1983) and is therefore only one of several contexts suitable for the study of children. Some of the different forms that families now take are families with both parents as wage-earners, single-parent families, unrelated persons living together, and what have come to be called "blended" families (also known as "reconstituted" or "new extended" families) created by the divorce and subsequent remarriage of one or both parents (Hetherington & Camara, 1984; Lamb, 1982b).

Besides these changes in family forms, fragmentation and isolation of the family have progressed. First, people today frequently move in search of work, resulting in the further lessening of the extended family (Packard, 1972). Many families therefore do not have the immediate access to the experience and counsel of their elders that they once had, nor the support system for child care they could once count on. Second, and more pronounced in its effects on children, has been a striking increase in the number of single-parent families. The number of single-parent families grew by nearly 2 million between 1970 and 1978 (Norton, 1979). Currently, one out of five children in the United States is being reared in a single-parent family; among blacks, it is one out of every two children (U.S. Census Bureau, 1986). Divorce, which we will focus on in more detail later in the chapter, is one reason cited for the increase in single-parent families (Hetherington & Camara, 1984). Living in a home without a father, or not seeing their father, and the experience of the divorce of their parents, are new and difficult conditions under which recent generations of children are growing up— and are conditions which bear scientific investigation by researchers. What are the developmental consequences of growing up in a single-parent family? What are the weaknesses and strengths of single-parent families, and how do these differ from the assumed weaknesses and strengths of the traditional family? These are some of the questions psychologists are likely to ask.

Child Day Care

The increase in the number of children whose parents are both employed and the associated need for child care are other changes that have profoundly influenced family life. What is especially significant about the increase in the number of children whose parents are employed is the change in women's participation in the labor force. Whereas women, and in particular mothers, tended in the past to be employed part-time and to move in and out of the labor force depending on the ages of their children, many many mothers today are employed full-time even when their children are very young. Currently 62% of women with children are employed outside the home (Joint Economic Committee, 1986). This figure represents a tenfold increase in maternal employment since the end of World War II, and it has not yet peaked; it is estimated that by 1990, 75% of mothers will be in the labor force (Urban Institute, 1982) and that the fastest growing subgroup of employed mothers will be—as it is currently—mothers with children under one year of age (Hayghe, 1984; Klein, 1985). In single-parent families and in families where both parents are employed, the potential impact of this trend on children is enormous, as families have to rely on out-of-home care for their children and to relegate the rearing of the children to people who are nonrelatives.

There are two major issues of concern related to out-of-home care for children: one, the availability of a sufficient number of substitute care facilities, and two, the quality of care provided in such facilities. Many parents, even those who can afford good-quality child care, have conflicting ideas about how to balance their employment and their family life, and often feel guilty and defensive about having to relegate the rearing of their children to other people (Zigler & Hall, in press). Such feelings emanate in part from the insufficient number of child-care settings in this country. This lack of child-care facilities is one of the most critical social issues facing the nation (Zigler & Muenchow, 1983) and was recognized as such as early as 1970. At that time it was stated that making available more day care services of good quality was the number one priority for our nation in alleviating the problems faced by many families (White House Conference on Children, 1970). However, the need for more day care services not only continues, but has been exacerbated. Thus families are experiencing a great deal of stress trying to accommodate the parents' work schedules to a variety of different child-care arrangements. When parents cannot make adequate arrangements, children are sometimes left alone at home, often in the care only of siblings not much older than they are. This is an especially acute problem with school-age children. Each day, two to four million children between the ages of 7 and 13 come home from school to an empty house (Child Care: Beginning a National Initiative, 1984). These "latchkey" children, so called because their house keys are often worn strung around their necks, are left to their own resources during critical hours of the day.

The issue of latchkey children is a controversial one, with researchers differing on the potential impact on the children of being left alone after school. Some researchers point out that there are no differences on several measures of social and psychological functioning between latchkey children and children whose parents are home when they come back from school (Rodman, Pratto & Nelson, 1985; Vandell & Corasaniti, 1985). Others argue that the latchkey experience may be a positive one for many children who learn to function independently at an early age (e.g., Korchin, 1981). However, several researchers contend that there may be possible negative influences associated with the latchkey phenomenon (Steinberg, 1985). Long and Long (1983) and Ginter (1981), for example, note that latchkey children are more fearful and anxious than other children their age who are supervised by adults. Garbarino (1981) emphasizes the safety hazards that confront latchkey children. In a study in Detroit, for instance, an investigator discovered that one sixth of the fires in that city involved an unattended child (Smock, 1977). Given the conflicting nature of viewpoints on the topic, it is obvious that the phenomenon of latchkey children in our society is an empirical issue that needs to be investigated further to ascertain if there may be repercussions for the social and emotional development of these children whose contact with adults is minimal. In the meantime, however, some accommodations need to be made to provide school-age children with supervised settings to which they can go after school (School-Age Child Care Project, 1986).

Besides the need for child-care services, there is the issue of the quality of child care. Whereas the research indicates that the quality of care a young child receives makes a difference in terms of developmental outcome and psychological growth and development, most parents cannot afford to stay home to care for their own children; and often they do not earn enough to afford good-quality care if they work, since in many cases they need the earnings to meet basic family needs. In terms of the day care arrangements working parents utilize, the findings of a survey on such arrangements (O'Connell & Rogers, 1983) reveal that of the preschool children who are in out-of-home care, 18% are in day care centers and the remaining children are in family day care homes in which a nonrelative, sometimes herself a mother, takes care of several children in her own home. A national survey on substitute care for children under one year of age (Klein, 1985) indicates that less than 10% of infants in substitute care are in center-based day care and that the majority of such infants are cared for in private home settings. Although such data are valuable in revealing the types of substitute care arrangements made by parents of infants and young children, they do not provide any information on the care actually provided. Such information is important since studies have shown that many aspects of children's development are influenced by the quality of their day care environment (McCartney, 1984; McCartney, Scarr, Phillips, Grajek, & Schwarz, 1982). Howes and Rubenstein (1985), for example, have found that the quality of day care experience (as defined by adult:child ratio and the extent to which caregivers are able to engage in harmonious interactions with the children) significantly influences the individual experiences of children in day care.

Unfortunately, not much is known about the actual day care experiences of infants and young children, although in one early study on the topic (Keyserling, 1972) investigators noted that in some of the child-care settings studied, children received poor-quality care. The lack of information on the day care experiences of children stems in part from the fact that many studies on day care have focused thus far on the potential consequences of the day care experience on infants and children, as opposed to their actual experiences in day care. Additionally, what is known about the quality of care in either day care centers or family day care homes is available from licensed settings. However, many children are in centers or private homes which are informal and unlicensed and therefore not accountable to public authority, making reliable data on these children's actual day care experiences difficult to obtain. In fact, even among licensed day care facilities, standards for the quality of care provided are often lax or unenforced, so the fact that children are in a licensed day care setting does not necessarily provide an assurance that they receive good-quality care. In some states there are reasonable standards for the provision of quality care. In numerous other states, this is not the case (Young & Zigler, 1986). For example, in some states it is permissible for one adult to care for as many as 10 infants despite the fact that this staff:child ratio is not only potentially harmful in view of infants' need for individual attention, but also dangerous. In the case of fire, how could one caregiver bring 10 infants to safety?

Another aspect of the quality day care issue is related to the training of caregivers of infants and young children. The long-term consequences of day care, especially infant day care, are not yet known. However, from the research of the past few decades we know that an important factor in a child's development is the quality of interaction that the child has with the adults in his or her life. Children need to be reared in an environment that is not just safe but is nurturant as well. In the same vein, parents must be assured that their children are supervised by adults who are trained and competent in the task of child care. In 1972 the U.S. Office of Child Development, with the support of national organizations concerned with child development and welfare, established a consortium which set out to upgrade the quality of care children receive in day care centers. Known then as the Child Development Associate Consortium (CDAC), and now known as the CDA National Credential Program, this nonprofit organization—with the help of leading psychologists and early childhood educators—developed an assessment and credential system for child care workers (Ward, 1976). On the basis of this system we can now clearly delineate the qualities that are essential for effective caregiving in group situations. For example, providing quality care for young children does not only mean making nutritious meals available, but also involves an understanding on the part of the caregiver of the basic principles of child growth and development and of the importance of attending to the individual needs of each of the children.

The CDA project, in bringing research knowledge to bear on an emerging social problem, exemplifies the interface between social policy and child development research. Providing adequate and appropriate training for caregivers in an effort to ensure quality care for children is a major task facing policymakers today. Through the work of the CDA project staff, progress has been made in delineating the skills and competencies necessary for the care of preschool children in groups, and in the ability to formally recognize caregivers who possess such skills and competencies. Since its creation in 1972, the CDA project has been expanded to include the delineation of competencies necessary in the training and assessment of caregivers in infant day care centers, family day care homes, and school-age day care programs (Zigler & Kagan, 1981). In addition, the CDA effort has served as a catalyst for further research to ascertain what constitutes quality care and to examine the role of staff training and other factors in the overall quality of care provided in a day care setting. In a national study, it was determined that day care settings employing staff trained on the basis of the CDA competencies are more likely to offer good quality care than those which do not include such staff training (Roupp, Travers, Glantz, & Coelen, 1979). Howes and Rubenstein's (1985) more recent study indicates that the quality of care children receive, whether at home, in family day care, or in a day care center, is dependent upon the caregiver's ability to attend to the children's individual needs and to provide them with meaningful social interactions.

It is evident, given our discussion thus far, that many decisions regarding the type and quality of child day care facilities can be made on the basis of knowledge from child development research. This can help clarify policy options (Zigler & Muenchow, 1983) and provide directions for the operation of programs (Provence, 1982). Beyond the need for a sound empirical base upon which we can make policy and programmatic decisions, research is also needed in order that we may ascertain the impact of attendance in day care on children's development. Reviews of the day care literature (Clarke-Stewart & Fein, 1983) point to the many gains that have been made in the research on day care. However, our understanding of the impact of day care attendance on child development is still somewhat limited because many studies focus on a single question: Is day care attendance potentially harmful to children? However, this research question may be too narrow in focus. For instance, in a study on day care children's responsiveness to adults, Robertson (1982) found that the type of care (home or day care), interacting with other factors, significantly influenced children's behavior in three ways: (a) it influenced the children's responsiveness to adults, with specific effect depending on socioeconomic status and sex; (b) it influenced the cooperativeness and obedience of boys in school, but not of girls; and (c) it affected the academic achievement ratings given middle-socioeconomic status subjects but not lower-socioeconomic status subjects. In a review of the research on infant day care, Gamble and Zigler (1986) also found that although studies have thus far given infant day care a clean bill of health, there are some indications that male infants who experience stresses in family life and who are also placed in day care are vulnerable to the negative influence of the day care experience. These and other recent reviews cannot yet offer conclusive evidence on the effect of day care on infants, but they point to the fact that the impact of day care on different children's development is likely to vary based on the type of care provided as well as the individual children and families involved. Therefore researchers now recognize that their task is not simply to find out whether or not day care is harmful to children, but what facets of the day care experience can mediate or enhance such effects and for which individual children.

Children of Divorce

Other basic research studies which have widespread social implications are those related to children of divorce. The divorce rate has stabilized somewhat in recent years. Still, close to half of all marriages end in divorce (Cherlin, 1981), and in 60% of these marriages children are involved (Select Committee on Children, Youth, and Families, 1983).

Some researchers regard divorce positively, noting that the high rate of divorce per se is not a matter of concern since it means that there are now fewer unhappy, destructive families which stay together for the sake of the children or for some other reason (Bane, 1976). Although divorce may be considered a positive solution to destructive family functioning, it is also a critical experience that can have negative consequences for the entire family, especially the children. This point is made on the basis of several reports which have been issued by two major research projects on the impact of divorce on children, one project headed by Mavis Hetherington and her colleagues, the other by Judith Wallerstein and Joan Kelly from the Marin County (California) Mental Health Center. Several other researchers have contributed to our knowledge of the impact of divorce on children; among them are Joseph Goldstein, Anna Freud, and Albert Solnit, whose work, described later in the chapter, is a vivid example of the synthesis of theoretical principles organized in such a way that they are applicable to specific practical situations.

To summarize the research findings to date, it appears that for children, the divorce of their parents is not a single event but rather a sequence of experiences, each one representing a transition and each requiring adjustments (Wallerstein, 1985; Wallerstein & Kelly, 1979). The transitions center around the shift from the family life prior to the divorce; the disequilibrium and disorganization immediately following the divorce; the experimentation with a variety of coping mechanisms, living arrangements, and relationships; and the eventual reorganization, and attainment of equilibrium. Households in which divorce has occurred are characterized by greatly increased disorganization and by marked changes in the management of children, including inconsistency of discipline, diminished communication and nurturance, and the holding of fewer expectations of mature behavior from the children (Hetherington, Cox, & Cox, 1978, 1981).

Almost all children are found to experience divorce and the transition periods that follow it as painful experiences (Guidubaldi, Cleminshaw, Perry, & Mcloughlin, 1983; Kurdek & Sieski, 1980). Even children who eventually recognize the divorce of their parents as constructive, initially undergo considerable stress with the breakup of the family. However, studies indicate that children

vary widely in their reaction and adjustment to divorce: Some are actively negative, whereas others are more subdued in their reaction, and some also change in
their school performance during the adjustment period following the divorce
(Jurdek & Siesky, 1979, 1980). The fact that so many children in this nation are
involved in divorce, and the fact that divorce has become socially acceptable,
have not been found to alleviate the pain; this was documented in a book by and
for the children of divorce (Rofes, 1980).

Parents also undergo emotional, psychological, and economic stresses following the divorce (Kurdek & Blisk, 1983). Researchers have found, for example,
that often the parents' distress is so acute that they neglect to attend to the
children, to recognize their children's painful experience with the divorce,
and/or to prepare the children for the marital breakup. This is especially so when
young children are involved (Kurdek & Siesky, 1979). Researchers further note
that the intensity and duration of the emotional and psychological distress a child
may suffer due to the divorce are related to the psychological status of the
custodial parent, and the availability and involvement of the noncustodial parent
(Guidubaldi, Cleminshaw, Perry, Nastasi, & Lightel, 1986; Hess & Camara,
1979).

Custody Issues.   The most vulnerable children of divorce are those who are
involved in legal battles between their divorcing parents on custody issues and
visitation rights. These legal battles can continue indefinitely because any decision on any of the issues is modifiable by the courts. The courts attempt to make
custody decisions on the basis of the "best interests of the child." However, in
practice, the explication of this principle is far from easy. Judges and lawyers
often are not able to determine what the best interests of the child may be, and
they have little help in this regard because few psychologists or other mental
health professionals look on the court as an arena of their interest. When the
courts have psychological services attached to them, they are often understaffed
or staffed by people who are not trained to work with children (Wallerstein &
Kelly, 1979). Goldstein, Freud, and Solnit (1973, 1979) have made some attempt to provide guidance for decisions on custody issues. On the basis of
principles of developmental psychology and psychiatry, the authors recommend,
for example, that decisions regarding child custody be resolved in accelerated
proceedings instead of long, drawn-out procedures; that they have final effect
and not be reversible; and that they award full custody of the children to the
"psychological parent." However, there is difficulty in applying some of these
ideas because the terms used (e.g., "psychological parent") are not sufficiently
explicit (Thompson, 1986). Additionally, there is controversy surrounding Goldstein et al.'s recommendations (e.g., Benedek & Benedek, 1977); many psychologists emphasize the value inherent in the child's maintaining a close relationship
with both parents (e.g., Guidubaldi et al., 1986), a point which contradicts the
suggestions made by Goldstein et al. Although the work of these authors is not

fully accepted in practice, their efforts are important, as they have paved the way for others to think about the use of knowledge and theoretical principles in establishing some criteria for such practical decisions as those involved in child custody cases.

Mediating the Negative Consequences of Divorce.   What we have described is admittedly only a brief summary of the research literature on the impact of divorce on children. Numerous other issues related to divorce have been studied, and there are several important research questions that remain to be investigated (see Hetherington & Camara, 1984). However, the brief review presented here should be sufficient for the reader to realize that the research on divorce has widespread implications. An understanding of how and when divorce affects children is important not only to research and clinical psychologists but also to others who come in contact with children and families. Teachers, for instance, need to be alerted to these findings so that they can be sensitive to any changes in children's behavior in school, and can offer children and parents appropriate advice and guidelines about possible ways they can cope with the changes going on in their lives (Kurdek, 1981; Kurdek & Siesky, 1979). Pediatricians should also be alerted to these findings, for the same reasons. Most significantly, lawyers and judges who have primary and extensive involvement in divorce cases should be made aware of the research and its implications. Ideally, psychological support for parents and children should be offered immediately when divorce proceedings are begun. An important development in divorce cases is the use of mediators rather than lawyers, and the settling of cases outside the confines of the courtroom insofar as possible (Bahr, 1981). The increasing use of mediators, who are often psychologists or social workers with access to legal advice, is admittedly due to the high legal costs of divorce. Families who have used divorce mediation, however, consider the psychological support associated with the method—for the parents as well as the children—to be one of its major benefits (Bahr, 1981).

Family Support Programs

The need for support is expressed not only by individuals who experience divorce, but by many others who encounter different types of stressful life events. Numerous families—for example, those who have premature babies (Friedman & Sigman, 1980; Goldberg & DiVitto, 1983) or handicapped ones (Field, Goldberg, Stern, & Sostek, 1980), or who have experienced the illness or death of family members—have difficulty coping with and adjusting to the circumstances in their lives, and are in need of some type of support. Likewise, there are many people who need assistance if they are to effectively discipline, but at the same time nurture, their children; or if they are to cope with transitional problems they encounter in helping their teenagers with problems, such as those involving drugs (York & York, 1983).

In response to the widespread need for such assistance, a host of family support programs has been developed and implemented in recent years. The programs range from informal, grass-roots, self-help services such as Parents Anonymous and Parents Without Partners (Whittaker & Garbarino, 1983), to more formal types of services which include professional assistance. Often these programs are referred to as a ''new breed'' of programs in that they are rooted in the premise that the most effective way to create and sustain benefits for children is to improve their family and community environment. However, Zigler and Freedman (1987a) point out that this premise is hardly new and can be traced to Project Head Start (discussed in detail in the next section). Project Head Start was initiated over two decades ago in an effort to enhance the lives of young children. It was and continues to be an innovative program which includes a cycle of experimentation and revision that helps ascertain which types of services are best suited for and have the most impact on which children. As a result of this cycle of experimentation and revision, and of recent research interest in the ecological approach to the study of children, the conventional wisdom about how to enhance children's growth and development has shifted from child-centered programs to programs which focus not only on the child but on the family as a whole (Bronfenbrenner & Weiss, 1983; Zigler & Berman, 1983).

Although the development of family support programs is conceptually traced to previously developed social programs, family support programs differ from other types in a number of ways. The most important of these is that many family support programs were not created through government initiative, as in the case of Project Head Start and many other social programs. Rather, they began as grass-roots efforts initiated and sustained by people in response to stressful situations in their lives, and in the absence of any other form of social support. In discussing the development of such programs, Zigler and Weiss (1985) note that these programs are diverse, differing in the types of service they render and the populations they serve; but that they share a commitment to provide emotional, informational, and instrumental assistance to family members, thus enabling them to cope with whatever problems they may have.

Primary Prevention.   In helping individuals in these ways, family support programs exemplify a primary prevention strategy which focuses on preventing mental health disorders from arising (Caplan, 1974). Numerous research studies designed to identify factors which place individuals at risk for mental health disorders reveal a clear and consistent relation between adaptive difficulties and heightened levels of stress (Bloom, 1979; Cowen, 1980). Several other studies have also helped establish that both personal and situational variables may mediate this relation, and may enable individuals who are vulnerable to life stresses to become better able to cope (Dohrenwend, 1978; Sandler, 1980). One such variable is social support. Social support has been found to improve an individual's ability to withstand stress (Cassel, 1976), to mediate the consequences of life crises (Gore, 1980), and to enhance general adjustment and well-being. Such social support systems, according to Caplan (1974), should not be conceived of as the propping up of someone who is in danger of falling. Rather, they refer to efforts to augment an individual's strengths in order to facilitate mastery of the environment. Caplan (1974) further points out that social support as a means of primary prevention in mental health does not denote a one-time intervention but rather an enduring pattern of continuous or intermittent ties that help maintain the psychological and physical integrity of the individual.

Families, like individuals, have a certain life course in which, at particular points, stresses and crises are the natural state of affairs. At those times, support programs can be invaluable in helping family members to utilize their strengths, and rally to cope with problems, thus warding off severe family dysfunction and mental health disorders (Riessman, 1986). Although family support programs have this primary prevention potential, the question of whether or not they prevent mental health disorders—and if so, to what extent— are as yet unanswered. The fact is, the growth and proliferation of such programs has not been matched by evaluations of their efficacy. Weiss (1985) and Zigler and Freedman (1987b) suggest that one reason for this may be that these programs were not recognized by researchers until recently and have been, in fact, one of the best-kept secrets of our nation (Whittaker & Garbarino, 1983).

The lack of evaluation data is a characteristic not only of family support programs but of other types of primary prevention programs as well. This point is made by Cowen (1986) in his review of a monograph (Price & Smith, 1985) on the evaluation of prevention programs. Cowen points out in this review that evaluation data are imperative, being needed to separate some of the many good and effective preventive programs now being tried from others that may be less effective and simply "maintained by inertia or falsely placed conviction." Addressing problems posed by the lack of evaluation data regarding family support programs, Zigler and Freedman (1987b) point out that although these programs are growing at a rapid rate, they are doing so without any clear indication as to which direction their course of growth should take. On an even more practical level, Cowen (1986) notes that the future of prevention programs in general and family support programs in particular depends on evaluations of their effectiveness, since the funding of programs is often based on a single issue: Are these programs beneficial?

The evaluation of family support and other prevention programs is not a simple task, however. In many cases, these programs have no explicitly stated goals, thus rendering evaluation a difficult process (Zigler & Freedman, 1987b). In other cases, the programs are still in the formative stage which, according to some (e.g., Campbell, 1987), also renders evaluation difficult. These and other problems associated with the evaluation of social programs are discussed in detail in the following section. Suffice it to add here that these problems are not insurmountable but instead represent new vistas for research, and challenges to developmental psychologists to contribute to, as well as learn from, the partnership between research and practice.

DESIGN AND EVALUATION OF SOCIAL PROGRAMS

The fact that developmental psychologists can contribute to as well as learn from the partnership between research and practice is especially evident in the use of social science research in the design and evaluation of social programs. Beginning in the 1960s, a wide range of such programs has been implemented, many having the general goal of improving children's lives. It is beyond the scope of this chapter to describe many of the programs that have been developed (for a historical perspective on the field of early intervention, see Salkind, 1983 and Zigler & Berman, 1983). However, we will focus in much of our discussion on one such program, Project Head Start, because its wide scope and commitment to experimentation have permitted an evolutionary approach to the task of designing effective interventions for children and families, and have allowed it to serve as a stable base from which to develop a number of early intervention service models and methods (for an annotated history of Head Start, see Zigler & Valentine, 1979).

Project Head Start began in the summer of 1965 as part of the "War on Poverty," which was a massive effort to eradicate social class inequities in the United States. One facet of this effort was preschool intervention, which, it was hoped, would provide young children with an innoculation against the ills resulting from poverty. Project Head Start was different from other intervention efforts of the early sixties in that its planners were careful to avoid using a deficit model based on the notion of "cultural deprivation" or "cultural disadvantage" (Zigler & Berman, 1983). The focus in the deficit model is to provide poor children with learning experiences supposedly lacking in their impoverished environments. In contrast, Project Head Start focused on a cultural relativistic approach which respected the children's many cultures. One way this was achieved was through parent participation (Valentine & Stark, 1979). This included parents' work in the daily activities of the program and their involvement in the planning and administration of Head Start centers in the community. Parent participation has by now become an important and often required aspect of programs for children. In the early years of Head Start, however, it was regarded as a significant break from past practices in which paid professionals dictated the operation of programs. Several incidental benefits of parent involvement have been realized (A Review of Head Start Research, 1982). One such benefit is suggested by a finding of the Coleman report (Coleman et al., 1966) that children's school performance improved when they felt more control over their lives. Children's locus of control was associated first with family background and second with variance in school performance. It was found that because parents' attitudes are likely to influence those of their children, parental participation in decision-making could promote both parents' and children's feelings of control and lead to increased effort, performance, and self-satisfaction on the part of the children.

Head Start has further differed from other early intervention efforts in that it has been a source of learning for developmental psychologists and for scientists from other disciplines, and is often regarded as a national laboratory for the design of effective programs for children and adults (Zigler & Seitz, 1982b). Continued experimentation in Head Start has led to a number of innovative approaches to early intervention, exemplified in the changes that have taken place in the program since its inception. These changes are reflected in many other early intervention programs and in our general understanding of these. Over the years there has been, for instance, disillusionment with early childhood as a critical period for intervention (e.g., Clarke & Clarke, 1976). By extending the provision of Head Start services to include earlier as well as later stages of development, which was made possible by Head Start's Home Start and Follow Through efforts (Rhine, 1981), we have come to appreciate the importance of continuous intervention from one stage of life to the next (Seitz, 1982). Another example is the Child and Family Resource Program (CFRP) which is a Head Start demonstration project that has contributed to the emergence of family support programs discussed earlier. The underlying concepts of the CFRP are that children need to be served at different developmental stages, and that effective early intervention rests not in a single program designed to aid children, or to remediate any one particular problem, but in a host of family support services (Comptroller General, 1979). Thus the CFRP serves families with children from the prenatal period through age eight by linking them to existing community services, depending on the families' particular needs. Other Head Start innovations which have made significant contributions to services and programs for children include the Head Start Handicapped Children's Effort, an attempt to deal sensitively with mainstreaming handicapped children even before they reach school age. Head Start has also been a source of innovation in its adoption of the Child Development Associate program as the basis upon which to train and assess child care workers. Finally, as will become apparent in the next section, a major contribution of Project Head Start can be seen in its focus on evaluation, which resulted in the use of social competence instead of IQ score changes as the criterion by which to evaluate the success of early intervention programs.

Evaluation of Head Start and Other Social Programs

Indeed, the evaluation of Head Start and other social programs has been an important element of such programs and has been used to justify their usefulness. For many years, the argument for the need for early intervention programs for certain populations, and the question of how effective these are, have been addressed in academic journals of developmental psychology and other disciplines and constituted primarily a scientific interest (Salkind, 1983) in the effects of programs on children's growth and development. Over the years, however, we have learned that this perspective alone is not sufficient: We should also include in any evaluation effort a policy perspective. That is, we should address the concerns of taxpayers and policymakers about the costs and benefits of such programs.

The recognition on the part of researchers of the need to address both the scientific and policy issues inherent in social program evaluation has greatly increased our understanding of the ways in which these programs affect children, and improved our ability to document these through a variety of evaluation methodologies. Several methods have thus emerged that have been applied to evaluation research, and some problems have been encountered in that area. These problems are important. They have resulted not only in the search for and application of more valid evaluation methodologies and more realistic expectations of what evaluation studies can and cannot tell us, but also in changes in theoretical issues related to children's development (Travers & Light, 1982).

Methods in Evaluation Research.   Given the different perspectives associated with the evaluation of social programs, a useful definition of evaluation, incorporating both the scientific and policy perspectives, is offered by Travers and Light (1982). They define evaluation as the systematic inquiry into the operations of a program, the services it delivers, the process by which those services are provided, the costs involved, the characteristics of the population served, and the outcome or the impact of the program on its participants.

There are two types of evaluation associated with social services. The first is called *process evaluation*. Process evaluation refers to the assessment of the actual implementation of a program or service. An example of this is the monitoring effort in Head Start programs to guarantee that each Head Start center delivers the services mandated by the program. The second type of evaluation is *outcome evaluation*. This involves the assessment of the verifiable impact of the program or service, and is important as a source of knowledge and direction. It provides us with information about which programs work and which do not. This is especially relevant to policymakers who are faced with the many unmet needs of America's children, and the limited public funds for helping them, and who must decide whether to continue existing programs or to allocate funds to new ones that hold the promise of achieving a specific end. Since outcome evaluation involves investigation of the consequences of programs that attempt to alter key variables in people's lives, it also has the potential of adding to our store of basic knowledge and may lead to discoveries about human behavior.

The classic design for outcome evaluation studies has been the experimental model. In this model, an experimental and a control group are chosen at random from the target population—one group that receives a program and another that does not. Measures are taken of the relevant criterion variable (for example, IQ score) both before the program starts and after it ends. Any differences between the two groups at the end of the program are used to determine the program's success or failure. The experimental model presents some restrictions in the evaluation of social programs since these programs are not always developed or implemented in such a way as to allow for sufficient control of all the variables (Abt, 1974). What is more, the exclusive use of this model may fail to yield important or useful information that cannot be derived from experimental studies: What are the needs of the participants? Has the program secured community acceptance? The need for answers to these and other questions has led to the use of a variety of quasi-experimental and nonexperimental designs in the evaluation of programs (Campbell & Erlebacher, 1970).

Besides the changes in the design of evaluation studies, the validity and utility of evaluation studies have also been improved through the use of different methods of analysis. One of these methods is known as *secondary analysis* (Cook, 1974), which is the reanalysis of data for purposes of answering the original research question with better statistical techniques, or of answering new questions with old data; *primary* analysis, on the other hand, is the original analysis of data in a research study. Another method is meta-analysis (Glass, McGraw, & Smith, 1981), which is the statistical analysis of the summary of findings of many empirical studies. An example is the study by the System Development Corporation (Coulson et al., 1972) of data collected by regional Head Start Evaluation and Research Centers between 1966 and 1968. The data used in the study came from nine quasi-experimental programs that were part of a systematic planned variation study originally designed to assess the effects of different approaches in Head Start programs on children of different characteristics. Both these methods of analysis provide an added dimension to evaluation research, thus enhancing the ability of researchers to document some of the strengths and weaknesses of social programs.

Other evaluation methodologies have been developed because of recognition of the need to address the concerns of taxpayers and policymakers about programs. Examples of such evaluation methodologies are cost-effectiveness analysis and cost–benefit analysis. Salkind (1983) discusses these two methodologies, noting the differences between them. Cost-effectiveness analysis is used when the outcomes or benefits of a program or policy cannot be measured in dollars. Karnes, Teska, Hodgins, and Badger (1970), for example, reported a positive change in parents' ratings of their children's school performance as a function of participation in an early childhood program. This change is considered a beneficial outcome since it indicates greater parent involvement in the child's education, and greater understanding of the child's school performance; but effectiveness in this case can be measured only in units other than dollars. Cost–benefit analysis looks at both the costs of the program and the benefits associated with the program in terms of dollars, usually expressed as the ''amount of money invested'' and the ''amount of money returned.''

In response to economic realities and the pressure to demonstrate to taxpayers and policymakers the return to society of public investments, social scientists have become involved in the development of cost–benefit analyses that have proved to be meaningful to both psychologists and legislators. One of these is the Economic Analysis of the Ypsilanti Perry Preschool Project (Weber, Foster, & Weikart, 1978). In the study, the benefits and costs for the experimental group were compared with those of the control group, using the human capital approach of economics. The economic benefits of the preschool program were quantified; then, by comparing the costs of the program with these economic benefits, the rate of return on the investment was calculated. The study was based on a small sample, and, the researchers note, the computations required making some broad assumptions about the applicability of census data to the studied cohorts. Nonetheless, the results showed that the benefits to society outweighed the costs of the program. The economic benefits to society were derived from: (a) less costly education (that is, fewer children of the experimental group repeated a grade and/or were placed in special education programs); (b) higher projected lifetime earnings for this group; and (c) time release from child-care responsibilities for the parents of the children in the experimental group.

Similar findings on other intervention programs were obtained by the Consortium for Longitudinal Studies (1981), which pooled the information from several of the older and more complete early childhood education studies and, using the Economic Analysis described above, demonstrated the cost-effectiveness of such programs in the long run. In another compilation of the program findings, longitudinal data, and cost measures of selected early intervention programs, Antley (1982) also demonstrated the cost-effectiveness of several early intervention programs.

In addition to having refined evaluation methodologies, psychologists have delineated what are now known to be essential elements in any effective evaluation study (see Guttentag & Struening, 1975; Struening & Guttentag, 1974). Since it is beyond the scope of this chapter to enumerate these elements, we will briefly highlight several of the major principles that have emerged over the past 20 years of evaluations of early intervention.

The first principle is that programs must be evaluated broadly rather than by laboratory measures only. As noted by Travers and Light (1982), the choice of measures and/or research designs should be based on an assessment of the full range of possibilities in light of the goals and circumstances of the particular program under evaluation. To this end, researchers are urged to give careful consideration to several types of information that may illuminate the working of programs. Examples of such information are the characteristics of the quality of life of the children in these programs; descriptions of their social environment, such as the adults they come in contact with, who have the greatest potential for enhancing or thwarting the children's development; and the relationships between program clients and staff. This type of information can not only yield important data on the actual operation of the program but can also enhance our understanding of the variations in effectiveness within and across programs. An interesting example is the evaluation of the High/Scope preschool programs (Schweinhart, Weikart, & Larner, 1986). In the course of revealing that program benefits may extend to such developmental aspects as the reduction in the rate of juvenile delinquency, it showed also that a particular model of preschool intervention (namely, the open framework model which encourages children to engage in self-initiated activities) is more successful than are other models which require children to respond to activities planned and initiated by the teacher.

Related to the above is a second principle which is that both process and outcome evaluation are necessary. As defined earlier, process evaluation is a check to determine whether services are actually delivered, and how this is done. Outcome evaluation is an assessment of the impact of programs. Neither type of evaluation by itself is sufficient. For example, despite the fact that Head Start centers vary enormously from one locale to another, researchers in early studies compared—on a national basis—graduates of Head Start with children who had not attended Head Start (Cicirelli, 1969). There was undoubtedly as much variation within the groups as there was between them but the studies failed to document this. Over the years, it has become common practice to monitor the activities that actually occur in intervention programs and to compare differences within programs (e.g., Huston-Stein, Friedrich-Cofer, & Susman, 1977), as the use of both process evaluation and outcome evaluation can yield valuable lessons about the intervention.

The third principle is that because the effects of early intervention are complex, oversimplification in their assessment must be avoided. As will become apparent in the following section, researchers—using what has since come to be regarded as a narrow interpretation of evaluation results—hastened to declare that early intervention programs such as Head Start were failures. However, we now know that program evaluation is not a simple matter. Indeed, researchers—in their quest to find out not only *if* a social program is a success or failure, but *why* it is a success or failure—are learning to specify particular populations, particular ages, and particular modes of service delivery systems, and what the particular intervention means in relation to such mediating factors, rather than expecting to find that the program is either a ''success'' or a ''failure.''

What We Have Learned from Program Evaluation.   Besides learning a great deal about how to design and interpret the results of evaluation studies, developmental psychologists have also been able to clarify and enhance their understanding of a number of developmental issues. In our discussion of some of what psychologists have learned in this regard, we will focus on the evaluation of Project Head Start, which in many ways became the test of whether early intervention efforts could be successful. The most noted of Head Start evaluations was the Westinghouse report (1969), which was the first large-scale study to examine the impact of Head Start on later school achievement. There were shortcomings to this evaluation. First, the evaluation criteria did not reflect the fundamental goals of Head Start; and second, as we have now come to appreciate, its reliance on the IQ as a measure of success presented problems.

The Westinghouse study involved the assessment of children enrolled in summer Head Start programs between 1965 and 1968. Much has been written about the study and its impact (e.g., Cicirelli, 1974; Datta, 1974, 1979). Briefly summarized, the findings of the study indicated that the IQ improvements associated with children's participation in Head Start programs tend to "fade out." Although the Westinghouse study had numerous methodological problems (see Campbell & Erlebacher, 1970; Smith & Bissell, 1970; White, 1970), many people were quick to declare, on the basis of this one study, that public spending for early intervention is a waste of resources. So strong was the negative feeling generated by the Westinghouse study in regard to early intervention programs, that evidence about Head Start's positive outcomes rarely came to light. For example, even though a later study (Kirschner, 1970) pointed to several important contributions of the Head Start program, these findings were not widely acknowledged at the time.

Since the Westinghouse report, there has accumulated an extensive amount of literature discussing and even refuting its findings (e.g., Campbell & Erlebacher, 1970; Ryan, 1974). The problems associated with the study, however, have led to our greater understanding of evaluation research in general and the refinement of the methodologies involved. We have come to appreciate, for example, that our ability to perform outcome evaluation depends on the degree to which the goals of the program are well presented and held constant throughout the life of the program (Zigler & Trickett, 1978). The programs included in the cost–benefit analyses mentioned earlier had stated, at the outset, the explicit educational goals to be attained by the children involved. However, in the case of Project Head Start, the goals originally presented were vague, and were later changed; and various of its most promising components were not highlighted.

The same problem arose with another social program, the nutritional program for Women, Infants and Children (WIC). Approximately $200 million a year is spent in this program for the provision of dairy products to pregnant women and young children. Numerous evaluations of this program have attested to its effectiveness and importance in reducing developmental disabilities among children (Hicks, Langham, & Takenaka, 1982; Kotelchuck, Schwartz, Anderka, & Finison, 1981, 1984). However, researchers and advocates of the WIC program have had a difficult time convincing policymakers of the effectiveness of the program as a result of the failure to enunciate at the outset what WIC's circumscribed and measurable goal might be; whether to improve the nutritional status of pregnant women and young children, thereby preventing the serious disorders associated with malnutrition, or whether to eliminate poverty (Solkoff, 1977).

Another problem that has emerged in relation to evaluation is the selection of outcome measures. The most often utilized outcome measure during the past 20 years of early childhood intervention programs has been the IQ score, or the magnitude of change in a child's IQ score. Using the IQ score as a measure in the evaluation of programs afforded the opportunity to avoid the rigors of goal-sensitive outcome evaluation by concluding that a program was a success if it resulted in higher IQs, and a failure if it did not (Zigler & Trickett, 1978). Various theoretical and methodological problems are associated with the use of the IQ score in this way (Cronbach, 1971; McClelland, 1973). Despite the reservations that have been voiced about the use of the IQ score as an outcome measure, it is still widely used in evaluation efforts. There are several reasons for the initial popularity of the IQ score and for its continued use. One is historic; early intervention efforts in many cases were initiated in order to examine the degree to which IQ scores can be influenced by life experiences (e.g., Garber & Heber, 1977; Gordon, 1973; Gray & Klaus, 1965; Karnes et al., 1970; Levenstein & Sunley, 1968; Skeels, 1966). Another reason for the popularity of the IQ score is that standard IQ tests are well-developed instruments. Their psychometric properties are well documented, a factor which allows a user to avoid difficult measurement problems. The IQ tests are also readily available and easy to administer, an advantage which is further enhanced if other tests are employed (e.g., the Peabody Picture Vocabulary Test, the Otis-Lennon Mental Ability Test), because high correlation is found between such 10-minute tests and the longer Stanford–Binet Intelligence Scale or the Weschler Intelligence Scale for Children.

Also, no other test has been found to be related to so many behaviors of theoretical and practical significance (Kohlberg & Zigler, 1967; Mischel, 1968). Because early childhood intervention programs are popularly regarded as efforts to prepare children for school, the fact that the IQ is the best available predictor of school performance is a compelling rationale for its use as an assessment criterion. Beyond the school issue, if compensatory education programs are directed at correcting deficiencies across a broad array of cognitive abilities, the best single measure of the success of such programs is improvement on the IQ test, which reflects a broad spectrum of such abilities. Finally, once it became obvious that the most common outcome of just about any intervention program was a 10-point increase in the IQ score, the IQ test became an instant success as a tool for demonstrating the effectiveness of early intervention. However, over the years developmental psychologists have acquired more insight into the cause of the IQ changes resulting from participation in early childhood intervention programs such as Head Start. Considerable empirical evidence has shown that these changes in IQ reflect motivational changes that influence test performance, rather than changes in the actual nature of formal cognitive functioning (Seitz, Abelson, Levine, & Zigler, 1975; Zigler, Abelson, & Seitz, 1973; Zigler, Abelson, Trickett, & Seitz, 1980. Zigler & Butterfield, 1968).

Given some of the advantages associated with the use of the IQ score as an outcome measure, it is useful at this point to reflect on what the IQ test actually measures, as well as on some of its limitations. As is elaborated in other contexts (see Zigler & Trickett, 1978), the IQ test should not be viewed solely as a measure of formal cognition, but rather as a measure of behavior that is influenced by three empirically related but conceptually distinct collections of variables. First, the IQ test measures formal cognitive processes such as abstracting ability, reasoning, and speed of visual information processing (see Chapter 6). Second, the IQ test is an achievement test that is highly influenced by the child's particular experiences. This is an important point because in some situations the child's experiences are a major disadvantage. For example, if we ask children what a "gown" is and they reply that they do not know, it is easy to assume that there is something inadequate about their memory storage and/or retrieval systems which are aspects of their formal cognitive systems. However, if the children have never in their experience encountered a gown, they will fail the item even though there may be nothing wrong with their memory. Also, as Laosa (1984) points out, disadvantaged children's poor performance on measures of abilities is often evident at a young age and may be attributed to a combination of influences associated with their low socioeconomic level and, in the case of Chicano children in particular, their language minority status.

Intelligence test performance is also influenced by a variety of motivational and/or personality variables that have little to do with either formal cognition or achievement variables. This point is made on the basis of studies with infants and preschool children. Lamb (1982a), for example, notes that there is a correlation between infant sociability and cognitive performance, although he acknowledges that no firm conclusions regarding the relationship can yet be made. Zigler, Abelson, and Seitz (1973) tested disadvantaged preschool children and found that children's familiarity with the examiner and with the testing situation significantly affected their performance on the test. Zigler and Trickett (1978) explain that among economically disadvantaged children there is a tendency to answer questions with the standard reply "I don't know." This reply is not necessarily reflective of a lack of ability, nor of a lack of knowledge, but may be indicative of the children's desire to terminate or minimize their interactions with the examiner. Why this is so is not exactly clear, but it could be because the children dislike the examiner, or because they dislike the testing situation, or both. Clearly, given the demands of our society, children who adopt the "I don't know" strategy are not likely to utilize their cognitive systems optimally; moreover, if they continue with this strategy, they are unlikely to obtain those rewards—such as high grades in school and desirable jobs after school—that society dispenses to those who behave in the manner it prefers.

Policy Implications.   It is this tripartite conception of IQ test performance that explains why performance on the test is a successful predictor of a wide variety of behaviors and thus, if conceptualized and used properly, may be useful in the evaluation of programs. However, along with some of the disadvantages we have highlighted that are associated with use of the IQ test, there is a controversy surrounding its use in the evaluation and prediction of children's performance (e.g., Jensen, 1979). Therefore, alternative assessment instruments have been considered and to some extent developed. An example of these is the "generative tests" developed to assess the value and impact of the High/Scope Cognitively Oriented Curriculum (Weikart, 1982). In generative tests, which were created in order to avoid some of the testing problems associated with the use of IQ tests with disadvantaged children, the children themselves provide both questions and answers, and have full control over the sophistication of their responses. Another example is the Learning Potential Assessment Device (Feuerstein, 1980), which is an approach to the assessment of the cognitive modifiability of children.

In addition, it has been proposed (Zigler, 1970, 1973) that social competence rather than IQ should be used as the major measure of the success of early intervention efforts. The relationship between IQ and social competence has been made explicit in other contexts (e.g., Zigler & Trickett, 1978) and is implied in our preceding discussion on what the IQ test measures. However, there are problems associated with the use of social competence measures. One of these is a definitional problem that stems from the lack of agreement among psychologists as to what social competence is (Anderson & Messick, 1974) and therefore what a social competence index should consist of. Some psychologists contend, however. that we have sufficient knowledge of human development to warrant at the very least an arbitrary definition of social competence. It is suggested (Zigler & Seitz, 1982a; Zigler & Trickett, 1978) that a social competence index should include the following: first, measures of physical health and well-being, including appropriate weight for age, innoculation history, and so on; second a measure of formal cognitive ability; third, achievement measures such as the Caldwell Preschool Inventory or the Peabody Individual Achievement Test and/or a variety of school-age achievement tests; and fourth, measurement of motivational and emotional variables which may include (a) effectance motivation, including indicators of preference for challenging tasks, curiosity, variation-seeking, and mastery motivation; (b) outer-directedness and degree of imitation in problem solving; (c) positive responsiveness to social reinforcement; (d) wariness of adults; (e) verbal attention-seeking behavior; (f) locus of control, measured for both parents and children; (g) expectancy of success; (h) aspects of self-image and measures of learned helplessness; and (i) attitude toward school.

Zigler and his colleagues (Zigler & Seitz, 1982a; Zigler & Trickett, 1978) emphasize not only the importance of developing and utilizing a social competence measure, but also the policy implications entailed in the use of such a measure in evaluating social programs. They note in particular that such a measure is needed as an alternative to the use of IQ tests in determining the effectiveness of programs aimed at a disadvantaged population.

THE LINK BETWEEN CHILD DEVELOPMENT
RESEARCH AND SOCIAL POLICY

Numerous other psychologists include in their research reports not only findings of studies, but also the policy implications of their work. In his studies on young Chicano children, Laosa (1984), for example, makes a link between research and policy as he underscores "the urgent need for an effective implementation of policies aimed at eliminating ethnic group inequalities in socioeconomic level" (p. 1196). His recommendation is made on the basis of research with Chicano and non-Hispanic white preschool children which has shown that even before they enter school, Chicano children are at a disadvantage on a number of characteristics such as verbal skills, which are required for successful adaptation to the school environment. (Laosa, 1982, 1984). It is Laosa's contention that a policy approach, if it is to be effective, must attempt to implement not only programs that serve to eliminate ethnic group inequalities, but also programs designed to overcome the disadvantages associated with language. He stresses, in fact, that "policies that accomplish one but not the other of these [policy] goals, no matter how effectively, will fail to completely eliminate the ethnic group's disparity in children's performance" (Laosa, 1984, p. 1196).

These recommendations for policies made on the basis of research findings exemplify researchers' increased involvement in the policy arena and their recognition of the reciprocity that exists between research and policy. DeLone (1982) emphasizes this reciprocity, noting that any policy designed to facilitate human development must be based on good theory and an understanding of what development is and how it occurs; and that it must be a theory that can be translated into action, which he defines as a set of resource allocations and decisions that will lead to the desired outcomes provided by the theory. It is his contention that, in relation to policy, a theory is no better than its application and vice versa. Acknowledging the axiom that social policy should be based on science, Bronfenbrenner (1974) proposes that, particularly in the field of developmental psychology, science also needs social policy not only as a guide for organizational activities but also to provide what he regards as the two essential elements in any scientific endeavor, *vitality* and *validity*.

ENCOURAGING THE USE OF RESEARCH
IN THE POLICY ARENA:
THE ROLE OF DEVELOPMENTAL PSYCHOLOGISTS

Understanding the Problems in the Use of Research in Policy

The reciprocity between research and policy is observed not only in relation to developmental psychology but also in relation to other branches of psychology (Task Force on Psychology and Public Policy, 1986) and other disciplines as

618

well (DeMartini & Whitbeck, 1986; Weiss & Gruber, 1984). However, researchers' increased involvement in the policy arena is not as yet widely accepted, and there are several problems that impede the utilization of research knowledge in policy. This point is underscored by Maccoby, Kahn, & Everett (1983) who note that:

> The relationship between researchers and policymakers is essentially an uneasy one. Policymakers sometimes see researchers as impractical, and may be skeptical about policy recommendations coming from researchers who seem not to understand the complexities of achieving a consensus among rival constituencies or administering programs once they have been legislated. Researchers, on the other hand, often see policymakers as disingenuous and too willing to compromise on matters where compromise does not seem justified on the basis of research evidence. (p. 80)

Meltsner (1986) also observes that although the use of social science research for policymaking is by now relatively well established, it is frequently distrusted. In part, the distrust stems from the general assumption that social knowledge is value-free whereas policies are made in a value-laden context. However, this is a misleading characterization of research and policy, as scientific research often takes on the values of the investigators. This is evident, for example, in the questions researchers ask, the methodologies they employ, and their interpretation and presentation of data.

Another problem in the utilization of social science research in policy settings is related to the face that social scientists are perceived as unable to provide clear answers to policy questions; or, looked at from another perspective, that policymakers are not asking questions in a way that would lead to valid and reliable research (Maccoby, Kahn, & Everett, 1983). This problem arises because of unrealistic expectations on the part of policymakers about the types of questions which social science can answer, and the number of studies that need to be conducted to arrive at appropriate answers. Those who expect single studies to have an impact on policy are likely to be disappointed, for the effects of such studies are usually small or nonexistent (Cohen & Garet, 1975; Cohen & Weiss, 1977; Rich & Caplan, 1976). Nevertheless, there are times when studies on a particular topic can illuminate a policy direction. For instance, the studies conducted by the Children's Defense Fund on foster care provided a clear policy option—the provision of financial subsidies to encourage the adoption of children in foster care—which was eventually enacted into law (the Child Welfare Act of 1980). Even in this case, however, researchers point out that once a policy is enacted and implemented, further research is needed to verify its impact (Maccoby et al., 1983) as unanticipated consequences may arise.

In many cases, the proliferation of research studies on a particular topic may result not in a more adequate or definitive answer to a policy question, but rather in additional confusion (Cohen & Garet, 1975; Cohen & Weiss, 1977); this is because the research can be both contradictory and complex and therefore may not provide a consensus from which to draw undisputed solutions. Even in such cases, however, the use of research studies can be advantageous in that it can lead to a clarification of differences and perspectives as well as improved research methodologies. For instance, after the primarily negative findings of the Westinghouse evaluation of Head Start were published in 1969, questions arose about underlying assumptions, subject selection biases, methodologies, and program goals. The results of this questioning included, as we have shown, improved methodological and statistical techniques in program evaluation, the use of a wider range of methodologies, and an interest in outcome variables other than school achievement in evaluation efforts.

Strategies for Change

Understanding some of these and other problems that often impede the use of research in policy is important if research is to be utilized and to have a major impact on policies. This point is made by Lindblom (1986) who has identified four general guidelines for researchers to follow in order to encourage more widespread use of research in policy: (a) that researchers be concerned in a nonpartisan way with the values and interests of the whole society rather than with one segment of it; (b) that they take a practical approach and suggest policies that are feasible and have a chance of winning political support; (c) that they become cognizant of and responsible to the policy process; and (d) that they respond to the needs of policymakers and provide them with recommendations for action on the basis of available research.

Others (e.g., the Task Force on Psychologists and Public Policy, 1986) make similar recommendations. It is also suggested that social scientists should participate in a broad-based lobby in behalf of children (Blom, Keith, & Tomber, 1984), and that they identify appropriate leverage points within government and work through these to develop and implement policies for children (Takanishi, DeLeon, & Pallak, 1983; Zigler & Finn, 1981). These suggestions are made in light of the fact that while federal efforts in behalf of children and their families are extensive and varied, it is difficult to identify any overarching and consistent goals for the support of children in America. Programs have been enacted piecemeal over an extended period of time, with little apparent attention to their collective impact or their interrelations. As Steiner notes (1976), "public involvement in [this] field is federal agency-by-federal agency, congressional committee-by-congressional committee" (p. vii). This state of affairs exists also in state and local-level policies and services for children and families. Additionally, the lack of coordinated effort is only one problem. Other problems include the inadequate allocation of funds for child and family services, and policies and programs that are contradictory to what we know about children from the research on child development (Hayes, 1982).

One such contradiction is exemplified in the foster care system. We know from many years of accumulated research that a child suffers in the absence of a sense of continuity and consistency in his or her environment. When children need out-of-home placements, therefore, it is important that their lives be stabilized and that a permanent and supportive home for them be found. Beneficial programs for children at risk within their own family situations would include preventive family support services. If children must be removed from their families, they should be placed in the least restrictive environments, preferably with relatives and near their families. Reviews of children in the foster care system should be made periodically, and, if the children are not returned to their families, termination of parental rights should be hastened and adoption of those children encouraged (Cranston, 1979). Despite these possible solutions and the fact that they are cost-effective (Zigler & Finn, 1982), many children remain adrift in the foster care system in this country where they are subject to being moved from one home to another for indefinite periods. Recent improvements in this regard have been made as the result of the enactment of the Child Welfare Act of 1980 which ensures modifications in the way foster children are treated (Edna McConnell Clarke Foundation, 1984). Still, there are numerous localities where this is not enforced.

Our ability to address those problems rests in the efforts of social scientists to inform not only policymakers but, even more important, the general public, regarding the needs of children (McCall, Gregory, & Murray, 1984; Zigler & Finn, 1981). No society acts until it has a sense of the *immediacy* of a particular problem. This has been illustrated in the founding of what was called, in the mid-sixties, the "Great Society." During that time, social issues were covered in major newspapers and were in the forefront of national attention. There were daily stories on welfare mothers, reports on poverty, and expositions on hunger in the United States. Hence there was sympathy for the poor and support for the "War on Poverty" and its associated programs. Today there is less interest in social issues, with the result that public recognition of the needs of children is limited.

There are indications, however, that developmental psychologists are becoming aware of the need for public education on issues related to children (McCall, Gregory, & Murray, 1984). For many years it has been our pattern as researchers to function in isolation and to discuss human problems, as well as possible solutions for them, with each other either at professional conferences or by means of professional journals. Most researchers' assumptions about the audience they reach and influence were probably fairly modest. That is, they hoped their colleagues would notice their work, appreciate the implications, and carry the ideas one step further. Now this approach is changing. Researchers in the field of developmental psychology are acknowledging the need to disseminate their knowledge in the context of the popular media, not only by presenting research findings to policymakers but also indirectly, through addressing more general changes in viewpoint regarding a topic or an issue (Stevenson & Siegel, 1984). An example of this type of activity by researchers is the creation of a committee chaired by Robert McCall on the role of research and the media within the Society for Research in Child Development. In an article, McCall and his colleagues (McCall, Gregory, & Murray, 1984) summarize some of the procedures in the knowledge dissemination process, and illuminate the sorts of skills researchers need in order to communicate research findings to the public or other interested parties. Carol Weiss (1985) also documents the recognition among social scientists of the need to disseminate research findings in the popular media, noting that scientists seem to be generally satisfied with the way journalists represent their research findings.

Finally, in delineating the role of applied researchers in the area of social science and social policy, Ballard, Brosz, and Parker (1981) note that there are several requirements for the successful application of knowledge to social problems. Among these are the need for early and continued collaboration between researchers and policymakers in order to establish and maintain trust, and the need for scientific credibility on the part of the researchers. This latter requirement cannot be overemphasized. Whereas applied researchers must pay attention to approaches toward the utilization of their research, they must also maintain credibility in the scientific community. Academic credibility facilitates the application of social science knowledge—including theories, methods, and data bases—to social problems. In an effort to ensure the use of our research in practical ways that can help children and families, we must always ensure that we maintain a disciplinary and professional identity as scientists.

INTEGRATION OF CHILD DEVELOPMENT RESEARCH AND SOCIAL POLICY: BEYOND THE PUBLIC SECTOR

Thus far in the chapter we have illustrated the link between child development research and social policy largely as it is relevant to policies made at the federal government level. During the past two decades, the federal government was responsible for most of the initiatives related to programs for children and families. There are trends, however, which indicate that the role of the federal government will diminish in the coming years, not only in terms of the amount of money to be allocated for social services but also in terms of providing the direction those services will take (Hayes, 1982). These trends include the deficits in the national budget, the political temper of the times to allocate increasingly smaller amounts of money for social services, and public support in favor of less government intervention.

Although these developments are associated with a certain amount of optimism regarding the potential for increased activity at the state and local levels (Finn, 1981), the reality of dwindling government funds in general means that we must look beyond the public sector for the support of needy children and families. There are possibilities that developmental psychologists can look to in the private sector's support of family life. In this respect researchers can form an alliance with executives in industry who have the ability to institute changes that will have positive effects on children and families.

Work and Family Life

One way in which the private sector can exert its influence to benefit children and families is in the area of work and family life. With the two-paycheck family now the norm rather than the exception, and with the increase in single-parent households, the impact of the workplace on family life becomes a relevant issue. The relation between the two institutions has been the subject of several recent studies which emphasize an important point: Work and family life are not separate worlds as had been assumed, but are, rather, interdependent and overlapping, with functions and behavioral rules in each system influencing processes in the other (Fernandez, 1986; Kanter, 1977; Pleck & Staines, 1985; Staines & Pleck, 1983). This interplay between the worlds of work and family life, and its effect on children, are very much within the realm of concern of developmental psychologists.

To the extent that there are children present, life for the dual-career family is stressful. Day care arrangements must be made for the infant and preschool child; before- and after-school facilities have to be found for the older child; school vacations and days when a child is sick bring with them the need for yet other solutions. Since worker satisfaction and productivity have been found to be a function of family stability and of other processes within the family system (Kanter, 1977), it behooves industry to create policies that can help families. Such policies may include help with day care arrangements or provisions regarding flexible work schedules. Staines and Pleck (1986), for example, found that flexibility in work schedules acts as "a buffer against" the stresses associated with work and family life.

However, the role of industry in supporting employers in this regard has been slow to develop, although several corporations have made attempts to accommodate the needs of families (BNA Special Report, 1986; United Nations Association, 1986). Among these attempts have been changes in the work structure to allow flexible working arrangements (Kuhne & Blair, 1978), part-time work opportunities (Schwartz, 1974), and job-sharing (Olmsted, 1979). Companies are required by law to offer maternity leaves (Bureau of Business Practice, 1979). At best, these maternity leaves are for three months, although schoolteachers, for example, are able to take up to a year's leave of absence without pay in order to stay with their newborn infants. As a nation, however, we lag far behind other countries in the development of pronatal policies (Zigler & Muenchow, 1983). According to Kamerman and Kahn (1976), European nations, in order to facilitate childrearing, make provisions for six to twelve months of maternity *or* paternity leave *with* pay, and facilities for child care are available in cases where both parents choose to work. Research questions that need to be addressed regarding these changes in work schedules and employee benefits include the impact of the changes not only on productivity but on children and families. Do parents who take advantage of flexible working arrangements actually spend more time with their children? Do these working arrangements facilitate the reduction of stress in parents? If they had the option for maternity and paternity leaves, would parents use them?

For the past several years, corporations' responsibilities for the provision of day care services to their employees has been discussed. Several major corporations in the United States have instituted a variety of child day care programs. Stride Rite Corporation in Boston is one of several corporations that has a company-based day care center as one of its employee benefits packages. Employees pay for day care at the rate of 10% of their salary to a maximum of $25 a week (McIntyre, 1978). Several other companies have followed suit, although some have found that providing day care benefits or subsidizing on-site centers is too expensive. In these cases, several businesses—for example, a hospital, a telephone company, and a factory—could together support a day care program at a location central to where their employees work. This would prove convenient to the employees, as well as inexpensive, since several businesses would be contributing to the cost of each center and part of the costs may be paid by the employees themselves. Some initiatives in this regard have been taken in a project known as the Day Care Partnership Initiatives (*Child Care Action News,* 1986). Developed in 1985, this project involves the creation of 14 employer-sponsored child-care programs in Massachusetts made possible through partnerships with businesses, schools, public housing authorities, and local governments.

Several other suggestions on the role of industry in facilitating family life are elaborated on in other contexts (Zigler & Finn, 1982, 1981). These include helping promote interdependence among families within neighborhoods, as well as the provision of referral centers or networks of family support systems which, in view of the information presented in our earlier discussion on the status of family life, are important resources for the support of the family. However, unless executives in the private sector are alerted to the needs of families in their employ, as well as to some ways in which these needs can be met, it is unlikely that much progress will be made in this regard. The role of developmental psychologists in this area should include, therefore, not only research on aspects of work and family life but also dissemination of the findings to individuals in the private sector who have the power to change policy.

SUMMARY AND CONCLUSION

In our discussion of applied developmental psychology we have described the reciprocity that exists between applied and basic research, and we have highlighted the opportunities for new learning that are offered by applied settings as well as the contributions that developmental psychologists can make in the arena of policy. Our discussion has centered on the possibilities for research into children's development in view of the economic and demographic changes our society is experiencing, as well as on research related to the design and evaluation of social programs.

It is clear from this discussion not only that developmental psychologists have opportunities to learn from research in social settings and thereby to contribute to the improvement of human life, but also that, if they are to be effective, applied developmental psychologists cannot work entirely within their own discipline. This is true of both the acquisition and the implementation of knowledge wherein the principles taken from basic research and the collaboration with policymakers can significantly influence applied developmental psychology, and the potential inherent in the field to help meet the needs of children.

It is also evident from our discussion that there are tensions and uncertainties in the emerging efforts to integrate child development research and social policy. While these are not insurmountable (Masters, 1983), they nonetheless influence decisions by researchers to address policy issues in their work or to consider the social relevance of their research (Thompson, 1986). Fortunately, there is considerable encouragement and support today for developmental psychologists to engage in research that has social utility and to focus on the practical implications of their studies. This trend is evidenced, for example, by the growing number of child development and social policy centers in several universities (Masters, 1983), as well as in the inclusion of policy courses in numerous graduate and undergraduate programs in developmental psychology (Thompson, 1985; Zigler & Finn-Stevenson, 1987). The purpose in both these cases is to provide comprehensive training for developmental psychologists and other professionals in issues related to policy. The effort to train researchers at the intersection of child development research and social policy is, as yet, relatively new and subject to considerable variance among programs. But it should give impetus to more widespread efforts among researchers to resolve the needs of children and families by participating in the policy process. As to the direction such efforts would take, our suggestions include, first, the collaboration of developmental psychologists with public and private sector policymakers in the development of programs and policies based on principles taken from child development research; and, second, recognizing that our role as psychologists includes not only generating new knowledge through research but also sharing it with the general public. Through such activities we can anticipate, over time, an enhancement of our understanding of human development and an increased awareness of our obligation to be responsive to the developmental needs of children and families.

REFERENCES

Abt, C. C. (1974). Social programs evaluation: Research allocation strategies for maximizing policy payoffs. In C. C. Abt (Ed.), *The evaluation of social programs*. Beverly Hills, CA: Sage Publications.

Anderson, S., & Messick, S. (1974). Social competency in young children. *Developmental Psychology. 10*, 282–293.

Antley, T. R. (1982). *A case for early intervention: Summary of program findings, longitudinal data, and cost-effectiveness.* Seattle, WA: Model Preschool Center Outreach Program, Experimental Education Unit.

Bahr, S. J. (Winter 1981). Divorce mediation: An evaluation of an alternative divorce policy. *The Networker, 2*(2), 1. (Available from the Bush Center in Child Development and Social Policy, Yale University, New Haven, CT.).

Ballard, S. C., Brosz, A. R., & Parker, L. B. (1981). Social science and social policy: Roles of the applied researcher. In J. Grum & S. Wasby (Eds.), *The analysis of policy impact.* Lexington, MA: Lexington Books, D. C. Heath & Co.

Bane, M. J. (1976). Marital disruption and the lives of children. *Journal of Social Issues, 32*, 103–117.

Benedek, R. S., & Benedek, E. P. (1977). Post-divorce visitation: A child's right. *Journal of the American Academy of Child Psychiatry, 16*, 256–271.

Blom, G. E., Keith, J. G., & Tomber, I. (1984). Child and family advocacy: Addressing the rights and responsibilities of child, family, and society. In R. P. Boger, G. E. Blom, & L. E. Lezotte (Eds.), *Child nurturance: Vol. 4. Child nurturing in the 1980s.* New York: Plenum.

Bloom, B. L. (1979). Prevention of mental disorders: Recent advances in theory and practice. *Community Mental Health Journal, 15*, 179–191.

BNA (Bureau of National Affairs). (1986). *Special report. Work and family: A changing dynamic.* Rockville, MD: author.

Brim, O. G., & Dustan, J. (1983). Translating research into policy for children: The private foundation experience. *American Psychologist, 38*, 85–90.

Bronfenbrenner, U. (1974). Developmental research, public policy, and the ecology of childhood. *Child Development, 45*, 1–5.

Bronfenbrenner, U. (1979). *The ecology of human development.* Cambridge, MA: Harvard University Press.

Bronfenbrenner, U., & Weiss, H. (1983). Beyond policies without people: An ecological perspective on child and family policy. In E. Zigler, S. L. Kagan, & E. Klugman (Eds.), *Children, families, and government: Perspectives on American policy.* Cambridge, MA: Harvard University Press.

Bryant, G. (1972). Evaluation of basic research in the context of mission orientation. *American Psychologist, 27*, 947–950.

Bureau of Business Practice. (1979). *Fair Employment Practice Guidelines, 1979, 170*(9).

Campbell, D. T. (1987). An experimenting society in the interface between evaluation and service provider. In S. Kagan, D. Powell, B. Weissbourd, & E. Zigler (Eds.), *Family support programs: The state of the art.* New Haven, CT: Yale University Press.

Campbell, D. T., & Erlebacher, A. (1970). How regression artifacts in quasi-experimental evaluations can mistakenly make compensatory education look harmful. In J. Hellmuth (Ed.), *The disadvantaged child: Vol. 3. Compensatory education: A national debate.* New York: Brunner/Mazel.

Caplan, G. (1974). *Support systems and community mental health.* New York: Behavioral Publications.

Caplan, N. S. (1975). The use of social science information by federal executives. In G. Lyon (Ed.), *Social research and public policies.* Hanover, NH: Dartmouth College.

Cassel, J. (1976). The contributions of the social environment to host resistance. *American Journal of Epidemiology, 104*, 107–123.

Cherlin, A. J. (1981). *Marriage, divorce, remarriage.* Cambridge, MA: Harvard University Press.

Child Care Action News. (1986). Day care partnership. *Child Care Action News, 3*(5), 2.

Cicirelli, V. G. (1969). *The impact of Head Start: An evaluation of the effects of Head Start on children's cognitive and affective development.* Washington, DC: National Bureau of Standards, Institute for Applied Technology.

Cicirelli, V. G. (1974). Westinghouse summary—The impact of Head Start. In C. C. Abt (Ed.), *The evaluation of social programs.* Beverly Hills, CA: Sage Publications.

Clarke, A. M., & Clarke, A. O. B. (1976). *Early experience: Myth and evidence.* London: Open Books.

Clarke-Stewart, K. A., & Fein, G. G. (1983). Early childhood programs. In P. H. Mussen (Ed.), *Handbook of child psychology* (4th ed.); Vol. 2: M. M. Haith & J. J. Campos (Eds.), *Infancy and developmental psychobiology.* New York: Wiley.

Cohen, D. K., & Garet, M. A. (1975). Reforming education policy with applied social research. *Harvard Educational Review, 45,* 17–43.

Cohen, D. K., & Weiss, J. A. (1977). Social science and social policy: Schools and race. In C. H. Weiss (Ed.), *Using social research in public policy making.* Lexington, MA: Lexington Books.

Coleman, J. S., Campbell, E., Hobson, C., McPartland, J., Mood, A., Weinfeld, F., & York, R. (1966). *Equality of educational opportunity.* Washington, DC: U.S. Government Printing Office.

Comptroller General of the United States. (1979). *Report to the Congress: Early childhood and family development programs improve the quality of life for low income families.* (Document No. [HRD] 79-40). Washington, DC: U. S. Government Printing Office.

Consortium for Longitudinal Studies. (1981). Lasting effects of early education. *Monographs of the Society for Research in Child Development.*

Cook, T. D. (1974). The potential and limitations of secondary evaluations. In M. A. Apple et al. (Eds.). *Educational evaluation: Analysis and responsibility.* Berkeley, CA: McCutchan.

Coulson, J. M. et al. (1972). *Effects of different Head Start program approaches on children of different characteristics: A report on analyses of data from 1966–67 and 1967–68 national evaluations.* Technical Memorandum TM-4862-001/00 (EDO-70859). Santa Monica, CA: Systems Development Corporations.

Cowen. E. L. (1980). The wooing of primary prevention. *American Journal of Community Psychology, 5,* 258–284.

Cowen, E. L. (1986). Expanding horizons in prevention research. *Contemporary Psychology, 31,* 260–261.

Cranston, A. (1979). (Testimony). *Proposals related to social and child welfare services, adoption assistance and foster care.* Senate Committee on Finance, Subcommittee on Public Assistance. Ninety-sixth Congress.

Cronbach, L. I. (1971). Five decades of public controversy over mental testing. *American Psychologist, 30,* 1–14.

Datta, L. (1974). The impact of the Westinghouse/Ohio evaluation of Project Head Start: An examination of the immediate and longer term effects and how they came about. In C. C. Abt (Ed.), *The evaluation of social programs.* Beverly Hills, CA: Sage.

Datta, L. (1979). Another spring and other hopes: Some findings from national evaluations of Project Head Start. In E. Zigler & J. Valentine (Eds.), *Project Head Start: A legacy of the war on poverty.* New York: Free Press.

DeLone, R. H. (1982). Early childhood development as a policy goal: An overview of choices. In L. Bond & J. Joffe (Eds.), *Facilitating infant and early childhood development.* Hanover, NH: University Press of New England.

DeMartini, J. R., & Whitbeck, L. B. (1986). Knowledge use as knowledge creation. *Knowledge: Creation, Diffusion, Utilization, 7,* 383–396.

Dillon, R. F., & Sternberg, R. J. (1986). *Cognition and instruction.* New York: Academic Press.

Dohrenwend, B. S. (1978). Social stress and community psychology. *American Journal of Community Psychology, 6,* 1–14.

Eccles, J. A., & Hoffman, L. W. (1984). Sex roles, socialization, and occupational behavoir. In H. W. Stevenson & A. E. Siegel (Eds.), *Child development research and social policy.* Chicago: University of Chicago Press.

Edna McConnell Clarke Foundation. (1985). *Keeping families together: The case for family preservation.* New York: Edna McConnell Clarke Foundation.

Fernandez, J. (1986). *Child care and corporate productivity.* Lexington, MA: D.C. Heath.

Feuerstein, R. (1980). *Instrumental enrichment: An intervention program for cognitive and modifiability.* Baltimore, MD: University Park Press.

Field, T. M., Goldberg, S., Stern, S., & Sostek, A. M. (Eds). (1980). *High-risk infants and children: Adult and peer interaction.* New York: Academic Press.

Finn, M. (1981). Surviving the budget cuts: A public policy report. *Young Children, 37,* 1.

Friedman, S. L., & Sigman, M. (Eds.). (1980). *Preterm birth and psychological development.* New York: Academic Press.

Gamble, T. J., & Zigler. E. (1986). Effects of infant day care: Another look at the evidence. *American Journal of Orthopsychiatry, 56,* 26–42.

Garbarino, J. (1981, February). Latchkey children: How much of a problem? *Education Digest,* 14–16.

Garber, H., & Heber, R. (1977). The Milwaukee Project. In P. Mittler (Ed.), *Research to practice in mental retardation.* Baltimore, MD: University Park Press.

Garner, R. (1972). The acquisition and application of knowledge: A symbiotic relation. *American Psychologist, 27,* 941–946.

Ginter, M. A. (1981). *An exploratory study of the "latchkey child": Children who care for themselves.* Unpublished manuscript, Yale University, New Haven, CT.

Glass, G. V., McGraw, B., & Smith, M. (1981). *Meta-analysis in social research.* Beverly Hills, CA: Sage Publications.

Goldberg, S., & DiVitto, B. A. (1983). *Born too soon: Pre-term birth and early development.* New York: W. H. Freeman.

Goldstein, J., Freud, A., & Solnit, A. (1973). *Beyond the best interests of the child.* New York: Free Press.

Goldstein, J., Freud, A., & Solnit, A. (1979). *Before the best interests of the child.* New York: Free Press.

Gordon, I. J. (1973). *An early intervention project: A longitudinal look.* Gainesville, FL: University of Florida, Institute for Development of Human Resources.

Gore, S. (1980). Stress-buffering functions of social supports: An appraisal and clarification of research models. In B. S. Dohrenwend & B. P. Dohrenwend (Eds.), *Stressful life events: Their nature and effects.* New York: Wiley.

Gray, S. W., & Klaus, R. A. (1965). An experimental preschool program for culturally deprived children. *Child Development, 36,* 887–898.

Guidubaldi, J., & Cleminshaw, H. (1983). Divorce, family health, and child adjustment. *Family Relations, 34,* 35–41.

Guidubaldi, J., Cleminshaw, H. K., Perry, J. D., & Mcloughlin, C. S. (1983). The effects of divorce on child development. *School Psychology Review, 12,* 300–323.

Guidubaldi, J., Cleminshaw, H. D., Perry, J. D., Nastasi, B. K., & Lightel, J. (1986). The role of selected family environment factors in children's post-divorce adjustment. *Family Relations, 35,* 141–151.

Guttentag, M., & Struening, E. L. (1975). *Handbook of evaluation research* (Vol. 2). Beverly Hills, CA: Sage Publications.

Harlow, H. F. (1963). The maternal affectional system. In B. M. Foss (Ed.), *Determinants of infant behavior* (Vol. 3). New York: Wiley.

Hayes, C. D. (1982). *Making policies for children: A study of the federal process.* Washington, DC: National Academy Press.

Hayghe, H. (1984, December). Working mothers reach record numbers in 1984. *Monthly Labor Review,* 31–34.

Hess, R. D., & Camara, K. A. (1979). Post-divorce relationships as mediating factors in the consequences of divorce for children. *Journal of Social Issues, 35,* 79–96.

Hetherington, E. M., & Camara, K. A. (1984). Families in transition: The processes of dissolution and reconstitution. In R. D. Parke (Ed.), *Review of child development research: Vol. 7. The family.* Chicago: University of Chicago Press.

Hetherington, E. M., Cox, M., & Cox, R. (1978). The aftermath of divorce. In J. Stevens & M. Mathews (Eds.), *Mother–child/father–child relationships.* Washington, DC: National Association for the Education of Young Children.

Hetherington, E. M., Cox, M., & Cox, R. (1981). *Divorce and remarriage.* Paper presented at the meeting of the Society for Research in Child Development, Boston.

Hicks, L. E., Langham, R. A., & Takenaka, J. (1982). Cognitive and health measures following early nutritional supplementation: A sibling study. *American Journal of Public Health, 72*(10), 1110–1118.

Howes, C., & Rubenstein, J. L. (1985). Determinants of toddlers' experience in day care: Age of entry and quality of setting. *Child Care Quarterly, 14,* 140–151.

Huston-Stein, A., Friedrich-Cofer, & Susman, E. J. (1977). The relation of classroom structure to social behavior, imaginative play and self-regulation of economically disadvantaged children. *Child Development, 48,* 908–916.

Jensen, A. R. (1979). *Educational differences.* London: Methuen.

Joint Economic Committee. (May 10, 1986). Press release: Obey releases report on working mothers. Washington, DC: U.S. Congress.

Jones, E., & Prescott, E. A. (May, 1982). Day care: Short- or long-term solution? *Annals/AAPSS,* 461.

Kamerman, S. B., & Kahn, A. J. (1976). *European family policy currents: The question of families with very young children.* Unpublished manuscript, Columbia University School of Social Work.

Kamerman, S., & Kahn, A. (1979). The day care debate: A wider view. *Public Interest, 54,* 76–93.

Kanter, R. M. (1977). *Work and family in the United States: A critical review and agenda for research and policy.* New York: Russell Sage Foundation.

Karnes, M. B., Teska, J. A., Hodgins, A., & Badger, E. (1970). Educational intervention at home for mothers of disadvantaged infants. *Child Development, 41,* 925–935.

Keyserling, M. D. (1972). *Windows on day care.* New York: National Council of Jewish Women.

Kirschner Associates, Albuquerque, New Mexico. (May, 1970). *A national survey of the impacts of Head Start centers on community institutions.* (EDO45195). Washington, DC: Office of Economic Opportunity.

Klein, R. P. (1985). Caregiving arrangements by employed women with children under 1 year of age. *Developmental Psychology, 21,* 403–406.

Kohlberg, L., & Zigler, E. (1967). The impact of cognitive maturity on the development of sex-role attitudes in the years four to eight. *Genetic Psychology Monographs, 75,* 89–165.

Korchin, S. (1981, February 16). Quoted in *Newsweek,* p. 97.

Kotelchuck, M., Schwartz, J. B., Anderka, N. T. & Finison, K. F. (1981). *Final Report: 1980 Massachusetts Special Supplemental Food Program for Women, Infants and Children Evaluation Project.* Submitted to Food and Nutrition Service, USDA. Washington, DC.

Kotelchuck, M., Schwartz, J. B., Anderka, N. T. & Finison, K. F. (October, 1984). WIC participation and pregnancy outcomes: Massachusetts Statewide Evaluation Project. *American Journal of Public Health, 74,* 1084–1092.

Kuhne, R., & Blair, C. (April, 1978). Changing the workweek. *Business Horizons, 21*(2).

Kurdek, L. A. (1981). An integrative perspective on children's divorce adjustment. *American Psychologist, 36,* 856–866.

Kurdek, L. A., & Blisk, D. (1983). Dimensions and correlates of mother's divorce experiences. *Journal of Divorce, 6,* 1–24.

Kurdek, L. A., & Siesky, A. E., Jr. (1979). An interview study of parents' perceptions of their children's reactions and adjustments to divorce. *Journal of Divorce, 3,* 5–17.

Kurdek, L. A., & Siesky, A. E., Jr. (1980). Effects of divorce on children: The relationship between parent and child perspectives. *Journal of Divorce, 4,* 85–99.

Lamb, M. E. (1981). The development of father-infant relationships. In M. E. Lamb (Ed.). *The role of the father in child development* (2nd ed.). New York: Wiley.

Lamb, M. E. (1982a). Individual differences in infant sociability: Their origins and implications for cognitive development. In H. W. Reese & L. P. Lipsitt (Eds.), *Advances in child development and behavior* (Vol. 16) (pp. 213–239). New York: Academic Press.

Lamb, M. E. (Ed.). (1982b). *Nontraditional families: Parenting and childrearing.* Hillsdale, NJ: Lawrence Erlbaum Associates.

Lamb, M. E. (Ed.). (1986). *The father's role: Applied perspectives.* New York: Wiley.

Laosa, L. M. (1982). School, occupation, culture, and family: The impact of parental schooling on the parent-child relationship. *Journal of Educational Psychology, 74,* 791–827.

Laosa, L. M. (1984). Ethnic, socioeconomic, and home language influences upon early performance on measures of ability. *Journal of Educational Psychology, 76,* 1178–1198.

Leishman, K. (1980). When kids are home alone: How mothers make sure they're safe. *Working Mother, 3,* 21–25.

Levenstein, P., & Sunley, R. (1968). Stimulation of verbal interaction between disadvantaged mothers and children. *American Journal of Orthopsychiatry, 38,* 116–121.

Levitin, T. E. (1979). Children of divorce: An introduction. *Journal of Social Issues, 35,* 1–5.

Lindblom, C. E. (1986). Who needs what social research for policymaking? *Knowledge: Creation, Diffusion, Utilization, 7,* 345–366.

Long, L., & Long, T. (1983). *The handbook for latchkey children and their parents.* New York: Arbor House.

Maccoby, E. E., Kahn, A. J., & Everett, B. A. (1983). The role of psychological research in the formation of policies affecting children. *American Psychologist, 38,* 80–84.

Masters, J. C. (1983). Models for training and research in child development and social policy. In G. Whitehurst (Ed.), *Annals of Child Development* (Vol. 1). Greenwich, CT: JAI Press.

McCall, R. B., Gregory, T. G., & Murray, J. P. (1984). Communicating developmental research results to the general public through television. *Developmental Psychology, 20,* 45–54.

McCartney, K. (1984). Effect of quality of day care environment on children's language development. *Developmental Psychology, 20,* 244–260.

McCartney, K., Scarr, S., Phillips, D., Grajek, S. and Schwartz, J. C. (1982). Environmental differences among day care centers and their effects on children's development. In E. Zigler & E. Gordon (Eds.), *Day care: Scientific and social policy issues.* Boston: Auburn House.

McClelland, D. C. (1973). Testing for competence rather than for intelligence. *American Psychologist, 28,* 1–14.

McIntyre, K. J. (1978, December 11). Day care: An employer benefit, too. *Business Insurance,* 11–36.

Meltsner, A. J. (1986). The seven deadly sins of policy analysis. *Knowledge: Creation, Diffusion, Utilization, 7,* 367–382.

Mischel, W. (1968). *Personality and assessment.* New York: Wiley.

Norton, A. (1979). Portrait of the one-parent family. *The National Elementary Principal, 59,* 32–35.

Olmsted, B. (1979, May-June). Job sharing: An emerging work-style. *International Labour Review, 118*(3).

Packard, V. (1972). *A nation of strangers.* New York: Simon & Schuster.

Parke, R., & Peterson, J. L. (1981). Indicators of social change: Developments in the United States. *Accounting Organization and Society, 6,* 323–329.

Pleck, J., & Staines, G. L. (1985). Work schedules and family life in two-earner couples. *Journal of Family Issues, 6,* 61–82.

Price, R. H., & Smith, S. (1985). *A guide to evaluating prevention programs in mental health.* Rockville, MD: National Institute of Mental Health.

Provence, S. (1982). Infant day care: The relationship between theory and practice. In E. Zigler & E. Gordon (Eds.), *Day care: Scientific and social policy issues.* Boston: Auburn House.

A Review of Head Start Research Since 1970. (1982). Prepared by C.S.R. Inc. for the Administration for Children, Youth and Families, Department of Health and Human Services, Contract #185-81-C-026. Draft Copy.

Riessman, F. (1986). Support groups as preventive intervention. In M. Kessler & S. E. Goldston (Eds.), *A decade of progress in primary prevention.* Hanover, NH: University Press of New England.

Rhine, W. R. (1981). *Making schools more effective: New directions from Follow Through.* New York: Academic Press.

Rich, R. F., & Caplan, N. (1976). *Instrumental and conceptual use of social science knowledge in policy-making at the national level: Means/ends matching versus understanding.* Unpublished manuscript, University of Michigan.

Robertson, A. (1982). Day care and children's responsiveness to adults. In E. Zigler & E. Gordon (Eds.), *Day care: Scientific and social policy issues.* Boston: Auburn House.

Rodman, H., Pratto, D. J., & Nelson, R. S. (1985). Child care arrangements and children's functioning: A comparison of self-care and adult-care children. *Developmental Psychology, 21,* 413–418.

Rofes, E. (Ed.). (1980). *The kids' book of divorce: By, for and about kids.* New York: Vintage Books.

Roupp, R., Travers, J., Glantz, F., & Coelen, C. (1979). *Children at the center: Final report of the National Day Care Study* (Vol. 1). Cambridge, MA: Abt Books.

Ryan, S. (Ed.). (1974). *A report on longitudinal evaluations of preschool programs: Vol. 1. Longitudinal evaluation* (Pub. No. [OTTO] 72-54). Washington, DC: U.S. Department of Health, Education and Welfare.

Salkind, N. J. (1983). The effectiveness of early intervention. In E. M. Goetz & K. E. Allen (Eds.), *Early childhood education: Special environmental, policy, and legal considerations.* Gaithersburg, MD: Aspen Systems Corp.

Sandler, I. N. (1980). Social support resources, stress and maladjustment of poor children. *American Journal of Community Psychology, 8,* 41–52.

School-Age Child Care Project. (1982). School-age child care. In E. Zigler & E. Gordon (Eds.), *Day care: Scientific and social policy issues.* Boston: Auburn House.

School-Age Child Care Project, Wellesley College Center for Research on Women. (1986, Spring). When school is out and nobody's home: The center's school-age child care project. *Research Reports, 5*(2).

Schwartz, F. N. (May, 1974). New work patterns for better use of womanpower. *Management Review,* 4–12.

Schweinhart, L. J., Weikart, D. P., & Larner, M. B. (1986). Program report on the consequences of three preschool curriculum models through age 15. *Early Childhood Research Quarterly, 1,* 15–45.

Seitz, V. (1982). A methodological comment on "the problem of infant day care." In E. Zigler & E. Gordon (Eds.), *Day care: Scientific and social policy issues.* Boston: Auburn House.

Seitz, V., Abelson, W. D., Levine, E., & Zigler, E. (1975). Effects of place of testing on the Peabody Picture Vocabulary Test scores of disadvantaged Head Start and non-Head Start children. *Child Development, 46,* 481–486.

Select Committee on Children, Youth, and Families (Ninety-eighth Congress, First Session). (May,

1983). *U.S. children and their families: Current conditions and recent trends.* Washington, DC: U.S. Government Printing Office.

Select Committee on Children, Youth, and Families (Ninety-eighth Congress, Second Session). (April, 1984). *Child care: Beginning a national initiative.* Washington, DC: U.S. Government Printing Office.

Skeels, H. M. (1966). Adult status of children with contrasting early life experiences: A follow-up study. *Monographs of the Society for Research in Child Development, 31* (3, Serial No. 105).

Smith, M. S., & Bissell, J. S. (1970). Report analysis: The impact of Head Start. *Harvard Educational Review, 40,* 51–104.

Smock, S. M. (1977). *The children: The shape of child care.* Detroit: Wayne State University Press.

Solkoff, J. (1977, June 11). Strictly from hunger. *New Republic,* 13–15.

Staines, G. L., & Pleck, J. H. (1986). Work schedule flexibility and family life. *Journal of Occupational Behaviour, 7,* 147–153.

Staines, G. L., & Pleck, J. H. (1983). *The impact of work schedules on the family.* Ann Arbor, MI: Institute for Social Research.

Steinberg, L. (1985). *Latchkey children and susceptibility to peer pressure.* Unpublished manuscript, University of Wisconsin, Madison.

Steiner, G. (1976). *The children's cause.* Washington, DC: Brookings Institution.

Stevenson, H. W., & Siegel, A. E. (Eds.). (1984). *Child development research and social policy.* Chicago: University of Chicago Press.

Struening, E. L., & Guttentag, M. (Eds.). (1974). *Handbook of evaluation research* (Vol. 1). Beverly Hills, CA: Sage Publications.

Takanishi, R., DeLeon, P., & Pallak, M. S. (1983). Psychology and public policy affecting children, youth, and families. *American Psychologist, 38,* 67–69.

Tallman, I. (1979). Implementation of a national family policy: The role of the social scientist. *Journal of Marriage and the Family, 41*(3).

Task Force on Psychology and Public Policy. (1986). Psychology and public policy. *American Psychologist, 41,* 914–921.

Thompson, R. A. (1985, Winter). Teaching child development courses from a social policy perspective. *The Networker, 6*(2), 1, 6. (Available from the Bush Center in Child Development and Social Policy, Psychology Dept., Box 11A Yale Station, New Haven, CT.)

Thompson, R. A. (Summer, 1986). Applying research insights to legal policy issues. *The Networker, 7*(4), 1, 8. (Available from the Bush Center in Child Development and Social Policy, Psychology Dept., Box 11A Yale Station, New Haven, CT.)

Travers, J. R., & Light, R. J. (Eds.), (1982). *Learning from experience: Evaluating early childhood demonstration programs.* Washington, DC: National Academy Press.

United Nations Association. (1986). *Work and family in the United States: A policy initiative.* UNA–USA, 300 East 42nd Street, New York, N.Y.

Urban Institute. (1982). *The subtle revolution: Women at work.* Washington, DC: Urban Institute.

Valentine, J., & Stark, E. (1979). The social context of parent involvement in Head Start. In E. Zigler & J. Valentine (Eds.), *Project Head Start: A legacy of the war on poverty.* New York: Free Press.

Vandell, D. L., & Corasaniti, M. A. (1985, May). *After-school care: Choices and outcomes for third-graders.* Paper presented at the meeting of the American Association for the Advancement of Science, Los Angeles.

Wallerstein, J. S., & Kelly, J. B. (1979). Children and divorce: A review. *Social Work, 24,* 468–475.

Wallerstein, J. S. (1985). Children of divorce: Preliminary report of a ten-year follow-up of older children and adolescents. *Journal of the American Academy of Child Psychiatry, 24,* 545–553.

Ward, E. H. (1976). COA: Credentialing for day care. *Voice for Children, 9*(5), 15.

Watson, A. (1969). The children of Armageddon: Problems of children following divorce. *Syracuse Law Review, 21,* 231–239.

Weber, C. U., Foster, P. S., & Weikart, D. P. (1978). An economic analysis of the Ypsilanti Perry Preschool Project. *Monographs of the High/Scope Educational Research Foundation* (Series No. 5).

Weikart, D. (1982). Preschool education for disadvantaged children. In J. Travers & R. Light (Eds.), *Learning from experience: Evaluating early childhood demonstration programs.* Washington, DC: National Academy Press.

Weiss, C. H. (1985). Media report card for social science. *Society, 22*(3), 39–47.

Weiss, C. H., & Bucavalas, M. J. (1977). The challenge of social research to decision making. In C. H. Weiss (Ed.), *Using social science research in public policy making.* Lexington, MA: Lexington Books.

Weiss, J. A., & Gruber, J. E. (1984). Using knowledge for control in fragmented policy arenas. *Journal of Policy Analysis and Management, 3,* 225–247.

Weisz, J. R. (1978). Transcontextual validity in developmental research. *Child Development, 49,* 1–12.

Westinghouse Learning Corporation (1969, June). *The impact of Head Start: An evaluation of the effects of Head Start on children's cognitive and affective development.* Executive Summary (EDO 36321). Washington, DC: Clearinghouse for Federal Scientific and Technical Information.

White, S. (1970). The national impact study of Head Start. In J. Hellmuth (Ed.), *The disadvantaged child: Vol 3. Compensatory education: A national debate.* New York: Brunner/Mazel.

White House Conference on Children. (1970). *Report to the president.* Washington, DC: U.S. Government Printing Office.

Whittaker, J., & Garbarino, J. (1983). *Social support networks: Informal helping in the human services.* New York: Aldine.

Winick, M. (1976). *Malnutrition and brain development.* New York: Oxford University Press.

York, P., & York, D. (1983). *Toughlove: A self-help manual for parents troubled by teenage behavior.* Sellersville, PA: Community Service Foundation.

Young, K. T., & Zigler, E. (1986). Infant and toddler day care: Regulations and policy implications. *American Journal of Orthopsychiatry, 56,* 43–55.

Zigler, E. (1963). Metatheoretical issues in developmental psychology. In M. Marx (Ed.), *Theories in contemporary psychology.* New York: Macmillan.

Zigler, E. (1970). The environmental mystique: Training the intellect versus development of the child. *Childhood Education, 46,* 402–414.

Zigler, E. (1973). Project Head Start: Success or failure? *Learning, 1,* 43–47.

Zigler, E. (1980). Welcoming a new journal. *Journal of Applied Developmental Psychology, 1,* 1, 1–6.

Zigler, E., Abelson, W. D., & Seitz, V. (1973). Motivational factors in the performance of economically disadvantaged children on the Peabody Picture Vocabulary Test. *Child Development, 44,* 294–303.

Zigler, E., Abelson, W. D., Trickett, P. E., & Seitz, V. (1980). *Is intervention really necessary to raise disadvantaged children's IQ scores?* Unpublished manuscript, Yale University, New Haven, CT.

Zigler, E., & Berman, W. (1983). Discerning the future of early childhood intervention. *American Psychologist, 38,* 894–906.

Zigler, E., & Butterfield, E. C. (1968). Motivational aspects of changes in IQ test performance of culturally deprived nursery school children. *Child Development, 39,* 1–14.

Zigler, E., & Finn, M. (1981, May). From problem to solution: Changing public policy as it affects children and families. *Young Children, 36,* 31–32, 55–59.

Zigler, E., & Finn, M. (1982). A vision of child care in the 1980s. In L. Bond and J. Joffe (Eds.), *Facilitating infant and early childhood development* (pp. 443–465). Hanover, NH: University Press of New England.

Zigler, E., & Finn-Stevenson, M. (1987). *Children: Development and social issues*. Lexington, MA: D.C. Heath.

Zigler, E., & Freedman, J. (1987a). Head Start: A pioneer of family support. In S. Kagan, D. Powell, B. Weissbourd, & E. Zigler (Eds.), *Family support programs: The state of the art*. New Haven, CT: Yale University Press.

Zigler, E., & Freedman, J. (1987b). Evaluating family support programs. In S. Kagan, D. Powell, B. Weissbourd, & E. Zigler (Eds.), *Family support programs: The state of the art*. New Haven, CT: Yale University Press.

Zigler, E., & Gordon, E. (Eds.). (1982). *Day care: Scientific and social policy issues*. Boston: Auburn House.

Zigler, E., & Hall, N. (in press). Day care: An overview for pediatricians. *Pediatrics*.

Zigler, E., & Kagan, S. L. (1981, July). The Child Development Associate: A challenge for the 1980s. *Young Children, 36*, 10–15.

Zigler, E., Kagan, S. L., & Klugman, E. (Eds.). (1983). *Children, families, and government: Perspectives on American social policy*. New York: Cambridge University Press.

Zigler, E., & Muenchow, S. (1983). Infant day care and infant-care leaves: A policy vacuum. *American Psychologist, 38*, 91–94.

Zigler, E., & Seitz, V. (1982a). Future research on socialization and personality development. In E. Zigler, M. Lamb, & I. Child (Eds.), *Socialization and personality development* (2nd ed.). New York: Oxford University Press.

Zigler, E., & Seitz, V. (May 1982b). Head Start as a national laboratory. *Annals of the American Academy of Political and Social Science, 461*, 81–90.

Zigler, E., & Trickett, P. E. (1978). IQ, social competence, and evaluation of early childhood intervention programs. *American Psychologist, 33*, 789–798.

Zigler, E., & Valentine, J. (Eds.). (1979). *Project Head Start: A legacy of the War on Poverty*. New York: Free Press.

Zigler, E., & Weiss, H. (1985). Family support systems: An ecological approach to child development. In N. Rapoport (Ed.), *Children, youth, and families: The action-research relationship*. New York: Cambridge University Press.

Zill, N., Sigal, H., & Brim, O. G., Jr. (1983). Development of childhood social indicators. In E. Zigler, S. L. Kagan, & E. Klugman (Eds.), *Children, families, and government: Perspectives on American social policy*. New York: Cambridge University Press.

Author Index

A

Abbott, C., 113, *140*
Abelson, R., 476, 477, *486*
Abelson, W. D., 62, *83*, 615, 616, *631*, *633*
Abikoff, H., 572, *588*
Abramov, I., 166, 180, *196*
Abramovitch, R., 393, 394, *397*, *406*, 531, *544*
Abt, C. C., 611, *625*
Achenbach, T. M., 88, 130, *140*, 553, 554, 557, 560, 561, 562, 563, 564, 567, 571, 580, 583, 585, *588*, *589*
Acredolo, L. P., 178, *196*, 242, *256*
Adams, R. J., 181, *196*
Adamson, L., 369, *409*
Adelson, J., 537, *543*
Adler, T., 449, *453*
Ager, J. W., 118n, 128, *140*
Agras, W. S., 465, *491*
Ahn, R., 467, *488*
Ahrens, R., 365, *397*
Ainsworth, M. D. S., 98, *140*, 364, 365, 366, 382, 383, *397*, *399*, *408*
Ajzen, I., 485, *486*
Albin, M., 388, *405*
Alexander, J. F., 574, *588*, *590*

Alexander, K., 181, *200*
Allison, P. D., 112, *140*
Allport, G. W., 96n, *140*
Als, H., 369, *409*
Altemeier, W. A., 392, *407*, *409*
Althaus, M., 560, *588*
Altmann, J., 100, *140*
Ambron, S. R., 500, *541*
Ambrose, J., 367, *397*
American Academy of Child Psychiatry, 553, *588*
American Psychiatric Association, 554, 557, *588*
American Psychological Association, 90, *140*
Amsel, E., 237, 242, *258*, *259*
Anastasi, A., 89, *140*
Anderka, N. T., 614, *629*
Anders, T. F., 556, 562, 582, *590*
Anderson, E. P., 382, *399*
Anderson, J. E., 6, *39*, 268, *289*
Anderson, J. G., 135, *140*
Anderson, J. R., 275, 278, *289*
Anderson, L. R., 118n, 128, *140*
Anderson, N., 242, *256*
Anderson, S., 617, *626*
Angell, J. R., 14, *39*
Ansul, S. E., 380, *407*

635

C

127–128
132

Foss, D. J., 317, *352*
Foster, P. S., 612, *632*
Foster, S. L., 99, *142*
Fowles, J., 440, 441, *452*
Fox, D. E., 336, *353*
Fox, N., 382, *401*
Fox, R., 180, *199*, 366, *401*
Fraiberg, S., 65, *81*, 368, 369, *401*
Frame, C. L., 472, *488*
Frane, J. W., 130, *142*
Frank, L. K., 6, 11, *42*
Frankel, K. A., 383, 385, *398*, 465, *487*
Fraser, S. C., 480, *492*
Frederiksen, J. R., 284, *291*
Freedman, D. G., 369, 371, 389, 390, 391, *401*
Freedman, J., 521, 536, *543*, 606, 607, *633*, *634*
Freedman, N. C., 391, *401*
Freeman-Moir, D. J., 20, *40*
Freiberg, K., 479, *492*
Freud, A., 567, *589*, 604, *628*
Freud, S., 7, 13, 22, 23, *42*, 361, 374, *401*, 517, 519, 530, 537, *543*, 566, *589*
Frey, K. S., 442, 444, 445, 446, 447, 448, *454*, *459*
Freyd, P., 312, *352*
Friedman, S. L., 605, *628*
Friedrich, L. K., 59, 61, *81*, *83*, 478, *494*, 535, 536, *543*
Friedrich-Cofer, 613, *629*
Frieze, I. H., 411, 422, 424, 425, 429, *454*
Frisch, H. L., *454*
Frodi, A. M., 369, 388, *401*, *404*
Frodi, M., 378, 388, *404*
Fromkin, V. A., 321n, *352*
Frommer, E. A., 558, *589*
Frost, N., 272, 273, *292*
Fujimura, O., 164, *202*
Fulker, D. W., 465, 466, *493*
Furby, L., 71, 75, 80, *81*, 88, *142*
Furrow, D., 320, *352*

G

Gabarino, J., 600
Gabrielli, W. F., 465, *492*
Gaensbauer, T. J., 365, 380, 387, *400*, *401*, *404*

Gaertner, S. L., 470, *493*, 516, *543*
Gagné, R., 225, *257*
Galambos, R., 170, *200*, *203*
Galanter, E., 270, 271, *293*
Gallagher, J. M., 283, *291*
Gallagher, K., 395, *401*
Gallatin, J. E., 18, *42*
Gallimore, R., 392, *410*
Gallistel, C. R., 277, *291*
Galton, F., 24, 26, 27, *43*, 261, 267, *291*
Gamble, T. J., 602, *628*
Games, P. A., 126, *143*
Garbarino, J., 606, 607, *628*, *633*
Garber, H., 615, *628*
Garcia, J., 173, *199*
Gardner, W., 120, *143*, 382, 384, 385, 395, *404*, *405*
Garet, M. A., 619, *627*
Garner, R., 596, *628*
Garrett, C. S., 440, 441, *454*
Garrett, H. E., 264, *291*
Garrett, M. F., 301, 307, 321n, *350*, *352*
Gaughran, J., 389, *398*
Gautier, M., 552, *590*
Gautier, T., 430, *455*
Gay, J., 33, *41*
Geary, P. S., 579, *591*
Geer, J. H., 516, *543*
Geiser, S., 125, *143*
Geisheker, E., 479, *489*
Gelfand, D. M., 102, *143*, 477, *494*
Gelman, R., 237, 241, *257*, 277, *291*, 310, 314, *355*, *356*
Gelman, S. A., 442, *454*
Gengerelli, J. A., 5, 6, *43*
Gentner, D., 310, *352*
George, C., 476, *489*
Georgoudi, M., 8, 29, 31, *48*
Gesell, A. L., 4, 5, 19, *43*, *257*
Gewirtz, J. L., 94, *143*, 368, 373, 375, *401*, *407*
Ghiselin, M. T., 9, 15, 30, *43*
Gholson, B., 225, *257*
Gibbs, E. D., 394, *402*, *408*
Gibbs, J. C., 472, *487*, 497, 503, 506, *542*, *544*
Gibson, E. J., 157, 177, 178, 186, 187, 188, 195, *199*, *200*
Gibson, J. J., 187, *200*
Gilbert, J. H. V., 164, *204*
Giles, H., 440, 441, *451–452*

Subject Index

Page numbers followed by n indicate footnotes.

A

Abnormal behavior, *see* Psychopathology
Absolute threshold, 166
Achievement, sex roles and, 418
Acoustic wave, form extraction from,
  language learning and, 316–327
Action directives, language learning and, 314
Adaptational theory, *see* Ethological-
  adaptational theory
Adaptive behavior, longitudinal course of,
  585–587
Adolescence (Hall), 17
Adolescents, conjoint family therapy and, 574
Adoption studies, temperament and, individual
  differences in, 390
Affective-cognitive synthesis, moral develop-
  ment and, 523–526
Affects, *see* Emotions
Age, intellectual development and, 263–266,
  267–269, 288
  flexibility and, 284–285
  higher order comprehension and, 282–284
  information processing and, 281–282
  metacomponents and, 280–281
Age differences
  comparisons of individuals with, 65–68, 69
    cohort sequential designs and, 67–68

cross-sectional studies and, 65–66
cross-sequential designs and, 68
longitudinal studies and, 66–67
scores adjusted for, 88–89
trend analysis and, 73
Age-graded influences, normative, 35, 36
Aggression
  definition of, 462
  social-information processing model of, 471
Aggressive behavior, 461, 463–464
  biological factors in, 464–465
  empathy and, 468
  interpersonal problem-solving skills and,
    470–472
  moral reasoning and, 472–474
  multi-factor model of, 483–486
  peer influences on, 531–532
  sex roles and, 419, 464
  socialization of, 475–479
    discipline in, 475–478
    familial patterns in, 482–483
    nondisciplinary, 478–479
  television and, 478, 534–536
Aging, perceptual development and, 188–190
Allocentric information, spatial perception
  and, 179
Altruism, 461, *see also* Prosocial behavior
  biological factors in, 465–466

Morphemes, 338–339, *see also* Language learning

Moses and Monothesism (Freud), 23

Mother(s), *see also* Parental *entries*
language learning and, 314–316, 327–328, 344–347
working, child day care and, 599

Motion perception, habituation and, 179–180

Motivational attributes, coping with novelty and, 286

Multidimensional contingency table analysis, 120–121

Multidisciplinary approach, life-span perspective and, 36–37

Multiple comparison tests, 126

Multivariate analysis of variance (MANOVA), 72, 73, 128–129, 132

Multivariate regression analysis, 128–129

N

Nativism
cognitive development and, 207–209
empiricism versus, perceptual development and, 154–161
perceptual development and, 151–152, 152n, 154

Naturally formed groups
correlational studies and, 63–64
representativeness in, 68, 70–71

Naturalness, continuum of, 58–59

Natural selection, 12

Nature-nurture controversy, 4–5, 152
perceptual development and, 161–164, 190–191

Neoconstructivism, 229–230

Nervous system, perceptual development and, 166–170

Neurophysiology, perceptual development and, 167

Newborn(s), *see* Infant(s)

Nomethetic approach, 96n

Non-normative life-event influences, 35–36

Normative influences, 35–36

Normative scores, 96, 97

Novelty, coping with, 286–287

Nuclear conflicts, 578–579

Null hypothesis testing, 114–118

Nurturance, prosocial behavior socialization and, 481–482

Nurture and nature, *see* Nature-nurture controversy

O

Object orientation, perception of, habituation and, 177–178

Oblimax factor rotation, 131

Observation, 52–55
of children's social behavior, 98–102
context of, 99–101
data quality in, 101–102
what to observe in, 99
closed methods of, 52–54, 100–101
functions of, 54–55
learning by, sex-role development and, 438–439
open methods of, 52, 100
reliability of, 54

Old age, perceptual development and, 188–190

Olfactory sensitivity, in infancy, 173, 174–175

Operant conditioning, 363
behavior therapies and, 571
sex-role development and, 434

Operative aspect of cognition, 576–577

Organicism, 7

Organismic model, roots of, 16, 17–22

Orientation, perception of, habituation and, 177–178

Origin of the Species, The (Darwin), 16

Orthogenetic principle, 22

Outcome evaluation, 610

Outliers, 102

P

Paired-associate learning, 211–212

Parent(s), *see also* Mother(s)
divorce of, children and, 603–605
as model, moral development and, 529–530

Parental imitation, types of, 388

Parental treatment, sex-role development and, 435–437

Parsimony principle, 211

Partial correlation, 110

Path diagrams, 133–134

Pedagogical Seminary, 17